# Lecture Notes in Computer Science 3713

Commenced Publication in 1973
Founding and Former Series Editors:
Gerhard Goos, Juris Hartmanis, and Jan van Leeuwen

Lionel Briand   Clay Williams (Eds.)

# Model Driven Engineering Languages and Systems

8th International Conference, MoDELS 2005
Montego Bay, Jamaica, October 2-7, 2005
Proceedings

 Springer

Volume Editors

Lionel Briand
Carleton University
Department of Systems and Computer Engineering
1125 Colonel By Drive, K1S 5B6 Ottawa, Canada
E-mail: briand@sce.carleton.ca

Clay Williams
IBM T.J. Watson Research Center
Software Quality and Testing
19 Skylane Drive, Room 2N-F07, Hawthorne, NY 10532, USA
E-mail: clay@us.ibm.com

Library of Congress Control Number: 2005932806

CR Subject Classification (1998): D.2, D.3, K.6, I.6

ISSN       0302-9743
ISBN-10    3-540-29010-9 Springer Berlin Heidelberg New York
ISBN-13    978-3-540-29010-0 Springer Berlin Heidelberg New York

Springer is a part of Springer Science+Business Media

springeronline.com

© Springer-Verlag Berlin Heidelberg 2005
Printed in Germany

Typesetting: Camera-ready by author, data conversion by Boller Mediendesign
Printed on acid-free paper     SPIN: 11557432     06/3142     5 4 3 2 1 0

# Preface

The MoDELS (Model Driven Engineering, Languages, and Systems) conference is a continuation of the successful series of ≪UML≫ conferences. This volume contains the final versions of the technical papers presented at MoDELS 2005 in Montego Bay, Jamaica, October 2–7, 2005.

The ≪UML≫ series began in 1988 at Mulhouse, France when the Unified Modeling Language was relatively new. Since then the conferences have been annually, with an increase in both attendance and the breadth of the work presented at the conferences. The appearance of new research areas and topics in prior conferences was the motivation for renaming the conference to reflect the broader mission the conferences were enabling. Among the new areas taking their place alongside UML and related standards, such as Model Driven Architecture (MDA), are model refactoring, aspect oriented modeling, and model quality control.

The call for papers for MoDELS 2005 resulted in the submission of 215 abstracts and 166 papers. Each submission was reviewed by at least 3 referees assigned from the set of 51 Program Committee members. After several rounds of discussion within the Program Committee, 46 papers (40 scientific papers and 6 experience papers) were selected for publication. The Program Committee also selected a paper for the Best Paper MoDELS 2005 Award. The paper is by Friedrich Steimann and is titled "Domain Models are Aspect Free."

The review process was managed using the VirtualChair reviewing system, developed by Vahid Garousi at Carleton University, Ottawa, Canada.

In addition to the presentations of the papers, the MoDELS 2005 scientific program included 2 keynote talks, "Model Driven Development for Distributed Real-Time and Embedded Systems", given by Douglas C. Schmidt (Vanderbilt University), and "Domain-Specific Modeling: No One Size Fits All" by Juha-Pekka Tolvanen (MetaCase). The conference also included 10 workshops, 6 tutorials, a Doctoral Symposium, an Educators Symposium, and a Poster/Demo Session.

We would like to thank all of the people who submitted papers and proposals for workshops and tutorials, as well as the excellent Program Committee members who reviewed these submissions. We also thank the invited speakers, the other members of the conference committees, the individuals who helped with the website and publicity, and the members of the Local Organizing Committee who helped make the conference run smoothly and made the local arrangements. Finally, we thank the sponsors for their generous support of MoDELS 2005.

Lionel Briand, Geri Georg, Stuart Kent, Ezra Mugisa, Clay Williams

# Organization

## Executive Commitee

| | |
|---|---|
| General Chair | Stuart Kent (Microsoft, UK) |
| Conference Co-chairs | Geri Georg (Colorado State U., USA) |
| | Ezra Mugisa (U. of the West Indies, Jamaica) |
| Program Chair | Lionel Briand (Carleton U., Canada and Simula Research Labs, Norway) |
| Experience Track Chair | Clay Williams (IBM Watson Research Center, USA) |
| Tutorial Chair | Gianna Reggio (U. of Genoa, Italy) |
| Workshop Chair | Jean-Michel Bruel (U. of Pau, France) |
| Panel Chair | Siobhán Clarke (Trinity College, Ireland) |
| Publication Chair | Vahid Garousi (Carleton U., Canada) |

## Organizing Team

| | |
|---|---|
| Publicity Co-chairs | João Araújo (New U. of Lisbon, Portugal) |
| | Emanuel Grant (U. of North Dakota, USA) |
| Local Arrangements Chair | Charmaine DeLisser (U. of Tech., Jamaica) |
| Doctoral Symposium Chair | Jeff Gray (U. of Alabama, USA) |
| Poster Chair | Felix Akinladejo (U. of Tech., Jamaica) |
| Tool Exhibition Chair | Gunjan Mansingh (U. of the West Indies, Jamaica) |
| Web Site Chair | Sudipto Ghosh (Colorado State U., USA) |
| Registration Chair | Robert France (Colorado State U., USA) |
| Treasurer | Robert France (Colorado State U., USA) |
| Paper Submission Chair | Vahid Garousi (Carleton U., Canada) |

## Program Committee

| | |
|---|---|
| Mehmet Aksit (Netherlands) | Alessandra Cavarra (UK) |
| Omar Aldawud (USA) | Betty H.C. Cheng (USA) |
| Ambrosio Toval Alvarez (Spain) | Steve Cook (UK) |
| Erik Arisholm (Norway) | Stphane Ducasse (Switzerland) |
| Colin Atkinson (Germany) | Gregor Engels (Germany) |
| Thomas Baar (Switzerland) | Sudipto Ghosh (USA) |
| Doo-Hwan Bae (Korea) | Martin Gogolla (Germany) |
| Antonia Bertolino (Italy) | Hassan Gomaa (USA) |
| Jean-Michel Bruel (France) | Jean Hartmann (USA) |
| Christian Bunse (Germany) | Hong Mei (China) |

Heinrich Hussmann (Germany)
Ashish Jain (USA)
Jean-Marc Jézéquel (France)
Philippe Kruchten (Canada)
Yvan Labiche (Canada)
Timothy C. Lethbridge (Canada)
Jonathan I. Maletic (USA)
Tom Mens (Belgium)
Richard Mitchell (UK)
Ana Moreira (Portugal)
Pierre-Alain Muller (France)
Oscar Nierstrasz (Switzerland)
Ivan Porres (Finland)
Alexander Pretschner (Switzerland)
Kerry Raymond (Australia)
Gianna Reggio (Italy)

Jaffar-Ur Rehman (Pakistan)
Laurent Rioux (France)
Bernhard Rumpe (Germany)
Peter H. Schmitt (Germany)
Andy Schuerr (Germany)
Mark Schulte (USA)
Bran Selic (Canada)
Liu Shaoying (Japan)
Perdita Stevens (UK)
Tong Sun (USA)
Francois Terrier (France)
Jos Warmer (Netherlands)
Ben Watson (USA)
Thomas Weigert (USA)
Jon Whittle (USA)

## Sponsors

ACM Special Interest Group on Software
Engineering
(www.acm.org)

IEEE Computer Society
(www.computer.org)

## Corporate Donors

Microsoft Corporation
(www.microsoft.com)

IBM
(www.ibm.com)

Digicel Jamaica
(www.digiceljamaica.com)

 Springer

Springer
(www.springeronline.com)

## Academic Supporters

Carleton University
(www.carleton.ca)

Colorado State University
(www.colostate.edu)

University of North Dakota
(www.und.edu)

University of the West Indies at Mona
(www.mona.uwi.edu)

University of Technology, Jamaica
(www.utech.edu.jm)

## Additional Referees

| | | |
|---|---|---|
| Marcus Alanen | Benoit Baudry | Maura Cerioli |
| Ilham Alloui | Hanna Bauerdick | Alexey Cherchago |
| Carsten Amelunxen | Nicolas Belloir | Kyoung-Sik Choi |
| Bente Anda | Alexandre Bergel | Yunja Choi |
| João Araújo | Gregory P. Bischoff | Sorana Cimpan |
| Gabriela Arévalo | Nieves Brisaboa | Michael L. Collard |
| Richard Atterer | Antonio Bucchiarone | Philippe Desfray |
| Bjrn Axenath | Fabian Buettner | Natalia Dragan |
| Manuel Barrio | Donggang Cao | Keith Duddy |
| Devasis Bassu | Eric Cariou | Francisco Duran |

Pascal Dürr
James Dzidek
Marina Egea
Jo M. Fernandes
Franck Fleurey
Frdric Fondement
Alexander Förster
Jaime Gomez
Miguel Goulão
Orla Greevy
Hans Groenniger
Nabil Hameurlain
Ulrich Hannemann
Michel Hassenforder
Jan Hendrik Hausmann
Manuel Hilty
Karsten Hoelscher
Paul Holleis
Jang-Eui Hong
Gang Huang
Johannes Jakob
Eshref Januzaj
Sang-Uk Jeon
Huzefa Kagdi
Harmen Kastenberg
Stuart Kent
Alexander Königs
Holger Krahn
Matthias Kranz

Ivan Kurtev
Yves Le Traon
Johan Lilius
Arne Lindow
Hui Liu
Moussa Lo
Marc Lohmann
Francisco Javier Lucas
Christoph Lueth
Haohai Ma
David Mak
Esperanza Marcos
Eve McGregor
Victor Nicola
Joaqun Nicolás
Erika Olimpiew
Ying Pan
Christian Peper
Jean-Marc Perronne
Luigia Petre
Andrea Polini
Raghu Reddy
Tobias Rötschke
Enrico Rukzio
Jose Saez
Belen Vela Sanchez
Stefan Sauer
Tim Schattkowsky
Martin Schindler

Markus Schmidt
Daniel Schneider
Michael Shepherd
Devon Simmonds
Jocelyn Simmonds
Bonita Simoes
Karsten Sohr
Eunjee Song
Hasan Szer
Jim Steel
Gerson Sunyé
Andrew Sutton
Bedir Tekinerdogan
Bernard Thirion
Laurent Thiry
Trung Dinh Trong
Hervé Verjus
Cristina Vigueras
Hendrik Voigt
Alan Cameron Wills
Gerald Winter
Kyoung-A Yoon
Rabih Zbib
Lu Zhang
Haiyan Zhao
Tewfik Ziadi
Paul Ziemann

# Table of Contents

## Quality Control

## MDA I

## Automation I

## UML 2.0

## Industrial Experience

## Crosscutting Concerns

## Modeling Strategies I

# MDA II

# Automation II

# Modeling Strategies II

# Workshops, Tutorials and Panels

# Keynote Address I:
# Model Driven Development for Distributed
# Real-Time and Embedded Systems

Douglas C. Schmidt

Vanderbilt University, USA
schmidt@dre.vanderbilt.edu

## Abstract

Despite advances in standards-based commercial-off-the-shelf (COTS) technologies, key challenges must be addressed before COTS software can be used to build mission-critical DRE systems effectively and productively. For example, developers of DRE systems continue to use ad hoc means to develop, configure, and deploy their applications and middleware due to the lack of formally analyzable and verifiable building block components.

This talk will describe how Model Driven Development (MDD) techniques and tools can be used to specify, analyze, optimize, synthesize, validate, and deploy product-line architectures (PLAs) and standards-compliant middleware platforms that can be customized for the needs of next-generation DRE systems. MDD is an emerging paradigm that combines:

- Domain-specific modeling languages (DSMLs), which provide programming notations that formalize the process of specifying application logic and quality of service (QoS)-related requirements in a PLA.
- Metamodeling, which define type systems that precisely express key characteristics and constraints associated with DSMLs for PLAs in particular application domains, such as software defined radios, avionics, vehtronics, and process automation.
- Model transformations and synthesis techniques that automate and ensure the consistency of software implementations with analysis information associated with functional and QoS requirements captured by models of PLA structure and behavior.

This talk will compare and contrast various model-based approaches (e.g., MIC, MDD, MDA, etc) to developing PLA-based DRE systems. It will also illustrate how MDD techniques and tools have been successfully integrated with standards-based QoS-enabled component middleware to develop PLAs that significantly improve the quality and productivity associated with developing next-generation mission-critical DRE systems. Concrete examples from avionics, process control, software defined radios, and warehouse management systems will be used to illustrate key points.

L. Briand and C. Williams (Eds.): MoDELS 2005, LNCS 3713, pp. 1–1, 2005.

# Activity Diagram Patterns for Modeling Quality Constraints in Business Processes

Alexander Foerster, Gregor Engels, Tim Schattkowsky

University of Paderborn, Germany
{alfo|engels|timschat}@uni-paderborn.de

**Abstract.** Quality management is an important aspect of business processes. Organizations must implement quality requirements, e.g., according to standards like ISO 9001. Existing approaches on business process modeling provide no explicit means to enforce such requirements. UML Activity Diagrams are a well recognized way of representing those business processes. In this paper, we present an approach for enforcing quality requirements in such business processes through the application of process quality patterns to Activity Diagrams. These patterns are defined using a pattern description language, being a light-weight extension of UML Activity Diagrams. Accordingly, such patterns can be used in forward-engineering of business processes that incorporate quality constraints right from the beginning.

Keywords: UML Activity Diagrams, Business Process, Process Quality, ISO 9001

## 1. Introduction

Total Quality Management (TQM) is a management concept which is an increasingly hot issue in most organizations. Businesses have become more and more competitive and the concentration on customer satisfaction is a key trait. Due to the increasing competitiveness of the markets, the customers formulate high expectations on products and services like user friendliness, reliability, security etc. The implementation of a TQM system in an organization is one answer to this situation since it puts the customer's demands in the first place and incorporates profound means of customer satisfaction.

The ISO 9001 standard [11] is one of the most popular TQM systems world-wide. It is in itself very process oriented and includes many quality related demands on business processes. In an organization with TQM, modeling business processes means that the process developer has to consider the quality requirements of the TQM system. We will present an approach how such quality requirements can be easily and thoroughly formulated and enforced. The approach is based on deriving business process patterns from the text of the ISO 9001 standard and applying these patterns to existing business processes.

A pattern based approach has many advantages. Using patterns is a common technology in software engineering. With design patterns, proven concepts and solutions can be easily described and communicated. Their application can significantly improve the quality of software models. Complex models can be easier

L. Briand and C. Williams (Eds.): MoDELS 2005, LNCS 3713, pp. 2-16, 2005.

understood and handled if the included patterns are known. These are only some advantages of the general concept of design patterns that we want to transfer to the world of business processes.

In our approach, we make use of UML Activity Diagrams as modeling language of choice for business processes. Therefore, the formulation of quality patterns will also be based on UML Activity Diagrams as modeling paradigm. Since they were not intentionally designed especially for the formulation of quality patterns, some aspects of the quality patterns cannot be satisfactorily modeled by them, as we will show further below. As a solution, we developed a pattern description language that is a light-weight extension of UML Activity Diagrams.

Fig. 1 shows an abstract model of a business process. If we assume that this process was created by the application of a quality management pattern to an original core business process, the resulting process contains Actions that have a different origin or belong to different aspects of the business process. Some Actions belong to the original core business process whereas others may fulfill only technical purposes or are part of the quality management system. These Actions are weaved together and can interleave each other in the final business process as shown by the different textures in Fig. 1. This means that the Actions and control flows of the original business process and the pattern have to be mixed together. Enforcing quality requirements with quality management patterns requires defined rules on how exactly a pattern must be applied to an existing business process. In addition to that, the pattern has to be a most exact formulation of the quality requirements. The formulation of quality patterns and the pattern application process is unfortunately neither easy nor straight-forward; we will provide an impression of that in the next example.

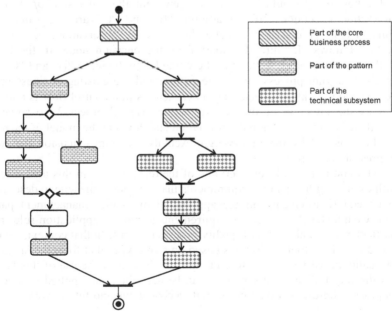

**Fig. 1.** Example behavior model including Actions that belong to different aspects of a business process

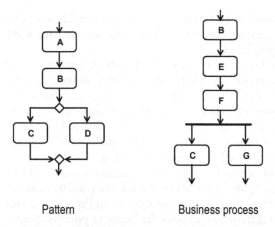

Pattern                          Business process

**Fig. 2.** Simple example of a pattern and a business process

Fig. 2 shows two simple workflows, the left shall be regarded as the pattern; the right shall be regarded as an excerpt of an existing business process in an organization. Let us assume the process modeler wants to apply the pattern on the left to the process on the right. The question is how exactly that can be done. Obviously, there are some distinct connection points which are the similar Actions in both processes, namely "B" and "C". Assuming that pattern application means to build one single united process and therefore one single united control flow from both Activities, we have to determine if the "B"s and "C"s of both processes have to be mapped to one single Action "B" and "C" in the resulting process. Another conceivable possibility would be that they represent the same *kind of* Action but different Action executions. If we assume "B" and "C" are the same Action executions in both processes, we make the following observation: in the pattern process, "C" follows "B" directly, apart from the decision node. In the business process, there are two other Actions in the control flow between "B" and "C". In an effort to create a joint process out of the pattern and the existing business process, how does the modeler know if inserting other Actions in a control flow is allowed or forbidden by the intention of the pattern or the original process? To solve these problems, there has to be additional information laid down in the model of the pattern. This can be achieved by the light-weight Activity Diagram extension that we are going to present in this paper.

The next section gives a brief overview of the related work in this area. Section 3 starts with examining the quality requirements that we want to be able to describe. We develop general requirements on the application of quality management patterns. After that, we transfer these general requirements to pattern application rules related to the particular model elements of quality process patterns. In that context, we define extensions to UML Activity Diagrams based on stereotypes that form the language to describe quality process patterns. In section 4 we show how the use of this language improves the way how a quality pattern can be described and applied to a concrete business process, before section 5 closes with a conclusion and future work.

## 2. Related Work

The pattern concept in computer science is well known when it comes to design patterns as presented in [9] and [10]. These design patterns are intended to describe good practice and proven solutions for common problems in object-oriented software design. These behaviors take place in a different context and are situated on a different level of abstraction than the business processes and patterns here.

In recent years, investigation of the pattern approach for application to the design of processes has begun. Especially workflows as automated processes controlled by computerized workflow management systems have been in the focus of interest for process patterns. Van der Aalst et al. provide an extensive coverage of workflow patterns in [1]. Their intention is mainly to demonstrate the expressiveness and capabilities of existing workflow management systems and their process description languages. Unlike our approach, their process patterns cover mainly technical concepts like all kinds of different basic and complex control flows and they are focused on Petri-nets.

In other works, Basten and van der Aalst aim at providing a theoretical foundation for the definition of inheritance of dynamic behavior of objects based on object life cycles [5]. There, four different inheritance rules based on hiding and blocking of transitions in transition systems are defined. The paper imparts a theoretical background for a possible way of defining the semantics of behavior inheritance. It is focused on behavior in form of object life cycles and studies inheritance in a process-algebraic setting and in a Petri-net framework. In [2], the theoretical framework of [5] is transferred to UML behavior models like sequence diagrams, state charts and activity diagrams. As in [5], this paper also focuses on modeling object life cycles and omits the particularities of business processes. However, the application of these inheritance concepts in the context of actual scenarios, e.g. to model patterns or quality constraints, is not clarified.

Some approaches consider the application of process patterns to software development processes. In [6], Coplien defines a pattern language for this kind of processes. Riehle gives the reader some advice on how to use such software process patterns in [13]. Finally, Ambler presents a broad collection of useful patterns for software design in [3] and [4]. However, these cover only specific aspects and usually omit the discussion of the actual application to existing processes.

An interesting discussion about analysis patterns and business objects can be found in [8] which claims that in the first category are patterns with a suggestive character that just give the idea but the designer is free to tweak the pattern any way he wants when he applies the pattern. In contrast to that, business objects are considered to have a prescriptive character, so they cannot be easily altered by the developer. Possible changes are based on what the writer of the business objects allows the designer to alter. This notion of a pattern is much closer to our notion of quality patterns since we want to be able to enforce properties of the resulting process instead of suggesting them.

## 3. Describing Quality Constraints with Process Patterns

Our approach is based on a visual language for describing quality process patterns based on UML Activity Diagrams. Such Activity Diagrams are well suited to express for example detailed process models that are ready for execution. In contrast to that, patterns describe processes that contain merely action roles and incomplete or loose temporal/logical relationships between Actions and high-level constraints. These are going to be substituted by concrete process elements from the application domain when the pattern is applied.

When modeling patterns, we want to follow the *principle of least constraint*; this means to describe everything that is elementary for the pattern without risking to lay down properties of the resulting process that are not elementary parts of the pattern. This principle of least constraint is a necessary prerequisite to enable the highest possible flexibility when applying the pattern.

In this section, we will show how quality requirements can be directly derived from standards like ISO 9001 and used as a basis for the definition of quality patterns using our pattern description language.

### 3.1 Deriving Patterns from Quality Requirements of the ISO 9001

A central part of a TQM system is quality control. This means that the result of a production process has to be compared to predefined quality objectives. The textual formulation of the requirements of quality control in the ISO 9001 standard is composed of different parts of the standard's text:

> "The organization shall monitor and measure the characteristics of the product to verify that product requirements have been met." [11]

> "7.1 Planning of product realization [...]
> In planning product realization, the organization shall determine the following, as appropriate:

> a)   quality objectives and requirements for the product;
> b)   the need to establish processes, documents, and provide resources specific to the product;
> c)   required verification, validation, monitoring, inspection and test activities specific to the product and the criteria for product acceptance;
> d)   records needed to provide evidence that the realization processes and resulting product meet requirements (see 4.2.4)." [11]

> "The organization shall ensure that product which does not conform to product requirements is identified and controlled to prevent its unintended use or delivery. [...] The organization shall deal with nonconforming product by one or more of the following ways
> a)   by taking action to eliminate the detected nonconformity;
> [...]" [11]

This description of quality requirements is still rather informal. At first we will state more precisely in natural language what steps have to be performed to fulfill the requirements of the given problem:

- Quality tests have to be performed in the processes in which products for external customers are produced.
- Quality objectives have to be defined before the production process starts.
- The quality objectives have to be communicated to the persons conducting the production process before the production process starts. *(This requirement results partly from other parts of the ISO 9001)*
- The quality of the product has to be measured and compared to the quality objectives.
- In case that the quality objectives are not met the detected nonconformities have to be eliminated. *(This requirement results partly from other parts of the ISO 9001)*
- Quality related information has to be collected and sent to the quality management department for statistical analysis, systemic improvements etc. *(This requirement results partly from other parts of the ISO 9001)*

In our approach, such requirements are the basis for the definition of quality patterns for processes to enforce these requirements. The application of such a pattern to an existing business process means merging two control flow structures into one, in other words weaving them together, leaving both processes "intact".

It must be ensured that the original behavior is preserved. All Actions of the pattern as well as all Actions of the business process have to be preserved when applying the pattern, although they might coincide in the resulting process. Furthermore, the partial order defined for Actions by both the pattern and the original business process has to be preserved when applying the pattern. However, the actual interleaving of Actions from the pattern and the original business process may vary.

## 3.2 Pattern Application and Activity Diagram Extensions

In order to explain the application of the model elements of quality patterns to an existing business process, we will see many diagrams in this section in which we have to distinguish between the pattern Activity Diagram and the model Activity Diagram, which contains the applied pattern. We will depict this in the following figures by adding the labels "Pattern:" and "Model:" to the Activity Diagrams.

Applying a pattern means that there exists a mapping between the pattern model elements and the model elements of the resulting process in which the pattern can be found again. We will depict this mapping using arrows with solid arrowheads. Fig. 3 shows an example of such a diagram in which Actions "A" and "B" have been specialized by Actions "A1" and "B2" and the relative order relationship between "A" and "B" (which we will explain further below) has become an ActivityEdge at the model level after applying the pattern.

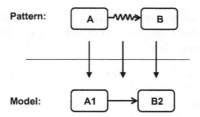

**Fig. 3.** Mapping between Pattern Level and Model Level

An Action in an Activity Diagram is usually notated as a rounded rectangle containing a label. Since "Action" is an abstract class in the UML 2.0 metamodel, we assume that Actions in a business process normally refer to "CallBehaviorActions". The Behavior itself is not further specified. In a business process, an Action is often something like "Send Invoice" or "Assemble Product", which refers to a Behavior that is complex but does not need further explanation in the context of the actual business process. So the text that is written into the rectangle symbolizing an Action is in fact the *name* of a Behavior.

When a pattern is applied, the pattern Actions are mapped to Actions of the resulting model where the pattern can be found again expressing that the two Actions refer to the same Behavior. There is a problem since the pattern and the model Activity Diagram have most likely been devised by different persons with different "Behavior" namespaces. To make a mapping possible, the process developer is responsible for determining similar Behaviors from both namespaces, so without loss of generality we assume that the "Behavior" namespaces are already synchronized.

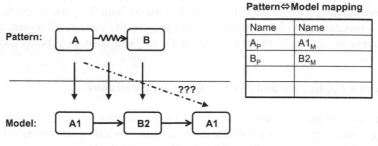

Pattern⇔Model mapping

| Name | Name |
|------|------|
| $A_P$ | $A1_M$ |
| $B_P$ | $B2_M$ |
|  |  |
|  |  |

**Fig. 4.** Wrong pattern/model mapping

Actions referring to the same Behavior can occur multiple times in the same Activity Diagram. For example one Action at the pattern level is mapped to one Action at the model level which occurs multiple times but we want to express that only one of them is referred to in the pattern. This means that the mapping between the pattern Actions and the model Actions as in Fig. 4 can not simply be done by creating a relation

(Pattern Action name) ⇔ (Model Action name)

but the mapping has to be done based on individual Actions.

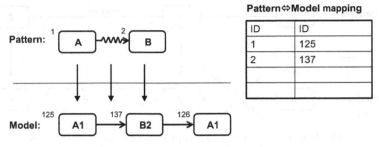

Fig. 5. Correct pattern/model mapping

As solution, the individual occurrences of the Actions have to be considered. The mapping can for example be defined upon individual Action IDs. In Fig. 5 the Action IDs are depicted as small numbers close to the upper left corner of the Action symbol. In our example these IDs are numeric, but other representations are also possible as long as they are unique. Now the correct mapping between pattern and model Actions has to be made using the IDs as shown in Fig. 5.

Up to now, we have mapped Actions that refer to the exact same Behavior. Since patterns usually describe more generic processes, the pattern Actions and the Behaviors they refer to are also usually more generic than those at the model level. Therefore, pattern Actions can, when the pattern is applied to a concrete business process, be replaced by model Actions referring to a specialized Behavior or sub-processes. Activity diagrams at the model level describe rather fixed temporal and logical relationships between Actions. In pattern Activity Diagrams the designer of the pattern wants to have the possibility to describe flexible relationships between Actions in some situations and strict relationships between Actions in other situations.

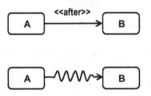

Fig. 6. Presentation option for the <<after>> stereotype

In the last subsection we have pointed out that pattern workflows have to be adapted to the actual business process when they are applied to it; especially sometimes Actions have to be inserted into the control flow of each original Activity Diagram. In other situations the designer might also want to express that Actions have to directly follow each other. A normal ActivityEdge in a pattern Activity Diagram means that Actions are tightly connected and there may no other Actions or control flows be inserted between them. For the flexible alternative, we introduce a stereotype of an ActivityEdge called <<after>>. This stereotype expresses a kind of temporal/logical order relationship or in other words a control flow path, which means that there may be other Actions in between. We also suggest a visualization option as shown in Fig. 6. A visual interpretation of the semantics of the <<after>> stereotype can be found in Fig. 7.

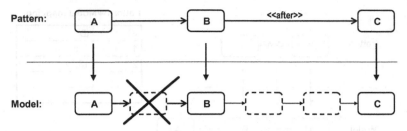

**Fig. 7.** Visualization of the semantics of the <<after>> stereotype

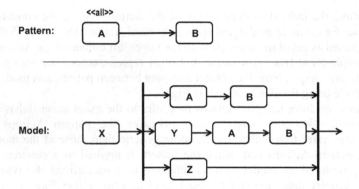

**Fig. 8.** Referring to all Actions referencing the same Behavior

**Fig. 9.** Presentation option for the <<all>> stereotype

As we have already seen, Actions referencing the same Behavior can occur multiple times in a process. If all occurrences of an Action referencing the same Behavior shall be referred to in the pattern at the same time, this can be expressed using the stereotype <<all>> as in Fig. 8 or writing a multi-action as in Fig. 9. For example, Action "A" of the pattern in Fig. 8 refers to all Actions "A" at the model level as far as the application of the pattern goes, that way all execution instances of "A" in the model have to be directly followed by Action "B". So the model instance shown in Fig. 8 is a correct application of the (very academic and simplified) "pattern".

Now we can take a look on some special cases that occur in connection with control nodes, i.e. parallel split/parallel join and decision/merge. Fig. 10 shows abstractly how the sequence "A"→"B" (with <<after>> stereotype) could be applied to become a parallel join (Model 3) or a parallel split (Model 4). Model 3 is a correct specialization of the pattern since "B" still has to be executed after "A". The fact that the execution has to wait between "A" and "B" until the synchronization with the other control flow takes place makes no difference for the order relationship between "A" and "B". Model 4 is also a correct specialization of the pattern since the fact that another control flow is forked between "A" and "B" also makes no difference to the fact that "B" is executed after "A".

Fig. 11 shows how decision and merge control nodes are treated in the pattern application process. The problem with the pattern application in Model 5 is that we cannot guarantee that "B" is executed after "A" or even at all. But since "B" is definitely executed in the pattern after "A", we regard this as a wrong application. The same is true for Model 6 where we cannot guarantee that Action "A" is executed before "B" or at all. So neither Model 5 nor Model 6 is a correct application of the pattern. Thus, if a conditional control flow is desired in the resulting process model after the pattern application, there has to be a conditional construction (split/merge/condition) in the pattern process, too.

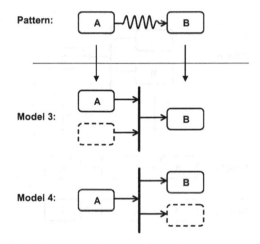

**Fig. 10.** Pattern application and parallel control flows

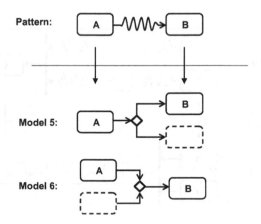

**Fig. 11.** Pattern application and conditional constructs

Parallel constructions in the pattern should generally be sustained when applying the pattern. Parallelism in pattern processes can however be just an expression of the fact that the order in which Actions are executed is irrelevant. According to the UML 2.0 specification [11], no real concurrency is enforced. This means for the application of patterns containing parallel control flows that they can potentially be serialized when applying the pattern, if needed. Fig. 12 shows an example; both Model 7 and Model 8 are valid instances of the pattern. Parallel control flows can also be partly serialized as shown in Fig. 13. Note that this may become problematic if parallel Actions have side effects that mutually affect each other.

This concludes the analysis of the modeling elements of quality pattern Activity Diagrams. In the next section we will apply our findings to a concrete example from the ISO 9001.

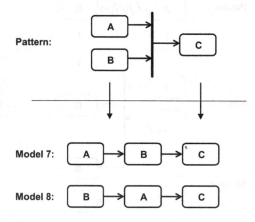

**Fig. 12.** Parallel constructs in the pattern being serialized

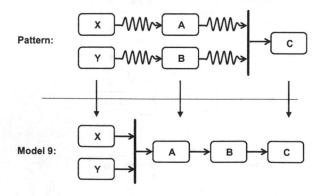

**Fig. 13.** Parallel constructs in the pattern partly serialized

## 4. Example

In the last section we made rather theoretical observations about process patterns and their application. In section 3.1 we have already presented some excerpts from the ISO 9001 standard's text. We can now make use of the new stereotypes to reflect the quality requirements stated in the standard's text.

From the ISO excerpts we can derive the pattern "Quality control" which is shown in Fig. 14. As the next step, we are going to apply this pattern to a concrete business process which is in our case a production process. We chose a heavily simplified model of an "Incremental software development" process as example of a business process, as shown in Fig. 15.

Without the concept of path-like ActivityEdges with the <<after>> stereotype, only one very simple way of applying the pattern to the business process would be possible: the "Incremental software development process" as a whole could be viewed as a specialization of the Action "Execute Production Process" of the pattern. That would mean that the whole existing business process would become a sub-activity of "Execute Production Process". This is certainly a possible application of the pattern, but it is questionable if this was intended by the ISO 9001 standard.

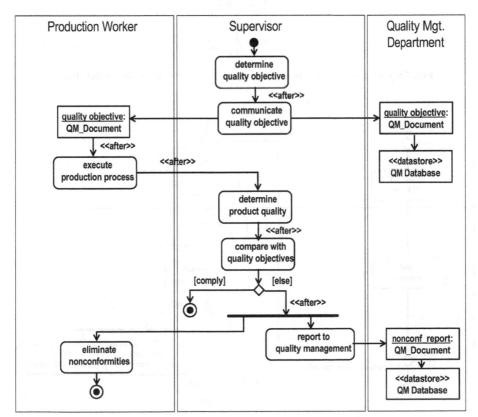

**Fig. 14.** Example pattern "Quality Control"

With the new stereotypes included at many places in the processes of Fig. 14, there open up completely new possibilities of pattern application. A comparision with the actual process example in Fig. 15 shows a number of similarities between the concrete business process and the pattern. Some Actions of the business process can be seen as specialization of actions of the pattern and the control structures have distinct similarities, too.

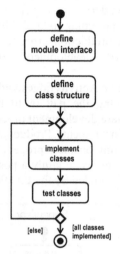

**Fig. 15:** Concrete business process (simplified incremental software development)

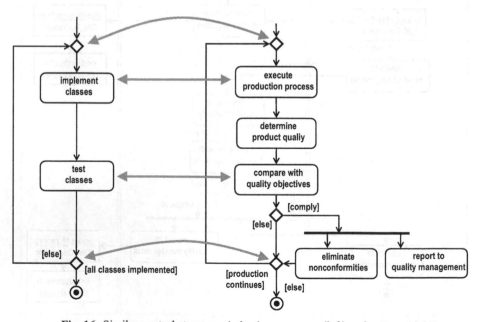

**Fig. 16:** Similar control structures in business process (left) and pattern (right)

In both processes,

- The actual "production" takes place in a loop.
- The Action "Implement classes" is main "production" task and could therefore be viewed as a specialization of the Action "Execute production process" of the pattern.
- The Action "Test classes" can be seen as a specialization of "Determine product quality" of the pattern.

Fig. 16 depicts these similarities between the pattern process and the original business process graphically. Now, having the stereotyped ActivityEdges and the possibility to add Actions into the control flows of both processes, we can weave both processes much more tightly together as it would be possible without these concepts as shown in Fig. 17.

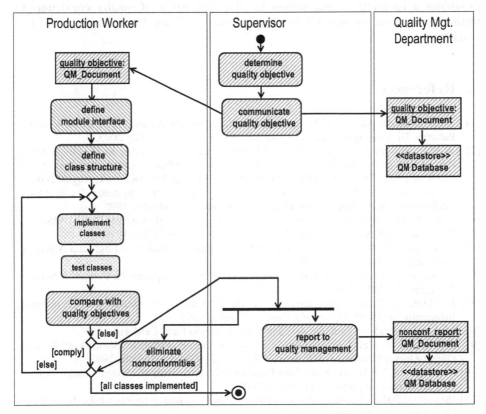

**Fig. 17:** More sophisticated application of the pattern

## 5. Conclusion and Future Work

Standards like ISO 9001 can be used as a source for deriving quality patterns. However, we have shown that Activity Diagrams cannot be applied directly to capture such patterns. Thus, we have introduced light-weight extensions captured by stereotypes to overcome the shortcomings on expressiveness for this particular application. We elucidated rules and properties that have to be taken care of when applying a quality management process pattern in general. Finally, we have formulated an example that demonstrates the new possibilities that arise from the application of these extensions.

Further research will include the application of our approach to other TQM systems and an evaluation in a real word process context. Furthermore, in this paper we have seen the concept of quality patterns rather in a forward-engineering perspective. Forthcoming works will also be more focused on quality pattern matching and recognition in existing business processes. Thus, we finally aim at providing a complete formal notion for the application of quality constraints to business processes as we did in previous work [7] for the refinement of state machines.

## 6. References

[1]   W.M.P. van der Aalst, A.H.M. ter Hofstede, B. Kiepuszewski, and A.P. Barros: Workflow Patterns. Distributed and Parallel Databases. 14(3), pages 5-51, July 2003.

[2]   W.M.P. van der Aalst: Inheritance of Dynamic Behavior in UML. In D. Moldt, editor, Proceedings of the Second Workshop on Modelling of Objects, Components and Agents (MOCA 2002), volume 561 of DAIMI, pages 105-120, Aarhus, Denmark, August 2002.

[3]   S. W. Ambler: Process Patterns - Building Large-Scale Systems Using Object Technology. SIGS Books/Cambridge University Press, Cambridge 1998.

[4]   S. W. Ambler: More Process Patterns - Delivering Large-Scale Systems Using Object Technology. SIGS Books/Cambridge University Press, Cambridge 1999.

[5]   T. Basten, W.M.P. van der Aalst: Inheritance of Behavior. Journal of Logic and Algebraic Programming, 47(2):47-145, 2001.

[6]   J. Coplien: A Generative Development-Process Pattern Language. In Coplien & Schmidt 1995, pp. 183-238, 1995.

[7]   J. Ebert, G. Engels: Specialization of Object Life Cycle Definitions. Fachberichte Informatik Nr. 19/95, Universität Koblenz-Landau, 1997.

[8]   M. Fowler: Analysis Patterns. Addison Wesley, Menlo Park, California, 1997.

[9]   E. Gamma, R. Helm, R. Johnson, J. Vlissides: Design Patterns, Elements of Reusable Object-Oriented Software. Addison-Wesley, Reading, Massachusetts, 1995.

[10]  D. Gross and E.S.K. Yu: From Non-Functional Requirements to Design through Patterns. Requirements Engineering, 6(1):18-36, 2001.

[11]  ISO 9001:2001: Quality Management Systems – Requirements. ISO International Organization for Standardization. 2001.

[12]  Object Management Group, The: UML 2.0 Superstructure, 2005. Version 2.0. http://www.omg.org/cgi-bin/doc?ptc/2004-10-02. Last visited: 03-23-05.

[13]  D. Riehle, H. Zullighoven: Understanding and Using Patterns. Software Development. Theory and Practice of Object Systems. 2(1):3-13, 1996.

# UML4SPM: A UML2.0-Based Metamodel for Software Process Modelling[i]

Reda Bendraou[1], Marie-Pierre Gervais[1,2], and Xavier Blanc[1]

[1] Laboratoire d'Informatique de Paris 6 (LIP6), [2] University Paris X
LIP6 - 8 rue du Capitaine Scott - F75015 PARIS
{Reda.Bendraou, Marie-Pierre.Gervais, Xavier.Blanc}@lip6.fr

**Abstract.** In the context of Model Driven Development, models play a central role. Since models can nowadays be executed, they are used not only for description but also for production [32][30][24]. In the field of software process modelling, the current version of the OMG SPEM standard (ver1.1) has not yet reached the level required for the specification of executable models. The purpose of SPEM1.1 was limited at providing process descriptions to be read by humans and to be supported by tools, but not to be executed. Therefore, the OMG issued a new RFP in order to improve SPEM1.1 [35]. Since we intend to participate in the next major revision of SPEM, namely SPEM2.0, in this work, we: 1) compare SPEM1.1 both with primary process model elements (i.e. Activity, Product, Role,...) and with basic requirements that any Process Modelling Language should support (i.e. expressiveness, understandability, executability,....); 2) identify its major limitations and advantages and 3) propose a new UML2.0-based metamodel for software process modelling named: UML4SPM. It extends a subset of UML2.0 concepts - with no impact on the standard - in order to fit software process modelling.

**Key words:** MDD, Software Process Modelling, Process Modelling Languages, SP Metamodel.

## 1 Introduction

The Model Driven Development (MDD) vision comes with a set of recommendations in order to manage the complexity of software development. The main one is to promote an approach where extensive models are created before source code is written. A primary example of MDD is the OMG's (Object Management Group) Model Driven Architecture (MDA) approach [23]. The MDA promotes model engineering rather than object engineering in order to ease code production in a cost-effective manner. It pushes beyond the original bounds of the Unified Modelling Language (UML) by providing open specifications that support the formal modelling of most aspects of the software life cycle. Currently, MDA provides a growing family of standards that now includes the UML v2.0 (UML 2.0 Superstructure adopted, UML2.0 Infrastructure in finalization) [37], the Meta Object Facility (MOF v1.4, v2.0 in finalization) [26] and the Software Process Engineering Metamodel (SPEM v1.1, RFP for SPEM2.0) [34] [35] which is devoted to software development process specifications.

L. Briand and C. Williams (Eds.): MoDELS 2005, LNCS 3713, pp. 17–38, 2005.

As software development process is the backbone of the software development lifecycle, software development processes and software engineering standards have gained more and more importance in the software industry. Actually, it has been wildly accepted that, the quality of any software product cannot be ensured simply by inspecting the product itself or by performing the traditional verification and validation approach (V&V) [2] [11], but relates to both, the production process that is carried out and to actors involved in this production process [27]. Therefore, software companies recognized the need of capturing processes they follow for building software, good practices and their know-how in a standard way. The term *Software Process Modelling* is used to describe the production of models of defined software development processes. A *Process Model* is an abstract description of an actual or proposed process. It represents selected process elements that are considered important to the purpose of the model and can be executed by a human or a machine [6]. Process models are described with *Process Modelling Languages* (PMLs). A Process Modelling Language (PML) is defined in terms of a notation, a syntax and semantics, often suitable for computational processing. Process modelling is a very diverse and complex area. Requirements for *PMLs* in order to support modelling and executing of software processes are both functional (e.g. expressiveness, abstraction, executability...) and non functional (e.g., commercial support) [5].

In this paper, we focus on PML and more precisely, on SPEM. Thus, as a first step of this work, we present primary requirements identified in [7] [16] that any PML should support which are: *Formality, Expressiveness, Understandability, Abstraction, Executability, Modularization, Analyzability, Reflection, and Multiple conceptual perspectives*. Then, we evaluate these requirements in respect with SPEM1.1. This helped us to identify its major limitations and advantages.

As a second stage, we show how to improve the current metamodel of SPEM1.1. This is done by: 1)    introducing basic concepts (e.g. Activity, Product, Role...) that process modelling languages should provide as defined in [4] [10] [21]; 2) Discussing how a subset of UML2.0 concepts and those we introduce provide these process model elements and how they can be used for modelling software processes.

The paper is organized as follows: Section 2 introduces basic concepts in the field of software engineering and lists requirements that should be supported by PMLs. Section 3 gives a brief description of the main concepts of SPEM1.1 and presents its limitations according to requirements highlighted in Section 2. In Section 4, we present our metamodel for software process engineering, named: UML4SPEM. It extends a subset of UML2.0 concepts by adding some features and elements related to software development processes in an MDA context. Then, we compare our metamodel to primary process model elements and to PMLs requirements. We then show how it overcomes major SPEM1.1 limitations. Execution of process models is out of the scope of this paper. Section 5 presents related work and Section 6 introduces perspectives of this work.

# 2   Software Engineering

In this section, we give a brief reminder of basic concepts in the area of Software Engineering. Then, we present primary elements of Process Models as well as requirements that PMLs should support.

## 2.1   Definitions

As introduced by Humphrey [15], "*Software Engineering refers to the disciplined application of engineering, scientific, and mathematical principles and methods to the economical production of quality software*". Here, the term quality refers to the degree to which a product meets its user's needs. While "*The Software Engineering Process is the total set of software engineering activities needed to transform user's requirements into software*". This process may include, as appropriate activities of: requirement specifications, design, implementation, verification, installation, operational support, and documentation. *Process Models (PMs)* are precisely seen as a "*representation of a networked sequence of these activities, objects, transformations, and events that embody strategies for accomplishing software evolution*" [14]. Advantage of process models is that they are built in some known modelling language, namely: *Process Modelling Languages (PMLs)*. This allows the process model to be validated against a known set of rules and makes it easier to edit and to maintain. This also facilitates collaborative work between different teams and subcontractors (offshore). A PML should offer a sufficient set of concepts i.e., a vocabulary that covers the real-word software production process. In the following we introduce them.

## 2.2   Primary Process Model Elements

In [4] [5] [10] and [21] a set of software process model elements has been identified. They establish that any PLM should be able to express six primary process elements[i]. We give here an essential summary of each element:

- **Activity**: A concurrent process step, operating on artifacts and coupled to a human or a production tool. It can be at different levels i.e., activities can be decomposed.
- **Product**: Software artifact inputs or outputs of activities.
- **Role**: Defines rights and responsibilities of the human involved in the software activity.
- **Human**: Human are process agents who may be organized in teams. It has skills and authority and can fulfil a set of roles.
- **Tool**: Relates to any tool used by the software process, may be batch (i.e. compilers, links, parsers...) or interactive (i.e. textual editors, graphical CASE tools...).
- **Evolution Support:** Support for static or dynamic variability of the process model. This means that most previous lifecycle phases must be repeatable "on the fly" (during process execution). As a consequence of this, the PML must offer at least support for the evolution of the process model. This support has to be ensured

---

[i] For brevity reasons, we prefer redirect the reader into papers referenced above

technically (i.e. reflection or interpretation) and conceptually (by a defined metamodel) [7].

As a process model consists of a set of these process elements together with additional constraints controlling how they may be interrelated, a PML has to provide language features to model these basic elements as well as their interrelationships. This is considered as the first requirement of a PML i.e., *Expressiveness* (cf. definition below).

## 2.3 Basic PMLs Requirements

PMLs have to support some well-known requirements which are very similar to those of programming languages [28]. In [7] and [16] essential ones are introduced in the context of PMLs. They are:

- **Formality**: The syntax and semantics of a PML may be defined formally, i.e. precisely, or informally, i.e. intuitively. Formal PMLs support, for example, reasoning about developed models, analyzing of the precisely defined properties of a model, or transforming models in a consistent manner.
- **Understandability**: It dependents on the possible process model's users. Users with a computer science background will find easier to understand a model written in a PML that resembles a programming language. Those with other backgrounds may prefer graphic representations based on familiar metaphors.
- **Expressiveness**: Indicates whether all aspects of a process model may be directly modelled by language features of the PML or have, for example, to be expressed by means of additional comments.
- **Abstraction** and **Modularization**: The PML may offer modelling-in-the-large concepts, such as Abstraction and Modularization, to structure a process model into sub-models connected by certain relationships. Abstraction concepts may support the definition of more general, abstract
sub-models which are customized within a concrete process model. In addition, a PML may offer the possibility of distinguishing between generic and specific process models.
- **Executability**: The PML may support the definition of operational models. These are executable.
- **Analyzability**: The PML may support the definition of descriptive models, e.g. predicate logic expressions. Such models are easily analyzable.
- **Reflection:** The PML may directly support the evolution of process models. In this case there are parameterization, dynamic binding, persistency and versioning issues to be addressed.
- **Multiple conceptual perspectives/views**: The PML may support the definition of views of certain perspectives of a process model. This implies mechanisms to integrate different views of a process model into an overall process model.

PMLs can be evaluated according to these requirements. However, some desired requirements are in conflict and so it is not possible to address all of them within one PML [1] [29]. Thus, fundamentally different PMLs and notations may be needed to cover such diversity in scope.

In the next section, we evaluate if the SPEM1.1 standard deals with these requirements as well as with primary process model elements.

# 3   SPEM 1.1

## 3.1   SPEM1.1 Presentation

SPEM introduces common concepts and modelling structure to construct models of software development processes [34]. SPEM1.1 uses some basic modelling concepts from UML1.4 to describe rules, constraints, vocabulary, and notation to be used in defining process models [38]. Thus SPEM1.1 meta-model is defined as an extension of a subset of UML1.4, expressed in the *SPEM_Foundation* package. The *SPEM_Extensions* package which extends the *SPEM_Foundation* package, adds the constructs and semantics required for software process engineering. It owns five packages; each package addresses a specific concern of the software process definition.

The building block of the SPEM metamodel is the *Process Structure* package (figure 1). It defines the main structural elements from which a process description may be constructed. In the following, we compare them with primary process model elements.

## 3.2   Comparison of SPEM1.1 with Primary Process Model Elements

- **Activity**: In SPEM1.1, an *Activity* is the main subclass of *WorkDefinition*. It describes a piece of work performed by one *ProcessRole* and may consist of atomic elements called *Steps*.
- **Product**: A *WorkProduct* in SPEM is anything produced, consumed, or modified by a process.

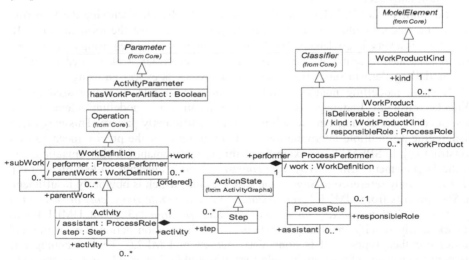

**Figure 1.** The process Structure package, the core of SPEM1.1 metamodel for process definitions.

It describes one class of artifacts produced in a process and has a *WorkProductKind* that describes a category of artifact, such as Text Document, UML Model, Executable, Code Library, and so on.

- **Role**: in SPEM, a *ProcessRole* is a subclass of *ProcessPerformer* and defines responsibilities and roles over specific *WorkProducts* and *Activities*.

Whether SPEM1.1 defines the notion of *ProcessRole* (Role), it does not provide the one of **Human** who can undertake this Role. Moreover, concepts equivalent to **Tool** and **Evolution Support** are not provided by the standard. In SPEM1.1, software processes are described in static models and there is no support for their evolution during execution-time.

Table 1 summarizes correspondences between primary process model elements and those offered by SPEM1.1. It shows that **Human**, **Tool** and **Evolution Support** notions are lacking in SPEM1.1.

| Basic process model elements | SPEM1.1 |
|---|---|
| Activity | WorkDefintion /Activity |
| Product | WorkProduct |
| Role | ProcessRole |
| Human | - |
| Tool | - |
| Evolution | - |

**Table 1.** Comparison between primary process elements and SPEM1.1 elements.

### 3.3    Evaluation of SPEM1.1 Towards Basic PMLs Requirements

In this section, SPEM1.1 is evaluated with respect to requirements on process modelling languages.

- **Formality**: As SPEM1.1 extends a sub set of UML1.4, discussing the formality i.e., syntax and semantics of SPEM1.1 partly comes to discuss the formality of UML 1.4 which is a very large debate. The UML semantics is described using a metamodel that is presented in terms of three views: the abstract syntax, well-formedness rules, and modelling element semantics. The abstract syntax is expressed using a subset of UML static modelling notations and well-formedness rules are expressed in the Object Constraint Language (OCL). The semantics of modelling elements are described in natural language, which may not be sufficiently precise. This may cause disagreements, multiple interpretations and confusion over the precise meaning of a construct [9]. In SPEM1.1, an example of this lack of semantic is the semantic given to the *Step* element: *"An Activity may consist of atomic elements called: Steps"* [34]. This is the only reference to *Step* in the specification, which is obviously insufficient. A *Step* inherits from UML1.4 *ActionState*. *"An action state represents the execution of an atomic action, typically the invocation of an operation"* [38]. But, UML1.4 does not explicitly specify, neither parameters of the invocation action (i.e., name and value) nor their types as it is done with *Actions* in UML2.0. Then, mapping this element to an executable or analyzable format would be impossible and useless. Let's also consider the concept of *ProcessPerformer*. The standard defines the

*ProcessPerformer* as a performer for a set of *WorkDefinitions*. It also states that *ProcessPerformer* represents abstractly the "whole process" or one of its components. Definitively, we can clearly note that this definition is confusing. One obvious question would be: what is the practical use of a *ProcessPerformer*? Is it used as a *container* for *WorkDefinitions* or as a *role,* responsible for specific activities? In the latter case, what is the difference with the *ProcessRole* concept? We believe that a container of *WorkDefinitions* and *roles* are totally two separate concepts that should be expressed separately.

• **Understandability**: SPEM1.1 uses UML notation. This is considered as an advantage as UML has attractive features: it is standard, graphical, intuitive, and easy to be understood. Besides, a wide community of software developers is familiar with UML and uses a UML case tool environment. UML being so popular and widely used, SPEM has an important competitive advantage compared to any specialized PML [8].

• **Expressiveness**: In this point, we address expressiveness of SPEM1.1 concepts to model software processes and not UML1.4 expressiveness. We have seen in section 3.2., that SPEM1.1 doesn't provide concepts like Human, Tool or Evolution support. In the following, we present other limitations related to the expressiveness criterion:

**a)** In SPEM1.1, a *WorkProduct* inherits from the UML1.4 *Classifier* and is used as a parameter into or from *Activities* (*WorkDefinition* in general). Nevertheless, we can't know which *Steps* of the *Activity* are going to act on *WorkProducts* nor responsible roles of these *Steps*. We think that it would be useful to affect *WorkProducts* to *Steps* rather than to *Activities* for more exhaustive process automation. Also, we believe that we have to provide designers with the possibility to  specify and to personalize their own *WorkProducts* in order to be domain or method specific. The *WorkProduct* class has some fixed properties such as *name, isDeliverable,* or *kind* and it is not possible to add more properties for the *WorkProduct*. Indeed, with the appearance of the MDA, some specific *WorkProducts* emerge. Examples are models, model transformation rules and so on. These *WorkProducts* have different properties each, which can't be resumed by a *name* and a *boolean* that indicates either it is a *deliverable* or not as it is in SPEM1.1.

**b)** During software development process, depending on some results, developers would need to interact and to impose choices about activities to be executed. Human interactions are lacking by SPEM1.1.

**c)** Finally, project managers would also like to have some additional features on process definitions in order to monitor and to capture process metrics during execution-time. Examples of these features could be duration time of an activity, its priority and its thrown exceptions. The current specification does not provide any of those facilities.

• **Abstraction**: As the OMG has chosen an OO approach for modelling software processes [34], SPEM1.1. provides *Abstraction* thanks to the *Generalization/ Specialization* mechanism. Indeed, a process model defined by SPEM1.1 can be customized using the inheritance i.e., specialization mechanism in order to fit specific domains or user's requirements. Thus, in the specialized process model, we can add new attributes to new classes that inherit basic ones as well as new references. This allows taking advantage of existing process models while adapting them to an appropriate domain.

- **Modularization**: One of the major lacks of SPEM1.1 is *ProcessComponent* compositions. A *ProcessComponent* is a chunk of process description that is internally consistent and may be reused with other *ProcessComponents* to assemble a complete process. However, developers who want to combine two or more *ProcessComponents* in order to get one coherent process, have to carry out a *unification* procedure. Indeed, to combine for instance two *ProcessComponents* P1 and P2, at least the output *WorkProducts* from P1 must be *unified* i.e., made identical with the inputs to P2. Other elements may possibly be *unified* in addition, such as *ProcessRoles*. Composition of *ProcessComponents* can be fully automated only if they originate from a common family so that the unification is obviously capable of being automated. Otherwise, the unification would involve human intervention that normally would consist of some re-writing of the elements, and possibly associated elements, to be unified. This could be manageable in case of the combination of two simple *ProcessComponents*. However in case of complex *ProcessComponents,* it becomes increasingly difficult. When outsourcing and offshore appear as a new way working for companies, it is important to address this lack.

- **Executability**: Nowadays, companies are looking for how to extensively automate all parts participating in software production, among them the development process itself. However, SPEM1.1 provides as actions of a development activity, the concept of *Step,* which only represents the name of the action that developer has to perform (e.g., Step x: Check model consistency). This could help for process description but it is so far of its execution. We agree that execution of process models is outside the scope of SPEM1.1. However, we hardly believe that it should provide concepts that enable the specification of executable action semantics within process models. UML2.0 offers this possibility thanks to the *Actions* packages. It gives precise execution semantics to actions, by defining their effect as well as their typed inputs and outputs. This may help in mapping them into executable actions in some well-known OO languages such as Java or C++ [8].

- **Analyzability**: SPEM1.1 is defined as a MOF metamodel, based on a subset of UML. This is considered as an advantage as MOF definitions are machine processable. Specifically, the MOF standard dictates how MOF models and instances of MOF models may be rendered in XML format (schemas and XML documents, respectively), and how interfaces to repositories for models can be derived from MOF definitions of the languages in which those models are expressed [20] [19]. This helps in manipulating SPEM1.1 models i.e., creation, suppression or modification, in checking their conformance to the SPEM1.1 metamodel and in analyzing them from different process perspectives (e.g. to get *ProcessRole* for the *Activity*: *x*, or *Steps* owned by the *Activity*: *y*, how many *WorkProducts* are used by the *WorkDefinition*: *z*, and so on).

- **Reflection**: Reflection is about whether SPEM1.1 supports process models evolution (static or dynamic) or not. In fact, SPEM1.1 doesn't provide mechanisms for dynamic evolution of process models. Static evolution is offered by manipulating process models outside execution-time.

- **Multiple conceptual perspectives/views**: Another considerable advantage for SPEM is that is defined both as a metamodel and as a UML profile, which allows

SPEM modelers to use the UML as a concrete notation. Thus, SPEM both defines modelling capacities dedicated to the software process domain, and gains the benefit of the expressiveness of UML. For example, Use Case modelling, which is sometimes used for modelling processes, is not defined as a specific SPEM facility, but can be inherited from UML. Other UML diagrams i.e., Class, Package, Sequence, State chart and Activity diagrams can be used by SPEM1.1 with some restrictions. For instance, SPEM1.1 allows the use of UML Sequence diagrams to illustrate interaction patterns among SPEM model element instances with the restriction that only stick arrowheads should be used [34]. Table 2 summarizes the result of the evaluation of SPEM1.1 with respect to basic PML requirements.

| Basic PML Requirements | SPEM1.1 |
|---|---|
| Formality | -Lacks of a precise semantic of some elements (*Step, ProcessPerformer*...). |
| Expressiveness | -Lacks of some process model elements (Human, Tool and Evolution Support); <br><br> -*WorkProducts* are used as parameters of *Activities* and not of *Steps*(useless for process automation) <br><br> -Impossibility of defining explicit *WorkProducts* properties; <br> -Lacks of human interactions and decision points; <br><br> -Lacks of some features on process elements in order to capture process metrics, exceptions. |
| Understandability | -Good. Uses UML as a notation |
| Abstraction | -Good. As an OO PML, SPEM1.1 offers Generalization/Specialization mechanism to deal with Abstraction. |
| Modularization | -Lacks of *ProcessComponent* compositions. Need of a *Unification* mechanism. |
| Executability | -Major Lack. SPEM1.1 models are not executable. It was outside the scope of the specification. |
| Analyzability | -Good. Possibility to manipulate process models and to analyze them thanks to MOF repositories. |
| Reflection | -Lack |
| Multiple conceptual perspectives/views | -Good. Thanks to the possibility of using UML diagrams as SPEM1.1 is a UML profile. |

**Table 2.** Evaluation of SPEM1.1 with respect to basic requirements of PMLs.

As we can notice, SPEM1.1 suffers from several lacks at different levels of PML requirements. Principal ones are: *Formality, Expressiveness, Modularization, Executability* and *Reflection*, whereas it has serious advantages in *Understandability, Abstraction, Analyzability* and *Multiple conceptual perspectives/views*.

In the next section we introduce our solution and show how it overcomes these lacks.

# 4    UML4SPM: A UML2.0-Based Metamodel for Software Process Modelling

As intent to overcome SPEM1.1 limitations, our proposition for modelling software processes comes in form of a MOF-compliant metamodel named: UML4SPM. It takes advantages of the expressiveness of UML2.0 by extending a subset of its elements suitable for process modelling. By adopting UML2.0 as a basis of our metamodel, we will take advantage of:

o    The expressiveness of the new UML2.0 for modelling executable action semantics within activities and in orchestring them;
o    The fact that UML is currently the most widely used modeling language in the industry;
o    Tool supports and facilities;
o    Notations and diagrams offered by the standard ;
o    Easier adoption by UML and SPEM1.1modelers;

## 4.1    Metamodel Presentation

As in SPEM1.1, UML4SPM comes in form of package hierarchies. The outermost level contains two packages: the *SPEM_Foundation* package and the *SPEM_Extensions* package (see figure 2).

The *SPEM_Foundation* package contains all UML2.0 packages required as a basis for defining software process models. Main ones relate to *Activities*, *Actions*, *Behavior* and *Kernel* packages. The *SPEM_Extensions* package holds packages that extend UML2.0 and add the constructs and semantics required for software process modelling i.e., the *ProcessStructure* package and the *WorkProducts* package. Figure 3 point out how concepts of both packages are interconnected. It gives a global overview of UML4SPM Lighted boxes of the figure represent UML2.0 classes. Shaded boxes represent those we specified and that inherit UML2.0 classes. We start the description of the metamodel by *SPEM_Extensions* packages.

### *Process Structure Package*

The *ProcessStructure* package is the core of UML4SPM. Its main class is the *Process* class (figure 3).    A *Process* inherits form UML2.0 *BehavioredClassifier*. A *BehavioredClassifier is* a *Classifier* that has *Behavior* specifications defined in its namespace. One of these may specify the classifier's behavior itself which will be invoked when an instance of the *BehavioredClassifier* is created. One advantage is that the *Process*'s behavior can be represented by state machines; this adds more control on the *Process* lifecycle. Another advantage, being a *Classifier,* a *Process* can be categorized and can own (encapsulate) other *Classifiers* such as *WorkProducts* as well as *ActivityPerformer* on these *WorkProducts*. A *Process* has a *name* and is governed by a *Lifecycle*. It is composed of *SoftwareActivities*, which extends the UML2.0 *Activity*. A *Process* may be defined by a *meta-process* thanks to the *metaProcAssoc* association. A *SoftwareActivity* may be an *Activity* or a *Phase* depending on the value of the *Kind* attribute.

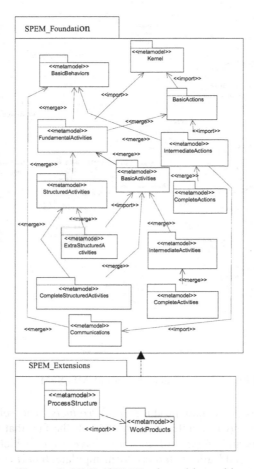

**Figure 2.** UML4SPM Package hierarchies

As mentioned previously, we need to have some features within activity descriptions that help in monitoring and in getting metrics on development processes. Thus, we define a new property named *weigh* within *SoftwareActivity*.

It represents its importance in the development process (e.g. collecting user's requirements = 30%) and a *TimeLimit* class linked to the *SoftwareActivity* class with the *starts at, ends at* associations and witch represents time estimations defined by the team. Based on these metrics, project managers may affect more time and resources to *Activities* having a high *weight*. A *SoftwareActivity* contains *Actions*. An *Action* takes a set of inputs and converts them into a set of outputs, though either or both sets may be empty. Input to, respectively, output from, an *Action* is a typed element. It represents the *Pin* of the *Action*. A *Pin* is typed by a *Classifier*. A *SoftwareActivity* has one or more *ActivityPerformer* who are in charge of the *SoftwareActivity* and more particularly of *Actions* owned by it. An *ActivityPerformer* can be a *ResponsibleRole* or a *SoftwareTool* (i.e. compilers, model transformation engines...). A *ResponsibleRole* describes the rights and responsibilities of the *Human* who will be in charge of the *Activity*. A *Human* may be an agent or a team; it has a *name*, a *skill(s)* and an

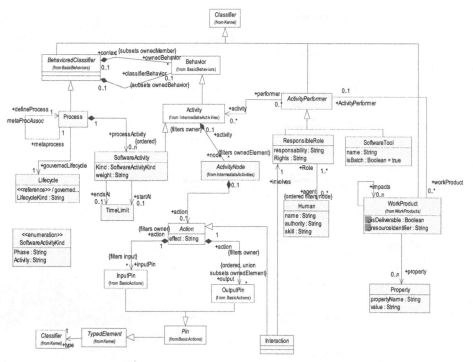

**Figure 3**. A global overview of UML4SPM

*authority. Actions* consume and produce *WorkProducts*. The relation between an *Action* and *WorkProducts* it handles is made through the fact that *WorkProducts* are *Classifiers* and *Inputs* and *Outputs* of an *Action* have a type which is specified by a *Classifier* too. This would allow *Actions* to manipulate *WorkProducts* as easily as calling a method while passing it parameters in usual OO programming languages.

### WorkProducts Package

A *WorkProduct* is the specification of a physical piece of information that is produced, consumed, or modified by a software process. In UML4SPM, we decide to add a new property to the *WorkProduct* class, the *resourceIdentifier* property (figure 4). It represents a unique identifier of the *WorkProduct* and helps in its localization. Then, during process executions, it should be up to a naming service to resolve the identifier in order to locate the *WorkProduct*. *WorkProduct* is specified as a concrete class. It may have *Properties* defined by a *name* and a *value*. This adds more flexibility (see figure 4). Thus, developers could specify new *WorkProducts* with specific properties depending on their needs. The modification of a *WorkProduct* may affect one or more *WorkProducts*. This property is defined thanks to the *impacts* association.

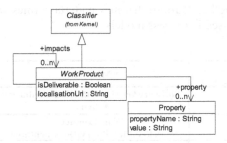

**Figure 4.** The WorkProducts package

*Additional Actions*

As pointed out earlier, a software development process can't be fully automated. Developer involvements are necessary during development phases. Considering this need of human interactions, we add the concept of *Interaction*. An *Interaction* is an *Action*. It involves a *ResponsibleRole* and is associated with a *Guide* in order to help *ResponsibleRole* in taking decisions and guides its design choices (see above figure 3). Finally, having in mind that processes may need some tool facilities during execution-time, we decide to extend the *Actions* model. The *CallToolServiceAction* is a *CallAction* (see figure 5). It has *InputPins* which represent the arguments of the call and *OutputPins* as call results. We make the assumption that a *ToolService* has a *name* and a set of typed parameters. One constrain on the *CallToolServiceAction*, would be that *CallToolServiceAction* arguments fits to *ToolService* parameters (in number and type). The model of the tool (list of services, parameters of services, binding mode...) is outside the scope of this work [3].

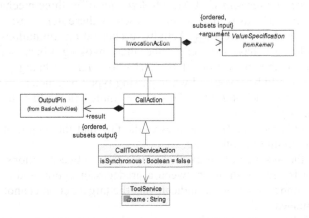

**Figure 5.** The CallToolServiceAction

**4.2    Comparison of UML4SPM with Respect to Basic Process Model Elements**

Table 3 compares UML4SPM elements with basic process model elements introduced in Section 2. The concept of **Tool** (*SoftwareTool*) which will be in charge of performing activities as well as **Human** that may undertake roles within the software process can now be expressed in process models.

| Basic Process model Elements | UML4SPM |
|---|---|
| Activity | SoftwareActivity with Kind attribute= Activity |
| Product | WorkProduct (Model/Guide/Library/Documentation) |
| Role | ResponsibleRole |
| Human | Human |
| Tool | SoftwareTool |
| Evolution support | Only static evolution. Dynamic evolution as further work |

**Table 3.** Comparison of primary process elements with UML4SPM

## 4.3    Evaluation of UML4SPM Towards Primary PMLs Requirements

In this section, we only address requirements that were lacking by SPEM1.1. As a first stage, we particularly focus on *Expressiveness, Modularization, Executability* and *Formality. Reflection* will be addressed in a further work. Requirements for *Understandability,      Abstraction,      Analyzability* and *Multiple     conceptual perspectives/views* are taking into account since UML4SPM, as SPEM1.1, is UML based (cf. Section 3.3).

• **Expressiveness**: In SPEM1.1 the ability to orchestrate process *Activities* and *Steps* was ensured thanks to the *Precedes* dependency. Kinds of precedence were: *start-start, finish-start or finish-finish.* UML2.0 *Activities* offer three mechanisms for the orchestration of *Activities* as well as *Actions* owned by these *Activities*:
- The *CallBehaviorAction* overcomes Activity orchestration limitations. It is a *callAction* that invokes a behavior directly rather than invoking a behavioral feature that, in turn, results in the invocation of that behavior. *Activity* being a *Behavior*, therefore, an *Activity* could be invocated while passing typed parameters to be treated by *Actions* owned by the *Activity*. This adds more flexibility for *Activity* orchestrations (figure 6).
- *Object flow* connects object nodes. It expresses the fact that the output of an action could be used like an input of another one.
- *Control flow*: In the absence of an explicit *object flow* between actions, a *control flow* indicates an ordering constraint between a predecessor action and a successor action. It explicitly connects *Actions* to indicate that the target action cannot start until the source action finishes.
- Concerning flexibility, decision points are not taken into account by SPEM1.1. UML2.0 offers the possibility to specify decision points thanks to *DecisionNodes*. A *Decision Node* is a *Control Node* that chooses between outgoing flows in order to invoke the appropriate behavior. *Guards* are fixed on those flows to drive behavior invocations. In order to express concurrency as well as synchronization, UML2.0 defines respectively, *ForkNode* and *JoinNode*. A *ForkNode* splits a flow into multiple concurrent flows while a *JoinNode* synchronizes them.

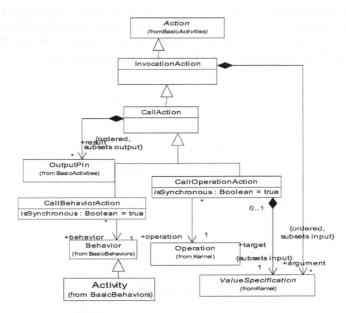

**Figure 6.** The CallBehaviorAction for Activity orchestrations

- The UML2.0 *Activity* metamodel defines seven levels with increasing expressiveness: *FundamentalActivities, BasicActivities, IntermediateActivities, CompleteActivities, StructuredActivities, CompleteStructured-Activities, and ExtraStructuredActivities.* The fundamental level defines activities as containing nodes, which includes actions. The second level i.e. *IntermediateActivities* provides the way to specify *concurrency* and *synchronization* through *ControlNodes* (*ForkNode, JoinNode*).

This would allow activities to be launched concurrently or for an activity before starting, to wait for other activity completions. The *StructuredActivities* level supports modelling of traditional structured programming constructs, such as loops and conditionals, as an addition to the basic non-structured activity sequencing.
- In UML2.0 *Activity* metamodel, another facility is offered to process modelers. It is about how to support exception handling during *Action* executions. This is ensured within the ("*ExtraStructuredActivities*") level. As in programming languages, an *Action* can be handled by exception handlers.
- Finally, the lack of some process model elements (tool, human), of human interaction, of explicit *WorkProduct* and features for process metrics was addressed while defining UML4SPM (see Section 4.1).
• **Modularization**: When SPEM1.1 offers process component compositions through *unification* procedure, UML2.0 provides a more powerful way to deal with that.
Let's have two *Process Components* PC1 and PC2 (see figure 7). PC1 is in charge to realize a UML class diagram. PC2 has to transform a UML Class Diagram to a Relational Database Diagram. These two processes were specified separately, so *WorkProducts* and *roles* might have different names. If a process modeler decides to

compose these two process components, he will have to unify output-WorkProducts from PC1(i.e., *ClassD*) in order to be in conformity with inputs-WorkProducts of PC2(i.e., *UmlCD*). Likewise, he has to explicitly link activities from PC2 within PC1. Because of these limitations, *unification* procedure can't be automated.

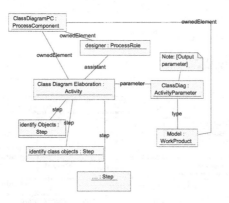

*PC1: Class Diagram Process Component*

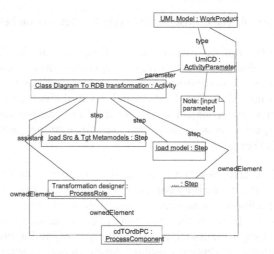

*PC2: Class DiagramToRDBTransformation Process Component*

**Figure 7.** Two SPEM1.1 process components

Considering that a UML2.0 *Activity* can define an internally consistent process, Activities can be seen as a *Process Components*. The UML2.0 *CallBehaviorAction* allows to *Activities* to be interconnected in a practical way. The advantage of this construct is that *Activity* behaviors are invoked as it is done for methods in classical programming languages. Making this way, modelers don't have to carry out the *unification* of PC1 outputs with PC2 inputs. In Java for instance, parameters of a method call can have another name in the operation signature. *CallBehaviorAction* being a *CallAction,* casting of parameters is done implicitly when activities are invoked thanks to the abstraction given by *InputPins* and *OutputPins* concepts. The previous example is used in order to demonstrate how *CallBehaviorAction* allows process component compositions see figure 8.Shaded boxes of the figure represent the "class diagram realization" *Activity*. In the figure we can see how output of an *Action* (i.e., a *ClassDiagram*) can be used as an input of *CallBehaviorAction*. The lighted boxes of the figure represent "*ClassDiagram-ToRDBTransformation*" *Activity*. The two activities are interconnected thanks to *ActivityParameterNode* and no unification procedure is needed. Then, process component compositions (Activities composition in this case) can be automated. They can even be specified at execution-time. This offers more flexibility and spares many efforts to process modelers.

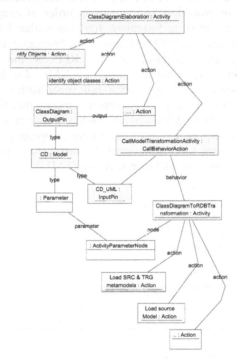

**Figure 8.** Activity interconnections thanks to CallBehaviorAction.

- **Executability**: In UML2.0, the intent of *Activity* construct has changed fairly radically from UML1.x. Activities are not only used to model processes, they also now have some features necessary to support the automation of these processes [36]. Comparing the UML2.0 *Activity* and *Action* constructs with those of SPEM1.1 *WorkDefinition* (more particularly the *Activity*) and *Step* respectively, we found some significant variations. While an activity *Step* in SPEM1.1 is just defined by a name (e.g. Check for model consistency), UML2.0 offers the possibility to specify *inputs* of the *Action*, its *effect* on these inputs and the *outputs* resulting of the action execution. We illustrate this in an example in figure 9. *CallOperationAction* is an *Action* that transmits an operation call request to the target object, where it may cause the invocation of associated behavior. As additional features, *CallOperationAction* specifies the operation to be invoked by the action execution as well as the target object to which the request is sent. Besides, UML2.0 offers four *Actions* packages (*BasicActions, IntermediateActions, Structured Actions* and *CompleteActions*) in order to express most semantic of executable actions that we can find in programming languages (*CallAction, LinkAction, CreateObjectAction, StructuralFeatureAction, ValueSepcification-Action* and so on). Thus, the specification of software process models with executable action semantics is rendered possible. By the same way, the rigorous semantics given to *Actions* within the new UML2.0 standard tends to be more precise than previous versions of UML. Indeed, the *Activity* and *Action* constructs in UML2.0 are more sophisticated than *Activity* and *Step* in SPEM1.1 This facility makes possible the automation of mapping software process models towards programming languages or workflow formalisms in order to execute them. Some works was already done as intent to formalize *Activities* within UML2.0 [13] [36]. Furthermore, the OMG issues a new RFP (Request For Proposal) named: *Executable UML Foundation* [33]. The objective of this RFP is the definition of a computationally complete and compact subset of UML 2.0 to be known as "Executable UML Foundation", along with a full specification of the execution semantics of this subset. "Computationally complete" means that the subset shall be sufficiently expressive to allow definition of models that can be executed on a computer either through interpretation or as equivalent computer programs generated from the models through some kind of automated transfor-mations. We believe that all these efforts will reduce the lack of **Formality** in SPEM1.1.

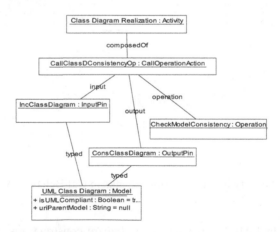

**Figure 9.** Instance of CallOperationAction

Table 4 summarizes the result of comparing UML4SPM with basic PML requirements. As we can notice, our metamodel overcomes major SPEM1.1 lacks requirements of *Understan-dability, Abstraction, Analyzability and Multiple conceptual perspectives/views* are fulfilled as UML4SPM is UML based.

| Basic PML Requirements | SPEM1.1 | UML4SPM |
|---|---|---|
| Formality | -Lacks of a precise semantic of some elements (e.g. *Step, ProcessPerformer*). | -Formality provided thanks to the precise and executable semantics of *Actions* within UML2.0 |
| Expressiveness | -Lacks of some process model elements (Human, Tool and Evolution Support); <br> -Lacks of efficient mechanism for *Activity* and *Step* orchestrations; <br> -*WorkProducts* are used as parameters of *Activties* and not of *Steps*(useless for process automation); <br> -Lacks of explicit *WorkProducts* (models, libraries…); <br><br> -Lacks of human interactions and decision points <br><br> -Lacks of some features on process elements in order to capture process metrics, exceptions; | -*SoftwareTool* and *Human* elements provided to overcome this lack <br> -Three mechanisms for *Action* and *Activity* orchestrations: *Control Flow, Object Flow* and the *CallBeaviorAction*. <br> - *WorkProducts* are used as typed parameters by *Actions;* <br> -Definition of explicit *WorkProduct* (*Model, Guide, Library and Documentation*); *urilLocalization* attribute for *WorkProducts*; *WorkProduct* as a concrete class with the possibility to specify new properties. <br> - Class *Interaction* defined for human decisions as well as *Decision, Fork and Join Nodes* thanks to UML2.0 <br> - *TimeLimit, SoftwareActivity weight* for process metrics; the possibility to handle exceptions thanks to *ExceptionHandler* in *ExtraStructuredActivities* |
| Modularization | -Lacks of *ProcessComponent* compositions mechanism. Need of a *Unification* mechanism. | -*Process Component* composition/integration thanks to the *CallBehaviorAction* from/to *Activities* |
| Executability | -SPEM1.1 models are not executable. It was outside the scope of the specification. | -Use/extends of *Activities* and *Actions* packages of UML2.0 makes possible the specification of executable software process models |
| Reflection | -Lacks | - Will be addressed in a further work. |

**Table 4.** Comparison of UML4SPM with PML requirements and with SPEM1.1 lacks

# 5    Related Work

In this Section, we only deal with existing approaches that extend the UML meta-model for software process modelling. Taxonomy of recent PMLs is given in [39]. In PROMENADE [12], a UML metamodel is extended to allow modeling of both the static and the dynamic aspects of software processes. The static aspect of software processes is given by means of a conceptual model. It defines the elements that participate in a software PMs and which extend UML ones. The dynamic aspect of software processes consists of the way in which model is enacted (e.g. the ordering of tasks). PROMENADE introduced both proactive control-flow (e.g., enactment of some actions according to pre-establish plan) and reactive control-flow (e.g., enactment of some actions in response to events). Authors were induced to introduce these mechanisms in order to deal with the lack of expressiveness in UML1.4 activity diagrams [31]. Nevertheless, PROMENADE does not provide the possibility to specify *Tasks* with executable semantics. It lacks of evolution support as well as of the *Interaction* element (i.e., human intervention) which is primordial due to the variability and no-rigidity nature of software processes.

[18] Presents an approach which describes in UML, the dynamic part of the model using class diagrams with stereotyped associations for showing the control and data flow. The metamodel is defined by attaching stereotypes to model elements. However, stereotypes and other UML extension mechanisms have proven several

limitations in order to define a metamodel. A well-known is the lack of standard semantics. As in [18], [22] proposes the use of the stereotype mechanism of UML to extend activity diagrams in the context of business process modelling. The new diagrams can express the required activity properties (computer support to the activity, duration...) but no new control paradigm is provided. In [17], authors select class and state diagrams as main constructs to describe processes. Tasks are represented as objects that can be created and manipulated as needed. Activities (tasks) are represented as "task packages" which encapsulate the interface of a task (i.e., offered behavior) and "realization packages" which define how the task is realized in terms of other lower level tasks. In the corresponding class diagrams, stereotypes are used to represent the input and output of each task, as well as the flow of control and data between tasks which is missing in UML1.4 activity diagrams. The internal behavior of tasks is described by a predetermined and un-modifiable state diagram. Compared to previous approaches, this one is clearly more focused on adapting UML to the capabilities and semantics of the virtual machine that will be used to enact the process. Therefore, the process is described at a low level of abstraction. However, it is not apparent how roles that participate in the process are described and how they are associated to the various activities to be executed, or how possible parallelisms between activities, synchronizations and decision points are expressed. This, together with the replacement of activity diagrams with massively stereotyped class diagrams makes the resulting process description less natural for UML users. In [8] Di Nitto et at., propose a formalization of the semantics of the UML subset and present the translation of UML process models into code, which can be enacted in a process-centered environment. However, as in PROMENADE, authors did not consider modeling the interface with human agents and/or the development tools used in the process. Likewise, no semantics for executable actions is defined in PM

# 6    Conclusion

One important challenge in the area of software process modelling is the development of a standard PML. As principal requirements, the PML has to promote expressiveness, understandability, and executability. In this paper, we introduced a UML2.0-based metamodel for software process modelling named: UML4SPM. It extends a subset of UML2.0 by adding constructs and semantics required for defining process models. We compared it with primary PMLs requirements. UML4SPM has proven that it fulfils all of them except *Reflection*, which will be addressed in a further work. As a result, it allows the specification of understandable process models with executable action semantics. Another contribution of this work was the identification of SPEM1.1 limitations and advantages which may help in the next revision of the standard, namely: SPEM2.0. One perspectives of this work is to address the *Reflection* requirement in UML4SPM. Then, a case study will be elaborated and evaluated within the MODELWARE project [25], which this work is part of. We will also investigate the possible use of a UML virtual machine in order to execute UML4SPM process models.

# 7 References

[1] Ambriola V., Conradi R. and Fuggetta A. *"Experiences and Issues in Building and Using Process centered Software Engineering Environments"*, Internal draft paper, Politecnico di Milano, September 1994.

[2] ANSI/IEEE Std 1012-1986, *"IEEE Standard for Software Verification and Validation Plans"*, The Institute of Electrical and Electronics Engineers, Inc., February 10, 1987.

[3] Blanc X., Gervais M.P., and Sriplakich P. *"Model Bus: Towards the Interoperability of Modelling Tools"*, in Proc. of the Model Driven Architecture: Foundations and Applications (MDAFA 2004), Linköping University, Sweden, June 2004.

[4] Conradi R., Fernström C., Fuggetta A. and Snowdon R. *"Towards a Reference Framework for Process Concepts"*, in Proc. Of the 2nd European Workshop on Software Process Technology (EWSPT'92), Trondheim, Norway, September 1992, LNCS Vol. 635.

[5] Conradi R., Liu C. *"Process Modelling Languages: One or Many?"*, in Proc. of the 4th European Workshop on Software Process Technology (EWSPT'95), Noordwijkerhout, The Netherlands, April 1995, LNCS, Vol. 913.

[6] Curtis B., Kellner M., and Over J. *"Process Modelling"*, Communications of the ACM Vol. 35, Num. 9, September 1992.

[7] Derniame J.C., Kaba B.A. and Wastell D. *"Process Modelling Languages"*: in *"Software Process: Principles, Methodology, and Technology"*, LNCS Vol. 1500/1999.

[8] Di Nitto E. et at. *"Deriving executable process descriptions from UML"*, in Proc. of the 24th Inter. Conf. on Software Engineering (ICSE'02), Orlando, Florida 2002, ACM Press.

[9] Evans A.S., S.Kent. *"Meta-modelling semantics of UML: the pUML approach"*, in Proc. of the 2nd Inter. Conf. on the Unified Modelling Language, 1999, Colorado, LNCS Vol. 1723.

[10] Feiler P.H., Humphrey Watts. S. *"Software process development and enactment"*, in Proc. of 2nd Inter. Conf. on the Software Process, Berlin, 1993, IEEE Computer Society Press.

[11] FIPS PUB 132, *"Guideline for Software Verification and Validation Plans"*, U.S. Department of Commerce/National Bureau of Standards (U.S.), November 19, 1987.

[12] Franch X., Ribó J. M. *"Using UML for Modelling the Static Part of a Software Process"*, in Proc. of UML '99, Forth Collins CO, USA, LNCS, Vol.1723.

[13] Hausmann J.H., Störrle H., *"Towards a Formal Semantics of UML 2.0 Activities"*, in Proc. of the German Software Engineering Conference (SE'05).

[14] Humphrey Watts S. *"Process Models in Software Engineering"*, Encyclopedia of Software Engineering, 2nd Edition, John Wiley and Sons, Inc, New York, December 2001.

[15] Humphrey Watts S. *"The Software Engineering Process: Definition and Scope"*, in Proc. of the 4th International Software Process Workshop on Representing and Enacting the Software Process, Devon, United Kingdom, 1989.

[16] Jaccheri M.L., Baldi M., Divitini M., *"Evaluating the Requirements for Software Process Modelling Languages and Systems"*, in Proc. of Process support for Distributed Team-based Software Development (PDTSD'99), Orlando, Florida, USA, August 1999.

[17] Jager D., Schleicher A., and Westfechtel B. *"Using UML for Software Process Modelling"*, in Proc. of ESEC/FSE'99,Toulouse, France, LNCS Vol.1687, September 1999.

[18] Jäger D., Schleicher A., Westfechtel B." *Object-Oriented Software Process Modeling"*, in the Proc. of the 7th European Software Engineering Conference (ESEC), Toulouse, September 1999.

[19] JMI1.0, *"Java Metadata Interface Specification"*, Java Community process document JSR040, June 2002, at http://www.jcp.org.

[20] Kent S. *"Model Driven Engineering"*, in Proc. of the 3rd Inter. Conf. on Formal Method (IFM 2002), Turku, Finland, May 2002, LNCS Vol. 2335.

[21] Lonchamp J. *"A structured conceptual and terminological framework for software process engineering"*, in Proc. of the $2^{nd}$ Inter.1 Conf. on Software Process, Berlin, 1993, IEEE Computer Society Press.

[22] McLeod, G. *"Extending UML for Entreprise and Business Process Modeling"*, in Proc. of the UML 98' Workshop, Mulhouse, France (1998).

[23] MDA. *"Model Driven Architecture (MDA)"*, OMG TC document ormsc/2001-07-01, July 2001, at http://www.omg.org.

[24] Mellor S. J., Balcer M. J., Balcer M. *"Executable UML: A Foundation for Model-Driven Architecture"*, Pearson Education, July 2002.

[25] MODELWARE Project, at http://www.modelware-ist.org

[26] MOF 1.4. *"Meta-Object Facility"*, OMG document formal/2002-04-03, April 2002, at http://www.omg.org.

[27] Montangero C., Derniame J.C., and Kaba B.A., Warboys B. *"The software process: Modelling and technology"*, LNCS GmbH. Vol. 1500/1999.

[28] Osterweil L., *"Software Processes Are Software Too"* in Proc. of the 9th Inter. Conf. on Software Engineering (ICSE'9), New York, 1987, ACM Press.

[29] Perry D. E., Editor, *Proc. of the 5th Inter. Software Process Workshop (ISPW'5)*, Kennebunkport, Maine, USA, October 1989, IEEE Computer Society Press.

[30] Raistrick C., Francis P. and Wright J. *"Model Driven Architecture With Executable UML"*, Cambridge University Press, March 2004.

[31] Ribó J. M., Franch X. *" A Precedence-based Approach for Proactive Control in Software Process Modelling"*, in Proc. of the Conf. on Software Engineering and Knowledge Engineering (SEKE-2002), Ischia (Italy), ACM Press, September 2002.

[32] Riehle D., et at. *"The Architecture of a UML Virtual Machine"*, n Proc. of the 2001 Conf. on Object-Oriented Programming Systems, Languages, and Applications (OOPSLA '01), ACM Press, 2001.

[33] Semantics of a Foundational Subset for Executable UML Models RFP, *OMG document ad/05-04-02*, April 2005, at: http://www.omg.org/docs/ad/05-04-02.pdf, page last visit June 17, 2005

[34] SPEM1.1, *"Software Process Engineering Metamodel"*, OMG document formal/02-11/14, November 2002, at http://www.omg.org.

[35] SPEM2.0 RFP, *"Software Process Engineering Metamodel"*, OMG document ad/2004-11-04, November 2004, at http://www.omg.org/docs/ad/04-11-04.pdf, page last visit April 4, 2005.

[36] Störrle H. *"Semantics of UML2.0 Activities with Data-Flow"*, in Proc. of the Visual Languages and Formal Methods Workshop (VLFM'04), Rome, Italy, Septembre 2004.

[37] UML2.0 Superstructure, *"Unified Modelling Language"*, adopted specification, OMG document ptc/04-10-02, October 2004, at http://www.omg.org.

[38] UML1.4, *"Unified Modelling Language"*, OMG document formal/01-09-67, September 2001, at http://www.omg.org.

[39] Zameli, K. Z., Lee, P.A. *"Taxonomy of Process Modelling Languages"*, in Proc. of the ACS/IEEE Inter. Conf. on Computer Systems and Applications (AICCSA'01) Beirut, Lebanon, June 2001.

# Realizing Model Driven Security for Inter-organizational Workflows with WS-CDL and UML 2.0

## Bringing Web Services, Security and UML Together

Michael Hafner, Ruth Breu

Universität Innsbruck, Institut für Informatik, Techniker Straße 21a,
A – 6020 Innsbruck
{m.hafner, ruth.breu}@uibk.ac.at

**Abstract.** The growing popularity of standards related to Web services, Web services security and workflows boosted the implementation of powerful infrastructures supporting interoperability for inter-organizational workflows. Nevertheless, the realization of such workflows is a very complex task, in many aspects still bound to low-level technical knowledge and error-prone. We provide a framework for the realization and the management of security-critical workflows based on the paradigm of Model Driven Security. The framework complies with a hierarchical stack of Web services specifications and related technologies. In this paper, we introduce a UML based approach for the modeling of security-critical inter-organizational workflows and map it to the Web Services Choreography Description Language. Our approach is based on a set of security patterns, which are integrated into UML class and activity diagrams. A tool translates the models into executable artifacts configuring a reference architecture based on Web services.

## 1 Introduction

Collaboration protocols or choreographies specify the communication processes between collaborating partners. Modern businesses and governments implement such processes based on Web services centric architectures. Although Web services security standards, building on SOAP, WSDL, and UDDI provide some guidance for the integration of security into B2B applications and workflows, they remain very close to the technical level and hence almost unintelligible to the domain expert [1].

Even in case of a satisfying implementation of security requirements, the costs of continually adapting workflows to match changing business requirements are very often too high. The workflows remain static. Because of the low level of abstraction, security requirements are often not aligned to the business goals.

Model driven software development is particularly suited to cases, where a plethora of standards and complex technologies require highly specialized technical knowledge for the implementation. Relying on Model Driven Approaches that integrate an array of well-known security protocols, best practices, patterns, and algorithms with formally proven correctness is a matter of cost-effectiveness. The

L. Briand and C. Williams (Eds.): MoDELS 2005, LNCS 3713, pp. 39–53, 2005.

automatic generation of executable software for target architectures allows for an agile approach to the implementation and a responsive high-level management of secure inter-organizational workflows.

We present a UML based modeling language that supports the formal specification of secure inter-organizational workflows in a peer-to-peer environment. Our approach offers a standardized but intuitive means to model graphically collaboration protocols with additional security semantics. As we provide an extensible meta-model, the models can be enriched with workflow and security semantics. As the integration of widespread standards fosters interoperability, we show how the models can systematically be mapped to a choreography standard like the *Web Services Choreography Description language* (WS-CDL) [2]. The actors of an inter-organizational process can take the formal WS-CDL choreography definition to check the compliance of their internal processes to the requirements of the choreography, to generate public interfaces or to control correct proceeding during run-time.

Section 2 provides some background information on Web services standards our work is based upon. We sketch the problem context by introducing an e-government case study and give an overview on related work. In section 3, we present our UML-based framework and map it to the W3C standard WS-CDL. Section 4 gives an outlook and draws a brief conclusion.

## 2     Background

### 2.1     Technologies and Standards

**Model Driven Architecture.** The growing popularity of standards related to Web services, workflows and security fosters the implementation of powerful infrastructures supporting interoperability for inter-organizational workflows. The paradigm of Model Driven Architecture (MDA) makes it possible to realize their full potential. The OMG [3] is promoting the approach of Model Driven Architecture as a means for the reduction of development costs and the improvement of application quality. MDA defines two types of models, a Platform Independent Model (PIM), and a Platform Specific Model (PSM). The PSM describes the system on its intended platform (e.g. J2EE or .Net), whereas the PIM – specified using a well-defined modelling language such as UML - captures the domain level knowledge and abstracts from implementation details of the target PSM. Applying the MDA approach means the transformation of a PIM into a PSM. Model Driven Security Architectures (e.g. [4]) extend the MDA approach in the sense that the PIM integrates security requirements and the PSM specifies the security infrastructure. Security Requirements are mapped onto the platform.

**Web Services Composition.** Businesses provide value-added services through composition of basic or elemental Web services using service composition languages. Often the services are offered by different companies. A Web services composition consists of multiple invocations of other Web services in a specific order. A composition takes the form either of an orchestration or of a choreography. An orchestration describes how Web services interact with each other at the message level, including the business logic and the execution order of the interactions from the viewpoint of the partner controlling the workflow execution. A choreography or a business protocol describes the interaction between business partners in terms of the sequence of messages that are exchanged in a "peer-to-peer" fashion. There is no central control of workflow execution.

The Business Process Execution Language for Web Services (WS-BPEL) is an XML-based language to compose workflows on top of atomic Web services [5]. It provides mechanisms to define executable business processes and, with limitations, abstract business protocols. BPML [7] is quite similar to WS-BPEL as it supports Web services standards, but it is considered as semantically weaker.

Collaboration protocols like WSCI [39], ebXML [8] and WS-CDL [2] provide the means to specify distributed collaborations by offering a global view on collaborating services. ebXML comprises a powerful set of standards for the specification of B2B protocols but it is not compatible to the Web services concept [9].

**Web Services Security.** Currently a comprehensive set of Web services security standards is emerging [6]. OASIS has proposed WS-Security, a security extension built on top of the SOAP Protocol [10]. The extension uses the XML encryption and signature mechanism to add security features to SOAP messages ([11], [12]). This way, security mechanisms can be integrated into the header and the body of a SOAP message, and be sent via any transport channel without compromising security. Beside transport level security extensions, a variety of standards provides means to manage and exchange security policies. XACML [13] is a standard to define access control for resources in a system. Sun has proposed a specific profile for XACML – called Web Services Policy Language - to define the reconcilement of access rights between partners. The Security Assertion Markup Language [14] is a standard for the exchange of security tokens (e.g. Certificates). WS-Policy [15] allows for the definition of protocol level security requirements. WS-Security Policy [40] is a complementary standard to WS-Policy and specifies how actors can assert to potential partners their policies with respect to specific WS-Security mechanisms. WS-Trust [41] enables token interoperability. It provides a request/response protocol for the exchange, the issuance and the validation of security tokens by a trusted third party.

### 2.2 Problem Context

Our research efforts are driven by case studies in various industries. We illustrate our methodology for the systematic design and realization of security-critical inter-organizational workflows with a portion of a workflow-scenario drawn from the e-government use case *"Municipal Tax Collection"* which describes the Web services based interaction between a business agent (the Tax Advisor) and a public service provider (the Municipality).

In Austria, wages paid to employees of an enterprise are subject to the municipal tax. Corporations have to send an annual statement via their tax advisor to the municipality, which in turn is responsible for collecting the tax by the end of March of the following year. The municipality checks the declaration of the annual statement and calculates the tax duties. As a result, a notification with the amount of tax duties is sent to the tax advisor by mail.

We elaborated the case within the project SECTINO, a joint research project between the research group Quality Engineering at the University of Innsbruck and the Austrian Research Centre Seibersdorf. The project's vision was defined as the development of a framework supporting the systematic realization of e-government related workflows with a special emphasis on security requirements. We specified the project's deliverables in terms of prototypical implementations of an MDA framework in an industrial context. The case studies provide valuable practical context for the definition of problems related to Model Driven Security, which are of scientific interest. We identified five major topics of interest to our research agenda:

1. The modeling of distributed inter-organizational business processes
2. The integration of security requirements at an abstract model level
3. The transformation of the "virtual workflow" emerging out of the collaboration between the actors to executable workflow stubs for the distributed nodes
4. The transformation of the security requirements specified at the model level into executable artifacts that configure the reference architecture
5. The specification of a component-based reference architecture that provides the runtime environment based on Web services standards

In [21] and [38], we define the main model views and steps for the development of security-critical inter-organizational business processes (topic 2). In [17] we extend the concepts of Model Driven Architecture to provide Model Driven Security and we provide a detailed description of model dependencies (topic 4). We present the framework for the realization of security-critical workflows by applying it to an e-government project in [16]. In [18] we specify a component-based security architecture integrating several Web services security standards for the realization and management of security-critical workflows (topic 5). We describe the mapping between the models themselves and to the components of the target reference architecture in [19] (topic 3).

In this paper, we describe a UML-based approach for the platform and standards independent modeling of security-critical inter-organizational workflows, thereby tackling the last open issue (topic 1). It takes into account the mapping to standards for the modeling of collaboration protocols – like WS-CDL in our case – as well as the mapping to the technologies of the target reference architecture, which we built on Web services technologies (SOAP, WSDL, BPEL4WS, XACML, etc.).

## 2.3    Related Work

**Workflow.** A big community is currently working on issues related to inter-organizational workflow management systems [24], [25], [26], [27], [28]. A number of contributions discuss standards for specifying service choreographies (e.g., [9], [42]) and propose formal foundations (e.g., [25], [48]). In [9] Bernauer et al. discuss the semantic shortcomings of WSDL-based language concepts and analyze security and workflow semantics related issues that arise when modeling B2B protocols. The paper provides a methodical comparison of WSDL- and ebXML-based approaches.

**Workflow Security.** Security extensions for workflow management systems are treated in [29], [30], [31] and [32] - although at a quite technical level. Some contributions propose approaches for integrating security at different levels of abstraction in the system development cycle, but the full potential of a model driven approach, linking abstract domain-level models to their technical implementation, is not yet exploited ([20], [21].

**Model Driven Security.** A model driven approach that is close to the idea of our framework is [4]. It introduces the concept of Model Driven Security for a software development process that allows for the integration of security requirements through system models and supports the generation of security infrastructures. However, this approach focuses exclusively on business logic, whereas we concentrate on inter-organizational workflow management.

**Tools.** In [22] Mantell describes an implementation, where a local workflow is modeled in a case-tool, exported via XMI-files to a development environment and automatically translated into executable code for a BPEL-Engine based on Web services [23]. Nevertheless, the approach does not provide any facilities for the integration of security requirements at the modeling level nor does it support the specification of global workflows by means of peer-to-peer interactions as suggested by the concept of abstract processes in [5].

## 3  Modeling Inter-organizational Workflow Security with UML

In the following, we give an overview of the UML-based framework (Sect. 3.1). We then focus on the Global Workflow Model, which models the collaboration protocol and integrates the security requirements (Sect. 3.2). We map the generic, language independent UML-framework to the WS-CDL, a language for the specification of collaboration protocols (Sect. 3.3).

### 3.1  Model Views and Reference Architecture

**Model Views.** We define a *workflow* as a network of partners cooperating in a controlled way by calling services and exchanging documents. Our approach is based on two orthogonal views: the *Interface View* and the *Workflow View* (Figure 1a). The latter is further divided into the *Global Workflow Model* (GWfM) specifying the message exchange protocol between cooperating partners as well as additional requirements related to security or quality of service and the *Local Workflow Model* (LWfM) that describes an executable process. In practical terms, this means that the partners agree on a particular workflow scenario by specifying the messages they exchange and the services which every one of them agreed to contribute to the "virtual" global workflow in compliance with additional constraints (e.g., security requirements). In this way – through peer-to-peer interaction – the local workflows should exactly realize the behavior as specified in the GWfM. Formal approaches based on Petri Nets prove the consistency of the overall process [33].

The *Interface View* represents a contractual agreement between the parties to provide a set of services based on the minimum set of technical and domain level constraints and thereby links the GWfM to the LWfM. It describes the interface of every partner independently of its usage scenario and consists of four sub-models: the *Role*, the *Interface*, the *Access* and the *Document Model*. The *Document Model* is a

UML class diagram describing the data type view of the partner. We talk of documents because we do not interpret this class diagram in the usual object oriented setting but in the context of XML schema [35]. The *Interface* Model contains a set of abstract (UML-) operations representing services the component offers to its clients. The types of the parameters are either basic types or classes in the Document Model. Additionally, pre- and post-conditions (in OCL style) may specify the behavior of the abstract services. The *Role Model* describes the roles having access to the services. The *Access Model* describes the conditions under which a certain role has the permission to call a service. The permissions are written in SECTET-PL [44] in a predicative style over the structures of the Document Model. We provide an in-depth view on model dependencies in [16].

The GWfM and the models of the Interface View carry all information needed by the security components in the hosting environments at the partner nodes to implement their part of the workflow, the LWfM. In the present paper, we assume that the partners have already implemented the application logic according to some LWfM and made it available through a Web service interface.

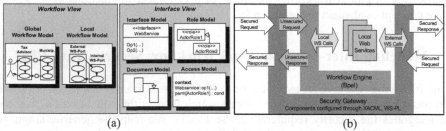

(a)                                                      (b)

**Fig. 1.** UML Model Views (a) and Schematic View on Target Architecture (b)

**Target Reference Architecture.** The overall architecture is based on the data-flow model of XACML [13]. The target architecture (Figure 1b) wraps a set of local Web services that implement the workflow. Since we strongly focus our approach on Web services technologies, which is a widespread technology with strong vendor support, we consider WS-BPEL as an appropriate standard to model executable processes. A workflow engine, based on WS-BPEL (as e.g. BizTalk from Microsoft) orchestrates the sequence of calls to local and external services as specified by the LWfM.

In order to guarantee the secure exchange of messages between cooperating partners, security components "wrap" the workflow engine. Depending on its functionality, every security component implements a specific Web services security standard. At the core, a security gateway takes care of implementing requirements related to message integrity, confidentiality and non-repudiation. It intercepts incoming SOAP messages and applies basic security processing to the message structure. It extracts tokens from the inbound SOAP messages, decrypts elements and checks the validity of signatures. Accordingly, the gateway adds tokens to, encrypts and signs elements in outbound messages according to some security policy as specified in the GWfM. The component implements standards like XML-Encryption, XML-Digital signature and WS-Security. After the basic processing, the gateway queries a Policy Decision Point in order to check inbound messages for compliance to the security requirements. The Policy Decision Point is configured via XACML policy files. Interacting with other security components, the gateway provides authentication facilities, checks for authorization depending on dynamic constraints, establishes a message-level security context and provides logging facilities. All configuration data for the security components is generated from the respective models views. We provide technical details on the target architecture in [18].

## 3.2  Modeling Secure Inter-Organizational Workflows

In the following section, we show how a security-critical, inter-organizational workflow is modeled with an intuitive graphical notation based on a set of platform independent UML 2.0 diagrams [34]. Activity and class diagrams are used to define the GWfM (3.2.1) and its orthogonal view the Interface Model (3.2.2). In Section 3.3 we map the models to WS-CDL, a Web services based standard for the specification of collaboration protocols.

### 3.2.1  The Global Workflow Model

The GWfM captures information required by a collaboration protocol standard like WS-CDL or BPSS / ebXML. Figure 2 shows the document exchange between the two public service providers. The exchange has to comply with the security requirements of confidentiality, integrity and non-repudiation. In the sequel, key words describing workflow semantics are in **boldface Times,** UML 2.0 elements are in *boldface, italicized Times* and technical syntax is in `Courier`.

**Partners** are modeled as *Swimlanes*. **Actions** correspond to business logic at a partner node, which either is made accessible to the outside through Web services interfaces or makes calls to some partner's interface. Sequences orchestrate actions by a *Control Flow* and represent a workflow local to the partner node. Internal processing steps of the local workflow at the partner nodes remain hidden. **Interactions** in Web services based environments have the semantics of remote procedure calls, where one partner requests a service that another one may provide. In the GWfM they are always depicted as crossing domain boundaries and are modeled as a *Message Flow* crossing the swimlanes from the party calling the service to the one offering it. They start with a send action on the calling partner's side and end with a receive action on the provider's side. In case of a synchronous invocation, where the control flow is blocked until he gets an answer from the service provider, the receive action on the caller's side is omitted. The message flow returns to the initial send action which in turn is handed back the control flow. **Messages** travel as instances of XML-documents through an *Object Node,* which acts as their logical container. The security requirements integrity, confidentiality and non-repudiation qualify the instance of the message (or parts of it) flowing in the specific interaction. The *Value Specification* of the constraint consists of attributes assigned to a document node corresponding to the document parts to be encrypted and signed.

The security requirements are assigned to object nodes and described in the form of navigation expression through the associated document model (red boxes in figure 2). In general, the requirement of confidentiality is associated with one or more document nodes. It carries information about permissions to view the information, as the security gateway encrypts the node with the corresponding public key of the recipient. Accordingly, integrity means that the gateway signs the document at the domain boundaries, whereas non-repudiation triggers a protocol, which requires the gateways to exchange signed message receipts.

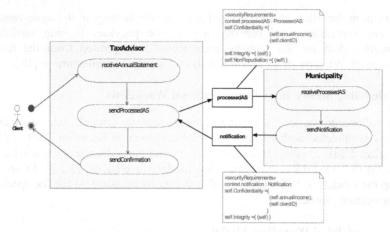

**Fig. 2.** Global Workflow Model with Security Requirements

### 3.2.2     Interface Model

The Interface View describes the partner nodes as components offering a set of services with given properties and permissions. The four sub-models correspond to the public part of the local application logic, which is accessible to the inter-organizational workflow. Table 1 shows the mappings of the model elements of the Interface View to their representation in UML.

**Table 1.** Model Elements of InterfaceView Mapped to UML Stereotypes.

| InterfaceView Model Type | UML Model Element | UML Stereotype |
| --- | --- | --- |
| InterfaceView | Package | <<interfaceView>> |
| InterfaceModel | Package | <<interfaceModel>> |
| Interface | Class | <<interface>> |
| RoleModel | Package | <<roleModel>> |
| Role | Class | <<role>> |
| DocumentModel | Package | <<documentModel>> |
| MessageTypeModel | Package | <<messageType>> |
| Message | Class | <<messageType>> |
| DocumentTypeModel | Package | <<documentType>> |
| Document | Class | <<documentType>> |
| DataTypeModel | Package | <<dataType>> |
| Information | Classe | <<dataType>> |
| AccessModel | Constraint | <<accessConstraint>> |

Figure 3(a) represents the InterfaceView with the document exchange (`processedAS` and `notification`) in the interaction `sendProcessedAS` between the roles `TaxAdvisor` and `Municipality` as specified in the GWfM (Fig. 2). In this case, the Municipality implements the **AS_Service** interface. The Tax Advisor implements the callback interface **AS_Callback** for receiving the `notification`. The Document Model in Figure 3(b) represents the data type view of a component's interface.

The model consists of three conceptual layers. The Data and the Document Layer model the application data relevant to the domain modeler. The Data Layer adds facilities to reference information units of a document and specifies datatypes (e.g., client ID), that are the building blocks for the document layer (e.g., annual statement).

The Message Layer adds technical information to the message body. Protocol-specific message classes (e.g. SOAP Envelope, Header and Body) are referenced through stereotyped classes. For example a <<soapHeader>> class carries technical, protocol and security related information that is used by the security infrastructure (routing information, security tokens, encryption algorithms etc.) using the SOAP protocol. Message Layer information is usually generated and added during the transformation process and remains hidden to the business analyst.

Instances of the Document Model correspond to the messages traveling between the actors in the GWfM. Security requirements at this level of abstraction involve the support of a role model and the specification of access rights for particular Web service operations. We describe access rights formally and platform-independently using an OCL dialect. The predicative specification is transformed into an XACML-policy file via automatic generation. A more detailed description of the corresponding sub models can be found in [36].

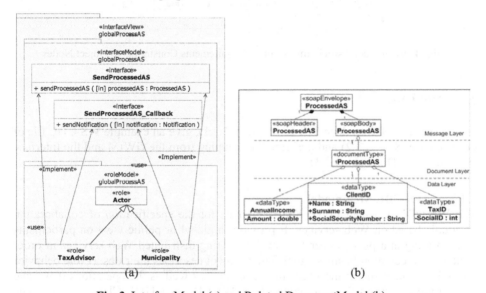

**Fig. 3.** InterfaceModel (a) and Related DocumentModel (b)

### 3.2.3    Integrating Security into the GWfM

The security requirements integrity, confidentiality and non-repudiation are associated with the *Object Node* (see figure 2 in section 3.2.1). Hence, they only qualify the document instance flowing in the specific interaction.

The *Value Specification* of the constraint consists of attributes assigned to a set of element nodes, which correspond to the document parts to be encrypted and signed. Figure 4 shows the metamodel for the integration of the basic security requirements confidentiality, integrity and non-repudiation into the GWfM. A *Constraint* stereotyped **<<SecurityRequirements>>** is associated to the constrained element *Object Node*, which acts as a container for a message instance. The *Value Specification* of the constraint consists of attributes assigned to a set of element nodes corresponding to the document parts to be encrypted and signed. Every requirement may be associated with one or more document nodes.

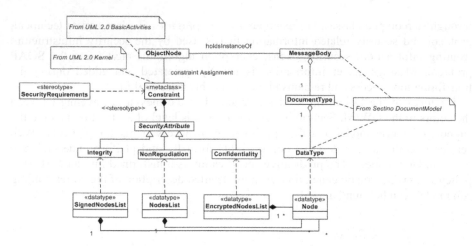

**Fig. 4.** Metamodel Associating Security Requirements Constraints to Object Nodes

### 3.3   WS-CDL

In this section, we introduce WS-CDL (Sect. 3.3.1), give an example WS-CDL file of our use case (Sect. 3.3.2) and describe the mapping from the GWfM and the Interface View to WS-CDL (Sect. 3.3.3).

#### 3.3.1   WS-CDL Metamodel

The WS-CDL is a declarative XML-language for the specification of collaboration protocols based on Web services. It provides a global or public view on participants collaborating in a peer-to-peer fashion by offering distributed Web services in order to achieve a common business goal. The protocol describes their observable behavior through the order of the messages they exchange as well as the operations they have offer. Figure 5 shows the main concepts of WS-CDL as a UML Class Diagram. The `Package` element is the root of every chorography definition. A Choreography Package aggregates a set of WS-CDL type definitions and provides a namespace for the definitions. It contains eight basic entities. In the following, we confine ourselves to those basic entities and concepts that are necessary to capture the information in the Interface and GWfM of our use case scenario (grey shaded boxes in Figure 5).

The core of every collaboration is defined by the `Choreography` entity, which specifies a set of peer-to-peer interactions. The `Interaction` element is the basic building block of a choreography. It participates in a `RelationshipType` referencing the two partners via `RoleTypes` (the sender is specified as `FromRole` and the receiver as `ToRole`) and declares the interaction pattern in an `Action` attribute (`Request` or `Response`) and the name of the `Operation` associated with this interaction. The `Exchange` element describes the message flow between two parties by associating specific WS-CDL–functions inside an Xpath-expression to a `Variable` of type as declared in `InformationType`, which references either a WSDL Message Type or a Schema Element.

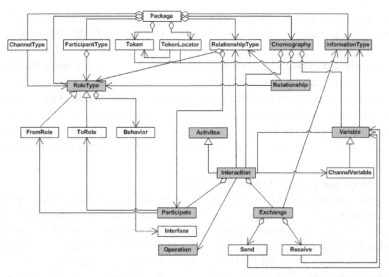

**Fig. 5.** Class Diagram Showing Relationships of WS-CDL Entities

### 3.3.2   WS-CDL Example

Taking our example choreography "Municipal Tax Collection", listing 1 shows the main concepts of WS-CDL in two parts:    the *package information* and the *choreography definition*.

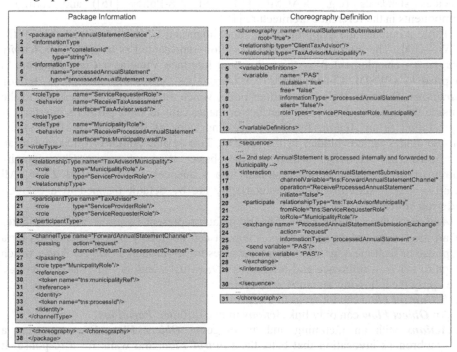

**Fig. 6.** Part of Global Workflow captured in WS-CDL Choreography Entity

The *choreography definition* in Figure 6 shows the part of the WS-CDL file that specifies the interaction between the TaxAdvisor and the Municipality. The `Choreography` {1} defines a `Relationship` {4} of type `TaxAdvisorMunicipality`, whose `RelationShipType` has been declared as part of the `Package` entity in the *package information* part {16-19}. The element associates two roles (`ServiceRequestorRole` and `Municipality`) according to their `RoleType` definitions, which defines one or more observable `behavior` attribute and an optional WSDL `interface` type associated to the role. Additional `relationshipTypes` may be added for modeling multi-party collaborations.

### 3.3.3    Mapping the GWfM to WS-CDL

The mapping of the GWfM and the Interface Model to an XML-based choreography definition language (e.g. a WS-CDL file) allows the actors to verify that their internal processes match the requirements for a participation in the collaboration. Additionally, they can generate public interfaces and code skeletons of executable workflow languages (e.g., BEPL4WS) that tie in their internal workflows to support the global workflow. The names of the model elements conform to the uniform technical and syntactical specifications the partners agreed upon during the design phase (e.g., parameter format, interaction protocol, notation names of the complementary roles, the service interfaces and the parameters, operation semantics etc.).

The security requirements are integrated into the GWfM as UML artifacts and directly translated into a set of executable XML code files that comply with Web services standards (e.g., XACML [13] and WS-Policy [15]) and configure components in the reference architecture [18].

Table 2 outlines the mapping of the most important UML elements of the GWfM to WS-CDL. The inter-organizational workflow represented as an UML 2.0 *Activity Diagram* - complemented by the orthogonal Interface View as a *Class Diagram* is mapped to a WSDL Choreography `Package`. `RoleTypes` are modeled as *Activity Partitions*. Business logic at a partner node, which either is made accessible to the outside through a Web services interface or makes calls to some partner's interface, is represented as an *Action*. Internal processing steps of the local workflow at the partner nodes remain hidden in the GWfM. Two related *Actions* correspond to an `Interaction` Activity, which is the basic atom of every Choreography composition. Actions are orchestrated into sequences by a *Control Flow*. All `Interaction` Activities in a choreography are by default mapped to a `choice` ordering structure.

*Actions* with an *Object Flow Edge* by default represent `request` action attributes of an `Exchange` inside an `Interaction`. It can optionally be complemented by a response or fault message. Document instances travel through an *Object Node*, which maps to a `Token` reference and references a `Variable` and an `InformationType`. We apply the following semantic restrictions:
1. A *Control Flow* cannot cross its *Partition*.
2. An *Object Flow* can only link *Actions* in two different *Partitions*.
3. *Actions* with an incoming and an outgoing *Object Flow Edge* represent a synchronous invocation that halts the *Control Flow* and waits for a response. It maps to an `Interaction` with two `Exchange` definitions: one with a `request`

`Action` attribute and one with a `respond Action` attribute in an `Interaction` that can be complemented by a response or fault message.

4. An `Interaction` activity is marked as a Choreography Initiator when the `initiate` attribute is set to "true". This is represented by an ***Action Object Flow Edge*** coming from an ***Initial Node.***

**Table 2.** Mapping of Activity Diagrams to WS-CDL

| UML 2.0 Activity Diagram to WS-CDL Mapping | | |
|---|---|---|
| AD - Node Type | AD Notation | WS-CDL |
| Activity | Activity Name | Package<br>Choreography |
| Activity Partitions | TaxAdvisor     Municipality | RoleTypes<br><br>or ParticipantTypes |
| Two Actions linked by an Object Flow | Forward AS → processed AS → ReceiveAS | Interaction<br>Participate Element (fromRole, toRole)<br>Exchange Element Action (variable) |
| Activity Partitions linked by Object Flow | TaxAdvisor     Municipality | RelationshipType<br>Behavior<br>RoleTypes |
| Object Node | processed AS | Token, Tokenlocator<br>Variable Definition<br>InformationType (WSDL/XSD) Reference |

### 3.3.4    Mapping the Interface View in UML to WS-CDL

The package **<<interfaceView>>** (See Figure 3(a), Section 3.2.2) contains all **<<interfaceModel>>** elements that map to `relationshipType` declarations in a WS-CDL `package` and to `relationship` elements in a `choreography`. The **<<interface>>** `AS_Service` maps to a `request` action attribute of an `exchange` element inside of an `interaction` block and to a corresponding `operation` attribute. The **<<interface>>** `AS_Callback` maps to an associated `response` action attribute of the same `exchange` element. A **<<role>>** maps to a `roleType`. **<<datatype>>** and **<<documentType>>** (See Figure 3(b), Section 3.2.2) map to `informationType` and optional associated WSDL Message type or Schema element. Instances of documents are associated to `variables`.

## 4    Conclusion and Outlook

We do not aim to contribute a novel formal approach on how to model inter-organizational workflows. Nor do we want to develop a new security technology or to specify a new choreography standard. Instead, focusing on Web services technology, we use existing technology and standards to realize our vision of Model Driven Architecture in the context of inter-organizational workflows with a special emphasis on security. We hope to boost the acceptance of Web services technologies and standards in business areas, where security is critical and all stakeholders, from the domain expert to the technician, need to have the same understanding of security requirements.

As requirements of real-life scenarios drive our research activities, we are currently working along two lines of actions. On the one hand, we push the stepwise implementation of our MDA approach by developing custom modeling tools and plug-ins as well as implementing the components of the reference architecture. On the other hand, we are formalizing the current results and extending our research efforts towards more complex security issues. Currently, we are analyzing the application of the Qualified Signature in e-government and more complex security patterns like non-repudiation, rights delegation and authorization [36].

# References

1.  A. Nadalin, et al., "Web Services Security: SOAP Message Security 1.0 (WS Security 2004)". OASIS Standard 200401, March 2004.
2.  N. Kavantzas et al., "Web Services Choreography Description Language Version 1.0". W3C Working Draft 17 December 2004.
3.  J. Miller et al. (ed.), "MDA Guide Version 1.0.1". OMG, 2003.
4.  T. Lodderstedt et al., "SecureUML: A UML-Based Modeling Language for Model-Driven Security". In: J.-M. Jézéquel et al. (eds.), *Proc. of the 5th Int. Conf. on the Unified Modeling Language*, Springer, 2002.
5.  IBM, Microsoft, BEA Systems, SAP AG, Siebel Systems, "Specification: Business Process Execution Language for Web Services Version 1.1". IBM, 2003.
6.  C. Gutiérez et al., "Web Service Security: is the Problem solved?". In: *Proc of the 2nd Int Workshop on Security In Inf. Sys., WOSIS 2004, in conj. with ICEIS 2004, Porto*, 2004.
7.  BPMI, "BPML 1.0 Specification". BPMI, 2002.
8.  OASIS, "ebXML Business Process Specification Schema Version 1.01". OASIS, 2001.
9.  M. Bernauer et al., "Comparing WSDL-based and ebXML-based Approaches for B2B Protocol Specification". In: *Proc. of the 1st Int. Conf. on Service-Oriented Computing (ICSOC)*, Trento, 2003.
10. N. Mitra, N., "SOAP Version 1.2 Part 1: Messaging Framework". W3C Recommendation 24 June 2003.
11. Eastlake, D. (ed.), et al., "XML-Signature Syntax and Processing". W3C Recommendation 12 February 2002.
12. Eastlake, D. (ed.), et al., "XML Encryption Syntax and Processing". W3C Recommendation 10 December 2002".
13. T. Moses (ed.), et al., "XACML Profile for Web-Services". XACML TC Working draft, Version 04, September 29, 2003.
14. P. Mishra (ed.), et al., "Conformance Requirements for the OASIS Security Assertion Markup Language (SAML) V2.0". Committee Draft 02, 24 September 2004.
15. S. Bajaj, et al., "Web Services Policy Framework (WS-Policy)". September 2004.
16. R. Breu, M. Hafner, B. Weber, A. Novak, "Model Driven Security for Inter-Organizational Workflows in E-Government". In: *Proc. TCGOV 2005*, TED, ISBN 3-540-25016-6.
17. R. Breu, M. Hafner, B. Weber, "Modeling and Realizing Security-Critical Inter-Organizational Workflows", In: W. Dosch, N. Debnath (Eds.), *Proc. IASSE 2004*, ISCA, ISBN 1-880843-52-X.
18. M. Hafner, R. Breu, M. Breu, "A Security Architecture for Inter-Organizational Workflows: Putting Security Standards for Web Services Together". In: C. S. Chen et al. (Eds.): *Proc. ICEIS 2005*, INSTICC, ISBN 972-8865-19-8, 2005.
19. M. Hafner, R. Breu, M. Breu, A. Nowak, "Modeling Inter-organizational Workflow Security in a Peer-to-Peer Environment". Accepted for ICWS 2005.
20. A. Hall, R. Chapman, "Correctness by construction developing a commercial secure system". *IEEE Software 19 (2002) 1*, 2002, pp. 18-25.
21. R. Breu, K. Burger, M. Hafner, G. Popp, "Towards a Systematic Development of Secure Systems". *Inf. Systems Security 13 (2004) 3*, Auerbach, New York, 2004, pp. 5-13.
22. K. Mantell, "From UML to BPEL". IBM-developerWorks, 2003.

23. IBM, "Business Process Execution Language for Web Services Java™ Run Time (BPWS4J)". IBM, 2002.
24. W.M.P. van der Aalst, M. Weske, "The P2P approach to Interorganizational Workflows". In K.R. Dittrich et al. (eds.): *Proc. of the 13th Int. Conf. on Adv. Information Systems Eng. (CAiSE'01)*, Springer, Berlin, 2001, pp. 140-156.
25. W.M.P. van der Aalst, "Loosely Coupled Interorganizational Workflows: Modeling and Analyzing Workflows Crossing Organizational Boundaries". *Information and Management 37 (2000) 2*, pp. 67-75.
26. Z. Luo, et al., "Exception Handling in Workflow Systems". *Applied Intelligence 13 (2000) 2*, pp. 125-147.
27. P. Grefen, et al., "CrossFlow: cross-organizational workflow management in dynamic virtual enterprises". *International Journal of Computer Systems Science & Engineering 15 (2000) 5*, pp. 277-290.
28. F. Casati and M. Shan, "Event-based Interaction Management for Composite E-Services in eFlow". *Information Systems Frontiers 4 (2002) 1*, pp. 19-31.
29. V. Atluri, W.K. Huang, "Enforcing Mandatory and Discretionary Security in Workflow Management Systems". *Proc. of the 5th Europ. Symp. on Research in Comp. Sec., 1996*.
30. E. Gudes, et al., "Modelling, Specifying and Implementing Workflow Security in Cyberspace". *Journal of Computer Security 7 (1999) 4*, pp. 287-315.
31. W. K. Huang, V. Atluri, "SecureFlow: A secure Web-enabled Workflow Management System". *ACM Workshop on Role-Based Access Control 1999*, pp. 83-94.
32. J. Wainer, et al., "W-RBAC – A Workflow Security Model Incorporating Controlled Overriding of Constraints". *International Journal of Cooperative Information Systems. 12 (2003) 4*, pp. 455-485.
33. W.M.P. Van der Aalst, "Loosely Coupled Interorganizational Workflows: Modeling and Analyzing Workflows Crossing Organizational Boundaries". *Information and Management 37 (2000) 2*, pp. 67-75.
34. OMG, "UML 2.0 Superstructure Specification ". OMG, 2002.
35. D. Carlson, "Modeling XML Applications with UML: Practical E-Business Applications". Addison Wesley, Boston, 2001.
36. M. Alam, M. Breu, R. Breu, "Model Driven Security for Web Services". In: *Proc. of the 8th International Multi-topic Conference* (INMIC 2004), IEEE, Lahore, 2004.
37. Austrian Signature Act (Signaturgesetz - SigG), Art. 1 of the Act published in the *Austrian Federal Law Gazette*, part I, Nr. 190/1999.
38. R. Breu, M. Breu, M. Hafner, A. Nowak, "Web Service Engineering - Advancing A New Software Engineering Discipline". Accepted for ICWE 2005.
39. BEA, Intalio, Sun Microsystems, SAP, "Web Service Choreography Interface (WSCI)". August 2002.
40. G. Della-Libera et al, "Web Services Security Policy Language (WS-SecurityPolicy)". December 2002.
41. S. Anderson et al., "Web Services Trust Language (WS-Trust)". February 2005.
42. A. Barros et al., "A Critical Overview of the Web Services Choreography Description Language (WS-CDL)". BPTrends Newsletter, Volume 3, Number 3, March 1, 2005.
43. R. M. Dijkman, M. Dumas, "Service-Oriented Design: A Multi-Viewpoint Approach". Int. Journal of Cooperative Information Systems 13(4): 337-368 (2004).
44. M. Alam, R. Breu, M. Hafner, "Modeling permissions in a (U/X)ML world". Submitted to ECMDA 2005, Nuremberg, Germany.

# Code Generation from UML Models with Semantic Variation Points*

Franck Chauvel[1] and Jean-Marc Jézéquel[2]

[1] VALORIA
[2] INRIA & Université de Rennes 1

**Abstract.** UML semantic variation points provide intentional degrees of freedom for the interpretation of the metamodel semantics. The interest of semantic variation points is that UML now becomes a family of languages sharing lot of commonalities and some variabilities that one can customize for a given application domain. In this paper, we propose to reify the various semantic variation points of UML 2.0 statecharts into models of their own to avoid hardcoding the semantic choices in the tools. We do the same for various implementation choices. Then, along the line of the OMG's Model Driven Architecture, these semantic and implementation models are processed along with a source UML model (that can be seen as a PIM) to provide a target UML model (a PSM) where all semantic and implementation choice are made explicit. This target model can in turn serve as a basis for a consistent use of code generation, simulation, model-checking or test generation tools.

## 1 Introduction

UML (Unified Modeling Language) has been widely critized in the past for its fuziness, making it difficult to build code generators, simulation, model-checking or test generation tools working in a consistent manner. Many tool vendors are nevertheless producing useful tools, some of them even have reach a certain level of industrial acceptance. The interest of having a *unified* modeling language is however questionable if the meaning of a UML model depends on which tool is used for any given purpose. With the advent of UML 2.0 [14] though, many of previous version UML fuziness issues have been solved, and some of the rest have been encapsulated into the notion of *semantic variation points*.

A semantic variation point is a point of variation in the semantics of a metamodel. It provides an intentional degree of freedom for the interpretation of the metamodel semantics. For instance, we find on page 40 of [14] *The precise lifecycle semantics of aggregation is a semantic variation point*. The interest of semantic variation points is that UML now becomes a family of languages sharing lot of commonalities and some variabilities that one can customize for a

---

* This work has been partially supported by the Amadeus project of Région Bretagne and by the Artist2 Network of Excellence on Embedded Systems Design (IST-004527).

L. Briand and C. Williams (Eds.): MoDELS 2005, LNCS 3713, pp. 54–68, 2005.

given application domain. This makes a lot of sense, because for instance the type of behavior one would expect from the statecharts of books in a library business application has some differences with the statecharts of a CD player in a real-time system. Furthermore the code one wants to see generated definitively does not look the same.

Similarly to working with product lines [18], the challenge of the tool builders is then obviously to capitalize on commonalities while making it possible to customize their tools with respect to the choosen variants. We propose to reify these semantic variation points as well as possible implementation choices into models of their own. Then along the line of the OMG's Model Driven Architecture [15], these models are processed along with a source UML model (that can be seen as a PIM) to provide a target UML model (a PSM) where all semantic and implementation choice are made explicit. This target model can in turn serve as a basis for a consistent use of code generation, simulation, model-checking or test generation tools. In this paper we concentrate on behavioral aspects described through UML 2.0 statecharts. Section 2 introduces the running example of a CD player modeled as a statechart at a PIM level. It then discusses semantic variation points for UML statecharts and proposes a model $M_s$ for them. Section 3 discusses several implementation techniques for UML statecharts and also proposes a model $M_i$ for them. Section 4 describes how a PSM can be automatically obtained from these three models, (the PIM, $M_s$ and $M_i$) through model transformations. Section 5 discusses related works, and Section 6 concludes and present some perspectives to this work.

# 2   Semantic Variation Points for UML 2.0 Statecharts

Let's consider a simple CD player supporting three main functionalities: one can open the player and play a CD, as well as suspend and resume the playing. Furthermore, if the playing is suspended (in pause) for more than 10 minutes, the player automatically stops. This is modeled with a simple statechart [6,8] as illustrated in Figure 1.

Before dealing with semantic variation points let's have a look at the UML Statecharts meta-model which is shown on figure 2. UML 2.0 Statecharts define a set of concepts that can be used to define finite state-transitions systems.

Numerous semantics have already been developed to precisely define the meaning of statecharts notations (see Von der Beek's impressive catalog [3]). Along this line, UML 2.0 defines yet another semantics for statecharts, or more precisely a family of semantics since it lets a number of issues open. These semantic variation points mainly concern 3 aspects: time management (synchronous vs. asynchronous), the event selection policy, and the transition selection policy.

## 2.1   Time Management

With respect to the statechart progression, time can be either synchronous or asynchronous.

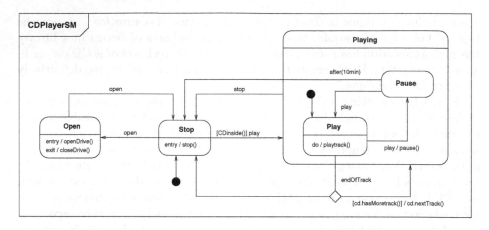

**Fig. 1.** Behavior of a CD player

**Under the asynchronous hypothesis,** time is discrete. On each step, the statechart processes events that have occurred between the current and the previous step. The statechart thus needs to store incoming events into some sort of collection. Depending on the policy choosen for event processsing (see below) this collection might be a queue, a bag or a stack or even something more exotic.

**Under the synchronous hypothesis,** time is continuous. As soon as an event occurs, it is processed in zero time. So, there is no more need of any data structure to store events.

## 2.2   Event Management

Different kinds of events can be considered. Events can be internal/external or discrete/continuous.

Events are called external if they are produced by an object different from the target object. Let's consider two objects $O_1$ and $O_2$ where $O_2$ reacts when event $e_1$ occurs. In the context of $O_2$, $e_1$ is an external event because it was produced by object $O_1$. If it were produced by $O_2$ itself, it would have been viewed as an internal event.

Events are either discrete if they trigger only one transition during their life cycle, or continuous otherwise. In UML 2.0, we also have deferred events: a state may specify a set of event types that may be deferred in that state. If an event occurs in a state where it cannot trigger any transitions, then it should not be discarded if its type matches one of the types in the deferred event set of that state. Instead, it should remain in the event pool while another non-deferred event is dispatched instead.

Using deferred events can lead to conflict: for instance when a substate defers an event while the composite state consumes it, or vice versa. In case of a composite orthogonal state, substates of orthogonal regions may also introduce

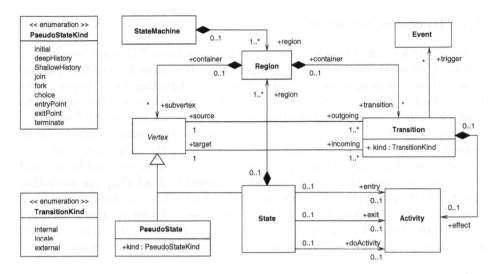

**Fig. 2.** Excerpt of the UML 2.0 Statecharts Meta-Model

deferral conflicts. To solve this kind of conflict, UML 2.0 consider that nested states override composite state and a consumer state overrides a deferring state when conflict appears between two orthogonal regions.

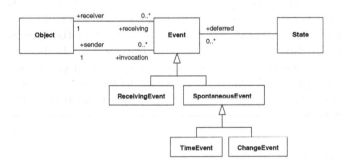

**Fig. 3.** Events in UML 2.0

One other variation point in UML is the way to select an event in the event pool. It is explicitly listed as a semantic variation point in the UML 2.0. In fact, there are many ways to do this. The structure can be a queue and so events are selected by incoming order. It can also be a stack if the most recent event is selected. We can also use any priority systems or a mail box system to define more powerful selection policies.

## 2.3 Transition Management

Using a composite state (such as the "playing" state in our CD player) can lead to conflicts among transitions. To solve this, the UML defines a transition priority system based on source states, with transitions originating from deeper states having higher priority. For example, if $s_2$ is a substate of $s_1$ then transitions originating from $s_2$ have higher priority than transitions originating from $s_1$.

This kind of priority system does not solve every conflicts. For example, consider the case of two transitions originating from the same state, triggered by the same event, but with different guards. If that event occurs and both guard conditions are true, then only one transition should be fired. Only one transition can be fired simultaneously except for concurrent state's regions. So we need a way to decide between two conflicting transitions. There are two main ways to solve this kind of conflicts: we can either always choose the same arbitrary transition or use a randomized choice (for fairness purposes for example).

## 2.4 Modeling Statechart Semantic Variation Points

To explicitly express these semantic variation points, we need a model describing the various event selection policies and transition policies. This model can be seen as a reification of the part of the semantics which is subject to variability, with the variability itself modeled using standard OO features such as inheritance and delegation (see Figure 6).

Harel [8] describes the operational semantics of statecharts based on the description of a *run-to-completion* step as it shown in figure 4.

The way this procedure is called depends on whether the time model is synchronous or asynchronous. Under the asynchronous hypothesis, time is discrete and so the *step* procedure must be triggered by a third party mechanism like a clock for example. Under the synchronous hypothesis, time is continuous and this procedure must be encapsulated into an infinite loop to process events as soon as they occur.

```
procedure step()
begin
   eventSet := eventPool.select();
   anEvent := eventSet.choice();
   transitionSet := getFirableTransition(anEvent).select();
   aTransition := transitionSet.choice();
   aTransition.fire();
end.
```

**Fig. 4.** The run-to-completion procedure

With respect to the semantic variation points described above, this *run-to-completion* procedure looks like a GoF's *Template Method* [4], that is the skeleton of an algorithm in an operation, deferring some steps to subclasses. The steps we want to be able to redefine here are the following:

1. We apply some priority scheme in order to determine which event we want to process (cf. operation "*eventPool.select()*" on figure 4).
2. Since this priority scheme might return more than one event (events of the same priority), we then need to choose the one we actually process (cf. operation "*eventPool.choice()*").
3. With this event, we now can select the set of firable transitions (cf. operation "*getFirableTransition(anEvent)*").
4. On this transition set, we apply some other priority scheme to first resolve simple cases of non-determinism (cf. operation "*transitionSet.select()*"), and then if this is not enough to get only one transition, we need to decide between selected transitions.
5. finally, fire the transition.

All the semantic variation points are then encapsulated in the operations *select* and *choice* called on event sets and transition sets. So to model state-charts semantics we need to add some behavior behind these operations. Quite straightforwardly, we can use the *Strategy* pattern [4] twice to define both an event management policy and a transition management policy. Each one is described with both a selection policy and a conflict resolution policy (See figure 6).

Event and transition management can be explicitly described with an action language such as the Action Semantics. In figure 5, we use the Kermeta Language [12] to describe the semantic of our "select" operation. Kermeta is an object-oriented meta-language and so is well suited to define semantics into meta-models. So, to define a new event selection policy for example, one just needs to extends the "event selection Policy" and to redefine the *select()* operation (See figure 6). For instance, we can define a new event selection policy where TimeOut events have an higher priority than other events as described in the example below.

---

```
class MyEventSelection inherits EventSelectionPolicy
{
  method select() : OrderedSet<Event> is
  do
    result := eventPool.select{e | TimeEvent.isInstance(e)}.first()
  end
}
```

---

**Fig. 5.** A event selection policy defined with *KerMeta*

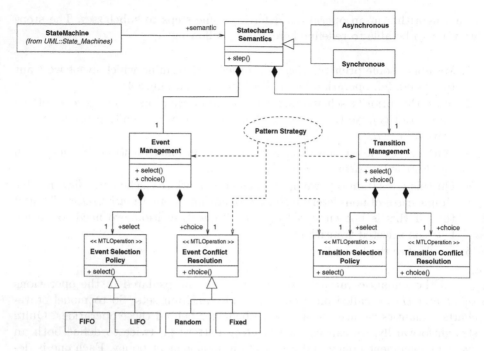

**Fig. 6.** Model of the UML Statecharts Semantic Variation Points

# 3   Implementing UML Statecharts

Even if we would have settled on a single possible semantics for statecharts, there can still be many ways to implement them. There are indeed many trade-off to make to handle non-functional issues such as execution time, memory footprint, flexibility, maintainability, possibility of dynamic upgrade and so on. For example, if we need a compact and efficient implementation, we might want to use enumerated values representing states and events. If we rather want a more flexible solution, we might prefer to resort to the State Pattern and/or the Command Pattern [4]. In this section, we propose to model these implementation choices in the same spirit as for the modeling of semantic variation points.

## 3.1   Enumeration Vs. Reification

For each of the statechart notions, such as states, events, or transitions, we typically face the choice of either hard code it (into static tables or switch blocs) for maximum efficiency, or reify it for maximum flexibility (using the State Pattern, the Command Pattern, and reifying transitions).

The easiest way to manage states is to represent them with an enumeration. In our example, this type would be "open, stop, playing Play, playing Pause". Note that this solution is not however very well suited for hierarchical state-charts, because it requires to first flatten the state hierarchy. Another solution is to reify the possible states into a specific class hierarchy through the application of the state pattern [4]. See the right side of Figure 7 for an illustration of the application of the state pattern to our CD player statechart. This solution would even allow us to dynamically add new states, which could be very useful to modify a system behavior without stopping it.

Using an enumeration to manage events requires to put the statechart progression mechanism into a specific method called for instance *"processEvent(e : event)"*. Its role is to select the right transition using two "switch" statements. Alternatively we can reify events using the Command Pattern [4]. Then, the progression mechanism is distributed into event classes through object-oriented method dispatch. If the states have not been reified, we still need to select the right state with a "switch" statement.

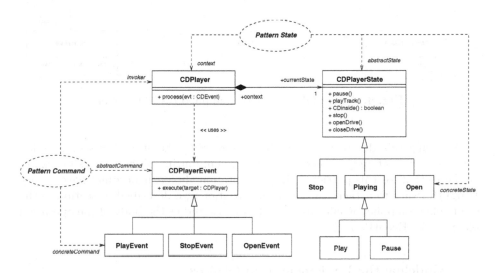

**Fig. 7.** Implementing CD player using states and events reification

It is also possible to reify both states and events as illustrated in Figure 7. Then, the progression mechanism is distributed into the event classes and the state classes. In fact, here, we use a double dispatch to select the right behavior according to the event and the current state.

We might go as far as also reifying the transition concept. There are some patterns indeed reifying most of the statechart notions (like Tomura's statecharts pattern [16]), including guard condition, actions, etc.

## 3.2   Statechart Progession

Beyond states, events and transitions, we also have to care for variations about the implementation of the statechart "engine", i.e. the method that makes it progress by selecting which transition must be triggered according to events and to the current state. The basic choice here is whether the engine is shared accross multiple statecharts or whether it is statechart specific. In the former case, a single statechart can be considered as a passive reactive object with the event dispatching being performed from outside. In the later case we can resort to the Active Object pattern and encapsulate all the internal mechanisms behind a proxy object, as illustrated in Figure8.

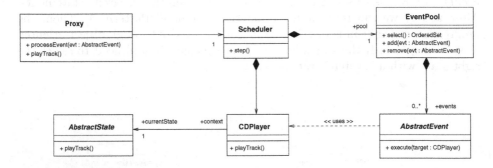

**Fig. 8.** Active-Object Pattern applied on CD Player

Applying this design patterns allow us to reify the statecharts progression mechanism by defining a scheduler object manipulating object events for example. Note that for this particular implementation choice, it becomes particularly straightforward to attach the semantic variations we described in section 2: the event selection policy would just have to be inserted as the body of the operation select of the EventPool class.

### 3.3   Modeling the Implementation Choices

In previous sections, we have defined various semantics and implementation choices but we still need to link these choices to our initial statemachine. To help doing that, the UML provides an extension mechanism called a "profile". A profile can be seen as a lightweight extension to the meta-model which adds extra-information to meta-classes. To do this, a profile can contains "stereotype" and "tagged values". Stereotypes are a way to represent boolean information like "is an interface" whereas "tagged values" can be parameterizad by values.

The profile we provide is a way to specify required choices on a statemachine. An example is given in the figure 9. Here, the CDPlayer statemachine would use a FIFO policy for handling events for example.

**eventSelection** this tagged value allows the specification of the required event selection policy. It correspond to the *select()* operation in the procedure *step()* in figure 4. The value is a string which identifies the event selection policy in the semantic model.

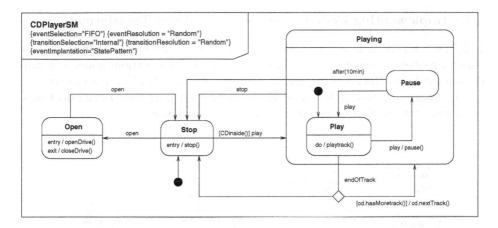

**Fig. 9.** The CDPlayerSM with some stereotypes specifying semantic

**eventResolution** this tagged value is used to specify a way to resolve conflict between events. It corresponds to the *choice()* operation in the procedure *step()* in Figure 4. The value is a string which identifies the concrete conflictResolution policy in the semantic model.

**transitionSelection** this tagged value is used to specify the required transition selection. It corresponds to the *choice()* operation in the procedure *step()* in Figure 4. The value is a string which identifies the concrete transition selction policy in the semantic model.

**transitionResolution** this tagged value is used to specify a way to resolve conflict between firable transitions. It corresponds to the *choice()* operation in the procedure *step()* in Figure 4. The value is a string which identifies the concrete conflictResolution policy in the semantic model.

**eventImplantation** this tagged value represent the technic used to specify implantation of event. This is an enumerate value, which can be "enumerate" or "reify" to used a command pattern.

**stateImplantation** this tagged value represent the technic used to specify implantation of state. This is an enumerate value, which can be "enumerate" or "reify" to used a state pattern.

## 4   Processing Semantics and Implementation Variants Through Model Transformations

We can now combine the description of a statecharts, its semantics choices and implementation choices in a consistent manner for various software engineering activities such as automatic code generation, simulation, model-checking and test generation.

## 4.1    Implementing Code Generation as a Model Transformation

For that we need a model transformation language and engine able to process these 3 models as input, and produce either an implementation model or a validation model. In the following, we describe how we used MTL [13], an imperative object oriented language based on KerMeta for that purpose. Our model transformation can be divided in three main steps (See figure 10).

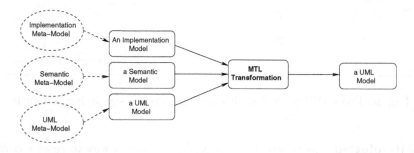

**Fig. 10.** Processing Statecharts, Semantics and Implementation models to provide a PSM model

Firstly, we search input models for semantic and implementation choices. An abstract factory is then used to dynamically select and configure the needed transformations, most of which are actually quite simple pattern applications [5].

In a second step, we apply the selected patterns. Defining a general way to apply design patterns is a non-trivial issue, but we face here only a subset of this problem: we just need to apply (or not apply) 3 patterns in a specific order, which slightly reduce the combinatory aspect of the problem. So we start with either a direct implementation or with the active-object pattern to define a common structure to implement statecharts mechanisms. Then, depending on the previous choice, we can apply (or not apply) the state and command patterns in an orthogonal way. (See figure 11 for the result of the application of the 3 patterns in a row).

Anyway, we have obtained a detailed model where the statecharts progression mechanism has been fully reified. So, we can easily attach the statecharts semantics by filling the corresponding methods. For example, the semantics specified by the user for the event selection policy would go into the *select* method of the class *Pool* (See figure 11). To do that, we used the MTL language at the meta-model level to describe semantic choices in the input semantic model. As for KerMeta on which it is based, MTL can also be used at the model-level as a kind of simple action language for UML, making it easy to translate the description of the semantics into its implementation.

Finally, our model is refined to the point where each statecharts concept has been mapped onto structural OO notions like classes or operations. An example of behavior of this output model is presented on the figure 12. It can

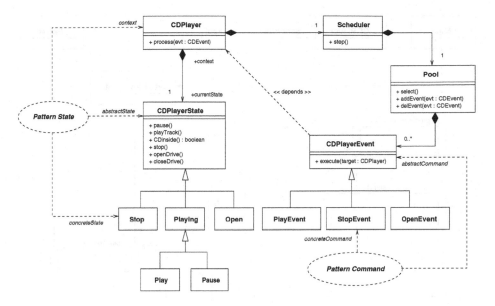

**Fig. 11.** Output model of the transformation

then be directly translated into executable code using any off-the-self UML code generator, including the MTL one. Indeed, using MTL to describe operation bodies allows us to re-use the MTL Java code generator to generate for free an executable Java code corresponding to our input model.

## 4.2 Handling UML Variability into UMLAUT NG

UMLAUT NG [9] is an object-oriented framework dedicated to model transformations in a MOF based context. It provides both a library of model transformations specific to UML models (e.g.; UML2RDBMS which translate a UML model to a relational model) as well as composition operators. UMLAUT NG was designed as an open tool working with several flavors of XMI, in order to be easily connected to various CASE tools.

UMLAUT NG also provides a way to connect MDD to formal technics initially developed for SDL, Lotos and others. UMLAUT NG supports model transformations for transforming UML models into labelled transition systems (LTS), to be used with the CADP tool box which provides tools for model checking, simulation, test synthesis and vizualization of the state spaces.

The integration into UMLAUT NG of our approach at reifying statecharts semantic variation points makes it possible to uncouple all of these tools from a specific choice of the statechart semantics. It can be seen as an easy way to specialize a complex tool chain towards a specific domain (e.g.; small embedded devices) where a particular interpretation of the statechart semantics is preferred.

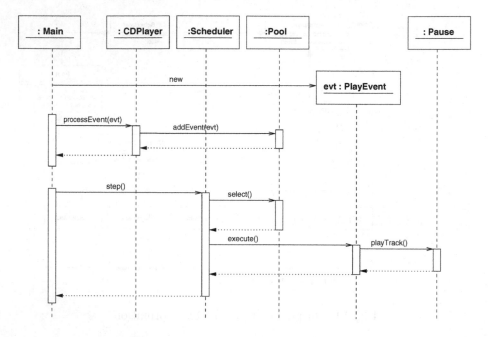

**Fig. 12.** Behavior of the output model

## 5   Related Works

The work of [3] has been one of the starting point of our work. Indeed, many papers try to define a formal semantics for Statecharts and especially for UML-Statecharts. Among this works, M.Von der Beeck [17] proposes a structured operational semantics for UML Statecharts. Borger provide another semantics based on abstract StatesMachines [1]. All these works contribute to give a formal ground to UML at the price of choosing a particular semantics, which might be adequate for a particular application domain, but not that much for others, which is the basic reason why the UML provides semantic variation points. In this paper we specifically address this semantic variation point issue.

Building on formal semantics, many tools are able to simulate UML models and specially statecharts [7]. Another example is *iUML* of Kennedy Carter [2] which includes a modeler and a simulator based on the ASL language. Most of these tools are based on more or less formalized semantics and do not take into account semantic variation points.

Another way to execute UML models is to generate executable code directly from models. In an MDA perspective, many models transformations are required to get code from high level models. This process starts at the highest level with the platform independent model (PIM) and continues until a Plateform Specific Model (PSM) is generated. We believe that actual code generation should be used only when a model is low level enough to be directly translated to C++ or Java. However most of dedicated code generation tools provide code generation directly from e.g. statecharts. For instance Tanaka [11,10] proposes an UML to Java code generation from statecharts diagrams (based on the state pattern with events reified as method calls), or Rhapsody, a UML Case tool, proposes a code generator where events and states are selected using a switch statement (which is a relevant choice for its commercial target which is the real-time domain). These code generators tends to hard code semantic and implementation choices, making them difficult or even irrelevant to use outside of their sometimes very narrow domain. On this aspect, the main contribution of our work consists in providing a way to uncouple semantics issues and implementation choices from code generation, and let them open-ended. Users can always add a particular semantics and choose a particular implementation technics by extending the existing framework.

## 6  Conclusion and Future Works

The interest of semantic variation points in UML is that it now becomes a family of languages sharing lot of commonalities and some variabilities that one can customize for a given application domain. In this paper, we have proposed to reify the various semantic variation points of UML 2.0 statecharts into models of their own to avoid hardcoding the semantic choices in the tools. We did the same for various implementation choices. Through model transformations, these semantic and implementation models are then processed along with a source UML model to provide a target UML model where all semantic and implementation choice are made explicit. We have shown how this target model can in turn serve as a basis for a consistent use of code generation, simulation, model-checking or test generation tools.

This process has been implemented within our UMLAUT framework for model transformations, along with others tools such as statecharts generation from sequences diagrams or sequences diagram generation from textual requirements. Even if a a complete chain of model transformations from requirements to executable code is not a realistic approach, UMLAUT aims at providing building blocks that can be customized for a specific model driven design and validation process.

In the future, we plan to use the same approach to reify other semantic variation points in the UML2.0 metamodel. In the UML2.0 component model for example, we can find some open issues like the semantics of method dispatch, interfaces conformity or the support of QoS attributes. It could be interesting to describe these semantic choices as we did for statecharts and to merge them with a component model to get a PSM model.

## References

1. Egon Börger, Alessandra Cavarra, and Elvinia Riccobene. On formalizing UML state machines using ASM. *Information & Software Technology*, 46(5):287–292, 2004.

2. Kennedy Carter. iUMLite tool suite and ASL language. from Kennedy Carter's website (http://www.kc.com).

3. Michael Von der Beeck. A comparison of statecharts variants. In L. De Roever and J. Vytopil, editors, *In Formal technics in Real-Time and Fault-tolerant Systems*, volume 863 of *Lecture Notes in Computer Science*, pages 128–148, New-York, 1994. Springer Verlag.

4. Gamma, Erich, Helm, Richard, Johnson, Ralph, and Vlissides, John. *Design Patterns: Elements of Reusable Object-Oriented Software*. Addison-Wesley Longman Publishing Co., Inc., 1995.

5. Alain Le Guennec, Gerson Sunyé, and Jean-Marc Jézéquel. Precise modeling of design patterns. In *Proceedings of UML 2000*, volume 1939 of *LNCS*, pages 482–496. Springer Verlag, 2000.

6. David Harel. Statecharts: A visual formalism for complex systems. *Science of Computer Programming*, 8(3):231–274, June 1987.

7. David Harel and Eran Gery. Executable object modeling with statecharts. In *ICSE '96: Proceedings of the 18th international conference on Software engineering*, pages 246–257. IEEE Computer Society, 1996.

8. Harel, David and Naamad, Amnon. The STATEMATE Semantics of Statecharts. *ACM Transactions on Software Engineering and Methodology*, 5(4):293–333, october 1996.

9. Wai-Ming Ho, Jean-Marc Jézéquel, Alain Le Guennec, and François Pennaneac'h. UMLAUT: an extendible UML transformation framework. In *Proc. Automated Software Engineering, ASE'99, Florida*, October 1999.

10. Jauhar, Ali and Tanaka, Jiro. Implementation of the Dynamic Behavior of Object Oriented System. In *Third World Conference on Integrated Design and Process Technology (IDPT'98)*, volume 4, Berlin, Germany, July 1998.

11. Jauhar, Ali and Tanaka, Jiro. Implementing the dynamic behavior represented as multiple state diagrams and activity diagrams. *Journal of Computer Science & Information Management (JCSIM)*, 2(1):24–36, 2001.

12. Franck Fleurey Pierre-Alain Muller and Jean-Marc Jézéquel. Weaving executability into object-oriented meta-languages. In *Proceedings of UML MoDELs 2005, Jamaica*, LNCS. Springer Verlag, 2005. to be published.

13. Damien Pollet, Didier Vojtisek, and Jean-Marc Jézéquel. OCL as a core UML transformation language. WITUML 2002 Position paper, Malaga, Spain, jun 2002. http://ctp.di.fct.unl.pt/ ja/wituml02.htm.

14. UML Revision Task Force RTF. UML draft version 2.0 specification, April 2003.

15. Soley, Richard and OMG Staff Group. Model Driven Architecture. White papers, Object Management Group, Novembre 2000.

16. Toyoaki Tomura and Satoshi Kanai. Developing simulation models of open distributed control system by using object-oriented structural and behavioral patterns. In *ISORC*, pages 428–437, 2001.

17. Michael von der Beeck. A structured operational semantics for UML-statecharts. *Software and System Modeling*, 1(2):130–141, 2002.

18. Twefik Ziadi. *Manipulation de lignes de produits en UML*. PhD thesis, Universit de Rennes 1, 2004.

# Composing Domain-Specific Languages for Wide-Scope Software Engineering Applications

Jacky Estublier, German Vega, Anca Daniela Ionita

LSR-IMAG, 220, rue de la Chimie BP5338041 Grenoble Cedex 9, France
{jacky.estublier, german.vega, Anca.Ionita}@imag.fr
http://www-imag.fr

**Abstract.** Domain-Specific Languages (DSL) offer many advantages over general languages, but their narrow scope makes them really effective only in very focused domains, for example Product Lines. The recent Model Driven Engineering (MDE) approach seeks to provide a technology to compose and combine models coming from different metamodels. Adapted to DSL, it means that it should be possible to compose "programs" written in different DSLs, which will enable the use of the DSL approach to build applications spanning different domains. The paper presents the Mélusine environment, where such a composition technology has been developed and experimented.

## 1 Introduction

Most domain engineering approaches emphasize domain modeling as an important mechanism for the development of product families. Domain-specific modeling addresses this issue by designing languages specifically tailored to directly represent the concepts of an application domain.

Domain-Specific Languages (DSL) [1] have several advantages over general purpose languages:

- They raise the level of abstraction, by proposing constructs directly related to application domain concepts.
- They provide a notation (graphical or not) close to the practitioners' natural way of thinking.
- They propose specialized tools (like optimizers, analyzers, editors) that embed much domain knowledge and thus provide better support for practitioners, which are not necessarily professional software engineers.
- They enable the partial automation of large parts of the development process, increasing productivity.

General-purpose languages propose generic, low-level concepts, so that developing an application requires lengthy and heavy programming, but they can be used for a very large range of applications, such that the development of high quality environments and tools becomes economically feasible.

In contrast, to be effective, a DSL must target a narrow and well-scoped domain; given the cost of the upfront domain analysis and of the development of the environment and tools, DSLs become economically viable only if many applications are to be

L. Briand and C. Williams (Eds.): MoDELS 2005, LNCS 3713, pp. 69–83, 2005.

built inside the targeted domain. This compromise is the major limitation of DSL in practice. This limitation can be overcome in two ways :

• reduce the cost of developing tools,
• develop a large number of applications in the domain.

Programming languages address the first point, generating the tools from a formal DSL specification; Product Lines address the second point, emphasizing variations and features. In this paper, we present an alternative and complementary approach, based on the development of generic reusable domains which can be composed for developing wide-scope applications. We illustrate the approach by our environment - Mélusine - in which these solutions have been implemented and tested in real size industrial projects.

The paper is organized as follows: section 2 gives some background information and places our approach in the context of language and MDE technologies, section 3 presents our conceptual domain approach, section 4 is devoted to the subject of domain composition and evolution; the paper ends with related works and conclusions.

## 2   Languages and Models

Domain-Specific Languages (DSL) is a technology that takes its roots in two technological domains: programming languages and models. Their strength and weaknesses are briefly analyzed in this section, before taking a closer look at DSL.

### 2.1   The Language and Compiler Technology

Programming languages heavily rely on a technology based on grammars. A grammar G is a finite set of production rules. A language L(G) is defined by induction, as the set of sentences obtained by the reflexive and transitive closure of the derivation relationship, from an axiom. A sentence s is said to conform to the grammar G if there exists at least one sequence of derivations, from the axiom, that produces s; s is said to pertain to L(G).

In this sense, a grammar can be seen as the model of a programming language and the language as the set of all possible sentences (programs) conforming to that model (Fig.1).

The main lesson from the language domain is that grammars themselves can be seen as sentences in a (meta) language (e.g., EBNF - Extended Backus-Naur Form), defined by another (meta) grammar and compiled by another (meta) compiler. This meta-compiler can automatically generate, for a given grammar, the corresponding syntactic analyzer. For example, this is how Yacc and Lex work [2]. Yacc defines a metamodel for algebraic grammars; since it is formally defined, the algorithms can be proved to be correct and can also be optimized.

The success in languages can be measured by the fact that, on one side, compilers are now trusted and efficient and, on the other side, (simple) languages can be easily built, using meta-compilers. The major lessons are the following:

• Formal meta-grammars enable creating generators, making it easy to produce reliable compilers.

- Conformity is checked, based on the grammar.
- The semantic domain consists of logic and mathematics.

## 2.2 Modeling: The MDE Approach

MDE, as depicted in Fig. 1, presents many similarities to languages, except that the meta-meta level is not a grammar definition language, like EBNF, but a model definition language, like MOF.

The first fundamental difference is that modeling focuses on the relationship between the model and the modeled system, while languages do not consider directly the relationship between a program and reality. In fact, many definitions of model refer to this relationship, a model is usually defined as *"a simplification of a system built with an intended goal in mind. The model should be able to answer questions in place of the actual system "* [3].

It is important to notice that the *Model_of* relationship is also fundamental to DSL. Indeed, some of the alleged benefits of DSL stem from the fact that there is a close, intentionally, direct link between the program and the modeled reality in the domain.

Interestingly enough, current work in MDE has shifted its emphasis from *Model_of* to *Conform_to* [4] and recognizes that a metamodel is *"a model that defines the language for expressing a model"* [5].

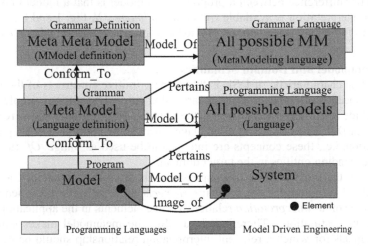

**Fig. 1.** MDE fundamental relationships

In contrast with programming languages, MDE makes the assumption that a single model can have different views and that the target system is described by many different models, possibly in different metamodels. Therefore, instead of considering a single source and target language, MDE considers that many source models can produce one or more new models.

## 2.3  Domain-Specific Languages (DSL)

DSL can thus be seen from a programming language or from an MDE perspective. The fundamental difference lies in the relationship between a model (a program) and the modeled system (the meaning of the program).

### 2.3.1  Model Meaning and Program Semantics

Consider the following Java method (seen as a model):

$$\text{int m(int c, int d) \{return c*10 + d;\}} . \qquad (1)$$

Its metamodel is the definition of the Java language [6]. Java syntax is defined through a grammar; formal semantics can be defined through denotations toward some mathematical semantic domain. Method m is a (valid) Java program, therefore it satisfies *Conform_to* for the Java specification and, as such, is perfectly defined; however, m gives no information about its "real world" meaning. A virtual machine (the JVM – Java Virtual Machine) recognizes the Java concepts, but ignores what the program means. In this example, a possible *meaning* for m could be that it computes the speed of an object, occuring during c time, with d initial speed. *Interpretation* of 10 is earth acceleration (9.81 ms$^2$); *interpretation* of c is a time in seconds, etc. This simple example shows that formal semantics (i.e., models and metamodels, per se) do not give any information on the meaning of the modeled system.

The major difference between a program and a model is that a model makes sense only if an interpretation is available (relationship *Image_Of,* Fig. 1 and Fig. 2), while a program's formal semantics do not provide any information about what it *means*.

### 2.3.2  Metamodel and Domain Semantics

An important characteristic of DSL is that some primitive constructs of the language have an embedded *interpretation* in the target domain. A DSL for our simple example could include a primitive construct for the concept of *speed* with its corresponding operators. A DSL can be seen as a language where some concepts have a predefined interpretation, i.e., these concepts are intended to be used as *Image_Of* (see Fig. 2) their corresponding entities in the target domain.

Following the programming language approach, from the metamodel, a parser is developed, which identifies the language *elements*. In a DSL, these elements constitute the range of an *interpretation* relationship; the elements in the application domain constitute its destination.  Therefore, in a DSL, the metamodel makes explicit the model elements for which a relevant interpretation relationship should be established toward the domain elements.

*To a large extent, a DSL metamodel is a model of the application domain.*

In semiotics and linguistics, semantics is defined as "*the study that relates signs to things in the world*" [7]. From that point of view, the interpretation relationship can be considered the semantics of a DSL. We will call it the *domain semantics*. In summary, we can identify the following important characteristics of a DSL:

- The metamodel is a model of the domain.
- Semantics can be defined with respect to (1) a mathematical domain (formal semantics) and (2) the application domain (domain semantics).

The domain semantics identifies the model entities that are *Image_of* entities in the system and defines their behavior. These entities and their relationships constitute the structural part of the model. The interpretation relationship allows interpreting this structure as a description of the target system structure at a given point in time. *The structural part of a model is a model of a state of the system.*

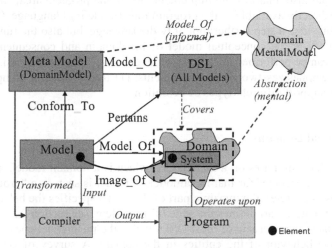

**Fig. 2.** The DSL Approach

The formal semantics serve essentially to specify the behavior, i.e., the operations on the model entities that change the structure of the model. The interpretation relationship allows interpreting this model change as a system change. *The behavioral part of the model is a model of the system dynamics,* i.e., it describes how the system (is supposed to) evolve.

## 2.4   The Composition and Evolution Problems

The application domain evolves under market and technology pressures and, therefore, the domain model should evolve accordingly. Unfortunately, most tools are based on the domain model and changes have dramatic consequences: rewrite the compiler, editors, translators, programs (models) and so on. In practice, the cost of such changes is so high that they are not performed. It is not easy to extend the compiler, nor the other associated tools, even for simple changes.

A similar scenario arises when we try to compose different domains. While the composition can be clearly specified at the domain model level, it is not easy to specify the corresponding modifications at the compiler level. Indeed, the difficulties are not at the meta and model levels; the problems arise at the implementation level, because there is another level of abstraction. This problem is well known and extensible (DSL) languages and/or composition of existing DSLs [9] have been proposed. These technologies have not been successfully deployed yet.

# 3 The Mélusine Approach

Our approach to domain composition and evolution follows the underlying trend in DSL and MDE: perform as many activities as possible at the level of the domain model, not at the implementation level. Both DSL and MDE propose to perform not only design, but also a part of the implementation in the problem area, since problem concepts are directly available in the programming (modeling) language. Our proposition pushes this idea a step further: not only the language, but also the run-time architecture is based on the conceptual model of the domain and consequently, domain composition can be performed at an abstract level, using high-level domain concepts.

Mélusine emphasizes two new requirements: (1) Reuse existing components and tools and (2) Support different types of evolution.

## 3.1 Conceptual Domains

As in DSL, Mélusine relies on a metamodel, which is a domain model, and assumes that there is an interpreter for that metamodel. A model is seen as a "program" interpreted by this interpreter; the dynamic part of the model specifies the behavior of entities and the structural part defines the state of the system, see section 2.3.2.

An important characteristic of most DSLs is that the metamodel encapsulates most (if not all) the behavior of the entities in the domain. A survey of DSLs [10] has shown that most DSLs do not provide constructs for user-defined abstractions: only 15% of the surveyed languages provide user defined types and roughly one third provide user-defined functions. This is interesting because in many DSLs, when developing a model, there is no need (and no way) to specify the behavior of the system; this behavior is implicit in the constructs of the language. Most of the time the model represents only the structural part of the application and simply parameterizes the predefined behavior.

The fact a model is purely structural has important consequences:
1. It is relatively easy to fully generate, from the metamodel, a model editor and a model does not need any programming.
2. The system behavior (how it evolves) is mainly defined by the behavior of the predefined domain concepts, implemented by the domain interpreter.
3. Domains can be composed by composing their interpreters, without modifying the existing models.

## 3.2 Domain-Specific Virtual Machines

A straightforward implementation of a domain interpreter is to transform each metamodel concept into a class and the concept behavior into methods of these classes (plus some technical classes, not discussed here). In this case, the structural part of the model is simply transformed into instances of these classes and considered as the initial state of the interpreter. As this transformation is a bijection, there is an isomorphism between the model and the program state and, therefore, the program state is also a model of the target system. Since execution is based on the domain model, the

program state evolves in accordance with the behavior of the associated domain entities (see Fig. 3). This implementation is not only straightforward - and supported by most UML environments - but also has two important properties:
1. At any time, the state of the program is a model of the target system.
2. The interpreter is a domain virtual machine.
The former property is fundamental for DSL composition (see section 4). The latter is important, since it gives a way to solve reuse and evolution issues. Indeed, since the interpreter implementation is based on the domain semantics, its behavior is defined only in terms of changes of the instances that are images of domain elements. *It is a formal execution.* The execution, in this case, does not rely on lower level libraries or languages, as is usually the case in DSL technology (Fig. 2), nor on a transformation toward lower level "platform dependent" models, as in MDE. A very important property of this approach is that *the interpreter is independent from actual components, tools and platforms.*

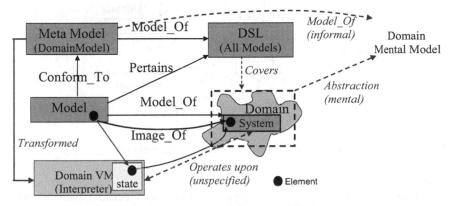

**Fig. 3.** Domain modeling and Mélusine

## 3.3  Virtual Machine Implementation

Formal execution means the execution only changes the state of abstract entities (Java objects) but, most often, such a change "means" that its "image" in the system (either software or physical) must change its state accordingly. Conversely, if the state of the system changes, the model should be updated accordingly. In other words, formal interpretation is not sufficient, abstract actions should be mapped to actual software components, devices and so on.

In order to reuse existing software artifacts, Mélusine supports a bottom-up approach, defining the concepts of role and tool [11]. A role is an abstract interface for a class of tools. A tool is any piece of software, (a COTS, a legacy application, a component, a library, a physical device and so on), local or distant, that can play a role (directly or through a wrapper).

The *Mapping* expresses the relationship between a state change in a model entity (a Java object) and the correspondent change for its image in the "real" system (a tool executing an action, a device activations) and so on. Conversely, the mapping changes the model entity state to keep them synchronized with changes in the "real" system.

Our requirement is to keep the interpreter independent from mapping. For this purpose, mapping is performed in the Mélusine environment by transparently translating it into aspects, in the AOP (Aspect Oriented Programming) sense. This is easy to do, because the formal interpretation directly changes the state of the model entities; it is enough to capture the methods that change the (Java) model entities and to call the corresponding mapping. Our AOP machine [12] inserts byte code in the interpreter, to execute the aspect in accordance with the mapping specification (Fig. 4).

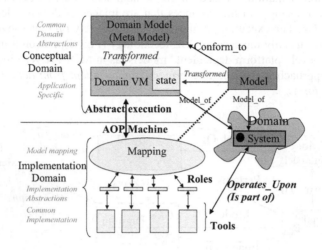

**Fig. 4.** Conceptual domain and implementation

In our solution:
- the interpreter and the models are independent from any specific implementation,
- the mapping is defined at a high level, between the model and roles (abstract tools),
- actual tools implement abstract services (roles) and can be changed at any time.

Our domain-layered architecture emphasizes the reuse of tools, models and interpreters and enables each actor (analyst, designer, implementer, administrator) to work with tools and concepts at its level of abstraction.

Reusing a domain model implies being able to combine it with other domains in order to cope with wider scope applications (see section 4 about domain composition) and to adapt it to specific requirements (see section 5 about domain evolution).

## 4   Domain Composition

Our approach to domain composition is built on the insight that composition is easily expressed at the conceptual level (see section 2.4), and that most of the reuse benefits can be achieved if one can use the existing domains and their models without modifying them.

Domain composition (section 4.1) consists of defining concepts and relationships that are valid for all the applications in the new composite domain. The new behavior is implemented in the composition virtual machine (section 4.2) by synchronizing its execution with the corresponding sub-domain interpreters. Then the domain models can be easily composed  (section 4.3).

## 4.1  Domain Model Composition

The composition is initially defined at the conceptual level, by identifying relation-ships that must be established between existing domains and potentially new concepts and behavior, specific to the composition (see the upper part of Fig. 5).

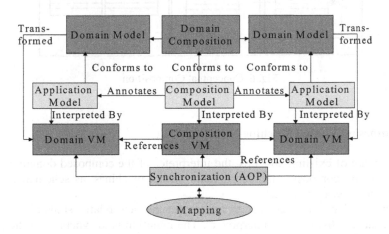

**Fig. 5.** Conceptual Domain Composition

Because domain models are designed independently, they often contain similar concepts, defined in different ways, since each domain corresponds to a specific con-cern and outlines the characteristics relevant for this concern only. Two types of rela-tionships can then be established between concepts present in two different domain models: associations (in the UML sense) and correspondences, relating similar or overlapping concepts [13]. For example, Fig. 6 shows some of the new relationships defined for the composition of the Process and Resource domains. The *association* Project/Resource models the resources assigned to the project, while Activ-ity/Human indicates the person in charge of an activity; they are usually class asso-ciations that capture some emerging behavior of the composition. The relationships Process/Project and Task/Activity are *correspondences* between overlapping con-cepts in different domains, in the sense that they can be considered as different as-pects of a single unified concept in the composed domain. The example illustrates an important property: domain composition may involve more than two domains. The human resources assigned to an activity must be selected from the available resources of the project; this is a constraint that covers the three composed domains.

A crucial point to highlight is that conceptual composition defines the metamodel of the composed domain. This new metamodel comprises the concepts and associa-tions existing in the sub-domains, the added relationships and, eventually, new emerging concepts. As for any other domain, an interpreter must be implemented for this new metamodel and appropriate models must be developed for the new composed domain (section 4.3).

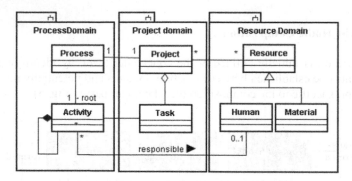

**Fig. 6.** Conceptual Composition

## 4.2  Composing Virtual Machine

To foster reuse of existing domains, the interpreter of the composed domain must be implemented by composing the sub-domain virtual machines, as schematically presented in the lower part of Fig. 5.

It turns out that it is necessary to implement the new relationships and behavior without changing the existing interpreters. The intention is to synchronize the execution of several independent virtual machines (sub-domain interpreters). Note that the new virtual machine is allowed to explicitly reference existing classes and associations in the sub-domain interpreters, but not the other way around.

To implement this synchronization, AOP technology is used again, defining aspects that capture the methods representing significant events in the sub-domain interpreters and calling the appropriate methods in the composition domain interpreter, that implements the behavior of the new classes and relationships. This approach may look low level, but this is not the case because, as pointed out in section 3.2, the state of the virtual machine is a model of the target system and the captured events are meaningful in the new conceptual model.

To illustrate this claim, the sample of program presented below shows the synchronization between Process and Resource domains (this is the real, complete code, extracted from an operational document management application). The new behavior to be implemented is assigning a human to be responsible for a particular activity. The aspect assignActivity captures, in the process virtual machine, the signals representing that an activity has become ready; the aspect calls the composite virtual machine (class ActivityAssignationManager) that itself calls the resource virtual machine to display a list of humans playing the associated role and changes the responsible.

```
import apel.motor.model.*;
aspect assignActivity(int newState) of Activity {
  when  newState == Activity.READY;
```

```
  body( JAVA ) {
    activityAssignationMaager.assignActivity(instance);
    }
}
public class ActivityAssignationManager {
  public ActivityAssignationManager () {
    resource = Domains.getRoot("resourceEngine");
  }
  public Vector getPotentialHumans(String roleName) {
    Role theRole = resource.getRole(roleName);
    return resource.getHumanIds(theRole);
  }
  public void assignActivity (Activity activity) {
    String user = showAssignDialog(activity.getName(),
      getPotentialHumans(activity.getRole()));
    return activity.setResponsible(user);
  }
}
```

The classes in the composition virtual machine are similar to other domains, they capture abstract concepts of the composition and, as shown in Fig. 4, may require a mapping to lower level software, components, devices and so on, just as for other domains, see section 3.3.

Composing virtual machines is not necessarily easy, but not too complex either, because each interpreter is a direct implementation of the corresponding domain concept and therefore, the composition is performed at the conceptual level of the composite domain. This is much easier than trying to change the existing interpreters or to implement a new one. In our experience, a typical composition interpreter is very tiny; for instance, in the document management application, the composition interpreter is about 15% (in LOC) of all composed domain virtual machines.

### 4.3  Model Composition

The composite domain has its own metamodel, meaning that we may need to develop new models conforming to this metamodel. These models can refer to existing sub-domains models and can make the links between them explicit. For example, for the document management composite domain presented in section 4.2, the data circulating in the data flows defined in a process model should be associated with actual product definitions in the product data management domain; more specifically, the entity called *doc* in the process model is the document *specifProjectX* in the Product domain. This information is captured by the composite model and is interpreted by the composition virtual machine (see the code of class ActivityAssignationManager in the previous section).

There is an important point to highlight: the existing models have not changed at all, but a new model was defined that relates the existing sub-domain models. The experience shows that this is very easy to do and allows models to be reused. Since the domain itself evolves, its model has to incorporate the novelties introduced in the real domain.

## 4.4  Domain Evolution

Some variations in the domain can be expressed without having to change the domain model. A *feature* captures *optional domain behavior*; they are implemented in the same way as mappings, by capturing domain behavior and adding/substituting it with the actual feature behavior. In this way, the domain model, the interpreter and models are totally unchanged. For example, the Process domain has *trace, mail_notification* and *persistent* features. They can be selected or not for each application in the domain.

*Extensions* are new concepts, added to the domain and linked by associations with the domain model concepts. These concepts, with their semantics, behavior and implementation, make sense only in connection with the domain model.

This is in contrast with domain composition, where each domain is independent and makes sense by itself. Nevertheless, the technology we use to define and implement extensions is the same as for domain composition [14].

## 5  Related Work

The idea of extending or specializing a language by modifying its interpreter has been actively studied in the context of Meta Object Protocols [15] and reflective programming languages. In this context, the formal domain interpreter can be seen as the meta level, the actual tools and components as the base level and the mapping as the causal link between the two. An important difference in our approach is that the meta level is directly related to the domain (domain semantics) and not (only) to the formal semantics. Another difference is that we develop the two levels separately, in order to be able to evolve them independently, and we use AOP to keep them synchronized.

More generally, our approach is based on the idea that a domain presents two interfaces: when used in the development of a particular application, only the model editor is visible, the domain model and its interpreter are hidden. When composed or extended, the conceptual model is exposed like a white box. In this regard, our work can be related to the idea of open implementations [16][17] and more particularly to the ideas of open design programming languages [18]. The domain-specific virtual machine can also be related to the idea of a UML virtual machine [19]. The difference is that, instead of implementing a low-level UML action language, we implement the behavior of the high-level domain concepts.

Composing modeling languages by composing their corresponding metamodels is also considered in [20], but the approach is limited to the generation of the model editor and does not consider the domain behavior and run-time environment. Fritsch and Renz [21] present a meta-level architecture for the development of product lines based on several related DSLs, similarly Barry et Al. [22] present an example of composition of Process and Product Data Management software, by composing metamodels. Although very similar to our approach, both are limited to a particular domain. We have generalized the approach and have applied it systematically in very different domains.

The problem of metamodel evolution and adaptation and its impact on the corresponding interpreters has been stated in [23] and an approach for metamodel evolution based on a transformation language is presented in [24]. These approaches are based on the idea of refactoring the metamodel and automating the impact on the existing models and interpreters. Our approach is based on the idea of modularly defining the metamodel and reusing the existing models and interpreters. The two approaches complement each other very well.

Another solution other than DSL would be to use a general modeling language, such as UML 2.0 [5], that offers support for:

- *Evolution*, with the possibility to introduce variability (through templates, power-types for creating metamodels and semantic variation points like model annotations) and extensions (with inheritance, stereotypes, constraints and tagged values);
- *Reuse*, with patterns, stereotyped packages like model libraries or frameworks and the facility to merge packages (models), by introducing a generalization for classifiers with the same name;
- *Domain-specific concepts*, with profiles, that allow for the definition of stereotypes grouping property extensions.

UML was not adopted, because defining a DSL is simpler than defining a profile. A profile, even if extending only a metamodel subset, requires conformity with the huge UML semantics and checking this conformity is not entirely supported by existing tools. From the point of view of code generation, model transformation often needs supplementary marking models [25] and restriction to UML subsets. Executable UML [26] goes forward, by creating an UML profile and adding actions for a detailed definition of the behavior, such as to be executed. Models for different subject matters are woven together by an executable UML compiler that, unlike Mélusine, keeps all the burden of general languages. Apart from making the composition at the meta level, between small DSLs, the flexibility added by our approach also comes from its layered architecture, which separates the models from their implementation tools and allows domain extensibility.

A possible solution for directly manipulating the domain concepts is expected to be given by future tools, for example, based on MOF [27], allowing users to define entirely new languages via metamodels. In the meantime, the Eclipse Modeling Framework (EMF) seems to be closer to our needs, proposing Ecore meta-metamodel, similar to MOF and expressing models as XML schemas, UML class diagrams or annonated Java [28]. EMF provides all the facilities and extensibility of Eclipse and also offers a number of tools to support automatic editor generation and round-trip engineering, while still leaving the user the possibility to write code that remains outside models.

# 6 Conclusion

Our work is based on a simple idea: DSL is a good engineering approach, but it is limited by its narrow scope; so, composing DSLs would permit implementing wide-scope applications, while retaining the strong points of DSLs. Unfortunately, this simple idea is far from trivial if one seeks a solution answering the question: how is it possible to *compose DSLs*, but still *reuse* existing components and tools and support different types of *evolution*.

We have spent a number of years answering this question, implementing (re-implementing) solutions, and validating them in real scale industrial applications. The lesson we have learned is that no single technology or technical approach alone can solve these issues. Indeed, our approach puts together ideas coming from DSL, MDE, programming languages, AOP and component technologies.

AOP, as well as components, are implementation techniques, not engineering approaches. Nevertheless, AOP is our corner stone implementation solution, because it allows both reuse and evolution.

Our approach is typical of MDE, but, in contrast with the main stream, our technology allows for the composition of independent models and metamodels by defining relationships among their concepts. This composition technology is a practical and high-level way to compose DSLs, defining a new, extended DSL, that can be further composed itself. Furthermore, as this approach uses formal interpretation and AOP techniques, it is possible to reuse the existing domains (interpreters, models and so on) without changing them. Finally, the introduction of features and extensions at the conceptual level and the explicit mappings and roles at the implementation level, provide large evolution capabilities.

Composing DSLs in the general case is very difficult, but it becomes a practical and promising software engineering approach when supported by a methodology and a specific environment, like Mélusine, providing high-level modeling, generation, evolution and reuse.

**Acknowledgements**: The work of Anca Daniela Ionita is supported by a Marie Curie Intra-European Fellowship, within the 6th European Community Framework Programme.

# References

1. D. S. Wile., Supporting the DSL Spectrum, Journal of Computing and Information Technology, CIT 9, 2001 (4) 263-287
3. Levine, John R., Tony Mason and Doug Brown [1992]. Lex & Yacc. O'Reilly & Associates, Inc. Sebastopol, California
3. Bézivin, J., Gerbé O., "Towards a Precise Definition of the OMG/MDA Framework", ASE'01, Novembre 2001
4. Favre J.M., "Towards a Basic Theory to Model Model Driven Engineering", 3rd Workshop in Software Model Engineering, WiSME 2004, http://www-adele.imag.fr/~jmfavre
5. OMG, "UML 2.0 Superstructure Specification", August 2003
6. Gosling J., Joy B., & Steele G., The Java Language Specification, Addison Wesley, 1997
7. J.F. Sowa, Ontology, Metadata, and Semiotics, in B. Ganter & G. W. Mineau, eds., *Conceptual Structures: Logical, Linguistic, and Computational Issues*, Lecture Notes in AI #1867, Springer-Verlag, Berlin, 2000, pp. 55-81
8. R.A. Falbo, G. Guizzardi, K.C. Duarte, An ontological approach to domain engineering, *Proc. of the 14thInt. Conf. on Software Eng. and Knowledge Eng.*, Ischia, Italy, 2002, ISBN:1-58113-556-4, pp. 351 – 358
9. R. Prieto-Diaz, Domain Analysis: An Introduction, *Software Engineering Notes*, Vol. 15, No. 2, April 1990
10. S. Thibault, "Langages Dédiés : Conception, Implémentation et Application", Ph.D. Thesis Université de Rennes1, 1998

11. T. Le-Anh, J. Villalobos, J. Estublier. Multi-level Composition for Software Federations. In Proceedings of the 6th European Joint Conferences on Theory and Practice of Software (ETAPS 2003) Workshop on Software Composition, April 2003

12. F. Duclos, J. Estublier, R. Sanlaville "Separation of Concerns and The Extended Object Machine." Submitted to Journal Advise. http://www-adele.imag.fr/Les.Publications/BD/ADVICE2004Est.html

13. J. Estublier, A.D. Ionita, Extending UML for Model Composition, *Australian Software Engineering Conference*, 29 March – 1 April, Brisbane, Australia

14. J. Estublier, J. Villalobos, T. Le-Ahn, S. Sanlaville, G. Vega. An Approach and Framework for Extensible Process Support System. . In Proceedings of the 9th European Workshop on Software Process Technology (EWSPT 2003), September 2003

15. G. Kiczales, J. des Rivières, D. Bobrow. The Art of the Metaobject Protocol. MIT Press, Cambridge Massachusetts, 5th Printing 1999

16. G. Kiczales. Beyond the black box: Open Implementation, IEEE Software, Vol. 13 Issue 1, January 1996

17. C. Maeda, A. Lee, G. Murphy, G. Kizales. Open Implementation Analysis and Design, ACM SIGSOFT Software Engineering Notes, Vol. 22 Issue 3, May 1997

18. P. Steyaert. Open Design of Object Oriented Languages. PhD thesis, Vrije Universiteit Brussel, 1994.

19. D. Riehle, S. Fraleigh, D. Bucka-Lassen, N. Omorogbe. The Architecture of a UML virtual machine, Proceedings of the 16th ACM SIGPLAN Conference on Object oriented programming, systems, languages, and applications OOPSLA 2001, Tampa Bay, USA, October 2001

20. G. Karsai, M. Maroti, A. Ledeczi, J. Gray, J. Sztipanovits. Composition and Cloning in Modeling and Meta-Modeling, IEEE Transactions on Control System Technology, Vol. 12 No. 2, March 2004

21. C. Fritsch, B. Renz. Four Mechanisms for Adaptable Systems A Meta-level Approach to Building a Software Product Line. Proceedings of the 3rd International Software Product Lines Conference, SPLC 2004, Boston, USA, August 2004

22. A. Barry, N. Baker, J.-M. Le Goff, R. McClatchey, J.-P. Vialle. Meta-Data based design of Workflow Systems. Proceedings of Workshop on Meta-data and Active Object Model pattern mining, OOPSLA 1998, Vancouver, Canada. October 1998

23. J. Zhang, J. Gray. A generative approach to model interpreter evolution. Proceedings of Workshop on Domain Specific Modeling, OOPSLA 2004, Vancouver, Canada. October 2004

24. J. Sprinkle, G. Karsai. A Domain-Specific Visual Language For Domain Model Evolution. Journal of Visual Languages and Computing, vol. 15, no. 2, April 2004.

25. S. Mellor, K. Scott, A. Uhl, D. Weise. MDA Distilled: Principles of Model-driven Architecture, Addison-Wesley, 2004

26. S. Mellor, M. Balcer. Executable UML: A Foundation for Model Driven Architecture. Addison-Wesley, 2002

27. OMG, "Meta Object Facility (MOF) 2.0 Core Specification", October 2003

28. F. Budinsky, D. Steinberg, E. Merks, R. Ellersick, T. Grose, "Eclipse Modeling Framework", Addison Wesley, 200

# Model Typing for Improving Reuse in Model-Driven Engineering

Jim Steel and Jean-Marc Jézéquel

Irisa (INRIA & University of Rennes)
Campus Universitaire de Beaulieu
35042 Rennes CEDEX, France

**Abstract.** Where object-oriented languages deal with objects as described by classes, model-driven development uses models, as graphs of interconnected objects, described by metamodels. A number of new languages have been and continue to be developed for this model-based paradigm, both for model transformation and for general programming using models. Many of these use single-object approaches to typing, derived from solutions found in object-oriented systems, while others use metamodels as model types, but without a clear notion of polymorphism. Both of these approaches lead to brittle and overly restrictive reuse characteristics. In this paper we propose a simple extension to object-oriented typing to better cater for a model-oriented context, including a simple strategy for typing models as a collection of interconnected objects. Using a simple example we show how this extended approach permits more flexible reuse, while preserving type safety.

## 1 Introduction

From the perspective of the data structures involved, model-driven computing can be seen as a progression from object-oriented computing. Models are, in essence, composed of objects linked together using first-class bidirectional relationships, where the structure of the objects and the relationships between them are typically defined by a MOF, or MOF-like, metamodel. The presence of these relationships has the effect that model structures are much more tightly coupled than object structures.

For this reason, it is hardly surprising that the majority of approaches to developing languages for manipulating models have adopted formalisms based on those found in object-oriented programming languages.

The study of languages for manipulating these model structures is active. In 2001, the OMG issued an RFP soliciting languages for defining model transformations, as mappings between models. In response, many languages have been developed, using variously logic-based[10], pattern-based [13], and graph-transformation [14] approaches. Concurrently, a number of efforts are being undertaken to develop or extend programming languages to better deal with models as data structures [2, 17].

L. Briand and C. Williams (Eds.): MoDELS 2005, LNCS 3713, pp. 84–96, 2005.

The vast majority of these efforts have chosen to use type systems developed for use within object-oriented development. However, as discussed in [8] and mentioned in [16], the use of such type systems in a model-oriented context renders programs somewhat brittle with respect to changes in the metamodel.

Most importantly, however, is that these systems do not truly allow the user to specify their transformations or programs in terms of models and types of models, but rather in terms of objects within models. This is counter-intuitive to the user.

To resolve this, we discuss necessary extensions to object-oriented typing to deal with the relationships defined in MOF metamodels. Using this extended notion of object typing, we propose a definition of a model type, including a definition of substitutability of model types and a discussion of reflection and inference of model types.

In section 2, we provide a background on typing and models and the role of typing in model-driven engineering, including a motivating example. Following this, in section 3 we present a definition of model types with a rule for model type substitutability, including an illustration using the example. Section 4 discusses the implication of this definition for the related issues of model type reflection and model type inference. Section 5 discusses a number of related works from the domains of both MDE and type systems.

## 2   Background

Generally speaking, a type can be understood as a set of values on which a related set of operations can be performed successfully. Once types have been defined, it is possible to use them in operation specifications of the form: if some input of type X is given, then the output will have type Y. Type safety is the guarantee that no run-time error will result from the application of the operation to the wrong object or value. A type system is a set of rules for checking type safety (a process usually called type checking since it is often required that enough information about the typing assumptions has been given explicitly by the designer or programmer, so that type checking becomes mostly a large bookkeeping process).

Type checking is said to be static when it is performed without program execution (typically at compile-time or bind-time). It aims at ensuring once and for all that there is no possibility of interaction errors (of the kind addressed by the type system). Not all errors can be addressed by type systems, especially since one usually requires that type checking is easy; e.g., with static type checking it is difficult to rule out in advance all risks of division-by-zero errors.

Type systems allow checking substitutability when services are combined: by comparing the data types in a service interface, and the data types desired by its caller, one can predict whether an interaction error is possible (e.g. producing a run-time error such as "Method not understood"). Conformance is generally defined as the weakest (i.e., least restrictive) substitutability relation that guarantees type safety. Necessary conditions (applying recursively) are that a caller must not invoke any operation not supported by the service, and the service must not return any exception not handled by the caller. Conformance has a property called contravariance: the types of the input parameters of a service must conform in opposite to the types of its result parameters.

## 2.1   Example

We consider as a motivating example a simple model transformation that takes as input a state machine and produces a lookup table showing the correspondence between the current state, an arriving event, and the resultant state. The input metamodel for this transformation is presented in figure 1. The output metamodel, not shown, can be assumed to be a simple database language, but in any case we will focus on the conformance of the input type.

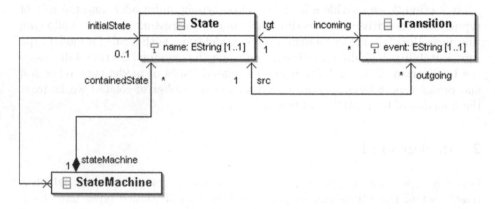

**Fig. 1.** Simple State Machine Metamodel

The choice of which language is used to implement the transformation, and even of which paradigm of language to use, is immaterial. Also immaterial is the choice as to whether the input and output types of the transformation are derived (inferred) or explicitly declared. (This choice is discussed further in section 4).

Having given this metamodel as the nominal input for the transformation, we consider that there are a number of variants of state machines whose instances might also be interesting as potential inputs to the transformation.

Initially, we might consider changing to the multiplicity of the "initial" reference from 0..1 to 0..*, for state machines with multiple start states (Figure 2), or from 0..1 to 1..1, mandating that each state machine have exactly one start state (Figure 3). Alternatively, we might apply the composite pattern by adding an inheritance of State by StateMachine, for composite state machines (Figure 4). Finally, we might consider the addition of a FinalState class as a new subclass of State (Figure 5).

The question is, then, does the initial transformation written for models conforming to Figure 1 still work with models conforming to these variant metamodels?

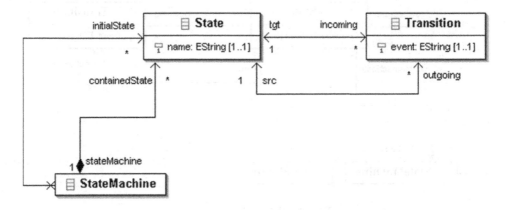

**Fig. 2.** State Machine Metamodel with multiple start states

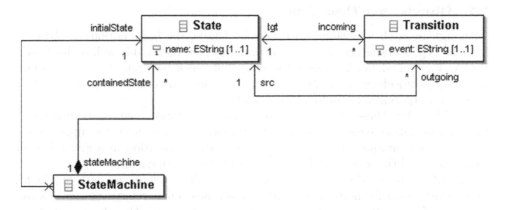

**Fig. 3.** State Machine Metamodel with mandatory start states

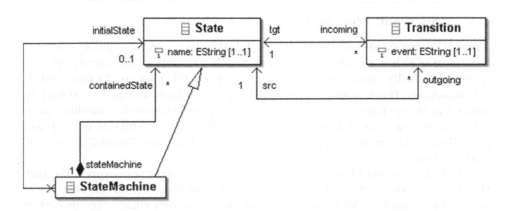

**Fig. 4.** Composite State Machine Metamodel

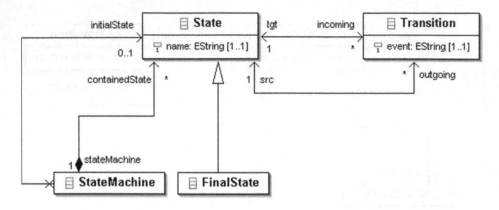

**Fig. 5.** With Final States

## 2.2 Objects, and Their Types

Although research is ongoing into the fine details, the basic notions of objects and the type systems that describe them are by now reasonably well-understood [1]. As mentioned briefly above, the main difference between the objects seen in classical object-oriented systems and the objects used within models is the presence of (potentially) bidirectional relationships.

In MOF 1.x, these were defined as binary associations, which in turn contained association ends, which defined characteristics such as the upper and lower bounds, uniqueness and orderedness of the association in a given direction. Navigabilities were specified by the addition of references.

In MOF 2.0, relationships are defined as a pair of references, each of which defines the details formerly kept by association ends. These references may link to another reference, thus forming a bidirectional relationship. This change entails a subtle change of expressivity but, in effect, yields the same type of relationships.

## 2.3 Models and Metamodels

The MOF specifications, unlike those of UML, have never included a formal definition of either a model or a metamodel. By convention, and intuitively, the latter has usually been used as a synonym for a MOF package. In many MOF 1.x implementations, a model was defined as a "package instance", a term not defined in the specifications, but an intuitive concept that could contain objects instantiated from any class within a given MOF package. While intuitive, these definitions were somewhat limiting for situations where cross-"model" references were common.

MOF 2.0 has introduced the notion of an extent, and made explicit the fact that extents may contain objects instantiated from classes from different packages. This recognises the increasing abundance of models which reference other models; these are intuitively, and may now be considered as, single models. However, this leaves us without a firm idea of a metamodel, since we can no longer be guaranteed that all objects within an extent will possess a type contained by a single package.

Beyond these conventions, there are two general approaches to defining a concept of a model. The first, that taken by UML, is to designate some class as being a root node for the model, whereby the model thus consists of instances of that class and all objects contained by (or perhaps reachable from) that object. However, this does not work in the case of models which lack a single root element, as is common in cases such as models containing tags or models of, for example, collaborative processes[12]. The alternative and more general approach, the one evident as Extent in MOF 2.0, is to define a model as just a set of objects.

Taking this second definition, the obvious choice for the type of a model is the set of the object types of all the contained objects. The details of such a definition are given in the next section.

## 2.4   Typing in Model-Driven Engineering

The application of typing in model-driven engineering is seen at a number of levels.

At a fine-grained level, languages that manipulate and explore models need to be able to reason about the types of the objects and properties that they are regarding within the models. For this level of granularity, an object-based approach to typing is probably more natural and appropriate.

From a broader perspective, there is also a need to reason about the types of artifacts handled by the transformations, programs, repositories and other model-related services. It is at this level that an appropriate type system should allow us to reason about the construction of coherent systems from the services available to us. While it is possible to define the models handled by these services in terms of the types of the objects that they accept, we argue that this is not a natural approach, since these services intuitively accept models as input, and not objects.

Having established that services might accept and produce models, it follows that they should specify a type for these models. Furthermore, having established these type declarations, it is also useful to find a semantic for substitutability that allows the maximum possible flexibility and reuse, while still assuring that the services do not receive models whose elements they do not understand.

For example, the sample transformation described in section 2.1 can be said to accept state machines as input, and should accept as many of the noted variants as possible, provided that at no point the transformation attempts an action on the model that is not possible.

## 3   Model Types and Model Type Substitutability

In this section we provide a simple structure for the type of a model and discuss the conditions under which one model type may be substituted for another.

This includes an analysis of the dependence of model typing upon object typing, and the extensions necessary for object typing to function correctly in this new context. We demonstrate the application of model types using the example presented earlier.

## 3.1 Model Types

The previous section defines a model type as the set of object types for all the objects contained in a model. However, this is a definition based on reflection, and the aim of model types is rather targeted at transformation or model-based programming languages, where reflection will not be the dominant manner of determining types. Therefore, we need to redefine our model type more basically.

So what structures do we have? Normal MOF reflection upon an object yields a MOF class. While literature on type systems, such as [11], suggests that a type is not the same thing as a class, MOF is something of a special case. Since MOF is a signature language, i.e. unable to specify behaviour, a MOF class is in fact more analogous to a type than to a class in type system terminology. We therefore content ourselves to define a model type as a set of MOF classes (and, of course, the references that they contain).

In the example presented in section 2.1, the model type required for our transformation is in essence the metamodel shown in figure 1. In fact, the only significant difference between model types and metamodels is the structuring provided by packages and relationships between packages.

## 3.2 Model-Type Checking

Under what conditions may one model type, i.e. set of object types, be considered conformant, or substitutable, for another? Quite simply, each object type in the required set must be "understood" by the candidate set. Clearly, this returns to a situation of object type conformance.

**Object-Type Conformance** The presence of relationships, in whichever form, defined between classes has little effect on the overall approach on the typing of objects. The structure of an object type remains the same. Indeed, if one considers a relationship as a mutually dependent pair of references, they do not differ fundamentallly from the properties seen commonly in object-oriented systems. There is, of course, a stronger prevalence of cyclic dependencies between the conformance of classes. For example, consider a class C1 in a relationship A1, consisting of two references R1 and R2, with another class C2. For a class C1' to be considered a subtype of C1, it must participate in a relationship A1' with a class C2' that is a subtype of C2, which fact depends on the original comparison of C1' and C1.

As has been already presented in [15], there are many possible approaches to the type conformance of object types in a model-based context, ranging from the currently-predominant approach based on subclass-based conformance, as in Java, to structural conformance. As is also presented in [15], these must be extended to ensure that the covariance (for operation return types and property types) and contravariance (for parameter types) rules take into account the structural differences such as multiplicities on associations (using subsumption and inverse subsumption respectively).

However, to use these approaches when typing a model as a collection of objects, there are additional requirements that must be met which do not appear when evaluating object type conformance in isolation. Specifically, there are certain rules pertaining to the preservation of the identity of classes when assessing conformance of relationships. These rules are most evident in resultant axioms such as:

1. A reflexive relationship may not be satisfied by a non-reflexive relationship.

2. Similarly, a non-reflexive relationship may not be satisfied by a reflexive relationship.

Having added this constraint, the choice remains open as to which algorithm one uses when assessing object type conformance. So as to avoid confusing our examples by using metamodel extension techniques, we will proceed using the structural conformance proposed in [15], with appropriate extensions for the above constraint.

**Model-Type Conformance** Using our object type conformance rule, the question of whether a required model type may be satisfied by a provided model type is determined by checking whether for each required object type, there exists a conformant object type in the provided type.

It is very important to note here the reason for avoiding a reflective definition of model type. In particular, in requiring that each object type exist in the provided model type, we do not mandate that there exist an instance of each object type. Put more simply, there is a difference between the absence of an object of a given type in a model and the absence of the object's type in the model's model type. The model type of a state machine without transitions would still contain the Transition class.

This difference poses no problems if we remain within the domain of transformations or programs with manifest typing, but may become problematic for dynamically determining the type of a model using reflection, or for a language that determines its input or output model types using inference. These problems are discussed in section 4.

### 3.3   Details and Demonstration

The approach for testing model type conformance discussed above may be summarised by the following steps:

– For each class (object type) in the required model type, find all conformant object types in the provided model type. Using structural conformance from [15], this means that

- Each operation on the required class must be satisfied by a conformant operation according to covariance on return type, contravariance on parameter types and appropriate subsumptions of multiplicities
- Each property on the required class must be satisfied by a conformant property according to covariance on type, subsumption on multiplicity, etc
- Eliminate conformant provided types which violate the identity rules described above
- Ensure that for each class in the required model type, there remains at least one conformant type in the provided model type.

More formally, conformance of a provided model type $MT_p$ to a required model type $MT_r$ may be defined as follows.

First, we establish the object type conformance relation $image(MT_r.types \rightarrow MT_p.types)$, such that:

$\forall C_p : Class \in MT_p, \ \forall C_r : Class \in MT_r,$
$C_p \in image(C_r) \Longleftrightarrow$

$\quad \forall O_r : Operation \ \in C_r.allOperations(),$
$\quad \exists O_p : Operation \ \in C_p.allOperations() \ —$
$\quad\quad O_p.name = O_r.name,$ and
$\quad\quad O_p.type \ \leq O_r.type$ (return type covariance), and
$\quad\quad O_p.multiplicity \subseteq O_r.multipicity$ (return type multiplicity subsumption), and
$\quad\quad \forall Pa_r : Parameter \in O_r.ownedParameter,$
$\quad\quad \exists Pa_p : Parameter \in O_r.ownedParameter \ —$
$\quad\quad\quad Pa_r.type \leq Pa_p.type$ (parameter type contravariance), and
$\quad\quad\quad Pa_r.multiplicity \subseteq Pa_p.multipicity$ (parameter multiplicity subsumption (inverse))
$\quad \forall Pr_r : Property \in C_r.allProperties(),$
$\quad \exists Pr_p : Property \in C_p.allProperties() \ —$
$\quad\quad Pr_p.type \leq Pr_r.type$ (property type covariance), and
$\quad\quad Pr_p.multiplicity \subseteq Pr_r.multipicity$ (property multiplicity subsumption), and
$\quad\quad Pr_r.isReadOnly = false \Rightarrow Pr_p.isReadOnly = false$

Having established this relation $image(MT_r.types \rightarrow MT_p.types)$, check the identity constraints described above, by ensuring that:

$\forall C_r \in MT_r, \ image(C_r) \neq \emptyset$ (each required class has a conformant)
$\forall C_r \in MT_r, \forall P_r \in C_r.allProperties(),$

$\quad P_r.type = C_r \Rightarrow image(P_r.type) = image(C_r),$ (reflexive properties are satisfied by reflexive properties) and
$\quad P_r.type \neq C_r \Rightarrow image(P_r.type) \cap image(C_r) = \emptyset$ (non-reflexive properties are satisfied by non-reflexive properties)

| ȓ conforms to → | Simple | Mult-St | Mand-St | Comp | Final |
|---|---|---|---|---|---|
| Simple (Figure 1) | YES | YES | NO | NO | YES |
| Multiple-Start (Figure 2) | NO | YES | NO | NO | NO |
| Mandatory-Start (Figure 3) | YES | YES | YES | NO | YES |
| Composite (Figure 4) | YES | YES | NO | YES | YES |
| With-Final-States (Figure 5) | YES | YES | NO | NO | YES |

**Table 1.** Model Type Conformance Relation for State Machine Variants

Applying these steps to the example metamodels provided in section 2.1, we obtain the model type conformance relation shown in Table 1.

In this relation we can see that the addition of new classes (FinalState) and the broadening of multiplicity constraints have not broken the subtyping relationship, but that tightening of multiplicities has. It is notable also that composite state charts are found to be subtypes of simple state charts, although the reverse might have been more intuitive. The effect of using structural conformance is seen by the conformance of simple state charts to those with final states.

## 4   Further Considerations

Having considered the general idea of types for models and presented an approach for verifying the conformance of model types, we now proceed to discuss two related issues, those of model type reflection and model type inference.

### 4.1   Model Type Reflection

Reflection is one of the key features of model-driven engineering. The ability to ask an object about what features it provides allows for the creation of generic tools that work regardless of the metamodel from which the object was instantiated. Many services such as XML and textual serialization and deserialization, model repositories, and code generators, already make extensive use of object reflection.

Having added an idea of a model type, it is clearly necessary to consider the problem of model type reflection. That is, if a user provides a model to a service, it should be possible to determine the type of the model by looking at the types of the objects that it contains.

As discussed, the main difficulty with model reflection is the difference between the presence of an object of a given type within a model and the presence of the object type in the model's type. This problem makes it impossible to simply determine (using object reflection) the object type of each member of the model and return that as the type of the model.

Intuitively, the problem requires finding all classes that may be associated with the objects already present in the model. As a general problem, this requires a form of existential quantification, which is something not available in current MDE tools. In lieu of this, an alternative is to use bounded existential quantification, such as searching for all referring object types within a given set of packages, e.g. those already containing object types obtained from object reflection. This is, however, a partial solution that requires further consideration.

### 4.2   Model Type Inference

A closely related issue to model type reflection is that of model type inference.

In the example transformation presented earlier, we deliberately did not discuss how the input model type was determined, in order to remain independent of the choice of language used for implementing the transformation language. There are two alternatives for determining this type. In manifest typing, as is commonly seen in languages such as Java and C#, for example, types are defined by the user. By contrast, in languages such as ML, types are inferred from the code written by the user.

One can imagine that a similar approach could be used by a model transformation language. A transformation or program whose definition constructs models from a limited set of classes might be able to determine its output model type from the statements creating the objects. Obviously, this has a lot in common with the reflection problem discussed above, and one would imagine that, having determined the classes used in the definition, similar techniques might be used to determine more accurately the complete model type.

While model typing and model type reflection are problems that can be considered largely independent of the choice of model transformation or programming language, model type inference is clearly not. Inference on transformations defined using a rule/pattern-based language such as XMorph[7] will require a different solution to inference on programs defined using a more imperative language such as MTL[17].

## 5   Related Work

The problem of organising models, transformations, programs and other development artifacts to form coherent model-driven systems is a field just beginning to attract attention. In [5], the authors discuss a model bus, for describing model services and mediating access to them including automation of coercion of models to ensure compatibility. In [3], the idea is presented of a megamodel, a system or registry of models and the relations that exist between them, most significantly those of conformance and representation.

The study of type systems for object systems is a well-researched field. More recently, a number of works have begun to extend this field towards type systems for more tightly coupled systems of objects.

In [4], the authors present an extension to Java to provide for first-class relationships between classes, including a formal definition for the resultant type system. Their proposal includes a notion of relationship subtyping based on set membership, which bears a resemblance to the idea of association subsetting presented in the UML 2.0 Infrastructure.

In [8], the authors present a system for checking the type compatibility of constraints on object models expressed in Alloy, a language similar in purpose to OCL. They propose an algorithm using bounding types and base types to determine whether an expression has meaning with respect to a given object model. Since this approach is based on the UML class diagram metamodel, which bears significant structural similarity to that of MOF, this algorithm would apply straight-forwardly to MOF metamodels.

Both of these works discuss, albeit from different perspectives, the problem of checking the types of objects defined in the context of an object model that is more tightly coupled than those traditionally used in object systems. However, in each case, they consider only the typing of objects, and not of models as a whole. By contrast, the extension presented here attempts, as much as possible, to make orthogonal the question of typing the objects within a system, and to address rather the problem of typing the model as a set of objects. Indeed, our approach depends upon the existence of an object-typing algorithm that is able to handle the presence of first-class relationships, and thus these works can be seen as complementary.

There is also a body of work within the type system community on the grouping of object types. In [9] and [6], the authors propose respectively "family polymorphism" and "type groups". However, although the type structures are similar to those used in our approach, the problem under study in these works is one of object typing, particularly of binary and reflective functions, which, due to the simple type systems currently predominant in model-driven development, does not pertain to our domain. Furthermore, their approach is, once again, designed to aid in the typing of single objects (albeit objects whose types are dependent on other types in a group), and not for typing models as sets of objects. In light of this, these works might also be seen as complementary, if MOF models in fact required the sophisticated checks that they provide.

# 6 Conclusion

The lack of proper mechanisms for typing operations on models such as model transformations leads to brittle and overly restrictive reuse characteristics. In this paper we have proposed a simple extension to object-oriented typing to better cater for a model-oriented context, including a simple strategy for typing models as a collection of interconnected objects. Using a simple example we have shown how this extended approach permits more flexible reuse of model transformations accross various meta-models, while preserving type safety. We have proposed a simple algorithm for checking the conformance of model types, independently of any given transformation language. A prototype implementation of this algorithm is being implemented on the Eclipse/EMF platform, with the goal of testing its usefulness in several contexts, such as Model-Bus tool interoperability or Q/V/T transformations.

# References

[1] Martín Abadi and Luca Cardelli. *A Theory of Objects*. Springer, 1996.

[2] Mariano Belaunde and Mikael Peltier. From edoc components to ccm components: A precise mapping specification. In *FASE*, pages 143–158, 2002.

[3] Jean Bézivin, Frédéric Jouault, and Patrick Valduriez. On the need for meg-amodels. In *OOPSLA and GPCE Workshop on Best Practices for Model Driven Software Development*.

[4] Gavin Bierman and Alisdair Wren. First-class relationships in an object-oriented language. In *Foundations of Object-Oriented Languages (FOOL 2005)*.

[5] Xavier Blanc, Marie-Pierre Gervais, and Prawee Sriplakich. Model bus : Towards the interoperability of modelling tools. In *Model Driven Architecture: Foundations and Applications (MDAFA 2004)*.

[6] Kim B. Bruce. Some challenging typing issues in object-oriented languages. *Electr. Notes Theor. Comput. Sci.*, 82(7), 2003.

[7] Keith Duddy, Anna Gerber, Michael J. Lawley, Kerry Raymond, and Jim Steel. Declarative transformation for object-oriented models. In P. van Bommel, editor, *Transformation of Knowledge, Information, and Data: Theory and Applications*. Idea Group Publishing, 2004.

[8] Jonathan Edwards, Daniel Jackson, and Emina Torlak. A type system for object models. In *SIGSOFT '04/FSE-12: Proceedings of the 12th ACM SIGSOFT twelfth international symposium on Foundations of software engineering*, pages 189–199. ACM Press, 2004.

[9] Erik Ernst. Family polymorphism. In *ECOOP '01: Proceedings of the 15th European Conference on Object-Oriented Programming*, pages 303–326. Springer-Verlag, 2001.

[10] Anna Gerber, Michael J. Lawley, Kerry Raymond, Jim Steel, and Andrew Wood. Transformation: The missing link of MDA. In *Proc. 1st International Conference on Graph Transformation, ICGT'02*, volume 2505 of *Lecture Notes in Computer Science*, pages 90–105. Springer Verlag, 2002.

[11] W. LaLonde and John Pugh. Subclassing ≠ subtyping ≠ is-a. *Journal of Object-Oriented Programming*, 3(5):57–62, January 1991.

[12] Object Management Group. Enterprise collaboration architecture (ECA). OMG Document no. formal/2004-02-01, 2004.

[13] QVT-Merge Group. Revised submission for MOF 2.0 Query/Views/Transformations RFP. OMG document number ad/2005-03-02, March 2005.

[14] Shane Sendall. Combining generative and graph transformation techniques for model transformation: An effective alliance? In *Proceedings of 2nd OOPSLA Workshop on Generative Techniques in the context of Model Driven Architecture*, 2003.

[15] Jim Steel and Jean-Marc Jézéquel. Typing relationships in MDA. In D.H. Akehurst, editor, *Second European Workshop on Model-Driven Architecture (EWMDA-2)*, 2004.

[16] Jim Steel and Michael Lawley. Model-based test driven development of the tefkat model-transformation engine. In *15th International Symposium on Software Reliability Engineering (ISSRE 2004)*, pages 151–160, 2004.

[17] Didier Vojtisek and Jean-Marc Jézéquel. MTL and umlaut NG - engine and framework for model transformation. *ERCIM news*, 2004.

# UML Vs. Classical Vs. Rhapsody Statecharts: Not All Models Are Created Equal

Michelle L. Crane and Juergen Dingel

School of Computing, Queen's University
Kingston, Ontario, Canada
{crane,dingel}@queensu.ca

**Abstract.** State machines, represented by statecharts or statechart diagrams, are an important formalism for behavioural modelling. According to the research literature, the most popular statechart formalisms appear to be Classical, UML, and that implemented by RHAPSODY. These three formalisms seem to be very similar; however, there are several key syntactic and semantic differences. These differences are enough that a model written in one formalism could be ill-formed in another formalism. Worse, a model from one formalism might actually be well-formed in another, but be interpreted differently due to the semantic differences. This paper summarizes the results of a comparative study of these three formalisms with the help of several illustrative examples. Then, we present a classification of the differences together with a comprehensive overview.

## 1 Introduction

Model driven development (MDD) is a software development process that has been gaining in popularity in recent years. MDD focuses on the models, or abstractions of the software system, rather than on the final programs [20]; these models are transformed, automatically or manually, into code. Executable models are a key component of MDD, as well as such concepts as automatic transformation of models, validation of models, and standardization to enable interoperability of different MDD tools (e.g., OMG's Model Driven Architecture initiative). Within MDD, state machines are a popular way of modelling the behaviour of systems.

With respect to state machines, the most popular formalisms, as represented in the research literature, are UML statechart diagrams (as specified in UML 2.0 [18]), Classical Harel statecharts (implemented in STATEMATE [9, 11]), and a newer object-oriented version of Harel's statecharts (implemented in RHAPSODY [8]). These three formalisms appear to be very similar. For instance, at first glance, a model written in one formalism could be easily ported to one of the other two formalisms. However, there are some subtle syntactic and semantic differences between the formalisms which can lead to pitfalls. Consider, for example, the state machines shown in Fig. 1. The two machines are identical, except for the notation used to represent static choice. Fig. 1(a) makes use of a junction (small filled circle); this machine is well-formed in the Classical and

L. Briand and C. Williams (Eds.): MoDELS 2005, LNCS 3713, pp. 97–112, 2005.

UML formalisms. Fig. 1(b) shows a condition construct (circled 'C'), which is used by both the Classical and RHAPSODY formalisms. Ignoring the notation difference for a minute, this model is well-formed in all three formalisms. However, the behaviour exhibited by the state machine is different for all three. When the state machine first starts, it moves to state A, at which point the variable $x = 0$. All three formalisms agree on this point. What they do not agree on is what happens when event e occurs. In the Classical formalism, the state machine moves to state D. In the UML formalism, the state machine moves to state B. Finally, in the RHAPSODY formalism, the state machine moves to state C.

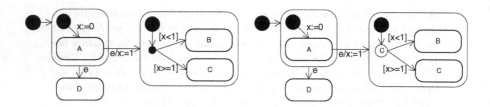

(a) Junction (small filled circle) used for static choice. Model is well-formed in Classical and UML formalisms

(b) Conditional (circled 'C') used for static choice. Model is well-formed in Classical and RHAPSODY formalisms

**Fig. 1.** Ignoring notation differences, this model is well-formed in all three formalisms, but is interpreted differently in all three. The classical state machine moves to D because the priority of conflicting transitions is handled differently (see Section 3.2). In UML, the junction is a static choice, i.e., the guards are evaluated with the information available at the beginning of the entire transition. Here, $x = 0$, so the state machine moves to B. In RHAPSODY, the conditional is also a static choice, but the fact that it is enclosed in a composite state causes it to behave as a dynamic choice (see Section 3.7). The initial transition is a 'microstep'; variables are evaluated at the beginning of each microstep. $x = 1$ when the conditional is reached and the state machine moves to C. State machine inspired by [8]

The fact that there can be three distinct interpretations of one state machine indicates that there is a lack of standardization between the three formalisms. It also indicates that the task of transforming, or porting, a model from one formalism to another may not be straightforward. Therefore, it is worthwhile to study the syntactic and semantic differences between the most popular formalisms. In this paper, we present a detailed comparison of these three formalisms, including several illustrative examples. Our results are of interest to modellers, customers, and tool developers because they summarize the differences between the three most popular formalisms and thus help to avoid the pitfalls of incorrectly interpreted models. On the one hand, modelling and transformation tools must correctly implement the syntax and semantics of a formalism (or more than one, if the tool is expected to import/export models). On the other hand, the modellers and customers who make use of models to communicate must also be conversant in these details in order to communicate effectively.

This paper is organized as follows: Section 2 briefly describes state machines and the three formalisms. Section 3 contains a detailed comparison of syntactic constructs and semantic concepts which differ between the three formalisms, while a tabular summary is presented in Section 4. Section 5 discusses related work. Finally, Section 6 contains the conclusion and contributions of this work.

## 2   State Machines, Statecharts and Statechart Diagrams

A finite state machine (FSM) is a model of computation that "specifies the sequence of states an object goes through during its lifetime in response to events, together with its responses to those events" [2, Ch. 2]. FSMs are very useful for representing reactive systems. The term 'finite state machine' refers to the model of computation, but not the diagram representing it; instead, the traditional name for a diagram representing a FSM is 'state diagram' or 'state transition diagram'.

In the late 1980's Harel defined a "visual formalism for describing states and transitions in a modular fashion, enabling clustering, orthogonality, and refinement, and encouraging 'zoom' capabilities...between levels of abstraction" [5]. These new *statecharts* were essentially state transition diagrams with the addition of hierarchy (also known as depth), orthogonality (also known as concurrency) and broadcast communications [5, 14]. Other publications by Harel and other authors quickly followed, defining a preliminary semantics for the statecharts formalism [10, 19]. Far from being a final product, the statecharts formalism evolved over the years, spawning many variants. In fact, as of 1994, there were at least 20 variants of these statecharts [22]. In 1996, Harel revisited the formalism, modifying some of the previous semantics [6, 9]. These statecharts are often referred to in the research literature as simply *statecharts*, *Harel statecharts*, or *classical statecharts*. Because of the fact that the semantics of statecharts has evolved over the years, and the fact that there are so many variants, it is necessary to define unambiguously which statecharts we refer to. For the purposes of this paper, the term *Classical statecharts* will be used to represent Harel's original statecharts syntax with the newest semantics, as documented in [6, 9, 11]. Although Harel himself states that there is no official semantics for his statecharts [9], Classical statecharts are actually implemented in I-Logix's STATEMATE tool, to which Harel has contributed.

The Unified Modeling Language (UML) has become the *de facto* industry standard for general-purpose modelling; it can be used for "specifying, constructing and documenting the artifacts of a system" [17, Part I]. The UML is a visual modelling language; different diagram types (sub-languages) can be used to model various parts of the system under consideration. These diagram types can be sub-divided into structural and behavioural views. In addition, behavioural diagrams can be further sub-divided into inter-object and intra-object behavioural views. UML statechart diagrams are one diagram type that can be used to model intra-object behaviour, i.e., how individual model elements behave. A statechart diagram is used to represent a state machine. The syntax and semantics of UML state machines have remained reasonably consistent throughout UML's history, although there are occasionally minor modifications. We concern ourselves with the latest draft of the UML 2.0 Superstructure specification [18].

UML statechart diagrams are an object-based variant of Classical statecharts [18, 16, 4]. An alternative object-based variant is one to which Harel himself has contributed: the statechart formalism implemented in I-Logix's RHAPSODY tool. This formalism was created after the introduction of UML 1.1. Actually, the RHAPSODY formalism is more closely related to the UML formalism than to its Classical ancestor. In fact, there was cooperation between the RHAPSODY and UML development teams, resulting in cross-pollination between the two formalisms [7, 21]. For the purposes of this paper, we concern ourselves with RHAPSODY as it is documented in [7, 8].

## 3    Detailed Comparison

In general, all three formalisms are similar. Basically, statecharts[1] are directed graphs, consisting of states and transitions between them. Transitions may have labels of the form event[guard]/action. All three formalisms support both orthogonal (AND) and sequential (OR) composite states.

These basic similarities aside, there are several syntactic and semantic differences between the three formalisms. The syntactic differences concern how various syntactic constructs are represented and their well-formedness constraints, while the semantic differences are caused by variations in basic semantic concepts. These differences can be divided into three categories, based on the type and severity of errors that they can cause when porting statecharts from one formalism to another. Note that a particular syntactic construct or semantic concept can result in differences in more than one category.

**Notation** A construct may be common to all three formalisms and yet be represented with alternative notation. For example, a final state in UML is represented as "a circle surrounding a smaller solid filled circle" [18], while the Classical and RHAPSODY formalisms make use of a circled 'T'. This category is the least critical; after a simple notation translation, a model would be compatible with the target formalism(s).

**Well-Formedness** Differences in this category are more important; they result in models that are well-formed in one or two formalisms, but not in all three. For instance, a construct may not be available in a particular formalism, or a formalism may enforce additional or different constraints on a common

---

[1] In the interests of simplicity, we refer to the diagrams of all three formalisms as *statecharts* and use the term *state machine* when referring to the model of computation.

construct. A model could be checked for compatibility with simple syntax or well-formedness checking. Translation and re-working of a model may make it compatible with the target formalism(s); however, not all models can be made fully compatible with all formalisms. For example, event triggers are not permitted after pseudo-states in UML; however, it may be possible to re-work the state machine to conform to this restriction. On the other hand, simultaneous events cannot be handled simultaneously in UML; it may not be possible to re-work a Classical state machine to mimic this behaviour without using simultaneous events.

**Executable Behaviour** This is the most critical category of differences, and the most insidious. A model may be well-formed in more than one formalism and yet not behave exactly the same. This type of incompatibility would not be found by simple syntax or well-formedness checking. In essence, an incompatible model would 'compile', but its executable behaviour would be other than expected, sometimes the opposite of the intended behaviour.

In order to more fully understand these categories and the potential problems associated with each, we now examine several syntactic constructs and semantic concepts in detail. We start with the semantic concepts because, in general, they affect multiple constructs and the overall understanding of the models. Several of the more interesting syntactic constructs are then examined.

## 3.1   Synchrony Hypothesis

**Synchrony and Zero Time** The *(perfect) synchrony hypothesis* [1] states that a system must react immediately to external events and that the corresponding output must occur at the same time [22]. The zero-time assumption follows from the synchrony hypothesis and implies that transitions take zero time to execute [16]. In general, Classical statecharts support both the synchrony hypothesis and the zero-time assumption [22, 16].[2]

In UML, a transition *may* take time [16], although no assumptions are actually made, allowing for models with either zero- or fixed-execution time [18, Sect. 13.3.30]. The RHAPSODY formalism mirrors that of UML in that a "step does not necessarily take zero time" [8]. Therefore, with respect to the zero-time assumption, it is theoretically possible that both the UML and RHAPSODY formalisms adhere to the synchrony hypothesis.

**Synchrony and Simultaneous Events** By the synchrony hypothesis, Classical statecharts must be able to react immediately to external events. They can do so, supported by the fact that different events may occur simultaneously, and be acted upon simultaneously, in Classical statecharts [15]. However, neither the UML nor RHAPSODY formalisms support the synchrony hypothesis in

---

[2] Note that Classical statecharts semantics, as implemented in STATEMATE, supports two time models: asynchronous and synchronous. Only the asynchronous time model supports zero-time transitions [9].

this regard. Instead, both formalisms adhere to the concept of run-to-completion (RTC), which means that each event is handled completely before the next event is processed.[3]

It is thus impossible in a UML or RHAPSODY statechart for different events to be handled simultaneously.[4] For example, consider the statechart in Fig. 2. Assume that the state machine is currently in states A and C and that events e1 and e2 occur simultaneously. If this were a Classical statechart, then both events would be handled simultaneously (since they do not conflict) and the machine would move to states B and D in one step. However, in the other two formalisms, only one event can be handled at a time. Therefore, the state machine would next move to either states A and D or B and C, depending on which event was handled.

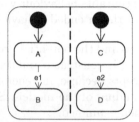

**Fig. 2.** Statechart with potentially simultaneous events

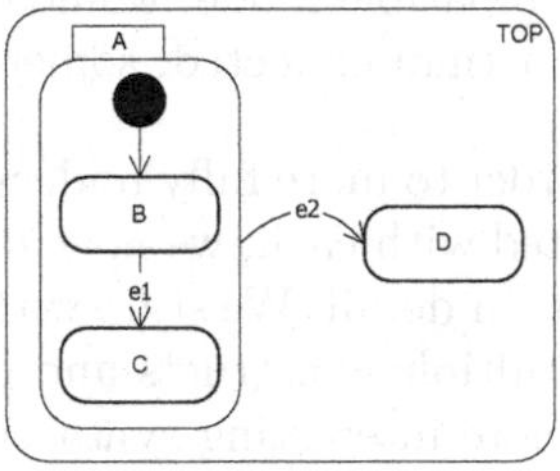

**Fig. 3.** Statechart with potentially conflicting transitions

## 3.2  Priorities of Conflicting Transitions

It is possible in all three formalisms to have conflicting transitions, i.e., a set of enabled transitions that cannot all be fired due to conflict in their results. For example, consider the statechart in Fig. 3. Assume that the machine is currently in state B and that events e1 and e2 are generated. The two transitions enabled by these events are in conflict because their effects conflict. For instance, if the transition labelled e2 is taken, the state machine moves to state D, and the transition labelled e1 cannot be taken.

One of the most serious differences between the UML/RHAPSODY and Classical formalisms is the handling of conflicting transitions. In Classical statecharts, the *scope* of a transition is the lowest OR-state neither exited nor entered by that transition [9, 15]. Priority is given to the transition with the highest scope. In the case of the statechart in Fig. 3, the scope of the transition labelled e1

---

[3] In UML, "event occurrences are detected, dispatched, and then processed...one at a time" [18, Sect. 15.3.12]. In RHAPSODY, events are handled "one by one, in order" [7].

[4] It is however, possible for the same event to be handled simultaneously in different regions of an orthogonal composite state.

is state A, while the scope of the transition labelled e2 is the state TOP. Since priority is given to the transition with the highest scope, event e2 is handled; therefore, the state machine moves to state D.

In UML, a "transition originating from a substate has higher priority than a conflicting transition originating from any of its containing states" [18, Sect. 15.3.12]. In RHAPSODY, lower level states also get priority [7]. In this case, the transition labelled e1 originates from state B, which is a substate of state A, the origin of the transition labelled e2. Since priority is given to the substates, event e1 is handled; therefore, the state machine moves to state C in both UML and RHAPSODY.

The rationale behind the different priority schemes is not well-documented, although it has been suggested that the lowest-first priority scheme espoused by both UML and RHAPSODY is more object-oriented. In other words, this priority scheme allows substates to override superstates in a way that is similar to how subclass operations/methods can override those of the superclass [8].

## 3.3  Order of Execution of Actions

In all three formalisms, is it possible to list multiple actions (or behaviours) on a transition between two states, as shown in Fig. 4. Assume that the state machine is in state A, $x = 0$, and event e occurs. In Classical statecharts, actions on a transition are executed in parallel, rather than in sequence [9]. Therefore, at state B, $x = 1$ and $y = 0$, because both actions were executed simultaneously. In UML however, the behaviour expression "may be an action sequence comprising a number of distinct actions" and "behaviors are executed in sequence following their linear order" [18, Sect. 15.3.14]. Similarly, in RHAPSODY, "actions are guaranteed to be performed in sequential order" [8]. For both UML and RHAPSODY therefore, at state B, $x = 1$ and $y = 5$.

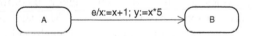

**Fig. 4.** Transition with a list of actions [9]

## 3.4  Fork and Join

Fork and join constructs are common to all three formalisms, although the notation is slightly different in Classical/RHAPSODY than in UML. Published work on the Classical and RHAPSODY formalisms show forks and joins as simply arrows with either multiple sources or multiple targets. The UML specification, as well as the RHAPSODY 6.0 tool itself [13], show separate fork and join constructs, which break the transitions into incoming and outgoing transitions.

In addition to the notational differences between the formalisms, there are several well-formedness differences. For example, actions (or any labelling) are not permitted on the outgoing transitions of a fork in RHAPSODY. Thus, the UML statechart in Fig. 5 would be ill-formed in RHAPSODY, even with the alternate notation taken into account.

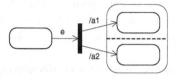

**Fig. 5.** This UML fork would be ill-formed in RHAPSODY

**Fig. 6.** This Classical fork would be ill-formed in both UML and RHAPSODY

As another example, the Classical statechart in Fig. 6 would be ill-formed in both UML and RHAPSODY. In the first place, RHAPSODY does not allow the labelling of transitions leaving a fork. UML does allow the placement of actions on these transitions, but not event triggers. However, there is a much more fundamental semantic difference between the Classical and the other two formalisms. In the Classical formalism, the fork transition would only be taken if all three events e, e1 and e2 were to occur simultaneously, which is possible since the Classical formalism allows for simultaneous events. On the other hand, both UML and RHAPSODY adhere to the RTC assumption; therefore, only one event can be handled at a time.

The Classical statechart in Fig. 7 would be ill-formed in UML because UML does not allow for event triggers after the join pseudo-state. In addition, the obvious solution of simply moving the event trigger to the incoming transitions would not work; UML does not allow for event triggers incoming to join pseudo-states. In fact, joins are not explicitly triggered in UML; they are only used with completion events [21], i.e., leaving the last state in each region of an orthogonal state. Finally, the UML statechart in Fig. 8 would be ill-formed in RHAPSODY, since RHAPSODY does not allow for any labels on transitions coming into a join.

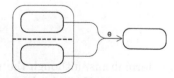

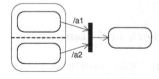

**Fig. 7.** This Classical join would be ill-formed in UML

**Fig. 8.** This UML join would be ill-formed in RHAPSODY

## 3.5   Junction

Junction constructs are common to all three formalisms, although there are some well-formedness differences. For example, the Classical statechart in Fig. 9 is ill-formed in UML. However, it is possible to make the statechart compatible by simply moving the event trigger to the transitions coming into the junction. In fact, each incoming transition may even have a different event trigger.

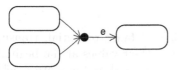

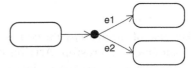

**Fig. 9.** This Classical junction can be made compatible to UML

**Fig. 10.** This Classical junction would be ill-formed in UML and RHAPSODY

In addition, the RTC assumption also affects the compatibility of the junction construct. For example, the Classical statechart in Fig. 10 is ill-formed in both UML and RHAPSODY. The transition in question will only be triggered if both events e1 and e2 occur at the same time, which is possible with Classical statecharts but not with UML or RHAPSODY. In addition, UML does not allow for event triggers on transitions outgoing from a pseudo-state. Finally, RHAPSODY does not allow for more than one outgoing transition from a junction.

## 3.6   Conditional

Classical and RHAPSODY statecharts support a specific conditional construct, such as that shown in Fig. 11. This construct simply represents a *static* choice, i.e., the guards on the outgoing transitions are evaluated before the transition is taken. The conditional construct no longer exists in UML,[5] but its semantics can be mimicked with the standard junction pseudo-state, as shown in Fig. 12.

## 3.7   Choice

UML does allow for a *dynamic* choice pseudo-state, which is not equivalent to the Classical/RHAPSODY conditional construct. Consider the UML statechart in Fig. 13. When the state machine starts, it moves to state A and $x = 0$. When event e occurs, the action on the transition is executed *before* the guards on the outgoing transitions are evaluated. The state machine will thus move to state C.

Although neither the Classical nor RHAPSODY formalisms support this dynamic choice construct, it is possible to simulate it at least in RHAPSODY. Consider the RHAPSODY statechart in Fig. 14. In this case, the fact that RHAPSODY

---

[5] The conditional construct was removed from UML 1.3, since it is equivalent to a junction [3, Sect. 3.4.3].

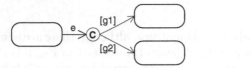

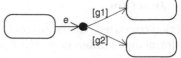

**Fig. 11.** Conditional construct supported by Classical and RHAPSODY formalisms

**Fig. 12.** UML supports the same static choice by using the junction pseudo-state

makes use of *microsteps* [8] comes into play. The default, or initial, transition is considered a microstep. Attributes are assigned their values at the beginning of each microstep, so the assignment $x := 1$ is executed as the state machine enters the composite state. Once the conditional is reached, $x = 1$, so the state machine would move to state C.

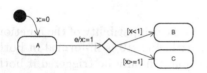

**Fig. 13.** UML supports dynamic choice

**Fig. 14.** Dynamic choice can be simulated in RHAPSODY

It is very important to note that even if the conditional in Fig. 14 were replaced by UML's static choice construct (junction), the state machine would not behave identically in UML. UML does not make use of microsteps, and the action along the transition will not be considered when the guards are evaluated [21]. If this state machine were to be evaluated in UML, it would move to state B.

### 3.8   More on Compound Transitions

In Classical statecharts, any composition of pseudo-states, simple transitions, guards and labels is permitted, but these transition compositions are constrained for practical purposes in UML state machines [16]. Therefore, there are some Classical statecharts which cannot be easily converted to UML. Consider, for example, the statecharts below. Fig. 15(a) shows a compound transition between two states. Both transitions are labelled with an event trigger and an action. In the Classical formalism, the transition coming into the junction cannot be executed without also executing the transition coming out of the junction [9]. Therefore, this compound transition is equivalent to the single transition in Fig. 15(b), which is labelled with the conjunction of two events, and a pair of resultant actions.

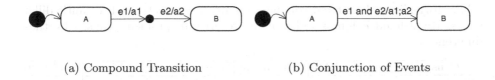

(a) Compound Transition                    (b) Conjunction of Events

**Fig. 15.** Sample compound transition from Classical statecharts and its equivalent single transition (with conjunction of events) [9]

Neither of these equivalent state machines would be well-formed in UML. On the one hand, the state machine in Fig. 15(b) cannot be interpreted because UML does not allow for the conjunction of events. On the other hand, the state machine in Fig. 15(a) also cannot be interpreted because UML does not allow for triggers on transitions leaving a pseudo-state [18, Sect. 15.3.14].

## 4   Comparison Summary

Table 1 summarizes the findings of the previous section, as well as results for some other syntactic constructs. The left-hand columns of the table summarize the syntactic and semantic differences. UML 2.0 is used as the baseline, with Classical and RHAPSODY both being compared to it. The right-hand columns indicate in which potential problem categories each construct and concept fall:

- The notation category indicates differences which can be easily managed, i.e., a model in one formalism can be easily ported to the other formalisms with a simple notation translation.
- Differences in the well-formedness category are more serious. Sometimes it will be possible to modify a model to make it compatible to another formalism, e.g., the UML statechart in Fig. 12 represents the Classical/RHAPSODY statechart in Fig. 11. Unfortunately, not all models can be made compatible, e.g., the Classical statechart in Fig. 7 cannot be translated into an equivalent UML statechart.
- Finally, differences in execution behaviour are the most serious of all. This is not because they imply a model cannot be ported to another formalism, but because a model designed with constructs/concepts from this category can be well-formed in more than one formalism and yet behave differently in each. The statecharts in Fig. 1 are prime examples of this particular pitfall.

Obviously, problems caused by well-formedness differences can also cause problems in execution behaviour. For example, a UML statechart with deferred events[6] would be ill-formed in the other two formalisms. However, if the deferred

---

[6] Normally, when an event occurs, it either matches the event trigger on some transition and is handled, or it does not match any trigger and is ignored. However, the use of deferred events allows the state machine to recognize certain events (which do not trigger transitions) and postpone responding to them.

**Table 1.** Summary of differences between Classical, UML and RHAPSODY statechart formalisms. Left-hand columns summarize syntactic and semantic differences. Right-hand columns indicate the severity of problems caused by these differences

| Construct/Concept | UML | Class. | RHAP. | Note | Notation | Well-Form. | Behaviour |
|---|---|---|---|---|---|---|---|
| Syntax | | | | | | | |
| States | | | | | | | |
|   entry/exit actions | ● | ⊙ | ● | 1 | | | ✓ |
|   do-activity | ● | ⊙ | ⊙ | 2 | | ✓ | |
|   deferred events | ● | ⊗ | ⊗ | | | ✓ | |
| Pseudo-states | | | | | | | |
|   initial | ● | ● | ● | 3 | | | |
|   final | ● | ● | ● | 4 | ✓ | | |
|   fork | ● | ⊙ | ⊙ | 5 | ✓ | ✓ | |
|   join | ● | ⊙ | ⊙ | 5 | ✓ | ✓ | |
|   shallow history | ● | ⊙ | ⊗ | 6 | | ✓ | |
|   deep history | ● | ⊙ | ⊙ | 6 | | ✓ | |
|   junction (static) | ● | ● | ⊙ | 7 | | ✓ | ✓ |
|   conditional (static) | ⊗ | + | + | 8 | ✓ | | ✓ |
|   choice (dynamic) | ● | ⊗ | ⊗ | | | ✓ | |
| Transitions | | | | | | | |
|   event trigger | ● | ⊙ | ⊙ | 9 | | ✓ | |
|   action (behaviour) | ● | ⊙ | ● | 1 | | | ✓ |
|   completion | ● | ⊘ | ⊘ | 10 | | | |
| Semantics | | | | | | | |
|   simultaneous events | ⊗ | + | ⊗ | 11 | ✓ | | ✓ |
|   simultaneous actions | ⊗ | + | ⊗ | 12 | | | ✓ |
|   priority | ● | ⊙ | ● | 13 | | | ✓ |

1  Multiple actions are permitted on a transition (or as entry/exit actions) in all formalisms; see Section 3.3 for how execution of these actions differs.
2  Classical and RHAPSODY offer a 'static reaction' construct, which may also have triggers and guards. In addition, Classical statecharts allow multiple (potentially simultaneous) static reactions for a particular state [11, Sect. 6.1.1].
3  Called 'default' [9].
4  Called 'termination connector'; symbol is a circled 'T' [11, 7].
5  Notation is slightly different. See Section 3.4.
6  UML allows history in orthogonal states. RHAPSODY does not support shallow history.
7  Not used for static choice in RHAPSODY. See Section 3.5.
8  Equivalent to junction; removed from UML [3, Sect. 3.4.3]. See Section 3.6.
9  Classical allows conjunction and negation of triggers [23], as well as disjunction. UML does not permit conjunction or negation [23, 16]. RHAPSODY does not support conjunction [7] or disjunction [12], or presumably, negation.
10  Completion events and transitions are not mentioned in Classical or RHAPSODY statecharts; although null transitions are permitted.
11  See Section 3.1.
12  See Section 3.3.
13  See Section 3.2.

Legend for Left-Hand Columns

| Symbol | Description |
|---|---|
| ● | supported, with little or no difference from UML 2.0 |
| ⊙ | supported, with considerable difference from UML 2.0 |
| ⊗ | definitely not supported (direct evidence) |
| ⊘ | presumably not supported (indirect evidence) |
| + | not supported by UML, but supported by other formalism(s) |

events were simply removed, the state machine would not behave as expected. In this case, the execution behaviour problem would not be indicated in Table 1, since the well-formedness problem itself alerts modellers of the mismatch and thus encourages them to ensure that a ported model is well-formed and behaves as expected. Instead, the behavioural problems indicated in Table 1 are *in addition* to any notational or well-formedness problems for that construct/concept, and not caused by them.

Not only does this table present a comprehensive summary of the differences between the three formalisms, but it also brings to light several facts, such as:

- RHAPSODY is much syntactically and semantically closer to UML than to its Classical ancestor, especially with respect to behavioural semantics. This means that models can be more easily ported between UML and RHAPSODY than between either of these formalisms and Classical statecharts.
- UML is the only formalism that allows for dynamic choice.
- Many of the well-formedness and execution behaviour differences are indirectly caused by the fact that UML and RHAPSODY do not support simultaneous events or actions, e.g., with respect to do-activities, forks, joins, junctions, and event triggers.
- Although the priority scheme between the Classical and UML/Rhapsody formalisms is inverted, it does not cause any notation or well-formedness problems with the syntactic constructs. In other words, the fact that a model would behave differently due to the opposite priority schemes would not be found by a syntax or well-formedness checker.

## 5   Related Work

The UML 2.0 Semantics Project is an international collaboration including IBM (Canada, Germany, Israel), Queen's University (Canada), the Technical University of Munich (Germany), and the Technical University of Braunschweig (Germany). The purpose of this project is to define a formal semantics of UML 2.0. Under the auspices of this project, we have initiated an effort to survey, categorize and compare semantic approaches for formalizing state machine behaviour. In order to critique these approaches, we needed a detailed understanding of the syntax and intended semantics of state machines. During our literature review, it became apparent that Classical, UML and RHAPSODY statecharts could not be considered equivalent, even though at first glance, they appear almost identical.

Unfortunately, although there is much research relating to these formalisms, there is no definitive comparison between them. The most detailed comparison is a bulleted list in an older UML specification [16, Sect. 2.12.5.4], which is not even included in the new UML 2.0 specification. Other sources offer one- or two-line high-level comparisons between Classical and UML statecharts, without going into great detail. The bulk of the research presented in this paper is thus a result of detailed inspection of the UML specification [18], as well as key documents relating to the Classical [5, 6, 9, 11] and RHAPSODY [7, 8] formalisms.

It should be noted that there are several other statechart-like formalisms linked to specific tools, such as RoseRT, AnyStates, LabVIEW, SmartState, etc. We have not considered these latter formalisms for two reasons: 1) many of these tool-specific formalisms claim to support UML and thus could be considered a subset of the UML formalism; and 2) these tools are not very well represented in the research literature.

# 6　Conclusion

There are currently three popular formalisms for modelling state machines: UML statechart diagrams, Classical statecharts and RHAPSODY statecharts. Modellers may adhere to MDD without being restricted to one particular formalism. In general, the similarities between Classical statecharts, UML statechart diagrams, and the statecharts implemented by the RHAPSODY tool are enough to imply to the non-expert that a state machine modelled in one formalism can be interpreted in the other formalisms. Unfortunately, this is not necessarily the case; there are enough syntactic and semantic differences between the formalisms to cause problems when sharing models.

Some problems are caused by simple notation differences and can be solved with a translation. Some problems cause well-formedness issues; occasionally, these problems can be solved with translation or re-working of the model. Occasionally, these problems cannot be solved, but at least their presence can be identified by syntax or well-formedness checks. Finally, some problems cannot be identified by such checks; these are the most insidious problems and result in well-formed models which behave differently in different formalisms.

The results of this research are of interest to modellers, tool developers, and end users of statecharts and statechart diagrams for the following reasons:

- Modellers should be aware of how their models will be interpreted in different formalisms. This is especially important with respect to execution behaviour issues, where a modeller might be expecting a different behaviour than that exhibited by a model. In the same vein, statecharts can be used as a communication medium between modellers and their customers, or end users. Users may interpret these models differently, based on an alternate formalism with which they are familiar. Indeed, the users may not even be aware that their interpretation is different, leading to a modeller/customer disconnect, which may not be noticed.
- Similarly, models might be shared between modellers, or ported from one modelling environment to another. If the participants are not aware of the potential problems of notation, well-formedness and execution behaviour, these models cannot be shared or ported accurately.
- Finally, tool developers should also be aware of these differences and potential problems in order to gear their tools to particular formalisms. Tool developers may also offer import/export capabilities; our work indicates the parts of a model that must be translated or otherwise modified. In addition,

the development of syntax and well-formedness checkers can benefit from knowledge of these differences.

Future work on this particular topic includes adding in the formalisms supported by tools such as RoseRT, AnyStates, LabVIEW, SmartState, etc. Another possible avenue is to investigate the possibility of creating automatic or guided translations between the different formalisms.

## Acknowledgements

We would like to acknowledge the invaluable assistance of Bran Selic from IBM Rational Software Canada. This research is supported by the Natural Sciences and Engineering Research Council of Canada and the IBM Centers for Advanced Studies.

## References

[1] G. Berry and G. Gonthier. The ESTEREL synchronous programming language: design, semantics, implementation. *Science of Comp. Prog.*, 19:87–152, 1992.

[2] G. Booch, J. Rumbaugh, and I. Jacobson. *The Unified Modeling Language User Guide*. Addison-Wesley, 1999.

[3] B.P. Douglass. *Real Time UML*. Object Technology Series. Addison-Wesley, third edition, 2004.

[4] M. Gogolla and F. Parisi-Presicce. State diagrams in UML: A formal semantics using graph transformations. In *Proc. Workshop on Precise Semantics for Modelling Techniques*, pages 55–72. Technische Universität München, TUM-I9803, 1998.

[5] D. Harel. Statecharts: A visual formalism for complex systems. *Science of Computer Programming*, 8(3):231–274, 1987.

[6] D. Harel. Some thoughts on statecharts, 13 years later. In *Proceedings of the 9th International Conference on Computer Aided Verification (CAV'97)*, LNCS 1254, pages 226–231. Springer, 1997.

[7] D. Harel and E. Gery. Executable object modeling with statecharts. *Computer*, 30(7):31–42, 1997.

[8] D. Harel and H. Kugler. The RHAPSODY semantics of statecharts (on, on the executable core of the UML) (preliminary version). In *SoftSpez Final Report*, LNCS 3147, pages 325–354. Springer, 2004.

[9] D. Harel and A. Naamad. The STATEMATE semantics of statecharts. *ACM Transactions on Software Engineering and Methodology*, 5(4):293–333, 1996.

[10] D. Harel, A. Pnueli, J.P. Schmidt, and R. Sherman. On the formal semantics of statecharts. In *Proc. of the 2nd IEEE Symposium on Logic in Computer Science*, pages 54–64. Computer Society Press of the IEEE, 1987.

[11] D. Harel and M. Politi. *Modeling Reactive Systems with Statecharts: the STATEMATE Approach*. McGraw-Hill, 1998.

[12] I-Logix. *Rhapsody 6.0 User Guide*.

[13] I-Logix. *Tutorial for Rhapsody in J (Release 4.1 MR2)*, 2003.

[14] G. Lüttgen, M. von der Beeck, and R. Cleaveland. A compositional approach to statecharts semantics. In *Proc.8th ACM SIGSOFT Int'll Symposium on Foundations of Software Engineering*, pages 120–129. ACM Press, 2000.

[15] E. Mikk. *Semantics and Verification of Statecharts.* PhD thesis, Christian-Albrechts University of Kiel, 2000. Bericht Nr. 2011.

[16] OMG. OMG Unified Modeling Language specification. Adopted Formal Specification formal/03-03-01, Object Management Group, 2003. Version 1.5.

[17] OMG. UML 2.0 infrastructure specification. Technical Report ptc/03-09-15, Object Management Group, 2004.

[18] OMG. UML 2.0 superstructure specification. Technical Report ptc/04-10-02, Object Management Group, 2004.

[19] A. Pnueli and M. Shalev. What is in a step: On the semantics of statecharts. In *Proc. Int'l Conf. on Theoretical Aspects of Computer Software*, LNCS 526, pages 244–264. Springer, 1991.

[20] B. Selic. The pragmatics of model-driven development. *IEEE Software*, 20(5):19–25, 2003.

[21] Bran Selic. Personal Communication, March 2005.

[22] M. von der Beeck. A comparison of statecharts variants. In *Formal Techniques in Real-Time and Fault-Tolerant Systems*, LNCS 863, pages 128–148. Springer, 1994.

[23] M. von der Beeck. A structured operational semantics for UML-statecharts. *Software and Systems Modeling*, 1(2):130–141, 2002.

# Evaluating the Effect of Composite States on the Understandability of UML Statechart Diagrams

José A. Cruz-Lemus[1], Marcela Genero[1], M. Esperanza Manso[2] and Mario Piattini[1]

[1]ALARCOS Research Group, Department of Computer Science
University of Castilla – La Mancha
Paseo de la Universidad, 4 13071 Ciudad Real (Spain)
{JoseAntonio.Cruz, Marcela.Genero, Mario.Piattini}@uclm.es
[2]GIRO Research Group, Department of Computer Science
University of Valladolid
Campus Miguel Delibes, E.T.I.C. 47011 Valladolid (Spain)
manso@infor.uva.es

**Abstract.** UML statechart diagrams have become an important technique for describing the dynamic behavior of a software system. They are also a significant element of OO design, especially in code generation frameworks such as Model Driven Architecture (MDA). In previous works we have defined a set of metrics for evaluating structural properties of UML statechart diagrams and have validated them as early understandability indicators, through a family of controlled experiments. Those experiments have also revealed that the number of composite states had, apparently, no influence on the understandability of the diagrams. This fact seemed a bit suspicious to us and we decided to go a step further. So in this work we present a controlled experiment and a replication, focusing on the effect of composite states on the understandability of UML statechart diagrams. The results of the experiment confirm, to some extent, our intuition that the use of composite states improves the understandability of the diagrams, so long as the subjects of the experiment have had some previous experience in using them. There are educational implications here, as our results justify giving extra emphasis to the use of composite states in UML statechart diagrams in Software Engineering courses.

## 1. Introduction

Modeling is at the core of many disciplines, but it is especially important in engineering because it facilitates the communication and construction of complex things from smaller parts [14]. Models help us understand a complex problem and its potential solutions through abstraction. It seems obvious, therefore that software systems, which are often among the most complex of all engineering systems, can benefit greatly from using models and modeling techniques [12]. Over the last three decades, the abstraction level has not only risen from implementation over design to analysis; there is also a recent interest in code generation frameworks such as the Model Driven Architecture (MDA) [9] proposed by the Object Management Group (OMG). To the extent that code generation is used, it seems likely that factors which

L. Briand and C. Williams (Eds.): MoDELS 2005, LNCS 3713, pp. 113-125, 2005.
© Springer-Verlag Berlin Heidelberg 2005

influence evolvability on the implementation level, such as the naming of variables and a badly structured program code, will become less relevant. Hence, in this context, the evolvability of information systems would be more and more determined by that of the models [15].

Linked to the idea of models which are capable of evolution, UML statechart diagrams have become an important technique for describing of the dynamic aspects of a software system and are also an important element of OO design documents [4].

According to [12], in order to be useful and effective, an engineering model must possess, to a sufficient degree, the following five key characteristics: abstraction, understandability, accuracy, predictiveness and inexpensiveness .

The motivation for this research comes from the fact that in a previous work [3] we have studied the relationship between many of the constructs of the UML statechart diagrams and the effect that they have on the understandability of the diagrams themselves. To do so, we had previously defined and validated, both theoretically and empirically, a set of metrics [2] for evaluating the structural properties of UML statechart diagrams, based on UML v.1.4 [8]. But in all these works we have found that the effect of composite states on the understandability of the UML statechart diagrams was unclear. A composite state is a state that contains other states within it. When the behavior of a class is quite complicated, using composite states may be useful, as we can join those simple states that are part of a larger common one. Intuitively, grouping into a composite state those that are highly related could help to improve the understandability of a diagram.

In this work we will focus on the evaluation of the effect that a construct of the UML meta-model [8] has on one of the afore-mentioned .characteristics. More specifically, we will evaluate the effect that composite states have on the understandability of UML statechart diagrams, which are of the most commonly used diagrams when modeling using UML and which are part of the main UML diagrams set established in [5].

In order to clarify these impressions, we have designed and performed a controlled experiment and a replication so as to evaluate whether the use of composite states really does improve the understandability of the diagrams, as may be thought intuitively. In this work we will present the experimental process and the conclusion that has been reached after the performance of the experiment.

In section 2, we define our research question and formulate the work hypotheses. Later, we test these hypotheses in the experiment and its replication as reported in section 3. In section 4 we discuss the validity threats to our experiments. Finally, section 5 sets out the conclusions reached and the future work that is planned.

## 2. Research Question and Hypotheses

As the main goal of the current work is to ascertain if the use of composite states can make the UML statechart diagrams easier to understand, our research question can be stated as:

*Does the use of composite states improve the understandability of UML statechart diagrams?*

Based on previous experiments [3] and on our intuition and experience working with UML statechart diagrams, we think that the answer to this question should be a 'yes', especially when the person that is trying to understand the UML statechart diagram is used to working with this modeling language and this kind of diagram.

In order to evaluate our research question, we carried out a controlled experiment and a replication. In these experiments, we considered the efficiency of the subjects in understanding the diagrams, i.e. the relationship between how accurately they solve the required tasks and how quickly they do this. The *understandability efficiency* was defined as correct answers given by the subjects divided by the time spent on answering the questions related to an UML statechart diagram. This was used to evaluate the property we have previously mentioned: the efficiency of the subjects.

On the basis of our research question we formulated the following experimental hypotheses:

- $H_0$: the use of composite states does not improve the understandability efficiency of an UML statechart diagram.
- $H_1$: the use of composite states improves the understandability efficiency of an UML statechart diagram.

## 3. Experimental Process

In this section, we describe a controlled experiment and a replication that we carried out for testing the hypotheses stated in the previous section. All the experimental process is based on the guidelines outlined in [16].

### 3.1. First Experiment

This experiment took place at the University of Murcia (Spain) in February 2005. Its main features are the following:

**Subjects.** 55 Computer Science students from the University of Murcia participated in this experiment.

The tasks to be performed did not require high levels of industrial experience, so experiments with students could be considered as appropriate [1, 6]. Moreover, students are the next generation of people entering this profession , so they are close to the population under study [7]. Besides, working with students implies a set of advantages [15], such as the fact that the prior knowledge of the students is rather homogeneous. The availability of a large number of subjects is another plus point.

All the subjects were in the fourth year of Computer Science and had received a complete Software Engineering course in which they had studied modeling techniques, including UML. They also received a short training session before the performance of the experiment, in which the main constructs of UML statechart diagrams were commented on and where two examples of the tasks to be performed by them were explained by the conductor of the experiment. So we consider that the level of experience they brought to the experiment was acceptable.

**Experimental design.** We selected a factorial with interaction confounded. Our dependent variable was the understandability of UML statechart diagrams and we would measure this through the previously introduced measure *understandability efficiency*. Our independent variables were the Universe of Discourse (UoD) to which the diagrams were related and the use or not of composite states (CS) in the diagram.

We used two different Universes of Discourses (UoD's): an ATM machine and a phone call. For each of them, we presented two different diagrams, conceptually identical. One of the diagrams included composite state(s) and the other did not.

As each subject would receive two diagrams, one with and another without composite states, and each of them related to a different UoD, we obtained two different groups as shown in Table 1. The diagrams of each group were given to the subjects in different orders. For instance, in group A, the subjects first had to solve the tasks related to an ATM machine without composite states and, after that, those related to a phone call with composite states or exactly the same tasks for the same diagrams but in an inverse order (phone call with composite states and then ATM machine without composite states).

**Table 1.** Overview of the experimental design

|  | Universe of Discourse | |
| --- | --- | --- |
|  | **ATM machine** | **Phone call** |
| **Without composite states** | Group A | Group B |
| **With composite states** | Group B | Group A |

Group A was performed by 28 subjects and group B 27 subjects.

**Experimental task.** As commented previously, we used two different UoD's, one modeled the behavior of an ATM machine and the other the behavior of a phone call. These UoD's were quite usual and not exceptional at all, so that there was no need for extra effort in understanding the diagrams.

Each diagram had a test which contained 6 questions which were conceptually similar and set out in the same order. In fact, in both diagrams of each UoD, the questions were the same. The questions inquired about what state would be reached after the triggering of some events which were in a given state. Another question asked which state would be reached after a certain sequence of events and guard conditions. There was a final inquiry as to what sequence was the minimum possible for going from one given state to another. The subjects had to note down the times at which they started and finished answering the questions, as well as providing the answers to the questions themselves.

An example of the experimental material given to the subjects can be found in Appendix A, at the end of the present work.

**Experimental procedure.** The experiment started with a twenty-five-minute introductory session in which the conductor briefly explained the behavior of the elements of an UML statechart diagram. After that, the materials for the experiment were randomly distributed to the subjects.

In order to increase the motivation and interest of the subjects, they were explained that the exercises that they were going to perform could be similar to those that would find in their exam at the end of the term.

At this point two examples in shortened version were performed by the supervisor, who explained the correct answer to each question and the way of noting down the starting and finishing times properly.

**Data analysis and interpretation[1].** First we carried out an analysis of the descriptive statistics of the data. We obtained the results shown in the box-plot of figure 1 and eliminated the extreme and atypical data, obtaining the results displayed in Table 2. In this table, we show the descriptive statistics of the valid data for the diagrams that used composite states and of those that did not.

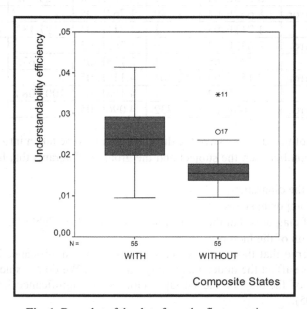

**Fig. 1.** Box-plot of the data from the first experiment

**Table 2.** Descriptive statistics of the understandability efficiency (first experiment)

| CS | N | Mean | S.E. | Min. | Max. | Skew. | Kurtosis |
|---|---|---|---|---|---|---|---|
| With | 55 | 0.024165 | 0.007447 | 0.00947 | 0.04138 | 0.1659 | -0.5494 |
| Without | 51 | 0.015269 | 0.002809 | 0.00962 | 0.02151 | 0.0721 | -0.3164 |

---

[1] All the data analysis was carried out by means of SPSS [13]

Table 2 shows that these subjects, who were quite familiar with the use of UML statechart diagrams, obtained much better results for efficiency when working with those diagrams that used composite states.

After this, we decided to perform an ANOVA, because this type of analysis allows us to analyze the interaction between the independent variables under study when the measurement of the dependent variable is repeated [10].

The results of the ANOVA which was performed for the understandability efficiency are shown in Table 3. The last column of Table 3 represents the level of significance, which will allow us to reject or accept the hypothesis we have formulated.

**Table 3.** ANOVA results for understandability efficiency in the first experiment

| Source | Sum of Squares | df | Mean Squared | F | Significance level |
|---|---|---|---|---|---|
| Subject (Group) | 2.137E-03 | 51 | 4.190E-05 | 2.378 | 0.001 |
| Error | 8.632E-04 | 49 | 1.762E-05 | | |
| UoD | 3.555E-04 | 1 | 3.555E-04 | 20.182 | 0.000 |
| Error | 8.632E-04 | 49 | 1.762E-05 | | |
| CS | 1.711E-03 | 1 | 1.711E-03 | 97.133 | 0.000 |
| Error | 8.632E-04 | 49 | 1.762E-05 | | |
| Group | 8.334E-05 | 1 | 2.778E-05 | 0.675 | 0.572 |
| Error | 2.154E-03 | 52.301 | 4.119E-05 | | |
| Interaction | 4.108E-02 | 1 | 4.108E-02 | 1003.084 | 0.000 |
| Error | 2.160E-03 | 52.732 | 4.096E-05 | | |

In each row of the table we have the different factors to be taken into account:
– The interaction between the subject and the group of diagrams that he/she has performed.
– The UoD of the diagrams.
– The use of composite states.
– The group of diagrams that the subject has performed (see Table 1).
– The interaction of the factors.

We can observe that there exist several factors whose significance level is below 0.05; hence these affect the understandability efficiency. We do not study the effect of the interaction of factors nor the Group factor as the significance level for this is 0.572 (over 0.05).

We are especially interested in the CS factor, which indicates if a diagram uses this kind of constructor or not. In this case, its value is below 0.05, which implies that the use of composite states affects the understandability efficiency.

In figure 2, we can also observe the profile plot of the data, which indicates that independently of the UoD, using composite states in the diagrams makes the understandability efficiency increase.

Combining the results obtained in Table 2. and figure 2, we can reject the hypothesis $H_0$, which asserted that the use of composite states did not improve the understandability efficiency of an UML statechart diagram.

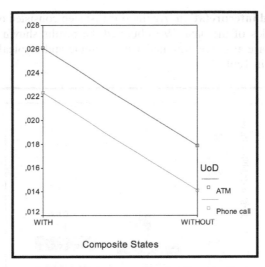

**Fig. 2.** Understandability efficiency profile plot from the first experiment

## 3.2. Experiment Replication

This replication took place at the University of Alicante (Spain) in March 2005. As most of its features are similar to those we have commented on before for the first experiment, we will go over only the differences between them:

- In this case the subjects were 178 Computer Science students from the University of Alicante.
- In order to increase the interest and motivation of the subjects, they would be granted with some extra points in the exam at the end of the term. Anyway, they participated voluntarily and some of the students decided not to perform the experiment.
- The skill of the subjects using UML for modeling, especially UML statechart diagrams, was much lower in this replication, as most of them had only a few months of experience, and they had not worked with some UML meta-model constructs (e.g. composite states) yet. They received the same training session as in the original experiment before performing the replication, but even with this, their experience level was much lower, compared to the first group of subjects.
- Due to space limitations in the classrooms where the replication took place, the subjects were divided into two groups of 92 and 86 subjects respectively and they performed the experiment at a different time. To be more specific, the second group finished one hour later, but there was no interaction between the subjects of both groups.
- The materials for the experiment were given out randomly to the subjects and a half of them (89 subjects) performed each possible option (A and B).

**Data analysis and interpretation.** Again, our first step consisted of an analysis of the descriptive statistics of the data. We obtained the results shown in the box-plot of figure 3. In this case also, we eliminated the extreme and atypical data and obtained the results shown in Table 4.

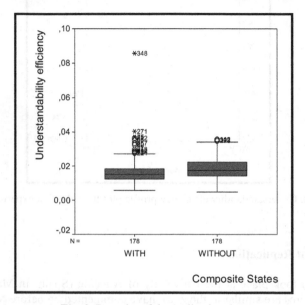

**Fig. 3.** Box-plot of the replication data

**Table 4.** Descriptive statistics of the understandability efficiency (replication)

| CS | N | Mean | S.E. | Min. | Max. | Skew. | Kurtosis |
|---|---|---|---|---|---|---|---|
| With | 160 | 0.014956 | 0.003720 | 0.00580 | 0.02449 | 0.3205 | -0.1812 |
| Without | 173 | 0.018106 | 0.005440 | 0.00496 | 0.03109 | 0.3649 | -0.3192 |

In this case, the results were better for the diagrams which did not use composite states. The lack of experience of the subjects working with this kind of UML diagram was a key factor in obtaining these results. Anyway, although the subjects had scarcely worked with composite states, the difference in the mean values are much smaller than in the case of the first experiment, where the diagrams that used composite states were much more efficiently understood than the others.

In the replication, we also applied an ANOVA and obtained the results shown in Table 5.

Again, we do not study the effect of the interaction of sources nor the Group factor, as the significance level for this is 0.129 and the test power was 0.451. In this case, the value of the factor CS is also below 0.05, as happened in the experiment. So, again in the replication, the results show that using composite states in UML statechart diagrams affects their understandability efficiency. In this case the effect is negative and makes the understandability decrease, but as we have remarked before, this effect is a consequence of the lack of experience that the subjects had.

**Table 5.** ANOVA results for understandability efficiency in the replication

| Source | Sum of Squares | df | Mean squared | F | Signifi-cance level |
|---|---|---|---|---|---|
| Subject (Group) | 3.759E-03 | 176 | 2.136E-05 | 1.649 | 0.001 |
| Error | 1.981E-03 | 153 | 1.295E-05 | | |
| UoD | 1.606E-03 | 1 | 1.606E-03 | 124.044 | 0.000 |
| Error | 1.981E-03 | 153 | 1.295E-05 | | |
| CS | 6.283E-04 | 1 | 6.283E-04 | 48.519 | 0.000 |
| Error | 1.981E-03 | 153 | 1.295E-05 | | |
| Group | 4.827E-05 | 1 | 4.827E-05 | 2.326 | 0.129 |
| Error | 3.994E-03 | 192.445 | 2.075E-05 | | |
| Interaction | 8.737E-02 | 1 | 8.737E-02 | 4210.117 | 0.000 |
| Error | 3.994E-03 | 192.445 | 2.075E-05 | | |

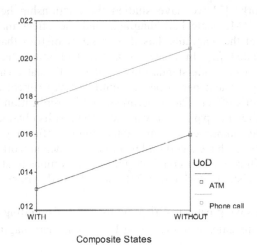

**Fig. 4.** Understandability efficiency profile plot from the replication

## 4. Threats to Validity

We must keep in mind a number of validity issues that are typically related to experiments of this type.

First, the subjects were not professional modelers. Obviously, we would expect much better results if the subjects were more experienced. However, the limited diffi-culty of the tasks and the different UoD's make the students become suitable experi-mental subjects, as they are much easier to work with than some others.. Nevertheless, further replications of these experiments using people already working in this profes-sion would be really interesting.

Secondly, the diagrams that have been used represent relatively simple models and it is possible that if real-projects data were used, we could obtain different results.

In order to alleviate possible effects of learning and fatigue, we counterbalanced the order in which treatment combinations were given to the subjects; furthermore, the subjects were assigned at random to each possible treatment order sequence. To minimize plagiarism, the experiment conductor encouraged an honest performance of the experiment and was present in the room throughout.

Finally, in order to decrease a possible 'session effect', in the replication the subjects were randomly assigned to the session in which they performed the experimental tasks.

## 5. Conclusions and Future Work

The appearance of the MDA, and hence the emphasis to be put on the models, has favored that UML statechart diagrams have become an important technique in the describing of the dynamic aspects of a software system.

In previous works [3] we have studied the relationship between many of the constructs of the UML statechart diagrams and the effect that they have on the understandability of the diagrams, based on a set of metrics that we had previously defined and validated [2]. In these works we had found that the effect of the composite states on the understandability of the UML statechart diagrams was not clear. So we designed and performed a controlled experiment and a replication in order to evaluate this effect. The experiment and its replication were carried out by students of two different Spanish Universities. The results obtained show that the use of composite states improves the understandability efficiency of UML statechart diagrams if the subjects have a certain level of experience in working with this kind of UML diagrams. Thus, we can conclude that using composite states when modeling the behavior of systems through UML statechart diagrams makes them more understandable.

These findings give greater justification than ever for putting special emphasis on the use of composite states when teaching UML statechart diagrams in Software Engineering courses.

In spite of these encouraging findings, we considered them to be preliminary. Further validation is needed, to be performed with experienced practitioners, as well as by taking data from real projects. When we have obtained conclusive results about the effect of composite states on the understandability of UML statechart diagrams, we will investigate the optimal nesting level within the composite states.

It could also be interesting testing the hypotheses again but using other experimental design in which the effect of interaction is not confounded, in order to obtain more knowledge about it.

Once UML 2 [11] is adopted as standard by the OMG we will study the metamodel corresponding to the statechart diagrams, in order to find out if the findings presented in the present work are also valid for this version of the language. In addition, we will investigate whether our proposed metrics [2] could be used as maintainability indicators of UML statechart diagrams.

## Acknowledgements

This research is part of the MESSENGER project (PCC-03-003-1) financed by 'Consejería de Ciencia y Tecnología de la Junta de Comunidades de Castilla-La Mancha (Spain)', the CALIPO project supported by 'Dirección General de Investigación del Ministerio de Ciencia y Tecnología (Spain)' (TIC2003-07804-C05-03) and the DIESEL project (TIN2004-03145), financed by 'MEC-FEDER'.

The authors would like give their sincere thanks to Professor Ambrosio Toval from the University of Murcia and Professor Cristina Cachero from the University of Alicante for allowing us to perform the above experiments with their students.

## References

1. Basili, V., Shull, F. and Lanubile, F.: Building Knowledge through Families of Experiments. IEEE Transactions on Software Engineering, Vol. 25(1999) 456-473
2. Cruz-Lemus, J. A., Genero, M. and Piattini, M.: Metrics for UML Statechart Diagrams. In: Metrics for Software Conceptual Models. Genero, Piattini and Calero (eds.), Imperial College Press, UK (2005)
3. Cruz-Lemus, J. A., Maes, A., Genero, M., Poels, G. and Piattini, M.: Analyzing Data Extracted from a Family of Experiments for Evaluating UML Statechart Diagrams Understandability. Research Working Paper, University of Ghent (to appear) (2005)
4. Denger, C. and Ciolkowski, M.: High Quality Statecharts through Tailored. Perspective-Based Inspections. Proc. of 29th EUROMICRO Conference "New Waves in System Architecture". Belek, Turkey. (2003) 316-325
5. Erickson, J. and Siau, K.: Theoretical and Practical Complexity of UML. Proc. of 10th Americas Conference on Information Systems. New York, USA. (2004) 1669-1674
6. Höst, M., Regnell, B. and Wohlin, C.: Using Students as Subjects - a Comparative Study of Students & Professionals in Lead-Time Impact Assessment. Proc. of 4th Conference on Empirical Assessment & Evaluation in Software Engineering (EASE 2000). Keele, UK. (2000) 201-214
7. Kitchenham, B., Pfleeger, S., Pickard, L., Jones, P., Hoaglin, D., El-Emam, K. and Rosenberg, J.: Preliminary Guidelines for Empirical Research in Software Engineering. IEEE Transactions on Software Engineering, 28 Vol. 8. (2002) 721-734
8. Object Management Group: UML Revision Task Force. OMG Unified Modeling Language Specification, v.1.4. document formal/01-09-67. (2001)
9. Object Management Group: MDA - The OMG Model Driven Architecture. (2002)
10. Reynoso, L., Genero, M. and Piattini, M.: Measuring OCL Expressions: An approach based on Cognitive Techniques. In: Metrics for Software Conceptual Models, Genero, Piattini and Calero (eds.), Imperial College Press, UK. (2005)
11. Rumbaugh, J., Jacobson, I. and Booch, G.: The Unified Modeling Language Reference Manual, Second Edition. Addison-Wesley. (2005)
12. Selic, B.: The Pragmatics of Model-Driven Development. IEEE Software, 20 Vol. 5. (2003) 19-25.
13. SPSS: SPSS 11.5, Syntax Reference Guide, Chicago, USA, SPSS Inc. (2002)
14. Thomas, D.: MDA: Revenge of the Modelers or UML Utopia? IEEE Software, 21 Vol. 3. (2004) 15-17
15. Verelst, J.: The Influence of the Level of Abstraction on the Evolvability of Conceptual Models of Information Systems. Proc. of 3rd International Symposium on Empirical Software Engineering (ISESE 2004). Redondo Beach, USA. (2004) 17-26.

16. Wohlin, C., Runeson, P., Hast, M., Ohlsson, M.C., Regnell, B. and Wesslen, A.: Experimentation in Software Engineering: an Introduction. Kluwer Academic Publisher. (2000)

# Appendix A. An Example of the Experimental Material

In this appendix we show part of the experimental material handed out to the subjects in the experiments. These two diagrams model a phone call; the first one (figure 5) uses composite states and the second (figure 6) does not. The complete original (in Spanish) material can be found at http://alarcos.inf-cr.uclm.es/

The following text sets out the questions that had to be solved by the experimental subjects. In this study, the questions were the same for both diagrams.

## QUESTIONNAIRE (PHONE CALL DIAGRAM)

CHECK TIME (HH:MM:SS):     __ : __ : __

Please solve the following questions related to the diagram shown on the following page. This diagram models the **behavior of a phone call:**

1. If we are in the state DIALING and the event *Dial digit* occurs, which state do we reach?
2. If we are in the state OBTAINING LINE and the event *Time exhausted* occurs, which state do we reach?
3. Starting in the state DIALING, which state do we reach if the following sequence of events occurs?
   *Number dialed [Number valid]*
   *On-line*
   *Destination answers*
4. Starting in the state CONNECTED, which state do we reach if the following sequence of events occurs?
   *New call*
   *On-line*
   *Hang up*

5. Write down the minimum sequence of events and conditions needed, to go from the state DIALING to the state DISCONNECTED:

6. Write down the minimum sequence of events and conditions needed, to go from the state CONNECTING to the state BUSY:

CHECK TIME (HH:MM:SS):     __ : __ : __

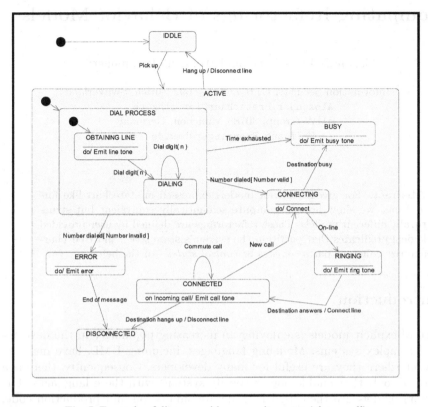

**Fig. 5.** Example of diagram with composite states (phone call)

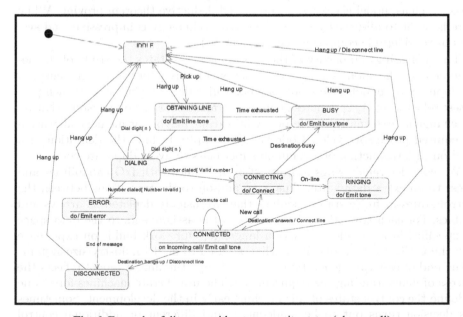

**Fig. 6.** Example of diagram without composite states (phone call)

# Computing Refactorings of Behavior Models

Alexander Pretschner[1] and Wolfgang Prenninger[2]

[1] Information Security, ETH Zürich, 8092 Zürich, Switzerland
Alexander.Pretschner@inf.ethz.ch
[2] BMW Group, 80788 München, Germany
Wolfgang.Prenninger@bmw.de

**Abstract.** For given behavior models expressed in statechart-like formalisms, we show how to compute semantically equivalent but structurally different models. These refactorings are defined by user-provided logical predicates that partition the system's state space and that characterize coherent parts—*modes* or *control states*—of the behavior.

## 1 Introduction

The use of explicit models is enjoying an increasing popularity in the development of complex systems. Modeling languages, including UML, have matured to a point where they are useful for many developers. Consequently, there is a plethora of tools that enable one to specify systems with these languages. The (behavior) models are then used to generate simulation and production code, code skeletons, or test cases. They are also subjected to formal verification technology such as model checking or automated deductive theorem proving. While there is no fit to all needs yet, the respective technology is impressive, and systems of considerable complexity can be handled.

The increasing complexity of these systems necessitates the study of the development of the models itself. The context of this paper is the incremental development of models. We study one particular development step in such processes: refactoring [1, 2] denotes structural transformations of a system that do not change its externally visible behavior, except maybe for memory allocation or required processor cycles. Code-based examples include the definition of a function or introduction of a common super class to avoid duplicate code.

We consider refactorings of finite state machines with I/O capabilities and access to an extra data state. This is an add-on to the transitions between the control states in finite state machines that are usually depicted as arrows and bubbles. For each transition, the guard and the assignments to the data space are specified in a well-defined action language. Our work builds on experience with the CASE tool AutoFocus [3] that we used to model industry-size systems to the end of test case generation (e.g., [4, 5, 6]). Building a model reflects the process of understanding the requirements. The use of state machines forces one to define the control states of this machine early in the development. Sometimes this decision turns out to be inadequate, and different or additional control

L. Briand and C. Williams (Eds.): MoDELS 2005, LNCS 3713, pp. 126–141, 2005.

states have to be defined. In the worst case, with current tools, the complete state machine has to be redrawn, a tedious and error-prone task.

Control states can be interpreted as names of predicates over the state space. Given a state machine and a set of such predicates, we show how to compute the transitions (arrows) between the corresponding new control states. Consider a state machine that models a stack: one control state with three looping transitions: *push*, *pop*, and *get*. Given two predicates that specify that the stack is empty ($p$) or not empty ($q$), we show how to compute the transitions between $p$ and $q$. Our main motivation for refactorings of the said kind is the insight that the control states of a behavior model were inadequately chosen. A further motivation is the desire for complementary views on the system [7]. We do not discuss how to pick $p$ and $q$. The approach is prototypically implemented.

We present our ideas on the grounds of the simple example of a stack. As a proof of concept, we show how our techniques have been used in the case study of an automotive network controller [4]. We concentrate on one single flat state machine: parallel composition and hierarchical states are not in the scope.

Our work is based on a development process that uses tables like those in SCR [8, 9, 10]. Unless they grow too large, tables are easy to understand, and one of their important advantages is that they are comparably easy to manipulate. Tool support for manipulating and checking consistency or completeness of different flavors of tables has been around for some time [11, 10]. On the other hand, tables are not always utterly convincing to customers who sometimes prefer equivalent graphically displayed executable state machines. We also found that converting tables into a different representation, namely that of equivalent state transition diagrams, is a valuable aid in reviewing the models. In sum, we believe that both tables and graphically represented state machines are valuable in the development process of models. This is consistent with the findings of Parnas and his colleagues that there is a need for more than one kind of tables [12, 13].

To summarize, we tackle the following *problem*. In the context of incremental development, assume a state machine, or a table, and a partitioning of the state space, to be given. How can we compute an equivalent state machine with a set of control states characterized by a set of predicates? The *solution* is the formal definition of the transformation and its prototypical implementation. Our *contribution* is, to our knowledge, the first formal treatment of refactorings of behavior models on the grounds of partitions of the state space. Our approach generalizes to other formalisms as well. Statecharts, for instance, may in principle arbitrarily access the data definitions of a UML model. By translating the statechart into the (standard) formalism given in this paper, we can directly apply our approach, provided that only direct assignments (and output) are allowed in the action part of a transition

Section 2 presents the formalism of this paper and defines the notions of rule systems, state machines, state transition diagrams, and tables. Section 3 considers the development steps in incremental development processes of behavior models, given by both tables and state transition diagrams. Given a partitioning of the state space, Section 4 shows how to compute refactorings and briefly considers the implementation. Section 5 presents the application of the approach in an industrial case study. Sections 6 and 7 present related work and conclude.

## 2    Modeling Constructs

In this section, we define the notion of *rule systems*. Roughly, rule systems are programs in a language of guarded commands. *Tables* are textual representations of rule systems. *State machines* are a special kind of rule systems with *state transition diagrams* as their graphical representation. The usefulness of and need for these different representations will become apparent later. Before precisely formulating our refactoring steps, we have to introduce some formalism.

**Preliminaries**  The formalism borrows from Breitling and Philipps [14]. Let $V$ denote a finite set of typed variables. A valuation $\beta$ maps a variable to a term of its type. $A_V$ is the set of all valuations for a set $V$. Let $free(\Phi)$ denote the set of free variables in a logical formula $\Phi$. In case an assertion $\Phi$ evaluates to true when all $v \in free(\Phi)$ are replaced by $\beta(v)$, we write $\beta \models \Phi$.

Variable names also occur in primed form (intuition given in the next paragraph on rule systems). For instance, if $v$ is a variable, then priming yields a new variable, $v'$. Natural extensions apply (1) to sets of variables: $V' = \{v'|v \in V\}$, (2) to valuations: for $\beta \in A_V$, we have $\beta' \in A_{V'}$ with $\beta'(v') = \beta(v)$ for all $v \in V$, and (3) to assertions: if $\Phi$ is an assertion, then $\Phi'$ is the assertion that results from priming all variables in $free(\Phi)$. Unprimed valuations assign values to unprimed variables only, and primed valuations assign values to primed variables only. If an assertion $\Phi$ contains both primed and unprimed variables, two valuations are needed for evaluations. We write $\beta, \gamma' \models \Phi$ in case $\Phi$ evaluates to true when all unprimed variables $v$ in $free(\Phi)$ are replaced by $\beta(v)$, and all primed variables $v'$ are replaced by $\gamma'(v')$. Two valuations $\beta, \gamma \in A_V$ coincide on a subset $W \subseteq V$, denoted $\beta \overset{W}{=} \gamma$, if $\forall v \in W \bullet \beta(v) = \gamma(v)$. Extensions naturally apply to sequences of valuations—$\beta_1\beta_2\ldots \overset{W}{=} \gamma_1\gamma_2\ldots$ denotes $\beta_k \overset{W}{=} \gamma_k$ for all $k$—and to sets of sequences: for two sets of sequences of valuations $Y_1$ and $Y_2$, $Y_1 \overset{W}{=} Y_2$ denotes $\forall y_1 \in Y_1 \exists y_2 \in Y_2 \bullet y_1 \overset{W}{=} y_2$ and $\forall y_2 \in Y_2 \exists y_1 \in Y_1 \bullet y_2 \overset{W}{=} y_1$.

$T(\Sigma, X)$ denotes the set of terms over a signature $\Sigma$ and a set $X$ of variables. We assume a fixed signature to be given—the names of the functions defined in the action language and used in guards and assignments. The type of a term $t$ is denoted by $type(t)$. Two terms are unifiable ($l \cong r$) iff $\exists \beta \in A_{V_l \cup V_r} \bullet \beta(l) = \beta(r)$, where $V_l$ and $V_r$ are the sets of variables in $l$ and $r$, respectively, and $V_l \cap V_r = \emptyset$.

Given a predicate $p$, $p[f_w/w]_{w \in W}$ denotes the replacement of all variables $w$ in $W$ by terms $f_w$ of the same type. $p'[f_w/w']_{w \in W}$ applies the same notion to replacing primed variables. Finally, function composition is denoted by $\circ$, $\forall x \bullet (f \circ g)(x) = f(g(x))$. The identity mapping is called $id$.

**Rule Systems**  A *rule system* is a tuple $R = (V, S, T)$. $V$ consists of disjoint sets of typed variables, $I, O, L$. They denote input, output, and local variables, respectively. A *state* of $R$ is a valuation $\beta \in A_V$ that type-correctly maps all variables in $V$ to ground terms. $\beta \in A_L$ is called a *data state* of $R$.

$S$ is an assertion with $free(S) \subseteq V$. It describes the *initial state(s)*, and we require $S$ to be satisfiable: $\exists \beta \in A_V \bullet \beta \models S$.

$T$ is a set of *transitions*. Each $t \in T$ is an assertion with $free(t) \subseteq V \cup V'$. It relates states to successor states. Unprimed variables are evaluated in the current state, and primed variables are evaluated in the successor state.

We require all transitions in $T$ to be of the form $in \wedge g \wedge a \wedge out$. $in$ and $out$ read input values and compute and write output values, respectively. $g$ is a guard; it defines conditions on the input and the current values of the variables in $L$. $a$ assigns new values to the variables in $L$. More precisely, $in$ is a statement of the form $\bigwedge_{i \in I} i \cong \pi_i$ where $\pi_i$ is a pattern that may contain free *transition-local* variables, $H_t$, with $H_t \cap V = \emptyset$. We assume $\pi_i \in \mathcal{T}(\Sigma, H_t)$ and $type(\pi_i) = type(i)$. The idea is that these variables are bound at runtime, and the values can be used in the computation of guards, output values, and assignments. We naturally extend the notions of states by stipulating that states be elements of $A_{V \cup H_R}$ where $H_R = \bigcup_{t \in T} H_t$. The guard $g$ is a conjunction of predicates over $H_t \cup L$, with $type(g) = Bool$. The assignment $a \equiv \bigwedge_{l \in L} l' = f_l$ type-correctly assigns values to the variables in $L'$, and it may do so by referring to the variables in $L \cup H_t$: $f_l \in \mathcal{T}(\Sigma, L \cup H_t)$ with $type(f_l) = type(l)$. Finally, $out \equiv \bigwedge_{o \in O} o' = f_o$ assigns values to the output variables, $O'$. It may refer to the variables in $L \cup H_t$: $f_o \in \mathcal{T}(\Sigma, L \cup H_t)$ with $type(f_o) = type(o)$. $\varepsilon$ denotes the absence of signals both for input and output channels; types are lifted correspondingly.

Without loss of generality, we will assume that the action language for guards and assignments is a simple first-order functional language without explicit quantifiers, i.e. all variables are free. The reason for this choice is that this is the language supported by the CASE tool AutoFocus which was used in our studies.

A *run* of a rule system is an infinite sequence of states, $\beta_1 \beta_2 \ldots$ with $\beta_i \in A_{V \cup H_R}$. The set of all runs, i.e., the semantics of a rule system, $R$, is denoted by $[\![R]\!]$. We require $\beta_1 \models S$ and $\forall o \in O \bullet \beta_1(o) = \varepsilon$—output can only be produced after or during the first transition. Subsequent valuations of a run, $\beta_n$ and $\beta_{n+1}$, are related by a transition in $T$: $\forall n \bullet \beta_n, \beta'_{n+1} \models \bigvee_{t \in T} t$. Clearly, there is room for many classical constraints such as causality [15], input enabledness [16], fairness, etc. Rule systems need not be total nor deterministic.

**State Machines, Tables, and State Transition Diagrams** A *state machine* is a rule system with a dedicated variable *state* of a finite type. It specifies the *control state* or *mode* of the state machine. We require an initial control state to be determined in the initial assertion $S$, each guard to contain a statement *state* $= \overline{src}$, and each assignment to contain a statement *state'* $= \overline{dst}$ where $\overline{src}$ and $\overline{dst}$ are the source and destination control states of the transition, respectively. By convention, we will use overlines for the names of control states. State machines are graphically represented by *state transition diagrams* (STDs)—bubbles (control states) and arrows (transitions). Two examples of (incomplete) STDs are given in Fig. 1. The black dot denotes the initial state.

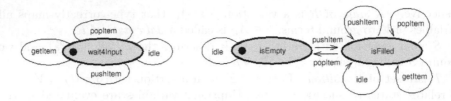

**Fig. 1.** Original STD of the stack (left); refactoring (right)

Every state machine is a rule system, but not each rule system is a state machine. However, there are many ways of transforming a rule system into a state machine. The simplest one is as follows: we add *state* of type $\{\bar{s}\}$ to $L$, add the conjunct *state* $= \bar{s}$ to the guard of each transition, and add the conjunct *state'* $= \bar{s}$ to the assignment of each transition (assuming *state* $\notin L$; otherwise we rename the old variable *state* before introducing the new one). Different ways of computing state machines from rule systems are the topic of this paper.

A *table* is the textual representation of a rule system in some tabular form. Parnas has devoted considerable work to the classification of tables [13]. For us, any tabular representation will do. An example of a table is given in Tab. 1.

| Name | Guard | Input | Output | Assignment |
|------|-------|-------|--------|------------|
| pushItem | true | e$\cong$ push(DATA) | a'=$\varepsilon$ | st'=list(DATA,st) |
| getItem | not(isE(st)) | e$\cong$ get | a'=ft(st) | st'=st |
| popItem | not(isE(st)) | e$\cong$ pop | a'=$\varepsilon$ | st'=rt(st) |
| idle | true | e$\cong$ $\varepsilon$ | a'=$\varepsilon$ | st'=st |

**Table 1.** Behavior of a stack

**Example** Consider the specification of a stack of integers. We assume a component with one input channel $I = \{e\}$ with $type(e) = \{push(Int), get, pop, \varepsilon\}$, and one output channel, $O = \{a\}$ with $type(a) = Int \cup \{\varepsilon\}$. There is one local variable, $L = \{st\}$. Using functional notation, its type is recursively defined by `data d_st = empty | list(Int, d_st)`. Three functions are defined: `isE(X) = (X == empty)`, `ft(list(X,Y)) = X`, and `rt(list(X,Y)) = Y`. One transition-local variable is used in the example, namely `DATA` in transition *pushItem*.

By adding a further local variable *state* of $type(state) = \{\overline{wait4Input}\}$ to the set $L$ of local variables, we generate a state machine from the rule system by also adding trivial statements *state* $= \overline{wait4Input}$ and *state'* $= \overline{wait4Input}$ to guard and assignment of each row of Tab. 1. Fig. 1, left, shows the STD that corresponds to the state machine of the stack example.

# 3   Incremental Development

*Increments* denote different development stages of a system, or model, respectively. To be as flexible as possible, we do not impose any constraints on these steps (except for enforceable consistency conditions that we do not discuss here).

**Development Process** Our experience with building large models boils down to the following process. Existing (informal) requirements specifications are read: a first understanding of the system's behavior is gained. One is capable of writing down statement such as "if a certain input occurs under certain conditions, then the system's state changes as follows, by outputting certain values". These rules are preliminary in that they are likely to be corrected later on. Reading the requirements documents also tends to lead to a first natural partitioning of the state space; for instance, one might find it natural to have a partitioning into *on* and *off* states in the model of an embedded system.

We found it useful not to exclusively use the graphical STDs in these early stages of development. Instead, tables turned out to be tremendously useful. The reason is that modifications in STDs are rather tedious: because the control states of the state machine change, transitions or parts of transitions have to be copied or removed multiple times. This is an error-prone and tedious task.

Nonetheless, there is no doubt that STDs are highly useful. Debugging is sometimes easier with executable STDs than with tables. For demonstration purposes with customers and domain experts, we found STDs to yield a good basis for discussion. In addition, the graphical layout helps one to identify symmetries, or missing symmetries which lead to corrections of the model (Section 5).

**Modifications and Refactorings** Development steps can alter interfaces, or they alter the behavior. We do not consider architectural modifications such as the addition of components here [15, 17, 18]. *Interface modifications* add or delete input or output channels to or from a system. If, before deletion, the name of a channel does not occur in a system's description, its removal does not change the system's behavior, and neither does the introduction of a new channel. *Behavior modifications* consist of removals and additions of traces of a model. Syntactically, this is achieved by inserting, modifying, or deleting transitions in $T$, possibly by taking into account extensions of $L$.

An increment $\tilde{R}$ of a rule system $R$ with $[\![R]\!] \stackrel{I \cup O}{=} [\![\tilde{R}]\!]$ is called a *refactoring* of $R$. This assumes that $R$ and $\tilde{R}$ define the same external interface $I = \tilde{I}$ and $O = \tilde{O}$: refactorings do not modify the interface of a component. An increment that is no refactoring is called a *modification*. In our incremental development process that relies on both tables (rule systems) and STDs (state machines), there are hence four different kinds of development steps: refactorings of state machines ($\rho_S \in \{\rho | [\![R]\!] \stackrel{I \cup O}{=} [\![\rho(R)]\!]$ *and* $R$ *is a state machine*$\}$), refactorings of rule systems ($\rho_R \in \{\rho | [\![R]\!] \stackrel{I \cup O}{=} [\![\rho(R)]\!]$ *and* $R$ *is a rule system*$\}$), and modifications of rule systems and state machines (both denoted by $\delta$ in Fig. 2). Modifications modify, add, or delete transitions, possibly with alterations of $L$.

Let $\tau$ and $\tau^{-1}$ denote transformations from rule systems into state machines, and vice versa. Fig. 2 illustrates the relationship between the development steps. As development progresses from top to bottom, modifications take place. Within each row, usually different refactorings of both tables and state machines are considered, and the further can be transformed into the latter, and vice versa.

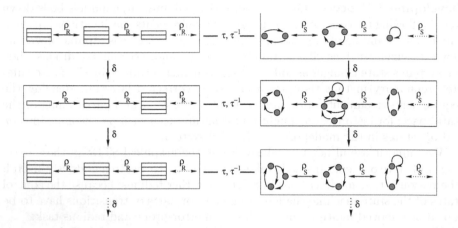

**Fig. 2.** Incremental Development

In the next section, we will describe how to compute refactorings of rule systems, $\rho_R$. Since state machines are rule systems, this also caters for refactorings of state machines. However, for reasons that we will be able to explain only after refactorings have been made precise, it is not always desirable to let $\tau^{-1} = id$.

Refactorings of rule systems that are not state machines appear to be of moderate value: they remain textual, and we have discussed the benefits of graphical representations in Section 1. Methodologically, one would prefer to get a state machine (in fact, an STD) from a refactored rule system (in fact, a table) in one step. Consequently, we will focus on combinations of (1) refactorings of rule systems (tables) and (2) transformations from rule systems (tables) into state machines (STDs). As we will see in the next section, it is sufficient to consider refactorings of state machines defined by $\rho_S = \tau \circ \rho_R \circ \tau^{-1}$. The only reason for having included refactorings of rule systems into the left part of Fig. 2 is precisely that we compute refactorings of state machines by relying on these $\rho_R$.

## 4 Refactorings

In our stack example, one might want to transform the specification into an equivalent one with two control states: one specifies that the stack is empty, and the other one specifies that it is not. The problem then consists of computing the transitions between these two control states.

| Name | Guard | Input | Output | Assignment |
|---|---|---|---|---|
| ~~pushItem~~ | ~~isE(st) ∧ isE(list(DATA,st))~~ | ~~e≅push(DATA)~~ | | ~~st'=list(DATA,st)~~ |
| pushItem | isE(st) ∧ not(isE(list(DATA,st))) | e≅push(DATA) | | st'=list(DATA,st) |
| ~~pushItem~~ | ~~not(isE(st)) ∧ isE(list(DATA,st))~~ | ~~e≅push(DATA)~~ | | ~~st'=list(DATA,st)~~ |
| pushItem | not(isE(st)) ∧ not(isE(list(DATA,st))) | e≅push(DATA) | | st'=list(DATA,st) |
| ~~getItem~~ | ~~not(isE(st)) ∧ isE(st) ∧ isE(st)~~ | ~~e≅get~~ | ~~a'=ft(st)~~ | |
| ~~getItem~~ | ~~not(isE(st)) ∧ isE(st) ∧ not(isE(st))~~ | ~~e≅get~~ | ~~a'=ft(st)~~ | |
| ~~getItem~~ | ~~not(isE(st)) ∧ not(isE(st) ∧ isE(st))~~ | ~~e≅get~~ | ~~a'=ft(st)~~ | |
| getItem | not(isE(st)) ∧ not(isE(st)) ∧ not(isE(st)) | e≅get | a'=ft(st) | |
| ~~popItem~~ | ~~not(isE(st)) ∧ isE(st) ∧ isE(rt(st))~~ | ~~e≅pop~~ | | ~~st'=rt(st)~~ |
| ~~popItem~~ | ~~not(isE(st)) ∧ isE(st) ∧ not(isE(rt(st)))~~ | ~~e≅pop~~ | | ~~st'=rt(st)~~ |
| popItem | not(isE(st)) ∧ not(isE(st)) ∧ isE(rt(st)) | e≅pop | | st'=rt(st) |
| popItem | not(isE(st)) ∧ not(isE(st)) ∧ not(isE(rt(st))) | e≅pop | | st'=rt(st) |
| idle | isE(st) ∧ isE(st) | e≅ε | | |
| ~~idle~~ | ~~isE(st) ∧ not(isE(st))~~ | ~~e≅ε~~ | | |
| ~~idle~~ | ~~not(isE(st)) ∧ isE(st)~~ | ~~e≅ε~~ | | |
| idle | not(isE(st)) ∧ not(isE(st)) | e≅ε | | |

**Table 2.** Refactored behavior

In this paper, the idea of refactoring state machines or rule systems is to define a set of predicates that partition the data space. In general, whether a set of predicates forms a partitioning is undecidable. In our case studies, however, we could easily see whether or not a set of predicates formed a partitioning. Each of these predicates corresponds to one control state of the refactored model: control states are projections of the data space (defined as the set of all possible valuations of all variables). Once the partitioning predicates have been defined, one must compute the transitions between the corresponding states.

To get an intuition of this computation, assume a set of predicates, $P$, that partition the data space, and that do not constrain input nor output values. The elements of $P$ will form the control states of the refactored model. Let $p, q \in P$. Transitions (arrows in the graphical representation) from $p$ to $q$ for each pair $p, q$ are computed as follows. For each guard $g$ of a row in the table, we compute the intersection between $p$ and $g$, i.e. $p \wedge g$. We also need to make sure that $q$ is compatible with the assignment $a \equiv \bigwedge_{l \in L} l' = f_l$ of the transition, i.e. that $q$ holds if the assignment has been computed. Overall, the predicate $g \wedge p \wedge q'[f_l/l']_{l \in L}$ has to be satisfiable. With $|P|$ new control states and $t$ transitions, the transformation requires the computation of $t \cdot |P|^2$ new transitions.

**Example** Consider the stack again. Suppose we want to derive a state machine with two control states characterized by the predicates $p \equiv isE(st)$ and $q \equiv not(isE(st))$. Clearly, $p$ and $q$ partition the data space. Tab. 2 shows the result of the refactoring where empty output ($a' = \varepsilon$) and trivial assignments ($st' = st$) are, for brevity's sake, omitted. Unsatisfiable transitions are canceled out.

For each transition of the original specification, four new transitions are computed: from $p$ to $p$, from $p$ to $q$, from $q$ to $p$, and from $q$ to $q$. For instance, the first row in the table corresponds to a transition from $p$ to $p$ that is defined by the old transition *pushItem*. *isE*($st$) checks if the source control state, $p$, is compatible with the old guard, *true*. *isE*($list(DATA, st)$) checks if the destination control state, $p$, is compatible with the old assignment, $st' = list(DATA, st)$. The conjunction of the two terms is unsatisfiable; the transition is canceled out.

As a second example, the tenth line of Tab. 2 is the transition from $p$ to $q$ w.r.t. the old transition *popItem*. $not(isE(st)) \wedge isE(st)$ checks the compatibility of the old guard, $g$, with the source control state, $p$. $not(isE(rt(st)))$ checks if the destination control state, $q$, is compatible with the old assignment. $p \wedge g$ are not satisfiable which is why this transition is also canceled out.

Fig. 1, right, shows the STD of the stack as defined by Tab. 2 that we assume to be extended by the respective assignments to *state* and *state'*. Transitions are abbreviated. *isFilled* denotes the control state that is defined by $not(isE(st))$.

**Formalization** We will now make the refactoring step precise. Let $P$ denote a finite set of predicates that partition the data space of a rule system $R = (V, S, T)$ with $V = I \cup O \cup L$ defined as above. The partitioning requirement means firstly that $P$ covers $A_L$, i.e. for all states $\beta$, we have $\beta \models \bigvee_{p \in P} p$. Secondly, the predicates in $P$ must be pairwise disjoint, i.e. $\forall p, q \in P \bullet p \neq q \Rightarrow \neg(p \wedge q)$. For convenience, we also require that all predicates in $P$ be satisfiable and an initial partition be uniquely defined, i.e. $\exists s \in P \bullet S \Rightarrow s$ because of the partitioning requirement. Refactoring a rule system $R = (V, S, T)$ w.r.t. a partitioning $P$ of the data space yields a rule system $\rho_R(R) = \tilde{R} = (V, S, \tilde{T})$ with

$$\tilde{T} := \left\{ in \ \wedge \ g \wedge p \wedge q'[f_l/l']_{l \in L} \ \wedge \ \bigwedge_{l \in L} l' = f_l \ \wedge \ \bigwedge_{o \in O} o' = f_o \ | \right.$$
$$\left. (in \ \wedge \ g \ \wedge \ \bigwedge_{l \in L} l' = f_l \ \wedge \ \bigwedge_{o \in O} o' = f_o) \in T \wedge \{p, q\} \subseteq P \right\}.$$

The proof that the transformation is indeed a refactoring, i.e. $[\![R]\!] \overset{I \cup O}{=} [\![\tilde{R}]\!]$, is given in Appendix A. The proof only requires $P$ to cover the state space; partitioning ensures that no internal nondeterminism is introduced.

If one wants to perform the refactoring and generate a state machine in one step (Section 3), then the following construction can be used. With a new variable $state \in \tilde{L}$ of $type(state) = \bigcup_{p \in P} \{\bar{p}\}$ we define $\tau \circ \rho_R((I \cup O \cup L, S, T)) = (I \cup O \cup L \cup \{state\}, \tilde{S}, \tilde{T})$ with $\tilde{S} = S \wedge state = \bar{s}$ for some $s \in P$ with $S \Rightarrow s$, and

$$\tilde{T} := \left\{ in \ \wedge \ g \wedge p \wedge q'[f_l/l']_{l \in L} \ \wedge \ state = \bar{p} \ \wedge \ state' = \bar{q} \ \wedge \ \bigwedge_{l \in L} l' = f_l \ \wedge \right.$$
$$\left. \bigwedge_{o \in O} o' = f_o \ | \ (in \ \wedge \ g \ \wedge \ \bigwedge_{l \in L} l' = f_l \ \wedge \ \bigwedge_{o \in O} o' = f_o) \in T \ \wedge \ \{p, q\} \subseteq P \right\}.$$

**Removing State Variables** Assume an iterative process where a state machine, or an STD, is generated, modified, re-transformed into a table which is subsequently modified, etc. Adding a new *state* variable for each transformation from a rule system to a state machine is likely to clutter the model (more precisely, guards and assignments of transitions). This is the only reason for not letting $\tau^{-1} = id$ (Section 3). It is not a conceptual but rather a practical problem: we would like the rule systems to be readable by humans, and thus contain as little redundancy as possible.

We will now characterize the operations that, upon application of $\tau^{-1}$ allow one to delete *state* variables in rule systems that were previously introduced by the application of $\tau$. As explained in Section 3, it is sufficient to focus on behavior modifications, and to ignore interface modifications.

The above construction of computing a refactoring and a state machine in one step shows that $state = \bar{p}$ whenever $p$ holds. Conversely, we have $state' = \bar{q}$ whenever $q'[f_l/l']_{l \in L}$ evaluates to true. In other words, the information on the explicit state variable is indeed redundant and can be removed (it is only used to decide whether or not to draw a transition arrow between two control states).

The same is true for modifications of existing transitions (including modifications of the data state $L - \{state\}$), and also for the deletion of transitions. New transitions between control states that are characterized by $p, q \in P$ are equally unproblematic if some implementing CASE tool adds $p \wedge q'[f_l/l']_{l \in L}$ to the guard of a transition from $\bar{p}$ to $\bar{q}$ (by removing assignments to *state* and *state'*; this is the—informal—definition of $\tau^{-1}$). The only problem occurs if a new control state plus transitions to or from it are added at the graphical level *without* giving a logical characterization of this control state. This is problematic because in this case, it is not possible to automatically modify guards and assignments as in the case of logically characterized control states.

In other words, if the CASE tool forbids the introduction of new control states at the *graphical level* when no logical characterization is provided and, instead, requires development steps of this kind to be performed at the *level of tables* only, then we can work with tables and STDs in parallel, without cluttering the model. In this case, refactorings of state machines are computed via $\rho_S = \tau \circ \rho_R \circ \tau^{-1}$ rather than via $\rho_R$.

**Implementation** As far as we know, there is no model-based CASE tool that integrates tables and STDs. We have used Excel and AutoFocus with ad-hoc translations between the two. While not yet integrated into the tool, the computation of refactorings is automated and includes (a) the—trivial—computation of refactored transitions (set $\tilde{T}$), and (b) their simplification, possibly to *false*. Step (b) is particularly important because the computed transitions should be readable by humans, and, as the examples of this paper show, there is a great potential for the removal of redundant parts. Our simplification algorithm implements the rules of Boolean algebra and includes a simple satisfiability checker. The latter is used to remove unsatisfiable disjuncts for formulas in disjunctive normal form. The problem is generally undecidable, but one could argue that (a) the cut-off of infinite data structure that can often be justified by domain knowledge, and (b) the simplicity of the involved functions—e.g., there is usually no mutual recursion, and most recursions turn out to be primitive—make manual decisions possible. Because our action language for guards and assignments is a functional language, we have implemented the simplifier in the functional logic language Curry [19] (the operational semantics of which relies on narrowing [20] which explains why it lends itself to satisfiability checking). With a restriction of all lists to a maximum length of 5, the example in the next section is computed in negligible time. We have not yet implemented a plugin that also takes into account automatic layouting of computed STDs.

## 5    Example: MOST NetworkMaster

This section illustrates the methodological benefits of our approach when applied to the behavior model of a network controller for automotive infotainment systems, the MOST NetworkMaster (NM) [21]. The model was the basis for model-based testing of an NM implementation [4]. The functionality of the network is divided into function blocks which reside on the network's devices. The NM is a special function block responsible for network management. Here we consider only the model of the NM's main service: setting up and maintaining the *central registry*. The central registry contains all function blocks and their associated network addresses currently available in the network.

We do not show any complex modeling details here and describe only the main local variables of the model. The model defines the variable *mode* which models the five modes of the NM: in mode *off* the NM is switched off; in mode *init* the NM performs a system configuration check during startup—all devices are asked for their function blocks; in mode *cfgOk* the NM has set up the network to normal operation, i.e. all devices are allowed to communicate freely; in mode *ncd* the NM performs a system configuration check after a network change, i.e. a device has left or jumped in the network; and in mode *delayed* the NM requests periodically devices which have not answered to any request yet. Furthermore the model defines the variable *wa* which stores the network address from which the NM expects an answer to its last request. There are four additional variables for storing the central registry and other informations about the system.

In an advanced modeling stage the NM's service is specified by a table with 17 rows where most guards contain four or five atoms. We transformed this table into different state machines for a review of the model. We choose the partitioning $P_1$ which divides the state space according to the five modes of the NM. Fig. 3, left, depicts the respective state machine. In addition, we choose a second partitioning $P_2$ which distinguishes between states (1) *requestingDevices* $\equiv$ $wa = empty \wedge mode \in \{init, ncd, delayed\}$ where the NM requests devices, (2) *waitForStatus* $\equiv wa \neq empty \wedge mode \in \{init, ncd, delayed\}$ where the NM waits for an answer, and the states (3) *off* and (4) *cfgOk* where the NM is in modes *off* or *cfgOk*. Fig. 3, right, depicts the state machine w.r.t. partitioning $P_2$.

$P_1$ allows us to study symmetries w.r.t. mode switching. For example, upon each network reset, the NM returns to mode *init* (transitions with names ending in *NotOk*). We would have detected an error in the model if one of these transitions had been missing. By means of $P_2$, we can observe that the NM can enter state *requestingDevices* from state *cfgOk* only if a network change occurs (transitions beginning with *NCD*) or if there are devices which have not answered yet (transition *swDelay*). There would be an error if there were further transitions.

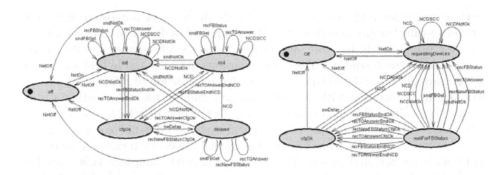

**Fig. 3.** STD of the NM w.r.t. partitioning $P_1$ (left); w.r.t. partitioning $P_2$ (right)

This example reveals that specific symmetries can be found and analyzed by building different abstract views of behavior models. By reviewing this kind of abstractions, the model can be analyzed easily if some transitions must or must not exist for symmetry considerations. The abstract view reveals relations in the model which would have stayed hidden in the detailed view of tables.

## 6   Related Work

*Refactorings:* Sunyé et al. consider the refactoring of statecharts on the grounds of hierarchical states [22]. Roughly, sets of states are merged, and the new transitions are computed. This differs from our work in that they do not consider arbitrary new definitions of states (our sets $P$ that cover the state space). In the context of inductive verification, Cheng considers refactoring a parameterized process into a set of constant processes [23]. In our context, this would amount to refactoring one state machine into more than one state machine. Van Gorp et al. propose extensions to the UML meta model such that pre- and postconditions for behavior-preserving transformations can be expressed [24]. This work is not concerned with refactorings of state machines. In a similar vein, Correa and Werner discuss refactorings of OCL expressions and class structures, without explicitly taking into account state machines [25]. Philipps and Rumpe present a set of transformation rules for data flow networks and formally show that the transformed system is a refinement of the original one [18]. Their work differs from ours in that we actually compute the refactoring of a behavior model.

*Tables and Incrementality:* Shen et al. [12] are concerned with transformations of tabular specifications of a system. They concentrate on transformations between different kinds of tables [13] rather than transforming tables into graphical representations in the form of extended state machines. Their transformations are refactorings in their own right. Prowell and Poore use incrementally discovered equivalence classes on I/O sequences to specify the I/O behavior of a system [26]. One could directly use such canonical sequences as states. Janicki and Sekerinski claim that this leads to complex state machines even for small systems [27]. In that paper, the trace assertion method is revisited, and by directly catering for certain signal interleavings, the authors propose to interpret certain so-called step-traces as states. Both approaches do not seem to see a need for refactorings at all, but they also advocate the use of different specifications.

*Logical Characterization:* The state invariants in timed and hybrid automata [28, 29] are directly related to our logical characterization of refactorings. However, we are concerned with discrete systems, and we use the invariants in a methodologically different manner, namely to the end of refactoring. Furthermore, state invariants in timed and hybrid systems need not cover the state space. Lamport uses TLA predicates—invariants—to characterize control states [7] in predicate-action diagrams. Except for the concrete language, this is similar to what we do in this paper. However, Lamport is not concerned with refactorings. Finally, the predicates that we use to characterize control states relate to the "reaffirmed invariants" in the context of STeP [30], namely local invariants $PC = i \Rightarrow I(i)$ that describe properties $I(i)$ at program location $i$ and that are defined on data variables only. These special invariants are dubbed "mode invariants" in the SCR context [31].

# 7  Conclusions and Future Work

The starting point of our work is the observation that current model-based CASE tools provide insufficient support for the incremental development of STDs when it comes to fundamental changes of the control states. These might become necessary if a better understanding of the systems suggests a different, more adequate, perspective on the state space. Refactorings of STDs are hence motivated by a better understanding of the system rather than by a "model smell" [1, p. 75].

We have shown a way of computing refactorings of state machines on the grounds of predicates that describe parts of the state space: local invariants. Our incremental development process is based on both tables and STDs. We have argued that there is room for both representations, and that it is beneficiary to use them in parallel: because of their clear structure, tables are sometimes easier to grasp—and STDs help with identifying symmetries and, possibly together with simulation traces in the form of sequence diagrams, also with conveying fundamental ideas behind the model. Refactoring tables that do not represent state machines appears to be of modest value. Benefits do become apparent when the simultaneous transformation into STDs is considered.

Because the computed refactorings are meant to be readable by humans, we have shown how refactoring steps can be performed with both representations while reducing to a minimum the number of conjuncts in guards that are introduced by the computation of a refactoring. We singled out one particular development step—the introduction of transitions from or to control states with no logical characterization—that should be performed at the level of tables rather than state machines.

Our experience with behavior models of embedded systems that we built to the end of generating test cases suggests that the cost of building and maintaining the models is likely to turn out as a critical parameter. In many cases, the potential of considerable reuse will drive the decision for or against this or comparable technologies. CASE tool support for (1) quick and easy development of new models and, in particular, (2) comfortable modification of existing models then appears as an indispensable prerequisite for cost-effectively handling their development. Refactorings of behavior models, like the work presented in this paper, are one step towards more comfortable and cheaper model-based development processes.

Future work is bound (1) to extended implementations of the satisfiability checker that is needed for the reduction of refactored transitions, (2) to the tight integration of our approach into a CASE tool that, in particular, must include the automatic layouting of computed STDs, and (3) to an extension to other formalisms, e.g., statecharts with OCL. While we believe that working with logical characterizations of control states is a viable option to refactoring state machines, we need more experience to identify situations where which model refactorings are of considerable methodological value, where not, and why.

*Acknowledgments* J. Philipps pointed us to Lamport's work on predicate-action diagrams. B. Schätz and B. Seybold provided useful comments on this paper.

# References

[1] Fowler, M.: Refactoring - Improving the Design of Existing Code. Addison Wesley (1999)
[2] Mens, T., Demeyer, S., Du Bois, B., Stenten, H., Van Gorp, P.: Refactoring: Current Research and Future Trends. In: Proc. ETAPS 2003 Workshop on Language Descriptions, Tools and Applications. (2003)
[3] Huber, F., Schätz, B., Einert, G.: Consistent Graphical Specification of Distributed Systems. In: Proc. Formal Methods Europe. (1997) 122 – 141
[4] Pretschner, A., Prenninger, W., Wagner, S., Kühnel, C., Baumgartner, M., Zölch, R., Sostawa, B., Stauner, T.: One evaluation of model-based testing and its automation. In: Proc. 27th Intl. Conf. on Software Engineering. (2005) 392–401
[5] Philipps, J., Pretschner, A., Slotosch, O., Aiglstorfer, E., Kriebel, S., Scholl, K.: Model-based test case generation for smart cards. In: Proc. 8th Intl. Workshop on Formal Methods for Industrial Critical Systems. (2003) 168–192
[6] Pretschner, A., Slotosch, O., Aiglstorfer, E., Kriebel, S.: Model Based Testing for Real—The Inhouse Card Case Study. J. STTT **5** (2004) 140–157
[7] Lamport, L.: TLA in Pictures. IEEE TSE **21** (1995) 768–775
[8] Heninger, K.: Specifying Software Requirements for Complex Systems: New Techniques and Their Application. IEEE TSE **SE-6** (1980) 2–13
[9] Parnas, D., Madey, J.: Functional Documents for Computer Systems. Science of Computer Programming **1** (1995) 41–61
[10] Heitmeyer, C., Jeffords, R., Labaw, B.: Automated Consistency Checking of Requirements Specifications. ACM Trans. on SW Eng. and Meth. **5** (1996) 231–261
[11] Parnas, D., Peters, D.: An Easily Extensible Toolset for Tabular Mathematical Expressions. In: Proc. TACAS'99. (1999) 345–359
[12] Shen, H., Zucker, J., Parnas, D.: Table transformation tools: Why and how. In: Proc. 11th Annual Conf. on Computer Assurance. (1996) 3–11

[13] Parnas, D.: Tabular Representations of Relations. Technical Report CRL-260, Telecommunications Research Institute of Ontario (1992)

[14] Breitling, M., Philipps, J.: Step by step to histories. In: Proc. Algebraic Methodology And Software Technology. Volume 1816 of Springer LNCS. (2000) 11–25

[15] Broy, M., Stølen, K.: Specification and Development of Interactive Systems – Focus on Streams, Interfaces, and Refinement. Springer (2001)

[16] Lynch, N., Tuttle, M.: Hierarchical correctness proofs for distributed algorithms. In: Proc. 6th annual ACM symp. on principles of distr. computing. (1987) 137–151

[17] Philipps, J., Rumpe, B.: Refinement of information flow architectures. In: Proc. ICFEM'97. (1997)

[18] Philipps, J., Rumpe, B.: Refinement of pipe and filter architectures. In: FM'99, LNCS 1708. (1999) 96–115

[19] Hanus, M.: Functional Logic Language Curry. Language Hompage: http://www.informatik.uni-kiel.de/~mh/curry/ (2005)

[20] Hanus, M.: The integration of functions into logic programming: From theory to practice. J. Logic Programming **19,20** (1994) 583–628

[21] MOST Cooperation: MOST Specification, Rev. 2.2. http://www.mostnet.de/downloads/Specifications/ (2002)

[22] Sunyé, G., Pollet, D., Le Traon, Y., Jézéquel, J.M.: Refactoring UML models. In: Proc. 4th Intl. Conf. on the Unified Modeling Language. (2001) 134–148

[23] Cheng, Y.P.: Refactoring design models for inductive verification. In: Proc. Intl. Symp. on Software Testing and Analysis. (2002) 164–168

[24] van Gorp, P., Stenten, H., Mens, T., Demeyer, S.: Towards Automating Source-Consistent UML Refactorings. In: Proc. UML. (2003) 144–158

[25] Correa, A., Werner, C.: Applying Refactoring Techniques to UML/OCL Models. In: Proc. 7th Intl. Conf. on the Unified Modeling Language. (2004) 173–187

[26] Prowell, S., Poore, J.: Foundations of Sequence-Based Software Specification. IEEE TSE **29** (2003) 1–13

[27] Janicki, R., Sekerinski, E.: Foundations of the Trace Assertion Method of Module Interface Specification. IEEE TSE **27** (2001) 577–598

[28] Lynch, N., Vaandrager, F.: Forward and backward simulations for timing-based systems. Volume 600 of Springer LNCS. (1991) 397–446

[29] Alur, R., Courcoubetis, C., Halbwachs, N., Henzinger, T., Ho, P.H., Nicollin, X., Olivero, A., Sifakis, J., Yovine, S.: The algorithmic analysis of hybrid systems. Theoretical Computer Science **138** (1995) 3–34

[30] Manna et al., Z.: STeP: the Stanford Temporal Prover. Technical Report STAN-CS-TR-94-1518, Dept. of Computer Science, Stanford University (1994)

[31] Jeffords, R., Heitmeyer, C.: Automatic Generation of State Invariants from Req. Specifications. In: Proc. 6th Intl. Symp. on Foundations of SW Engineering. (1998)

# A    Proof

We show that the given transformation w.r.t. a partitioning $P$ is indeed a refactoring, i.e., $[\![R]\!] \stackrel{I \cup O}{=} [\![\tilde{R}]\!]$. We prove the stronger claim, $[\![R]\!] = [\![\tilde{R}]\!]$. Restrictions to the I/O behavior are necessary only if the set of local data state variables, $L$, is modified. We have moved modifications of this set—more precisely, of state variable *state*—into the mappings $\tau$ and $\tau^{-1}$ that transform rule systems into state machines, and vice versa. We need to show that for all pairs of subsequent states, $\beta\gamma$, of runs in $R$, there is a transition $\tilde{t}$ of $\tilde{R}$ with $\beta, \gamma' \models \tilde{t}$, and vice versa. Both directions are proved by induction.

"$\subseteq$". In order to show $[\![R]\!] \subseteq [\![\tilde{R}]\!]$, we first show that the first state of a run of the further also is the first state of a run of the latter. This follows directly because $R$ and $\tilde{R}$ have the identical assertion $S$ for initial states.

For the induction step, consider two subsequent states $\beta$ and $\gamma$ of a run of $R$, i.e., $\ldots\beta\gamma\ldots \in [\![R]\!]$. By definition, there must be a transition $t \in T$ with $\beta, \gamma' \models t$ where $\beta, \gamma \in A_{V \cup H_t}$. Let $t \equiv in \wedge g \wedge a \wedge out$. We have to show that there are $p, q \in P$ with $\beta, \gamma' \models p \wedge q'[f_l/l']_{l \in L}$.

Since $P$ partitions the data space, $A_L$, there must be $p, q \in P$ s.t. $\beta \models p$ and $\gamma \models q$, or equivalently, $\gamma' \models q'$. By definition, $a \equiv \bigwedge_{l \in L} l' = f_l$, and because $t$ implies $a$, it is the case that $\beta, \gamma' \models t$ implies $\beta, \gamma' \models \bigwedge_{l \in L} l' = f_l$. Hence $\beta, \gamma' \models p \wedge q' \wedge \bigwedge_{l \in L} l' = f_l$.

By definition, we have $q'[f_l/l']_{l \in L} \equiv q' \wedge \bigwedge_{l \in L} l' = f_l$. Consequently, $\beta, \gamma' \models p \wedge q'[f_l/l']_{l \in L}$. $\beta, \gamma' \models t$ implies $\beta, \gamma' \models in \wedge g \wedge out$. Altogether, this yields $\beta, \gamma' \models in \wedge g \wedge p \wedge q'[f_l/l']_{l \in L} \wedge a \wedge out$. This shows that if $\gamma$ is reachable from an initial state $\beta$ in $R$, then this is also the case in $\tilde{R}$.

"$\supseteq$". In order to show $[\![R]\!] \supseteq [\![\tilde{R}]\!]$, we already know that the first state of a run of $\tilde{R}$ also is one of a run of $R$. Consider subsequent states $\beta, \gamma$ of a run of $\tilde{R}$. There is a $\tilde{t} \in \tilde{T}$ with $\beta, \gamma' \models \tilde{t}$. By construction of $\tilde{T}$, there also is a $t \in T$ with $\tilde{t} \Rightarrow t$, and consequently, $\beta, \gamma' \models t$.

# Dynamic Secure Aspect Modeling with UML: From Models to Code

Jan Jürjens[1]* and Siv Hilde Houmb[2]

[1] Software & Systems Engineering, Dep. of Informatics, TU Munich, Germany
http://www4.in.tum.de/~juerjens
[2] Department of Computer and Information Science,
Norwegian University of Science and Technology, Norway
siv.hilde.houmb@idi.ntnu.no

**Abstract.** Security engineering deals with modeling, analysis, and implementation of complex security mechanisms. The dynamic nature of such mechanisms makes it difficult to anticipate undesirable emergent behavior. In this work, we propose an approach to develop and analyze security-critical specifications and implementations using aspect-oriented modeling. Since we focus on the dynamic views of a system, our work is complementary to existing approaches to security aspects mostly concerned with static views. Our approach includes a link to implementations in so far as the code which is constructed from the models can be analyzed automatically for satisfaction of the security requirements stated in the UML diagrams. We present tool support for our approach.

## 1 Introduction

Constructing security-critical systems in a sound and well-founded way poses high challenges. To support this task, we propose an Aspect-Oriented Modeling (AOM, see e.g. [EAK+01, EAB02, FRGG04, LB04]) approach which separates complex security mechanisms (which implement the security aspect model) from the core functionality of the system (the primary model) in order to allow a security verification of the particularly security-critical parts, and also of the composed model.

Since security requirements such as secrecy, integrity and authenticity of data are always relative to an unpredictable adversary, they are difficult to even define precisely, let alone to implement correctly within the development of security-critical systems. Being able to consider security aspects already in the design phase, before a system is actually implemented, is advantageous: Removing security flaws in the design phase saves cost and time. Thus, the goal is to develop security-critical systems that are secure by design. Towards this goal, the security extension UMLsec for the Unified Modeling Language (UML) has been defined

---

* This work was partially funded by the German Federal Ministry of Education, Science, Research and Technology (BMBF) in the framework of the Verisoft project under grant 01 IS C38. The responsibility for this article lies with the author(s).

L. Briand and C. Williams (Eds.): MoDELS 2005, LNCS 3713, pp. 142–155, 2005.

in [Jür02, Jür04a]. It allows us to encapsulate knowledge on prudent security engineering as aspects and thereby make it available to developers which may not be specialized in security. In the current work, we present an approach which lets one weave in the security aspects specified as UMLsec stereotypes (such as secrecy) as concrete security mechanisms (such as a cryptographic protocol) on the modeling level. We demonstrate how to check whether the code which is meant to implement the models fulfills the security requirements by security verification with automated theorem provers (ATPs) for first-order logic. To support our approach, a tool is available over a web-interface and as open-source which, from control flow graphs generated from the source code and corresponding security requirements, automatically generates FOL logic formulas in the standard TPTP notation as input to a variety of ATP's [Jür04b].

In the next section, we give a short background on aspect-oriented modeling. In Sect. 3, we explain how one can specify security aspects in UMLsec models and how these are woven into the primary model using our approach. Section 4 explains our code analysis framework. Throughout the paper we demonstrate our approach using a variant of the Internet protocol Transport Layer Security (TLS). In Sect. 5, we report on experiences from using our approach in an industrial setting. After comparing our research with related work, we close with a discussion and an outlook on ongoing research.

# 2    Aspect-Oriented Modeling (AOM)

AOM techniques allow system developers to address crosscutting objectives, such as security requirements, separately from the core functional requirements during system design. An aspect-oriented design model consists of a set of aspects and a primary model. An aspect describes how a single objective is addressed in a design, and a primary model describes how core functional requirements are addressed. The aspects and the primary model are then composed before implementation or code generation. This is done by weaving the aspect and the primary model at the modeling level.

As illustrated in Fig. 1, aspect models consist of models describing the static and dynamic views. After weaving the security aspect with the primary model, our approach allows one to perform a security verification on the composed model. From the composed model, the code is constructed (either manually or by automatic generation). If one later performs changes in the code, as often necessary in industrial development, the primary and aspect models cannot be directly extracted from the code any more. Thus changes in the code cannot in general be un-weaved at the model level. Therefore, our approach furthermore allows us to directly verify the code constructed from the UML model and to make sure that, after the necessary manual adjustments, the code is still secure.

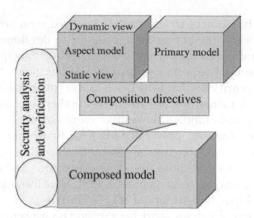

**Fig. 1.** Overview of the AOM approach for dynamic security aspects

# 3   Introducing Dynamic Security Aspects

## 3.1   Specifying Security Aspects

We can only shortly recall part of the UMLsec notation here for space reasons. A complete account can be found in [Jür02, Jür04a]. In Table 1 we give some of the stereotypes from UMLsec and in Table 2 the associated tags and corresponding adversary threats. The constraints connected to the stereotypes are formalized in first-order logic and can be verified by an automated first-order logic theorem prover, which is part of our UML analysis tool suite.

| Stereotype | Base Class | Tags | Constraints | Description |
|---|---|---|---|---|
| Internet | link | | | Internet connection |
| encrypted | link | | | encrypted connection |
| LAN | link | | | LAN connection |
| secure links | subsystem | | dependency security matched by links | enforces secure communication links |
| secrecy | dependency | | | assumes secrecy |
| secure dependency | subsystem | | « call », « send » respect data security | structural interaction data security |
| critical | object | secret | | critical object |
| no down-flow | subsystem | | prevents down-flow | information flow |
| data security | subsystem | | provides secrecy | basic datasec requirements |
| fair exchange | package | start,stop | after start eventually reach stop | enforce fair exchange |

**Table 1.** UMLsec stereotypes (excerpt)

The general system model used here is the one that builds the foundation for a semantics for part of UML currently in development in a project with IBM Rational Software [BJCR05].

The primary model is a set of UML models and the dynamic aspect are weaved in by including the stereotypes defined above.

## 3.2   Weaving in Dynamic Security Aspects

Aspects encapsulate properties (often non-functional ones) which crosscut a system, and we use transformations of UML models to "weave in" dynamic security aspects on the model level. The resulting UML models can be analyzed as to whether they actually satisfy the desired security requirements using automated tools [Jür05]. Secondly, one should make sure that the code constructed from the models (either manually or by code generation) still satisfies the security requirements shown on the model level. This is highly non-trivial, for example because different aspects may be woven into the same system which may interfere on the code level in an unforeseen way. To achieve it, one has in principle two options: One can either again verify the generated code against the desired security requirements, or one can prove that the code generation preserves the security requirements fulfilled on the model level. Although the second option would be conceptually more satisfying, a formal verification of a code generator of industrially relevant strength seems to be infeasible for the foreseeable future. Also, in many cases, completely automated code generation may not be practical anyway. We therefore followed the first option and extended our UML security analysis techniques from [Jür04b] to the code level (presently C code, while the analysis of Java code is in development). The analysis approach now takes the generated code and automatically verifies it against the intended security requirement, which has been woven in as dynamic aspects. This is explained in Sect. 4. This verification thus amounts to a *translation validation* of the weaving and code construction process. Note that performing the analysis both at the model and the code level is not overly redundant: the security analysis on the model level has the advantage that problem found can be corrected earlier when this requires less effort, and the security analysis on the code level is still necessary as argued above. Also, in practice generated code is very rarely be used without any changes, which again requires verification on the code level.

The model transformation resulting from the "weaving in" of a dynamic security aspect $p$ corresponds to a function $f_p$ which takes a UML specification

| Tag | Stereotype | Type | Multipl. | Description | Stereotype | Threats$_{default}()$ |
|-----|-----------|------|----------|-------------|-----------|----------------------|
| secret | critical | String | * | secret data | Internet | {delete,read,insert} |
| start | fair exchange | $\mathcal{P}(\text{String})$ | 1 | start states | encrypted | {delete} |
| stop | fair exchange | $\mathcal{P}(\text{String})$ | 1 | stop states | LAN | $\emptyset$ |

**Table 2.** UMLsec tags (excerpt); Threats from the *default* attacker

$S$ and returns a UML specification, namely the one obtained when applying $p$ to $S$. Technically, such a function can be presented by defining how it should act on certain subsystem instances[3], and by extending it to all possible UML specifications in a compositional way. Suppose that we have a set $S$ of subsystem instances such that none of the subsystem instances in $S$ is contained in any other subsystem instance in $S$. Suppose that for every subsystem instance $S \in S$ we are given a subsystem instance $f_p(S)$. Then for any UML specification $\mathcal{U}$, we can define $f_p(\mathcal{U})$ by substituting each occurrence of a subsystem instance $S \in S$ in $\mathcal{U}$ by $f_p(S)$. We demonstrate this by an example.

We consider the data secrecy aspect in the situation of communication over untrusted networks, as specified in Fig. 2. In the subsystem, the Sender object is supposed to accept a value in the variable d as an argument of the operation send and send it over the « encrypted » Internet link to the Receiver object, which delivers the value as a return value of the operation receive. According to the stereotype « critical » and the associated tag {secrecy}, the subsystem is supposed to preserve the secrecy of the variable d.

A well-known implementation of this aspect is to encrypt the traffic over the untrusted link using a key exchange protocol. As an example, we consider a simplified variant of the handshake protocol of the Internet protocol TLS in Fig. 4. The notation for the cryptographic algorithms is defined in Fig. 3.

The goal of the protocol is to let a sender send a secret over an untrusted communication link to a receiver in a way that provides secrecy, by using symmetric session keys.[4] The sender $S$ initiates the protocol by sending the message $\mathsf{request}(\mathsf{N}, \mathsf{K_S}, Sign_{K_S^{-1}}(\mathsf{S} :: \mathsf{K_S}))$ to the receiver $R$. If the condition $[\mathbf{snd}(\mathcal{E}xt_{K'}(\mathsf{c_S}))=\mathsf{K'}]$ holds, where $K'$ and $\mathsf{c_S}$ are the second and third arguments of the message received earlier (that is, if the key $K_S$ contained in the signature matches the one transmitted in the clear), $R$ sends the return message $\mathsf{return}(\{Sign_{K_R^{-1}}(\mathsf{K} :: \mathsf{N'})\}_{K'}, Sign_{K_{CA}^{-1}}(\mathsf{R} :: \mathsf{K_R}))$ back to $S$ (where $\mathsf{N'}$ is the first argument of the message received earlier). Then if the condition

$$[\mathbf{fst}(\mathcal{E}xt_{K_{CA}}(\mathsf{c_R}))=\mathsf{R} \wedge \mathbf{snd}(\mathcal{E}xt_{K''}(\mathcal{D}ec_{K_S^{-1}}(\mathsf{c_k})))=\mathsf{N}]$$

holds, where $\mathsf{c_R}$ and $\mathsf{c_k}$ are the two arguments of the message received by the sender, and $\mathsf{K''} ::= \mathbf{snd}(\mathcal{E}xt_{K_{CA}}(\mathsf{c_R}))$ (that is, the certificate is actually for $R$ and the correct nonce is returned), $S$ sends $\mathsf{transmit}(\{\mathsf{d}\}_k)$ to $R$, where $\mathsf{k} ::= \mathbf{fst}(\mathcal{E}xt_{K''}(\mathcal{D}ec_{K_S^{-1}}(\mathsf{c_k})))$. If any of the checks fail, the respective protocol participant stops the execution of the protocol.

Note that the receiver sends two return messages - the first matches the return trigger at the sender, the other is the return message for the receive message with which the receiver object was called by the receiving application at the receiver node.

---

[3] Although one could also define this on the type level, we prefer to remain on the instance level, since having access to instances gives us more fine-grained control.

[4] Note that in this simplified example, which should mainly demonstrate the idea of dynamic security aspect weaving, authentication is out of scope of our considerations.

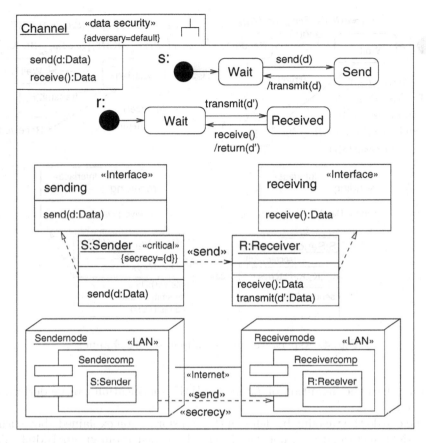

**Fig. 2.** Aspect weaving example: sender and receiver

- _ :: _                 (concatenation)
- **head**(_) and **tail**(_)    (head and tail of a concatenation)
- {_}_                  (encryption)
- $\mathcal{D}ec\_(\_)$              (decryption)
- $\mathcal{S}ign\_(\_)$            (signing)
- $\mathcal{E}xt\_(\_)$             (extracting from signature)

**Fig. 3.** Abstract Crypto Operations

To weave in this aspect $p$ in a formal way, we consider the set $S$ of subsystems derived from the subsystem in Fig. 2 by renaming: This means, we substitute any message, data, state, subsystem instance, node, or component name $n$ by a name $m$ at each occurrence, in a way such that name clashes are avoided. Then $f_p$ maps any subsystem instance $\mathcal{S} \in S$ to the subsystem instance derived from that given in Fig. 4 by the same renaming. This gives us a presentation of

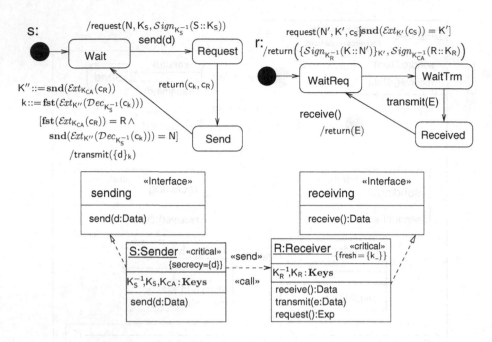

**Fig. 4.** Aspect weaving example: secure channel

$f_p$ from which the definition of $f_p$ on any UML specification can be derived as indicated above.

One can do the weaving by defining the transformation explained above using the model transformation framework BOTL developed at our group [BM03]. The overall tool-suite supporting our aspect-oriented modeling approach is given in Fig. 5. The tool-flow proceeds as follows. The developer creates a primary UML model and stores it in the XMI file format. The static checker checks that the security aspects formulated in the static views of the model are consistent. The dynamic checker weaves in the security aspects with the dynamic model. One can then verify the resulting UML model against the security requirements using the analysis engine (an automated theorem prover for first-order logic). One then constructs the code and also verify it against the security requirements using the theorem prover. The error analyzer uses the information received from the static and dynamic checkers to produce a text report for the developer describing the problems found, and a modified UML model, where the errors found are visualized.

## 4   Analyzing the Code

We define the translation of security protocol implementations to first-order logic formulas which allows automated analysis of the source code using automated first-order logic theorem provers. The source code is extracted as a control flow

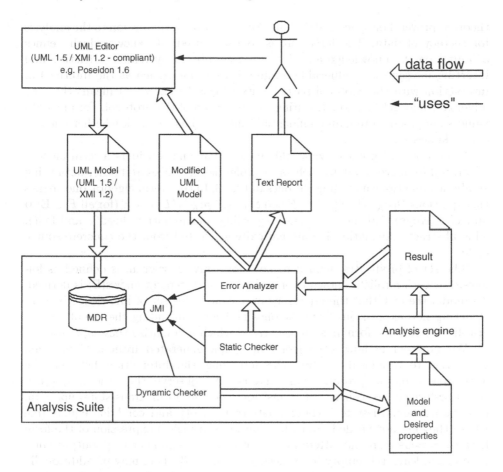

**Fig. 5.** UML verification framework: usage

graph using the aiCall tool [Abs04]. It is compiled to first-order logic axioms giving an abstract interpretation of the system behavior suitable for security analysis following the well-known Dolev-Yao adversary model [DY83]. The idea is that an adversary can read messages sent over the network and collect them in his knowledge set. He can merge and extract messages in the knowledge set and can delete or insert messages on the communication links. The security requirements are formalized with respect to this adversary model. For example, a data value remains secret from the adversary if it never appears in the knowledge set of the adversary. As with similar approaches such as [SFWW03], our approach works especially well with nicely structured code. For example, we apply an automated transformation which abstracts from pointers before applying our security analysis.

We explain the transformation from the control flow graph generated from the C program to first-order logic, which is given as input to the automated theorem prover. For space restrictions, we restrict our explanation to the analysis for secrecy of data. The idea here is to use a predicate knows which defines a bound on the knowledge an adversary may obtain by reading, deleting and inserting messages on vulnerable communication lines (such as the Internet) in interaction with the protocol participants. Precisely, knows($E$) means that the adversary may get to know $E$ during the execution of the protocol. For any data value $s$ supposed to remain confidential, one thus has to check whether one can derive knows($s$).

From a logical point of view, this means that one considers a term algebra generated from ground data such as variables, keys, nonces and other data using symbolic operations including the ones in Fig. 3. In that term algebra, one defines the equations $\mathcal{D}ec_{K^{-1}}(\{E\}_K) = E$ and $\mathcal{E}xt_K(Sign_{K^{-1}}(E)) = E$ (for all $E \in \mathbf{Exp}$ and $K \in \mathbf{Keys}$) and the usual laws regarding concatenation, head(), and tail(). This abstract information is automatically generated from the concrete source code.

The set of predicates defined to hold for a given program is defined as follows. For each publicly known expression E, the statement knows(E) is derived. To model the fact that the adversary may enlarge his set of knowledge by constructing new expressions from the ones he knows, including the use of cryptographic operations, formulas are generated which axiomatize these operations.

We now define how a control flow graph generated from a C program gives rise to a logical formula characterizing the interaction between the adversary and the protocol participants. We observe that the graph can be transformed to consist of transitions of the form trans(state, inpattern, condition, action, truestate), where inpattern is empty and condition equals true where they are not needed, and where action is a logical expression of the form localvar = value resp. outpattern in case of a local assignment resp. output command (and leaving it empty if not needed). If needed, there may be additionally another transition corresponding to the negation of the given condition, where we safely abstract from the negated condition (for logical reasons beyond this exposition).

Now assume that the source code gives rise to a transition TR1 = trans(s1, i1, c1, a1, t1) such that there is a second transition TR2 = trans(s2, i2, c2, a2, t2) where s2 = t1. If there is no such transition TR2, we define TR2 = trans(t1, [], true, [], t1) to simplify our presentation, where [] is the empty input or output pattern. Suppose that c1 is of the form cond($arg_1, \ldots, arg_n$). For i1, we define $\bar{i1}$ = knows(i1) in case i1 is nonempty and otherwise $\bar{i1}$ = true. For a1, we define $\bar{a1}$ = a1 in case a1 is of the form localvar = value and $\bar{a1}$ = knows(outpattern) in case a1 = outpattern (and $\bar{a1}$ = true in case a1 is empty). Then for TR1 we define the following predicate:

$$\mathrm{PRED(TR1)} \equiv \bar{i1}\&c1 \Rightarrow \bar{a1}\&\mathrm{PRED(TR2)} \tag{1}$$

The formula formalizes the fact that, if the adversary knows an expression he can assign to the variable i1 such that the condition c1 holds, then this implies

```
void TLS_Client (char* secret)
{  char Resp_1 [MSG_MAXLEN];
   char Resp_2 [MSG_MAXLEN];
   // allocate and prepare buffers
   memset (Resp1, 0x00, MSG_MAXLEN);
   memset (Resp2, 0x00, MSG_MAXLEN);
   // C->S: Init
   send (n, k_c, sign(conc(c, k_c), inv(k_c)));
   // S->C: Receive Server's respond
   recv (Resp_1, Resp_2);
   // Check Guards
   if ( (memcmp(fst(ext(Resp_2, k_ca)), s, MSG_MAXLEN) == 0) &&
        (memcmp(snd(ext(dec(Resp_1, inv(k_c))),
             snd(ext(Resp_2, k_ca)))), n, MSG_MAXLEN) == 0) )
   {  // C->S: Send Secret
      send (symenc(secret, fst(ext(dec(Resp_1,
      inv(k_c)), snd(ext(Resp_2, k_ca)))))); }}
```

**Fig. 6.** Fragment of abstracted client code

that a1 will hold according to the protocol, which means that either the equation localvar = value holds in case of an assignment, or the adversary gets to know outpattern, in case it is send out in a1. Also then the predicate for the succeeding transition TR2 will hold.

To construct the recursive definition above, we assume that the control flow graph is finite and cycle-free. As usual in static code analysis, loops are unfolded over a number of iterations provided by the user. The predicates PRED(TR) for all such transitions TR are then joined together using logical conjunctions and closed by forall-quantification over all free variables contained.

Figure 6 gives a simplified C implementation of the client side of the TLS variant considered earlier. From this, the control flow graph is generated automatically. Although the complete graph cannot be shown here, we show as an example a fragment of the client side in Fig. 7. The main part of the transformation of the client to the e-SETHEO input format TPTP is given in Fig. 8. We use the TPTP notation for the first-order logic formulas [SS01], which is the input notation for many automated theorem provers including the one we use (e-SETHEO [SW00]). Here & means logical conjunction and ![E1, E2] forall-quantification over E1, E2. The protocol itself is expressed by a for-all quantification over the variables which store the message arguments received.

Given this translation of the C code to first-order logic, one can now check using the automated theorem prover that the code constructed from the UMLsec aspect model still satisfies the desired security requirements. For example, if the prover can derive knows(secret) from the formulas generated by the protocol, the adversary may potentially get to know secret. Details on how to perform this analysis given the first-order logic formula are explained in [Jür05].

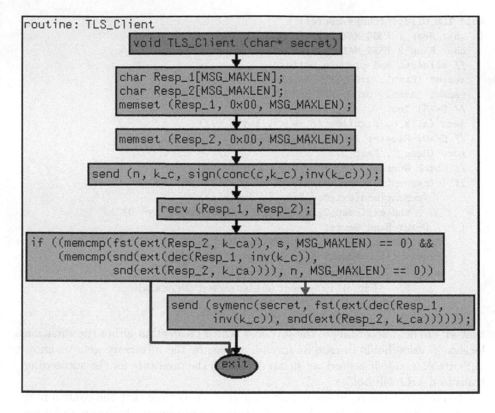

**Fig. 7.** Control graph for client

```
input_formula(protocol,axiom,(
 ![Resp_1, Resp_2] : (((knows(conc(n, conc(k_c,sign(conc(c,conc(k_c,eol)),inv(k_c)))))
        & ((knows(Resp_1) & knows(Resp_2)
        & equal(fst(ext(Resp_2,k_ca)),s)
        & equal(snd(ext(dec(Resp_1,inv(k_c)),snd(ext(Resp_2,k_ca)))),n))
     => knows(enc(secret,fst(ext(dec(Resp_1,inv(k_c)),snd(ext(Resp_2,k_ca)))))))))))))).
```

**Fig. 8.** Core protocol axiom for client

# 5   Industrial Application

We are currently applying our method in an industrial project with a major
German company. The goal is the correct development of a security-critical biometric authentication system which is supposed to control access to a protected
resource. Because the correct design of such cryptographic protocols and the correct use within the surrounding system is very difficult, our method was chosen
to support the development of the biometric authentication system. Our approach has already been applied at the specification level [Jür05] where several

severe security flaws had been found. We are currently applying the approach presented here to the source-code level for a prototypical implementation we constructed from the specification. The security analaysis results achieved so far are obtained with the automated theorem prover within less than a minute computing time on an AMD Athlon processor with 1533 MHz. tact frequency and 1024 MB RAM.

# 6   Related Work

In [FKGS04, FRGG04], aspect models are used to describe crosscutting solutions that address quality or non-functional concerns on the model level. A rigorous technique for specifying pattern solutions in UML is described. It is explained how to identify and compose multiple concerns, such as security and fault tolerance, and how to identify and solve conflicts between competing concerns. [GS04] proposes an approach which models application requirements and designs separately from security requirements and designs in the UML notation. Security requirements are captured in security use cases and encapsulated in security objects separately from the application requirements and objects. One of the benefits of aspect-oriented approaches is reuse of models or patterns and code. [EAK+01] discusses an approach to enhance reuse of code for requirements such as synchronization and scheduling. The authors present a formal design methodology to model the system's concerns based on aspect-orientation. Aspects of AOP are discussed more generally in [EAB02]. [LB04] focuses on the importance of subsystem (pattern) reusability. They propose an Aspect-Oriented Development Framework (AODF) where functional behaviors are encapsulated in each component and connector, while non-functional requirements are tuned separately. To support the modularity of non-functional requirements, they devise Aspectual Composition Rules (ACR) and Aspectual Collaborative Composition Rules (ACCR). Related to the source-code analysis side of our work, [MSRM04] addresses the problem of concept location using an advanced information retrieval method, Latent Semantic, that supports software maintenance and reverse engineering of source code.

Note that although dynamic aspects have been one major focus of aspect-oriented approaches in general, in the case of security, most approaches so far have not concentrated on an integrated approach for weaving in dynamic security aspects at the design level and for constructing and analyzing the code.

# 7   Conclusion

We explained how to develop and analyze specifications and implementations wrt. dynamic security aspects using aspect-oriented modeling. The approach separates complex security mechanisms from the core functionality to allow a security analysis and verification of the particularly security-critical parts and also of the composed model. Being able to consider security aspects already in the design phase (before a system is actually implemented) is advantageous, since removing security flaws in the design phase saves cost and time. In practice usually at least part of the code construction is still done manually and is thus again prone to security flaws. We therefore extended our approach to be able to check whether code obtained in the end actually fulfills the security requirements, using an automated security analysis with first-order logic theorem provers.

Experiences from the industrial application project mentioned in Sect. 5 indicate that our approach is quite suited to increase the security of systems developed in practice (exemplified also by the number of security flaws found and removed so far).

Since we focus on the dynamic views of a system, our work is complementary to existing approaches mostly concerned with static views. For future work, it would therefore be very interesting to try to integrate these approaches with the one proposed here. Note that although we concentrate on security aspects in this paper, which pose specific challenges (such as the correct use of cryptographic operations), our approach can be generalized to other non-functional aspects such as dependability by using a suitable extension of UML (see e.g. [Jür03]).

*Acknowledgements* Assistance from Mark Yampolskiy on the material for the example in this paper is very gratefully acknowledged.

# References

[Abs04]   AbsInt. aicall. http://www.aicall.de/, 2004.

[BJCR05]  M. Broy, J. Jürjens, V. Cengarle, and B. Rumpe. Towards a system model for UML. Technical report, TU Munich, 2005.

[BM03]    P. Braun and F. Marschall. The BOTL tool.
          http://www4.in.tum.de/~marschal/botl/index.htm, 2003.

[DY83]    D. Dolev and A. Yao. On the security of public key protocols. *IEEE Transactions on Information Theory*, IT-29(2):198–208, 1983.

[EAB02]   T. Elrad, O. Aldawud, and A. Bader. Aspect-oriented modeling: Bridging the gap between implementation and design. In Don S. Batory, Charles Consel, and Walid Taha, editors, *GPCE*, volume 2487 of *Lecture Notes in Computer Science*, pages 189–201. Springer, 2002.

[EAK+01]  T. Elrad, M. Aksit, G. Kiczales, K.J. Lieberherr, and H. Ossher. Discussing aspects of AOP. *Commun. ACM*, 44(10):33–38, 2001.

[FKGS04]  R.B. France, D. Kim, S. Ghosh, and E. Song. A UML-based pattern specification technique. *IEEE Trans. Software Eng.*, 30(3):193–206, 2004.

[FRGG04]  R.B. France, I. Ray, G. Georg, and S. Ghosh. Aspect-oriented approach to early design modelling. *IEE Proceedings - Software*, 151(4):173–186, 2004.

[GS04]    H. Gomaa and M.E. Shin. Modeling complex systems by separating application and security concerns. In *ICECCS*, pages 19–28. IEEE Computer Society, 2004.

[Jür02]   J. Jürjens. UMLsec: Extending UML for secure systems development. In J.-M. Jézéquel, H. Hußmann, and S. Cook, editors, *UML 2002 – The Unified Modeling Language*, volume 2460 of *LNCS*, pages 412–425. Springer, 2002.

[Jür03]   J. Jürjens. Developing safety-critical systems with UML. In P. Stevens, editor, *The Unified Modeling Language (UML 2003)*, volume 2863 of *LNCS*, pages 360–372. Springer, 2003.

[Jür04a]  J. Jürjens. *Secure Systems Development with UML*. Springer, 2004.

[Jür04b]  J. Jürjens. Security analysis tool (webinterface and download), 2004.
http://www4.in.tum.de/csduml/interface.

[Jür05]   J. Jürjens. Sound methods and effective tools for model-based security engineering with UML. In *27th International Conference on Software Engineering
(ICSE 2005)*. IEEE Computer Society, 2005.

[LB04]    J.-S. Lee and D.-H. Bae. An aspect-oriented framework for developing
component-based software with the collaboration-based architectural style.
*Information & Software Technology*, 46(2):81–97, 2004.

[MSRM04] A. Marcus, A. Sergeyev, V. Rajlich, and J.I. Maletic. An information
retrieval approach to concept location in source code. In *WCRE*, pages 214–
223. IEEE Computer Society, 2004.

[SFWW03] J. Schumann, B. Fischer, M.W. Whalen, and J. Whittle. Certification
support for automatically generated programs. In *HICSS*, page 337, 2003.

[SS01]    G. Sutcliffe and C. Suttner. The TPTP problem library for automated theorem proving, 2001. Available at http://www.tptp.org.

[SW00]    G. Stenz and A. Wolf. E-SETHEO: An automated[3] theorem prover. In
R. Dyckhoff, editor, *TABLEAUX 2000*, volume 1847 of *LNCS*, pages 436–
440. Springer, 2000.

# Performance Analysis of UML Models Using Aspect-Oriented Modeling Techniques

Hui Shen and Dorina C. Petriu

Carleton University, Department of Systems and Computer Engineering
Ottawa, ON Canada, K1S 5B6
{hshen,petriu}@sce.carleton.ca

**Abstract.** Aspect-Oriented Modeling (AOM) techniques allow software designers to isolate and address separately solutions for crosscutting concerns (such as security, reliability, new functional features, etc.) This paper proposes an approach for analyzing the performance effects of a given aspect on the overall system performance, after the composition of the aspect model with the primary model of a system. Performance analysis of UML models is enabled by the "UML Performance Profile for Schedulability, Performance and Time" (SPT) standardized by OMG, which defines a set of quantitative performance annotations to be added to a UML model. The first step of the proposed approach is to add performance annotations to both the primary model and to the aspect model(s). An aspect model is generic at first, and therefore its performance annotations must be parameterized. A generic model will be converted into a context-specific aspect model with concrete values assigned to its performance annotations. The latter is composed with the primary model, generating a complete annotated UML model. By using existing techniques, the complete model is transformed automatically into a Layered Queueing Network (LQN) performance model, which can be analyzed with existing solvers. The proposed approach is illustrated with a case study system, whose primary model is enhanced with some security features by using AOM. The LQN model of the primary system was validated against measurements in previous work. The performance effects of the security aspect under consideration are analyzed in two design alternatives by using the LQN model of the composed system.

## 1. Introduction

Aspect-Oriented Modeling (AOM) techniques allow software designers to conceptualize, describe and communicate separately solutions for crosscutting concerns (such as security, reliability, new functional features, etc.) An aspect-oriented architecture model produced by AOM consists of a base architecture model called the *primary model*, which reflects core design decisions, and a set of *aspect models*, each reflecting a concern that crosscuts the primary model [3]. In order to build the complete solution for a system, different aspect models will be composed with the primary system model. Current AOM research is addressing the following problems: using aspects to describe crosscutting concern solutions [3, 13]; describing aspect models at different levels of abstractions (e.g., generic and mechanism specific) [5]; composition of as-

L. Briand and C. Williams (Eds.): MoDELS 2005, LNCS 3713, pp. 156–170, 2005.
© Springer-Verlag Berlin Heidelberg 2005

pect and primary models [3, 17, 2]; automation of the AOM approach [8]; analysis of composed models to identify and resolve conflicts and undesirable properties that may arise as a result of the composition [5, 3].

According to [7], there are two broad categories of concerns: a *concrete concern* can be directly realized by some model elements that specifically address it (e.g., security), whereas a *qualitative concern* is based on intrinsic qualities of a system (e.g., performance). This paper proposes an approach for analyzing the system-level performance effects of a concrete concern realized as an aspect model, after its composition with the primary model. In other words, it becomes possible to analyze the combined effects of any concrete concern with a specific qualitative concern (i.e., performance). In order to avoid confusion, the term "aspect model" will be used in the rest of the paper for the concrete concern only.

Over the years, many modeling formalisms, methods and tools have been developed for performance analysis. The challenge is not to reinvent new analysis methods for UML models, but to bridge the gap between UML-based software development tools and different existing performance analysis tools.

Software Performance Engineering (SPE) is a methodology introduced in [16] that promotes the integration of performance analysis into the software development process from the early stages and continuing throughout the whole software life cycle. The "UML Performance Profile for Schedulability, Performance and Time" (SPT) standardized by OMG enables the application of the SPE methodology to systems developed with UML [14]. The SPT Profile defines a set of quantitative performance annotations (such as resource demands made by different software execution steps and visit ratios) to be added to a given UML model. An annotated UML model can be transformed into a performance model and analyzed with known analysis techniques and tools. Since the introduction of SPE, there has been a significant effort to integrate performance analysis into the software development process by using different performance modeling paradigms: queueing networks, Petri nets, stochastic process algebras, simulation, etc. [1]. The performance modeling formalism used in this paper is the Layered Queueing Model (LQN) [18]. The transformation from UML to LQN used in this paper was developed in previous research for systems designed without AOM [10, 6, 9, 12, 19].

The paper is organized as follows: section 2 presents the overview of the proposed approach; section 3 describes how performance annotations are added to aspect and primary models and how are handled during the composition, which is approached as a graph rewriting problem; and section 4 analyzes the performance effects of a concrete aspect under consideration and discusses different design alternatives. The case study used throughout the paper is an existing application, named the Document Exchange Server (DES) that was implemented and measured in previous work [12]. DES is enhanced in this paper with some security features by using AOM. The approach for defining generic and context-specific aspect models and for combining the aspect with the primary model is inspired from the work of France et al. [3, 5]. The original contribution of this paper is two-fold: a) adding performance analysis to UML models developed with AOM, and b) approaching the composition of the behavioural representation from the aspect and primary models as a graph rewriting problem applied to activity diagrams with composite activities.

## 2.  Overview of the Proposed Approach

The long-term goal of the research presented in this paper is to provide tool support to software developers who are using AOM techniques for assessing the performance effects of different aspect realizations early in the development cycle. This paper is just the first step on the road toward such a goal. Fig. 1 illustrates the high-level view of the proposed approach.

A primary model and one or more generic aspect models with performance annotations, produced with an UML tool, are exported to XMI. The first phase is to instantiate the generic aspect model, producing a context-specific one as in [3, 5], by following a set of binding rules provided by the designer. The binding rules are augmented with instructions on how to transform the parametric annotations of the generic aspect model into concrete ones. The next step is to compose the context-specific aspect model(s) with the primary model, according to a set of composition directives. The result is a composed annotated UML, which can be transformed automatically into a performance model (LQN in this case) by using the transformation techniques from [19]. The LQN model is analyzed with an existing solver for different workloads and conditions, and the analysis results are used to draw conclusions about different design alternatives. The process will be eventually completed with a feedback path, shown with dotted arrows, whereby the performance results are inserted into predefined annotation placeholders in the XMI file of the composed model, which will be imported back in the UML tool for display. The composed model can be also imported directly into the UML tool for display without performance results.

The focus of this paper is on the instantiation and composition steps, and especially on the treatment of performance annotations. The paper also illustrates the application of the proposed approach to enhance an existing application, the Document Exchange Server, with some security features (namely authorization). The LQN model of the primary system was previously validated against measurements in [12]. The performance effects of the aspect under consideration are analyzed in the paper by solving the LQN model of the composed system for two design alternatives.

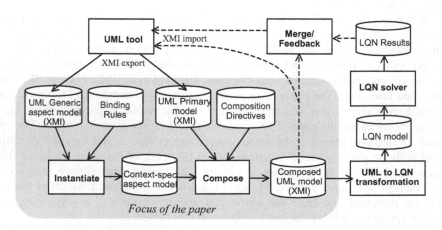

**Fig. 1.** Approach for performance analysis of UML models using AOM

## 3.  Aspect Oriented Models with Performance Annotations

The SPT Profile [14] contains the Performance Subprofile that identifies the main basic abstractions used in performance analysis. Scenarios define response paths through the system, and can have QoS requirements such as response times or throughput. Each scenario is executed by a workload, which can be closed or open, and has the usual characteristics (number of clients or arrival rate, etc.) Scenarios are composed of scenario steps that can be joined in sequence, loops, branches, fork/joins, etc. A step may be an elementary operation at the lowest level of granularity, or may be a complex sub-scenario. Each step has a mean number of repetitions, a host execution demand, other demand to resources and its own QoS characteristics. Resources are another basic abstraction, and can be active or passive, each with their own attributes. A more detailed description of the way to apply the Performance Subprofile is given in [11]. Please note that SPT was standardized for UML 1.4; until SPT will be upgraded for UML 2, we apply its stereotypes to UML 2.

### 3.1.  Primary Model

The primary UML model contains different views necessary for performance evaluation [10]:
– High-level software architecture represented by one or more class or components diagrams showing the concurrent (distributed) component instances (Fig. 2).

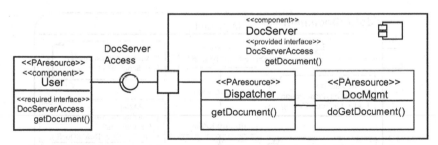

**Fig. 2.** DES primary model: component diagram with performance annotations

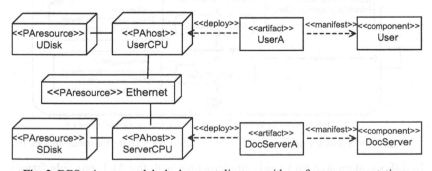

**Fig. 3.** DES primary model: deployment diagram with performance annotations

- Deployment of high-level software components to hardware devices (Fig. 3).
- One or more key performance scenarios annotated with performance information according to the SPT Profile [14], modeled by interaction or activity diagrams [11]. In the paper we consider the scenario modeled by the activity diagrams in Fig. 4.

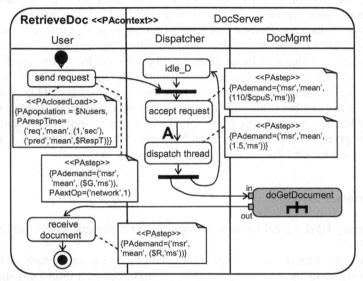

(a) DES primary model: high level activity diagram for RetrieveDoc scenario

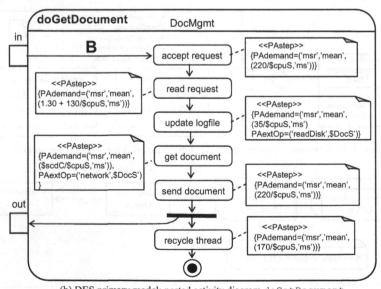

(b) DES primary model: nested activity diagram doGetDocument

**Fig. 4.** DES primary model: scenario RetrieveDoc with performance annotations

The DES system was previously implemented with the ACE reusable frameworks [15], and its LQN model was validated against measurements [12]. DES consists of a document exchange server and multiple clients. There are two types of users: regular users and system administrator. A regular user can get the document directory from the server, upload new documents and retrieve documents stored at the server. In this case study, we will focus on the scenario for retrieving a document, `RetrieveDoc`, as the key scenario for performance analysis. The UML model shown here does not represent the complete design of the DES system, just the elements necessary for performance analysis. The performance annotations are shown in notes in Figures 2 to 4 to make them visible. Due to space limitations, we give here just a brief overview of the most important stereotypes and attributes.

The high-level architecture contains two components, `User` and `DocServer` communicating through the interface `DocServerAccess`, which contains the operation `getDocument()`. The server component is multithreaded, containing a `Dispatcher` thread that accepts the requests and dispatches them to a number of worker threads named `DocMgmt`, organized in a thread pool. In Fig. 2, the stereotype `<<PAresource>>` is used to indicate those software units that are running under their own thread of control (in this case, the user component and each server thread). DES is deployed on a distributed system connected through a local area network, as shown in Fig. 3. The shared documents are stored on the server's local disk. A processor is modeled by the stereotype `<<PAhost>>`, which has attributes that define its scheduling policy, processing rate, context switching time and performance measures such as utilization and throughput. Other non-processing hardware devices that introduce contention in the software may be modeled as `<<PAresource>>`.

The activity diagram for the `RetrieveDoc` scenario (Fig. 4) shows that the `Dispatcher` loops infinitely, going back to accepting a new request once the previous one was dispatched. The detailed processing of the operation `doGetDocument()` performed by a `DocMgmt` thread is encapsulated in the composite activity given in Fig.4.b, which has an input pin `in` and an output pin `out`. The call of this operation is shown in gray in the main activity diagram from Fig.4.a. The labels A and B are used to mark possible insertion points for the aspect behaviour during model composition, as discussed later in section 3.4.

The main activity diagram is stereotyped as an SPT analysis context `<<PAcontext>>`, and each activity as a scenario step `<<PAstep>>`. The first step carries the workload stereotype `<<PAclosedLoad>>` with a given number of users $Nusers, and the scenario overall performance measures, which can be required ('req'), measured ('msr'), estimated ('assm') or predicted ('pred'). (Note that in SPT variable names begin with '$'.) For example, the scenario from Fig. 4 has a required mean response time of 1 second for the specified number of users $Nusers, and the response time predicted by the LQN model will be stored in the variable $RespT, as indicated in the following tagged value:

PArespTime=(('req',mean,(1, 'sec')),('pred',mean,$RespT))

A PAdemand tagged value indicates the execution time on the host processor for the respective step. For instance, the activity `accept request` from Fig. 4.b has:

PAdemand=('msr','mean,(220/$cpuS, 'ms'))

which indicates that the mean measured value of the CPU demand is given by the expression (220/$cpuS) in milliseconds, where the variable $cpuS is the frequency of the host processor in MHz. The variables used in performance annotations capture application or platform-specific performance values. The following variables used in the example are dependent on the disk I/O mechanism and the document size:

$gcdC = CPU demand for getting a document from the disk

$scdC = CPU demand for sending a document to the network

The following variables are application dependent:

$RP = the size of a request message in data packets

$DocP = document size in data packets (given by the ratio between the document size and network packet size rounded up to the closest integer).

## 3.2. Generic Aspect Model

AOM is applied in this paper to extend the original DES system with a security related crosscutting concern, whereby only authorized clients are allowed to get documents from the DES server. The approach for expressing the solution to this concern as an aspect was inspired from [3], where a *generic aspect model* that describes the general structure and behaviour of a generic authorization solution is defined with UML 2 templates. More precisely, in [3] the generic aspect structure is modeled with classifier templates (classes or structured classes) and the behaviour with interaction templates. The generic aspect model is instantiated to get a *context-specific aspect model* by binding the template parameters to application-specific values.

Our approach is similar to [3], except that the software architecture is modeled with component templates (with offered and required interfaces), and the behaviour with activity templates, as shown in Fig.5. We are making use of the UML 2 feature that all subclasses of Classifier - such as Class, Collaboration, Component, Interface - and all subclasses of Behavior - such as Activity, Interaction - are templateable. Components and/or structured classes allow for a clear separation between their external use and their internal structure/behaviour, and are more suitable than the traditional class diagrams for representing the kind of systems for which performance analysis is important (usually distributed and/or concurrent systems). We chose activity diagrams rather than interaction diagrams because of their ability to describe both inter- and intra-object behaviour as flows of actions, and to express concurrency more naturally, like in Petri nets. We propose to approach the behaviour composition as a graph rewriting problem applied to activity diagrams, as described in section 3.4.

Fig. 5.a shows that there are three kinds of components in the generic aspect model: |Client, |Server and |AuthorizationRep. (Note that we use the same notation for template parameters as in [3], i.e., a parameter name begins with a '|'). The |Server component provides the interface |ServerAccess containing the operation template |operation, and requires the interface |Authorization-Access containing the operation template |checkAuth. The aspect model does not know anything about the internal structure of |Server, nor any details about the actual functionality of |operation, which are given in the primary model.

The generic aspect model shows that, when a request for |operation arrives from |Client to |Server, the latter must check with the component |AuthorizationRep whether the client is authorized to perform the |operation. More exactly, |Server invokes |checkAuth, waits for the reply, and then verifies the result. If this indicates a not authorized access, then |Server

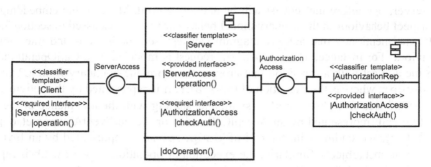

(a) Generic Authorization aspect model: component diagram

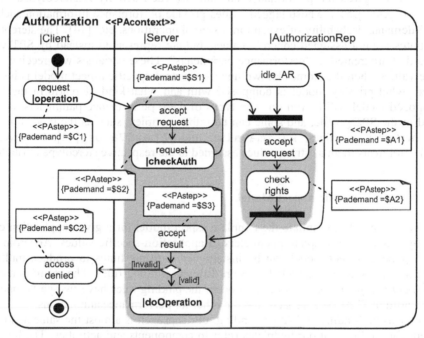

(b) Generic Authorization aspect model: activity diagram

**Fig. 5.** Generic aspect model with parametric performance annotations

will reply to |Client that the access is denied; otherwise, it delegates the actual execution of the required functionality to |doOperation (which will be detailed only in the primary model). The signatures and parameters of the operation templates are similar to those from [3] and are not described here due to space limitations.

It is worthwhile to mention here that the behaviour model from Fig. 5.b contains two kinds of activities: some represent the new functionality associated with the aspect (such as checking the access rights and letting the client know when the access is denied) and others represent "embedding" activities, which show where to insert the new behaviour relative to the primary model behaviour. In our example, the new authorization functionality must take place every time when the client sends a request to the server, but before the request will be actually served. More on the embedding of the aspect behaviour in the primary model behaviour will be discussed in section 3.4.

It was mentioned that activity diagram can represent both intra- and inter-object behaviour. For instance, an |operation request is modeled by a CallOperationAction metaobject with a transition that crosses the swimlane boundary from |Client to |Server, whereas the execution of |operation is represented by the activities in the shaded area from |Server's swimlane, starting with the acceptance of the respective call (represented by an AcceptCallAction or AcceptEventAction metaobject in UML 2), and ending with the call of |doOperation (represented by an InvocationAction metaobject). Similarly, the execution of operation |checkAuth is represented by the shaded area from the swimlane of |AuthorizationRep.

In what regards the performance annotations, each activity is stereotyped as an SPT <<PAstep>>, whose tagged values provide performance information such as CPU demand, probability of execution, external operations, etc. [14]. The stereotype attributes are not assigned concrete values, but are represented instead by SPT variables that are treated as "performance parameters". These variables will receive concrete values when it becomes known how the context-specific aspect model is instantiated, what primary model is composed with and what kind of platform the final composed model will be run on. The types of these performance parameters are defined in the SPT profile, and some can be rather complex, such as the types for time and performance values, PAtimeValue and PAperfValue [14]. However, a UML tool treats them as string values assigned to the respective stereotype attributes.

### 3.3. Context-Specific Aspect Model

The next step is to instantiate the template aspect model for a given application context by binding the template parameters to application-specific values. According to [5], a generic aspect model can be instantiated multiple times to produce multiple context-specific aspect models based on different binding rules. The result is a *context-specific aspect model*. In our approach, the binding rules have two parts: one for the "traditional" AOM approach, and the other for performance annotations.

In terms of "traditional" AOM binding, our approach is almost the same as in [3], except for the fact that our templates refer to components and activities. The binding rules for operation signatures, similar to [3], and are not shown here due to space limitations. The bindings for structural elements used in our case study, listed here as *(formal parameter, actual parameter)* pairs, would be normally given in a UML diagram:

- Component bindings: (|Client, User); (|Server, DocServer); (|AuthorizationRep, **DocAuthorizationRep**)
- Interface bindings: (|ServerAccess, DocServerAccess); (|AuthorizationAccess, **DocAuthorizationAccess**);
- Operation bindings: (|operation, getDocument); (|doOperation, doGetDocument); (|checkAuth, **checkDocAuth**).

In the structural view, some of the component (operation) templates are bound to actual counterparts that exist in the application context, while others are bound to new components/interfaces/operations (shown in boldface in the above list). For instance,

`DocAuthorizationRep,` along to its interfaces and operations, is a new component that does not have a counterpart in the primary model of the application.

There is another issue concerning the model structure that has to be resolved during the creation of the context-specific model: the allocation of the software components to hardware resources. This is important for performance analysis. The rule is as follows: if a component template is bound to an existing component, then the host processor is already known from the primary model. However, for new components, the designer has to specify the deployment explicitly (either on existing nodes or on new ones).

The instantiation of the template activity diagram has two parts: one is concerned with binding activity templates from the generic to the application-specific context, and the other with assigning concrete values to the "performance parameters" identified in the previous section as part of the performance annotations. The binding of activity templates will be done according to the binding of the corresponding operation templates from the structural view. For instance, the activity template that requests |`operation` will be bound to an activity that requests `getDocument`, and so on. The activity diagram of the context-specific model is represented in Fig. 6.a.

The issue of binding "performance parameters" cannot be solved through the UML 2 template mechanism, because it requires the "binding" of new values to stereotype attributes. For instance, the variable `$A1` from Fig. 5.b, which represents the tagged value `PAdemand` of the step `accept_request`, should be assigned the value

$$(\text{'assm','mean', (220/\$cpuS, 'ms'))}$$

of type `PAperfValue`defined in SPT. We propose to use an auxiliary XML file for "performance bindings" which gives all the values to be assigned to the performance parameters representing stereotype attributes in the generic aspect model.

Choosing the values to be assigned to the performance parameters of the context-specific aspect model is not a simple problem; some difficulties are related to performance evaluation issues rather than to UML modeling. In general, it is difficult to estimate quantitative resource demands for each activity in the design phase, when an implementation does not exist and measurements cannot be performed yet. Several approaches are used by the performance analysts to come up with reasonable estimates in the early design stages: expert experience with previous versions or with similar software, understanding of the algorithm complexity, measurements of reused software, measurements of existing libraries, or using time budgets. As the project advances, early estimate can be replaced with measured values for the most critical parts. However, this is not to say that performance analysis should be deferred until late in the lifecycle, when the system is implemented and can be measured, because by then it may be too late to correct costly performance mistakes frozen in the code (see [16] for more details on software performance engineering).

## 3.4. Model Composition

The role of model composition is to integrate a context-specific aspect model with the primary model in all three relevant views: architecture, deployment and behaviour.

Composing the software architecture is not as difficult as composing the behaviour. The context-specific aspect model contains either components that exist in the primary model or new ones, with well-defined interfaces. The composed model will contain the union of all the components from the two models. It is however possible that a component in the aspect model does not contain the level of details from the primary model (for example, `DocServer` is multithreaded in the primary model only). A recursive approach, similar to that at the system level, will be applied to compose the internal structure of each component in turn. The composition at the deployment level, which is also a structural view, can be tackled in a similar way, adding new nodes to he ones that exist already in the primary model.

The composition of the behaviour view is more challenging. Conceptually, we propose to approach the composition of activity diagrams as a graph-rewriting problem, where a subgraph $X$ found inside of a larger host graph $H$ is isolated and replaced by another subgraph $Y$. Subgraph $X$ is described by the left-hand-side and $Y$ by the right-hand side of a rewriting rule, which also specifies how to embed (i.e., connect) $Y$ within the host graph $H$. In our case, the host graph is the activity diagram of the primary model, $Y$ is the subset of activities from the context-specific model that bring new functionality to the whole, and $X$ is an element of the host $H$ that pinpoints the insertion place. The proposed approach is illustrated in Fig. 6.

Fig. 6.a shows the activity diagram for the behaviour of the context-specific model, which contains two kinds of activities, as already mentioned in section 3.2: a) new functionality introduced by the aspect (the shaded area in Fig. 6.a), and b) "embedding" activities repeated from the primary model that indicate where to insert the new functionality (the non-shaded area). We propose to isolate the activities from the shaded area and to encapsulate them in a UML 2 *complete structured activity* with input and output pins, which corresponds to the connecting points between the new functionality from the shaded area with the embedding activities from the non-shaded area, as shown in Fig. 6.b. In this case, there is only one input and one output pin, but in general more than one input/output pins may be necessary. The designer has the responsibility to indicate which sub-area of the aspect model contains new functionality and should be converted into a complete structured activity, to play the role of $Y$ in the rewriting rule.

The role of $X$ is played by an element from the activity diagram of the primary model that indicates the insertion place. In our case study, we have considered two design alternatives: i) insert the authorization checking functionality in the `Dispatcher` thread in Fig.4.a, point A, and ii) insert it in the `DocMgmt` thread in Fig. 4.b, point B. As shown in the next section, the choice of the insertion point will have a strong impact on the overall performance without changing in any way the aspect model or its performance annotations.

The outcome of the composition for Design A is illustrated by the component diagram in Fig. 7.a and the activity diagram in Fig. 7.b. The composed deployment diagram is not given, as it is very similar to the deployment of the primary model from Fig. 3.

## 4. Performance Analysis

This section presents the performance analysis experiments conducted with the LQN models obtained from: a) the primary model, b) the composed model for design A, and c) the composed model for design B. The LQN models were obtained with the

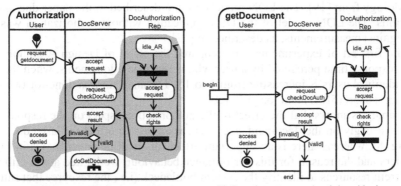

(a) Context-specific aspect model behaviour    (b) Complete structured activity with pins

**Fig. 6.** Generating a complete structured activity with pins that contains the aspect model sub-behaviour to be inserted into the primary model behaviour

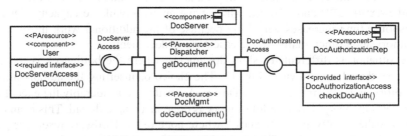

(a) Composed DES model: component diagram

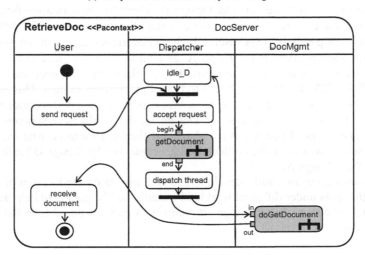

(b) Composed DES model: high-level activity diagram

**Fig. 7.** Composed DES model

methodology from [19]. The LQN models are not described in the paper due to space limitations. The LQN model of the DES application without authorization was validated against measurements, as described in [12].

In the first set of experiments, we compared the effect of Design A authorization on the response time perceived by a user who is retrieving documents, when the number of identical users is increasing from 1 to 15. The analysis was done for two document sizes: short (5K B) and long (50 KB).

The analysis shows that the effect of the authorization aspect on the response time depends strongly on the document size: there is almost no effect for large documents (see Fig. 8), whereas there is an important effect for small documents (see in Fig. 9). To understand the reason for this performance behaviour, we looked at the utilization of different resources to identify the system bottleneck (i.e., the resource that saturates first, has the longest waiting queue and limits the system throughput). For large documents, the bottleneck device is the Local Area Network, which is utilized close to 100% for 15 users, as shown in Fig. 10. Other resources, such as `ServerCPU` and `SDisk` are utilized much less than the network (only about 55% for 15 users). However, the new authorization functionality adds no extra load on the network, but uses instead `ServerCPU` and `SDisk`, which have enough available capacity. Therefore the response time increases very little because of the additional work introduced by the authorization functionality in the case of long documents.

The situation is different for short documents, where the bottleneck is the `Dispatcher` thread, as shown in Fig. 11. The choice of inserting the authorization responsibility in the `Dispatcher` in Design A serializes considerably the execution of the requests in the system, as a lot of work is done in a single thread. This is an example of so called "software bottleneck", where none of the hardware resources gets to be fully utilized due to the low concurrency levels in the software. In order to solve the software bottleneck, we consider Design B, where the authorization functionality is inserted in each of the `DocMgmt` threads (i.e., the authorization for different request is done in parallel). This insures higher concurrency levels in the system and gives better response time than Design A, as long as `DocAuthorizationRep` is also able to process requests concurrently. Fig. 12 shows that for small messages, the response time of Design B is very close to that of the primary system. This is an illustration of the fact that a small design difference may have a big performance impact.

Fig. 13 shows that in the case of Design B, the hardware resources (such as ServerCPU) are indeed utilized at a higher level than in Design A, whereas the Dispatcher thread is no longer the bottleneck. This explains why Design B has better performance than Design A.

Performance analysis allows developers to gain insight on the location of performance trouble spots under different workload conditions. The goal is to help developers to evaluate and choose better design alternatives as early as possible in the development process.

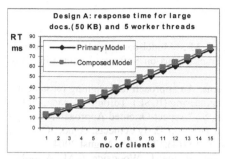

**Fig. 8.** Design A: Response time for the retrieval of large documents

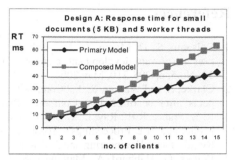

**Fig. 9.** Design A: Response time for the retrieval of small documents

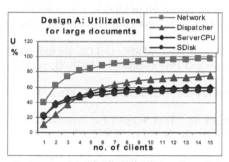

**Fig.10.** Design A: Utilization of resources for the retrieval of large documents

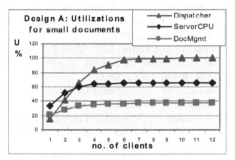

**Fig.11.** Design A: Utilization of resources for the retrieval of small documents

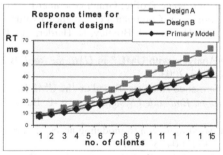

**Fig.12.** Response times for different designs alternatives

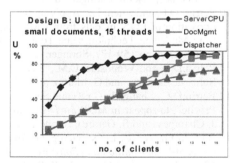

**Fig.13.** Design B: Utilization of resources for the retrieval of small documents

## 5. Conclusions

This paper proposes an approach for combining Aspect Oriented Modeling techniques with performance analysis of UML models. The long-term goal of the research is to provide tool support to software developers who are using AOM techniques for assessing the performance effects of different aspect realizations early in the development cycle. There is ongoing work to develop fully the proposed approach and to build a tool prototype.

# References

1. Balsamo, S., Di Marco, A., Inverardi, P., Simeoni, M., "Model-based performance prediction in software development: a survey" IEEE Transactions on Software Engineering, Vol 30, No.5, pp.295-310, May 2004.
2. Clarke, S. and Walker, R. J., "Composition patterns: An approach to designing reusable aspects", In Proc. of 23rd Int. Conf. on Software Engineering (ICSE), Toronto, Canada, 2001.
3. R. B. France, R.B., Ray, I. ,.Georg, G. and Ghosh, S., "Aspect-Oriented Approach to Design Modeling," IEE Proceedings - Software, Special Issue on Early Aspects: Aspect-Oriented Requirements Engineering and Architecture Design, 151(4):173--185, August 2004.
4. Franks, G., Hubbard, A., Majumdar, S., Petriu, D.C., Rolia, J., Woodside, C.M., A toolset for Performance Engineering and Software Design of Client-Server Systems, Performance Evaluation, Vol. 24, Nb. 1-2 (1995) 117-135.
5. Georg, G., France, R. and Ray, I. "An Aspect-Based Approach to Modeling Security Concerns".In Proceedings of the Workshop on Critical Systems Development with UML, Dresden, Germany, 2002.
6. Gu, G., and Petriu, D.C. "XSLT Transformation from UML Models to LQN Performance Models", Proc. of 3rd Int. Workshop on Software and Performance WOSP'2002, pp.227-234, Rome, Italy, 2002.
7. Kande, M., "A Concern-Oriented Approach to Software Architecture", PhD thesis, EPFL, Lausanne, Switzerland, 2003.
8. Mekerke, F., Georg, G., France, R., and Alexander, R. "Tool Support for Aspect-Oriented Design", In Advances in Object-Oriented Information Systems: OOIS2002 Workshops. Springer-Verlag, 2002.
9. Petriu, D.B. and Woodside, C.M., "A Metamodel for Generating Performance Models from UML Designs," in In Proc. «UML» 2004 - Modelling Languages and Applications, 7th Int. Conference, Lisbon, Portugal, vol. LNCS 3273, Springer 2004, pp. 41-53.
10. Petriu, D.C. and Shen, H. "Applying the UML Performance Profile: Graph Grammar based derivation of LQN models from UML specifications", in Computer Performance Evaluation: Modelling Techniques and Tools, (T. Fields, P. Harrison, J. Bradley, U. Harder, Eds.) LNCS 2324, pp.159-177, Springer, 2002.
11. Petriu,D.C. and Woodside, C.M., "Performance Analysis with UML," in *UML for Real*, B. Selic, L. Lavagno, and G. Martin, pp. 221-240 Kluwer, 2003.
12. Petriu,D.C., Zhang, J., Gu, G and Shen, H., "Performance Analysis Based on the UML SPT Profile", to appear in *MDD for Distributed Real-time Embedded Systems* (Eds. J.-P. Babau, J. Champeau and S. Gérard), Hermes, Paris, 2005.
13. Ray, I., France, R., Li, N., Georg, G. An aspect-based approach to modeling access control concerns", *Information and Software Technology*, 46 (2004) 575–587.
14. Object Management Group, *UML Profile for Schedulability, Performance, and Time Specification*, OMG Adopted Specification ptc/02-03-02, July 1, 2002.
15. Schmidt, D.C., Huston, *S. D., C++ Network Programming Vol 2: Systematic Reuse with ACE and Frameworks*, Addison-Wesley, 2002.
16. Smith, C.U., *Performance Engineering of Software Systems*, Addison Wesley, 1990.
17. Straw, G., Georg, G., Song, E., Ghosh, S., France, R., Bieman, J.M., "Model Composition Directives", In Proc. «UML» 2004 - Modelling Languages and Applications, 7th Int. Conference, Lisbon, Portugal, LNCS 3273, pp 84-97, Springer 2004.
18. Woodside, C.M., Neilson, J.E., Petriu, D.C., Majumdar, S., "The Stochastic Rendezvous Network Model for Performance of Synchronous Client-Server-like Distributed Software", in *IEEE Transactions on Computers*, Vol.44, Nb.1, pp. 20-34, 1995.
19. Woodside, C.M, Petriu, D.C., Petriu, D.B., Shen, H, Israr, T., and Merseguer, J. " Performance by Unified Model Analysis (PUMA)", In Proc. 5th Int. Workshop on Software and Performance WOSP'2005, Palma, Spain, July 2005.

# Domain Models Are Aspect Free

Friedrich Steimann

Fachbereich Informatik, Lehrgebiet Programmiersysteme
Fernuniversität in Hagen
Universitätsstraße 1, D-58097 Hagen
steimann@acm.org

**Abstract.** Proponents of aspect orientation have successfully seeded the impression that aspects — like objects — are so fundamental a notion that they should pervade all phases and artefacts of the software development process. Aspect orientation has therefore proliferated from programming to design to analysis to requirements, sparing neither software processes nor their favourite languages. Since modelling plays an important role in software engineering, much effort is currently being invested in making modelling languages aspect ready. However, based on an observed lack of examples for domain level (or functional) aspects this paper argues the case against the omnipresence of aspects, particularly the existence of aspects in domain models, and offers some informal arguments as well as a semiformal proof in favour of the claims made.

## 1 Introduction

Since the term AOP came public at ECOOP in 1997 [1], workshops and conferences on aspect-related matters have literally mushroomed. Today we witness attempts to rewrite large parts – if not all of software engineering to become aspect oriented: aspect-oriented design, aspect-oriented modelling, aspect-oriented requirements engineering, and so forth. One may ask oneself whether this enthusiasm is a sign of something revolutionary having been discovered, or just a symptom of the general pressure felt by the OO community to come up with something suitable to fill the hole called "post OO". Does aspect orientation really have the substance necessary to found a new software development paradigm, or is it just another term to feed the old buzzword-permutation based research proposal and PhD thesis generator?

That aspects can revolutionize software engineering analogous to the way objects did would require that aspects are an equally general notion, one that applies to the domains hosting computing problems as well as to the technology used to solve them. At first glance, this would seem case: when looking at a problem, we usually find that it has many aspects, that indeed every aspect comes with its own set of problems. We can even say that the objects of a domain themselves have different aspects, so that

---

[1] Popular precursors of (and contributors to) the AOP paradigm were Composition Filters [1], DEMETER [15], and Subject-Oriented Programming [12].

L. Briand and C. Williams (Eds.): MoDELS 2005, LNCS 3713, pp. 171-185, 2005.
© Springer-Verlag Berlin Heidelberg 2005

viewing aspects as a primitive concept of object-oriented software development would only seem natural.

Yet an aspect is immanently something observed of an object (or a problem), it is not itself one (or part of one). This is also reflected in natural language, where we usually speak of the aspects *of* something, not of the aspects *in* something. In fact, it seems that aspects reside one level above what is being looked at or, in other words, that aspects are a meta-level construct. Although aspects are not alone in this regard, I will argue below that this – together with a few other peculiarities – explains why we cannot expect to find aspects (at least not in the aspect-oriented sense) *in* any but a single, rather special problem domain.

The remainder of this paper is organized as follows. First I will identify different uses of the term aspect as relevant in the context of modelling. As I will argue, these uses are either better covered by other concepts or lie outside the subject of a domain model, i.e., do not refer directly to the modelled domain. Based on these findings I will attempt a theoretical argumentation explaining why aspects (in the aspect-oriented sense) are necessarily second-order constructs and hence extrinsic to the problem domain and its models, which focus on the nature (the intrinsic properties) of the things being looked at. A discussion of my claim with some of the relevant literature concludes my position.

## 2    Different Uses of the Term *Aspect* in Modelling

While technically the concept of an aspect is unambiguously defined by the aspect-oriented (modelling) language being used, conceptually it is not: people have different conceptions of what an aspect is and, consequently, of how and where it can be identified in a given subject matter. This is only natural since aspect is a general term in broad use not only in software engineering, but also in everyday conversation; like the term object before, it is readily adopted by everyone, but acceptance and popularity come at the price of precision.

What follows is a brief discussion of the different uses of the term *aspect* as found in software modelling. The discussion may be incomplete, yet I believe it covers the most important points being taken in the literature, and suffices to show that these kinds of aspects are either not needed for domain modelling, or lie outside its scope.

### 2.1   Aspects as Roles

Long before the term aspect-oriented programming was coined, it was discovered that objects can have different *facets*, *views*, *perspectives*, *roles*, or *aspects* [24]. The classic example of a class whose instances have many roles[2] is *Person*: *Employee*, *Employer*, *Customer*, *Student*, and so forth are all roles that can be played by a person. Many different ways to deal with roles have been proposed; most frequent are approaches that treat roles as subtypes, as supertypes, as a combination of both, or as ad-

---

[2] In order not to confuse aspects and roles (which basically mean the same thing in this subsection, but do not in the remainder of this paper), I use the term *role* here.

junct instances [24]. All share the same least intent: to let objects of *same type* have *different properties* in different contexts at different times.

There is however another important characteristic of the role concept: objects of *different types* having *same properties*. For instance, many things in a modelled domain may be billable (play the role of a *Billable*), but these things need not be naturally related. On the programming side, we have roles such as *Serializable, Comparable, Printable*, etc., which are implemented by the most different classes. Technically, these are all *role types* allowing assignment compatible objects of otherwise unrelated types to play the associated roles in the context of serialization, comparison, and printing, respectively. Conceptually, there is no difference between a document's being printable and a person's being employable; both require that the objects have certain properties that enable their functioning in the context defining the role. These properties are comprised in a corresponding role type.

Role types complement the natural partitioning of a problem domain (based on the natural types of objects, i.e., their classes) by one that is based on relationships and the contexts they produce. Given that roles partition a domain, one might argue that they crosscut it in the sense that they let several otherwise unrelated classes share same properties. However, although these properties are same, they are usually *realized differently*, reflecting the different nature of the objects possessing them – the roles are in fact polymorphic, meaning that they have different implementations. Factoring out different implementations to a single place as suggested by an aspect-oriented approach would seem inapt, since it would contradict basic object-oriented principles.[3] Instead, interfaces (specifying protocol, but lacking implementation) and multiple (interface) inheritance readily lend themselves to representing roles and role playing, respectively, with mixins stepping in to allow for the inheritance of code wherever deemed appropriate [25, 26].

In object-oriented software modelling, roles are tied to collaborations: they specify what it takes for a single object to contribute to fulfilling some joint system functionality [2, 17, 25]. Collaborations are based on interactions of objects; specification of such an interaction is typically not tied to a single role, but is distributed over all that contribute. Aspects on the other hand are typically defined independently of one another; in fact, the obliviousness property of aspect orientation [8] suggests that aspects have no mutual knowledge of each other.[4] It follows immediately that modelling the roles of a system as aspects works only in cases where roles are isolated and monomorphic.[5]

---

[3] In fact, it would effect to replacing the polymorphism of a role with a conditional (reversing the *Replace Conditional with Polymorphism* refactoring [9]): code treating objects of different types differently would not be attached to the types, but located in a single place, a conditional (typically a switch statement) branching on the type of an object. Although aspects could be made polymorphic [4], doing so does not better the situation, since the definition of role-playing objects would remain scattered.

[4] Note that aspects can apply to aspects, so that there may be some unilateral awareness. Also, aspects can model collaborations [2, 25], which includes the modelling of roles; the roles themselves however are no aspects.

[5] One might argue that there are roles whose implementation is the same throughout, so that they are naturally represented by aspects. For instance, "having an address" (role *Addressee*) is something that applies to the most different objects, but has the same implementation everywhere. However, this does not preclude *Addressee* from being modelled as a role, particu-

All this in not to say that aspect technology has nothing to contribute to role modelling. In fact, role-oriented modelling (in the spirit of OORAM [23]) requires some kind of weaving, since it is not sufficient that the objects (of the classes) playing the roles of a collaboration guarantee to conform to the interface specification (or contract) associated with each role: the way the state of the same object playing different roles at the same time is to be shared or kept separate must also be specified. Because roles of *different* collaborations are defined largely independently of each other, some kind of weaving has to be performed when merging the different roles into the implementation of one class. However, given that every class implements its roles differently (the general case), it is difficult to conceive how aspect weaving mechanisms could help without major modifications. Aspectual collaborations [15] address these problems in some detail, but use roles in the specification of aspects, without equating the two concepts (*cf.* related work in Section 5).

To summarize: a role is a named type specifying a cohesive set of properties whose specification is determined by the collaboration with other roles and whose implementation by different classes is typically polymorphic. An aspect on the other hand is neither a type, nor is it meaningful only in the context of another aspect, nor does is naturally introduce different implementations for different objects. Although conceptually a role of an object can be viewed as an aspect of it, this aspect is typically not one in the aspect-oriented sense.[6]

## 2.2 Aspects as Ordering Dimensions

Ever since Aristotle, taxonomical orderings have been regarded as useful for structuring complex domains. However, the problem with taxonomies is that they can be based on different criteria, which may be independent of each other. Different views (or aspects) on a domain may therefore lead to different orderings which, without one dominating the other, are difficult – if not impossible – to unify.

The introduction of polyhierachies (and multiple inheritance) combining several alternative classifications seems an immediate remedy. On closer inspection, however, they introduce more problems than they solve, since they tend to obscure the original orderings they are trying to combine – not without reason, major programming languages such as JAVA and SMALLTALK have abandoned the concept. The Unified Modeling Language UML [19] on the other hand has a special *discriminator* construct used to separate different dimensions ("partitionings") of a model's generalization/specialization hierarchies; however, as mere labelling this has no further-reaching effect on the structure of a model. In fact, keeping the dimensions separate and thus avoiding the dominance of one structure (the aspect-oriented way) seems to be the best bet for maintaining accessibility of the domain. However, this does not mean that domains come with aspects, as the following reasoning shows.

The archetypal domain having conflicting ordering principles is the taxonomy of species. Its traditional version is based on externally visible properties such as number

---

larly as this would allow its objects to participate in a *send* collaboration (with roles *Addresser* and *Addressee*), which the aspect does not. *Cf.* the discussion in Section 5.2 for more on this issue.

[6] A contrary, but not very convincing view is held in [11].

of legs, reproductive system, etc. Although the discovery of new species and even whole kingdoms requires reorganization from time to time, biologists have managed to keep the taxonomy in a strict tree form. Modern genetics however has made it possible to reconstruct the evolutionary development of the different species right from the first protists, thereby creating a taxonomy based on common ancestors rather than observables, which means that it cannot be forced into strict tree form. While both *evolution* and *similarity* can be viewed as different *aspects* structuring the same problem domain, we observe that neither of these aspects is itself an element of the domain. Aspects as ordering principles describe the order, not the domain; hence, they reside one level above what they order.[7]

## 2.3 Domain-Specific Aspects

It has been noted many times that literally all aspects discussed in the literature are technical in nature: authentication, caching, distribution, logging, persistence, synchronization, transaction management, etc. One may add that these are all rather universal aspects, an observation that naturally begs the question whether all aspects are general, or whether there is such a thing as a domain-specific aspect. A comparison with classes springs to mind: while we have general purpose, technical classes such as *String*, *Vector*, and *Exception* in a program, we usually also have domain-specific, non-technical classes such as *Account*, *Loan*, and *Currency*; in fact, the latter are the classes that are being modelled during the early phases of software development, since they represent the problem domain.

On closer inspection, it becomes clear that the standard aspects are aspects *of programming* rather than aspects of the domain the program is applied in: caching is a programming problem, as are logging, security, transaction management, etc.[8] In fact, we can observe that these aspects are aspects of the solution and its artefacts, not of the original problem. While this explains why the aspects are all technical (programming is a technical matter, and looking at it from different perspectives necessarily reveals its technical aspects), it also sheds a different light on the term *domain specificity*: an aspect is considered domain-specific if it occurs only in few, rather special programming problems. Note that the same domain specificity can be observed of classes: *Thread* for instance is specific to domains that exhibit concurrency, and it is technical (part of the solution, unlike for instance *PatientRecord*, which is a domain-specific, non-technical class).

---

[7] This argumentation also applies to other abstraction mechanisms such as classification and composition: an object can be classified according to its natural type (e.g., a `Person`, not a `Thing`) or to its technical type (e.g., an `Object`, not a `Class`); it can be a component of another object in the same problem domain, or of a deployment, etc. None of these ordering dimensions are themselves part of the ordered domain.

[8] Having said this, we note that sometimes a technical aspect has a namesake in the problem domain: in the perennial ATM example, for instance, transactions and logs are entities that occur in the problem domain. However, these entities are in the same league as customers, accounts, and terminals: they are neither crosscutting nor do they exhibit other aspect-oriented peculiarities, so that they would preferably be considered (and implemented) as ordinary types.

Seen this way, we can expect to find new aspects while we address new problems (e.g., aspects of compiler construction, aspects of middleware, aspects of webs services, etc.), but these aspects will be domain-specific only in the sense that they address a programming problem that is specific to the domain – they are not themselves part of the domain. In fact, we can expect that every framework comes with its own set of aspects, and aspects will keep being discovered as long as technological advances are being made. But all of these aspects will be specific to the technical solution (the "domain", if you will), not to the concrete problem it is applied to.

## 2.4 Aspects of Modelling

Now if the aspects we find when programming are *aspects of programming*, not of the programmed problem, then we may expect that the aspects we find when modelling are really *aspects of modelling* (and not of the modelled problem). And indeed, the aspects we can immediately identify are aspects of such kind: a static and a dynamic aspect, a component view, a use case view, etc. The fact that it has aspects is part of the nature of modelling, as it is part of the nature of programming; however, this provides no evidence that there are aspects *in* the domain being programmed or modelled, unless in the rather special case that the modelled domain is *Modelling* itself.

As an aside, the fact that modelling has aspects implies that it requires some kind of weaving. In fact, since every model (model here defined as a single diagram) usually specifies only one tiny aspect of a modelled problem. I would conjecture that the weaving of diagrams (as partial models) is one of the key issues to be addressed if modelling is to deliver on its promises, MDA especially. I suspect that much can be learnt from AOP that can be extremely helpful in developing object-oriented modelling into a truly useful discipline, but I would expect none of this to relate to the level of the actual model, that is, to the conceptualization of a problem domain. This issue is picked up again in Section 4.

## 2.5 Aspects as Non-functional Requirements

Those who have given up on searching for functional aspects (or perhaps never did so) have retreated to the position that aspects model non-functional requirements. Non-functional requirements are often considered to be hard to express given the usual modelling languages (which might explain their absence from domain models); however, this is not necessarily so. For instance, that a banking transaction may only take a certain period of time would require that the modelling language has a notion of time, which is nothing too special in disciplines other than software engineering. Likewise, that a money withdrawal requires authentication can be expressed through an ordinary sequence diagram. In fact, that something is classified as a non-functional requirement does not preclude it from being part of a domain model – rather, it is the fact that it cannot be reified.

Modelling languages are usually first-order languages [5, 20]. This implies that statements about statements cannot be expressed unless the statements themselves become objects, that is, are reified. Aspects on the other hand are typically expressed as statements quantified over an infinite number of statements; in fact, non-functional requirement that might be expressed by an aspect are usually of the form "for all functional requirements of kind $x$, make sure that $y$". For instance, a statement of the form "make sure that all methods of a program that are called in the course of a transaction are logged" is something that cannot be expressed using the means of a first-order language, as will be argued below.

To conclude, one could be led to argue that aspects invariably express non-functional requirements, so if non-functional requirements are no elements of domain models, then neither are aspects. But even if one dismisses this argumentation (because certain non-functional requirements *can* be expressed using standard modelling languages), this does not imply that aspects can be found in domain models, since not all non-functional requirements are adequately expressed as aspects. In fact, as will be argued next, it is the very nature of aspects that makes them unsuitable for being included in domain models.

# 3   Proving Aspect-Freeness of Domain Models

Given that roles have properties that make them unsuitable for being modelled as aspects, that ordering dimensions are one level above the problem domain, and that the aspects we know of are really aspects of the solution and its technology rather than the underlying problem domain, are we ready to conclude that domains are aspect free? No, since it could be the case that there are aspects I have forgotten to mention or that we do not even know of yet. What is really needed is a positive argument making the claimed non-existence plausible or, better still, a proof of thereof.

Obviously, such a proof depends critically on two definitions: what a domain model is, and what an aspect is. Since both terms are in a rather broad use, definitions that are both precise and generally accepted are hard to find. I will therefore attempt a semiformal proof that builds on preconditions that should be easy to accept for a wide audience. That such a proof must remain debatable is a tribute to the diversity of the work in the field, and the many views held by the many authors. However, the proof should be seen in light of the observed absence of domain-level, or functional, aspects and as such as an explanation attempt in the tradition of natural science; questioning its soundness only leaves the observations unexplained, it does not make them wrong.

## 3.1   The First-Orderedness of Domain Models

There appears to be broad consensus in the conceptual, the data, and the software modelling community that the world be viewed as interrelated objects with attributes and behaviour. According to this view, objects are abstractions of real world entities (where we must be aware that even the concept of an entity is an invention of the mind), and their properties describe how entities appear, how they relate to others, and how they behave. While objects are the subjects of modelling, properties are "about" (or "above", which is the same word in German) them: not coincidentally, the most successful formalization of natural language, predicate logic, distinguishes between objects (zeroth-order expressions) and propositions about them (first-order expressions). As an aside, it is interesting to note that reality itself is free of propositions (it is only entities that exist), unless of course "reality" (the modelled domain) is language.

Being a picture of reality, a domain model consists of objects (representing the perceived entities of the real word) and propositions about them. In particular, a domain model contains no propositions about propositions, since these would describe the model rather than reality. Generally, there is broad consensus that *domain models are first order* (e.g., [5, 20]). Indeed, it appears that first order predicate logic is the natural language of domain models even in presence of object-orientation, i.e., typing, generalization, and inheritance. The following explains why this is so.

The standard semantics of object-oriented modelling maps the objects of a model to elements of the modelled domain. Types are mapped to unary predicates (called *type predicates*) serving as membership functions: an object *o* is an instance of type *T* iff $T(o)$ is true. Attributes correspond to functions associating certain elements (the objects) with others, their attribute values. Relationships between objects are mapped to binary or higher arity predicates, specifying tuples of elements that go together. Methods can be viewed as temporary relationships that objects engage in while collaborating; they introduce dynamics to a model in that they have the ability to alter existing relationships and attribute values as the result of their execution. [27]

The generalization of types expresses type inclusion, i.e., the fact that elements of one type are always (and necessarily) also elements of another type. More specifically, that *T* is a subtype of *U* maps to

$$\forall o : T(o) \rightarrow U(o) \tag{1}$$

where *o* ranges over all objects in the domain and *T* and *U* are the corresponding type predicates. From this, the semantics of generalization, the inheritance of properties, follows immediately: whatever is asserted of objects of type *U* must also hold for objects of type *T*.

Because sentences of the form of (1) occur repeatedly in object-oriented models (they express the type hierarchy), it is commonplace to introduce a special relationship, called generalization, whose instances (tuples) relate types (and thus predicates) rather than objects. In fact, in a model we would not write (1), but

$$T < U \tag{2}$$

or something alike. However, generalization as a relationship is only *extensionally* defined (i.e., by listing all its elements) – it rolls out to a finite set of first-order formulas in the style of (1).[9] And indeed, even though (2) suggests that that type *T* inherits the properties from type *U*, it is only the declaration of properties that is inherited (where the properties themselves pertain to the types' objects).

It is an interesting result of mathematical logic that many-sorted (typed) and also order-sorted (object-oriented) logic are no more expressive than their uni-sorted forerunner: as long as they do not quantify over propositions, they are all first order, i.e., their sentences consist of objects (zeroth order) and propositions about them (first order) [18]. Thus, the fact that a model is object-oriented does not negate that it is a pure domain model in the above sense. As it turns out, this is generally not the case for as-

---

[9]  In particular, generalization does not quantify over types (*cf.* Footnote 11 for a contrary position).

pect-oriented models, which typically quantify over open (potentially infinite, in any case *intensionally* defined) sets of propositions (*cf.* related work in Section 5, in particular [8]).

## 3.2   The Second-Orderedness of Aspects

Frankly, the claim is that aspect-oriented languages are essentially second-order languages, so that their models are no pure domain models in the above sense. The second order follows from the fact that it is necessary for an aspect to be able to make propositions about propositions. In ASPECTJ, this is reflected in the fact that an aspect definition usually contains clauses specifying *where* (or *when*) the aspect applies, and this specification involves variables (wildcards and other constructs) ranging over classes, methods, and control flow. Mathematically, this is comparable to a second-order predicate logic in which variables may range not only over objects, but also over predicates and functors. In fact, an aspect of AOP saying that a certain procedure or code fragment *a* (for *action* or *advice*) is to be executed with all methods satisfying some predicate *s* (for *selection*) translates to an expression of the form

$$\forall m(x_1,...,x_n) \in M : s(m(x_1,...,x_n)) \rightarrow \left(m(x_1,...,x_n) \rightarrow a(x_1,...,x_n)\right) \qquad (3)$$

where $M$ corresponds to the set of methods of a program. Note that (3) is not a first order formula: while $a$ is a first-order predicate specifying the advice of the aspect (the what), $s$ is a second-order predicate selecting certain methods (specifying the where) quantified over the predicate variable $m(...)$. Note that this way the specification of the advice $a$ has access to the parameters of the methods $m$ it applies to (but $a$ need not make use all parameters of $m$). Without resorting to the second order, the parameters of an aspect cannot be bound to the parameters of the methods they apply to; the aspect remains isolated and hence useless.

Theory aside, it is easy to see that in practice the processing of an aspect requires reasoning about and involves manipulation of a program, that AOP is *de facto* a meta-programming technique; this applies equally to aspect-oriented modelling. On the other hand, in order to actually do something every aspect must contain expressions (method calls etc.) that are on the same level as the items it is an aspect of. Since an aspect always (and necessarily) consists of both, a *what* and a *where/when* part, there can be no aspect without a meta-level.

On the other hand, postulating that there are (also) aspects in a first-order language (on the same level as other properties, namely types, attributes, relationships, and methods) would either force us to
a) explain what an aspect of an aspect is (or else exclude self-application of the concept), or would
b) require that the *where* part of these aspects applies to propositions one level below the other properties.
As for the latter: both modelling and programming usually start at the level of types; there are no propositions of a lower level so that the subject of first-order aspects would have to remain imaginary. As for the former: the only constellation in which I find aspects of aspects easy to conceive is if aspects are themselves the subject matter. However, these aspects must then be a weaker concept than the aspects of aspect ori-

entation, since there are no aspects they could be applied to (there is no lower level and applying them to themselves or to their second-order relatives would open the door for paradoxes or ill-definedness, as the history of mathematical logic has taught [29]). It follows that first-order aspects are unlikely to exist and, because pure domain models are first order, that these models are aspect free.

## 4     Possible Impact of Aspect Orientation on Domain Modelling

The immediate (and also rather dramatic) consequence of the absence of aspects from first-order languages is that it frees all modelling languages that are (and are to remain) first order from having to introduce aspects as an additional modelling construct. This may come as a disappointment to some, but should really be perceived as a relief rather than a setback, as the following argumentation shows.

The main advantage of graphical models (diagrams) over programs (text) is that they can express proximity in more than one dimension. In fact, literally all diagrams use lines to indicate the relatedness of concepts (represented by boxes and other shapes), thereby distinguishing conceptual proximity from the geometric one that results from diagram layout.[10] However, aspect orientation breaks with the proximity ("locality") concept of a language [8], so that the principal advantage of graphical over textual notations is lost. This explains why there seems to be no natural way of integrating aspects into UML as a complementary concept (see, e.g., [3, 4, 13] for attempts), an observation that should really come as no surprise, for subroutines (another language construct that breaks with locality [8]) cannot be represented naturally in flowcharts either. Seen this way, that everything can remain as is—at least for domain models—is good news.

Things get different, however, as soon as we switch from domain modelling to metamodelling. Metamodelling requires a second-order language (a language that can make statements about a language; *cf.* Section 5), in which aspects can be expressed. This might turn out to be extremely handy.

As mentioned in Section 2.4, modelling itself has many aspects; it could in fact be considered aspect oriented. An aspect language could be devised that allows one to model modelling much more adequately than the metamodelling languages used today (e.g., MOF or even UML); that allows the integration of functional and non-functional views, of static and dynamic views, of analysis, design, and even deployment views (which all could be considered aspects in this aspect-oriented metamodelling language) by suitable weaving techniques. The definition of such a metamodelling language would include aspects as a modelling concept but, as argued above, each concrete aspect would be a construct of the modelling language, not any domain modelled with it. It follows that only if a modelling language is itself considered the domain of modelling is it possible that we have an aspect *in* the domain. However, the discussion of metamodels and their languages is not what this paper is about.

---

[10] That related elements of a diagram are mostly also in geometric proximity of each other is a tribute to readability, but neither necessary nor always possible.

# 5   Related Work

## 5.1   Aspects and Second Order

In order to exclude certain paradoxical expressions involving negation and self-reference Russell introduced types to set theory and mathematical logics [29]. His type theory has led to the distinction of first and higher-order logics and – by generalizing the type concept – to the introduction of many and order-sorted logics (the latter being the logical pendant to the type systems of OOPLs such as C++ and JAVA). Interestingly, as stated before both many and order-sorted logics are first order [18].

Somewhat related to Russell's introduction of types is the work of Tarski and Carnap, who found in their investigations on the concept of truth that when speaking about sentences in a language we must cleanly separate between object and metalanguage [28]. According to this distinction, the former is the language used to speak about objects the in the world, while the later is used for the analysis of the former. Metalanguage is inherently more expressive than object language, since it must contain all sentences of the former plus a notion of truth and corresponding logical operations. Natural language permits paradoxes of Russell's kind only because object and metalanguage are the same. While all languages are products of the mind, the subject matter of object language is the real word, whereas that of metalanguage is itself language and as such un-real (in the literal sense of the word). Thus, metalanguages are not needed to model reality and, more important for the claim of this paper, concepts that can only be expressed by means of a metalanguage are not found in the modelled domain.

Filman and Friedman have identified "quantified programmatic assertions" ("quantification") as a "distinguishing characteristic of AOP" [8]. As it turns out, (3) is a formal paraphrase of their sentence

$$\text{"In programs } P \text{, whenever condition } C \text{ arises, perform action } A \text{" [8]} \qquad (4)$$

where $P$ corresponds to $M$ in (3), $C$ corresponds to $s(.)$, and $A$ to $a(...)$. That $C$ is formulated in terms of (the elements of) $P$ and thus second order is implicit in the surrounding text; obliviousness, the other defining characteristic of AOP, is also an implicit consequence of (4), since the elements of $P$ have no knowledge of the conditions $C$. According to Filman and Friedman, no language (construct) that lacks quantification or obliviousness can be called aspect-oriented; since quantification involves second-order statements, first-order languages are aspect free.[11]

Lopes et al. have also pointed out that the ability to reference parts of a program (the programmatic equivalence of linguistic anaphora) is a (if not the) key contribution of aspect orientation [17]. Being able to reference what has just been said or done, they argue, is the natural way of keeping specifications both concise and understandable. While I could not agree more with this, I note that this raises the program-

---

[11] Deviating from my argumentation in Section 3.1, the authors view mixins and even general inheritance as a form of quantification, since it induces statements of the form "for all classes inheriting from me, add ...". However, neither programs nor models actually quantify over the inheritance relationship; instead, they include explicit statements of inheritance so that the "quantification" is in fact a finite (and explicit) conjunction; in particular, as argued in Section 3.1, it is not second order.

ming language to the level of a metalanguage, since it involves sentences about sentences. The subject matter of these meta-sentences is programming artefacts, which are not themselves objects of the programmed domain.

## 5.2 Aspects and Roles

The relationship of aspects and roles has been investigated by several authors, for instance [10, 11, 14]. Most of this work regards roles as adjunct instances [24], separate objects which are the bearers of role-specific state and behaviour, but whose identity is amalgamated with that of the role player. This would make role-related properties extrinsic to the role-playing object (extrinsic in contrast to its own properties, which would be regarded as intrinsic). Contrary to this view, I argue that the role-playing ability of every object is intrinsic to it, since it must be made possible by its nature. In fact, I prefer to view roles as abstract data types specifying role-related properties and behaviour in the context of one or more collaborations, with the implementation being provided by classes (since different role player classes will implement roles – or provide role-specific features – differently). The role playing of an instance then amounts to that instance being assigned to a variable typed with the role (tantamount to the instance taking part in a collaboration), letting instances pick up and drop roles dynamically. Independent of how roles are being viewed, however, there seems to be consensus that there are only few rather special roles that can be covered by aspects ([10] and Section 2.1).

In contrast to its nature and its role-playing abilities (which, as argued above, should be regarded as the intrinsic properties of an object) aspects in the aspect-oriented sense add extrinsic properties and behaviour, namely features that are attached to objects by reason lying outside their nature.[12] This is why the definition of an aspect can be kept in one place, with second-order expressions specifying where these properties apply. It would appear that properties extrinsic to the objects of a domain are also extrinsic to the domain itself, since the domain consists of only objects and their interactions; one could maintain, though, that it is these interactions aspects focus on, but this has not become evident so far (*cf.* below).

As for the claimed lack of polymorphism of aspects (Section 2.1): Ernst and Lorenz have argued that late binding of advice could be introduced, for instance based on the actual (dynamic) type of the receiver of an intercepted method call [4]. However, Footnote 3 applies in full. In fact, Ernst's and Lorenz's exploration of the possibility to add late bound methods to a statically binding language via aspects ([4, Section 3.5]) is merely a theoretical contemplation and not meant to inspire the design of new programming languages based on late-bound advice rather than methods.

The relationship of aspects and collaborations (of which roles represent the paricipants) mentioned in Section 2.1 also deserves further discussion. The definition of an aspect and, in particular, *aspectual collaborations* [15] can involve roles, but these roles are not themselves aspects. Surely, one could argue that if roles are valid modelling elements, then it is hard to see why an aspect defining the roles should not

---

[12] Note that aspects can be used to implement adapters for classes (or entity types, see e.g. [20]) but this can also be done with adapter classes and makes sense only if the aspect weaver is more flexible than the compiler.

equally be considered as a domain-level concept. In fact, a collaboration of objects is identifiable at the same level as the objects themselves, and generalizing it (by introducing role types as placeholders for role players) does not raise it to a meta-level: for instance, *Printing* is a collaboration that is on the same (domain) level as its roles *Printer* and *Printed*. However, even though blending of collaborations and aspects is possible [15], the two are not the same concept (after all, not all aspects involve roles); a *Printing* aspect for instance would be largely infeasible, since the knowledge of how to print/be printed is intrinsic to the role-playing objects. The aspect could serve as a reification of the collaboration, but this does not seem to be what aspects were intended for. All that remains is to add extrinsic behaviour, which is likely to be extrinsic to the problem as well.

### 5.3   Early Aspects

Some authors (e.g., [1, 4, 22]) suggest methods for the discovery and handling of aspects in the non-functional and functional requirements of a software product ("early aspects"). However, the language of requirements is largely informal, as is the authors' notion of an aspect. That a functional requirement crosscuts several others does not suffice for it to be considered an aspect, at least not in the strict sense (such as elaborated here or in [8], as reflected in (3) and (4)). Instead, one could argue that "obliviousness" [8] is hardly a required property of a functional requirement, and that all "quantification" in the requirements list is over this (finite) list of requirements so that neither of the defining criteria of [8] for aspects is fulfilled. In fact, "candidate aspects" identified at the functional requirements level are formally indistinguishable from roles or plain old subroutine calls, and the claim of this paper is that in a domain model, they end as such.

## 6   Falsification of My Thesis

Of course my position could be proven wrong simply by providing counterexamples. However, I would conjecture that finding such examples is not as straightforward as it might seem, since in order to be sufficient a counterexample must fulfil the following criteria:
- the aspect must be an aspect in the aspect-oriented sense (in particular, it must not be a subroutine or a role);
- it must not be an artefact of the (technical) solution, but must be seen as representative of an element in the underlying problem domain; and
- its choice must have a certain arbitrariness about it so that the example provides evidence that there are more aspects of the same kind, be it in the same or in other domains.

# 7 Conclusion

Aspect-orientation has set off to augment all phases of software engineering – and their artefacts – with the notion of an aspect. This would include the analysis phase and with it object-oriented modelling of a problem domain. Although a full proof would require more rigorous reasoning (including complete formal definitions of both domain models and aspects, and widespread acceptance of these definitions), I believe to have made plausible that domain models are, under generally accepted preconditions, aspect free. This is in contrast to some of the published literature, which seems to suggest that so-called functional aspects exist in the same right and frequency as their more popular, non-functional siblings. As a result of my argumentation, domain modelling is freed from the felt obligation to become aspect oriented.

## Acknowledgments

The paper has profited from helpful comments from various anonymous reviewers. Thank you for taking the time!

## References

1. M Aksit, L Bergmans, S Vural "An object-oriented language-database integration model: the composition-filters approach" in: *ECOOP '92* (1992) 372–395.
2. M Aksit, K Wakita, J Bosch, L Bergmans, A Yonezawa "Abstracting object-interactions using composition-filters" in: R Guerraoui, O Nierstrasz, M Riveill (eds) *Object-Based Distributed Processing* ECOOP '93 Workshop, Springer LNCS 791 (1994) 152–184.
3. J Araújo, A Moreira, I Brito, A Rashid "Aspect-oriented requirements with UML" *Second International Workshop on Aspect-Oriented Modelling with UML* (2002).
4. ELA Baniassad, S Clarke "Theme: an approach for aspect-oriented analysis and design"in: ICSE 2004 (2004) 158–167.
5. J Edwards, D Jackson, E Torlak "A type system for object models" in: RN Taylor, MB Dwyer (eds.) *Proceedings of the 12th ACM SIGSOFT International Symposium on Foundations of Software Engineering* (ACM 2004) 189–199.
6. T Elrad, O Aldawud, A Bader "A UML profile for aspect oriented modeling" in: *OOPSLA 2001 workshop on Aspect Oriented Programming* (2001).
7. E Ernst, DH Lorenz "Aspects and polymorphism in AspectJ" in: *Proceedings of the 2nd International Conference on Aspect-Oriented Software Development* (ACM 2003) 150–157.
8. RE Filman, DP Friedman "Aspect-oriented programming is quantification and obliviousness" in: *OOPSLA Workshop on Advanced Separation of Concerns* (Minneapolis, 2000).
9. M Fowler *Refactorings: Improving the Design of Existing Code* (Addison-Wesley, 1999).
10. KB Graversen, K Østerbye "Aspect modelling as role modelling" in: *OOPSLA '02 Workshop on Tool Support for Aspect Oriented Software Development* (2002).
11. S Hanenberg, R Unland "Roles and aspects: similarities, differences, and synergetic potential" in: Z Bellahsène, D Patel, C Rolland (eds) *OOIS 2002* Springer LNCS 2425 (2002) 507–520.
12. WH Harrison, H Ossher "Subject-oriented programming (a critique of pure objects)" in: *8th OOPSLA* (1993) 411–428.

13. M Kande, J Kienzle, A Strohmeyer *From AOP to UML: towards an aspect-oriented architectural modeling approach* Technical Report, Swiss Federal Institute of Technololgy (Lausanne, 2003).
14. EA Kendall "Role model designs and implementations with Aspect-Oriented Programming" in: *OOPSLA* (1999) 353–369.
15. KJ Lieberherr, AJ Riel "Demeter: a case study of software growth through parameterized classes" in: *10$^{th}$ ICSE* (1988) 254–264.
16. KJ Lieberherr, DH Lorenz, J Ovlinger "Aspectual collaborations: combining modules and aspects" *The Computer Journal* 46:5 (2003) 542–565.
17. CV Lopes, P Dourish, DH Lorenz, K Lieberherr "Beyond AOP: toward naturalistic programming" in: *OOPSLA'03 Special Track on Onward! Seeking New Paradigms & New Thinking* (ACM 2003) 198–207.
18. A Oberschelp "Untersuchungen zur mehrsortigen Quantorenlogik" *Mathematische Annalen* 145 (1962) 297–333.
19. OMG *http://www.uml.org/*
20. B Paech, B Rumpe "A new concept of refinement used for behaviour modelling with automata" in: M Naftalin, BT Denvir, M Bertran (eds.) 2nd International Symposium of Formal Methods Europe Springer LNCS 873 (1994) 154–174.
21. A Rashid, P Sawyer, "Aspect-orientation and database systems: an effective customisation approach" *IEE Proceedings – Software* 148:5 (2001) 156–164.
22. A Rashid, P Sawyer, AMD Moreira, J Araújo "Early aspects: a model for Aspect-Oriented Requirements Engineering" *RE* (2002) 199–202.
23. T Reenskaug, P Wold, OA Lehene *Working with Objects – The OOram Software Engineering Method* (Addison-Wesley 1996).
24. F Steimann "On the representation of roles in object-oriented and conceptual modelling" *Data & Knowledge Engineering* 35:1 (2000) 83–106.
25. F Steimann "A radical revision of UML's role concept" in: A Evans, S Kent, and B Selic (eds) *UML 2000, Proceedings of the 3$^{rd}$ International Conference* (Springer 2000) 194–209.
26. F Steimann "Role = Interface: a merger of concepts" *Journal of Object-Oriented Programming* 14:4 (2001), 23–32.
27. F Steimann, T Kühne "A radical reduction of UML's core semantics" in: JM Jézéquel, H Hussmann, S Cook *UML 2002: Proceedings of the 5th International Conference* (Springer, 2002) 34–48.
28. A Tarski "The semantic conception of truth and the foundations of semantics" *Philosophy and Phenomenological Research* 4 (1944).
29. AN Whitehead, B Russell *Principia Mathematica* (Cambridge University Press, 1910).

# Representing and Applying Design Patterns: What Is the Problem?

Hafedh Mili & Ghizlane El-Boussaidi

Laboratoire de Recherches en Technologies du Commerce Électronique (LATECE)
Faculté des Sciences, Université du Québec à Montréal
B.P 8888, succursale Centre-Ville, Montréal (Québec) H3C 3P8, Canada
{hafedh.mili, el_boussaidi.ghizlane}@uqam.ca

**Abstract.** Design patterns embody proven solutions to recurring design problems. Ever since the gang of four popularized the concept, researchers have been trying to develop methods for representing design patterns, and applying them to modeling problems. To the best of our knowledge, none of the approaches proposed so far represents the design problem that the pattern is meant to solve, explicitly. An explicit representation of the problem has several advantages, including 1) a better characterization of the problem space addressed by the pattern—better than the textual description embodied in pattern documentation templates, 2) a more natural representation of the transformations embodied in the application of the pattern, and 3) a better handle on the automatic detection and application of patterns. In this paper, we describe the principles underlying our approach, and the current implementation in the Eclipse Modeling Framework™.

## 1 Introduction

Software development may be seen as a sequence of property-preserving transformations that are applied to a set of user requirements to produce a functional software that satisfies a number of quality requirements [16]. Researchers have long tried to describe those transformations precisely. However, doing so in a domain independent way has proved elusive because of the vast amounts of both domain and development knowledge that would be required. *Design maintenance systems* (see e.g. [3]) break the process of development by transformation into, i) *choosing* a transformation, which is a knowledge-intensive and complex task, but involving little labor, and ii) *applying* a chosen transformation, which is labor-intensive but knowledge poor. They, thus, focus on applying chosen transformations, and argue that, by changing the requirements a bit, they can update the design by reapplying the same set of transformations that were chosen for the initial requirements. To some extent, the design patterns movement takes an orthogonal approach to design maintenance systems : instead of focussing on small changes in the overall requirements, they focus on localized, recurrent design problems, whose solutions they codify [9].

L. Briand and C. Williams (Eds.): MoDELS 2005, LNCS 3713, pp. 186–200, 2005.

Since the publication of the gang of four book, several researchers have worked on providing support to developers for applying design patterns, including [4], [5], [6], [18], [1], and many more. Viewing design patterns as reusable artefacts, their usage requires [13] :

❑ Recognizing opportunity : recognizing the pattern as a potential solution to the problem at hand,

❑ Understanding the artefact : understanding the pattern, its structure, and the principles underlying it, and

❑ Adapting the artefact: in this case, applying the pattern to the problem at hand.

Each one of these tasks requires a particular representation of the pattern. To recognize opportunity, we need a representation of the problem solved by the pattern that we can match to a representation of the problem at hand. To understand the pattern, we need a representation that is intuitive, typically mixing text with a visual notation. The third task requires a representation of the transformation embodied in the pattern.

The approaches that we have studied have tackled either the understanding task, or the pattern application task (e. g. [2], [18], [17]), and sometimes both [7],[11]. Significant research in the software metrics area has addressed the opportunity aspects, but does little for pattern understanding, or for performing the subsequent refactoring—with a few exceptions, e.g. [19]. We know of no approach that tries to handle all three tasks. We argue that a representation of the design problem is required for all three tasks:

❑ We cannot ascertain the relevance of a design pattern to a design problem without a *formal characterization* of the design problems that the pattern is meant to solve,

❑ Proper understanding of the pattern requires that we understand the structure of our software (its models) *before* applying the pattern, and *after*

❑ The application (instantiation) of the pattern may be expressed declaratively as a mapping between a model of the problem and a model of the solution, that can be implemented by a generic transformation engine.

In this paper, we describe our approach for representing and applying design patterns. Section 2 presents the representation of the design problem, which is illustrated using the *bridge pattern*. We describe the model of the solution and the model of the transformation in section 3. We describe our EMF-based implementation in section 4. We compare our approach to related work and discuss the issue of assessing a pattern's applicability in section 5. We conclude in section 6.

## 2    Modeling the Design Problem

### 2.1    Example: The Bridge Pattern

Figure 1 illustrates a situation that warrants the bridge pattern [9]. Assume that we want to develop a program that manipulates graphical window objects, and that we want our program to be portable across OS platforms (MS Windows, Unix-based, etc.). A typical object-oriented design idiom consists of creating a root abstract class—call it *Window*—that defines *abstract* methods that specify the behavioral contract that the various implementations must provide. This solution is illustrated by the left hand-side of Figure 1. Assume now that we want to define new *types* of windows, e.g. square windows, which may provide additional behaviour (new methods) or refine existing ones (e.g. providing a more optimal implementation of some generic behavior). The extended design is shown on the right hand-side of Figure 1: a new subclass of *Window* has been created—*SquareWindow*—and new implementations of *SquareWindow* have been defined, one for each target platform.

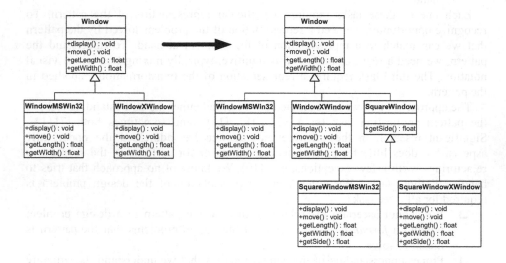

**Fig. 1.** An example problem solved by the bridge pattern.

The solution proposed by the *bridge pattern* consists of *decoupling implementations from abstractions* by putting them in separate class hierarchies that can evolve independently. In particular, new implementation classes are needed *only* in those cases where they provide new behaviour implementations. The example of Figure 2 shows a case where a new *abstraction* (*SquareWindow*) uses the same implementation as its parent (*Window*).

Figures 1 and 2 help explain the design pattern by showing a sample problem and the corresponding solution, i.e. a <problem, solution> *instance*. We would like to abstract, from this example, and from the textual pattern documentation, a representation of the problem solved by the bridge pattern that would support the three reuse tasks mentioned in the introduction. The subsequent subsections describe our representation.

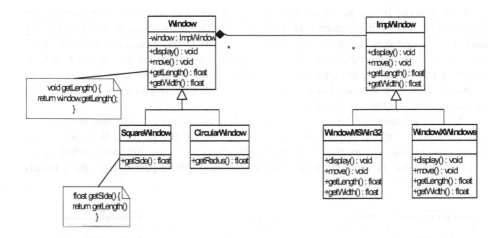

**Fig. 2.** The solution proposed by the Bridge pattern

## 2.2   A Metamodel of the Design Problem

Instances of the design problem solved by the bridge pattern are analysis and design
models of applications. To describe the *class* of problems solved by the pattern, we
will define a *problem meta-model*, i.e. a model whose instances are models such as
the one in Figure 1. Figure 3 shows a first-cut metamodel.

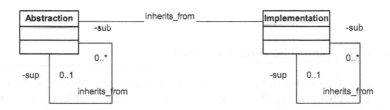

**Fig. 3.** A first-cut metamodel of the problem solved by *bridge*.

The classes *Abstraction* and *Implementation* are meta-classes in the sense that their
instances are classes such as *Window* or *WindowMSWin32*, respectively. The
associations labeled "inherits_from" represent *inheritance relationships that exist
between instances of the corresponding classes*. For example, such a relationship
exists between the two *abstractions SquareWindow* and *Window* (see Figure 1).
Similarly, there is an inheritance relationship between the *implementation
SquareWindowMSWin32* and the *abstraction SquareWindow*. Note that, for the time
being, we don't worry about what it means to be "an abstraction" or "an
implementation". We interpret these (meta)classes as simple tags for now; we later
discuss their semantics.

A metamodel of the problem should also include a description of the operations that are affected by the pattern. The operations of the *Abstraction*'s will be abstract, and the operations of the *Implementation*'s will be concrete. Further, each *Implementation* must implement all of the abstract operations of the *Abstraction* from which it inherits. We represent this constraint as a constraint between the association "inherits_from", between classes, and the association "implements", between the corresponding operations (Figure 4).

There is yet more to represent. We would normally need to capture return types and parameters of the operations that are affected by the pattern. We should also cover cases where *Abstraction*'s are not pure abstract classes, but may include some implementations. To keep the model simple, we will ignore parameters[1] and partially abstract classes.

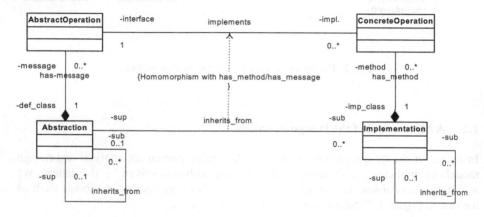

**Fig. 4.** A metamodel of the problem solved by the *Bridge* pattern. Take two.

## 2.3    The Missing Link: The Time Derivative!

To some extent, the various design patterns aim at shielding a client program from *changes* in the functionality, the environment, or the implementation of another program. Design patterns either make those changes transparent, or minimize their maintenance impact.

We argue that the *dynamic* nature of the problem to be solved is *an essential part* of the design problem, and as such, it needs to be captured explicitly. Consider the case of the *visitor* pattern. This pattern is applicable when a class hierarchy is stable, but the behaviours it supports (the set of methods) is not. Notice that if the set of behaviours is stable, but the set of types is not, plain class inheritance works just fine. Were we to use the same notation as in Figure 4, both situations would be characterized by the same metamodel, missing the essence of the problem.

---

[1] In our approach, what is not explicitly represented is assumed to be carried over, as is, from problem to solution. Thus, ignoring parameters in this case, simply means that they won't be modified by the application of the pattern, which is true for *Bridge*.

Accordingly, we decided to augment our problem metamodels by specifying those aspects that change. By studying the various kinds of time changes, we were able to reduce them all to changes in the cardinalities of some meta-level associations. For example, both the *Bridge* and the *Abstract factory* pattern handle cases where the number of subclasses of a given class is geared for frequent change. With *visitor* and *decorator*, the number of operations associated with a class is geared for change. *Template method* and *strategy* characterize cases where the number of *implementations* of a given operation is geared for change. And so forth. We represent these "time hotspots" by adding the symbol "++" to the cardinalities on the appropriate association ends. Figure 5 shows the new metamodel of the problem solved by *Bridge*. This model is saying that both the number of abstractions, and the number of implementations *per* abstraction, are geared for change.

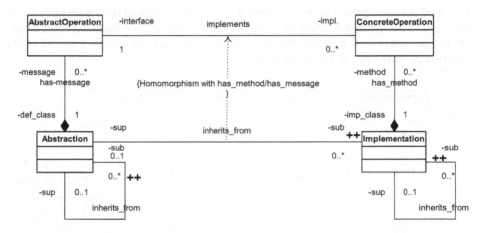

**Fig. 5.** A metamodel of the problem solved by Bridge, including the time hotspots.

## 2.4 A Language for Problem Metamodels

The previous example gave us some idea about the kinds of constructs needed by our language. Note that concepts such as *Abstraction* or *Implementation* are not part of the language primitives : the pattern designers (or documenters) can define any metaclass and give it the meaning they want. However, these metaclasses must inherit from the UML subset that is MOF compliant. Thus, while *Abstraction* and *Implementation* are specific to the bridge pattern[2], *because they represent classes, they must both be* (UML) *classifiers*. Similarly, while *AbstractOperation* and *ConcreteOperation* are specific to this pattern, the fact that they represent operations means that they must inherit from the UML/MOF Operation.

We have also introduced the notion of *family*, which represents a set of entities of the same type that share some characteristics, and that can be referenced or handled as

---

[2] Actually, the notion of *Abstraction* and *Implementation* are used in several patterns, and may be made part of a shared library of metaclasses.

a group. For example, we have the notion of *class family* that represents the set of subclasses of a given class, or what Odell calls *powertype* [14]. We also have the notion of *method families* that represents the set of methods that share some characteristic (name, signature, return type, etc.). Other than these two modifications, our metamodeling language is   similar to UML's metamodel. Our EMF™ implementation led us to make some adjustments, as we will see in section 4.

## 3   Representing the Solution and the Transformation

### 3.1   Representing the Solution

We used the same principles to represent the solutions produced by design patterns. In this regard, our approach is not much different from metamodel-based representations of design patterns, including [15], [1], [17], and [8]. Figure 6 shows a model of the solution provided by the bridge pattern.

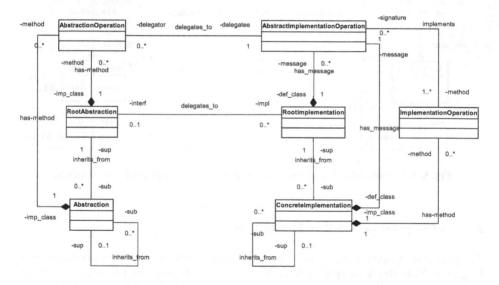

**Fig. 6.** A metamodel of the solution embodied by the bridge pattern.

The model is read as follows. We have a hierarchy of classes, representing abstractions (*RootAbstraction* and *Abstraction*), that delegates processing to another hierarchy of classes, representing implementations (*RootImplementation* and *ConcreteImplementation*). Note that we need to distinguish root classes from other classes in the tree, for both abstractions and implementations. Indeed, the root of the implementation hierarchy is *an abstract class* while its descendants are *concrete classes* that implement its interface. Interestingly, all of the classes of the abstraction hierarchy are *concrete classes* that delegate their processing to the corresponding methods on the implementation object.

Recall that, as was the case for the problem metamodel, the semantics of the classes *Abstraction* and *RootAbstraction* are specific to the Bridge pattern, and we are free to give them the meaning we want. Further, we don't have to use the same metaclasses that we used to describe the problem, since we will represent the transformation from problem to solution, explicitly. We discuss the representation of transformations in the next section.

The representation of solution models requires additional constructs that are not needed for problem models. One such construct is the notion of *constants* or *literals*. We have no need for literals in the bridge pattern, since all the operations that appear on the solution side come from the problem. However, some design patterns introduce methods and attributes that are supposed to appear as-is in the transformed model. For example, the Observer/Observable pattern requires that observable objects implement pattern-specific operations (notify(...), among others). Our representation language accommodates the representation of literals.


## 3.2    Representing the Mapping from Problems to Solutions

Applying a design pattern consists of transforming an *instance* of the class of problems solved by the pattern, to an *instance* of the class of solutions. Accordingly, we can *represent* this transformation as a mapping from elements of the problem metamodel (Figure 5) to elements of the solution metamodel (Figure 6). To *apply* the transformation to a sample input model—an analysis or a design-level UML model—we:

1)    *first* map the problem (meta)model to the input model, to identify those entities of the input model that match entities in the problem model, and

2)    *second*, produce the output model by transforming those so-matched entities (classes, associations, operations) according to the mapping, leaving the others unchanged.

In essence, the first step identifies the entities in the input model that play the *roles* described by the entities of the problem model. This step is typically referred to as *model marking*, and the outcome is a *marked* (input) *model*. In the case of the bridge pattern, we need to identify, in the input model, those classes that play the role of *Abstraction* and *Implementation*. The so-marked classes will be transformed according to the mapping.

Figure 7 shows a mapping metamodel, i.e. a model that represents mappings between problem models and solution models. A <problem model,solution model> mapping is represented by an instance of the class *ModelMapping*. For example, the mapping from the bridge problem model (Figure 5) to the bridge solution model (Figure 6) is represented by an instance of *ModelMapping*. An instance <model1,model2> of *ModelMapping* is an aggregation of, i) mappings between their classes (classes of model1 and classes of model2), and ii) mappings between their associations.    In turn, the mapping between two classes (an instance of *ClassMapping*) is an aggregation of, i) mappings between attributes (instances of *AttributeMapping*), and ii) mappings between operations (instances of *OperationMapping*). And so forth.

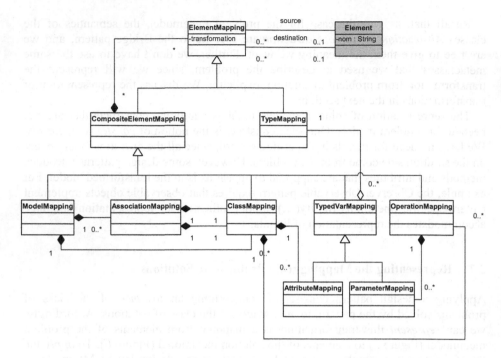

**Fig. 7.** A model for representing mappings between problem models and solution models.

All of the mapping classes inherit from *ElementMapping*. Each mapping has a source element, a destination element, and a description of how the source element is transformed into the destination element (attribute "transformation" of the class *ElementMapping*). The source and destination are instances of the class *Element* (with grey background), which represents MOF's *ModelElement*. A mapping with no source element means an element that is added by the application of the pattern. A mapping with no destination element means an element that is removed by the application of the pattern.

# 4    Implementation

We have implemented our representation of design patterns, and the transformation procedure in the Eclipse™ environment using the *Eclipse Modeling Framework™*. EMF is a modeling framework that supports code generation and XMI-based persistence. EMF includes a package—called *ECore*—that provides a simplified implementation of MOF. Section 4.1 describes the implementation of the various metamodels (problems, solutions, and mappings). The transformation algorithm is described in section 4.2.

## 4.1    Common Metamodel for Problems and Solutions

Figure 8 shows the common metamodel for representing problem models and solution models of design patterns. Initially, we planned to represent this metamodel as *an instance* of EMF's ECore package. This model would then be instantiated to describe problem models and solution models for specific patterns. Those models would, in turn, be instantiated to represent specific application models. Developers, working in the Eclipse environment with the EMF plug-in, would then *load* representations of various patterns (problem models, solution models, and mappings) from secondary storage, and apply them to the application models they are working on. However, EMF's built-in serialization mechanism supports the XMI serialization of only those models that have ECore (or an extension thereof) as a metamodel. Accordingly, instead of defining our pattern metamodel as an instance of ECore, we implemented it using an extension of ECore classes. Figure 8 shows the metamodel, which we will comment briefly. The ECore classes correspond closely to MOF entities (and to UML's meta-meta-model), and are greyed out.

First, in order to define a new metamodel, and thus, a new type of models, we have to define a subclass of *EPackage*, and register the new metaclasses within this subclass. In our case, this subclass is called *ModelPackage*. Figure 8 shows a class *ModelClass*, that extends the ECore class, *EClass*. *ModelClass* represents all the classes that appear within problem models or solution models. In our bridge example, the classes *Abstraction* and *Implementation*, from the problem model, and *RootAbstraction*, *Abstraction*, *RootImplementation*, and *Concrete-Implementation*, from the solution model, are all instances of *ModelClass*.

The class *ModelOperation* is used to represent all kinds of operations, be they virtual (abstract), concrete, or literal. Two boolean instance variables are used to distinguish between the various types: «abstract» and « literal ». Note also that we extended the ECore class *EReference* by our own *ModelReference* class in order to : 1) be able to represent inheritance relationships at the meta level (*SubtypeReference*), and 2) to represent the time variability of the cardinality, i.e. the so-called *time hotspots* (symbol ++ used in Figure 5).

## 4.2    Implementing the Transformation

We implemented model mappings in a similar fashion to problem and solution models : by extending ECore classes. As for the transformation algorithm itself, it takes three inputs:
   1)   the input model that we wish to transform, with properly marked entities
   2)   the mapping between the problem model and the solution model, and
   3)   the solution model

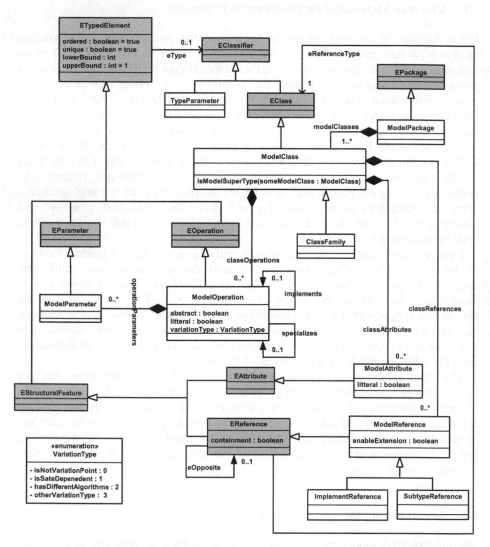

**Fig. 8.** Implementing the metamodel for pattern problem models and solution models in EMF.

The transformation engine uses a recursive algorithm, starting with aggregate, maps it to an empty aggregate on the destination side, and then recursively maps its components. For example, starting at the highest level, given the marked input model, we first generate an empty destination model, and then transform the classes in the input model, putting their transforms in the destination model. The same is true with classes, where we first generate en empty class, and then map its attributes and operations.

Notice that the same <problem --> solution> mapping may be applied to several entities in the input model. In the bridge pattern, for example, the mapping

*<Implementation --> ConcreteImplementation>* will be applied to all the classes in the input model that have been marked by the *Implementation* tag.

# 5    Discussion

## 5.1    Related Work

Ever since the publication of the GOF patterns, the representation and application of design patterns has received a lot of attention. Several approaches have been proposed, depending, in part, on the way design patterns are used. In the so-called *top-down* approach [6], developers *instantiate* a design pattern by specifying its components, as in [15] [6] [5] [1] [11] [8]; Budinsky et al.'s work on code generation by pattern instantiation may be seen as a special case [4]. The *bottom-up* approach consists of identifying perfect instances (hits) or imperfect ones (near hits) of specific design patterns, as in [5] [1], [10]. A hybrid approach attempts to re-engineer existing models to make them conform to a specific design pattern, as in [2] [5] [18]. Clearly, each one of these three usages has its own representational requirements.

Those approaches that set out to provide an explicit representation of design patterns were limited to the structural aspects (object model). Some approaches used meta-models to represent design patterns, while others simply offered a set of models, with no concern for a common, pattern-specific metamodel. In either case, the representation focused on the description of the *solution* : what the instantiated pattern will look like. This was the case for most of the top-down, forward-engineering approaches, which used design patterns as design templates that needed to be instantiated. However, we know of no approach that attempted to represent *the problem*; the work of Budinsky et al. may be the exception that confirms the rule [4]: the problem was described using natural language, according to the GOF pattern documentation template [9], but that description didn't lend itself to formal processing. To the best of our knowledge, our work is the only one that attempts to represent the problem explicitly. Such a representation enables us to *formally* characterize those situations where the pattern is appropriate. Such a representation would also enable us to specify the transformations that are embodied in the pattern. The time variability aspect—what we called *time hotspots*—is also unique to our approach, and we consider it to be a *central* aspect of the design problem solved by the design pattern.

With regard to the transformations, only those approaches that focussed on re-engineering existing models with patterns did provide an *explicit* representation for the transformation [2],[18],[19]. However, in such cases, the structure of the pattern itself is not explicit: it is embodied in the transformation. In our case, both the structure of the pattern, and the transformation embodied in its application, are represented explicitly. Further, the transformation is specified declaratively, making it possible to develop a generic, pattern-independent transformation engine (see section 4.2) that takes a marked input model, a pattern mapping model, and a pattern solution model, and produces a properly transformed output model.

## 5.2    Problem Model Semantics and Marking

In our current implementation, the entities that belong to problem models or solution models (e.g. *Abstraction, Implementation*) have no proper semantics. The only semantic constraints are inherent in their type (whether the entities represent a class or an operation) or in the relationships they have to other entities within a given problem (or solution) model. For example, if we look at the bridge problem model, we only know that *Abstraction's* have *AbstractOperation's*, and that *Implementation's* have *ConcreteOperations*, but we don't know what either concept means, beyond the fact that *Abstraction* and *Implementation* are classes, and *AbstractOperation* and *ConcreteOperations* are operations.

One way of capturing the semantics of these entities is to provide membership predicates for them that test a subset of the properties that are typically represented in input models, either directly—stored properties, such as the scope of a feature (instance versus class)—or implicitly –computed, such as the number of associated entities of a particular type. For example, we would define *AbstractOperation* as an operation that is, well, *abstract*, which is a property that is captured by the EMF metamodel—the class EOperation has such an attribute. Similary, *Abstraction* can be defined as a class whose methods are *all* abstract. Clearly, such a definition is useful in many patterns, and may be included in a *library* of such (meta)modeling concepts that are shared between several patterns. Pattern writers and documenters would have the option of using such concepts as is, extending them, or composing them—through mutiple inheritance.

We considered many languages for expressing membership predicates, including OCL, the early drafts of the (upcoming?) QVT standard (Query, View, Transformation), and a number of object-rule languages (e.g. JESS, ILOG JRules, OPSJ). We chose object-rule languages (and JRules in particular), because of their expressive power and because of the availability of mature, high performance tools for interpreting rules on Java objects. The following two rules, used to illustrate the syntax, show two ways of identifying abstract classes. We assume in this case that the class *Abstraction* is stored in a static member of our metaclass *ModelClass*, with the name ABSTRACTION.

```
rule mark_abstract_classes {
when {
      ?aClass: EClass (isAbstract());
} then {
      modify ?aClass {tag = ModelClass.ABSTRACTION;}
      }
}
rule mark_abstract_classes_from_operations {
when {
      ?aClass: EClass();
      not EOperation(isConcrete()) in ?aClass.getEOperations();
} then {
      modify ?aClass {tag = ModelClass.ABSTRACTION;}
      }
}
```

The first rule uses a simple test : the result of (actual) boolean method "boolean isAbstract()" on EClass. The second rule matches any EClass (any class in an input model) such that none of its operations are concrete[3], and marks it as an abstract class. Thanks to rule chaining, we could have tags that depend on complex patterns being built up incrementally, starting with simpler patterns. In fact, the entire problem model itself can be written as one (or several alternate) rule(s) that use pre-assigned tags [12].

There remains one aspect that membership predicates cannot capture: the *probable* evolution scenarios of the input model, which would make a design pattern a desirable alternative. This information is *dynamic* and will not be implicit in the input object model, which provides only a *snapshot* of the target application at the present time. There are two possible strategies for capturing this information. First, we make it a property that designers or analysts will have to enter before they can submit their models for marking. Experienced analysts and designers, with some knowledge of the application domain (e.g. a product line) will know this information but, conceivably, our tool can prompt analysts or designers for potential "time hotspots"—themselves following specific patterns. Second, we can look at consecutive versions of the same software to determine which parts have evolved and how, and use that information to identify the time hotspots. This second approach requires no judgement, but will only work for long-lived software whose source code, throughout several versions, is available.

# 6   Conclusion

Our work deals with providing developers with a repository of reusable model-based artifacts, and with the tools needed to assist them in using those artifacts. Developing with reuse involves three main tasks, 1) evaluating the opportunity of using an artifact for the problem at hand, 2) understanding that artifact, and 3) integrating the artifact—typically through model transformation—in the system at hand [13]. In this paper, we dealt specifically with the issue of representing and applying/enacting design patterns. Our approach relies on an explicit and precise description of the design problem solved by a given pattern. This description, provided in the form of a meta-model, supports the three reuse tasks.

Our approach is generic and consistent with model-driven engineering. Recognizing the opportunity for reusing a design artifact—design pattern in this case—remains a big challenge, similar to model marking in the context of MDA. One reason is that design problems come from non-functional requirements, which are usually not explicitly represented (or representable with available notations) in software models. To some extent, design patterns are point *solutions*, or *implementations*, for a general design *requirement*: provide model resilience through functional requirements change. Specifically, each design pattern addresses the general design requirement for a specific *functional pattern*, which can be characterized as the combination of a static structure, and an *evolution pattern*. To this

---

[3] There is no such method on org.eclipse.emf.ecore.EOperation. This is shown for illustration purposes only.

extent, we believe that our representation of design problems, which captures both the static structure of a functional pattern, and its evolution patterns, is a step in the right direction.

# References

1.  Albin-Amiot, H., Guéhéneuc, Y.G.: Meta-modeling Design Patterns: application to pattern detection and code synthesis. Proceedings of ECOOP Workshop on Automating OO Software Development Methods, 2001.
2.  Alencar, P.S.C., Cowan, D.D., Dong, J., Lucena, C.J.P.: A transformational Process-Based Formal Approach to Object-Oriented Design. Formal Methods Europe FME'97, 1997.
3.  Baxter, I.: Design Maintenance Systems. Communications of the ACM, vol. 35, no. 4, (1992) 73-89.
4.  Budinsky, F.J., Finnie, M.A., Vlissides, J.M., Yu, P.S.: Automatic Code Generation from Design Patterns. IBM Systems Journal, vol. 35, n° 2, (1996) 151-171.
5.  Eden, A.H., Gil, J., Hirshfeld, Y., Yehudai A.: Towards a mathematical foundation for design patterns. Technical report, dep. of information technology, Uppsala University, 1999.
6.  Florijn, G., Meijers, M., van-Winsen, P.: Tool support for object-oriented patterns. Lecture Notes in Computer Science, vol. 1241, (1997) 472-495.
7.  Fontoura, M., Lucena, C.: Extending UML to Improve the Representation of Design Patterns. Journal of OO Programming, vol. 13, n° 11 (2001).
8.  France, R., Kim, D.k., Ghosh, S., Song, E.: A UML-Based Pattern Specification Technique, IEEE Trans. on Software Engineering, vol. 30, n° 3, (2004) 193- 206.
9.  Gamma, E., Helm, R., Johnson, R., Vlissides, J.: Design Patterns: Elements of Reusable Object-Oriented Software. Addison-Wesley (1995).
10. Guéhéneuc, Y-G., Sahraoui, H.: des signatures numériques pour améliorer la recherche structurelle de patrons. Proceedings of Langages et Modèles à Objets 2005, Berne, Suisse, (2005).
11. Maplesden, D., Hosking, J., Grundy, J.: Design Pattern Modelling and Instantiation using DPML. Proceedings of 14th International Conference on Technology of OO Languages and Systems (2002).
12. Mili, H., El-Boussaidi, G.: Design patterns : recognizing opportunity through rule-based semantic marking. LATECE Technical report, LAT-2005-12 (2005).
13. Mili, H., Mili, A., Yacoub, S., Addy, E.: Reuse-Based Software Engineering: Techniques, Organization, and Control. John Wiley & Sons, (2002) ISBN 0-471-39819-5.
14. Odell, J.: Power Types. Journal of Object-Oriented Programming (JOOP), (1994).
15. Pagel, B-U., Winter, M.: Towards Pattern-Based Tools. Proc. of EuropLop (1996).
16. Partsch, H., Steinbruggen, R.: Program Transformation Systems. Computing Surveys, vol. 15, no. 3, (1983) 199-236.
17. Sanada, Y., Adams, R.: Representing Design Patterns and Frameworks in UML, Towards a Comprehensive Approach. Journal of Object Technology, vol. 1, n° 2, (2002)143-154.
18. Sunyé, G., Le Guennec, A., Jézéquel, J.M.: Design pattern application in UML. Proc. of the 14th Object Oriented Programming European Conference, (2000) 44-62.
19. Tahvildari, L., Kontogiannis, K.: Improving Design Quality Using Meta-Pattern Transformations: A Metric-Based Approach. The Journal of Software Maintenance and Evolution: Research and Practice, John Wiley Publishers, Volume 16, Issue 4-5, (2004) 331-361.

# Properties of Stereotypes from the Perspective of Their Role in Designs

Miroslaw Staron, Ludwik Kuzniarz

Department of Systems and Software Engineering
School of Engineering
Blekinge Institute of Technology
Ronneby, Sweden
(miroslaw.staron, ludwik.kuzniarz)@bth.se

**Abstract.** Stereotypes in object-oriented software development can be perceived in various ways and they can be used for various purposes. As a consequence of these variations, assessing quality of stereotypes needs to be purpose-specific. In this paper we identify eight types of stereotypes and provide a set of criteria for assessing quality of stereotypes. The criteria for each type are formed by a set of properties that characterizes its stereotypes. The identified types are based on the purpose of each stereotype (its role in designs) and its expressiveness. We identified the types of stereotypes and their properties in an empirical way by investigating stereotypes from UML profiles used in industrial software development. The properties are intended to be used in our further research for developing guidelines for creating and using stereotypes in a more efficient way.

## 1. Introduction

Extending a set of modeling abstractions with dedicated constructs for modeling specific purposes is an important issue in using the Unified Modeling Language (UML, [1, 2]) for model-driven development. This general-purpose language is known to have limitations and its extensions can be seen as a means of overcoming some of those issues. One of the extension mechanisms in UML is the notion of stereotype. *Stereotypes* are means of branding the existing UML modeling elements with new semantics and properties. The notion of stereotypes, however, was introduced into object-oriented software development before the creation of UML and MDA when the stereotypes were used in a different manner than in UML.

In order to properly create and use stereotypes, modelers should be able to assess whether their stereotypes are appropriate for the purpose – i.e. *assess the quality* of the stereotypes. Thus, we perceive the quality of stereotypes from one dimension which is fitness for the purpose. In order to assess the quality we elaborate the properties which the good stereotypes should possess. The criteria for quality assessment of stereotypes can created based on finding common properties of existing stereotypes which are known to be appropriate for their purposes (an alternative way is to arbitrarily set criteria for assessing the quality). The purposes, which were identified in our previous studies, are organized into categories according to the roles

L. Briand and C. Williams (Eds.): MoDELS 2005, LNCS 3713, pp. 201–216, 2005.

of stereotypes [3]. The identified properties of stereotypes can be used within a proposed lightweight process for assessing quality of stereotypes which is presented in Fig 1. The process is based on finding common properties of a set of reference stereotypes that are known to be well suited for their purpose. The stereotypes are presented as $S_R$. The criteria identified, based on investigation of $S_R$, are used to assess quality of other stereotypes (assessed stereotypes – $S_A$) in the process. In order to assess the quality of $S_A$ they must be classified (outlined in Sect. 7). The outcome of quality assessment process is an assertion whether the stereotype is good (i.e. appropriate for its purpose) or not.

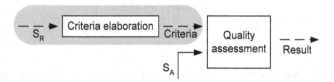

**Fig. 1.** A process of assessing quality of stereotypes

In this paper we focus on the way in which a set of criteria for assessing quality of stereotypes can be identified by extracting desired properties of good stereotypes (shadowed part in Fig. 1) hence we address the following research question:

> *How to elaborate quality assessment criteria for new stereotypes based on existing stereotypes which are known to be "good"?*

In this research question we identify the need for quality assessment criteria to be based on existing good practices of creating stereotypes. In our approach the identification of the properties, and their subsequent analysis, is done in an empirical way by investigating a set of 98 stereotypes used in practice. These stereotypes are grouped into profiles, which are standardized or used in companies developing UML tools and realizing the vision of model-driven software development. In the criteria elaboration we group stereotypes using categories from two classifications of stereotypes. Initially three classifications of stereotypes were considered: (i) according to their role, (ii) according to their usage scenarios [4, 5], and (iii) according to their expressiveness [6]. Based on our experiment it was found that only two classifications should be considered: (i) and (iii). Based on the results of classifying stereotypes we elaborated types of stereotypes. The *type* of a stereotype is a pair which consists of two categories to which the stereotype is classified – ($C_R$, $C_E$); where $C_E$ is a category in classification according to expressiveness and $C_R$ is a category in classification according to role. After elaborating the types we examined the stereotypes of each type thoroughly to identify common properties of stereotypes of each type. The properties of stereotypes we consider subsets of the following:

- kinds of data types of tag definitions (these kinds can be either data types defined in the UML metamodel or custom defined),
- kinds of the base classes the stereotype extends (concrete of abstract classes),
- kind of constraints the stereotype have,
- kind of concrete syntax (icons or guillements), and
- what kind of abstraction the stereotype should represent.

The first four properties are used to characterize stereotypes of each type. The last property is used to differentiate between types and is the basis for developing guidelines on how to choose a type of stereotype appropriate for the purpose under consideration. The guidelines are the core of our current work.

The outline of the paper is as follows. The most relevant related work in the field is presented in Sect. 2. In Sect. 3 we outline the evolution of the notion of stereotype in object-orientation and in Sect. 4 we describe the classifications used in our analysis. The design of the empirical investigation of stereotypes is presented in Sect. 5 which contains the identification of types of stereotypes. In Sect. 6 we present the properties of identified types of stereotypes. Sect. 7 suggests how the properties are to be used to assess the quality of stereotypes and Sect. 8 contains conclusions and outlines our further work.

## 2.  Related Work

Stereotypes have been given a special attention together with the idea of the Model Driven Architecture (MDA, [7]) which is gaining popularity. The idea of models being main assets in modern software development strives for more precise models and more flexible languages to create them. As stereotypes are the main extension mechanism providing some flexibility for UML, they were evaluated in several ways by analyzing different ways of using and defining them (e.g. [8-11]). Although the stereotypes are found to be very suitable for lightweight language customization, none of the analyses performs a formal empirical study on stereotypes, which is a presented in our research.

An alternative to using stereotypes for customizing UML is to extend the metamodel of UML – i.e. to facilitate the technique of metamodeling. There exists an extension of the classification of stereotypes according to expressiveness. It is a classification of various kinds of metamodel changes developed in [12] which attempts to classify the metamodel extensions into two categories: regular metamodel extensions and restrictive metamodel extensions. The classification can be used if one wants to extend our study from stereotypes to metamodel extensions.

The analysis methods for the auxiliary study presented in our paper are based on the analysis methods used in [13]. One of the results from the study (on defect classification) is that the poor agreement between classifiers can be caused by the fact that the classifiers are not the creators of the classified objects. To some extent this claim is valid in case of our study.

An empirical approach to verification of a small-scale classification schemes in the context of requirement engineering has been done in [14]. One of the outcomes of that study is that the classification result depends on the role of the classifier and that even classifiers that are well into the domain of the built system need a considerable time in order to classify a single requirement. Furthermore, a considerable amount of time was required for getting insight into the understanding of the differences between classifiers. The design of our study also used the same means of getting insight of the classification process performed by each subject in the auxiliary study.

## 3.   Stereotypes in UML

The idea of stereotyping was first introduced into software development by Rebecca Wirfs-Brock, who used the concept of stereotype to classify objects according to their "modus operandi" [15, 16]. Wirfs-Brock's original intention behind the usage of stereotypes was similar to the aforementioned view of stereotypes in other areas i.e. as a way of oversimplifying the view of objects' role or behavior. She used a fixed set of stereotypes, useful in characterizing the special roles of objects in the system.

An approach which is similar to Wirfs-Brock's of using stereotypes as a secondary classification of elements was adopted by the OPEN (Object-Oriented Process Environment and Notation) Modeling Language – OML [17]. Its designers perceived a stereotype as *"a facility for metaclassification"*. The initial set of stereotypes in the language was restricted (c.f. [17]), although it was divided into several groups of stereotypes (for example object, class and type stereotypes).

UML also contains a definition of stereotypes, but it specifies them as one of the possible extension mechanisms of the language. In UML, the stereotypes are a way of adding a new semantics to the existing model elements. They allow branding the existing model elements with new semantics, thus enabling them to "look" and "behave" as virtual instances of new model elements [2, 18]. They are no longer seen (at least directly in the specification) as a way of additional classification of model elements, according to their "modus operandi", but rather as a way of introducing new elements into the language, thus providing additional modeling abstractions (or providing means of adding secondary classification of the existing modeling abstractions – c.f. [9]).

During the evolution of UML (from version 1.1 [18] to 1.5 [2]), the definition of stereotypes in the UML metamodel has not changed significantly, although it underwent minor revisions due to the changes in the definition of other extension mechanisms (mostly *tagged values*, which evolved from being merely additional information for code generators in UML 1.1 specification towards virtual links between metamodel elements – tag definitions – in UML 1.3 and later). With a growing UML tool support for this mechanism the stereotypes are beginning to play a major role as a means of realizing the provision of UML as a family of languages rather than a one-fits-all modeling language [19].

In UML 2.0 [1], stereotypes are seen as a special kind of meta-classes that allow creating new modeling constructs. The constructs created in this way are intended to be as similar as possible to the original modeling constructs defined in the language specification. As far as the usage of stereotypes is concerned, the notion of stereotypes does not differ in UML 2.0 (compared with UML 1.x), but the way in which stereotypes are defined is more coherent with respect to the different levels in the four-layer metamodeling architecture.

## 4.   Classifications of Stereotypes

Two classifications of stereotypes are considered in the course of identifying properties of "good" stereotypes. The classifications are developed independently and classify stereotypes based on distinct criteria. The classifications are summarized in this section, while the details of them can be found in the papers where they are originally defined.

## 4.1.   Classification of Stereotypes According to Their Expressiveness

Berner et al. [6] examined the notion of stereotype independently from object orientation within the context of modeling languages with the focus on classifying stereotypes. Their work introduced a classification of stereotypes according to the expressiveness of the stereotype, i.e. according to the amount of changes in syntax and semantics they introduce to the base model element. In their work the authors distinguished between four categories of stereotypes (denoted as $C_E$ while defining the type of stereotype):

1. *Decorative stereotypes*, i.e. stereotypes which do not change the semantics of a language element, but change its concrete syntax (graphical representation),
2. *Descriptive stereotypes*, i.e. stereotypes which modify the abstract syntax of a language element and define the pragmatics of the newly introduced element without changing the semantics,
3. *Restrictive stereotypes* are descriptive stereotypes which modify the semantics of a language element,
4. *Redefining stereotypes*, which redefine a language element by changing its original semantics, w. r. t. syntax, they are similar to the restrictive stereotypes.

The classification attempts to address the complexity of a stereotype definition and provides guidelines for applying the different kinds of stereotypes. Although the classification addresses the problems of how stereotypes change the extended model element, it seems to neglect the problems of practical aspects of mechanisms for supporting stereotypes and the metamodeling levels that the stereotype definition concerns.

The classification aims in answering the question: "What changes does the stereotype make to the base model element?"

## 4.2.   Classification of Stereotypes According to Their Role

It is not always the case that the classifications presented above categorize the role of a stereotype in modeling. Therefore there is a need for a classification of stereotypes based on the usage of stereotypes in software development thus capturing this role. We use the classification to categorize the notion of stereotype within the context of practical usage and introduction of stereotypes into software development, especially customizing UML tools. The classification organizes the stereotypes into three categories (denoted as $C_R$ while defining the type of stereotype):

1. *Code Generation stereotypes*. They are aimed at making code generation rules for specific programming languages more precise and detailed, e.g. [20], intended to provide abstractions from a target programming language in order to model software using the "vocabulary" of the target programming language. Specific code generators are usually created together with the specific sets of stereotypes for code generation.

2. *Virtual Metamodel Extension stereotypes*. They are used to extend the set of UML modeling elements and perhaps to create a new "dialect" of UML, e.g. [21], intended to provide abstractions denoting new modeling constructs which are not present in the standard UML. For example these stereotypes can be used to add a "vocabulary" from another notation into UML (e.g. SPEM Profile, [22]).
3. *Model Simplification stereotypes*. They are used as an "oversimplification" of modeling elements (e.g. denoting the role of the stereotyped model element in the design), e.g. [16], intended to be created by individual modelers in an informal way. The majority of these stereotypes are used to distinguish between elements – denoting a specific purpose of the element or its role.

The detailed description of the categories is presented in [3]. The classification is based on the use of stereotypes in software development and in particular the purpose for which they are used in UML models. The proper categorization of a stereotype in this classification allows choosing the proper way of using the stereotype in UML tools.

The classification aids in answering the question – "What is the role of the stereotype in the design?"

## 5.    Investigation of Profiles

A previous step that we conducted of identifying the properties of stereotypes was a study on comparing the classifications of stereotypes. In that study we have found that only two classifications can be used for the purpose of evaluation of quality: (i) classification according to expressiveness, and (ii) classification according to role. The third classification (the classification according to usage scenarios [4, 5]) is not considered in our study as it was found that all stereotypes in the studied profiles were categorized into one category only – i.e. type classification category.

In this paper, the set of investigated stereotypes is extended to 98 stereotypes (compared to 68 stereotypes in the previous study). The stereotypes are part of established and standardized profiles by Object Management Group (OMG): UML Profile for Software Development Processes [2, pp. 4-3 to 4-9], UML Profile for CORBA [23]; UML Testing Profile. Furthermore, we investigated profiles developed by companies and used by them: JNX profiles used by a company which developed an MDA framework [20, 24]; and profiles available in a UML 2.0 tool (Telelogic Tau [25]): TTDApplicationBuilder profile, TTDExport profile, and TTDCppAppGeneration profile. The fact that the profiles are standardized and used in industry allows using them as a set of reference stereotypes in the lightweight process of assessing quality of stereotypes.

### 5.1.    Operation of the Study

The operation of the study is summarized in Fig. 2, where each oval represents a step taken during the study. Steps 1 and 5 are the main classification study. However, in order to increase the internal validity of the study, additional steps were required. Before classifying all stereotypes, the appropriateness of the classifier was verified by comparing the classifier's classification results to classifications of other subjects.

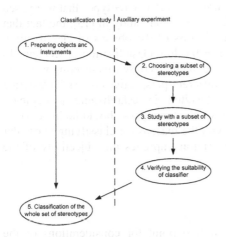

Fig. 2. Operation of the study.

Thus steps 2 through 4 are introduced as auxiliary steps used to verify the instruments before the classification study in step 5.

Using only one classifier during the study was caused by the fact the there is a substantial amount of time required to classify all stereotypes. This makes it hard to involve many subjects with appropriate knowledge for classification of all 98 stereotypes.

## 5.2.  Auxiliary Experiment

The auxiliary study was conducted with two additional subjects. The study was performed in an academic environment with doctoral students classifying a subset of thirteen stereotypes. The subjects (and the classifier) possessed the necessary knowledge of stereotypes and they also participated in other studies on stereotypes. They were sufficiently experienced in modeling, object orientation and programming. The study afforded us with the possibility to observe whether different individuals have different understandings of the criteria used in classifying stereotypes. The results from the classifications of three subjects were analyzed with Kappa statistics [26]. The Kappa statistics measures the agreement between pairs of the variables (in this case the classification results obtained from each subject). In order to use the statistics the categories were translated to numeric values on the nominal scale. The values of the Kappa statistics are presented in Table 1 for the two subjects in the study (denoted as S1 and S2) and the classifier performing the classification on the whole set of 98 stereotypes (denoted as C).

| Pair | Kappa value | Significance level | Agreement level (according to [26]) |
|------|-------------|--------------------|-------------------------------------|
| C – S1 | 0.24 | 0.0220 | Fair |
| C – S2 | 0.39 | 0.0001 | Fair |
| S1 – S2 | 0.09 | 0.4020 | Poor |

Table 1.  Summary of Kappa statistics

The results indicate that there is a poor agreement (statistically non-significant – the significance level is above 0.05) between subjects S1 and S2. However, the subjects' classifications are in fair agreement with the classification done by the classifier of the whole set of stereotypes (fair agreement with both subjects, significant at the levels of 0.022 and 0.0001 respectively for C-S1 and C-S2). The fact that the subjects were in agreement with the classifier supports the decision of choosing C as the classifier for the whole set of stereotypes at the same time minimizing the risk of obtaining an incorrect classification. Nevertheless, the fair agreement level indicates that there is a dose of personal judgment in the classification. This judgment can be caused by the fact that none of the subjects has developed these particular stereotypes that were used in the study. Furthermore, as it was also found in a similar study in [13], the fact that the subjects and the classifiers were not the creators of the objects of classification could be one of the factors that could result in the low classification agreement. In order to minimize the influence of a personal judgment, a consensus meeting was held after step 4. The objective was to discuss the different perspectives on each classified stereotype of each subject. The meeting resulted in establishing a common understanding of the different categories and which stereotypes should be included in them. Additionally the meeting provided us with the reasons for classifying particular stereotypes into each category. This in our opinion improves the objectivity of the classifier.

## 5.3.  Results of the Study

While analyzing types of stereotypes, the starting point for considerations of the properties is the purpose of the stereotype: i.e. investigating the appropriate category in the classification according to the role of stereotypes. After the consideration of the role of stereotypes, the properties of stereotypes from the perspective of the expressiveness of stereotypes need to be considered – i.e. investigating the appropriate category in the classification according to the expressiveness of stereotypes.

The results of the study are presented in Fig. 3. The nodes in the structure represent different groups of stereotypes and the edges represent the percentage of stereotypes that belong to the appropriate category in the node below. On the lowest level of the structure there are categories in the classification according to expressiveness. In the middle level there are categories in the classification according to the role of stereotypes. The top level node represents all stereotypes in the study.

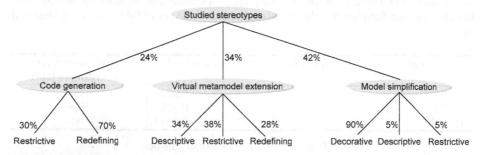

**Fig. 3.** Results of investigation of 98 stereotypes – grouping of stereotypes

The results of the study were the basis for elaborating types of stereotypes. Certain types of stereotypes, however, were not present in the study, e.g. (code generation, decorative). The results indicate that there exist some relationships between different categories in these classifications which make certain stereotypes (decorative) not usable for a certain purpose (code generation). The identified types of stereotypes are presented in Fig. 4 together with the percentage of stereotypes in this study that belong to each type.

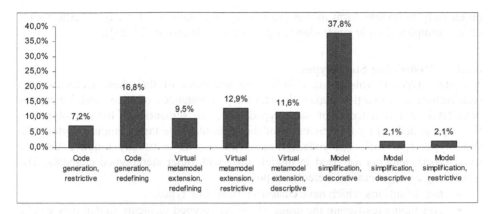

**Fig. 4.** Frequencies of types of stereotypes in the study

The figure shows that the most common type of stereotypes is type (model simplification, decorative). This observation shows that stereotypes are used to designate specific elements and their usage for altering the semantics of the extended elements is not very often.

## 6.    Properties of Types of Stereotypes

We examined stereotypes of each type by conducting a qualitative analysis of their definition and usage. Properties of each type of stereotype are presented in the following section grouped according to the role of stereotypes.

### 6.1.    Code Generation

Fig. 3 shows that there are two categories of code generation stereotypes, restrictive and redefining stereotypes. A close investigation of these two types: (code generation, restrictive) and (code generation, redefining). It shows that all code generation stereotypes possess common properties:

- base model elements (i.e. the elements the stereotype is extending) are usually concrete meta-classes from the UML metamodel as the concrete meta-classes have rules on how they should be used in the designs (some also have some standard code generation rules built into modeling tools),
- "templates" for code generation as part of the semantics of the stereotype; sometimes the "template" can be defined as a specific tagged value (provided that the code generator can interpret it), and
- no additional graphical icons defined for their presentation.

A way in which the templates for code generation are specified depends on the used code generator. The mechanisms of code generation should be investigated before creating code generation stereotypes (except, naturally, for profiles intended to be standardized – e.g. the UML Profile for CORBA – in which the templates can be

given only in textual form as the profiles are not dedicated for any specific tool –
other examples of code generation templates can be found in [27, 28]).

### 6.1.1.   Redefining Stereotypes

The stereotypes in this group redefine the semantics of their base elements. The
redefinition of semantics makes the stereotyped instances of base model elements
completely different from non-stereotyped ones. The semantics of the stereotypes of
this type is defined by the semantics of the element in the target language which the
stereotype represents. The redefinition of the semantics usually requires that the
stereotyped elements are used in models only with other stereotyped elements. The
redefining code generation stereotypes possess:

- tag definitions which have custom-defined data types,
- constraints restricting the usage of the stereotyped elements so that they can be
  used only with other stereotyped elements,
- semantics of the stereotyped elements that differs significantly from the
  semantics of the semantics of the model element being extended.

The data types of tag definitions are defined as part of the same profile. There exist
certain exceptions as not all tag definitions have custom defined data type. A few
stereotypes in the study had tag definitions which had standard data.

An example stereotype of this type is «CORBATypedef» from the UML profile for
CORBA. It is a stereotype that can be applied to classes. The stereotyped classes can
be used only with relation to classes that are stereotyped with other stereotypes from
the CORBA profile. Furthermore, the stereotyped classes cannot have attributes and
the code to be generated for the «CORBATypedef» stereotyped classes is very
different than the code to be generated from non-stereotyped classes.

### 6.1.2.   Restrictive Stereotypes

This type of stereotypes is used if an element in the target programming language is
similar to an existing model element in UML although it lacks certain properties.
Using model elements stereotyped with stereotypes of this type is allowed in most of
the cases when the base model element can be used, but there are restrictions on the
usage of the stereotyped elements(c.f. [6]). Stereotypes of this type have:

- tag definitions which types are custom-defined or built-in data types,
- constraints "restricting" the usage of the stereotyped elements in certain
  situations in which the base modeling element can be used,
- semantics making the semantics of the extended model element more precise.

The data types used for tag definitions can be both custom-defined (most often) or
built-in.

As example stereotype of this type is «CORBAStruct» from the UML Profile for
CORBA. The stereotype is applied to classes in UML and makes the semantics of
classes more precise, e.g. that all the attributes should be public. Its constraints state
that the «CORBAStruct» stereotyped class cannot be used in some situations when
the non-stereotyped class can be used.

## 6.2.   Virtual Metamodel Extension

Virtual metamodel extension stereotypes can be categorized into three categories in classification according to expressiveness: redefining, restrictive and descriptive. The virtual metamodel extension stereotypes are stereotypes that are used to add new constructs into UML.

### 6.2.1.   Redefining Stereotypes

Virtual metamodel extension stereotypes which are also redefining stereotypes are stereotypes that are intended to create a new (sub-) language based on UML. In many cases these stereotypes have been created based on metaclasses from another metamodel (further referred to as the defining metamodel). The defining metamodel specifies "a language" that is intended to be used as a member of the UML family of languages. Examples of this kind of metamodel-based profiles are the SPEM Profile or the UML Testing Profile [29]. They both have defining metamodels, which are then "translated" into UML profiles. The UML Profile for CORBA is similar, but the designers of the profile explicitly name the metamodel "virtual" and use only stereotypes in it.

The stereotypes of this type have:

- constraints stating that the stereotyped elements are allowed to be used only with other stereotyped elements,
- tag definitions (if defined) of custom-defined types (corresponding to attributes of the model element in the defining metamodel which is the basis for creating the stereotype),
- semantics of stereotypes in this group differs from the semantics of their base elements and is defined based on the defining metamodel (which is the base for abstractions denoted by stereotypes) and not the UML metamodel,
- base classes are concrete meta-classes in the UML metamodel as the redefinition of the semantics is usually restricted to only the concrete meta-class being extended, and
- icons with concrete syntax specified for the defining metamodel.

Examples of this type of stereotypes are stereotypes presented in [6] as typical redefining stereotypes, «actor» and «use case» in early versions of UML. These stereotypes change the meaning of the standard modeling elements (class) and in fact create a new kind of diagrams in UML (use case diagrams) which are different from class diagrams.

### 6.2.2.   Restrictive Stereotypes

The difference of this type in comparison to the previous type is that the semantics of the stereotypes is based on the semantics of the base model element, e.g. when the abstraction in the defining metamodel is based on an element in the UML metamodel. Just as the redefining virtual metamodel extension stereotypes they are based on defining metamodels. Thus the stereotypes in this group have:

- constraints restricting the usage of the stereotyped elements – they cannot always be used in places of the base model elements,

- base classes are most often (but not always) concrete meta-classes from the UML metamodel, the abstract meta-classes are rather uncommon as base classes for this type of stereotypes,
- tag definitions of custom-defined types (corresponding to attributes of the model element in the defining metamodel which is the basis for creating the stereotype),
- semantics making the semantics of the extended model element more precise, and
- icons with concrete syntax specified for the defining metamodel.

A representative of this type of stereotypes is «GRMdeploys» from the UML Profile for Performance, Schedulability and Time [30]. The stereotype restricts the usage of the stereotyped element in certain situations and the data type of the tag definition is custom-defined (defined as part of the same profile).

### 6.2.3.  Descriptive Stereotypes

Virtual metamodel extension stereotypes which are descriptive stereotypes are defined in order to make the structure of existing modeling elements more precise in a new context (although these stereotypes usually do not represent elements from any defining metamodel). They are characterized by:

- types of tag definitions being usually standard data types specified in the UML metamodel,
- base classes can be both abstract and concrete meta-classes from the UML metamodel,
- no constraints restricting the usage of the stereotyped elements, and
- usually no icons.

The tag definitions are usually used by external tools. An example stereotype of this type is the «GenericExport» stereotype from the TTDExport profile in Telelogic Tau G2. The intent of this stereotype is to provide means of connecting elements in the model with other artifacts, for example relating a class to a piece of Java code in Eclipse (but not for the generation of the code itself) or linking a class to a requirement in Telelogic DOORS.


### 6.3.  Model Simplification

Model simplification stereotypes are intended to be used for designating certain model elements. Thus they are usually the simplest of stereotypes and they merely change the concrete syntax of the stereotyped element. The name of the stereotype is usually the main element of its definition and it reveals the intention of the stereotype of all types of stereotypes for model simplification. Most of the stereotypes created for this purpose belong to the category of decorative stereotypes (90% of all model simplification stereotypes).  A common property of model simplification stereotypes is that their semantics is specified in a very loose form, e.g. only an intension of a decorative model simplification stereotype.

### 6.3.1.    Decorative Stereotypes

Most of the model simplification stereotypes are decorative stereotypes. They have the following properties:

- no tag definitions,
- no specific semantics, i.e. they are used for decoration of specific model elements, and
- icons associated with them to enable more effective recognition of stereotyped elements.

An example stereotype in this group is the stereotype «hidden» from the set of predefined stereotypes in Telelogic Tau G2. The stereotype means that the stereotyped elements should not be visible in a certain view in the tool. The stereotype does not add new properties to the extended model element, but it causes that stereotyped model elements are treated in a different way in model explorer in the tool (although they are treated in the same way as non-stereotypes model elements in models).

### 6.3.2.    Descriptive Stereotypes

Some model simplification stereotypes add properties to the stereotyped model elements. The tag definitions provide additional information about the "context" of making the element distinct. The properties of this group of stereotypes are:

- tag definitions which usually are of standard data types,
- no constraints, and
- no icons.

An example stereotype in this category is «commentedClass» from [5, p. 155] which provide means of adding information (as a tag definition) about authors of classes in UML designs thus making the stereotyped elements special in the design.

### 6.3.3.    Restrictive Stereotypes

Finally, there are also certain stereotypes, which to some extent restrict the usage of the stereotyped element though they are not intended to create a new modeling element (thus they are not virtual metamodel extension stereotypes). They are used to designate the elements and impose light restrictions on the elements denoting that the simplified element sometimes should not be used (the restrictions then designate the situations in which the stereotyped element should not be used). The restrictions are usually specified only informally. The properties of these stereotypes are:

- tag definitions which are usually of standard data types,
- constraints that restrict the usage of the stereotyped model element, and
- no icons.

An example stereotype which was found to be a restrictive model simplification in the study is «UseCasePackage» from the UML Profile for Software Development Processes [2, p. 4-4]. Applying the stereotype restricts the packages to be used only in specific contexts.

## 7.    Basic Guidelines on Assessing Quality

The elaborated properties of the types of stereotypes are to be used as assessment criteria. Modelers who use the properties for assessing quality of a particular stereotype should:
1) Find the type of the stereotype, i.e. answer the questions:
    a)    What is the purpose of the stereotype?
    b)    What changes the stereotype introduces to the base model element?
        i)    Does it redefine the semantics of the base model element (i.e. is it redefining)?
        ii)   Does it make the semantics of the base model element more precise (i.e. is it restrictive)?
        iii)  Does it add any tag definitions (i.e. is it descriptive)?
        iv)   If none of the above, then it is a decorative stereotype.
2) Check whether the stereotype has properties of the stereotypes of this type

The stereotypes which are of a good quality should possess the properties. These well-designed stereotypes save the effort for their maintenance since their definition is as easy as it is possible given their purpose. For example the model simplification stereotypes are very simple since they are used for simple purposes while the virtual metamodel extension stereotypes are more complex since they are dedicated for more advanced purposes.

There might be other types of stereotypes than the types found in the study although we made our best efforts to include stereotypes from various vendors and for diverse purposes in order to make the study as broad as possible. If the stereotype is of a type that is not included in the study it might be the case that the stereotype is too complex for the purpose it is supposed to serve (e.g. a redefining model simplification stereotype) and therefore it should be redesigned. Sometimes it is a case that a stereotype is intended to play two roles – then the stereotype should be redesigned and split into two stereotypes. It is important that the stereotypes are "coherent" in the sense that they are serving a single purpose and they are of a single type.

## 8.    Conclusions

Stereotypes play an important role in using UML in an effective way. The set of standard UML constructs is known to be insufficient for all purposes and the users of UML often create stereotypes to enrich their set of modeling elements. Since stereotypes are a notion which is defined by the users of the language and it is supposed to be instantiated in user models, thus being a part of the language, the quality assessment is specific. Furthermore, due to the fact that there are various reasons for which the stereotypes, these reasons influence the way in which the quality of stereotypes should be assessed. In this paper we provide a way in which a question "What is a good stereotype?" can be answered. This paper presents a part of the lightweight process for assessing quality of stereotypes and addresses the research question on how the existing stereotypes can be used for creating criteria for assessing quality of new stereotypes. It includes an investigation of a set of stereotypes used in industry aimed at identifying types of stereotypes. The types of stereotypes reflect the purpose for which the stereotypes are created and the changes which the stereotype introduces to its base model element.

The identified properties of stereotypes are designed to be used in assessing the quality of stereotypes that have already been created. The assessment is done in the final phase of creation of stereotypes. Currently in our research we focus on developing a set of guidelines for creating stereotypes which are appropriate for their purposes. The guidelines are intended to aid modelers to create "good" stereotypes for their purposes in a structured way. The intention of the guidelines are designed to be in a form of simple questions that would guide modelers through the process of creating the stereotype, beginning from an initial idea of what the stereotype is for and ending with the set of properties which the stereotype should possess. In our further research we intend to validate the method in a company creating a framework for model-driven software development.

# References

1. Object Management Group, "Unified Modeling Language Specification: Infrastructure Version 2.0", OMG, 2004, www.omg.org, last accessed 2004-02-20.
2. Object Management Group, "Unified Modeling Language Specification V. 1.5", OMG, 2003, www.omg.org, last accessed 2004-10-01.
3. Kuzniarz L. and Staron M., "On Practical Usage of Stereotypes in UML-Based Software Development", In the Proc. of Forum on Design and Specification Languages, Marseille, 2002, pp. 262-270.
4. Atkinson C., Kühne T., and Henderson-Sellers B., "Stereotypical Encounters of the Third Kind", In the Proc. of The 5th Int. Conf. on UML, Dresden, Germany, 2002, pp. 100-14.
5. Atkinson C., Kühne T., and Henderson-Sellers B., "Systematic Stereotype Usage", *Software and Systems Modeling*, vol. 2, 2003, pp. 153-163.
6. Berner S., Glinz M., and Joos S., "A Classification of Stereotypes for Object-Oriented Modeling Languages", In the Proc. of The 2nd Int. Conf. on UML, Fort Collins, CO, USA, 1999, pp. 249-64.
7. Miller J. and Mukerji J., "MDA Guide", OMG, 2003, http://www.omg.org/mda/, last accessed 2004-01-10.
8. Gogolla M. and Henderson-Sellers B., "Analysis of UML Stereotypes within the UML Metamodel", In the Proc. of The 5th Int. Conf. on UML, Dresden, Germany, 2002, pp. 84-99.
9. Atkinson C. and Kühne T., "Rearchitecting the UML Infrastructure", *ACM Trans. on Modeling and Comp. Simulation*, vol. 12, 2002, pp. 290-321.
10. Atkinson C. and Kühne T., "The Role of Metamodeling in MDA", In the Proc. of Workshop in Software Model Engineering, Dresden, Germany, 2002.
11. Atkinson C. and Kühne T., "Model-Driven Development: A Metamodeling Foundation", *IEEE Software*, vol. 20, 2003, pp. 36-41.
12. Schleicher A. and Westfechtel B., "Beyond Stereotyping: Metamodeling Approaches for the UML", In the Proc. of Hawaii Int. Conf. on Syst. Sciences, Maui, HI, USA, 2001, pp. 10-17.
13. Henningsson K., Wohlin, C., "Assuring Fault Classification Agreement - an Empirical Evaluation", *Proc.* Int. Symposium on Empirical Software Engineering, 2004, pp. 95-104.
14. Hertzum M., "Small-Scale Classification Schemes: A Field Study of Requirements Engineering", *Computer Supported Cooperative Work*, vol. 13, 2004, pp. 35-61.
15. Wirfs-Brock R., "Stereotyping: A Technique for Characterizing Objects and Their Interactions", *Object Magazine*, vol. 3, 1993, pp. 50-3.

16. Wirfs-Brock R., Wilkerson B., and Wiener L., "Responsibility-Driven Design: Adding to Your Conceptual Toolkit", *ROAD*, vol. 2, 1994, pp. 27-34.
17. Firesmith D. G., Henderson-Sellers B., and Graham I., "The Open Modeling Language (OML) Reference Manual", New York, Cambridge University Press/Sigs Books, 1998.
18. Object Management Group, "UML Specification ver. 1.1", OMG, 1997, www.omg.org, last accessed 2004-10-11.
19. Cook S., "The UML Family: Profiles, Prefaces and Packages", In the Proc. of The 3rd Int. Conf. on UML, York, UK, 2000, pp. 255-264.
20. Staron M., Kuzniarz L., and Wallin L., "A Case Study on Transformation Focused Industrial MDA Realization", In the Proc. of 3rd Workshop in Software Model Engineering, Lisbon, Portugal, 2004.
21. Evans A., Maskeri G., Sammut P., and Willians J. S., "Building Families of Languages for Model-Driven System Development", In the Proc. of 2nd Workshop in Software Model Engineering, San Francisco, CA, 2003.
22. Object Management Group, "Software Process Engineering Metamodel Specification 1.0", OMG, 2001, www.omg.org, last accessed 2004-02-01.
23. Object Management Group, "UML Profile for CORBA", OMG, 2002, www.omg.org, last accessed 2004-10-10.
24. Staron M., Kuzniarz L., and Wallin L., "Factors Determining Effective Realization of MDA in Industry", In the Proc. of 2nd Nordic Workshop on the Unified Modeling Language, Turku, Finland, 2004, pp. 79-91.
25. Telelogic, "Telelogic Tau G2", 2004, http://www.telelogic.com.
26. Altman D., "Practical Statistics for Medical Research", Chapman-Hall, 1991.
27. Kuzniarz L. and Ratajski J., "Code Generation Based on a Specific Stereotype", In the Proc. of Information Systems Modeling, Roznov, Chech Republic, 2002, pp. 119-128.
28. Sturm T., von Voss J., and Boger M., "Generating Code from UML with Velocity Templates", In the Proc. of The 5th Int. Conf. on UML, Dresden, Germany, 2002, pp. 150-161.
29. Object Management Group, "Unified Modeling Language: Testing Profile", OMG, 2004, www.omg.org, last accessed 2004-02-14.
30. Object Management Group, "UML Profile for Schedulability, Performance and Time", OMG, 2002, www.omg.org, last accessed 2003-09-20.

# A Modelling and Simulation Based Approach to Dependable System Design

Miriam Zia, Sadaf Mustafiz, Hans Vangheluwe, and Jörg Kienzle

School of Computer Science, McGill University
Montreal, Quebec, Canada
{mzia2, sadaf, hv, joerg} @cs.mcgill.ca

**Abstract.** Complex real-time system design needs to address dependability requirements, such as safety, reliability, and security. We introduce a modelling and simulation based approach which allows for the analysis and prediction of dependability constraints. Dependability can be improved by making use of fault tolerance techniques. The de-facto example in the real-time system literature of a pump control system in a mining environment is used to demonstrate our model-based approach. In particular, the system is modelled using the Discrete EVent system Specification (DEVS) formalism, and then extended to incorporate fault tolerance mechanisms. The modularity of the DEVS formalism facilitates this extension. The simulation demonstrates that the employed fault tolerance techniques are effective. That is, the system performs satisfactorily despite the presence of faults. This approach also makes it possible to make an informed choice between different fault tolerance techniques. Performance metrics are used to measure the reliability and safety of the system, and to evaluate the dependability achieved by the design. In our model-based development process, modelling, simulation and eventual deployment of the system are seamlessly integrated.

## 1 Introduction

Model-based approaches are used to represent the structure and behaviour of systems, which are becoming increasingly complex and involve a large number of components and domain-specific requirements [1][2]. Dependable systems, in particular, must satisfy a set of functional requirements, and in addition, must adhere to constraints which ensure correct behaviour of the system. Safety, security and reliability are a few such dependability requirements. The necessity for accomplishing these constraints has spawned new fields of research. The most prominent area is that of fault-tolerant systems, and the introduction of fault tolerance design in the software development process is an emerging topic.

We are interested in developing the model-based process illustrated in Fig. 1 for designing a dependable system. The process allows us to predict the behaviour of a specific system, and compare it to the behaviour of a fault-tolerant implementation of the same system. This is done through a sequence of manual activities. First, from functional requirements, a model is derived which represents the structure of a chosen system. A fault injection mechanism is also modelled as a means to generate faulty behaviour of the system. Simulation results indicate how the system performs in the

L. Briand and C. Williams (Eds.): MoDELS 2005, LNCS 3713, pp. 217–231, 2005.
© Springer-Verlag Berlin Heidelberg 2005

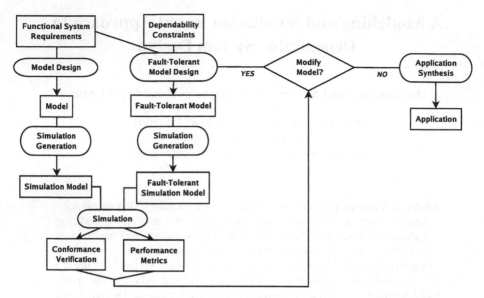

**Fig. 1.** The Model-based Process

presence of faults, and whether it conforms to the specified requirements. Secondly, from dependability constraints, a fault-tolerant model is created which includes techniques designed to improve on the initial system. A fault-tolerant simulation model is derived and simulated to gather performance data. This data reflects the dependability constraints that must be satisfied by the system.

Although research has been done in *formal modelling* and analysis of fault tolerance properties [3][4], either using natural language description of models, probabilistic models, figures of fault-trees or Markov models, we suggest using the formalism DEVS (*Discrete EVent System specification*). In our case study, the initial system as well as the fault tolerant system are translated into DEVS.

The paper is structured as follows. Section 2 presents essential background concepts relating to the DEVS formalism and to fault tolerance. Section 3 describes the real-time *Pump Control System* (PCS) chosen to demonstrate our process. We introduce its functional requirements and dependability constraints and briefly discuss why modelling and simulation is an appropriate approach, and why DEVS is an suitable modelling formalism. Section 4 introduces the model of the PCS, and the means by which fault injection is introduced in the system. A PCS failure situation is described in Section 5, and a fault-tolerant model is presented that counteracts this failure. Furthermore, safety and reliability are defined as the dependability constraints that are threatened by failure of the PCS. In Section 6, implementation-specific and experimental simulation framework details are outlined. Mathematical equations are presented to quantify the safety and reliability of the PCS, and results of the simulations are analyzed to compare the performance of the PCS in the two models. Finally, some general conclusions about our model-based process are drawn in Section 7.

## 2 Background

This section introduces the modelling formalism used in the case study, the *DEVS (Discrete EVent system Specification)* formalism and gives a brief overview of fault tolerance and the technique we apply in our work.

### 2.1 The DEVS Formalism

The DEVS formalism was introduced in the late seventies by Bernard Zeigler to develop a rigorous basis for the compositional modelling and simulation of discrete event systems [5][6]. The DEVS formalism has been successfully applied to the design and implementation of a plethora of different complex systems such as peer-to-peer networks [7], transportation systems [8], and complex natural systems [9]. In this section we briefly present the DEVS formalism.

A DEVS model is either *atomic* or *coupled*. An atomic model describes the behaviour of a reactive system. A coupled model is the composition of several submodels which can be atomic or coupled. Submodels have *ports*, which are connected by channels. Ports have a type: they are either *input* or *output* ports. Ports and channels allow a model to receive and send signals (events) from and to other models. A channel must go from an output port of some model to an input port of a different model, from an input port in a coupled model to an input port of one of its submodels, or from an output port of a submodel to an output port of its parent model.

An atomic model has, in addition to ports, a set of *states*, one of which is the *initial* state, and two types of transitions between states: *internal* and *external*. Associated with each state is a *time-advance* and an *output*.

**Atomic DEVS** [1]

An **atomic DEVS** is a tuple $(S, X, Y, \delta^{int}, \delta^{ext}, \lambda, \tau)$ where $S$ is a set of **states**, $X$ is a set of **input events**, $Y$ is a set of **output events**, $\delta^{int} : S \rightarrow S$ is the **internal transition function**, $\delta^{ext} : Q \times X \rightarrow S$ is the **external transition function**, $\lambda : S \rightarrow Y$ is the **output function** and $\tau : S \rightarrow \mathbb{R}_0^+$ is the **time-advance** function.

In this definition, $Q = \{(s, e) \in S \times \mathbb{R}^+ \mid 0 \leq e \leq \tau(s)\}$ is called the **total-state space**, for each $(s, e) \in Q$, $e$ is called the **elapsed-time**.[2]

Informally, the operational semantics of an atomic model are as follows: the atomic model starts in its initial state, and it will remain in any given state for as long as its corresponding time-advance specifies or until input is received on some port. If no input is received, when the time of the state expires, the model sends output as specified by $\lambda$ (before changing the state), and subsequently jumps to the new state as specified by $\delta^{int}$. On the other hand, if input is received before the time for the next internal transition expires, then it is $\delta^{ext}$ which is applied. The external transition depends on the current state, the time elapsed since the last transition and the inputs from the input ports.

The following definition formalises the concept of coupled DEVS models[3]

---

[1] For simplicity, we do not present a formalisation of the concept of "ports".

[2] $\mathbb{R}_0^+$ denotes the positive reals with zero included.

[3] For simplicity, this "formalisation" does not deal with ports, and it leaves out the proof of well-definedness for coupled models.

**Coupled DEVS**

A **coupled DEVS** named $D$ is a tuple $(X, Y, N, M, I, Z, select)$ where $X$ is a set of **input events**, $Y$ is a set of **output events**, $N$ is a set of **component names** such that $D \notin N$, $M = \{M_n \mid n \in N, M_n$ is a DEVS model (atomic or coupled) with input set $X_n$ and output set $Y_n\}$ is a set of DEVS **submodels**, $I = \{I_n \mid n \in N, I_n \subseteq N \cup \{D\}\}$ is a set of **influencer** sets for each component named $n$, $Z = \{Z_{i,n} \mid \forall n \in N, i \in I_n.Z_{i,n} : Y_i \to X_n$ or $Z_{D,n} : X \to X_n$ or $Z_{i,D} : Y_i \to Y\}$ is a set of **transfer functions** from each component $i$ to some component $n$, and $select : 2^N \to N$ is the **select** function.

Connectivity of submodels is expressed by the influencer set of each component. Note that for a given model $n$, this set includes not only the external models that provide inputs to $n$, but also its own internal submodels that produce its output (if $n$ is a coupled model.) Transfer functions represent output-to-input translations between components, and can be thought of as channels that make the appropriate type translations. The *select* function takes care of conflicts as explained below.

The semantics for a coupled model is, informally, the parallel composition of all the submodels. This is, each submodel in a coupled model is assumed to be an independent process, concurrent to the rest. There is no explicit method of synchronization between processes. Blocking does not occur except if it is explicitly modelled by the output function of a sender, and the external transition function of a receiver. There is however a *serialization* of events whenever there are two submodels that have a transition scheduled to be performed at the same time. Logically, the transitions are assumed to be done in that time instant, but its implementation on a sequential computer is serialized. The coupled model has a *select* function which chooses one of the models to undergo the transition first.

## 2.2 Fault Tolerance

Complex computer systems are increasingly built for highly critical tasks, from military and aerospace domains to industrial and commercials areas. They are critical in the sense that their failures may have severe consequences ranging from loss of business opportunities, physical damage, to more catastrophic loss, such as human lives. Systems with such responsibilities should be highly *dependable*. A number of varied means of achieving this goal have been established and should be considered jointly during hardware as well as software development: *fault prevention, fault removal, fault forecasting* and *fault tolerance* [10]. In particular, we will discuss fault tolerance in more detail in this section.

The idea of incorporating means for fault tolerance in order to achieve system dependability has developed considerably since the original work by von Neumann in the mid-1950s [11], and many techniques have been established. To discuss fault tolerance more meaningfully, a definition of *correct system behaviour* is needed: the specification. As long as the system satisfies the specification, it is considered to be behaving correctly. A failure can then be defined as an observable deviation from the system specification. An error is that part of the system state that leads to a failure. The error itself is caused by some defect in the system; those defects that cause observable errors are called *faults* [12]. Fault tolerance aims at preventing failures in the presence of hardware or software faults within the system. Therefore, as soon as an error has been detected, it must be corrected to ensure that a system continues to deliver its services and to avoid a potential failure later on in the execution.

These corrective measures need to be taken to keep the error from propagating to other parts of the system, thus preventing further damage. Once the error is under control, error recovery is applied and a correct error-free system state is restored. There are two basic recovery techniques [13]:

**Backward error recovery** replaces the erroneous system state with some previous correct state.

**Forward error recovery** attempts to construct a coherent, error-free system state by applying corrective actions to the current, erroneous state.

A popular form of forward error recovery is *Triple Modular Redundancy* (TMR). TMR uses three identical copies of a unit instead of one, and an intelligent, application-specific voting scheme which is applied to their output. In stateless cyclic systems, where one iteration of execution does not depend on the previous run, this mechanism allows for faults to be masked. This technique will be used in this case study to remedy the failure scenario discussed in section 5.1.

## 3   Modelling and Simulation Based Design: An Example

In Modelling and Simulation Based Design, all steps in the evolution from initial requirements to final system are explicitly modelled. Models at various stages of the process are each expressed in the most appropriate formalism. Transformations themselves are also modelled explicitly, so no knowledge is left implicit. Initially, the system is modelled in a formalism amenable to formal analysis and verification (covering all possible behaviours). Subsequently, simulation of the model is performed. The output of this simulation is processed by a checker, which checks it against a set of rules (derived from the requirements). An error found during this checking indicates an error in the design. Note that as even a large number of simulation runs may not cover all possible behaviours of the system, no positive statements about correctness of the model may be made. In the next phase, performance analysis is done to tune the model structure and parameters to satisfy performance requirements. Finally, code is synthesized from the model (if necessary), thus providing a continuous, traceable path from analysis model to deployed system. With appropriate model compilers, the simulation knowledge of the designer is limited to knowledge of suited formalisms (such as DEVS).

### 3.1   The Pump Control System Case Study

The system used to demonstrate our approach is a Pump Control System (PCS). The PCS has often been used in the real-time systems literature. For example, Burns and Lister used the PCS as a case study to discuss the TARDIS project [14]. We adopt the Pump Control System problem from [14], and with some abstractions, define it as our case study for modelling and simulation based design of a dependable system.

The basic task of the system is to pump to the surface the water that accumulates at the bottom of a mine shaft. The pump must be switched on when the *water-sensor* detects that the water has reached a *high-level* depth, and must be switched off when it detects that the level has been sufficiently reduced (*low-level*). In addition, the pump functionality depends on some atmospheric readings. A *methane-sensor* measures the level of methane in the environment: high levels may cause fire in the shaft if the pump is in operation. A *carbon monoxide-sensor* and an *air-flow sensor* also monitor the environment for critical readings (high for carbon monoxide and low for air-flow) which cause immediate evacuation of the shaft. Critical readings produced by all atmospheric sensors are sent to a human operator, but only critical methane readings cause the pump to switch off. To summarize, the pump is switched **ON** *if the water-level is high and methane-level is not critical, and is switched* **OFF** *if the water-level is low and pump is on; or if the pump is on and methane-level is critical.* The proposed architectural system structure for the PCS is illustrated in Fig. 2.

As all complex and critical applications, the PCS involves some important constraints, namely those of dependability, timing and security. This case study focuses on the dependability requirements defined for the PCS in [14] which dictate that the system is reliable and safe.

**Reliability** of the pump system is measured by the number of shifts that are lost if the pump does not operate when it should. In order to be considered reliable, our PCS should lose at most 1 shift in 1000.

**Safety** of the system is related to the probability that an explosion occurs as a result of the pump operating despite critical methane levels. In order to be considered safe, the probability of a possible explosion in our PCS should be less than $10^{-7}$ during the lifetime of the system.

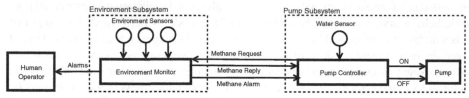

**Fig. 2.** The Pump Control System Logical Structure.

## 3.2   Why Use DEVS for the PCS?

The successful development of large-scale complex real-time systems commonly relies on system-theoretic modelling approaches, such as DEVS, or object-oriented approaches such as UML Real-Time. UML-RT is an extension to UML which, in addition to offering constructs to model relationships among components, incorporates the Real-Time Object-Oriented Modelling constructs and is used to model the structural and behavioural aspects of systems. The behaviour of the system is specified in StateCharts by the sequence of signal communication [15]. Contrary to DEVS, in StateCharts we cannot formally specify explicit timing in the specification of models. StateCharts are also based on multi-component specification and broadcast communication, and the lack of a complete formal definition of UML-RT StateChart semantics hinders the formal specification of structural information. Furthermore, although UML-RT offers important capabilities for modelling real-time systems, it does not provide semantics suitable for simulated time: it prohibits carrying out simulation studies. On the contrary, DEVS separates models from how they may be executed; therefore simulators can be independently developed and verified, thus increasing reusability, formal analysis, and model validation. In addition, DEVS allows the specification of both the structural and behavioural aspects of a system.

The PCS is a reactive discrete-event system: the system's state changes in reaction to external events, such as critical environmental readings. In addition, the PCS is composed of many different interacting subsystems. DEVS, being highly modularized and defining hierarchical coupling of modules, allows for the separation of concerns and a clean model of such a complex system. Since the aim of our approach is to improve the design of a real-time system, we can use the powerful simulation capabilities of DEVS to observe the faulty behaviour in the original PCS model and to predict the system's behaviour under different fault tolerance techniques. From the simulations one can gather statistical data on whether or not dependability requirements are met within the PCS, and evaluate alternative system designs. The above mentioned reasons make DEVS an appropriate modelling formalism for the Pump Control System.

## 4    Modelling the PCS

### 4.1    Building the DEVS Model of the PCS

Each subsystem illustrated in Fig. 2 (pump, environment, communication) is modelled as an atomic DEVS whose structure and behaviour encodes the functional requirements of the PCS (Fig. 3). Below is the general description of the system's model.

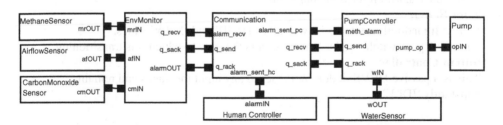

**Fig. 3.** The Pump Control System Modelled with the DEVS Formalism.

### Methane Sensor, Carbon Monoxide Sensor, Airflow Sensor

*States:* Sensor may either be 'READING' the level of gas or flow in the environment or 'IDLE' between readings.

*Output:* Upon transitioning from 'READING' to 'IDLE', the sensor outputs the level of gas or flow in the environment at that time.

**Environment monitor**

*States:* The monitor may either be processing sensor readings ('PROCESSING'), responding to a query ('QUERYING') or doing nothing ('IDLE').

*Output:* Upon receiving a query from the Pump Controller through the Communication channel, the monitor responds by sending an acknowledgement which contains a message stating the criticality of the methane level. Upon receiving critical readings from the environment sensors, it outputs alarms. All messages to and from the pump controller or to the human controller are sent through the Communication DEVS.

**Communication**

*States:* The communication channel may either be sending alarms ('SEND-ALARM'), sending a query to the environment monitor ('SEND-QUERY') or sending a query acknowledgement to the pump controller ('SEND-ACK'). When it completes either of these tasks, its state is 'IDLE'.

*Output:* Upon receiving a query from the Pump Controller, it forwards this query to the environment monitor, and once it receives the reply from the environment monitor, it propagates it to the pump controller. When it receives critical alarms, it delivers them to the human and pump controllers.

**Pump Controller**

*States:* It may either be processing a water sensor reading and sending an operation to the pump ('PROCESSING-WATER'), processing a methane alarm ('PROCESSING-ALARM'), processing a query acknowledgement ('PROCESSING-ACK'), or doing nothing ('IDLE').

*Output:* Upon receiving a low-water reading, the pump controller sends an "off" message to the pump to switch it off. If the controller receives a high-water reading, it turns the pump to ready mode and sends a query to the environment monitor: the controller only turns the pump on if the methane level is not critical. If an acknowledgement is received stating that the methane level is high, then the controller turns the pump off, otherwise, it turns it on. Similarly, when the controller receives a methane alarm, it turns the pump off.

**Water Sensor**

*States:* It randomly switches between the 'HIGH' and 'LOW' states.

*Output:* Upon switching, the sensor outputs the state to which it is transitioning.

**Human Controller**

This is a passive DEVS: it does not react to any input messages and remains constantly 'IDLE'.

## 4.2    Modelling of Fault Injection in the PCS

As dependability constraints need to be met in addition to functional requirements, a quantitative analysis method for assessing the dependability of the system must also be modelled. For this purpose, many methods have been defined, such as reliability block diagrams, analysis of non-deterministic state graph models, and fault simulation [10]. The latter is a universal approach combining techniques which assume a model of the system, a set of external input/output sequences applied to it, and the possibility to inject faults into it. Most of these techniques can be classified as fault injection techniques, which consist in adding faults to a system in order to analyze the behaviour. These faults make the system evolve towards different states which are recorded in order to assess the dependability constraints.

Therefore, in addition to modelling the PCS, a model for fault injection must be built. A fault injector could be described as an atomic entity on its own in the coupled DEVS model. However, modelling faults within a specific subsystem itself more accurately represents its real-world faulty behaviour. Our approach consists in provoking a sensor break-down on a periodic basis to simulate a fault which makes the Pump Control subsystem fail. For example, a fault in the methane sensor would generate faulty (noisy) methane readings of the environment, which would be propagated to the environment monitor, and through the communication subsystem to the pump controller. This wrong methane reading could possibly force the pump to shut off when it is not supposed to, or it might fail to cause a critical alarm to be raised. The simulation results should show how the performance varies over time in the absence and presence of faults.

We concentrate here on the consequence of the methane sensor failure on the safety and reliability requirements of the PCS (Section 5.1). To model faulty behaviour of a methane sensor $s$, we assign to it a probability $p$ of failure. We assume Byzantine failures, i.e. upon failing, sensors produce an erroneous result rather than no result at all. Therefore, $s$ fails by providing erroneous readings with probability $p$. In practice, a sensor has a very low failure probability, however in this case study, the simulated probability $p$ is chosen to be significantly higher to induce more erroneous states and observable failure of the system. For the methane sensor, we assume $p = 0.1$.

## 5  Modelling the Fault-Tolerant System

### 5.1  Failure Scenario in the PCS

Burns and Lister [14] describe four failure situations at the environment, communication and pump subsystems level for the PCS that affect the dependability. To illustrate our approach, we consider the situation in which the environment subsystem provides an incorrect methane reading (when asked by the pump subsystem). The case study focuses on the role of the environment subsystem on safety and reliability, thus upper-bounding the measure of dependability of the system by the dependability of the environment subsystem. We assume that no mechanical failures occur in the communication and pump subsystems and that they do not introduce erroneous state.

The environment subsystem fails in a noisy manner, i.e. it generates incorrect/noisy output. Since we only investigate hardware faults, we assume failures originate in the methane sensor: the subsystem provides incorrect methane readings if it receives such incorrect values from the sensor itself. Therefore, we can generalize the failure scenario to that of the methane sensor providing an incorrect methane reading.

**Safety of the System.** The safety requirement is threatened if the sensor outputs a falsely low methane reading which causes the pump to operate despite critical concentrations in the environment. This introduces a threat of explosion in the mine shaft. However, if the sensor outputs a false reading whose criticality is in accordance with the accurate reading, i.e. it is critical when the accurate reading is critical, and not critical when the accurate reading is not critical, then the system is still considered to be safe.

**Reliability of the System.** The reliability requirement is threatened if the sensor outputs a falsely high methane reading which causes the pump to shut down despite non-critical concentrations in the environment. This causes a loss of shift for the pump.

Safety and reliability can be improved by replication of the methane sensors and applying the TMR technique [14]. This method can also be used for the carbon monoxide and airflow sensors.

### 5.2 Modelling Fault Tolerance for the PCS

We change the PCS model to integrate fault tolerance based on TMR. A coupled DEVS containing three sets of methane sensors and a voter replace the sensor modelled in Fig. 3. In this case, even if one methane sensor fails, the correct reading can still be determined using the output of the other sensors, and a response from the voter is passed on to the environment monitor. This approach can also be applied to the carbon monoxide and airflow sensors. The fault-tolerant environment subsystem is shown in Fig. 4. In our experiment, we use two different types of voters, a *maximum* voter and a *majority* voter. The maximum voter is a PCS-specific voter in which the highest value received from the replicated sensors is considered as accurate. The interest in the highest value resides in the fact that the system must be safe: if the pump is switched on while methane levels are critical, safety is threatened. Thus, the maximum voter is an appropriate choice for this problem. The majority voter is a well-studied voter that given $n$ results selects the value of the majority. In our case, if majority cannot be decided, the voter falls back on the maximum value.

The fault injection in the sensors is modelled similarly to the PCS model. This allows us to compare the behaviour of the two systems and observe how the performance changes.

## 6   Simulation and Results

### 6.1   Performance Metrics Modelling

In the previous sections we showed how the PCS and the fault-tolerant PCS are modelled using DEVS. In order to perform dependability analysis, we model the safety and reliability as dependability metrics to be evaluated while the simulation runs. Each simulation keeps track of the total number of methane readings performed (*TotalMethaneReadings*). A reading $m_i$ is associated with a safety conformance index $s_i$ and a reliability conformance index $r_i$. These indices are equal to 0 if the reading causes a safety-threatening (for $s_i$) or reliability-threatening (for $r_i$) fault, and 1 otherwise. Then safety of the system can be determined by $\sum_{i=1}^{n} s_i$/TotalMethaneReadings, and reliability by $\sum_{i=1}^{n} r_i$/TotalMethaneReadings (where $n$ is equal to *TotalMethaneReadings*).

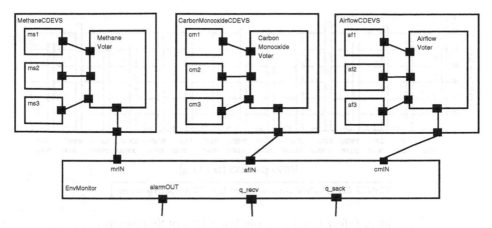

**Fig. 4.** Fault-tolerant Environment Subsystem of the Pump Control System

## 6.2 Implementation

Once the system and the constraints are modelled, they are implemented using the PythonDEVS package [16]. This package provides a simulation engine and a class architecture that allows hierarchical DEVS models to be easily defined. Using this framework, each atomic and coupled DEVS described in the model of the PCS, the fault-tolerant PCS using *maximum* voting, and the fault-tolerant PCS using majority voting, can be encoded into a Python class. Python is an interpreted object-oriented programming language, which offers high-level data types and a simple syntax. Its main advantage for the PCS case study is that it is an ideal language for quick and simple application development.

Each Python class representation of a DEVS has four functions defined in it: an internal transition function, an external transition function, an output function and a time-advance function. Next, simulation experiments are set-up to gather statistical data which is representative of the system's behaviour under the specified constraints. The following summarizes the experimental framework:

- **Time advances:** A methane reading is generated every 2s, carbon monoxide every 6s, airflow every 5s, and water level is checked every 10s.
- **Reading Interval:** All environmental readings are integers in the interval $[0, 10]$. We chose integers to avoid the errors common in voters when comparing floating point numbers.
- **Critical Readings:** The critical concentrations are defined in the reading interval to be 7 for methane, 5 for carbon monoxide and 3 for airflow.
- **Simulation Time:** Two sets of experiments are conducted. In the first set, each model is run for a duration of 2000 simulation time units (seconds). This process is repeated 5 times, starting from the same initial state. In the second set, each model is run for a duration of 75000 simulation units to satisfy the law of large numbers. As with the first set, this process is also repeated 5 times. For each of these runs, safety and reliability results are logged and analyzed.

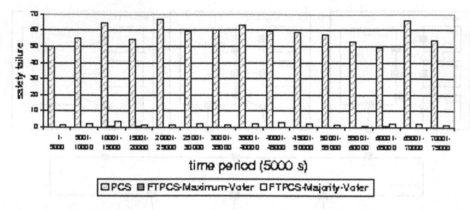

**Fig. 5.** Safety Results for the Second Set of Simulations.

## 6.3 Results

Since the results of the first set of simulations are comparable, only results of the second set are analyzed here. These results are an indicator of which voter is best suited for the PCS with regards to system safety and reliability.

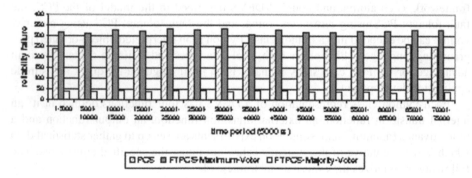

**Fig. 6.** Reliability Results for the Second Set of Simulations.

**Safety.** In the initial model, the average failure to satisfy the safety requirement is 2.32%, which is considerably high for a system in which failures are catastrophic in nature. In the fault-tolerant model using the maximum voter, the average safety rises to 99.99% (Fig. 5). It can be concluded that TMR with maximum voting reduces the occurrence of safety-threatening failures. However, there is a notable trade-off between safety and reliability here. This is not surprising as the choice of maximum voter was made to emphasize the safety requirement in such a critical system.

**Reliability.** In the initial model, the average failure to satisfy the reliability requirement is 10.09%, which is proportional to the probability that was associated with the methane sensor DEVS of 10% failure. In the implementation with the maximum voter, the reliability percentage falls even lower (Fig. 6). This is explained by the fact that the maximum voter always picks the highest value to output, be it accurate or false. For example, a case where the actual reading is 2, but the false reading received is 8, then 8 is voted to be the correct reading. This approach advocates safety of the system at the cost of reduced reliability of the sensors. In order to attain a fair balance between the safety and reliability requirements, the use of a majority voter is advised. The majority voter implementation results in an average reliability of 98.3%, but a slight decrease in the safety can be seen in Fig. 5. However, this is clearly a solid improvement on the original model and on the maximum voter, while still preserving safety.

## 6.4   Validation of Results

Over the years, a lot of work has been done on estimating software reliability based on probabilistic models. To compare our simulation-based approach to an analytic one, we perform a probabilistic assessment of the reliability based on the fault-tolerant model that uses majority voting and on the same assumptions as those used for our simulation. We assume that a methane sensor produces an integer reading $r \in [0, 10]$. The sensor either works correctly, or fails with a probability $p$ by outputting a random reading uniformly distributed between 0 and 10.

As discussed previously, reliability fails when a falsely critical reading is sent to the environment monitor although the actual reading is non-critical. There are three cases that lead to a wrong decision by the voter, and can be considered separately. The total probability of the voter failing to decide on the correct output is then equal to the probability that the correct reading is non-critical (which is 7/11) multiplied by the sum of the probabilities corresponding to the cases listed below:

- one sensor outputs a correct reading, two sensors output equal, critical and false reading: $3 * (1 - p) * (p * 4/11) * (p * 1/11)$
- all three sensors output wrong readings, but at least two are equal, critical and false reading: $p^3 * ((4/11)(1/11) + 2(7/11)(4/11)(1/11))$
- all three sensors output wrong distinct readings, and at least one is critical: $p^3 * (1 - 7/11 * 6/11 * 5/11) * (10/11 * 9/11)$

Since we assume that $p = 0.1$ for the methane sensor, this leads to a majority voter failure probability of 0.0061, or a reliability of 99.39%. The results of our simulation indicated a reliability of 98.3%, clearly comparable to the results derived from the analytic model.

This probabilistic assessment leads to exact and precise results, but in cases where the problem is non-linear, the equations may become very complex and impossible to solve. On the other hand, the approach presented in this paper is especially effective for complex systems for which deriving mathematical models is not feasible. One might argue that this approach requires extensive work in designing and encoding the models, and in analyzing the simulation results. However, models are easily derived from the requirements and logical structure of the system. Furthermore, the choice of modelling formalism and programming language make for a modular implementation, and if tools are available which automatically generate the applications, the process can be speedy. Lastly, simulation results are simple to analyze as they are derived from such simple equations as those described in Section 6.1. Mathematical models do not have these advantages. However, probabilistic models can be useful as a validation method for modelling and simulation based approaches as well as provide solutions to rare-event cases.

# 7 Conclusion

In most complex systems today, it is crucial to guarantee that the dependability requirements are successfully achieved. Methods should be provided which can accurately assess what level of dependability has been attained by a system. In this paper, we have presented a modelling and simulation-based development process targeted towards dependable systems, and have demonstrated it through an application to the safety-critical Pump Control System.

A continuity was maintained throughout the development process. We started from requirements, mapped these to a DEVS model, extended the model to consider the dependability constraints, defined performance metrics, implemented the model using the PythonDEVS framework, and performed simulations whose results reflected the safety and reliability of the system. DEVS is deemed the most appropriate formalism for modelling both the system under study and the fault tolerance techniques. This, as discrete-event models are clearly at the right abstraction level, and because of the compositionality of the DEVS formalism. Fault tolerance, more specifically TMR, was used as a means to achieve dependability. In this approach, two types of voters were used, and the simulation results were inspected to decide which voter best satisfied the dependability requirement. The results indicated that this outlined method improved the dependability levels of the example system.

We have shown how models can be useful for designing dependable systems: a model can be extended to address possible failures and to incorporate fault tolerance techniques that overcome them. This approach allows us to predict behaviour and estimate system dependability, and it enables an informed decision on which fault tolerance technique to apply. If such a step is taken during the analysis and design phase of any project, development cost is reduced as an optimal system is built right the first time, while fault tolerance is addressed earlier on in the development cycle, and simulation results emulate the expected behaviour of the dependable system.

We plan to further investigate a generic *process* for the analysis and design of dependable systems. Furthermore, we will use the fault-tolerant models to synthesize the final application.

# References

[1]  Gray, J., Rossi, M., Tolvanen, J.P., eds.: Domain-Specific Modeling with Visual Languages. Volume 15 of Journal of Visual Languages & Computing. Elsevier Science Publishers (2004)

[2] Vangheluwe, H., de Lara, J.: Domain-specific modelling for analysis and design of traffic networks. In Ingalls, R., Rossetti, M., Smith, J., Peters, B., eds.: Winter Simulation Conference, IEEE Computer Society (2004)

[3] Pfeifer, H., von Henke, F.W.: Formal modelling and analysis of fault tolerance properties in the time-triggered architecture. In: 5th Symposium on Formal Methods for Automation and Safety in Railway and Automotive Systems. (2004)

[4] Boue, J., Arlat, J., Crouzet, Y., Petillon, P.: Verification of fault tolerance by means of fault injection into VHDL simulation models. In: Contrat Esprit DeVa Project. (1996)

[5] Zeigler, B.P.: Multifacetted Modelling and Discrete Event Simulation. Academic Press (1984)

[6] Zeigler, B.P., Praehofer, H., Kim, T.G.: Theory of Modeling and Simulation, Second Edition. Integrating Discrete Event and Continuous Complex Dynamic Systems. Academic Press (2000)

[7] Cheon, S., Seo, C., Park, S., Zeigler, B.: Design and implementation of distributed DEVS simulation in a peer to peer network system. In: 2004 Advanced Simulation Technologies Conference, Design, Analysis, and Simulation of Distributed Systems Symposium 2004 (2004)

[8] Chi, S., Lee, J.: DEVS-based modeling and simulation for intelligent transportation systems. In Sarjoughian, H.S., Cellier, F.E., eds.: Discrete event modeling and simulation: A tapestry of systems and AI-based theories and methodologies. Springer-Verlag (2001) 215–227

[9] Filippi, J., Chiari, F., Bisgambiglia, P.: Using jDEVS for the modeling and simulation of natural complex systems. In: SCS AIS 2002 Conference on Simulation in Industry. Volume 1. (2002)

[10] Geffroy, J.C., Motet, G.: Design of Dependable Computing Systems. Kluwer Academic Publishers (2002)

[11] von Neumann, J.: Probabilistic logics and the synthesis of reliable organisms from unreliable components. In Shannon, C.E., McCarthy, J., eds.: Annals of Math Studies. Princeton University Press (1956) 43–98

[12] Laprie, J.C.: Dependable computing and fault tolerance : Concepts and terminology. In Meyer, J.F., Morgan, D.E., eds.: 15th FTCS. (1985)

[13] Lee, P.A., Anderson, T.: Fault tolerance - principles and practice. In: Dependable Computing and Fault-Tolerant Systems. 2nd edn. Springer Verlag (1990)

[14] Burns, A., Lister, A.: An architectural framework for timely and reliable distributed information systems (TARDIS): Description and case study. Technical report, University of York (1990)

[15] Huang, D., Sarjoughian, H.: Software and simulation modeling for real-time software-intensive system. In: Proceedings of the 8th IEEE International Symposium on DS-RT. (2004)

[16] Bolduc, J.S., Vangheluwe, H.L.: The modelling and simulation package pythonDEVS for classical hierarchical DEVS. Technical report, McGill University (2001)

# Extending Profiles with
# Stereotypes for Composite Concepts[1]

Dick Quartel, Remco Dijkman, Marten van Sinderen

Centre for Telematics and Information Technology, University of Twente,
PO Box 217, 7500 AE Enschede, The Netherlands
{D.A.C.Quartel, R.M.Dijkman, M.J.vanSinderen}@utwente.nl

**Abstract.** This paper proposes an extension of the UML 2.0 profiling mechanism. This extension facilitates a language designer to introduce composite concepts as separate conceptual and notational elements in a modelling language. Composite concepts are compositions of existing concepts. To facilitate the introduction of composite concepts, the notion of stereotype is extended. This extension defines how a composite concept can be specified and added to a language's metamodel, without modifying the existing metamodel. From the definition of the stereotype, rules can be derived for transforming a language element that represents a composite concept into a composition of language elements that represent the concepts that constitute the composite. Such a transformation facilitates tool developers to introduce tool support for composite concepts, e.g., by re-using existing tools that support the constituent concepts. To illustrate our ideas, example definitions of stereotypes and transformations for composite concepts are presented.

## 1 Introduction

The profiling mechanism, as defined in the UML 2.0 Infrastructure Specification [10], is a lightweight metamodel extension mechanism. It allows one to specialize any language, provided its metamodel is defined in the MOF, by specializing existing concepts that are represented in the metamodel of that language. By defining profiles on top of a general-purpose language one can re-use tools for the general-purpose language to support the languages that are defined by the profiles. Furthermore, one can develop dedicated languages for specific stages in the design process or specific application domains. Hence, the profiling mechanism combines the efficiency of general purpose languages with the intuitive clarity of dedicated languages.

We claim however that besides specialization, the profiling mechanism should support the extension of metamodels with composite concepts, i.e., concepts that are defined as compositions of existing concepts. In general, the introduction of composite concepts and associated language elements facilitates the task of a modeller and

---

[1] This work is part of the Freeband A-MUSE project (http://a-muse.freeband.nl), which is sponsored by the Dutch government under contract BSIK 03025.

L. Briand and C. Williams (Eds.): MoDELS 2005, LNCS 3713, pp. 232-247, 2005.

increases the clarity of models, because frequently occurring compositions of concepts can be replaced by composite concepts. In addition, the possibility of defining
composite concepts allows one to use a general-purpose language consisting of a
limited number of elementary and generic concepts. More complex concepts can then
be defined as compositions of those elementary and generic concepts. The benefit of
such an approach is that, on the one hand, it is easy to maintain consistency and tool
support for a limited set of elementary concepts, while, on the other hand, it provides
clarity and ease of use, because complex concepts can be defined directly and clearly.

For example, consider the extension of the UML 2.0 action semantics with a TimedOperationCall, which represents the handling of an operation call, including the possibility to set a maximal completion time. A timed operation call involves a number of
elementary actions, such as CallOperationAction, AcceptCallAction, ReplyAction and AcceptTimeEventAction (see also the elaboration of this example in section 3.3). This
means one has to be able to define which elementary actions are involved and how
these actions are related. This is however not possible by defining a timed operation
call as a stereotype of an existing concept using the current profiling mechanism.

The contribution of this paper is twofold. First, we propose an extension of the
UML 2.0 profiling mechanism with stereotypes for composite concepts. These stereotypes should leave the existing metamodel unmodified. Second, we describe how
rules can be derived from the stereotypes to transform a composite concept into the
corresponding composition of (elementary) concepts. Such transformation rules can
be used to generate tools supporting the dedicated modelling languages that use the
composite concepts, based on existing tools for the general-purpose language.

This paper is further structured as follows. Section 2 describes the profiling
mechanisms and the trade-off between profiling and metamodelling. Section 3 introduces stereotypes for specifying composite concepts. Section 4 explains how model
transformation can be used to implement these stereotypes. Section 5 illustrates some
applications of our ideas. And section 6 presents conclusions and future work.

## 2 Profiling

Profiling allows one to extend an existing language metamodel with specializations of
metaclasses and with constraints. The purpose of such an extension is to adapt a language for a particular application domain, development platform or design method.
For example, one may want to support specific concepts, notation or terminology. An
important restriction is that profiling does not allow one to modify the existing metamodel. Profiling in UML 2.0 can be applied to any MOF-compliant metamodel.

### 2.1 Profiles Package

Figure 1 depicts the Profiles package from the Infrastructure specification [10]. A
*profile* is a kind of package that extends an existing metamodel or profile. A profile
contains stereotypes. A *stereotype* extends (specializes) an existing metaclass or
stereotype. This *extension* is defined by a specialized association between the stereo-

type and the extended metaclass. Through the extension each instance of the stereotype is associated with an instance of the metaclass that it extends. A *profile application* defines which profiles have been applied to some package.

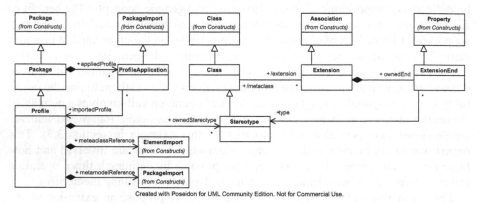

Fig. 1. The classes defined in the Profiles package.

Figure 2 depicts an example of the definition of an EJB profile. A profile is defined as a package stereotyped <<profile>>. A stereotype is denoted by the keyword <<stereotype>> above the stereotype name. An extension association is represented by a filled arrow pointing from the stereotype to the metaclass. The constraint {required} defines that the extension is required, which means that an instance of Bean, i.e., an instance of Entity or Session, must always be linked to an instance of Component. In general, constraints can be associated with stereotypes to specify rules and restrictions on their use. Just like a class, a stereotype may have properties (attributes). These properties extend the properties of the extended metaclass or stereotype. For example, attribute state of stereotype Session defines whether a session object is stateful or stateless. The values of stereotype properties are also referred to as *tagged values*. Package Conference illustrates how the EJB profile can be applied, which is represented by an import association stereotyped <<apply>>. Because state is a meta-attribute of stereotype Session, its value can not be set directly by the ConferenceManagement class, but can be set in a comment box that starts with the name of the stereotype.

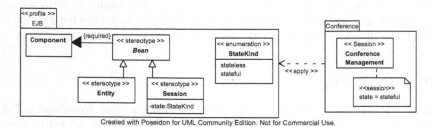

Fig. 2. Example of profiling.

We would like to stress that the Profiles package only provides a way to extend the metamodel, i.e., the abstract syntax, of some language. Language extension also involves the definition of the semantics and concrete syntax for the metamodel extension. This has to be done separately.

## 2.2  Profiling Versus Metamodelling

In general, two approaches to metamodel extension can be distinguished, which are often referred to as 'profiling' and 'metamodelling'. Profiling refers to the extension mechanism described in section 2.1. Metamodelling refers to the definition of metamodels. An essential difference between both approaches is that profiling starts from an existing metamodel and does not modify this metamodel, whereas metamodelling involves the creation of a new or the modification of an existing metamodel.

The metamodelling approach can always be used instead of profiling. Metamodelling has to be used in case some of the modelling concepts that have to be represented by the metamodel can not be obtained as specializations of existing concepts. Furthermore, if one has a stable set of modelling concepts, one may want to create a separate metamodel and develop dedicated tools, since this pays off by having better modelling and tool support.

Instead, the profiling approach is meant to provide a lightweight extension mechanism that is more easy to use by language developers and more easy to support by tools. This approach can only be used in case the required modelling concepts are specializations of existing concepts. From the MDA perspective this seems sufficient to facilitate the development of transformations from general models (PIMs) to more specific models (PSMs). However, a more expressive profiling mechanism may facilitate the MDA approach even further. In particular, we claim that an extension mechanism for composite concepts is useful and can be introduced while maintaining the lightweight character of profiling. Section 5 discusses some applications of such an extension mechanism for composite concepts.

The characteristic that an existing metamodel is left unmodified has been an important motivation to propose an extension of the profiling approach. The profiling approach avoids that an existing metamodel is compromised, helps to shield distinct language extensions from each other, and facilitates re-use of tool support. One could argue that the same benefits can be achieved by structuring metamodels and their extensions properly, but this would require much more expertise from the language developer. Furthermore, the choice to extend the profiling mechanism should not be considered as a (strong) preference for stereotypes to define language extensions. In fact, some of the ideas underlying the definition of stereotypes for composite concepts can also be used when following a metamodelling approach (see also section 3.3).

Several papers [1,2,3,4,8,15] discuss the principles of and problems associated with metamodelling and profiling in more detail.

# 3 Specification of Composite Concepts

A concept represents some system property that is considered essential in the development of (software) systems. Concepts form the building blocks for constructing models. A model consists of one or more concept instances, representing the system properties that are conceived by the developer and considered relevant in relation to the purpose of the model in the development process.

An *elementary concept* represents an elementary system property, and forms the smallest unit for constructing models. We define a *composite concept* as a composition of concept instances, where a concept can be an elementary or a composite concept. We define a *structure concept* as a composition of concepts (rather than concept instances). The difference between a structure concept and a composite concept is that, if we want to use a structure concept in a model, we still have to decide on what instances of its constituents we want to use and how we want to associate them. Consequently, a structure concept represents a set of composite concepts, i.e., one for each possible composition of instances of the structure concept.

Composite and structure concepts are commonly used during a development process, either explicitly or implicitly. Examples are compositions, patterns or groupings of model elements; e.g., a transaction that consists of multiple related operation calls is an example of a composite concept, and the StructuredActivityNode in UML's activities that represents a group of activity nodes and edges is an example of a structure concept.

## 3.1 Representing Composite and Structure Concepts

We represent a composite or structure concept as a class that is related to its constituents by composite aggregations. For example, figures 3(i) and 3(ii) depict metamodels representing the structure concepts ATask and BTask, respectively, which consist of the elementary concepts Action and Flow.

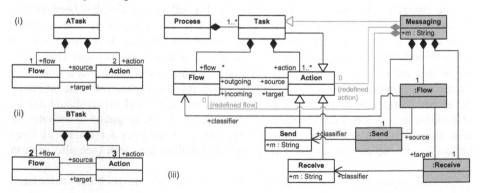

**Fig. 3.** Composite concepts.

One may be tempted to interpret the metamodel of figure 3(i) at an instance level, such that it represents: a task consisting of two actions that are related by a flow. However, the metamodel of figure 3(i) can only be interpreted at type level, such that it represents: a task consisting of two actions and a flow between (any) two actions. The difference between both interpretations becomes clearer in case of the metamodel of figure 3(ii), which represents: a task consisting of three actions and two flows, but does not define which actions are related by a flow. Also the metamodel of figure 3(i) does, strictly speaking, not define which actions are related by a flow.

We conclude that a composite aggregation between a structure concept and a constituent concept can be used to represent that an instance of the structure concept contains instances of the constituent concept, where the number of instances is determined by the multiplicity constraint. In addition, associations can be defined between the constituent concepts, but these associations represent associations at type level and can not be used to define associations between instances of the constituent concepts. Consequently, this way of specifying a structure concept does not allow one to define how the constituents of a composite concept are related at instance level.

To represent the instances that a composite concept consists of as well as their associations, we use the notion of *instantiation*. An instantiation represents a particular instance, but at a higher meta-level than the instance itself[2]. This allows one to define a composite concept as a composition of instantiations, which define the instances that should be created upon instantiation of the composite instance.

To represent instantiation, we use the UML metaclass InstanceSpecification, as defined in [10]. An InstanceSpecification represents an instance in a modelled system. Instances of any classifier can be specified, so not only instances of a class but also of an association. Furthermore, values can be specified for the structural features of the instance. Figure 3(iii) depicts the definition of composite concept Messaging, which consists of an instance of a Send action, a Receive action and a Flow, where Send and Receive are defined as specialized actions. An instance specification is expressed using the same notation as its classifier, with the classifier name replaced by the concatenation of the instance name (if any), a colon symbol and the classifier name. Constraints can be added, e.g., to specify that the contents of the message in the anonymous instances :Send and :Receive must be equal to the message specified in Messaging.

## 3.2  Extended Profiles Package

Figure 4 depicts an Extended Profiles package that supports the extension of metamodels with stereotypes for composite concepts. A composite concept is defined using the metaclasses CompositeStereotype, ConstituentClass(End), ConstituentAssociation(End), ClassInstantiation and AssociationInstantiation. A CompositeStereotype represents the composite concept and inherits from Stereotype to define that it extends an existing metaclass or stereotype. A ConstituentClass represents a composite aggregation between a composite stereotype and an instantiation of one of its constituent classes. An instantiation is defined as a kind of InstanceSpecification. Similarly a ConstituentAssociation represents a composite aggregation between a composite stereotype and an instantiation of one of its constituent associations. A ConstituentAssociation is related to the class instantiations that it will associate.

---

[2] In Merriam-Webster Online, *instantiate* is defined as "to represent (an abstraction) by a concrete instance".

The package defines how stereotypes can be defined, but does not enforce one to define how these stereotypes can be used in relation to existing metaclasses and stereotypes. However, both in case of a 'regular' stereotype and in case of a composite stereotype this is no issue, since a stereotype is defined as an extension of an existing metaclass, thereby 'inheriting' via the extended metaclass the associations that are defined between this metaclass and other metaclasses.

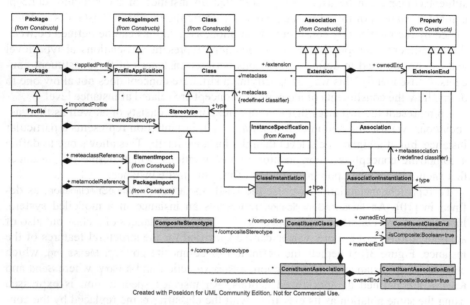

**Fig. 4**. The classes defined in the Extended Profiles package.

Hence, by extending an existing metaclass, a composite stereotype defines its possible associations with other existing metaclasses implicitly. The possible associations of the stereotype's constituents and these metaclasses are however not defined in this way. We call these associations the *context relations* of a stereotype. The context relations define how associations between the composite stereotype and other metaclasses must be replaced by associations between the composite's constituents and other meta-classes. We note, however, that associations between a composite's constituents and other meta-classes can only exist in the model, after the composite concept is replaced by its constituents. Otherwise, an inconsistent model may be the result. We represent context relations as OCL constraints. Since context relations represent changes to a model, we define the OCL constraints as constraints on operations that define these changes.

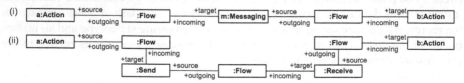

**Fig 5**. Example object models.

For example, consider the object model in figure 5(i). The context relations between the constituents of messaging task m and actions a and b are not defined by the definition of Messaging in figure 3(iii). We define the following context relations. Each association that relates an incoming flow to an instance of Messaging, must relate that incoming flow to the Send action of that instance instead. Each association that relates an instance of Messaging to an outgoing flow, must relate the flow to the Receive action of that instance instead. In addition, if a messaging concept instance is defined as part of a process or task, its constituents must be added to this process or task instead. Figure 5(ii) depicts the object model that results from replacing object m by the corresponding composition of elementary concept instances. We express the context relation regarding incoming flows in OCL as follows, where operation processContextRelations is assumed to implement the context relations when replacing a Messaging object by its constituents:

```
context Messaging::processContextRelations()
  post initial_actions:
    let incomingflows = self.incoming in
    self.Send.incoming->includesAll(incomingflows)    and
    incomingflows->forAll(f|f.target = self.Send)
```

## 3.3  Example: Operation Call with Time-Out

As an example we consider the definition of composite concept TimedOperationCall, as introduced in section 1. The activity diagram in figure 6 defines the behaviour of a timed operation call. For brevity, information aspects are not considered, which could be modelled through input and output pins.

When a timed operation call is invoked, actions CallOperationAction and AcceptTimeEventAction are enabled. CallOperationAction represents the transmission of an operation call request to the target object. The receipt of this request is represented by AcceptCallAction, which enables the actual handling of the operation call. ReplyAction represents the returning of the operation result, for which it uses return information produced by the AcceptCallAction. Action AcceptTimeEventAction represents the occurrence of a timeout after some time has expired. In this case an exception is generated through RaiseExceptionAction, which may interrupt the action sequence CallOperationAction, AcceptCallAction and ReplyAction.

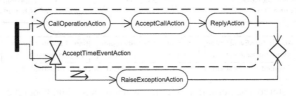

**Fig. 6.** Activity diagram of a TimedOperationCall.

Figure 7 depicts the metamodel definition of a timed operation call as a composite stereotype. The keywords <<composite>> and <<instantiate>> denote a composite stereotype and an instantiation, respectively. A line between two instantiations denotes the instantiation of an association between those instantiations. For clarity, a single Constituent association between TimedOperationCall and a grey box is used to represent all ConstituentClass and ConstituentAssociation associations between TimedOperationCall and the instantiations in the box.

Stereotype TimedOperationCall has been defined as an extension of metaclass StructuredActivityNode to define the way in which it can be composed with other metaclasses in the action semantics. Since an StructuredActivityNode is a kind of ActivityNode, it can be connected to other ActivityNodes via ActivityEdges. The context relations for TimedOperationCall are the following. An association that relates an incoming ActivityEdge to the TimedOperationCall must relate that ActivityEdge to the ForkNode that is labelled initial instead. An association that relates an outgoing ActivityEdge to the TimedOperationCall must relate that outgoing ActivityEdge to the MergeNode that is labelled final instead.

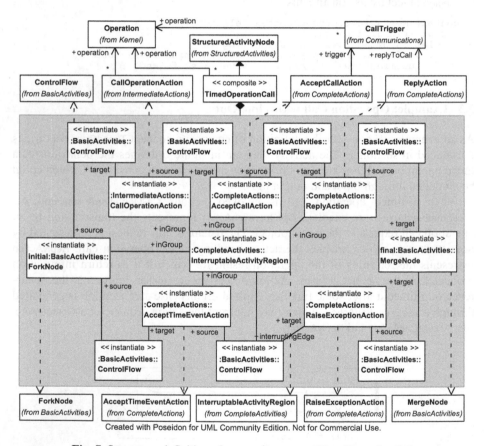

Created with Poseidon for UML Community Edition. Not for Commercial Use.

**Fig. 7.** Stereotype definition of composite concept TimedOperationCall.

**Metamodelling.** The composite concept of timed operation call can also be defined using metamodelling. We indicate two possible approaches to do this: a *constructive* and a *constraint-oriented* approach. In both approaches a TimedOperationCall is defined as a specialization of a StructuredActivityNode. Both approaches differ however in the way the composition is defined. The constructive approach defines the composition explicitly in terms of its constituents. This approach resembles the approach followed in section 3.3. The constraint-oriented approach defines the composition by adding OCL constraints to the composite concept, which define the constituents of the composition implicitly. We expect this approach is much more difficult to apply and understand than the constructive approach.

# 4 Transformation of Composite Concepts

In order to use design techniques that are defined on elementary concepts, such as simulation, analysis and validation, we have to transform each stereotype into the concept or concepts that it consists of. In this way, existing tools can largely be reused and the need for tool modification is minimized. Section 5 presents an example of how tool support can be extended through model transformation.

In this section we focus on the transformation of composite stereotypes. The transformation of 'regular' stereotypes as defined by the UML 2.0 Profile package is rather straightforward. Regular stereotypes can be transformed directly to the metaclasses they extend. We note, however, that in this transformation any specialized design information added by the stereotype is lost. It depends on the particular design technique whether this loss of information is acceptable and existing tools can be reused.

## 4.1 Transformation Rules

A composite stereotype completely defines how an instance of the corresponding composite concept is composed of instances of existing concepts and associations. In addition, context relations (see section 3.2) define how this composition is embedded in a model that contains the composite concept, i.e., how the constituent concept instances and associations are related to other concept instances in the model. This means that the definition of a composite concept, including its context relations, provide all the information that is required to define rules for transforming its instances to existing concept instances and associations. In principle, these rules can be derived automatically. The following transformation steps are distinguished:

1. creation of the constituent concept instances. For each instance of Constituent-Class, create an instance of the metaclass defined by the instantiation. In addition, each ConstituentClass may define the instance name and attribute values;
2. creation of associations between concept instances. For each instance of ConstituentAssociation, create an instance of the meta-association defined by the instantiation. Relate this instance to the classes to which the ConstituentAssociation is related via ConstituentClassEnd.
3. replacement of associations between the composite concept instance and other concept instances in the model by associations between the constituent concept instances as created in step 1 and the other concept instances. This replacement is defined by the context relations associated with the composite stereotype.

## 4.2  YATL

We use the transformation language YATL [9] to define transformations, because
tool support exists for this language and because it is compliant to the MOF. YATL
makes extensive use of the Object Constraint Language (OCL) [11], a language that
can be used to describe constraints on how concepts can be used. It can also be used
to query a design to verify that a constraint holds on that design or to yield a particular set of concept instances as indicated by the query. Here, we assume the reader is
familiar with the basic properties of OCL.

A YATL transformation has a name and consists of a set of transformation rules.
These rules are performed in the order in which they are invoked by the rule that is
declared the start rule. Each rule has a name, it optionally has a match part and it has a
body part. The match part identifies a MOF Class by its name and optionally defines an
OCL expression over that concept. The body part of the rule is evaluated over each
instance that is selected in the match part. For each execution of the body part self
takes the value of one of these instances.

The body part contains a sequence of statements that must be performed. A let
statement, let <name>: <classifier name>;, declares a variable by the given name of the
type given by the classifier name. An assignment statement, <expr$_1$> := <expr$_2$>, assigns
the value of <expr$_2$> to <expr$_1$>. A track statement is used to store and recall a temporary
relation between two concept instances. track(<ci$_1$>, <relation name>, <ci$_2$>) stores a relation between the concept instances <ci$_1$> and <ci$_2$> in the relation identified by <relation
name>. The relation must be functional, such that each <ci$_1$> can be assigned to at most
one other concept instance. track(<ci$_1$>, <relation name>, null) returns the concept instance
that is related to concept instance <ci$_1$> by the relation identified by <relation name>. A
tracking relation is visible in each rule in an entire transformation. A new statement,
new <class name>, creates a new instance of the Class by the specified name.

YATL transformations can be structured by defining them in the context of namespaces. A namespace identifies the Packages that contain the Classes that are the source
and the target of the transformation, respectively.

## 4.3  Example Transformation

As an example we have defined a YATL transformation for composite concept Messaging in figure 3(iii), which transforms a source model into a target model, such that
each instance of Messaging in the source model is replaced by its corresponding composition of elementary concept instances in the target model. We assume that the
metamodel of figure 3(iii) has been defined in a package named messagingpackage.
Furthermore, for convenience, directed composite aggregations have been used.

The following excerpt describes the main transformation rule, which consists of
the sequential invocation of 9 other rules. The first 7 rules basically define the copying of concept instances from the source model to the target model, excluding instances from the composite Messaging concept. For brevity, we don't illustrate these
rules here, but the complete transformation can be obtained from [16].

```
rule main () {
  pureaction2pureaction();
  sendaction2sendaction();
  receiveaction2receiveaction();
  taskaction2taskaction();
  flowrelation2flowrelation();
  taskcontainment2taskcontainment();
  process2process();
  messaging2basic();
  messagingassociations2basicassociations();
}
```

Rule `messaging2basic` defines the creation of the constituent concept instances and the associations between them. This corresponds to steps 1 and 2 from section 4.1.

```
rule messaging2basic match messagingpackage::Messaging () {
  let dstsend: messagingpackage::Send;
  let dstreceive: messagingpackage::Receive;
  let dstflow: messagingpackage::Flow;
  dstsend := new messagingpackage::Send;
  dstreceive := new messagingpackage::Receive;
  dstflow := new messagingpackage::Flow;
  dstsend.m := self.m;
  dstsend.outgoing := dstsend.outgoing->including(dstflow);
  dstreceive.m := self.m;
  dstreceive.incoming := dstreceive.incoming->including(dstflow);
  dstflow.source := dstsend;
  dstflow.target := dstreceive;
  track(self, tmessage2send, dstsend);
  track(self, tmessage2receive, dstreceive);
  track(self, tmessage2flow, dstflow);
}
```

Finally, rule `messagingassociations2basicassociations()` implements the context relations for Messaging. This corresponds to step 3 from section 4.1. The following code excerpt describes part of the rule, which defines that any incoming flow of a Messaging instance must be an incoming flow for its constituent Send instance. In addition, if a messaging concept instance is defined as part of a process or task, its constituents must be added to this process or task.

```
rule messagingassociations2basicassociation match
    messagingpackage::Messaging () {
  --if messaging is part of process p, its constituents are part of p
  let dstsend: messagingpackage::Send;
  let dstreceive: messagingpackage::Receive;
  let dstflow: messagingpackage::Flow;
  dstsend := track(self, tmessage2send, null);
  dstreceive := track(self, tmessage2receive, null);
  dstflow := track(self, tmessage2flow, null);
  foreach p: messagingpackage::Process in
      Process.allInstances()->select(p| p.task->includes(self)) do {
    let dstp: messagingpackage::Process;
    dstp := track(p, tprocess2process, null);
    dstp.task := dstp.task->including(dstsend);
    dstp.task := dstp.task->including(dstreceive);
  }
  --if messaging is part of a task t, its constituents are part of t
  foreach t: messagingpackage::Task in
      Task.allInstances()->select(t| t.action->includes(self)) do {
    let dstt: messagingpackage::Task;
    dstt := track(t, ttask2task, null);
    dstt.action := dstt.action->including(dstsend);
    dstt.action := dstt.action->including(dstreceive);
    dstt.flow := dstt.flow->including(dstflow);
  }
```

```
--if messaging has an incoming flow f, its send action has f
foreach f: messagingpackage::Flow in self.incoming do {
   let dstsend: messagingpackage::Send;
   dstsend := track(self, tmessage2send, null);
   let inflow: messagingpackage::Flow;
   inflow := new messagingpackage::Flow;
   inflow.target := dstsend;
   dstsend.incoming := dstsend.incoming->including(inflow);
   let srcsourceaction: messagingpackage::Action;
   srcsourceaction := f.source;
   if (f.source.oclIsTypeOf(messagingpackage::Messaging)) then
      let dstsourcemessage: messagingpackage::Messaging;
      dstsourcemessage :=
         track(srcsourcemessage, tmessage2receive, null);
      inflow.source := dstsourcemessage;
      dstsourcemessage.outgoing :=
         dstsourcemessage.outgoing->including(inflow)
   else
      let dstsourceaction: messagingpackage::Action;
      dstsourceaction:=track(srcsourceaction, taction2action, null);
      inflow.source := dstsourceaction;
      dstsourceaction.outgoing :=
         dstsourceaction.outgoing->including(inflow)
   endif;
}
```

# 5   Example Applications of the Extended Profiles Package

This section further motivates and illustrates the use of the Extended Profiles package by presenting two possible applications: (i) relating modelling languages and (ii) structuring modelling languages.

**Relating modelling languages**. In earlier work [5], we presented an approach to relate different viewpoints and viewpoint models via a basic viewpoint (see Figure 8). A conceptual model represents the set of concepts that is used in a particular viewpoint and forms the basis for modelling languages that are used to express models (views) of a system as conceived from this viewpoint. The approach is based on the assumption that the concepts from each viewpoint can be considered as extensions of a common set of basic, i.e., elementary and generic, modelling concepts, as represented by the basic viewpoint. Two types of extensions are considered: (i) a viewpoint concept is a specialization of a basic viewpoint concept, or (ii) a viewpoint concept is a composition of (possibly specialized) basic concepts. These assumptions allow one to map different models from the same or different viewpoints onto basic viewpoint models. In this way, relationships between different viewpoint models, e.g., refinement and consistency relationships, can be analysed within the scope of a

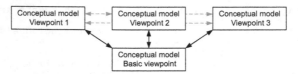

**Fig. 8**. Relating viewpoints via a basic viewpoint.

single conceptual model and by using the same set of analysis tools. By defining viewpoints as extensions (profiles) of a basic viewpoint, the Extended Profiles package provides a technique to implement the approach described above.

**Structuring modelling languages.** Another application of the Extended Profiles package is to structure and extend existing modelling languages, using the profiling mechanism. Using the Extended Profiles package we can structure a language into a small set of basic, i.e., elementary and generic, concepts and sets of composite (and specialized) concepts as extensions of those concepts. Having a small set of basic concepts helps to keep a language clear and consistent, while the definition of composite concepts helps us to increase the language's suitability and ease of use for some application domain. Although the existing profiling mechanism already helps us to structure a language in this way, the addition of composite stereotypes extends our possibilities.

An interesting case for this approach is UML, which consists of different languages supporting different modelling viewpoints. As is shown in [6], these languages can be divided into two main categories: structural languages (for class and component diagrams) and behavioural languages (for use case, collaboration, state, activity and sequence diagrams). Furthermore, it is shown that for each of these categories a basic conceptual model can be defined.

We also applied this structure to our behaviour modelling language ISDL [12, 13]. This language has originally been based on a small set of basic concepts [14]. To facilitate a designer in modelling frequently used compositions of ISDL concepts, we are currently introducing shorthand notations to express composite concepts more conveniently. Since each composite concept can be transformed into the basic concepts, we are able to reuse tools that we developed for the basic concepts to support the extended concepts. For example, in this way we have been able to reuse the ISDL simulator for ISDL models that contain instances of composite concepts. The same holds for our technique to assess the conformance between two ISDL models [16].


# 6  Conclusions

The use of the UML's 2.0 profiling mechanism allows one to combine the efficiency of general purpose languages with the intuitive clarity and ease of use of dedicated languages. Since the profiling mechanism leaves the language metamodel unmodified and introduces stereotypes as extensions of existing metamodel elements, modelling tool support can be reused. This benefit of profiling can be exploited further by allowing one to specify stereotypes for composite concepts, representing (frequently used) compositions of existing concepts. An extension of the UML's Profiles package is presented that supports the specification of composite stereotypes.

At the time of writing, we are not aware of other work that proposes metamodel extension mechanisms for composite concepts, particularly based on the UML profiling mechanism. However, many contributions can be found in literature on classifications of metamodel extension mechanisms and approaches, and on guidelines to use and interpret stereotypes [1,2,3,4,8,15]. This paper is orthogonal to this work and makes a further contribution by extending the use of stereotypes in a general way. The notion of composite stereotype we introduce can be seen as a restrictive kind of stereotype as described in [4]. Furthermore, this notion is used for type classification as described in [3], since it is meant to introduce new language elements. Although general metamodelling techniques can be used to support the introduction and application of composite concepts, we have extended the UML 2.0 Profiles package because it does not allow a language developer to modify an existing metamodel. But, in principle, this restriction can also be obtained through, or actually is, a restrictive form of metamodelling.

We believe that tool support for the specification of composite stereotypes as described in this paper can be developed rather easily. In addition, we have illustrated how transformation rules can be derived systematically from the specification of a composite stereotype to transform a composite concept instance to the composition of the constituent concept instances it represents. Such a transformation can be used to implement the composite concept using existing tool support.

A question that remains to be resolved is the expressive power of the proposed Extended Profiles package compared to metamodelling. To answer this question, the ideas presented in this paper should be applied to multiple cases from different application areas. In particular, attention should be paid to the systematic definition of the context relationships of a composite stereotype. This future work should lead to a precise set of rules for specifying stereotypes and deriving transformations, which should guarantee both the consistent use of stereotypes by language developers as well as the correct implementation of tool support.

# References

1. Atkinson, C. and Kühne, T. Strict Profiles: Why and How. In *Proceedings of <<UML>> 2000*, York, UK, October 2000, pp. 309-322.
2. Atkinson, C., et al. To Meta or Not to Meta – That is the Question. In *Journal of Object Oriented Programming*, Vol. 13, No. 8, December 2000, pp. 32-35.
3. Atkinsion, C. et al. Stereotypical Encounters of the Third Kind. In *Proceedings of <<UML>> 2002*, Dresden, Germany, September 2002, pp. 100-114.
4. Berner, S., et al. A Classification of Stereotypes for Object-Oriented Modeling Languages. In *Proceedings of <<UML>> '99*, Fort Collins, CO, USA, October 1999, pp. 249-264.
5. Dijkman, R.M., et al. An Approach to Relate Viewpoints and Modeling Languages. In *Proceedings of the 7th IEEE Enterprise Distributed Object Computing (EDOC) Conference*, Brisbane, Australia, pp. 14-27, 2003.
6. Evans, A., et al. A unified superstructure for UML. In *Journal of Object Technology*, Vol. 4, No. 1, January-February 2005, pp. 165-181.
7. ISDL. http://isdl.ctit.utwente.nl.
8. Jiang, Y., et al. On the Classification of UML's Meta Model Extension Mechanism. In *Proceedings of <<UML>> 2004*, Lisbon, Portugal, October 2004, pp. 54-68.
9. Patrascoiu, O. YATL: Yet Another Transformation Language. In *Proceedings of the 1st European MDA Workshop, MDA-IA*, pages 83-90. University of Twente, the Netherlands, January 2004.
10. OMG. UML 2.0 Infrastructure Specification. OMG Adopted Specification ptc/03-09-12.
11. OMG. UML 2.0 OCL Specification. OMG Adopted Specification ptc/03-10-14.

12. Quartel, D., et al. Methodological support for service-oriented design with ISDL. In *Proc. of the 2nd Int. Conf. on Service Oriented Computing*, New York City, NY, USA, 2004.
13. Quartel, D. et al. On architectural support for behavior refinement in distributed systems design. *Journal of Integrated Design and Process Science*, 6(1), March 2002.
14. Quartel, D. et al. On the role of basic design concepts in behaviour structuring. In *Computer Networks and ISDN Systems*, No. 29, 1997, pp. 413-436.
15. Schleicher, A. and Westfechtel, B. Beyond Stereotyping: Metamodeling Approaches for the UML. In: *Proceedings of HICSS 34*, 2001, pp. 3051-3060.
16. http://wwwhome.cs.utwente.nl/~dijkman/downloads/messagingtransformation.yatl.

# Transformation from CIM to PIM: A Feature-Oriented Component-Based Approach

Wei Zhang[1], Hong Mei[2], Haiyan Zhao[3], Jie Yang[4]

Institute of Software, School of Electronics Engineering and Computer Science,
Peking University, Beijing, 100871, China
{zhangw[1],zhhy[3],yangj[4]}@sei.pku.edu.cn, meih@pku.edu.cn[2]

**Abstract.** Model Transformation is a crucial part of Model-Driven Architecture (MDA). However, most of the current researches only focus on the transformation from PIM to PSM, and pay little attention to the CIM-to-PIM transformation. One of the results is that converting CIM to PIM will depend much on designers' personal experience or creativity, and thus the quality of PIM can not be well controlled. This paper presents a feature-oriented component-based approach to the CIM-to-PIM transformation. In this approach, *features* and *components* are adopted as the key elements of CIM and PIM, respectively. One important characteristic of this approach is that it provides a method to decompose the n-to-n relations between features and components into two groups of 1-to-n relations. The other important characteristic is that this approach proposes a way to create components by clustering responsibilities which are operationalized from features. These two characteristics partially resolve two basic problems related to the CIM-to-PIM transformation: one is the traceability problem between CIM and PIM, the other is the problem of CIM-based PIM construction.

## 1 Introduction

One crucial part of Model-Driven Architecture (MDA) is model transformation [16], i.e. transformation from CIM to PIM, or from PIM to PSM. In MDA, requirements for a system are modeled in CIM (Computation Independent Model). However, most of the current researches only focus on the transformation from PIM to PSM, and pay little attention to the CIM-to-PIM transformation. One possible reason of this phenomenon may be that there have been many mature technologies that can be adopted to represent PIM and PSM precisely (such as, UML [17], Software Architecture [6], CCM [15], EJB [19], and COM [14]), and many researchers believe it is possible to automate the transformation from PIM to PSM based on these technologies. Whereas, requirements modeled in CIM often lack a good structure, and it is thought to be impossible to automate the CIM-to-PIM transformation [11]. Consequently, MDA does not have enough capability to support the CIM-to-PIM transformation. One of the results is that converting CIM to PIM will depend much on designers' personal experience or creativity, and thus the quality of PIM can not be well controlled.

L. Briand and C. Williams (Eds.): MoDELS 2005, LNCS 3713, pp. 248-263, 2005.
© Springer-Verlag Berlin Heidelberg 2005

In this paper, we present an approach to transforming CIM to PIM in a feature-oriented component-based view. We use the *feature model* (consisting of a set of features and relationships between features) to structure requirements in CIM, and use the *software architecture* (consisting of a set of components and interactions between components) to organize elements at the PIM level. The feature model has been widely used in software reuse to capture the requirements of a set of similar systems [5, 7, 9, 10]. The entity-relationship structure and the explicit variability modeling of the feature model make it easy to be customized according to different reuse context [25]. The software architecture has long been recognized as a high-level design model to decompose a system into a set of computational elements and interactions between them [6, 1], and shows much chance of being adopted by UML2.0 [18]. Based on the research results in software reuse and software architecture, our approach mainly focuses on bridging the gap between CIM and PIM in a disciplined way, although not a fully automatic way.

Generally, there are two important problems related to model transformation. One is the traceability between the source and the sink model, that is, how the elements in the source model can be traced to elements in the sink model. It is the base for model transformation. The other is the problem of the sink model's construction, which means how the elements in the sink model are formed in transformation. It is the core of model transformation. In our approach, these two problems are incarnated into the problems concerning features and components, namely, how to trace features to components, and how to construct the software architecture based on the feature model.

To resolve these two problems, our approach introduces the concept of *responsibilities* as the connector between features and components. A responsibility is a cohesive set of program specifications from programmers' viewpoint, and can be used as a unit for work assignment.

Tracing features to components is complex. One important reason is the complex n-to-n relations between features and components [8]. By introducing responsibilities as the connector, the n-to-n relations are decomposed into two sets of 1-to-n relations. One set contains the 1-to-n relations between features and responsibilities, indicating that a feature can be generally *operationalized* into several responsibilities. The other contains the 1-to-n relations between components and responsibilities, showing that a component may be *assigned* several responsibilities. Based on the decomposition, tracing features to components can be done in a two-step way: first operationalizing features into responsibilities, then assigning responsibilities to components.

As to the software architecture's construction, we decompose it into two sub-problems, namely, *component construction* and *interaction identification*. Based on the 1-to-n relations between features/components and responsibilities, we propose a method of component construction by clustering responsibilities operationalized from features. We resolve the second sub-problem by analyzing interactions between responsibilities, and using them as the source of interactions between components.

The rest of this paper is organized as follows. Basic knowledge about the feature model is presented in Section 2. Section 3 gives the feature model of a simple document editor. Section 4 shows how to decouple the n-to-n relations between features and components. Section 5 presents a method of feature model based software architecture construction. Related work is discussed in Section 6. Finally, Section 7 concludes this paper with a short summary.

## 2   The Feature Model

In this section, we give some basic knowledge of the feature model, with the purpose of helping readers build a clear view on feature-oriented requirements modeling.

### 2.1   Definition of Features

Generally, the definition of a concept can be considered from two aspects: intension and extension. The intension describes the intrinsic qualities of a concept, while the extension characterizes the external embodiment. Many researches have given their definitions of features from either of the two aspects. For example, [20], [13] and [22] focus much on the intension aspect, defining a feature as a set of related requirements, while [9] and [8] emphasize the extension aspect, stating that a feature is a software-characteristic in the user or customer view. In this paper, we do not introduce any novel idea about features, but just combine these two aspects and give the following definition of features.

*In intension, a feature is a cohesive set of individual requirements.*

*In extension, a feature is a user/customer-visible characteristic of a software system.*

Then, requirements in CIM can be partitioned into a set of features.

### 2.2   Refinement

Refinements are binary relationships between features, which integrate features at different levels of abstraction into hierarchy structures. Hierarchy structures provide an effective way to describe complex systems.

**Table 1.** Refinement Definitions. This show informal definitions of three kinds of refinements

| Refinement | Informal Definition |
|---|---|
| Decomposition | *Refining a feature into its constituent features* |
| Characterization | *Refining a feature by identifying its attribute features* |
| Specialization | *Refining a general feature into a feature incorporating further details* |

Refinements can further be classified into three more concrete subclasses: *decomposition*, *characterization*, and *specialization*. Their informal definitions are given in Table 1. Some examples of them are depicted in Fig.1. The three kinds of refinement are differentiated by roles of features involved in them (see Table 2).

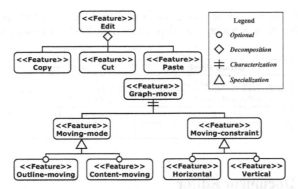

**Fig. 1.** Refinement Examples. This shows examples of three kinds of refinement, namely *decomposition*, *characterization*, and *specialization*

**Table 2.** Roles in Refinements. This table shows the different roles played by parents and children in different kinds of refinement. In a refinement, we call the feature at a higher level of abstraction the *parent*, and the other feature the *child*

| Refinement | Parent-Role | Child-Role |
|---|---|---|
| Decomposition | *Whole* | *Part* |
| Characterization | *Entity* | *Attribute* |
| Specialization | *General-Entity* | *Specialized-Entity* |

## 2.3 Constraint

Constraints are static relationships among binding-states of features. It provides a way to verify the results of requirements customization [25] and release planning [4]. Only those results that do not violate constraints on features can be treated as candidates of valid requirements subsets or releases. By explicitly modeling constraints, the feature model possesses a good quality of customization.

There are two important constraint categories, namely *binary constraints*, and *complex constraints*. Their formal definitions are given respectively in Table 3 and 4.

**Table 3.** Binary Constraints. Binary constraints are constraints on the binding-states of two features. This shows two kinds of basic binary constraint and their formal definitions

| Binary Constraint | Definition |
|---|---|
| *requires(a, b: Feature)* | $bound(a) \rightarrow bound(b)$ |
| *excludes(a, b: Feature)* | $\neg(bound(a) \wedge bound(b))$ |
| Where: $bound(a: Feature) =_{def} (a.binding\text{-}state = bound);$ | |

**Table 4.** Complex Constraints. Complex constraints are between two feature sets, which extend the parameters of binary constraints to group predicates. This shows two kinds of complex constraint and their formal definitions. Typical group predicates are listed in Table 5

| Complex Constraint | Definition |
|---|---|
| *requires(x, y: Group-Predicate)* | $x \rightarrow y$ |
| *excludes(x, y: Group-Predicate)* | $\neg(x \wedge y)$ |

**Table 5.** Group Predicates. Group predicates extend the parameter of the predicate *bound(a: Feature)* (see Table 3) to a feature set. This shows four kinds of group predicate and their formal definitions

| Group Predicate | Definition |
|---|---|
| *single-bound(P: set Feature)* | $\exists_{one}\, a \in P \bullet bound(a)$ |
| *all-bound(P: set Feature)* | $\forall\, a \in P \bullet bound(a)$ |
| *multi-bound(P: set Feature)* | $\exists_{some}\, a \in P \bullet bound(a)$ |
| *no-bound(P: set Feature)* | $\forall\, a \in P \bullet \neg bound(a)$ |

# 3   A Simple Document Editor

In this section, we introduce the feature model of a simple document editor, which will be used in the rest of this paper as an example to demonstrate our approach.

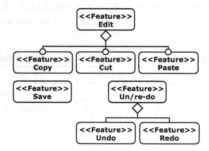

**Fig. 2.** The Refinement View. This shows all features in the simple document editor and refinements between these features

The simple document editor contains 8 features. The refinement view of its feature model is shown in Fig. 2. Each feature's description is listed in Table 6.

There is one complex constraint on these features:

    **requires (single-bound ({un/re-do}), multi-bound ({copy, cut, paste}));**

Its meaning is that feature *un/re-do*'s availability depends on one or more binding of features *copy*, *cut* and *paste*. That is, if none of the three features is bound, the binding of *un/re-do* will be not available to users.

**Table 6.** Descriptions of Features.

| Feature | Description |
|---|---|
| *Edit* | The collection of feature *copy*, *cut*, and *paste*. |
| *Copy* | Copy the selected text in the current document to the clipboard. |
| *Cut* | Cut the selected text in the current document to the clipboard. |
| *Paste* | Paste the text in the clipboard to the current position of the current document. |
| *Un/re-do* | The collection of feature *undo* and *redo*. |
| *Undo* | Undo the latest unsaved edit operation. |
| *Redo* | Redo the latest undo-ed and unsaved edit operation. |
| *Save* | Save the current document into a disk. |

# 4  Responsibilities

In this section, we introduce the concept of responsibilities and show how responsibilities can be used to decouple the complex n-to-n relations between features and components. At the end of this section, we introduce *resource containers* as a special kind of responsibility containers.

## 4.1  Definition of Responsibilities

The UML defines a responsibility as "a contract or obligation of a classifier" [17]. This definition clarifies the fact that a responsibility will be assigned to a classifier, for example, to a component in the software architecture. However, it does not tell us where a responsibility comes from, nor does it tell us the intension meaning of a responsibility.

Similar to features, we define responsibilities from two aspects:

*In intension, a responsibility is a cohesive set of program specifications.*
*In extension, a responsibility is a partial operationalization to certain requirements and can be used as a basic unit for work assignment to programmers.*

We define responsibilities as a concept at the level of program specifications and use it to partition program specifications for work assignment. We also think it is requirements that responsibilities come from, since the final purpose of building software is to satisfy requirements.

## 4.2  Decoupling the n-to-n Relations Between Features and Components

The purpose of introducing responsibilities is to decouple the n-to-n relations between features and components. These relations indicate that a feature may finally be implemented by a set of components, while a component may contribute to several features' implementation. The underlying idea of the decoupling is that besides the n-to-n relations, we should further point out the exact meaning of "*a feature has a relation with a component*", or "*a component contribute partly to a feature's implementation*". The decoupling is based on the following pattern:

    *Feature A has a relation with Component B.*

      ⇒ *Feature A assigns Responsibility A.B to Component B.*

Fig. 3 shows an example of decoupling the n-to-n relations between features and components by using this pattern.

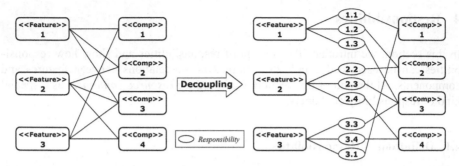

**Fig. 3.** A Decoupling Example. This shows how the n-to-n relations between features 1, 2, 3 and components 1, 2, 3, 4 are decoupled by responsibilities.

One result of the decoupling is that the original n-to-n relations between features and components are decomposed into two sets of 1-to-n relations. One set contains the 1-to-n relations between features and responsibilities. The essential of these relations is that "*a feature can be generally operationalized into a set of responsibilities*". The other set contains the 1-to-n relations between components and responsibilities, and the essential of them is that "*a component can be generally assigned several responsibilities*". In this sense, components can be viewed as a kind of responsibility containers.

Based on the decomposition, tracing features to components can be done following two steps: first operationalizing features into responsibilities, then assigning responsibilities to components. On the other hand, the decoupling also supports tracing back from components to features. This can be achieved just by changing the deduced part of the decoupling pattern into "*Component B is assigned Responsibility A.B from Feature A*". So we can see that, by introducing responsibilities, we find a more controllable way to create traceability between features and components.

### 4.3   Resource Containers: A Special Kind of Responsibility Containers

In features' operationalization, there are often responsibilities that consume or produce certain resources which are produced or will be consumed by other features. We introduce resource containers to structure resources related to features. Fig. 4 shows an example of resource containers in features' operationalization.

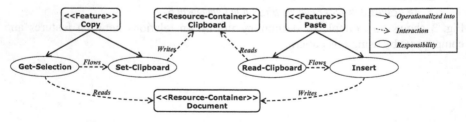

**Fig. 4.** An Example of Resource Containers. This shows the operationalization results of two features *copy* and *paste* in the simple document editor, and two resource containers (*clipboard* and *document*) related to the operationalization

Resource containers can be viewed as a special kind of responsibility containers, which are assigned responsibilities of passively accepting requests from environment for resource storing, querying and retrieving.

Another important role of resource containers is the medium of indirect interactions between features. An example of this can be found in Fig. 4, in which *set-clipboard* (operationalized from *copy*) writes information into resource container *clipboard*, while *read-clipboard* (operationalized from *paste*) reads information from it. That is, feature *copy* and *paste* interact indirectly through resource container *clipboard*.

## 5   Constructing Software Architecture

In section 4, we show how to create traceability between features and components, in the case that the feature model and software architecture have already existed. However, the real condition of transforming the feature model to the software architecture is that the later model does not exist. So, in transformation, we have to construct the software architecture based on the feature model.

In this section, we show how to construct components by clustering responsibilities operationalized from features, and how to identify interactions between components by analyzing interactions between responsibilities and using them as the source of interactions between components.

### 5.1   An Overview

An overview of transforming the feature model (CIM) to the software architecture (PIM) is depicted in Fig. 5. The principle of constructing components is based on the observation that "*a component can be generally assigned several responsibilities*" (see section 4). So, components can be treated as containers of responsibilities, and thus can be constructed by clustering responsibilities. Identifying interactions between components is guided by the following assumption: if two responsibilities are assigned to two different components, then any interactions between these two responsibilities will be developed into interactions between components.

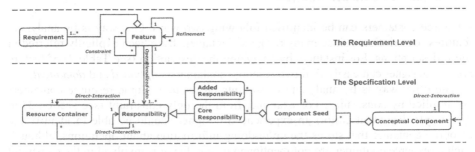

**Fig. 5.** An overview of transforming CIM to PIM.

The key concepts involved in the transformation can be categorized into two levels. First is the requirements level, at which requirements are organized into the feature model. Second is the specification level. At this level, program specifications are first be partitioned into responsibilities and resource containers, with a set of interactions between them. Then, responsibilities and resource containers are clustered into a set of conceptual components and interactions between these components.

In the remainder of this section, six basic aspects of the transformation are presented in six sub-sections, respectively. However, the order of these aspects is not essential. It is often the case that several of them should be considered simultaneously.

## 5.2 Feature Operationalization

The purpose of feature operationalization is to find a programmable way to implement requirements denoted by a feature. One basic way to feature operationalization is by analyzing a feature's description. For example, operationalizing feature *copy* follows this way. By analyzing the feature's description, an experienced designer can easily operationalize it into two responsibilities (see Fig. 4): *get-selection* which means "*getting the selected text from the current document*", and *set-clipboard* which means "*putting the selected text into the clipboard*".

When a feature has dependency on other features, its operationalization should also include responsibilities that this feature depends on other features to fulfill. For example, from the description of feature *undo*, we can find a requirement that only those unsaved operations can be undo-ed. Then, a responsibility *inform-saved* is identified, which means "*when the current document is saved, feature undo should be informed*". And *undo* depends on feature *save* to fulfill this responsibility.

Besides analyzing a feature's description, we can also find dependency between features from constraints on features. For example, from the constraint: *requires (single-bound ({un/re-do}), multi-bound ({copy, cut, paste}))*, a designer can identify responsibilities of "*recording information about each operation on the current document so that any operation can be undo-ed or redo-ed later*", responsibilities which are necessary for feature *un/re-do*'s implementation, and which *un/re-do* depends on the three features *copy*, *cut* and *paste* to fulfill respectively. From this example, we can see the value of constraints in feature operationalization.

## 5.3 Resource Container Analysis

Resource containers can be identified following two ways. One way is by analyzing features' descriptions, since many resource containers have been explicitly referred in these descriptions. For instance, by analyzing the description (see Table 7) of feature *copy*, a designer can easily find two resource containers: *clipboard* and *document*.

The other way is by analyzing constraints on features. Some resource containers are implied by constraints. For example, from the only constraint (see section 3) in the simple document editor, an experienced designer should be able to identify the resource container that stores the un/re-doing information about operations, although such a resource container are not mentioned by any features involved in the constraint. Here, we can see the value of constraints when identifying resource containers.

## 5.4 Interaction Analysis

Interaction analysis is a process tightly related to feature operationalization and re-source container analysis. Its purpose is to identify interactions between responsibili-ties /and resource containers. These interactions will be used later as the source of interactions between components. We use *IRR* to denote the set contains all these interactions. For an interaction *irr* in *IRR*, we use *irr.trigger* to denote the entity that triggers *irr* and thus plays an active role in *irr*, and *irr.triggee* the other entity which has a *passive* role.

At a low level, all these interactions are data flows between two entities. However, at some more semantic level, these interactions may be classified into more meaning-ful categories. For example, we can use *write, read, produce* or *consume* to character-ize interactions between responsibilities and resource containers. In section 5.6, we will give an interaction classification at the feature level. As an example, in Fig. 4, we can see interactions between responsibilities operationalized from feature *copy/paste*, and interactions between these responsibilities and related resource containers.

## 5.5 Component Seed Creation

The purpose of this step is to create seeds of components, so that responsibilities operationalized from features can be assigned to them, and conceptual components can be formed by clustering these seeds and resource containers.

In our approach, we adopt a simple rule to create component seeds, that is, creating one component seed for each feature. We use *ftr.cs* to denote the component seed of feature *ftr*, *cs.ftr* the feature that component seed *cs* is created for , and *cs.contains* the set of responsibilities assigned to component seed *cs*.

## 5.6 Responsibility Assignment

This step concerns assigning responsibilities operationalized from features to compo-nent seeds. For a responsibility *r*, we use *r.ftr* to denote the feature that *r* is operation-alized from, and *r.assignedTo* the component seed that *r* is assigned to.

**Definition: Core Responsibilities; Added responsibilities**

> A responsibility *r* is *a core responsibility*, iff *r.assignedTo* = *r.ftr.cs*.

> A responsibility r is *an added responsibility*, iff *r.assignedTo* ≠ *r.ftr.cs*.

In other words, a core responsibility *cr* can be fulfilled by the feature from which that *cr* is operationalized (namely *cr.ftr*), while an added responsibility *ar* is a responsibility that *ar.ftr* has to depend on another feature to fulfill.

The reason for assigning a responsibility *r* to a component seed other than *r.ftr.cs* is that the feature *r.ftr* depends on the data produced by feature *r.assignedTo.ftr*, whether directly or indirectly. For example, *r.assignedTo.ftr* sends an event directly to *r.ftr*, or *r.assignedTo.ftr* put some data into a resource container *rc* and later *r.ftr* reads data from *rc*.

Fig. 6 shows responsibilities assigned to component seed *copy.cs*, in which *get-selection* and *set-clipboard* are core responsibilities, and *record-copy-URI* is an added responsibility (where *URI* is the acronym for *un/re-doing infomation*) of *copy.cs* since *record-copy-URI* is only necessary to feature *un/re-do*'s implementation.

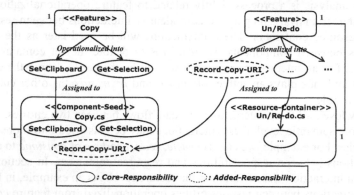

**Fig. 6.** An Example of Core and Added Responsibilities.

After responsibility assignment, the original interaction set *IRR* can be partitioned into three sets *IIS*, *IBS*, and *ISR*, where *IIS* denote the set of interactions inner component seeds, *IBS* the set of interactions between component seeds, and *ISR* the set of interactions between component seeds and resource containers. Due to page limitation, the formal definitions of the three sets are omitted here. We exclude interactions in *IIS* from our consideration since they have lost the chance to be developed into interactions between components.

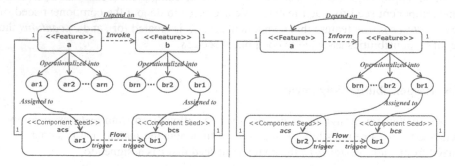

**Fig. 7.** Invoke and Inform.

Interactions in *IBS* can be classified into two categories: *Invoke_{IBS}* and *Inform_{IBS}*.

$Invoke_{IBS} =_{def} \{i \mid (i \in IBS) \wedge (i.trigger.ftr \neq i.triggee.ftr)\}$;

$Inform_{IBS} =_{def} \{i \mid (i \in IBS) \wedge (i.trigger.ftr = i.triggee.ftr)\}$;

The meaning of this classification should be understood at the feature level. The left part in Fig. 7 depicts a typical interaction in *Invoke_{IBS}*. At the low level, the interaction only models a data flow from responsibility *ar1* to *br1*, while at the feature level, it is an interaction in which feature *a* sends a command to *b* and *a* depend on *b* to behave according to this command, called "*a invokes b*". The right part in Fig. 7 depicts a typical interaction in *Inform_{IBS}*. At the low level, it models a data flow from responsibility *br2* to *br1*, while at the feature level, it is an interaction in which feature *a* sends an event to *b* to indicate certain condition has been satisfied, called "*a informs b*".

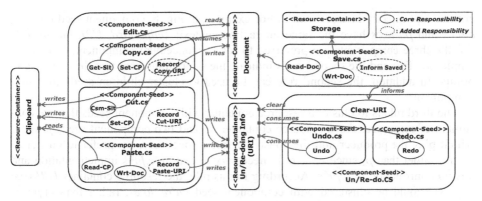

**Fig. 8.** The Result of Responsibility Assignment.

Interactions in *ISR* can also be classified into two similar categories: *Invoke_{ISR}* and *Inform_{ISR}*, where

$Invoke_{ISR} =_{def} \{i \mid (i \in ISR) \land (i.trigger$ is *Feature*$)\}$;

$Inform_{ISR} =_{def} \{i \mid (i \in ISR) \land (i.trigger$ is *Resource-Container*$)\}$;

This classification is based on the roles in an interaction *i* in *ISR*. When *i.trigger* is a feature, *i* is an interaction in which the feature depends on the resource container to fulfill a responsibility of resource storing, querying or retrieving, called "*i.trigger invokes i.triggee*". When *i.trigger* is a resource container, *i* is an interaction in which the resource container tells the feature certain condition about resources has been satisfied, called "*i.trigger informs i.triggee*".

Fig. 8 shows the result of responsibility assignment of the simple document editor. It contains 8 component seeds corresponding to the 8 features in the feature model, 4 resource containers identified by following the two ways in sub-section 5.3, and 15 interactions between them. For clarity, interactions inner component seeds are not included in this figure. Due to page limit, the descriptions of each responsibility arc not listed here.

## 5.7   Conceptual Component Analysis

The purpose of this step is to cluster component seeds and resource containers into components in the PIM, called conceptual components (to distinguish them from components that contain platform-specific information). For a component seed or a resource container *entity*, we use *entity.clusteredTo* to denote the conceptual component that *entity* belongs to.

Generally, there are three heuristic rules to decide which component seeds or/and resource containers should be clustered into a conceptual component. First rule is to consider the decomposition relationships (inherited from features) between component seeds and cluster a parent seed and all its children into a conceptual component. However, this rule provides no support to further cluster these children into subcomponents.

The second rule is to cluster component seeds with same interaction context into a conceptual component. The interaction context of a component seed consists of all entities that directly interact with it. For example, in Fig. 8, component seed *copy.cs*, *cut.cs* and *paste.cs* have the same interaction context: {*clipboard, URI, document*}. So, the three components are preferred to form a conceptual component. In this example, the first and the second rules indicate the same thing from two different viewpoints. In addition, the second rule can be used to cluster children seeds into subcomponents.

The third rule is to cluster a resource container with component seeds that are consumers of resources. For a resource container *rc*, and two component seeds *p* and *c* which play the producer and the consumer role respectively, we prefer to cluster *rc* with *c* rather than *p*, since *rc* is only necessary to feature *c.ftr*'s implementation and has no contribution to *p.ftr*'s. According to this rule, the resource container *URI* (see Fig. 8) should be clustered with component seed *un/re-do.cs*, rather than *copy.cs*, *cut.cs* and *paste.cs*.

There may also be such a situation, in which a resource container *rc* has several consumers, and these consumers should not be clustered into one component. In this case, *rc* may need to be further decomposed. Otherwise, we can just transform *rc* into a conceptual component without clustering it with other entities.

After clustering, only a subset of interactions in *IBS* and *ISR* are developed into interactions between conceptual components. We use *IBC* to denote this subset, which is defined as:

$$IBC =_{def} \{i \mid (i \in (IBS \cap ISR)) \wedge (i.trigger.clusteredTo \neq i.triggee.clusteredTo)\}$$

Fig. 9 shows the result of conceptual component analysis of the simple document editor. It contains 6 conceptual components identified based on the three rules above, and 6 component interactions, identified by clustering similar elements in *IBC*.

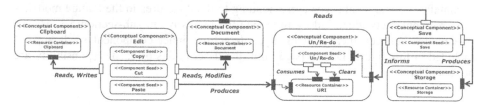

**Fig. 9.** The Result of Conceptual Component Analysis

# 6 Related Work

CRC cards [2], RDD (Responsibility-Driven Design) [23, 24], GRASP (General Responsibility Assignment Software Patterns) [12] are three responsibility-driven object-oriented design methods, in which responsibilities are assigned to objects in a domain model. Although these methods implicitly acknowledge the tight relation between responsibilities and requirements, none of them provides enough capabilities to organize requirements, or to maintain traceability between requirements and responsibilities/objects. These methods also depend much on the correctness and completeness of a pre-created domain object model. Our approach adopts the feature model to organize requirements, and uses responsibilities as the connector between requirements and design elements. Our approach focuses much on system functionality instead of object behavior, and is independent of any pre-created domain model. However, these methods do suggest an object-oriented way to implement these conceptual components in our approach.

UCM (Use Case Map) [3] also treats components as responsibility containers and assigns responsibilities to components. However, it doesn't point out where to find components, but presumes the pre-existence of components. On the contrary, our approach doesn't require the pre-existence of components. Components in our approach are constructed by clustering related responsibilities and resource containers. In addition, UCM doesn't make a distinction between *core* and *added* responsibilities. It only focuses on the time sequence between responsibilities, and doesn't distinguish between *invoke* and *inform* interactions.

[21] presents an approach to deriving software architecture from system goals. In this approach, agents in a system are treated as components in software architecture; responsibilities (called *operations*) are identified from goal specifications and assigned to agents; interactions between components are identified by considering the data dependencies among them. This approach may not work well when a software system contains only a few agents. Such a problem doesn't exist in our approach, since components in our approach are formed in a constructive way, instead of pre-appointed. An interesting characteristic of this approach is that it provides a set of formal patterns to ensure the correctness of goal operationaliztion, which is currently lacked in our approach.

## 7  Conclusions

This paper presents an approach to CIM-to-PIM transformation, in which, the feature model and the software architecture are adopted as CIM and PIM, respectively. This approach introduces *responsibilities* as the connector between features and components, that is, a feature can be generally operationalized into a set of responsibilities, and a component can be generally assigned several responsibilities. Then, this approach proposes a method to constructing software architecture based on the feature model. In this method, features are first operationalized into responsibilities, resource containers and interactions between them, then responsibilities and resource containers are clustered to form the software architecture at the PIM level. We think this approach provides a disciplined way to CIM-to-PIM transformation, although not a fully automatic way.

Future work includes the study of the issue of formal patterns in feature operationalization and component construction, applications to more complex case studies, and tool support for CIM-to-PIM transformation.

## Acknowledgements

The authors would like to thank the anonymous reviewers for their valuable comments and suggestions. This work is supported by the National Grand Fundamental

Research 973 Program of China under Grant No. 2002CB312003, the National Natural Science Foundation of China under Grant No.60233010, 60125206 and 90412011, and the Beijing Natural Science Foundation under Grant No. 4052018.

# References

1.  Allen, R., Garlan, D.: Formalizing Architectural Connection. In: Proceeding of 16th International Conference on Software Engineering. (1994) 71-80
2.  Beck, K., Cunningham, W.: A Laboratory for Teaching Object-Oriented Thinking. In: OOPLSA89, SIGPLAN Notices, Vol. 24. New Orleans, Louisiana (1989) 1-6
3.  Buhr, R.J.A.:Use Case Maps as Architectural Entities for Complex Systems. In: IEEE Transactions on Software Engineering, Vol. 24. IEEE Computer Society (1998) 1131-1155
4.  Carlshamre, P., Sandahl, K., Lindvall, M., Regnell, B., Natt och Dag, J.: An Industrial Survey of Requirements Interdependencies in Software Product Release Planning. In: Proceedings of 5th IEEE International Symposium on Requirements Engineering. IEEE Computer Society (2001) 84-91.
5.  Chastek, G., Donohoe, P., Kang, K.C, Thiel, S.: Product Line Analysis - A Practical Introduction. SEI-2001-TR-001, Software Engineering Institute, Carnegie Mellon University (2001)
6.  Garlan, D., Shaw, M.: An Introduction to Software Architecture. In: Ambriola, V., Tortora, G. (eds.): Advances in Software Engineering and Knowledge Engineering. Series on Software Engineering and Knowledge Engineering, Vol. 5. World Scientific Publishing Company, Singapore (1993) 1-39
7.  Griss, M.L., Favaro, J., d'Alessandro, M.: Integrating Feature Modeling with the RSEB. In: Proceedings of 5th International Conference on Software Reuse. IEEE Computer Society, Canada (1998) 76-85
8.  Griss, M.L.: Implementing Product-Line Features with Component Reuse. In: Proceedings of 6th International Conference on Software Reuse. IEEE Computer Society, 2000.
9.  Kang, K.C., Cohen, S.G., Hess, J.A., Novak, W.E., Peterson, A.S.: Feature-Oriented Domain Analysis Feasibility Study. SEI-90-TR-21, Software Engineering Institute, Carnegie Mellon University (1990)
10. Kang, K.C., Kim, S., Lee, J., Kim, K., Shin, E., Huh, M.: FORM - A Feature-Oriented Reuse Method with Domain-Specific Architecture. Annals of Software Engineering, Vol. 5. (1998) 143-168
11. Kleppe, A., Warmer, J., Bast, W.: MDA Explained-The Model Driven Architecture Practice and Promise. Addison Wesley (2003)
12. Larman, C.: Apply UML and Patterns: An Introduction to Object-Oriented Analysis and Design and the Unified Process. Prentice Hall (2001)
13. Mehta, A., Heineman, G.T.: Evolving Legacy System Features into Fine-Grained Components. In: Proceedings of the 24th International Conference on Software Engineering, IEEE Computer Society, Florida (2002) 417-427
14. Microsoft: Component Object Model. http://www.microsoft.com/com/.
15. Object Management Group: CORBA Component Model, v3.0. http://www.omg.org/technology/documents/formal/components.htm.
16. Object Management Group: MDA Guide Version 1.0.1. http://www.omg.org/mda/. (2003)
17. Object Management Group: UML 1.5 Specification. http://www.uml.org/. (2003)

18. Object Management Group: UML 2.0 Superstructure FTF convenience document. http://www.omg.org/cgi-bin/apps/doc?ptc/04-10-02.zip. (2004)
19. Sun Microsystems: EJB 2.1 Specification. http://java.sun.com/products/ejb/. (2002)
20. Turner, C.R., Fuggetta, A., Lavazza, L., Wolf, A.L.: A Conceptual Basis for Feature Engineering. Journal of Systems and Software, Vol. 49. (1999) 3-15
21. van Lamsweerde, A.: From System Goals to Software Architecture. In: Bernardo, M., Inverardi, P. (eds.): Formal Methods for Software Architectures. LNCS 2804. Springer-Verlag (2003) 25-43
22. Wiegers, K.E.: Software Requirements, Microsoft Press (1999)
23. Wirfs-Brock, R., Wilkerson, B.: Object-Oriented Design: A Responsibility-Driven Approach. In: OOPLSA89, SIGPLAN Notices, Vol. 24. New Orleans, Louisiana (1989) 71-76
24. Wirfs-Brock, R., McKean, A.: Object Design: Roles, Responsibilities, and Collaborations. Addison Wesley (2002)
25. Zhang, W., Zhao, H.Y., Mei, H.: A Propositional Logic-Based Method for Verification of Feature Models. In: Davies, J., Schulte, W., Barnett, M. (eds.): Formal Methods and Software Engineering. LNCS 3308. Springer-Verlag (2004) 115-130

# Weaving Executability into Object-Oriented Meta-languages

Pierre-Alain Muller, Franck Fleurey, and Jean-Marc Jézéquel

IRISA / INRIA Rennes
Campus Universitaire de Beaulieu
Avenue du Général Leclerc
35042 RENNES Cedex - France
{pa.muller, franck.fleurey, jean-marc.jezequel}@irisa.fr

**Abstract.** Nowadays, object-oriented meta-languages such as MOF (Meta-Object Facility) are increasingly used to specify domain-specific languages in the model-driven engineering community. However, these meta-languages focus on structural specifications and have no built-in support for specifications of operational semantics. In this paper we explore the idea of using aspect-oriented modeling to add precise action specifications with static type checking and genericity at the meta level, and examine related issues and possible solutions. We believe that such a combination would bring significant benefits to the community, such as the specification, simulation and testing of operational semantics of metamodels. We present requirements for such statically-typed meta-languages and rationales for the aforementioned benefits.

## 1 Introduction

In the model-driven engineering community, meta-languages such as MOF [11, 12], EMOF [12] or Ecore [3] are increasingly used to describe the metamodels of domain-specific languages. These meta-languages focus on structural specifications but have no built-in support for the definition of actions. Therefore, they cannot be used to precisely specify the operational semantics of metamodels. When such a precise semantics is needed, one has to resort to external languages, either imperative such as Java, or declarative such as OCL [14].

In this paper we explore the idea of using aspect-oriented modeling to build an executable meta-language by composing action metamodels with existing meta-languages. We examine how imperative control structures and iterators can be incorporated, while ensuring static typing capabilities and preserving compatibility with existing tools supporting MOF-like meta-languages (e.g.; Eclipse/EMF).

The intent of this paper is to describe why an executable meta-language would be valuable, to examine how such language could be composed using aspect-oriented modeling and then to expose how it may be promoted to become an executable meta-language.

This paper is organized as follows: Section 2 presents our motivations for adding action specifications in metamodels and justifies our proposal. Section 3 examines

L. Briand and C. Williams (Eds.): MoDELS 2005, LNCS 3713, pp. 264–278, 2005.
© Springer-Verlag Berlin Heidelberg 2005

how aspect-oriented modeling can be used to extend existing meta-data languages with action specifications and presents the metamodel of KerMeta (our experimental language). Section 4 shows how KerMeta is used to define a simple finite-state machine language. Section 5 examines some related works and finally the conclusion opens some general perspectives about aspect-oriented meta-modeling.

## 2 Motivations

In this section we present the rationales of our work. We explain why we believe that an action specification capability at the meta-level would be useful, and we examine some alternatives.

**Why do we need to extend meta-languages, aren't meta-data languages powerful enough?** MOF is an example of an object-oriented meta-data language, which provides support for metamodel modeling via object-oriented constructs such as classes, operations, attributes and relations. MOF defines operations, but not their implementation counterparts, which have to be described in text. The following example is excerpted from the MOF 2.0 Core Specification. The definition of the *isInstance* operation of the EMOF class *Type* (section 12.2.3 page 34) is given as follows:

*Operation **isInstance(element : Element) : Boolean***

*"Returns true if the element is an instance of this type or a subclass of this type. Returns false if the element is null".*

Such specification of the operational semantics of an operation is not easily amenable to automatic execution. Indeed, we need a real programming language, which goes beyond a meta-data description language. According to N. Wirth [20], a program is made of data structures + algorithms; so we propose to see executable metamodels as meta-data + actions. We see a lot of value in this capability, for instance for model transformations which involve strong algorithmic facets, e.g. the synthesis of state-machines from hierarchical message sequence charts [21].

The following specification given in our experimental language KerMeta is an example of executable specification which could be used in place of the previous textual description.

```
operation isInstance(element : Element) : Boolean is do
   // false if the element is null
   if element == void then result := false
   else
      // true if the element is an instance of this type
      // or a subclass of this type
      result := element.getMetaClass == self or
          element.getMetaClass.allSuperClasses.contains(self)
   end
end
```

**Fig. 1.** Executable specification of the *isInstance* operation of the EMOF *Type* class

**Why not use an existing programming language like Java?** Existing programming languages already provide a precise operational semantic for action specifications. Unfortunately, these languages provide both too much (e.g. interfaces), and too few (they lack concepts available in MOF, such as associations, enumerations, opposite properties, multiplicities, derived properties...).

There is no easy way to simultaneously restrict and extend such existing languages. Extension is difficult because of the typing mismatch between MOF and Java. Restriction is even more difficult, and we would have to stay with the existing language design choices for things such as single- or multiple-inheritance of classes, early- or late-binding, and schemes of method redefinition.

**Why not use the OCL language?** OCL (the Object Constraint Language) has been designed to express side-effect free constraints on UML models, and is also very well adapted for expressing queries and navigation expressions.

Provided that we would restrict OCL to work only on the subset of UML which could be aligned onto the MOF, we could use OCL to specify operations in terms of pre- and post-conditions. Nevertheless, and this was already pointed out by S. Mellor et al. [8], there is often a need to include some level of algorithmic specifications to ensure efficient implementation. This could be done by extending OCL with constructions such as assignment or object creation to support an imperative style for writing complex algorithms.

**Why not use the Action Semantics?** Like OCL, the Action Semantics is defined for UML models. The Action Semantics defines a minimal set of concepts useful to describe actions. Action languages are free to provide more sophisticated constructs, as long as these constructs can be translated into the basics concepts defined by the Action Semantics.

Executable meta-level languages and the UML Action Semantics are defined at different levels of abstraction. The Action Semantics defines fine-grained general purpose actions. Executable meta-languages define specific actions dedicated to metamodel specifications; e.g. the specification of the Action Semantics itself.

## 3 Using Aspect-Oriented Modeling to Extend a Meta-language

In this section, we examine how aspect weaving can be used to extend existing meta-languages. Fig. 2 shows how we use aspect-oriented modeling [5, 17] to compose the primary structural aspect (e.g. EMOF) with a behavioral aspect (which conforms to EMOF as well). The resulting metamodel is then further promoted to the M3 level, and can be substituted to EMOF. The composition process is designed to ensure that existing metamodels (such as UML), already defined in terms of EMOF, remain fully compatible with the new executable meta-language.

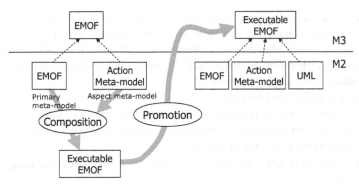

**Fig. 2.** Composing an action metamodel into the EMOF metamodel

The following paragraphs investigate how a meta-data language and a statically typed action language can be woven into a consistent executable meta-language. Section 3.1 motivates the choice of EMOF, section 3.2 lists the language constructs for precise action specification, section 3.3 presents how actions can be attached to EMOF operations and discusses the use of classical OO behavioral extension mechanisms. Sections 3.4 and 3.5 present several issues related to EMOF type system and some possible extensions to allow static typing of the action specifications. The discussion is illustrated by examples in KerMeta, our prototype language presented in section 3.6.

### 3.1 Choosing a Meta-data Language

The process described in this paper is directly applicable to any object-oriented meta-data language, such as the OMG MOFs (MOF 1.4, CMOF and EMOF) or Eclipse ECore. For our prototype language, we have chosen EMOF as the structural base for the executable meta-language. This decision is motivated by two main reasons: first because EMOF is standardized by the OMG and second as it is well-supported by tools such as Eclipse/EMF.

EMOF provides concepts for structuring data (package, classes, properties...), mechanisms for extending data structures (inheritance) and a type system (based on classes, primitive types and enumerations).

The following paragraphs will examine issues and solutions to integrate action specifications with those concepts and mechanisms.

### 3.2 Adding Imperative Control Structures

Adding imperative control structures into EMOF requires identifying how behavior can be attached to the structural constructions of the meta-language. As EMOF is already object-oriented, we have found that it is convenient to use class operations to hold this behavior specification.

Our work takes place in a software engineering context which includes relations with industrial partners who have very strong reliability concerns. In this context, static typing is a recognized best practice as it allows many kinds of early verifications, such as model-driven editing, testing and simulation.

Therefore, we have chosen to complement EMOF with imperative and statically-typed action specifications, which include the following control structures:

- Conditionals, loops and blocks.
- Local variable declarations.
- Call expressions for reading variables and properties or calling operations.
- Assignment expressions for assigning variables and properties.
- Literals expressions for primitive types,.
- Exception handling mechanism: exceptions can be raised and caught by rescue blocks.
- A limited form of lambda expressions which correspond to the implementation of OCL-like iterators such as *collect*, *select* or *reject* on collections.

Fig. 3 shows how behavior is attached to operations, using the property *body* of class *Operation* (to define the behavior of operations) and the properties *getterbody* and *setterbody* of class *Property* (to specify derived properties).

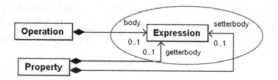

**Fig. 3.** Using operation bodies as join points between structure and behavior

However, this simple join point between data and behavior is not sufficient to define a full-fledged object-oriented executable meta-language, and a special attention has to be paid to ensure compatibility between extension mechanisms and type systems. The next subsections examine these points.

## 3.3 Adding Late Binding

Experience with the OO paradigm has demonstrated that operation redefinition is a useful and powerful mechanism to define the behavior of objects and support variability. However, EMOF does not provide semantics neither for operation call nor for operation inheritance and redefinition.

The issue of choosing semantics for operation overriding has been widely studied for the design of OO languages [1]. However, OO languages have not adopted a unique solution to this problem. For the sake of simplicity, in the current version of KerMeta we have chosen to implement invariant overriding (i.e. no specialization) and to exclude overloading.

EMOF provides multiple inheritance of classes. In the current version of KerMeta, we have chosen to include a minimal selection mechanism that allows the user to explicitly select the inherited method to override when several implementations of an operation are inherited. In the future, we plan to include a more general mechanism such as *traits* proposed by Schärli et al [15]. In any case, we believe that the conflict resolution mechanism should be explicitly stated by the programmer.

The following picture shows the extensions that we have made to the *Operation* class to support operation inheritance and redefinition (the red ellipses show what has been added).

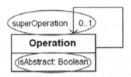

**Fig. 4.** Extensions to support operation inheritance and redefinition

### 3.4 Adding Genericity

As stated in section 2, an executable meta-language should include convenient model navigation capabilities. This section discusses the static typing of such navigation expressions.

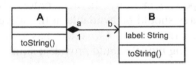

**Fig. 5.** A very simple metamodel

Fig. 5 presents a small metamodel which defines two classes *A* and *B* linked through an association. Let *myA* be an instance of class *A*; we need to write expressions such as:

$$myA.b.first.label$$

The type of *myA* is *A*, and according to EMOF the type of *myA.b* is *Set* whereas it should be *Set* of *B*. The type checking problem raised by this expression then concerns the type of *myA.b.first* that must be determined statically in order to check that it contains an attribute called *label* (*first* is supposed here to be an operation on sets which returns the first element of a set). Java, for instance, would ask the programmer to explicitly specify the expected type with static casts: *((B)myA.b.first).label*. More generally, the problem is that the type of what is returned by operations on collections depends on the contents of the collection at runtime. The following paragraphs detail two options for implementing static typing in this context.

**Option 1: Specific language constructions.** Collections (sets, ordered sets, bags and sequences) are introduced in the language, as in Xion [10] or MTL [19]. This can be viewed as an extension of the definition of arrays in OO languages such as Java 2.

This option requires syntactic and semantic language constructions specific to collections and the definition of corresponding policies in the type-checker. For this reason we did not chose this option for KerMeta.

**Option 2: Parameterized classes support.** Parameterized classes (generics) are included in the language. This way, typed collections can be defined like any other class. The concept of generics is now widely adopted in OO languages, including the recent versions of Java and C#, and it offers an elegant solution to static typing. However, the introduction of parameterized classes imposes some changes in the EMOF type system.

In EMOF a type can be a primitive type, an enumeration or a class. Adding type parameters on classes makes the link between classes and types more complex. For instance, a class *Collection<G>* defined with a type parameter *G* does not define a type *Collection* but engenders a family of types by binding *G* to actual types. In other words the type of a variable cannot simply be a *Collection* but must be a collection of something.

Fig. 6 shows the principle of weaving genericity into EMOF. Box A shows the original EMOF classes. Class *Class* inherits from class *Type* and contains a set of *Features*, i.e. properties and operations. Box B displays how genericity can be modeled. On one hand a parameterized class is modeled by a class *ClassDefinition* which contains a set of *TypeVariables* and a set of *Features*. On the other hand *ParametrizedClass* inherits from *Type*, references a *ClassDefinition* and is composed of a binding between the type variable of the class definition and actual types.

A careful weaving must be performed to obtain a model both compatible with EMOF and which supports genericity. In our context, "compatible with EMOF" means that EMOF features should be available in the woven model. As an example, since EMOF provides a class named *Class* that has two properties *isAbstract* and *ownedFeatures*, the resulting model should provide a similar structure.

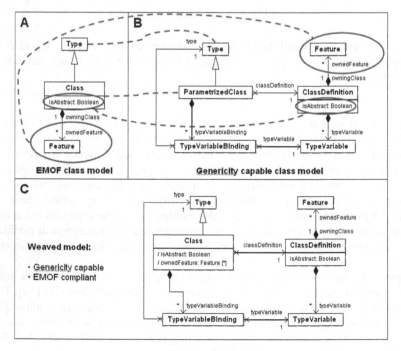

**Fig. 6.** Adding genericity to EMOF

Box C presents the result of the composition process. Classes such as *Type* or *Feature* play the role of join points between A and B models. EMOF class *Class* has been merged with classes *ClassDefinition* and *ParametrizedClass*. The name *Class* has been kept instead of *ParametrizedClass* to ensure EMOF compliance. Finally, some derived properties such as *isAbstract* and *ownedFeature* have been added to be fully-compatible with EMOF.

We have chosen this solution for the KerMeta language not only because it provides a general answer to the typing problem of navigation expressions but also, as presented in the next section, because it helps designing an elegant solution to the typing problem of OCL-like iterators.

## 3.5 Adding Function Objects (Typed Functions)

Iterators (such as *collect*, *select*, *reject* and *foreach*) are some of the most convenient constructions of OCL because they simplify a lot collection processing. The following expression (based on the metamodel described in Fig. 5) illustrates the kind of expressions that we want to type statically; the operation *toUpper* is supposed to be defined on String.

$$myA.b.collect\{\ o\ |\ o.label\ \}.first.toUpper\ .$$

Statically type checking such an expression raises two issues. First, in order to type-check the expression *o.label*, the type of variable *o* must be deduced from the type of the elements of the collection *myA.b*. Second, the type of the elements contained in the collection *myA.b.collect{ o | o.label }* depends on the type of the expression *o.label* in the body of *collect*.

In the following paragraphs, we examine two options to address these issues of typing.

**Option 1: Specific language constructions.** The problem can be addressed by defining iterators directly as constructions of the language. This is what is done in languages such as Xion, MTL, Java or C#. Iterators are implemented through specific statements such as *foreach* in C# and Java. This solution requires the set of iterators to be fixed during language design.

Each iterator needs to be specifically added to the language and specific rules for the type checker must be designed. Furthermore, this solution does not allow the programmer to easily define custom iterators or similar constructions on her classes. We thus rather propose a more general solution involving parameterized operations and an extension of the type system.

**Option 2: Function types and generic operations support.** The idea here is to extend the language to allow the definition of OCL-like iterators as regular operations in class *Collection*. In practice, this is implemented in dynamic OO languages such as Ruby [18] and in functional languages. This can be implemented in a statically typed OO language by extending the type system to support function types and by using generic operations.

The *collect* iterator for instance applies an expression to each element of a collection and collects the results. The operation *collect* has one parameter: an expression which is applied to each element of the collection. It returns a collection which contains the results of the application of the expression passed as parameter on each element of the collection. This example pin-points two major typing issues:

- The type of the parameter is a function. The language should then support function types.
- The return type depends on the type of the parameter. The language should support generic operations.

Using these concepts, iterators can be defined as regular operations. Fig. 7 presents the definition of the *collect* iterator in the class *Collection* of our prototype language.

```
abstract class Collection<G> {
[...]
    operation collect<T> (collector : <G -> T>) : Sequence<T> is do
        result := Sequence<T>.new
        from var it : Iterator<G> init iterator
        until it.isOff
        loop
            result.add( collector(it.next) )
        end
    end
[...]
}
```

**Fig. 7.** Using an operation to implement the collect iterator

Operation *collect* has a parameter *collector* which represents the expression to be applied to each element of the collection. The type of the parameter is a function type *<G -> T>*; the actual parameter should be a function applicable on the elements of the collection. *T* is a type parameter of the operation; it allows the expression of the link between the type of the parameters and the return type. Here the return type is a *Sequence* of *T*.

Fig. 8 shows how function types and generic operations can be added into EMOF, consistently with the adjustments made previously to support genericity.

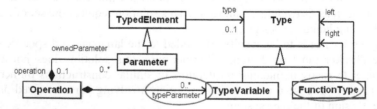

**Fig. 8.** Adding function objects and generic operations to EMOF

The class *TypeVariable* defines the generic formal type parameters of the operation, which must be used as the type of the formal parameters and return type of the operation. Actual types are bound to the generic formal type parameters for each call of the operation depending on the type of the actual parameters. In KerMeta, support for function types is provided by a sub-class *FunctionType* of EMOF class *Type*.

## 3.6 The Result: KerMeta

Fig. 9 shows an excerpt of the KerMeta metamodel, which results from the weaving of EMOF with our action specification metamodel. As detailed previously, it includes constructions that permit the static typing of KerMeta expressions in addition to EMOF constructions. The KerMeta metamodel can be divided in two parts,: structural and behavioral. The structural part is fully-compatible with EMOF. The behavioral part corresponds to class *Expression* and its sub-classes and is used for the specification of the operational semantics of metamodels.

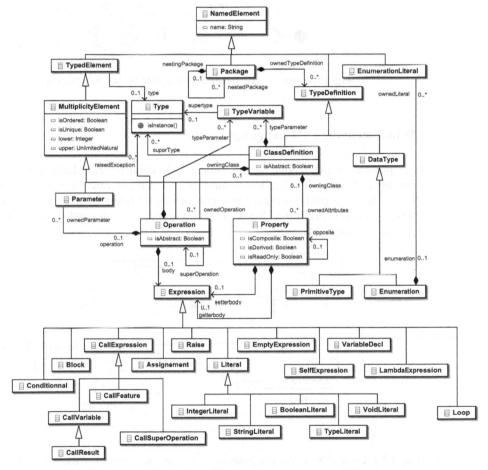

**Fig. 9.** Excerpt of the Kermeta metamodel

The next section presents an example of using KerMeta to define a simple state-machine language.

# 4 A Simple Example: A Language to Define Finite-State Machines

This section illustrates the benefits of an executable meta-language. The example is based on the definition of simple finite state-machines such as the one presented Fig. 10. Each state is labeled by a string, and each transition reads a character and writes another one. Section 4.1 shows how both the structure and the semantics of such a language can be defined and section 4.2 presents some simple example of how it can be used.

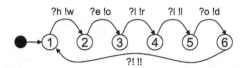

**Fig. 10.** A simple state machine to translate *"hello"* into *"world"*

## 4.1 Definition of the FSM Language

Fig. 11 presents a metamodel for this simple FSM (Finite-State Machines). An FSM is composed of states, it refers to an initial state and it can refer to a current state. A state has a name, it contains outgoing transitions and it refers to incoming transitions. A transition contains an input character and an output character and it refers both to a source and to a target state.

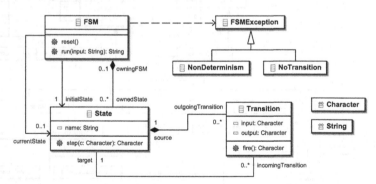

**Fig. 11.** Simple FSM metamodel

Fig. 12 presents the FSM metamodel in the textual syntax of KerMeta. The code highlighted in gray is derived from the class diagram represented in Fig. 11 and conforms to the structural part of KerMeta (and thus also to EMOF). The remaining part of the code represents the specification of the behavior of the operations (which could not be expressed in vanilla EMOF). The method *run* of the FSM reads its input string character by character. If the current state contains an outgoing transition which matches the read character then this transition is fired. If no transition or several transitions match the read character then an exception is raised. When a transition is fired the current state of the FSM becomes the target state of the transition.

```
01 : package fsm;
02 :
03 : require "kermeta/standard.kmt"
04 : using kermeta::standard
05 :
06 : // Some data types mapped to the kermeta standard library
07 : alias String : kermeta::standard::String;
08 : alias Character : kermeta::standard::Character;
09 :
10 : class FSM {
11 :    attribut ownedState : set State[0..*]#owningFSM
12 :    reference initialState : State[1..1]
13 :    reference currentState : State
14 :
15 :    operation run(input : String) : String raises FSMException is do
16 :        // reset if there is no current state
17 :        if currentState == void then reset end
18 :        // initialise result
19 :        result := ""
20 :        from var i : Integer init 0
21 :        until input.size == i
22 :        loop
23 :            result.append( currentState.step( input.charAt(i) ).toString )
24 :            i := i + 1
25 :        end
26 :    end
27 :    operation reset() : Void is do
28 :        currentState := initialState
29 :    end
30 : }
31 : class State {
32 :    attribut name : String
33 :    reference owningFSM : FSM#ownedState
34 :    attribut outgoingTransition : set Transition[0..*]#source
35 :    reference incomingTransition : set Transition[0..*]#target
36 :
37 :    operation step(c : Character) : Character raises FSMException is do
38 :        // Get the valid transitions
39 :        var validTransitions : Collection<Transition>
40 :        validTransitions := outgoingTransition.collect { t | t.input.equals(c) }
41 :        // Check if there is one and only one valid transition
42 :        if validTransitions.isEmpty then raise NoTransition.new end
43 :        if validTransitions.size > 1 then raise NonDeterminism.new end
44 :        // fire the transition
45 :        result := validTransitions.one.fire
46 :    end
47 : }
48 : class Transition {
49 :    reference source : State[1..1]#outgoingTransition
50 :    reference target : State[1..1]#incomingTransition
51 :    attribut output : Character
52 :    attribut input : Character
53 :
54 :    operation fire() : Character is do
55 :        // update FSM current state
56 :        source.owningFSM.currentState := target
57 :        result := output
58 :    end
59 : }
60 : abstract class FSMException {}
61 : class NonDeterminism inherits FSMException {}
62 : class NoTransition inherits FSMException {}
```

**Fig. 12.** Simple FSM in KerMeta concrete syntax

## 4.2 Benefits of Defining the FSM Language with an Executable Meta-language

The benefits of using KerMeta to describe a language such as the FSM language are two-fold. First, KerMeta is, by construction, compatible with EMOF which allows reusing existing EMOF tools to manipulate state machines. Fig. 13 (A) presents a screenshot of the model editor generated by EMF from the state machine metamodel.

Second, as KerMeta is executable, the state machines can be instantly simulated. Fig. 13 (B) presents a screenshot of the Kermeta interactive interpreter. The *require* statement is used to get access to a metamodel. The operation *system.load* loads a model from its representation in XMI (generated by the EMF generated editor).

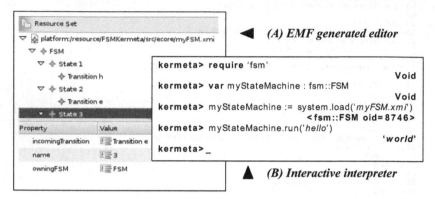

Fig. 13. KerMeta editor and interpreter

# 5 Related Works

Our work is related to many other works, and can be considered as some kind of synthesis of these works, in the specific context of model-driven engineering applied to language definition. The sections below include the major areas of related works.

**Grammars, graphs and generic environment generators.** Much of the concepts behind our work take their roots in the seminal work conducted in the late sixties on grammars and graphs and in the early eighties in the field of generic environment generators (such as Centaur [2]) that, when given the formal specification of a programming language (syntax and semantics), produce a language-specific environment. The generic environment generators sub-category has recently received significant industrial interest; this includes approaches such as Xactium [4], or Software Factories [7]. Among these efforts, it is Xactium which comes closer to our work. The major differences include the fact that we use aspect composition to generate the meta-meta level while preserving a clean separation of concerns, and that we have a fully static type system.

**Model-driven environments.** There are several ongoing efforts to promote the convergence of open-source model-driven environments, for instance: Modelware (http://www.modelware-ist.org/), TopCaseD (http://www.laas.fr/SPIP/spip-topcased/) and TopModL [9], and our work takes place in this context.

**Generative programming and domain-specific languages.** Generative programming aims at modeling and implementing system families in such a way that a given system can be automatically generated from a specification written in a domain-specific language. This includes multi-purpose model-aware languages such as Xion [10] or MTL [19], or model transformation languages such as QVT [13].

We share the vision of generative programming, and we use models to generate fully executable code which can be compiled. The Xion and MTL languages have had a direct impact on our work.

QVT is different as it addresses mappings between models. QVT works on structures, by specifying how one structure is mapped into another one; for instance translating a UML class diagram into a RDBMS schema. QVT is not suitable for the definition of the behavior of metamodels.

**Meta-CASE systems.** Meta-CASE systems, such as MetaEdit [16], Dome [6] or EMF [3], provide customized software engineering environments, separately from the main software components. The major difference with meta-CASE systems is that we remove the M3 level by the promotion process.

# 6 Conclusion

In this paper we have been discussing the rationales and benefits of weaving executability into meta-data languages. We have presented the benefits of defining the operational semantics of metamodels (using a statically-typed meta-language) for testing and simulation purposes.

We have explained how it is possible to design new executable meta-languages, using aspects to weave metamodels of existing meta-data languages with metamodels for precise action specifications. We have examined general issues related to meta-languages extensions, and we have presented several options to address these issues.

We have presented how to generate the metamodel of KerMeta, our experimental meta-language, and illustrated the benefits of static-typing and genericity, via an example featuring finite-state machines.

The same kind of process could be used to build tools such as parsers, code generators, interpreters or editors for specific languages. In fact each kind of tool requires a specific aspect to be composed with the metamodel of the language. For instance, a concrete syntax could be woven into the model of the language to allow the generation of a parser. Generally speaking, the idea is to define the aspect metamodel of the information which has to be composed in order to automatically obtain tools to work with domain-specific languages.

# References

1.  Abadi, M. and Cardelli, L. *A theory of objects*. New York: Springer, 1996.
2.  Borras, P., Clement, D., Despeyroux, T., Incerpi, J., Kahn, G., Lang, B. and Pascual, V. Centaur: the system. *Proceedings of the ACM SIGSOFT/SIGPLAN software engineering symposium on practical software development environments, 13* (5). 14 - 24.
3.  Budinsky, F., Steinberg, D., Merks, E., Ellersick, R. and Grose, T. *Eclipse Modeling Framework*. Addison Wesley Professional, 2003.

4.    Clark, T., Evans, A., Sammut, P. and Willans, J. Applied Metamodelling: A Foundation for Language Driven Development, http://albini.xactium.com, 2004.
5.    Clarke, S. Extending standard UML with model composition semantics. *Science of Computer Programming*, *44* (1). 71-100.
6.    Engstrom, E. and Krueger, J. Building and rapidly evolving domain-specific tools with DOME. *Proceedings of IEEE International Symposium on Computer-Aided Control System Design (CACSD 2000)*. 83-88.
7.    Greenfield, J., Short, K., Cook, S., Kent, S. and Crupi, J. *Software Factories: Assembling Applications with Patterns, Models, Frameworks, and Tools*. Wiley, 2004.
8.    Mellor, S., Tockey, S., Arthaud, R. and Leblanc, P. Action Language for UML: Proposal for a Precise Execution Semantics. *Proceedings of UML 98 (LNCS1618)*. 307-318.
9.    Muller, P.-A., Dumoulin, C., Fondement, F. and Hassenforder, M. The TopModL Initiative. in *UML Satellite Activities*, Springer, 2005, 242-245.
10.    Muller, P.-A., Studer, P., Fondement, F. and Bezivin, J. Platform independent Web Application Modeling and Development with Netsilon. *Accepted for publication in Journal on Software and Systems Modelling (SoSym)*. http://www.sciences.univ-nantes.fr/lina/atl/www/papers/netsilon_sosym.pdf.
11.    OMG. Meta Object Facility (MOF) Specification 1.4, Object Management Group, http://www.omg.org/cgi-bin/doc?formal/2002-04-03, 2002.
12.    OMG. MOF 2.0 Core Final Adopted Specification, Object Management Group, http://www.omg.org/cgi-bin/doc?ptc/03-10-04, 2004.
13.    OMG. Revised submission for MOF 2.0 Query/View/Transformation, Object Management Group (QVT-Merge Group), http://www.omg.org/cgi-bin/apps/doc?ad/2005-03-02, 2005.
14.    OMG. UML 2.0 Object Constraint Language (OCL) Final Adopted specification, Object Management Group, http://www.omg.org/cgi-bin/doc?ptc/2003-10-14, 2003.
15.    Scharli, N., Ducasse, S., Nierstrasz, O. and Black, A. Traits: Composable units of behavior. *Proceedings of ECOOP 2003*.
16.    Smolander, K., Lyytinen, K., Tahvanainen, V.-P. and Marttiin, P. MetaEdit: a flexible graphical environment for methodology modelling. *Proceedings of the third international conference on Advanced information systems engineering*.
17.    Straw, G., Georg, G., Song, E., Ghosh, S., France, R.B. and Bieman, J.M. Model Composition Directives. *Proceedings of the 7th International Conference Unified Modelling Language: Modelling Languages and Applications*. 84-97.
18.    Thomas, D., Fowler, C. and Hunt, A. *Programming Ruby - The Pragmatic Programmer's Guide, Second Edition*, 2004.
19.    Vojtisek, D. and Jézéquel, J.-M. MTL and Umlaut NG: Engine and Framework for Model Transformation. *ERCIM News*, *58*.
20.    Wirth, N. *Algorithms + data structures = programs*. Prentice-Hall, Englewood Cliffs, 1976.
21.    Ziadi, T., Hélouët, L. and Jézéquel, J.-M. Revisiting statechart synthesis with an algebraic approach. *Proceedings of the 26th International Conference on Software Engineering (ICSE 04)*.

# Keynote Address II:
# Domain-Specific Modeling: No One Size Fits All

Juha-Pekka Tolvanen

MetaCase, Finland
jpt@metacase.com

## Abstract

After 10 years of UML we have still not overcome the problems of the CASE tools of the 1980s. Imposing a "one size fits all" modeling language and generators has not significantly increased developers' productivity. Domain-Specific Modeling (DSM) provides a viable solution for improving development productivity by moving the focus from implementation concepts to problem domain concepts. With DSM, a new modeling language is created for each problem domain, with elements representing concepts from the domain world, not the code world. The DSM language follows domain abstractions and rules, guiding developers and allowing them to perceive themselves as working directly with domain concepts. When the domain is narrowed down to fit a single company's needs, domain-specific code generators can automatically produce full code straight from the models. Industrial experiences of this approach have consistently shown productivity increasing by a factor of 5-10.

This talk introduces DSM and shows a series of real-life examples from various fields of software product development, ranging from embedded cell phone software to B2B J2EE web sites. These cases illustrate a wide variety of design and generation requirements and demonstrate how different languages can support different kinds of modeling work. Having a modeling language focused on a given domain allows better code generation, optimization, error detection and reuse.

Defining a language and generator is usually considered a difficult task: this is certainly true if you try to make one language for everyone. The task eases considerably if you need make it for just one problem domain in one company - areas where you are the experts. In the second part of the talk we will explore the principles of creating DSM languages and generators: how to identify the necessary language constructs, different ways of building code generation, and how to deal with evolution of the DSM language.

L. Briand and C. Williams (Eds.): MoDELS 2005, LNCS 3713, pp. 279–279, 2005.
© Springer-Verlag Berlin Heidelberg 2005

# Refactoring OCL Annotated UML Class Diagrams*

Slaviša Marković and Thomas Baar

École Polytechnique Fédérale de Lausanne (EPFL)
School of Computer and Communication Sciences
CH-1015 Lausanne, Switzerland
{slavisa.markovic, thomas.baar}@epfl.ch

**Abstract.** Refactoring of UML class diagrams is an emerging research topic and heavily inspired by refactoring of program code written in object-oriented implementation languages. Current class diagram refactoring techniques concentrate on the diagrammatic part but neglect OCL constraints that might become syntactically incorrect by changing the underlying class diagram. This paper formalizes the most important refactoring rules for class diagrams and classifies them with respect to their impact on annotated OCL constraints. For refactoring rules, whose application on class diagrams could make attached OCL constraints incorrect, we formally describe how the OCL constraints have to be refactored to preserve their syntactical correctness. Our refactoring rules are defined in the graph-grammar based formalism proposed by the QVT Merge Group for the specification of model transformations.

## 1 Introduction

Modern software development processes, such as Rational Unified Process (RUP) [1] and eXtreme Programming (XP)[2] propagate the application of refactoring to support iterative software development. Refactoring (see [3] for an overview) is a structured technique to improve the quality of artifacts.

Artifacts produced in all phases of the software development lifecycle could become a subject of refactoring. However, existing techniques and tools mainly target the implementation code. Due to the increase in popularity of XP, the tool support for refactoring has been improved considerably over the last years. An up-to-date list of existing tools can be found at [4].

As the first author, Opdyke has tackled refactoring of implementation code in [5]. He defines refactorings as "... *reorganization plans that support change at an intermediate level*" and identifies 26 of such reorganization plans; now better known as refactoring rules. A refactoring rule for implementation code describes usually three main activities:

---

* This work was supported by Swiss National Scientific Research Fund under the reference number 2000-067917.

L. Briand and C. Williams (Eds.): MoDELS 2005, LNCS 3713, pp. 280–294, 2005.

1. Identify the parts of the program that should be refactored (code smells).
2. Improve the quality of the identified part by applying refactoring rules, e.g. the rule *MoveAttribute* moves one attribute to another class. As the result of this activity code smells such as *LargeClass* disappear.
3. Change the program at all other locations which are affected by the refactoring done in step 2. For example, if at some location in the code the moved attribute is accessed, this call became syntactically incorrect in step 2 and must be rewritten.

There are several catalogs of refactoring rules for different languages. The most complete and influential was published by Fowler in [6] for refactoring of Java code. The refactoring of artifacts more abstract than implementation code has become only recently a research topic. Some initial catalogs of refactoring rules for UML diagrams, mostly adaptations from the Java refactorings given by Fowler, are presented in [7, 8, 9]. Only few tools are currently available to support UML refactorings [10, 11]. None of these catalogs or tools takes OCL constraints into account, which might be attached to diagrams. Thus, applying these refactoring rules on diagrams that have constraints attached can make them syntactically incorrect. As spoken in terms of the above shown *MoveAttribute* example, the first two steps have been realized but the last step is ignored. The only refactoring approach of OCL we are aware of is by Correa and Werner [12], but here the focus is on improving badly structured OCL constraints and only to a very limited extent the relationship between OCL constraints and the underlying class diagram.

In this paper, the most important refactoring rules for class diagrams including attached OCL constraints are described formally. Not all class diagram refactoring rules have an impact on attached OCL constraints, so we first answer the question which of the rules for class diagrams can destroy the syntactical correctness of attached OCL constraints. If a rule has no impact on OCL we informally give the reasons for this. For the rules, whose application can influence the syntactical correctness of OCL constraints, we formalize the necessary changes on the OCL code. Up to now, we are not able to argue for all rules that they preserve the semantics of the refactored OCL constraint. This important topic will be addressed in our future research.

The formal description of refactoring rules is done on the level of the metamodel for UML and OCL. Unlike other approaches to describe refactoring rules formally [12, 7, 13] we do not use OCL pre/post-conditions for this purpose. The formalism of our choice is a slight adaptation of the QVT Merge Group [14] proposal to describe model transformations (note that refactoring can be seen as a special case of model transformation) that is based on graph grammars. Hence, our catalog of refactoring rules can also be seen as a case study for QVT.

In Sect. 2 we give preliminaries to understand our rules formally defined in Sect. 3. The insights gained during the formalization of the refactoring rules are summarized in Sect. 4 whereas Sect. 5 concludes the paper and gives an outlook of future research activities.

## 2     Description of Refactoring Rules with QVT

Model transformations are widely recognized now as the 'heart and soul' of model driven development [15]. The Object Management Group (OMG) is currently in the process to standardize the notation for the formal description of model transformations and has launched a corresponding *Query/Views/Transformations* Request for Proposals in 2002. In this paper, we mainly use the notation suggested by the QVT Merge Group in the subsequent proposal [14]. Since our aim is to refactor UML class diagrams annotated with OCL, our refactoring rules are based on the metamodels of UML and OCL. The following subsection recalls those parts of these metamodels that are used in our refactoring rules. Afterwards, a brief introduction to the QVT notation for model transformations is given.

### 2.1     Metamodels of UML/OCL

Metamodeling is a powerful technique to describe the abstract syntax of languages in a concise way. A metamodel for a language can roughly be seen as a class model whose classes and associations encode the concepts of the language and the relationships between them. Each syntactically correct sentence of the language can be represented in form of an instance of the metamodel.[1]

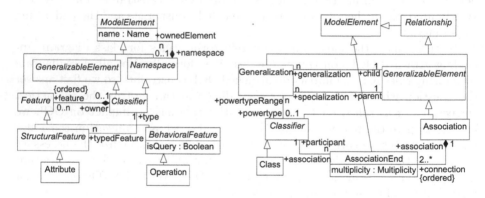

**Fig. 1.** Relevant parts of UML metamodel - Backbone and Relationships

Fig. 1 and Fig. 2 show relevant parts of the official metamodels for UML1.5 and OCL2.0 (for a complete definition see [16, 17]).[2] In addition to what is shown in Fig. 1 and Fig. 2, some of the refactoring rules refer to additional operations such as *Classifier.allParents:Set(Classifier)*. The definition for these operations are omitted here for the sake of brevity but can be found in the official metamodels [16, 17].

---

[1] In the remaining paper, such representations are called *MM-representations*.

[2] We have chosen UML1.5 as a basis, because in time of writing this paper, the OCL2.0 metamodel was not aligned yet to UML2.0 and still relied on UML1.5.

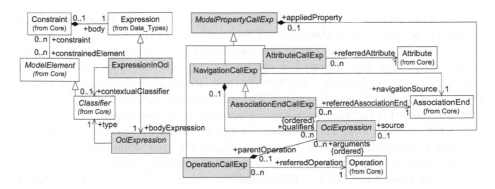

**Fig. 2.** Relevant part of OCL metamodel - Overview and ModelPropertyCallExp

## 2.2   Introduction to QVT

The QVT Merge Group proposal [14] aims at providing a standardized graphical notation to define model transformations.[3] A model transformation is defined as a set of *transformation rules* that, when applied on a source model, transform this into a target model. Source and target models are assumed to be represented as instances of metamodels. In general, QVT can handle the case of different metamodels for the source and target models but refactoring rules need only one metamodel for both source and target model.

A transformation rule in graphical notation consists of two patterns LHS (left hand side), RHS (right hand side) that are connected by a symbol indicating the transformation's type such as general transformation (←O→), relation (←◇→), or mapping (←▭▷). Optionally, a rule can have parameters and a when-clause comprising textual constraints.

The LHS and RHS patterns are denoted by a generalized form of object diagrams. In addition to the normal object diagrams, free variables can be used in order to indicate object identifiers and values of attributes. The same variable can occur both in LHS and RHS and refers – during the application of the rule – at all occurrences to the same value. Furthermore, links and objects in the pattern can be marked as non-existing (by a cross) what is read when applying the rule as a *negative matching condition*. In order to distinguish between objects/links occurring in the patterns and objects/links occurring in the concrete models we call the former ones as *pattern objects/links* and the later ones as *concrete objects/links*.

If a rule is applied on a source model (represented as an instance of the metamodel, i.e. as a graph), then each subgraph that matches with LHS is rewritten by a new subgraph derived from RHS under the same matching. A matching is an assignment of all variables occurring in LHS/RHS to concrete values. When applying a rule, the matching must obey the restrictions imposed by the when-

---

[3] The proposal defines also a purely textual notation that results, however, into less understandable transformation descriptions.

clause. This semantics of the QVT rules has the following consequences: If a pattern object appears in the rule's RHS but not in its LHS (i.e., in LHS there is no pattern object of the same class and identified by the same variable as in RHS) then – when applying the rule – a corresponding, concrete object is created. If there is a pattern object in LHS but not in RHS, then the matching object in the source model is deleted together with all 'dangling links'. Similarly, a link is created/deleted if the corresponding pattern link does not appear in both LHS and RHS (pattern links are identified by their role names and the pattern objects they connect). An attribute value is changed to the value derived from its specification in RHS under the current matching. Values of the attributes that are not mentioned in LHS and RHS remain unchanged. We have now explained the basic principle of rule applications and the fundamental constructs used in patterns. More complicated constructs will be explained later at the places they are needed.

As an example, suppose we want to describe the renaming of some model elements (such as attributes, operations, or classes) in UML models. As a first step, the model element, whose name should be changed, has to be selected. Then, its name can be changed to the new name if it is not already used by another model element of the same type in the same namespace.

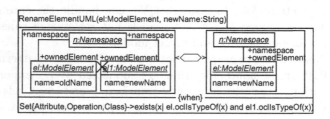

**Fig. 3.** Formalization of *RenameElement* refactoring

In the left pattern in Fig. 3, the model element *el* is selected by a parameter. If there is no other model element with a name equal to *newName* in the same namespace (indicated by the cross on *el1*), then the RHS pattern describes the change of the name of *el* to *newName*. Furthermore, the model elements *el* and *el1* must be both either attributes, operations, or classes. This is formalized by the when-clause.

## 3   A Catalog of UML/OCL Refactoring Rules

The rules presented below for refactoring of UML class diagrams and OCL are heavily inspired by refactoring rules for the static structure of Java programs given by Fowler in [6]. We took the freedom to change some rule names introduced by Fowler to indicate UML as their new application domain (e.g. *MoveMethod* became *MoveOperation*). Table 1 gives the list of the formalized rules. If the rule name has changed compared to the name used by Fowler, the original name is given in parentheses. In few cases, not only the name but also the semantics of the rule has slightly changed. Details on this are given at appropriate places in the text. Furthermore, Table 1 shows which of the rules have an influence on OCL. Note that two rules have an influence only either on the MM-representation or the textual notation of the OCL constraints.

**Table 1.** Overview of UML/OCL refactoring rules

| Refactoring rules | Influence on syntactical correctness of OCL constraints | |
|---|---|---|
| | MM-Representation | Textual Notation |
| *ExtractClass* | No | No |
| *ExtractSuperclass* | No | No |
| *RenameElement (RenameMethod)* | No | Yes |
| *MoveAttribute (MoveField)* | Yes | Yes |
| *MoveOperation (MoveMethod)* | Yes | Yes |
| *PullUpOperation (PullUpMethod)* | No | No |
| *PullUpAttribute (PullUpField)* | No | No |
| *PushDownOperation (PushDownMethod)* | Yes | Yes |
| *PushDownAttribute (PushDownField)* | Yes | No |

### 3.1   Rules Without Influence on OCL

**RenameElement** The rule *RenameElement* has been already used as an example in Sect. 2. Our version allows changing the name of many model elements (attributes, operations, and classes) whereas Fowler allows in [6] only renaming of methods.[4] This motivates the change of the rule name from *RenameMethod* to *RenameElement*.

At a first glance, renaming of an attribute requires to change all annotated OCL constraints where the attribute is used. However, these changes are required only for the textual notation. If the attached OCL constraint is seen as an instance of the OCL metamodel, then this instance remains the same. Note that the OCL metamodel *refers* only to the UML metamodel but does not comprise it. Thus, the change made in the underlying UML model is automatically propagated to all OCL expressions that use the changed UML element.

**PullUpAttribute/PullUpOperation** These two rules remove one attribute/ operation from a class and insert it into one of its superclasses, Fig. 4 shows a concrete example. We will concentrate our description on *PullUpAttribute*, the rule *PullUpOperation* is handled analogously.

---

[4] However, there is no principal obstacle for renaming other declarations in Java. The Eclipse tool [18], for example, provides capability for renaming other model elements, e.g. attributes.

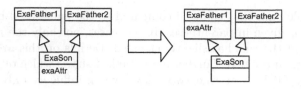

**Fig. 4.** Example for applying *PullUpAttribute*

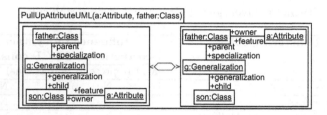

**Fig. 5.** *PullUpAttribute* refactoring rule

In Fig. 5, the pre-conditions to apply this rule are given: Attribute $a$ is owned by class *son* that must have a parent class *father*. The RHS pattern formalizes that the owner of attribute $a$ has changed from class *son* to class *father* (link from $a$ to *son* is deleted and to *father* created). Unlike the *PullUp* rules for Java, it is not necessary to state as a condition on the LHS, that in the pre-state the class *father* must not have an attribute with the same name as $a$. This is automatically imposed by a well-formedness rule in UML1.5 preventing a class to use names for its attributes which were already taken by one of its ancestor classes (cmp. Sect. 2.5.4.4 in [17]). If the class *father* had an attribute with the same name as attribute $a$ then this well-formedness rule would be broken for class *son*. Java is not so strict in this respect; e.g. names for private attributes can be reused in subclasses without problems.

The *PullUpAttribute* rule has no influence on OCL constraints because it widens the applicability of the moved attribute. The attribute `exaAttr` can only occur in attribute call expressions (*AttributeCallExp*) of form *exp*.`exaAttr`. Here, the type of expression *exp* must be compatible with the owner of the attribute *son*. After the refactoring, *exp*.`exaAttr` is still syntactically correct because the type of *exp* is also a subtype of *father* what is the new owner of the attribute.

**ExtractClass/ExtractSuperclass** The rule *ExtractClass* creates an empty class and connects it with a new association to the source class from where it is extracted. The multiplicity of the new association is 1 on both sides. The *ExtractSuperclass* rule creates an empty class as well but inserts it between the source class and one of its direct parent classes. Note that *Extract-Class/ExtractSuperclass* differ from the corresponding rules given by Fowler in [6]. Our rules are more atomic since they do not move features from the source class to the newly created class. In order to move features to the new class one could apply the refactorings *MoveAttribute/Operation* or *PullUpAttribute/Operation*.

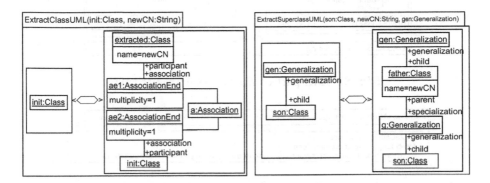

**Fig. 6.** *ExtractClass/ExtractSuperclass* refactoring rules

Applying the rules *ExtractClass/ExtractSuperclass* cannot alter the syntactical correctness of attached OCL constraints because both the rules merely introduce new model elements and do not delete or change old ones.

## 3.2   Rules with Influence on OCL

**PushDownAttribute** This rule is the counterpart of the rule *PullUpAttribute* from Fig. 5 and moves an attribute from the parent to some selected subclasses (see Fig. 7). As described by Fowler in [6] for the corresponding rule *PushDownField*, the attribute is moved only to such classes, where it is actually used.

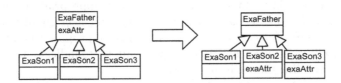

**Fig. 7.** Example for applying *PushDownAttribute*

The formalization of the *PushDownAttribute* rule is split into a UML and an OCL part shown in Fig. 8 and Fig. 9. It uses some elements of QVT that have not been explained yet as well as some 'private' elements that are missing in QVT.

Multiobjects as *gs* and *users* are already defined in QVT and represent a set of objects of the same type (here *Generalization* and *Class*). A multiobject that is linked to an ordinary pattern object – in our example, *gs* is linked to *father* – encodes the situation where all elements represented by the multiobject have actually a link to the object represented by the ordinary pattern object. Note

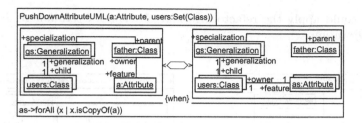

**Fig. 8.** UML part of *PushDownAttribute* rule

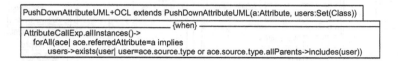

**Fig. 9.** OCL part of *PushDownAttribute* rule

that in Fig. 8 the variable *a* is passed as an parameter and thus *father* is implicitly determined as the owner of attribute *a*. The multiobject *gs* is determined as the set of generalizations which have *father* as the parent and which are linked with the elements represented by the multiobject *users* as their child. Note that the variable *users* is also passed as a variable to the rule in order to select the subclasses where the attribute *a* is moved to.

The multiplicity 1/1 at the link between *gs* and *users* is a 'private' pattern element and not included in the QVT Merge Group proposal yet. It was added here to enrich QVT's standard semantics of links between two multiobjects. The QVT semantics always assumes that such a link represents the situation where each element of the first multiobject is linked to every element of the second one, and vice versa. This standard semantics is not appropriate to describe the relationship between *gs* and *users* since each element of *gs* should be linked to exactly one element of *users*, and vice versa. Thus we propose to add multiplicities to pattern links between multiobjects what allows to indicate a non-standard semantics of such links in an intuitive way.

Another new element is the usage of operation *isCopyOf()* in the when-clause. Since the multiobject *as* occurs only in the RHS, we already know that all its elements are newly created. The multiplicity 1/1 between *as* and *users* let us further conclude, that for each element of *users* exactly one element of *as* is created. The when-clause and the intended semantics of *isCopyOf()* should ensure that each element of *as* is a shallow copy of attribute *a*. However, the elements of *as* have a different owner than *a* as indicated in RHS.

If *PushDownAttribute* is applied on a class diagram that has attached OCL constraints then we must ensure that in all constraints the attribute is never used in the superclass (*father*) nor in any class which is not compatible with at least one of the selected subclasses (*users*). This has been formalized by the rule shown in Fig. 9 that extends the rule of Fig. 8.

The rule *PushDownAttribute* does not cause changes of the OCL textual notation because instead of calling the attribute that is removed from the superclass, all calls now refer to a copy of this attribute at some of the subclasses. However, this refactoring causes changes on the MM-representation of OCL because every instance of *AttributeCallExp* that was calling the moved attribute has after the refactoring a new link to a newly created copy of the attribute in the subclasses.

**MoveAttribute** Applying the *MoveAttribute* rule helps to make a class smaller; an example of this refactoring is shown in Fig. 10.

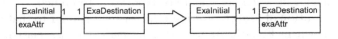

**Fig. 10.** Example for applying *MoveAttribute*

The attribute can only be moved to a class which is connected with the initial class by an association with multiplicity 1 at both ends. This allows objects of the initial class still to have access to the moved attribute after the refactoring. Not visible in the example but in the formalization in Fig. 11 is that neither the destination class nor one of its parents or children is allowed to have already an attribute with the same name as the moved attribute.

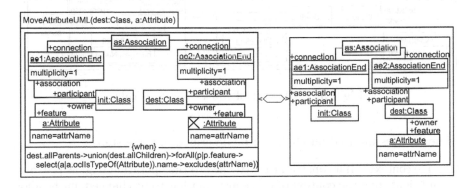

**Fig. 11.** UML part of *MoveAttribute* rule

Analogously to the changes of Java code described by Fowler for the corresponding refactoring *MoveField*, this rule must update OCL constraints on all locations where the moved attribute is applied. The necessary change of the OCL expressions can be seen as a kind of "Forward Navigation": Terms of form *exp*.exaAttr have to be rewritten as *exp*.destination.exaAttr. This change of OCL is formalized by the rule in Fig. 12.

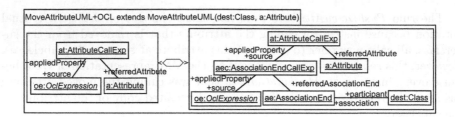

**Fig. 12.** OCL part of *MoveAttribute* rule

**MoveOperation** The rule *MoveOperation* is often applied when some class has too much behavior or when classes are collaborating too much.

The formalization of *MoveOperation* refactoring is similar to that of *MoveAttribute* and shown in Fig. 13. As for *MoveAttribute*, the association must have on both ends multiplicity 1. The main difference is that the name of the moved operation is now allowed to be already used in the parent classes of the destination since UML1.5 allows operations to be refined along the generalization hierarchy.

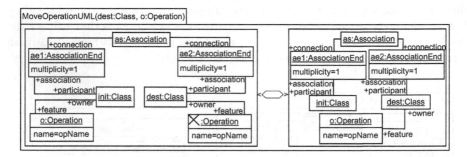

**Fig. 13.** UML part of *MoveOperation* rule

The changes induced on OCL can be described in three steps:

"Change context": If a constraint is attached to the operation (e.g. as pre/post-condition) then the context of this constraint has to be changed, in the above example from **context ExaInitial::exaOp()** to
**context ExaDestination::exaOp()**. Fowler describes in [6] informally this step as "Copy the code from the source method to the target". Note that in this step, we only copy the constraint body, the adaptations of the body will be done in the next steps.

"Backward navigation": After "Change context" the constraint attached to the moved operation still assumes variable **self** to be of type of the original class. At the new location, the variable **self** of the original class can be "simulated" by navigation from the destination class to the original class.

All occurrences of **self.**_propertyCallExp_ in the moved constraints[4] have to
be rewritten by **self.exaInitial.**_propertyCallExp_. This navigation is made
possible by the multiplicity 1 on the end of the original class. For this step,
Fowler says: "... create or use a reference from the target class to the source".

"Forward navigation": In case that the moved operation is a query we have to
redirect in all operation call expressions the operation reference. This means
to substitute all expressions _expression_.**exaOp()** by
_expression_.**exaDestination.exaOp()**. This step corresponds to "Turn the
source method into a delegating method" from Fowler's book.

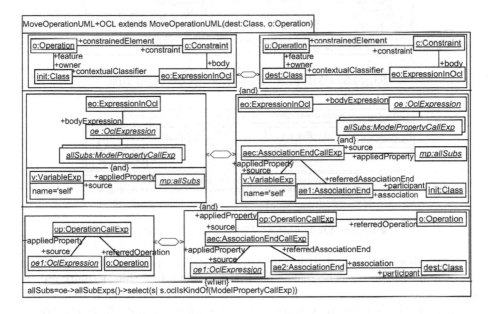

**Fig. 14.** OCL part of _MoveOperation_ rule

As shown in Fig. 14, the formalization of _MoveOperation_ refactoring is composed of three smaller transformations. The first sub-transformation is used to
change the context of one OCL expression. LHS and RHS in the rule differ only
in the class that represents the context for the attached OCL constraint.

In the second sub-transformation, the backward navigation is specified by
adding a new instance of _AssociationEndCallExp_ to the class from which the
operation has moved. The when-clause uses a new operation
_OclExpression.allSubExps:Set(OclExpression)_ that is not part of the OCL metamodel yet. The intended semantics of _allSubExps_ is to return all subexpressions
of the OclExpression it is applied to.

---

[4] Note that OCL allows in the textual notation to suppress **self**. Thus, **self** within
**self.**_propertyCallExp_ is sometimes given only implicitly.

The third sub-transformation describes "Forward navigation". The LHS pattern finds all occurrences where the moved operation is called. RHS specifies the insertion of an additional navigation to the destination class.

**PushDownOperation** This rule is very similar to *PushDownAttribute* but, somehow surprisingly, it has influence on the OCL textual notation.

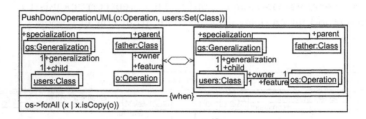

**Fig. 15.** UML part of *PushDownOperation* rule

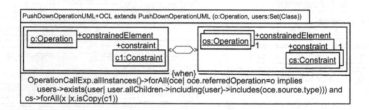

**Fig. 16.** OCL part of *PushDownOperation* rule

If the moved operation is a query and occurs in operation call expressions then the operation must be moved at least to all children that actually use the query.

No matter whether the moved operation is a query or not all its constraints have to be copied with an adapted context to the new operations in the selected subclasses (see Fig. 16).

## 4   Lessons Learned

The formalization of refactoring rules for UML/OCL has highlighted some advantages but also some missing elements of the graph-grammar based notation proposed by the QVT Merge Group in [14].

Since our refactoring rules are described in a graphical formalism they are much more accessible and understandable than existing formalizations of UML refactoring rules in form of pure OCL pre/post-conditions. Another advantage compared to purely OCL-based formalizations is the elegant solution of the *Frame problem* that is provided by the QVT semantics: only structures of the source model which match the LHS pattern of the rule are processed and substituted by the RHS under the same matching. The source model and the result of the refactoring can only differ in the elements that were made explicit in the RHS whereas an OCL formalization of the rules has to be read as "everything can change unless it is not explicitly stated that it remains the same".

Compared to corresponding refactoring rules for Java, the rules for UML and OCL are sometimes simpler to formulate because, for example, the visibility of model elements is ignored in the OCL syntax. Also the assumption in UML1.5 on the uniqueness of attributes names along the generalization hierarchy helps to keep the formulation of refactoring rules elegant. On the contrary, other concepts of UML such as multiple inheritance make the formulation of refactoring rules often more difficult.

Another interesting insight is that, not all class diagram refactoring rules can simply be classified in such a way that keep the OCL code untouched and in a way that can require a change in OCL. There is a group of rules in between which do not influence the OCL but whose applicability depends on some properties of the OCL constraints attached to the class diagram (e.g., in *PushDownAttribute* the LHS of the rule states that terms of a certain type do not appear).

**Proposed Change to QVT and OCL** We have encountered some elements that are missing in the current QVT proposal and OCL metamodel:

- Sometimes, it is inevitable to express, that an object is the (shallow) copy of another object but an operation such as *OclAny.isCopyOf(OclAny):Boolean* is not available in OCL yet although its semantics is clear.
- The pattern language of QVT should allow to express a 1-1 relationship between objects of two multiobjects. As an intuitive way, we propose to add multiplicities to links connecting two multiobjects.
- The operation *OclExpression.allSubExps():Set(OclExpression)* is needed to access all subexpressions of an expression and, thus, should be added to the OCL metamodel as an additional operation.

## 5    Conclusions and Future Work

In the literature, refactoring rules for UML class diagrams have been described so far only informally or in form of pure OCL pre/post-conditions. In this paper, we formalized these rules in a precise and very readable way by using the formalism proposed by the QVT Merge Group. As the main contribution, the impact of changing class diagrams on annotated OCL constraints has been investigated. For the rules having an impact on OCL, the class diagram refactoring rules have been extended by additional transformation rules for OCL expressions. The extended rules now allow keeping class diagrams, which are often subject of change, easily in sync with annotated OCL constraints. Note that the OCL constraints play an important role in modern model-based software development paradigms.

So far, we are only able to argue that the presented refactoring rules preserve the syntactical correctness of OCL constraints. In a next step we will investigate whether or not the given refactoring rules are also behavior preserving (or rather semantics preserving). As another activity, we are currently developing a tool that is capable to perform the described UML refactorings and propagate these refactorings to annotations given in OCL.

# References

[1]  Kruchten, P.: The Rational Unified Process: An Introduction. Addison-Wesley (2004)
[2]  Beck, K.: Extreme Programming Explained: Embrace Change. Addison-Wesley (2000)
[3]  Mens, T., Tourwé, T.: A survey of software refactoring. IEEE Trans. Software Eng. **30** (2004) 126–139
[4]  Refactoring community: Refactoring homepage. www.refactoring.com (2005)
[5]  Opdyke, W.F.: Refactoring: A Program Restructuring Aid in Designing Object-Oriented Application Frameworks. PhD thesis, University of Illinois at Urbana-Champaign (1992)
[6]  Fowler, M.: Refactoring: Improving the Design of Existing Programs. Addison-Wesley (1999)
[7]  Rumpe, B.: Agile Modellierung mit UML. Springer (2005) In German.
[8]  Astels, D.: Refactoring with UML. In: International Conference eXtreme Programming and Flexible Processes in Software Engineering. (2002) 67–70
[9]  Sunyé, G., Pennaneac'h, F., Ho, W.M., Guennec, A.L., Jézéquel, J.M.: Using UML action semantics for executable modeling and beyond. In Dittrich, K.R., Geppert, A., Norrie, M.C., eds.: CAiSE. Volume 2068 of LNCS., Springer (2001) 433–447
[10] Boger, M., Sturm, T., Fragemann, P.: Refactoring browser for UML. In: International Conference eXtreme Programming and Flexible Processes in Software Engineering. (2002) 77–81
[11] Porres, I.: Model refactorings as rule-based update transformations. In Stevens, P., Whittle, J., Booch, G., eds.: UML 2003 - The Unified Modeling Language, Modeling Languages and Applications, San Francisco, CA, USA. Volume 2863 of LNCS., Springer (2003) 159–174
[12] Correa, A., Werner, C.: Applying refactoring techniques to UML/OCL. In Baar, T., Strohmeier, A., Moreira, A., Mellor, S.J., eds.: UML 2004 - The Unified Modeling Language. Model Languages and Applications, Lisbon, Portugal. Volume 3273 of LNCS., Springer (2004) 173–187
[13] Gorp, P.V., Stenten, H., Mens, T., Demeyer, S.: Towards automating source-consistent UML refactorings. In Stevens, P., Whittle, J., Booch, G., eds.: UML 2003 - The Unified Modeling Language, Modeling Languages and Applications, San Francisco, CA, USA. Volume 2863 of LNCS., Springer (2003) 144–158
[14] OMG: Revised submission for MOF 2.0, Query/Views/Transformations, version 1.8. OMG Document ad/04-10-11 (2004)
[15] Sendall, S., Kozaczynski, W.: Model transformation: The heart and soul of model-driven software development. IEEE Software **20** (2003) 42–45
[16] OMG: UML 2.0 OCL Specification – OMG Final Adopted Specification. OMG Document ptc/03-10-14 (2003)
[17] OMG: UML 1.5 Specification. OMG Document formal/03-03-01 (2003)
[18] Eclipse community: Eclipse homepage. http: //www.eclipse.org (2005)

# Replicators: Transformations to Address Model Scalability

Jeff Gray[1], Yuehua Lin[1], Jing Zhang[1], Steve Nordstrom[2],
Aniruddha Gokhale[2], Sandeep Neema[2], and Swapna Gokhale[3]

[1] Dept. of Computer and Information Sciences, University of Alabama at Birmingham
Birmingham AL 35294-1170
{gray, liny, zhangj}@cis.uab.edu

[2] Institute for Software Integrated Systems, Vanderbilt University
Nashville TN 37235
{steve-o, gokhale, sandeep}@isis.vanderbilt.edu

[3] Dept. of Computer Science and Engineering, University of Connecticut
Storrs, CT 06269
ssg@engr.uconn.edu

**Abstract.** In Model Integrated Computing, it is desirable to evaluate different design alternatives as they relate to issues of scalability. A typical approach to address scalability is to create a base model that captures the key interactions of various components (i.e., the essential properties and connections among modeling entities). A collection of base models can be adorned with necessary information to characterize their replication. In current practice, replication is accomplished by scaling the base model manually. This is a time-consuming process that represents a source of error, especially when there are deep interactions between model components. As an alternative to the manual process, this paper presents the idea of a replicator, which is a model transformation that expands the number of elements from the base model and makes the correct connections among the generated modeling elements. The paper motivates the need for replicators through case studies taken from models supporting different domains.

## 1. Introduction

A powerful justification for the use of models concerns the flexibility and analysis that can be performed to explore various design alternatives. This is particularly true for distributed real-time and embedded (DRE) systems, which have many properties that are often conflicting (e.g., battery consumption versus memory size), where the analysis of system properties is often best provided at higher levels of abstraction [10]. A general metric for determining the effectiveness of a modeling toolsuite comprises the degree of effort required to make a change to a set of models. In previous work, we have shown how crosscutting concerns that are distributed across a model hierarchy can negatively affect the ability to explore design alternatives [9]. A

L. Briand and C. Williams (Eds.): MoDELS 2005, LNCS 3713, pp. 295–308, 2005.

form of alternative exploration involves experimenting with model structures by scaling up different portions of models and analyzing the result on scalability. This paper makes a contribution to model scalability and describes an approach that can be used to enable automated replication[1] to assist in rapidly scaling a model.

Scalability of modeling tools is of utmost concern to designers of large-scale DRE systems. From our personal experience, models can have multiple thousands of coarse grained components (others have reported similar experience, please see [11]). Modeling these components using traditional model creation techniques and tools can approach the limits of the effective capability of humans. The process of modeling a large DRE system with a domain-specific modeling language (DSML), or a tool like MatLab, is different than traditional UML modeling. In DRE systems modeling, the models consist of instances of all objects in the system, which can number into several thousand instances from a set of types defined in a meta-model (e.g., thousands of individual instantiations of a sensor type in a large sensor network model). The traditional class-based modeling of UML, and supporting tools, are typically not concerned with the same type of instance level focus.

The issue of scalability affects the performance of the modeling process, as well as the correctness of the model representation. Consider a base model consisting of a few modeling elements and their corresponding connections. To scale a base model to hundreds, or even thousands, of duplicated elements would require a lot of clicking and typing within the associated modeling tool. Furthermore, the tedious nature of manually replicating a base model may also be the source of many errors (e.g., forgetting to make a connection between two replicated modeling elements). A manual process to replication significantly hampers the ability to explore design alternatives within a model (e.g., after scaling a model to 800 modeling elements, it may be desired to scale back to only 500 elements, and then back up to 700 elements, in order to understand the impact of system size).

Often, large-scale system models leverage architectures that are already well suited toward scalability. Likewise, the modeling languages that specify such systems may embody similar patterns of scalability, and may lend themselves favorably toward a generative replication process. The contribution of this paper is automatic generation of large-scale system models from smaller, baseline specification models by applying basic transformation rules that govern the scaling [2] and replication behavior.

The rest of the paper is organized as follows: Section 2 provides an overview of the tools used in the paper, followed by an outline of the technical challenges of model replication in Section 3. Two case studies of model scalability using replicators are provided in Section 4. The conclusion offers summary remarks and a brief description of future work.

---

[1] The term "replicator" has specific meaning in object replication of distributed systems and in database replication. In the context of this paper, the term is used to refer to the duplication and proper connection of modeling elements to address scalability concerns.

# 2. Background: Supporting Technologies and Related Work

The implementation of the scalability approach described in this paper is tied to a specific set of tools, but we believe the general idea can be applied to many toolsuite combinations. The modeling tool and model transformation engine used in the work are overviewed in this section. The purpose of the paper is not to describe these tools in detail, but an introduction may be needed to understand the subsequent sections of the paper.

## 2.1 Model-Integrated Computing

A specific form of model-driven development, called Model-Integrated Computing (MIC) [17], has been refined at Vanderbilt University over the past decade to assist the creation and synthesis of computer-based systems. A key application area for MIC is those domains (such as embedded systems areas typified by automotive and avionics systems) that tightly integrate the computational structure of a system and its physical configuration. In such systems, MIC has been shown to be a powerful tool for providing adaptability in frequently changing environments. The Generic Modeling Environment (GME[2]) [12] is a meta-modeling tool based on MIC that can be configured and adapted from meta-level specifications (called the modeling paradigm) that describe the domain. An effort to make the GME MOF-compliant is detailed in [6]. Each meta-model describes a domain-specific modeling language (DSML). When using the GME, a modeling paradigm is loaded into the tool to define an environment containing all the modeling elements and valid relationships that can be constructed in a specific domain. A model compiler can be written and invoked from within the GME as a plug-in in order to synthesize a model into some other form (e.g., translation to code or simulation scripts). All of the modeling languages presented in the paper are developed and hosted within the GME.

## 2.2 C-SAW: A Model Transformation Engine

The paper advocates automated model transformation to address scalability concerns. The Constraint-Specification Aspect Weaver (C-SAW[3]) is the model transformation engine used in the case studies in Section 4. Originally, C-SAW was designed to address crosscutting modeling concerns [9], but has evolved into a general model transformation engine. C-SAW is a GME plug-in and is compatible with any meta-model; thus, it is domain-independent and can be used with any modeling language defined within the GME. The Embedded Constraint Language (ECL) is the language that we developed for C-SAW to specify transformations. The ECL is featured and briefly explained in Figures 3 and 5.

---

[2] The GME is an open-source meta-programmable tool that is available from the following website: http://escher.isis.vanderbilt.edu/tools/get_tool?GME
[3] The C-SAW plug-in, publications, and video demonstrations are available at the following website: http://www.cis.uab.edu/gray/Research/C-SAW/

## 2.3 Related Work

We are not aware of any other research that has investigated the application of model transformations to address scalability concerns like those illustrated in this paper. However, a large number of approaches to model transformation have been proposed by both academic and industrial researchers (example surveys can be found in [4, 15]). There is no specific reason that GME, ECL and C-SAW need to be used for the general notion of model replication promoted in this paper; we used this set of tools simply because they were most familiar to us and we had access to several DSMLs based on the combination of these tools. Other combinations of toolsuites are likely to offer similar capabilities.

There are several approaches to model transformation, such as graphical languages typified by graph grammars (e.g., GReAT [1] and Fujaba [7]), or a hybrid language (e.g., the ATLAS Transformation Language [3] and Yet Another Transformation Language [14]). Graphical transformation languages provide a visual notation to specify graphical patterns of the source and target models (e.g., a subgraph of a graph). However, it can be tedious to use purely graphical notations to describe complicated computation algorithms. As a result, it may require generation to a separate language to apply and execute the transformations. A hybrid language transformation combines declarative and imperative constructs inside the transformation language. Declarative constructs are used typically to specify source and target patterns as transformation rules (e.g., filtering model elements), and imperative constructs are used to implement sequences of instructions (e.g., assignment, looping and conditional constructs). However, embedding predefined patterns renders complicated syntax and semantics for a hybrid language.

With respect to model transformation standardization efforts, C-SAW was under development two years prior to the initiation of OMG's Query View Transformation (QVT) request for proposal. It seems reasonable to expect that the final QVT standard would be able to describe transformations similar in intent to those presented in this paper. For the purpose of exploring our research efforts, we have decided to continue our progress on developing C-SAW and later re-evaluate the merits of merging toward a standard.

# 3. Alternative Approaches to Model Replication

This section provides a discussion of key characteristics of a model replication technique. An overview of existing replication approaches is presented and a comparison of each approach is made with respect to the desired characteristics. The section offers an initial justification of the benefits of a model transformation engine to support scalability of models through replicating transformations.

## 3.1 Key Characteristics for a Replication Approach

An approach that supports model scalability through replication should have the following desirable characteristics: 1) retains the benefits of modeling, 2) general across multiple modeling languages, and 3) flexible to support user extensions. Each of these characteristics (C1 through C3) is discussed further in this subsection.

**C1. Retains the benefits of modeling:** As stated in Section 1, the power of modeling comes from the ability to perform analysis (e.g., model checking and verification of system properties) in a way that would otherwise be difficult at the implementation level. A second advantage is the opportunity to explore various design alternatives. A model replication technique should not remove these benefits. That is, the replication mechanism and tool support should not perform scalability in such a way that analysis and design exploration is not possible. This seems to be an obvious characteristic to desire, but we have observed replication approaches that void these fundamental benefits of modeling.

**C2. General across multiple modeling languages:** A replication technique that is generally applicable across multiple modeling languages can leverage the effort expended in creating the underlying transformation mechanism. A side benefit of such generality is that a class of users can become familiar with a common replicator technique that can be applied to many modeling languages they use.

**C3. Flexible to support user extensions:** Further reuse can be realized if the replicator supports multiple types of scalability concerns in a templatized fashion (e.g., the name, type, and size of the elements to be scaled are parameters to the replicator). The most flexible type of replication would allow alteration of the semantics of the replication more directly using a notation or language that can be manipulated by an end-user. In contrast, replicator techniques that are hard-coded and unable to be extended restrict the impact for reuse, thus limiting the value of the time spent on creating the replicator.

The next subsection will compare existing replicator approaches to these characteristics.

## 3.2 Existing Approaches to Support Model Replication

From our past experience in applying MIC to DRE modeling, the following categories of techniques represent alternative approaches to support replicators: 1) an intermediate phase of replication within a model compiler, 2) domain-specific model compiler for a particular modeling language, and 3) specification of a replicator using a model transformation engine. Each of these approaches is discussed in this subsection and compared to the desiderata mentioned in Section 3.1.

**A1. Intermediate stage of model compilation:** As a model compiler performs its translation, it typically traverses a parse tree (containing an internal representation of the model) through data structures and APIs provided by the host modeling tool. Several model compilers can be con-

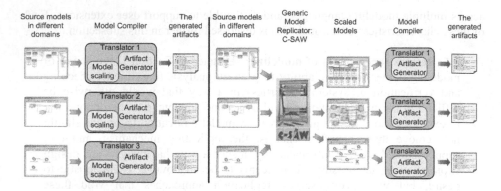

**Fig. 1.** Alternative Approaches for Scaling Models

constructed that generate different artifacts from the same model. One of our earlier ideas for scaling large models considered performing the replication as an intermediate stage of the model compiler. Prior to the generation phase of the compilation, the parse tree can be converted to an intermediate representation that can be expanded to address the desired scalability. This idea is represented in the left-hand side of Figure 1.

This is the least satisfying solution to replication and violates all three of the desired characteristics enumerated in Section 3.1. The most egregious violation is that the approach destroys the benefits of modeling. Because the replication is performed as a pre-processing phase in the model compiler, the replicated structures are never rendered back into the modeling tool itself. Thus, analysis and design alternatives are not made available to the end-user for further consideration. Furthermore, the pre-processing rules are hard-coded into the model compiler and offer little opportunity for reuse across other modeling languages. In general, this is the least flexible of all approaches that we considered.

**A2. Domain-specific model compiler to support replication:** A model compiler is not only capable of synthesizing to an external artifact, but is also able to alter the current model structure through API calls. Another approach to model scalability is to construct a model compiler that is capable of replicating the models as they appear in the host modeling tool. Such a model compiler has detailed knowledge of the specific modeling language, as well as the particular scalability concern. Unlike approach A1, this technique preserves the benefits of modeling because the end result of the replication provides visualization of the scaling, and the replicated models can be further analyzed and refined.

This approach has a few drawbacks as well. Because the replication rules are domain-specific and hard-coded into the model compiler, the developed replicator has limited use outside of the intended modeling language. Although generality across modeling languages is lost, some replicators based on this approach may have means to parameterize certain parts of the replication process (e.g., the replicator may request the size to scale, or the name of specific elements that are to be scaled).

**A3. Replication with a model transformation specification:** A special type of model compiler within the GME is a plug-in that can be applied to any meta-model (i.e., it is domain-independent). The C-SAW model transformation engine (see Section 2.2) is an example of a plug-in that can be applied to any modeling language. C-SAW executes as an interpreter and renders all transformations (as specified in the ECL) back into the host modeling tool. The ECL can be altered very rapidly to analyze the affect of different degrees of scalability (e.g., the affect on performance when the model is scaled from 256 to 512 nodes).

This third approach to replication advocates the use of a model transformation engine like C-SAW to perform the replication (please see the right-hand side of Figure 1 for an overview of the technique). This technique satisfies all of the desirable characteristics of a replicator: by definition, the C-SAW tool is applicable across many different modeling languages, and the replication strategy is specified in a way that can be easily modified, as opposed to a hard-coded rule in the approaches described in A1 and A2. With a model transformation engine, a code generator is still required for each domain (see "Artifact Generator" in the right-hand side of Figure 1), but the scalability issue is addressed independently of the modeling language. Our most recent efforts have explored technique A3 on several existing modeling languages as described in the next section.

# 4. Case Studies in Scalability with Model Replicators

In this section, the concept of model replicators is demonstrated on two separate example modeling languages that were created in GME for different domains. In each subsection, the DSML is briefly introduced, including a discussion of the scalability issues and how ECL model transformations solve the scalability problem. The DSMLs chosen are:

- System Integration Modeling Language, which has been used to model hardware configurations consisting of up to 5,000 processing nodes for high-energy physics applications at Fermi National Accelerator Lab.
- Event QoS Aspect Language, which has been used to configure a large collection of federated event channels for mission computing avionics applications.

In addition to the above cases studies, our initial exploration into scalability of models was performed for a different modeling language representing unmanned air vehicles to address various quality of service concerns related to transmitted video (e.g., bandwidth and frame size adjustment). Space limitations prohibit further discussion of this third example.

## 4.1 Scaling the System Integration Modeling Language

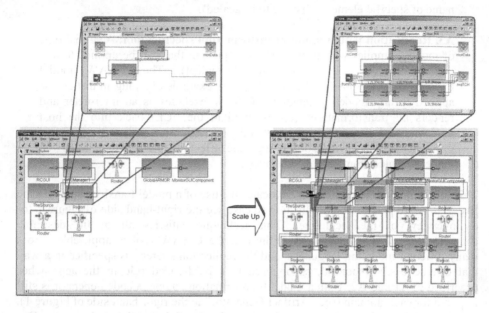

**Fig. 2.** Visual Example of SIML Scalability

The System Integration Modeling Language (SIML) is a language developed to specify configurations of large-scale fault tolerant data processing systems [16]. Features of SIML include hierarchical component decomposition and dataflow modeling with point-to-point and publish-subscribe communication between components. There are several rules defined by the SIML meta-model:

- A *system* model may be composed of several independent *regions*
- Each *region* model may be composed of several independent *local process groups*
- Each *local process group* model may include several primitive application models
- Each system, region, and local process group must have a representative *manager* that is responsible for mitigating failures in its area

The *local process group* is the set of processes that run the set of critical applications to perform the system's overall function. In a data processing network, the local process group would include the algorithmic tasks to perform as well as the data processing and transport tasks. A *region* is simply a collection of local process groups, and a *system* is defined as a collection of regions and possibly other supporting processes. As the SIML language itself is used to describe configurations of highly scalable architectures, it embodies some patterns of scalability as a by-product of the domain for which it was created. These patterns include the one-to-many relationship between system and regional managers, and also a one-to-many relationship between regional and local process group managers. These relationships are well defined. Because this relationship can be captured, it should be feasible to perform automatic generation of additional local process groups and/or regions to create larger and more elaborate system models.

Scaling up a system configuration using SIML can involve: 1) an increase in the number of regions, 2) an increase in the number of local process groups per region, or 3) both 1 and 2. The left-hand side of Figure 2 shows a simple SIML base model that captures a system composed of one region and one local node in that region (shown as an expansion of the parent region), utilizing a total of 15 physical modeling elements (several elements are dedicated to supporting applications not included in any region). Consider this example when the system is increased to 9 regions with 6 local process groups per region. Such replication involves the following:

- Replication of the local process group models
- Replication of entire region models and their contents
- Generation of communication connections between regional managers and newly created local managers
- Generation of additional communication connections between the system manager and new regional manager processes

The scaled model is shown in the right-hand side of Figure 2. This example scales to just 9 regions and 6 nodes per region simply because of the printed space to visualize the figure. In practice, SIML models have been scaled to 32- and 64-node models. However, the initial scaling in these cases was performed manually. The ultimate goal of the manual process was to scale to 2500 nodes. After 64 nodes, it was determined that scaling to further nodes would be too tedious to perform without proper automation through improved tool support. Even with just a small expansion, the manual application of the same process would require an extraordinary amount of manual effort (much mouse-clicking and typing) to bring about the requisite changes, and increase the potential for introducing error into the model (e.g., forgetting to add a required connection). If the design needs to be scaled forward or backward, a manual approach would require additional effort that would make the exploration of design alternatives impractical.

**ECL Transformation to Scale SIML:** The scalability illustrated in Figure 2 can be performed with a model transformation, as illustrated by the ECL specification shown in Figure 3. As a point of support for the effectiveness of replicators as transformations, this ECL specification was written in less than an hour by a user who was very familiar with ECL, but had studied the SIML meta-model for less than a few hours.

The ECL transformation specification is composed of an aspect and several strategies. An aspect serves as the starting point of a transformation, and a strategy is used to specify the computation entities to perform a particular transformations task. In Figure 3, the aspect "Start" (Line 1) invokes two strategies, "scaleUpNode" and "scaleUpRegion" in order to replicate the local process group node ("L2L3Node") within the region model, and the region itself. The strategy "scaleUpNode" (Line 7) discovers the "Region" model, sets up the context for the transformation, and calls the strategy "addNode" (Line 12) that will recursively increase the number of nodes based on the given name "L2L3Node." The new node instance is created on Line 18, which is followed by the construction of the communication connections between ports, regional managers and the newly created nodes (Line 21 to Line 23). Some other connections are omitted here for the sake of brevity. Two other strategies "scaleUpRegion" (Line 29) and "addRegion" (Line 34) follow the similar mechanism as above.

```
1   aspect Start()
2   {
3     scaleUpNode("L2L3Node", 5); //add 5 L2L3Nodes in the Region
4     scaleUpRegion("Region", 8); //add 8 Regions in the System
5   }
6
7   strategy scaleUpNode(node_name : string; max : integer)
8   {
9       rootFolder().findFolder("System").findModel("Region").addNode(node_name,max,1);
10  }
11
12  strategy addNode(node_name, max, idx : integer)              //recursively add nodes
13  {
14    declare node, new_node, input_port, node_input_port : object;
15
16    if (idx<=max) then
17        node := rootFolder().findFolder("System").findModel(node_name);
18        new_node := addInstance("Component", node_name, node);
19
20        //add connections to the new node; three similar connections are omitted here
21        input_port := findAtom("fromITCH");
22        node_input_port := new_node.findAtom("fromITCH");
23        addConnection("Interaction", input_port, node_input_port);
24
25        addNode(node_name, max, idx+1);
26    endif;
27  }
28
29  strategy scaleUpRegion(reg_name : string; max : integer)
30  {
31      rootFolder().findFolder("System").findModel("System").addRegion(reg_name,max,1);
32  }
33
34  strategy addRegion(region_name, max, idx : integer)          //recursively add regions
35  {
36    declare region, new_region, out_port, region_in_port, router, new_router : object;
37
38    if (idx<=max) then
39        region := rootFolder().findFolder("System").findModel(region_name);
40        new_region := addInstance("Component", region_name, region);
41
42        //add connections to the new region; four similar connections are omitted here
43        out_port := findModel("TheSource").findAtom("eventData");
44        region_in_port := new_region.findAtom("fromITCH");
45        addConnection("Interaction", out_port, region_in_port);
46
47        //add a new router and connect it to the new region
48        router := findAtom("Router");
49        new_router := copyAtom(router, "Router");
50        addConnection("Router2Component", new_router, new_region);
51
52        addRegion(region_name, max, idx+1);
53    endif;
54  }
```

**Fig. 3.** ECL Model Transformation to Perform Replication Shown in Figure 2

Flexibility of the replicator can be achieved in several ways. Lines 3 and 4 specify the magnitude of the scaling operation, as well as the names of the specific nodes and regions that are to be replicated. In addition to these parametric changes that can be made easily, the semantics of the replication can be changed because the transformation specified can be modified directly. This is not the case in approaches A1 and A2 from Section 3.2 because the replication semantics are hard-coded into the model compiler.

## 4.2 Scaling the Event QoS Aspect Language

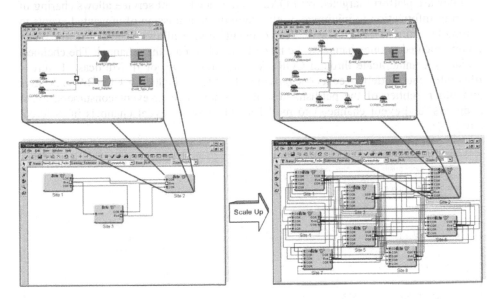

**Fig. 4.** Illustration of Replication in EQAL

The Event QoS Aspect Language (EQAL) [5] is a DSML for graphically specifying publisher-subscriber service configurations for large-scale DRE systems. Publisher-subscriber mechanisms, such as event-based communication models, are particularly relevant for large-scale DRE systems (e.g., avionics mission computing, distributed audio/video processing, and distributed interactive simulations) because they help reduce software dependencies and enhance system composability and evolution. In particular, the publisher-subscriber architecture of event-based communication allows application components to communicate anonymously and asynchronously. The publisher-subscriber communication model defines three software roles:

- *Publishers* generate events to be transmitted
- *Subscribers* receive events via hook operations
- *Event channels* accept events from publishers and deliver events to subscribers

The EQAL modeling environment consists of a GME meta-model that defines the concepts of publisher-subscriber systems, in addition to several model compilers that synthesize middleware configuration files from models. The EQAL model compilers automatically generate publisher-subscriber service configuration files and component property description files needed by the underlying middleware.

The EQAL meta-model defines a modeling paradigm for publisher-subscriber service configuration models, which specify quality of service (QoS) configurations, parameters, and constraints. For example, the EQAL meta-model contains a distinct set of modeling constructs for building a federation of real-time event services supported by the Component-Integrated ACE ORB (CIAO) [8], which is a component middleware platform targeted by EQAL. A federated event service allows sharing of filtering information to minimize or eliminate the transmission of unwanted events to a remote entity. Moreover, a federated event service allows events that are being communicated in one channel to be made available on another channel. The channels typically communicate through CORBA Gateways, UDP, or IP Multicast. Figure 4 illustrates the modeling concepts provided by EQAL including CORBA Gateways and other entities of the publish-subscribe paradigm (e.g., event consumers, event suppliers, and event channels) to model a federation of event channels in different sites.

```
1   //traverse the original sites to add CORBA_Gateways
2   //n is the number of the original sites
3   //m is the total number of sites after scaling
4   strategy traverseSites(n, i, m, j : integer)
5   {
6     declare id_str : string;
7     if (i <= n) then
8       id_str := intToString(i);
9       rootFolder().findModel("NewGateway_Federation").findModel("Site " + id_str)
10                                                      .addGateWay_r(m, j);
11      traverseSites(n, i+1, m, j);
12    endif;
13  }
14
15  //recursively add CORBA_Gateways to each existing site
16  strategy addGateWay_r(m, j: integer)
17  {
18    if (j<=m) then
19      addGateWay(j);
20      addGateWay_r(m, j+1);
21    endif;
22  }
23
24  //add one CORBA_Gateway and connect it to Event_Channel
25  strategy addGateWay(j: integer)
26  {
27    declare id_str : string;     declare ec, site_gw : object;
28    id_str := intToString(j);
29    addAtom("CORBA_Gateway", "CORBA_Gateway" + id_str); //create one CORBA_Gateway
30    ec := findModel("Event_Channel");  site_gw := findAtom("CORBA_Gateway" + id_str);
31    addConnection("LocalGateway_EC", site_gw, ec);
32  }
```

**Fig. 5.** ECL Fragment to Perform the First Step of Replication in EQAL

The scalability issues in EQAL arise when a small federation of event services must be scaled to a very large system, which usually accommodates a large number of publishers and subscribers. It is conceivable that EQAL modeling features, such as the event channel, the associated QoS attributes, connections and event correlations must be applied repeatedly to build a large scale federation of event services. Figure 4 shows a federated event service with 3 sites, which is then scaled up to federated event services with 8 sites. This scaling process includes three steps:

- Add 5 CORBA_Gateways to each original site
- Repeatedly replicate one site instance to add 5 more extra sites, each with 5 CORBA_Gateways
- Create the connections between all of the 8 sites

The above process can be automated with an ECL transformation that is applied to a base model with C-SAW. Figure 5 shows a fragment of the ECL specification for the first step, which adds more Gateways to the original sites. The other steps would follow similarly using ECL. The size of the replication in this example was kept to 5 sites so that the visualization could be rendered appropriately in Figure 4. The approach could be extended to scale to hundreds or thousands of sites and gateways.

## 5. Conclusion

This paper has demonstrated the effectiveness of using a general model transformation engine to specify replicators that assist in scaling models. Among the approaches to model scalability, a model transformation engine offers several benefits, such as domain-independence and improvements to productivity (when compared to either the corresponding manual effort, or the effort required to write plug-ins that are specific to a domain and scalability issue). The case studies presented in this paper highlight the ease of specification and the general flexibility provided across domains.

Transformation specifications, such as those used to specify the replicators in this paper, are written by humans and prone to error. To improve the robustness and reliability of model transformation, there is a need for testing and debugging support to assist in finding and correcting the errors in transformation specifications. Ongoing and future work on ECL focuses on the construction of testing and debugging utilities within C-SAW to ensure the correctness of the ECL transformation specifications [13].

## 6. Acknowledgments

This project was supported by the DARPA Program Composition for Embedded Systems (PCES) program and the National Science Foundation under CSR-SMA-0509342.

# References

1. Aditya Agrawal, Gábor Karsai, and Ákos Lédeczi, "An End-to-End Domain-Driven Software Development Framework," Object-Oriented Programming, Systems, Languages, and Applications (OOPSLA) – Domain-driven Track, Anaheim, CA, October 2003, pp. 8-15.
2. Don Batory, Jacob Neal Sarvela, and Axel Rauschmeyer, "Scaling Step-Wise Refinement," IEEE Transactions on Software Engineering, June 2004, pp. 355-371.
3. Jean Bézivin, F. Jouault, and P. Valduriez, "On the Need for MegaModels," OOPSLA Workshop on Best Practices for Model-Driven Software Development, Vancouver, BC, October 2004.
4. Krzysztof Czarnecki, and Simon Helsen, "Classification of Model Transformation Approaches," OOPSLA Workshop on Generative Techniques in the Context of Model-Driven Architecture, Anaheim, CA, October 2003.
5. George Edwards, Gan Deng, Douglas Schmidt, Aniruddha S. Gokhale, Bala Natarajan, "Model-Driven Configuration and Deployment of Component Middleware Publish/Subscribe Services," Generative Programming and Component Engineering (GPCE), Vancouver, BC, October 2004, pp. 337-360.
6. Matthew Emerson, Janos Sztipanovits, and Ted Bapty, "A MOF-Based Meta-modeling Environment," Journal of Universal Computer Science, October 2004, pp. 1357--1382.
7. The FUJABA Toolsuite, http://www.fujaba.com
8. Aniruddha Gokhale, Douglas Schmidt, Balachandran Natarajan, Jeff Gray, and Nanbor Wang, "Model-Driven Middleware," in Middleware for Communications, (Qusay Mahmoud, editor), John Wiley and Sons, 2004.
9. Jeff Gray, Ted Bapty, Sandeep Neema, and James Tuck, "Handling Crosscutting Constraints in Domain-Specific Modeling," Communications of the ACM, Oct. 2001, pp. 87-93.
10. John Hatcliff, William Deng, Matthew Dwyer, Georg Jung, Venkatesh Prasad Ranganath, "Cadena: An Integrated Development, Analysis, and Verification Environment for Component-based Systems," International Conference on Software Engineering, Portland, OR, May 2003, pp. 160-173.
11. Sven Johann and Alexander Egyed, "Instant and Incremental Transformation of Models," Automated Software Engineering, Linz, Austria, September 2004, pp. 362-365.
12. Ákos Lédeczi, Arpad Bakay, Miklos Maroti, Peter Volgyesi, Greg Nordstrom, Jonathan Sprinkle, and Gábor Karsai, "Composing Domain-Specific Design Environments," IEEE Computer, November 2001, pp. 44-51.
13. Yuehua Lin, Jing Zhang, and Jeff Gray, "A Framework for Testing Model Transformations," Model-Driven Software Development, Springer, 2005.
14. Octavian Patrascoiu, "Mapping EDOC to Web Services using YATL," 8th International IEEE EDOC Conference, Monterey, CA, September 2004, pp. 286-297.
15. Shane Sendall and Wojtek Kozaczynski, "Model Transformation – the Heart and Soul of Model-Driven Software Development," IEEE Software, Special Issue on Model Driven Software Development, September/October 2003 (Vol. 20, No. 5). pp. 42-45.
16. Shweta Shetty, Steve Nordstrom, Shikha Ahuja, Di Yao, Ted Bapty, and Sandeep Neema, "Systems Integration of Large Scale Autonomic Systems using Multiple Domain Specific Modeling Languages," Engineering of Autonomic Systems, Greenbelt, MD, April 2005.
17. Janos Sztipanovits and Gábor Karsai, "Model-Integrated Computing," IEEE Computer, April 1997, pp. 10-12.

# Simplifying Transformations
# of OCL Constraints

Martin Giese[1] and Daniel Larsson[2]

[1] Johann Radon Institute for Computational and Applied Mathematics
Altenbergerstr. 69, A-4040 Linz, Austria
martin.giese@oeaw.ac.at
[2] Chalmers University of Technology
Department of Computer Science and Engineering
S-412 96 Gothenburg, Sweden
danla@cs.chalmers.se

**Abstract.** With the advent of Model Driven Architecture, OCL constraints are no longer necessarily written by humans. They can be part of models that emerge from a chain of transformations. They might be the result of instantiating templates, of combining prefabricated parts, or of more general computation. Such generated specifications will often contain redundancies that reduce their readability. In this paper, we explore the possibilities of transforming OCL formulae to a simpler form through the repeated application of simple rules. We discuss the different kinds of rules that are needed, and we describe a prototypical implementation of the approach.

## 1 Introduction

The Object Constraint Language (OCL) [12] is designed with human authors and readers in mind. While some of today's UML tools allow attaching OCL constraints to diagrams and checking their syntax with a parser, there is practically no support for authoring OCL specifications. But writing good specifications is hard, and as the software to be specified becomes larger and more complex, designers will need tools that help them with that task.

OCL constraints might result from a transformation of a more abstract description of the system. For instance, constraints written at the analysis level might be transformed into design level constraints by some tool. Or a specification in some other graphical or logic-based formalism might be translated into OCL.

While tools performing such tasks have yet to be written, we already encounter tool-generated constraints in connection with an extension of the 'design pattern' instantiation mechanism provided by various case tools [2].[3] The idea is to let the user instantiate templates, pieces of class diagrams, which provide implementations for various design patterns. As part of the instantiation, one

---

[3] In the present work we employ Borland Together ControlCenter (TCC), see
http://www.borland.com/together/index.html.

L. Briand and C. Williams (Eds.): MoDELS 2005, LNCS 3713, pp. 309–323, 2005.
© Springer-Verlag Berlin Heidelberg 2005

can generate OCL constraints that capture certain properties of the pattern.[4] Due to the availability of the tool as part of the KeY system [1], we will use the design pattern instantiation scenario in the motivating example for this paper. See e.g. [7, 8] for other work involving tool-generated OCL constraints.

Whichever scenario we pick, the (semi-)automatically generated constraints will often contain redundancies that make them hard to read for humans. The topic of this paper is how OCL constraints can be simplified with the goal of making them more readable. We will propose a rule-based method where various simple rules get applied exhaustively.

In Sect. 2, we describe the context of this work and give a motivating example. We show in Sect. 3 how a generated constraint can be simplified. We then analyze the required simplification steps in Sect. 4. In Sect. 5, a prototypical implementation of our ideas within the KeY system is presented. Sect. 6 discusses related work. Finally, Sect. 7 concludes the paper with some remarks about future work.

## 2    Motivation

The KeY tool [1] is a CASE tool in which formal methods are integrated with contemporary software development techniques. Besides the usual tasks of a CASE tool of creating UML models and creating implementations in Java, KeY allows the developer to add formal specifications to a model in the form of OCL constraints. One of the main goals of the KeY project is to spread the use of formal methods in software development, and a crucial step in the use of formal methods is the authoring of formal specifications like OCL constraints.

Unfortunately, it is not easy to write useful formal specifications. This is one of the major obstacles in getting developers to use formal methods in software development. One possible solution to this problem would be to, somehow, *automatically generate* formal specifications out of some prior information. Ideally, we would like to go directly from an informal specification to a formal one, but the possibilities to do so are very limited. However, an experienced developer can often recognize parts of an informal specification as instances of certain *design patterns* and, given a specific design pattern, it is possible to generate a formal specification that expresses useful requirements associated with that pattern [2].

As software development is becoming more and more structured, using patterns, frameworks, and so on, it is very natural that authoring of formal specifications also follows that line. It is a good way of re-using and taking advantage of experienced developers' knowledge.

---

[4] Design patterns in the usual sense of the word [5] provide a vocabulary for communicating design ideas. They are relatively abstract entities, consisting of textual descriptions of why, when, and how to use them, and the consequences of using them. What is called "design pattern" in CASE tools like TCC is just mechanical instantiation of templates. It is nevertheless useful, and it is such a template mechanism we use as an example in this work.

How can we obtain a formal specification for a design pattern? The problem is that in order to write a useful specification we need some information that is not available until the pattern gets instantiated, i.e. applied to a concrete design. Until then we do not know:

- The name space of the modeled domain, i.e. we do not know the names of the classes, fields, methods, associations, etc. in the design to which the pattern is being applied.
- How the developer will modify the structure of the pattern, i.e. adding or removing classes, fields, methods, associations, etc.
- What *flavor* of the pattern the developer will use. By flavor we here mean that different instances of a specific design pattern can have different requirements associated with it regarding some details.

## 2.1 Example of Constraint Generation

Let us look at a concrete example to make this more clear. The intention of the *Observer* design pattern (taken from [5]), that is shown in Fig. 1, is to "define a one-to-many dependency between objects so that when one object changes state, all its dependents are notified and updated automatically." This pattern is useful when one needs to maintain consistency between related objects, but one does not want to achieve this by making the classes tightly coupled.

In modern CASE tools such as TCC, one can perform machine-assisted application of design patterns. The user then has to supply a mapping from the name space of the pattern to the name space of the modeled domain. Optionally, the user may choose to modify the structure of the pattern. In the KeY tool, the user can also choose what flavor of the pattern he wants to use. In the context of the Observer pattern we can, for instance, find the following "flavor component":

- *Should the observers be allowed to observe more than one subject?* In other words, what should be the multiplicity of the `subject` association-end: `0..1` or `0..*`? In some situations, observers need information from more than one source, and then it might be a good idea to let them observe more than one subject. For example, a spreadsheet may depend on more than one data source.

An *instance* of the Observer pattern is shown in Fig. 2. This example is from the design of a system that handles statistical data. The statistics can be viewed graphically, both as a pie chart and as a bar chart. We can see that what is called `ConcreteSubject` in the pattern is here called `Statistics`, the role-name `statistics` corresponds to the role-name `subject` in the pattern, and so on. We can also see that we here have two concrete observers (`PieChart` and `BarChart`) in contrast to the single one in the pattern (`ConcreteObserver`), so the original structure of the pattern has been slightly modified.

What flavor of the pattern would be useful for this particular instance? Let us assume that the GUI observers only need information from one `Statistics` object, i.e. the `subject` association-end has multiplicity `0..1`.

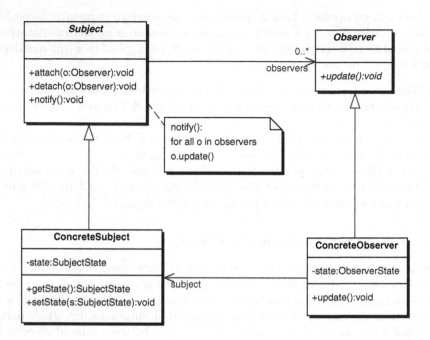

**Fig. 1.** The Observer pattern

Now, if we are going to write a formal specification for this design pattern, we need information that we do not obtain until the pattern is instantiated. A possible solution is to use *schemas*, as suggested in [2]. For each design pattern we want to specify, we design a schema from which we can generate formal specifications when the pattern is applied. A schema for (part of) the Observer pattern might look like this:

```
schema numOfSubjects(String flavor)
 ocl: context Observer inv:
      if flavor = 'one'
        then self.subject->size() <= 1
        else true
      endif
```

Here we have a parameterized version of one of the "flavor components", namely whether the `subject` association-end should have multiplicity `0..1` or `0..*`. The keyword `schema`, the name of the schema, optional flavor parameters, and the keyword `ocl:` are followed by the actual OCL constraint containing the flavor parameters. But there is a problem with this schema. There is no inheritance mechanism in the semantics of OCL, and this means that a formal specification will be generated for the abstract class `Observer` but not for the concrete ob-

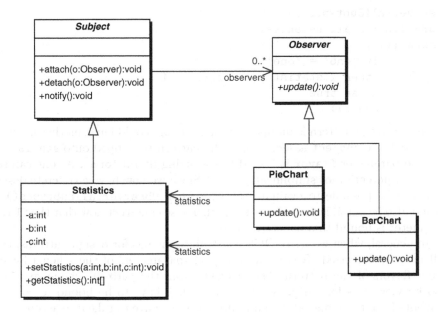

**Fig. 2.** An instance of the Observer pattern

server objects `PieChart` and `BarChart`. Writing a schema for `ConcreteObserver` instead, so that a specification is generated for each concrete observer in the model, does not solve the problem in general. If the developer introduces a hierarchy of observers including abstract super classes for subsets of the observers, then we have the same problem again. However, we can address the problem directly in our schema:

```
schema numOfSubjects(String flavor)
  ocl: Observer.allSubtypes()->
       forAll(s | s.allInstances()->
        forAll(i |
           if flavor = 'one'
             then i.subject->size() <= 1
             else true
           endif))
```

Now we quantify over all subtypes of `Observer`, and for each subtype we quantify over all instances of that subtype. This means that in essence we will get an invariant for each subtype. (The property `allSubtypes` is not pre-defined in OCL but can be expressed with the help of other operations. We just use it here to make the constraint more readable.) Here is the result of applying the Observer pattern to the model in Fig. 2 and using the schema above to generate a specification for the pattern instance:

```
Observer.allSubtypes()->
 forAll(s | s.allInstances()->
  forAll(i |
          if 'one' = 'one'
           then i.statistics->size() <= 1
           else true
          endif))
```

Observer in the pattern is mapped onto Observer (could have another name) in the model, the subject association in the pattern is mapped onto statistics, and the parameter flavor is bound to the string literal 'one'. As one can see, there is a potential for simplification here. Since we now have a concrete design, it should be possible to evaluate the expression Observer.allSubtypes(). It should also be possible to evaluate the if-then-else construct now that the flavor parameter is bound to a concrete value.

In general, when we write OCL constraint schemas for design patterns, they will be parameterized. We will have explicit parameters of the schema for different flavors of the pattern. The elements from the pattern's name space can also be viewed as formal parameters, since they have to be bound to concrete elements from the modeled domain. Moreover, we have to take into account possible structural modifications of the pattern. As we saw in the example, all this will lead to generated specifications containing redundant information. They become hard to read, hard to understand. The generated specifications need to be simplified.

## 3   Example

We shall now see how the previous example may be simplified through the application of several small simplification steps. The first step would be to recognize that 'one' = 'one' is always true, and may therefore be replaced by true:

```
Observer.allSubtypes()->
 forAll(s | s.allInstances()->
  forAll(i | if true
               then i.statistics->size() <= 1
               else true
              endif))
```

Next, an if-then-else construct with a condition known to be true may be replaced by its then-branch:

```
Observer.allSubtypes()->
 forAll(s | s.allInstances()->
  forAll(i | i.statistics->size() <= 1))
```

A further simplification becomes possible if we take information about the model into account, namely the subtypes of Observer in this particular instance of the pattern. In Fig. 2, there are only two subtypes, so we can simplify the constraint as follows:

```
Set{PieChart,BarChart}->
 forAll(s | s.allInstances()->
  forAll(i | i.statistics->size() <= 1))
```

The outer `forAll` application now ranges over a finite set of which we know all elements. We can therefore transform it into a conjunction:

```
    PieChart.allInstances()->forAll(i | i.statistics->size() <= 1)
and BarChart.allInstances()->forAll(i | i.statistics->size() <= 1)
```

Finally, a property that should hold for all instances of a class is usually stated as an invariant. One could therefore split up this constraint and add an invariant to both of the observer classes:

```
context PieChart inv: statistics->size() <= 1
context BarChar  inv: statistics->size() <= 1
```

These constraints are certainly much simpler and more natural than the original general form from the schema. On the other hand, the meaning is guaranteed to be the same, as none of the small transformations changed it.

As a second example, let us assume that **flavor** was bound to **many**. We then get the constraint

```
Observer.allSubtypes()->
 forAll(s | s.allInstances()->
  forAll(i | if 'many' = 'one'
             then i.statistics->size() <= 1
             else true
             endif))
```

The strings `'many'` and `'one'` are different, so the condition can be simplified to **false**:

```
Observer.allSubtypes()->
 forAll(s | s.allInstances()->
  forAll(i | if false
             then i.statistics->size() <= 1
             else true
             endif))
```

In this case, only the else-branch needs to be kept:

```
Observer.allSubtypes()->
 forAll(s | s.allInstances()->
  forAll(i | true))
```

A `forAll` expression with body **true** always evaluates to **true**, so we can simplify this to

```
Observer.allSubtypes()->
 forAll(s | true)
```

and finally to

```
true
```

In this case, the constraint gets simplified away completely, as it does not say anything about the case where `flavor` is not `'one'`.

Another example of a step-wise simplification is given in [2]. There, OCL constraints from an instantiation of the Composite pattern are simplified in a similar way as was presented here.

## 4    Analysis

The previous section shows how OCL constraints can be simplified considerably through the repeated application of small, simple rules. All rules require only local transformation of the constraint, no global analysis is needed. This suggests implementing our simplification using a kind of rewriting rule engine. Such a rule engine repeatedly tries to apply transformation rules on subexpressions of the input until no more rules are applicable. This is a well-known principle and our work can profit from the extensive research on term rewriting systems (see e.g. [4]).

In this section, we are going to have a closer look at the different kinds of rules that are needed to simplify OCL constraints.

### 4.1    Primitive Types

The most fundamental primitive type in OCL is of course the `Boolean` type. For this, general logic simplification steps are needed, like for instance rewriting `false and e` to `false`, `true and e` to `e`, etc. One can give this kind of rules for all logical connectives, including the if-then-else construct. The rule that simplifies `e=e` to `true` also belongs to this category.[5]

A more difficult question is how to handle the other data types built into OCL. For instance, one surely wants to have simplification rules that rewrite `2+3` to `5`. Simplifying `0+x` to `x` is also useful. But should one have rules capable of simplifying `(x+y)*(x+y) - (x-y)*(x-y)` to `4*x*y`? It is known from computer algebra research that the simplification of algebraic expressions is a complicated affair. We think that it depends very much on the application field whether an OCL simplifier should be able to handle this kind of problem. If one thinks of design pattern instantiation, then it seems unlikely that algebraic simplification would be useful. We limit ourselves to evaluation of concrete expressions and simple laws on neutral elements, units, etc., until we come across an application that makes more powerful simplification necessary. This holds for all the primitive data types of OCL, i.e. integers, reals, and strings.

---

[5] We have so far ignored the difficulties of handling `undefined` using an appropriate three-valued semantics.

## 4.2   Collection Types

In Sect. 3 we saw an example of how a `forAll` expression over a finite set can be rewritten to a conjunction. Many interesting simplifications are possible for collections. Here are some examples:

- Operations with finite sets can be simplified: `Set{a,b}->exists(x|p(x))` can be written as `p(a) or p(b)`.
- Some operations can be completely evaluated for concrete sets. For instance, `Set{1,2,3}->sum()` can be simplified to 6.
- Operations where the other parameters have a simple form can often by simplified: `s->forall(x|true)` can be rewritten to `true` and, if `s` is a `Bag`, `s->collect(x|x)` can be reduced to `s`.
- Special cases can be detected for some operations. For instance, one might rewrite `s->including(o)->includes(o)` to `true`.

As is the case for primitive types, no finite set of simplification rules can cover all cases. One should therefore pick a basic supply and extend it when applications make it necessary.

An common property of the collection operators in OCL is that they can all be expressed using the `iterate` construct. We can reduce the number of needed simplification rules for the various collection operators by translating them to an `iterate` expression and providing simplification rules only for that. For instance, the previously mentioned expression

`Set{a,b}->exists(x | p(x))`

can be written as

`Set{a,b}->iterate(x ; acc:Boolean = false | acc or p(x) )`

The iteration over the finite set can then be unrolled to

`(false or p(a)) or p(b)`

which is in turn simplified to

`p(a) or p(b)`

It turns out that most of the simplifications one might think of for `forAll`, `exists`, `collect`, etc., can actually be handled in this way. If one has $m$ simplification rules for $n$ operators, one can effectively replace $m \cdot n$ rules by $m + n$.

The drawback of this approach is what happens when the expression *cannot* be simplified further after translation to the `iterate` form: in that case, the latter form is certainly harder to read than the original. Our current solution to this problem is to provide a number of rules for the inverse transformation, i.e. to transform `iterate` expressions of certain forms to `forAll`, `exists`, etc. These rules are applied as a final step after all other simplifications. In other words, simplification proceeds in two phases. In the first phase, everything is translated to the `iterate` form and simplified as much as possible. In the second phase, remaining `iterate` expressions are translated back to the various simpler operators.

This approach leads to an interesting theoretical question, namely which properties the rule sets for the two phases should have to make the overall behaviour equivalent to that of a single phase with $m \cdot n$ rules.

## 4.3   Model Dependent Simplifications

The previously discussed simplification rules are not very specific to OCL. They would make sense in any formal language that provides the same data types. A peculiarity of OCL is that OCL constraints are always attached to UML diagrams. They cannot occur in isolation. Accordingly, we can identify simplification rules that depend on the model.

For instance, some of the properties (operations) defined by OCL refer to the operations and attributes available for a type, rather than to a state of the modeled system.[6] If the concrete model is known, these can often be evaluated. For instance, in our example, `PieChart.supertypes()` can be simplified to `Set{Observer}`. In contrast to the simplifications proposed in the previous sections, this requires knowledge of the model. Similarly, expressions involving the `attributes`, `operations`, etc., properties defined for `OclType` will usually be simplifiable once the model is known.

The use of information from the UML model is not limited to 'meta'-properties: another possibility might be to use the multiplicities of associations. For instance, if the association `assoc` has a multiplicity of $n$, then `o.assoc->size()` can be simplified to $n$.

The interesting issue here is how to organize the implementation of such simplifications. An implementation that uses a rule engine with a fixed set of syntactic rewrite rules would have to generate a considerable number of rules from the model. For instance, there would be a rule for each of the `OclType` properties for each class in the model. Even worse, simplification rules that involve two types, for instance for expressions involving `oclIsKindOf`, might need one rule for every *pair* of classes, so the rule set would grow quadratically in the size of the model. At the same time, most of these rules would not be needed for any particular simplification.

To avoid this waste of resources, a practical solution requires a rule engine that can obtain information from the model to determine the applicability and result of some of the rules. This is the approach we have chosen, using the rule engine's 'meta constructs' as described in the next section.

We have not yet discussed the final step in Sect. 3, where a single constraint is split up and distributed among the invariants of several classes. This could be done as a post-processing step, but we chose to incorporate it into our rule based mechanism. The simplification rules are not applied on raw constraints, but on lists of constraints with contexts. This allows us to formulate rules that add constraints to different classes.

---

[6] In other words, these properties return information about the state of the *metamodel*. Up to OCL 1.5, these were predefined on the type `OclType`. In OCL 2.0, they were removed to avoid inconsistencies between OCL and the UML metamodel. Our discussion is based on the properties as defined in OCL 1.5.

# 5 Implementation

We have implemented a prototype of a rule-based OCL simplifier and integrated it with the pattern-instantiation mechanism in KeY. It is now possible in KeY to generate OCL specifications for instances of certain design patterns, with the help of schemas, and then to use the simplifier to simplify the generated specifications. To parse the OCL expressions that need to be simplified, we use a parser and typechecker that has been developed at Chalmers University and is described in [9]. When implementing the OCL simplifier, we used the fact that we already had a rule-engine available: the theorem prover in the KeY tool. This theorem prover is based on *taclets* [3], which are a kind of generalized term rewriting rules that can be used to describe the rules of a logic calculus.

## 5.1 Taclets

Although the taclet concept was designed with theorem proving in mind, the design is so general that it is possible to use taclets for other purposes as well. After a few extensions of the implementation of the KeY taclet engine, we were able to use taclets to perform OCL simplification.[7] A rewrite taclet for OCL simplification can, for instance, look like this:

```
find(#e and true) replacewith(#e)
```

Here, #e is a *schema variable*, i.e. it stands for an arbitrary expression. This taclet is *applicable* to an OCL expression exp if the find-part of the taclet matches exp (i.e. if we can instantiate the schema variable so that exp and the find-part become identical). If we *apply* the taclet to exp, then exp will be replaced by the instantiated replacewith-part of the taclet. The schema variables used in a taclet must first be declared, meaning that they are given a type. In this way we can ensure that taclets are only applicable to expressions with matching types. New rules can easily be defined in a text file, using the notation above, and are then parsed into the KeY system. Our approach is to write a set of simplification rules, in the form of taclets, and then apply them to the generated OCL specifications.

Each OCL taclet contains a find-expression and a replacewith-expression, both consisting of OCL syntax extended with schema variables, *meta constructs*, and the *substitution operator*. Meta constructs are references to procedures that transform a given OCL expression into another one when a taclet is being applied. They are only allowed to appear in the replacewith-part and are used to extract information from the UML model, e.g. the subtyping hierarchy of classes. Most taclets do not need any meta constructs. The meaning of the substitution operator will be explained in the context of an example below. Here are some examples of taclets needed for OCL simplification:

---

[7] There exists a number of model transformation languages within the MDA framework, and one of them could probably have been used to express the OCL simplification. However, when our project started no tool support was available for these languages, and we therefore went for the taclet solution.

```
equals {find(#e = #e) replacewith(true)}

and_false {find(#e and false) replacewith(false)}

if_true {find(if true then #e1 else #e2 endif)
          replacewith(#e1)}
```

In the examples, all schema variables are prefixed with a '#' sign to distinguish them from the keywords in the syntax. It should be pointed out that in the current implementation, one cannot use proper OCL syntax in the taclets like in the examples. A special, taclet-tailored syntax has to be used instead. This is due to the difficulties in integrating the parser for the taclet language with an OCL parser. Of course, this technicality will be visible only to the author of the simplification rules, and not to the user of the simplifier.

## 5.2   Collections

In order to simplify OCL expressions, one has to have a way of dealing with OCL collections. The constructors for OCL collections (`Set{...}`, etc.) can enumerate any number of elements, i.e. they can be viewed as operators having a *variable arity*. Now, operators with variable arity are not very easy to handle in an efficient way when one wants to apply rules to them. Our solution to this is to represent collection literals in structures that resemble the list in functional programming languages. These structures are built using two constructors: `insert` that takes two arguments—the "first" element in the collection and the rest of the collection—and `empty` that represents the empty collection.

To be more precise, we have two collection constructors for each collection type: `insert_set` and `empty_set`, `insert_bag` and `empty_bag`, and so on. In that way we do not lose the type information. Using these collection constructors, it is easy to perform various operations on OCL collections. Instead of having to deal with variable arity, we use *induction* when designing our simplification rules: we have one base case rule for the empty collection, and one induction step rule, just as one defines functions operating on lists in functional programming languages. As an example for this representation, `Set{a, b, c}` becomes

```
insert_set(a, insert_set(b, insert_set(c, empty_set)))
```

We can now define taclets to transform a universal quantification over a concrete, finite set to a conjunction. In other words, we want to transform an expression like

```
insert_set(a, insert_set(b, insert_set(c, empty_set)))
  ->forAll(x | e(x))
```

to

```
e(a) and e(b) and e(c)
```

Below we see the two taclets needed to perform this transformation, one rule for the base case and one for the induction step:[8]

```
forAll2Conjunction_base {
    find(empty_set->forAll(#x | #exp))
    replacewith(true)}

forAll2Conjunction_step {
    find(insert_set(#head, #tail)->forAll(#x | #exp))
    replacewith({#x #head}#exp and #tail->forAll(#x | #exp))}
```

Here we can see the syntax for *substitution*, {x e}exp, which causes all free occurrences of x in exp to be replaced with e once the taclet is applied.

## 5.3   Type Inference

Another thing we must handle in our implementation is a certain degree of type inference. The type of an OCL expression is in most cases given directly by the top operator of the expression, but in some cases one has to infer the type of the expression from the types of its subexpressions. For example, the type of an expression with forAll() as top operator is always Boolean, while the type of the expression if b then e1 else e2 endif is the least common supertype of the types of e1 and e2. One way to implement a type system that handles this kind of type inference would be to design a general type inference algorithm, e.g. using unification, like the ones found in functional programming languages like ML and Haskell. However, combining such an algorithm with subtyping is a delicate matter. Moreover, there are relatively few, builtin OCL operations that need special treatment, and their number is fixed. Instead of using a general type inference algorithm, we have therefore chosen to hard-code the necessary inference directly in the representation of these OCL operations.

## 5.4   Status of Implementation

In order to perform OCL simplification using taclets we have extended the implementation of the KeY tool so that we can now, for instance, perform the simplification steps described in Sect. 3, and also what is needed for the problem described in [2]. We can perform basic simplifications, like x and true to x, but also more advanced tasks like extracting information from the model using meta constructs. We can also handle bound variables and express the substitution of such variables, which is needed to handle forAll, iterate, etc. Moreover, we have extended the pretty-printing module of KeY so that the simplified OCL expression can be displayed in proper OCL syntax. What remains to be done is to complete our set of taclets. So far we have only written simplification taclets for a few design pattern schemas.

---

[8] As mentioned in Sect. 4.2, this simplification would actually be performed via the iterate representation. To make our presentation simpler, we here give rules that simplify forAll-expressions directly.

Since it is possible to use the prover of the KeY system "stand-alone", without the CASE tool component, we expect to be able to produce a stand-alone version of our OCL simplifier as well.

# 6   Related Work

The idea to attach schematic OCL constraints to design patterns was first discussed in [2]. The need for simplification was recognized there, but not systematically investigated. This is done in the present paper, together with an implementation approach.

The authors have explored the idea of applying partial evaluation [10] techniques to simplification, but the approach turned out to be rather unfruitful, as discussed in Sect. 6 of [6].

# 7   Conclusion

We presented an approach to perform OCL simplification through repeated application of simple rules. Simplification of OCL constraints is often needed when the constraints have been automatically generated by instantiation of templates, by combination of constraint fragments, or by some other technique. On a higher level, we think that tool support for the generation of formal specifications is an important step on the way to make formal methods more accessible to software developers. In this paper we concentrated on how to simplify OCL constraints generated in the context of design pattern instantiation, i.e. constraints expressing requirements associated with the patterns.

We identified various kinds of rules that are needed for OCL simplification and pointed out differences to usual term rewriting systems. We also compared template instantiation and simplification of OCL constraints to program specialization.

Moreover, we implemented a prototype of an OCL simplifier by re-using the rule application mechanism of the theorem prover in the KeY tool. We described some of the technical issues that need to be solved in such an implementation.

An important body of future work will be to add simplification rules for the various operators and data types built into OCL. In connection with this, we will need to evaluate our approach in some significant case studies. The well-studied theory of rewrite systems [4] can be applied to show termination, uniqueness of simplification results, etc. The presence of variable binding operators (`forAll`, `iterate`, etc.) also makes the work on higher-order rewriting [11] relevant in this context.

An interesting direction for future research is to perform simplification under side conditions. For instance, one might have information that is separate from an OCL constraint, but lets one decide which branch of an if-then-else construct needs to be kept. This would be useful for the work presented in [7].

We believe that future software engineering tools will in an increasing degree generate models and OCL constraints, in addition to today's manual authoring. Simplifying these specifications for improved readability will be indispensable.

## Acknowledgment

The authors are thankful to Philipp Rümmer for his useful comments on a draft of this paper.

## References

[1] Wolfgang Ahrendt, Thomas Baar, Bernhard Beckert, Richard Bubel, Martin Giese, Reiner Hähnle, Wolfram Menzel, Wojciech Mostowski, Andreas Roth, Steffen Schlager, and Peter H. Schmitt. The KeY tool. *Software and Systems Modeling*, 4(1), 2005.

[2] Thomas Baar, Reiner Hähnle, Theo Sattler, and Peter H. Schmitt. Entwurfsmustergesteuerte Erzeugung von OCL-Constraints. In K. Mehlhorn and G. Snelting, editors, *Informatik 2000, 30. Jahrestagung der Gesellschaft für Infomatik*, pages 389–404. Springer, September 2000.

[3] Bernhard Beckert, Martin Giese, Elmar Habermalz, Reiner Hähnle, Andreas Roth, Philipp Rümmer, and Steffen Schlager. Taclets: A new paradigm for constructing interactive theorem provers. *Revista de la Real Academia de Ciencias Exactas, Físicas y Naturales, Serie A: Matemáticas (RACSAM)*, 98(1):17–53, 2004. Special Issue on Symbolic Computation in Logic and Artificial Intelligence.

[4] Nachum Dershowitz and David A. Plaisted. Rewriting. In Alan Robinson and Andrei Voronkov, editors, *Handbook of Automated Reasoning*, volume I, chapter 9, pages 535–610. Elsevier Science, 2001.

[5] Erich Gamma, Richard Helm, Ralph Johnson, and John Vlissides. *Design Patterns: Elements of Reusable Object-Oriented Software*. Addison-Wesley, 1995.

[6] Martin Giese, Reiner Hähnle, and Daniel Larsson. Rule-based simplification of OCL constraints. In Octavian Patrascoiu et al., editor, *Workshop on OCL and Model Driven Engineering at UML2004, Lisbon*, pages 84–98, 2004.

[7] Martin Giese and Rogardt Heldal. From informal to formal specifications in UML. In Thomas Baar, Alfred Strohmeier, Ana Moreira, and Stephen J. Mellor, editors, *Proc. of UML2004, Lisbon*, volume 3273 of *LNCS*, pages 197–211. Springer, 2004.

[8] Reiner Hähnle, Kristofer Johannisson, and Aarne Ranta. An authoring tool for informal and formal requirements specifications. In Ralf-Detlef Kutsche and Herbert Weber, editors, *Fundamental Approaches to Software Engineering (FASE), Part of Joint European Conferences on Theory and Practice of Software, ETAPS, Grenoble*, volume 2306 of *LNCS*, pages 233–248. Springer, 2002.

[9] Kristofer Johannisson. Disambiguating implicit constructions in OCL. In *Workshop on OCL and Model Driven Engineering at UML2004, Lisbon*, 2004.

[10] N.D. Jones, C.K. Gomard, and P. Sestoft. *Partial Evaluation and Automatic Program Generation*. Prentice Hall, 1993.

[11] Tobias Nipkow and Christian Prehofer. Higher-order rewriting and equational reasoning. In W. Bibel and P. Schmitt, editors, *Automated Deduction — A Basis for Applications. Volume I: Foundations*, volume 8 of *Applied Logic Series*, pages 399–430. Kluwer, 1998.

[12] J. Warmer and A. Kleppe. *The Object Constraint Language*. Object Technology. Addison-Wesley, second edition, 2003.

# Lessons Learned from Automated Analysis of Industrial UML Class Models (An Experience Report) * **

Betty H.C. Cheng[1], Ryan Stephenson[1], and Brian Berenbach[2]

[1] Software Engineering and Network Systems Laboratory
Department of Computer Science and Engineering
Michigan State University
East Lansing, Michigan 48824 USA
{chengb,steph146}@cse.msu.edu
[2] Siemens Corporate Research, Inc.
Brian.Berenbach@siemens.com

**Abstract.** Automated analysis of object-oriented design models can provide insight into the quality of a given software design. Data obtained from automated analysis, however, is often too complex to be easily understood by a designer. This paper examines the use of an automated analysis tool on industrial software UML class models, where one set of models was created as part of the design process and the other was obtained from reverse engineering code. The analysis was performed by DesignAdvisor, a tool developed by Siemens Corporate Research, that supports metrics-based analysis and detection of design guideline violations. The paper describes the lessons learned from using the automated analysis techniques to assess the quality of these models. We also assess the impact of design pattern use in the overall quality of the models. Based on our lessons learned, identify design guidelines that would minimize the occurrence of these errors.

## 1 Introduction

As software systems become more complex, it is important to have techniques and tools to support the systematic design and development processes. While university texts and courses cover the fundamentals of software design, they typically do not adequately deal with issues associated with large models developed by teams. The interactions between hundreds or thousands of classes make it difficult for a designer to develop an object-oriented system that is free of design-level errors. Designs quickly expand to the point where they cannot

---

* This work is supported in part by Siemens Corporate Research, NSF grants EIA-0000433, CDA-9700732, CCR-9901017, Department of the Navy, and Office of Naval Research under Grant No. N00014-01-1-0744, and in cooperation with Siemens Transportation and Detroit Diesel Corporation.
** Please contact B. Cheng for all correspondences

L. Briand and C. Williams (Eds.): MoDELS 2005, LNCS 3713, pp. 324–338, 2005.
© Springer-Verlag Berlin Heidelberg 2005

be fully understood by reviewing diagrams, and serious flaws (e.g. circular dependencies) may go unnoticed because of the sheer volume of material. Even processes specifically developed to support large scale designs tend to be incomplete and not fully scalable [1]. To help manage the complexity of these systems, a variety of automated analysis tools have been developed. This paper describes experiences in using the DesignAdvisor tool to analyze two large industrial-scale models from the transportation domain, as well as numerous smaller models for automotive embedded systems and client-server applications developed in an academic setting. We compare the kinds of design errors obtained from analyzing the models and identify guidelines for best interpreting the error analysis data when revising a design.

Several tools have been developed to analyze the Unified Modeling Language (UML) diagrams for errors, where UML has become the *de facto* standard for modeling object-oriented designs. For example, several tools use software metrics [2, 3, 4, 5, 6, 7] to find examples of high coupling and high complexity in a software design, both of which strongly correlate to software flaws during coding or implementation. In addition to analyzing metrics, DesignAdvisor [8] also attempts to identify violations of general design principles such as high cohesion and low coupling. While useful, automated model analysis poses several difficulties despite its ability to examine large models for design errors. Analysis may yield a large amount of data, as thousands of errors are reported when analyzing models. It is often unclear how these errors should be repaired or which of these errors are the most critical to the quality of a model.

Based on the automated analysis of industrial and academic models, we propose some strategies for improving the understandability of the output produced by the automated model analysis. We also identified design guidelines that will minimize the number of design errors found by DesignAdvisor. It should be noted that one of the key motivations for selecting DesignAdvisor for our studies is that we had direct access to the product developers and were able to add metrics and design heuristics to be analyzed. We also were able to influence the output and the presentation of the analysis results. Furthermore, DesignAdvisor has a rich set of measurements suitable for both analysis and design models. In addition, it focused on the underlying model and did not use diagrams to perform analysis. This feature made it effective in studying models that had been reverse engineered from code (where there were no diagrams). A previous paper [8] described heuristics for improving the quality of analysis models through rigor and measurement; DesignAdvisor can be used to analyze models for adherence to these design heuristics. This paper describes results obtained from using DesignAdvisor to analyze these measurements taken primarily from design models, and from models that have been reverse engineered from code.

The remainder of the paper is organized as follows. Section 2 gives background information about the analysis tool DesignAdvisor and the models on which automated analysis was performed. Section 3 describes the results of the automated analysis on the models. Section 4 overviews related work in the field of automated metrics-based model analysis. Section 5 describes lessons learned from the analyses and briefly discusses future work.

## 2    Background

In order to evaluate the utility of automated analysis performed on UML models of software designs, we used a model analyzer tool, DesignAdvisor [9], on two industrial case-studies as well as numerous smaller models to identify guidelines for developing good designs. This section describes the DesignAdvisor tool and the industrial models analyzed.

### 2.1    DesignAdvisor

The DesignAdvisor tool [9] developed by Siemens Corporate Research is an automated model analyzer built atop the Rational Rose$^{TM}$ CASE tool. The DesignAdvisor tool was developed specifically to analyze and measure the "goodness" of large, complex UML models. There are two types of analysis rules encoded in DesignAdvisor: rules that encode design guidelines and rules that capture metrics that have upper and lower bounds. DesignAdvisor produces error reports for a given model by analyzing artifacts and relationships between artifacts in that model, and determines whether a given artifact or relationship violates any of the design rules encoded in the tool. As an example of a design guideline rule, if two classes exist in a design model with an inheritance relationship between the two, and if the parent class is accessing the methods inside the child class, a "Parent has knowledge of Child" error would be reported for the offending parent class. In addition, DesignAdvisor performs a metrics analysis on artifacts in the model, essentially determining whether the number of classes, associations, or any other artifact violates a (user) predetermined upper or lower bound.

Since the DesignAdvisor tool (described below) looks at the underlying model rather than at diagrams, it is capable of reporting problems that would not be amenable to visual inspection. For example, if there are circular dependencies between classes that are in the code but that do not appear on any diagram(s), then DesignAdvisor is able to find them.

As with many types of automated analysis of models, it is possible for spurious errors. Causes for spurious errors include incomplete designs, lack of context information, or difference in notation conventions. DesignAdvisor provides two facilities for handling spurious errors: a rule can be turned off (globally affecting all artifacts), or the rule can be suppressed for a single model object. By turning off some rules and suppressing others for specific objects, DesignAdvisor can be "tuned" to provide developer-specific meaningful information without showing erroneous or spurious errors.

### 2.2    Industrial Models

Class diagrams from two large, industrial models provided by Siemens Transportation were used as case studies. Model A is an integrated model of complex signaling systems in the transportation domain, containing both analysis and design artifacts. The model contains 1105 classes. It serves as an example of an industrial design model, as it existed in the design phase of software development prior to the coding phase. Model B is also from the transportation domain. As only the Java code was available for review, this model was developed via a reverse-engineering of code using The Rational Rose$^{TM}$ CASE tool. The reverse-engineered model provided a view of a design model as it existed at the end of the design life-cycle, after all changes to the model have been completed and the model has been implemented into a software system. This model contains 1570 classes.

## 2.3   Student-Designed Models

In addition to the large industrial transportation models, two collections of smaller models from student projects were examined. The first collection comprised smaller models that made use of design patterns [10]. These models were all created as a project for a graduate-level software engineering course by inexperienced model designers. The models themselves represent either a simplified course enrollment system or a simple e-commerce system for purchasing books. These models contained between 18 and 30 classes.

The second collection of smaller models did not make use of design patterns. These models each contained 10-20 classes and were developed by undergraduates in an upper-level undergraduate software engineering course. The models represented industrial automotive embedded systems for controlling cruise control or power window systems.

# 3   Automated Analysis Results

Several experiments were performed using the DesignAdvisor tool to help validate the results obtained from the tool and design guidelines for UML models that help minimize errors. This section describes the results obtained from the DesignAdvisor tool for each model.

## 3.1   Analysis of Industrial Models

We obtained computer-generated error reports by running the DesignAdvisor tool on the transportation models Model A and Model B. For both models, the total number of errors found in each was high, up to an order of magnitude higher than the number of classes in each model! For Model A, 12534 errors were found dealing with classes and their relationships. For Model B, 3751 such errors were found. The unexpected high number of errors reported by DesignAdvisor prompted us to manually examine the errors for both models to determine the relative importance of errors to each model. In particular, the large number of errors for Model B posed the possibility that many of the errors found in the model were spurious, since System B was already deployed and had very few error reports from the field. Table 1 contains a summary of the design error analysis for Models A and B.

**Table 1.** Design errors reported in Models A and B, sorted by severity

| Error Description (total number of classes) | Model A (1105) | Model B (1570) |
|---|---|---|
| SEVERE ERRORS: | | |
| Abstract class not inherited | 8 | 82 |
| Circular association | 0 | 8 |
| Circular dependency | 102 | 0 |
| Abstract class inherits from concrete class | 6 | 34 |
| Class inherits from one or more non-base classes | 0 | 5 |
| Interface to class expected but defined improperly | 1 | 53 |
| Two methods exist in the model with the same signature | 1 | 0 |
| Two objects exist in the model with the same name | 5 | 23 |
| Parent accessing attributes/operations of child class | 0 | 2 |
| *Rate of total number of severe errors per class* | 0.11 | 0.13 |
| MODERATE ERRORS: | | |
| Number of associations above user-defined threshold | 5 | 21 |
| Number of attributes above user-defined threshold | 1 | 2 |
| Number of methods above user-defined threshold | 2 | 3 |
| Base artifact in an inheritance tree is concrete | 55 | 107 |
| Number of messages passed to a class above user-defined threshold | 0 | 5 |
| Multiple inheritance | 0 | 10 |
| Operation has more arguments than user-defined threshold | 0 | 44 |
| Base class in inheritance tree has publicly accessible attributes | 352 | 154 |
| *Rate of total number of moderate errors per class* | 0.37 | 0.22 |
| LOW SEVERITY ERRORS: | | |
| A dependency has no declared stereotype | 624 | 0 |
| Interface not used | 12 | 0 |
| Missing Associations | 144 | 132 |
| Missing Dependencies | 281 | 1061 |
| No classes are dependent on this class | 303 | 1061 |
| Operation missing postconditions | 4903 | NA |
| Operation missing preconditions | 4903 | NA |
| A class's methods or attributes are unused by other classes | 826 | 944 |
| *Rate of total number of low severity errors per class* | 10.85 | 2.03 |
| **Rate of total number of all error types per class** | 11.34 | 2.39 |

**Categorization of Errors.** Numerous design errors found in both models by DesignAdvisor were determined to be spurious. For both models, several errors implied that model artifacts were missing or unused in their respective models. After examining these errors in the models, it was determined that in both cases, these omissions were intentional on the part of their respective developers. For example, Model B contains 1570 classes. In DesignAdvisor's error report, 1061 "Missing Dependencies" and 1061 "Missing Inverse Dependency" (no classes dependent on this class) errors were reported for Model B.

It is immediately clear from examining the model manually that since few dependencies were included in the model due to the reverse engineering performed, these errors would occur. A human observer, upon recognizing this case, would most likely determine that the model was not faulty for not including dependencies; however, DesignAdvisor reported the errors anyway (the option exists to disable reporting of any given type of error at the user's request). This error, and other errors of seemingly intentional omission were determined to have little effect on the quality of the design.

Several more types of errors found by DesignAdvisor were determined to be of moderate severity. These errors frequently exhibited the following characteristic – that they were violations, but not fatal violations, of good software engineering practice. Maintaining a proper structure of inheritance, with each class inheriting from one abstract class, and not multiple concrete classes, is an example of such a practice. Violation of this practice is not, by itself, indicative of a flaw in the design, but such a violation *does* complicate the design and thus creates a potential for errors. Concrete inheritance and multiple inheritance also fall into this category of moderate errors. Violations of lower or upper bounds on complexity or coupling metrics were also represented in this category. A class that is too tightly coupled with another class need not necessarily cause design problems, but such a class is much more likely to introduce design difficulties than a class with a more nominal level of coupling [3].

Finally, errors that actually represent a fatal violation of software engineering practice were determined to have high severity. Errors such as circular associations, a parent class having knowledge of its child class, two different classes named with the same identifier, etc., represent errors of this magnitude; these types of errors are very likely to cause problems if not corrected.

*Analysis of Model A.* Model A had several design errors identifiable as being severe. On eight occasions, abstract classes existed without corresponding concrete classes. There were 102 circular dependencies present in the model. On six occasions, an abstract class inherited from a concrete class. At one point in the model, an interface is required by a stereotype but is not present. Five name collisions and one method signature collision were also identified.

Moderate errors in Model A involved inappropriate (but not illegal) use of inheritance constructs. There were 55 instances of a base artifact defined as a concrete class. There were 352 instances of public information provided by a class at the base level, as opposed to an inherited class. There were also a handful of metrics violations reported due to abnormally high numbers of associations, attributes, and methods within a single class.

Model A had a very large number of low severity errors, most likely due to the fact that the model was constructed for the early phase of design. Associations and dependencies were not indicated on some diagrams in the model. The majority of operations did not have pre- or post-conditions listed. Likewise, many dependencies were missing stereotypes. Finally, 826 classes had publicly accessible methods or attributes yet were not explicitly referenced as being used elsewhere in the model.

*Analysis of Model B.* Model B also had several design errors identifiable as severe. 82 abstract classes existed without corresponding concrete classes. There were eight circular associations present in the model. On 34 occasions, an abstract class inherited from a concrete class. There were 5 occurrences of a multiple inheritance construct inheriting from at least one concrete class. Stereotypes required interfaces that did not exist within the model 53 times. Name collisions occurred within the model 23 times. On 2 occasions, a parent class has knowledge of one of its child classes.

Several moderate errors found in Model B were due to violations found by the DesignAdvisor metrics analysis. Several classes had too many associations, attributes, methods, and messages. Base classes in inheritance trees were identified as concrete 107 times. Additionally, 10 occurrences of multiple inheritance and 154 occurrences of public information within a base class were present.

Since Model B was reverse engineered from code, several types of relationships, such as dependencies were not included. Their absence resulted in the large number of low severity errors. For example, there were 1061 occurrences of "Missing Dependency" and 1061 occurrences of "Missing Inverse Dependency", as dependencies were not generated during the reverse engineering process. 132 classes were also missing associations. In addition, 944 classes were flagged as "Unused Classes", meaning that during reverse engineering, external usage of these classes was not detected.

**Comparison of Model Analyses.** Models A and B represent designs at different stages of development. Model A represents a system that was in the midst of development at the time the design diagrams were constructed. Model B, however, represents a design that had already been coded, and the design model was obtained by reverse engineering from code. Three important differences were discovered when comparing the error analysis results of the two models.

First, Models A and B differ in the quantity and types of low severity errors. Model B had nearly all of its low severity errors due to its lack of dependencies, while Model A had many more missing model artifacts. This finding suggests that low severity errors do not imply errors in a model, but they are more indicative of an incomplete model. If a model is missing associations or dependencies in the early design phase, then they will often be added in later phases as the design evolves towards code.

Second, far more errors of moderate severity were found in the implemented Model B than in the diagram-only Model A. Violations of "complexity" metrics (having too many associations, methods, etc. attached to a class) occur in Model B but not in Model A. In addition, Model B exhibits multiple inheritance while Model A does not. The higher number of errors could once again emphasize a difference in design stage; creating a large, important class with many associations and methods may occur at coding time, when ensuring that all objects communicate becomes absolutely necessary.

Finally, both Model A and Model B had similar types and numbers of severe errors. Both models have one major problem (many circular dependencies in the case of Model A, and many failures to inherit from an abstract class in Model B) and several infrequent errors (such as one instance of name collision and several instances of a parent class having knowledge of a child class.) This finding implies that it is likely that severe errors are often generated early in the design process and not as a result of refining a design into code, as both models had similar quantities of errors despite representing different design phases.

The fact that Model B contains many severe design errors despite existing in the field with minimal error reports is also interesting. The types of errors examined and reported by DesignAdvisor relate exclusively to the quality of a software design, and can reveal poor design practice. However, poor design practice does not always translate into poor software when exhaustive testing is taken into account. The most likely explanation of the high number of design errors and low number of system failures in Model B is that exhaustive testing performed prior to deployment corrected many errors created by the poor design practices used.

**Impact of Design Patterns.**   An attempt was made to determine possible causes of the high error rates found by DesignAdvisor's automated analysis. Our goal was to determine whether the software design practices used in the industrial models obtained from Siemens influenced the type and quantity of errors reported by the DesignAdvisor tool. A detailed manual examination of the models was performed to identify the methodology used in designing the models. Several sections of the models, when examined, appeared to use design patterns [10] to facilitate their construction. In other sections, however, no obvious methodology was used. After comparing the sections of the models created using design patterns to the model sections with less obvious design methodology, we found that the sections designed with patterns display a significantly lower rate of error than both the overall model and the sections constructed with no obvious design methodology.

An examination of Model A provided by Siemens was performed to identify the methodologies used in the design of the various sections of the model. Upon examination, several classes in Model A are related by structural design patterns found in the literature [10] such as the composite pattern, decorator pattern, or facade pattern. For example, a section of Model A provides a simple interface to a complex subsystem involving observation in the model, a clear instance of a *Facade* pattern. Another section of the model involves the linkage of a diagnostic controller and its subclasses and a diagnostic filter and its subclasses in Model A via a single aggregation, an example of a *Bridge* pattern. Other sections of the model use less clear methodology. For example, a diagnostic utility in Model A involves a single controller containing the aggregation of 21 other diagnostic subsystems in the model. These clear differences in design methodology within the same model led to an obvious question – Did the sections of the model designed using design patterns have a lower rate of errors than the sections of the model that did not use patterns?

*Error Analysis.* We wanted to determine the impact on the error rate with and without the use of design patterns. For example, a section of Model A implements a bridge pattern linking a diagnostic subsystem to a diagnostic filter for that subsystem. This model section contains 11 classes and various linking relationships, and represents approximately 2% of the total size of Model A (650 classes). When DesignAdvisor analysis was performed on this subsection of Model A, 119 total errors were detected by the software, for an error rate of 10.8 errors per class. When factoring out low severity errors, 11 errors were found in the 11 classes for an error rate of one error per class. Recall that DesignAdvisor found 12534 errors in Model A as a whole and 633 errors of moderate or high severity, corresponding to error rates of 19.3 errors per class and .97 errors per class, respectively. The error rate of the model section implementing the Bridge pattern was thus found to have roughly 43% fewer errors per class than the model as a whole, and roughly the same percentage of moderate or severe errors per class.

When DesignAdvisor analyzed a model section not implemented by a design pattern, far different results were obtained. A section of Model A responsible for running diagnostics on the rest of the system consists of a master class linked to 21 diagnostic subsystems via aggregation. This model section contained 29 total classes, or roughly 3.5% of the total size of Model A. After DesignAdvisor analyzed this section of the model, 537 total errors were recognized, for an error rate of 18.5 errors per class. 64 errors of high or moderate severity were found, making the error rate for these types of errors 2.2 per class. This section of the model had roughly the same number of errors per class as Model A as a whole, and it had 220% higher rate of errors of moderate or high severity per class when compared to Model A taken as a whole.

## 3.2   Examination of Classroom Models

A collection of smaller models designed by software engineering students were examined by DesignAdvisor. Ten models of an e-commerce system were developed as part of a graduate software engineering course by designers of relative inexperience. Each of these models was required to make use of common design patterns [10]. Additionally, ten models of automotive subsystems were analyzed by DesignAdvisor. These models were developed by students in an upper-level undergraduate software engineering course. All twenty models contained between 10 and 30 classes.

We used DesignAdvisor to analyze the classes and relationships in each of the ten small e-commerce class project models using patterns to identify the error rate of the models. In each of the 10 models examined, the errors found by DesignAdvisor were very similar. No severe errors were found in any of the models. This result seems reasonable as none of the models required more than one diagram to display, and there were no naming violations or circular relationships identifiable through automated analysis.

Only a small number of moderate errors were found by the DesignAdvisor. Typically, the most egregious errors found include a failure to use abstract base classes in inheritance structures. The rate of severe/moderate errors per class was found to be between 0.15 and 0.35 in the case of all 10 models. Low priority errors were once again common due to the fact that not all features of a UML class model were used by the designers of the models. Several models either contained no dependencies or no associations between a single class in the model. In addition, the students were not required to include the attributes and operations of each of the classes in the models. Thus, DesignAdvisor found that none of the classes were used by other classes in the model. Overall, there were between 4 and 5 low-priority errors per class found by DesignAdvisor. The overall error rate for each model varied between 4.1 and 5.1 errors per class. This error rate is much lower than either of the subsections of the Siemens model. Therefore, for small systems, the impact of design patterns use is not sufficiently high to see a noticeable improvement in the quality of the designs.

DesignAdvisor found very similar results for the automotive embedded systems models (developed by the undergraduates) that did not use design patterns, with one significant exception. Most of the small models designed without patterns contained violations of coupling metrics, indicating that classes had too many incoming or outgoing associations. On average one in ten classes in the small models had these errors. The overall number of severe and moderate errors found in the models was similar to the rate in the models that used design patterns, as was the rate of error when looking at all errors reported by DesignAdvisor.

## 4    Related Work

Several approaches to automated model analysis already exist. Several researchers have proposed modifications to the Object Management Group UML standard [11]. By adding formalism to UML specifications, ambiguity in the UML specification could be eliminated thus allowing for easier mathematically-based analysis of design models [12, 13, 14, 15]. Riel [16] proposed improvement to design model heuristics to eliminate ambiguity in models. Improvements to existing model validation techniques have been proposed by Campbell et al. [17]. These techniques, in general, require defining formal UML semantics [12, 13, 14, 15] and a strong mathematical background [17] to benefit from these techniques. Model analysis using the DesignAdvisor tool, by contrast, requires no background in formal analysis and runs on conventional UML diagrams.

Several researchers have attempted to assess design quality via empirical means through the use of software metrics. Chidamber and Kemerer [2], as well as Eder [3] developed software metrics to identify coupling between objects in a system, and found a correlation between coupling in a software system and the probability of faults in a system. Lorenz and Kidd [5] developed a series of metrics identifying the complexity of classes and correlated complexity to the likelihood of software faults. Briand et al. [18] and Chae and Kwon [19] developed metrics to identify cohesion within classes, using the principle that highly cohesive classes contribute to an uncluttered design and thus fewer design flaws.

Several researchers [20, 21] have developed clustered metrics that attempt to measure complexity, cohesion, and complexity simultaneously to ascertain the "goodness" of a particular class. These metrics could be added to the DesignAdvsior to provide further capabilities during the analysis process.

# 5    Conclusions

After automatically analyzing the two industrial models, it was apparent that the results obtained, although very useful, required substantial effort to process into a useful form. This section presents important lessons learned that could benefit future automated analyses. And we conclude with suggestions for follow-on investigations.

## 5.1    Lessons Learned

As many errors reported by a model analysis tool are spurious, some method of ranking or prioritizing errors should be performed by a tool; obvious errors like "Parent has knowledge of child" should take precedence over less important errors, such as unused classes. It was apparent when analyzing both models that grouping errors based on the severity of the reported error would be useful. Groups could be chosen on the basis of ranking severe, moderate, and low priority errors as done above, or each error could be given individual rank according to the experience of the developer. Using this grouping or ranking, designers would be able to use the majority of their time reviewing designs in the parts of models most likely to contain errors (the classes with many identified severe or moderate errors), reducing the quantity of errors propagated into the coding and post-release phases of development.

Both Model A and Model B were relatively similar in size, yet had a difference in rate of detected errors that was roughly one order of magnitude (11.34 errors/class in Model A versus 2.39 errors/class in Model B). The rate of severe errors detected in Model A was similar to the rate of severe errors detected in Model B (0.11 for Model A versus 0.13 for Model B). The rate of moderate errors detected in Model A was also similar to the rate of moderate errors detected in Model B (0.37 for Model A versus 0.22 for Model B). The major contributor to the difference in error rates was due to the occurrence of low severity errors, where Model A had 10.85 errors/class and Model B had 2.03 errors/class. The only real substantial difference in the two models was the design phase each model represented, as Model B was reverse-engineered from code that was already deployed, while Model A was created from UML design diagrams. Both models otherwise were developed by designers of similar skill level in the same domain. The quantity of total errors is thus likely to be inversely correlated to the design phase during which the model is analyzed. During the design phase, it is more likely for incompleteness thus pushing the low severity error rate up dramatically. Given that the high severity rates are similar for both models at different design stages, the error rate is most likely not strongly correlated to design phase. This finding suggests that severe errors are very likely to be propagated through the design process.

To obtain further data as to the origin of severe errors, we used DesignAdvisor to analyze several small UML models serving as simple textbook implementations of design patterns [10]. Each model had 5 classes on average. For each model, DesignAdvisor reported no severe errors, no moderate errors, and approximately 20 low severity errors. DesignAdvisor then performed analysis on several small embedded systems models of approximately 20 classes each. DesignAdvisor once again reported no severe errors for these models, few errors of moderate severity, and numerous errors of low severity.

Since only the two industrial-scale models examined had instances of severe errors, the conclusion can be reached that as design complexity increases, the quantity of severe errors increases. In small designs, severe errors are unlikely to appear because they would be easily identifiable to the original designer. In larger, more complex designs, this detection is not necessarily possible as different portions of a design created by different developers may conflict with each other.

**Benefits of Automated Analysis.** The benefits of automated analysis seem obvious, and are readily apparent from the results of the DesignAdvisor analysis performed on large models. Automated analysis, when run on large models, has the potential to greatly increase the speed at which developers find and correct design errors. In the case of each small model, any errors in the design would likely be visible during a manual inspection requiring a relatively short time to fully examine the model, reducing the potential utility of automated analysis. However, the complex, industrial models take much longer to analyze manually and contain more difficult-to-find and necessary-to-correct errors, and thus benefit greatly from automated means of analysis.

**Utility of Metrics.** Despite expectations confirmed in the literature regarding coupling and complexity metrics that high coupling and high complexity correlate strongly to software errors, the number of instances where a class had violated an upper or lower bound defined by a metric did not correlate to the likelihood of a more severe error at that point in the design. In Model B, a class violated a complexity or coupling metric on 26 separate occasions, and the percentage of these classes involved in severe errors was similar to the percentage of classes involved in severe errors throughout the model. The most likely reason for this disparity is the design phase represented by Model B. It is possible and likely that errors in complex classes were corrected at some point during the design life-cycle. Metrics may provide a more proper correlation to design errors in models examined earlier in the design process.

**Utility of Patterns.** In general, it was found that the use of design patterns contributed greatly to the lower number of errors in the model sections in which the patterns were used. Sections of Model A that implement design patterns have lower rates per class of both overall errors and severe errors when compared to sections of Model A that do not contain a design pattern. In Model A, a section of the model implementing a bridge pattern had 43% fewer errors per class and 220% fewer severe errors per class than a section of Model A that did not implement a design pattern. Small models that use design patterns contain fewer errors than small models that do not, when considering metrics bounds violations. One clear design guideline can thus be determined from these experiments – The reuse of good designs (e.g., in the form of one or more design patterns) directly contributes to a reduction of design-level errors in large scale systems.

## 5.2   Future Work

Analysis of Models A and B has revealed several important conclusions regarding the relative importance of various errors in models. The most severe design errors, that is, errors in a model that are most likely to cause the corresponding software to fail, are typically introduced early in the design process. This phenomenon may be due to a misunderstanding of the requirements. These errors are less likely to be introduced in later phases, such as when trying to refine a design into programming language code. Examples of severe errors include "Circular Association" and "Parent has knowledge of Child". A second tier of errors, including errors reported by metrics analysis of a design, were found to be correlated to the maturity of a design. These errors of "moderate severity" described above increased in number as a design evolved closer to the coding phase. Examples of moderately severe errors include "Multiple Inheritance", which is reported but may not be an error, depending on the design parameters, and "Public Information in Base Class".

It is most likely that the error types recognized as "severe" for the two models tested will be "severe" for all models DesignAdvisor tests. Likewise, moderate and low severity errors will also be of correspondingly low or moderate priority for all models. Comparing the analysis of industrial scale models in other domains to the results of the analysis performed here would reaffirm the given priority grouping of errors. Finding software metrics that strongly correlated to severe errors could eliminate time-intensive checks for severe errors and target problematic sections of a large model for visual inspection. Furthermore, a mechanism that would allow users to declare priorities of errors in the output of an analysis tool could then be added, providing an immediate benefit in the readability of the tool's results. For example, in a generated list of errors found by DesignAdvisor, each error would be preceded by "low", "moderate", or "severe", based upon user declarations of each error type. These error quantities could then be normalized and combined via a function relating their relative severity, potentially giving the designer a single value representing the quality of the model.

# Acknowledgements

The authors gratefully acknowledge the feedback on this work from Laura Campbell and Sascha Konrad. In addition, the authors greatly appreciate the detailed and insightful comments from the anonymous reviewers of an earlier version of this paper.

This work is supported in part by Siemens Corporate Research, NSF grants EIA-0000433, CDA-9700732, CCR-9901017, Department of the Navy, and Office of Naval Research under Grant No. N00014-01-1-0744, and in cooperation with Siemens Transportation and Detroit Diesel Corporation.

# References

[1] Rational Software: The Rational Unified Process. (2002)

[2] Chidamber, S.R., Kemerer, C.F.: A metrics suite of object oriented design. IEEE Transactions on Software Engineering **20** (1994)

[3] Eder, J., Kappel, G., Schrefl, M.: Coupling and cohesion in object-oriented systems. In: Conference on Information and Knowledge Management, Baltimore, USA. (1992)

[4] Li, W., Henry, S.: Object-oriented metrics that predict maintainability. Journal of Systems and Software **23** (1993) 111–122

[5] Lorenz, M., Kidd, J.: Object-Oriented Software Metrics: A Practical Guide. Prentice Hall (1994)

[6] Harrison, R., Counsell, S., Nithi, R.: Coupling metrics for object-oriented design. In: 5th International Symposium on Software Metrics. (1998) 150–157

[7] Tahvildari, L., Kontogiannis, K.: A metric-based approach to enhance design quality through meta-pattern transformations. In: Seventh European Conference on Software Maintenance and Reengineering. (2003) 183,192

[8] Berenbach, B.: The evaluation of large, complex UML analysis and design models. In: 26th IEEE International Conference on Software Engineering (ICSE04). (2004)

[9] Berenbach, B., Hartman, J.: DesignAdvisor, A UML-based Architectural Design Tool. Siemens Corporate Research. (2002)

[10] Gamma, E., Helm, R., Johnson, R., Vlissides, J.: Design Patterns: Elements of Reusable Object-Oriented Software. Addison-Wesley (1995)

[11] The Object Modelling Group: OMG Unified Modelling Specification Version 1.5. Object Management Group, Needham MA (2003)

[12] Babin, G., Lustman, F.: Formal data and behavior requirements engineering: a scenario based approach. In: 3rd annual IASTED International Conference on Software Engineering and Applications. (1999) 119–125

[13] Jackson, M.: Formalism and informality in RE. In: Fifth IEEE International Symposium on Requirements Engineering. (2001) 269

[14] Li, X., Liu, Z., He, J.: Formal and use-case driven requirement analysis in UML. In: 25th Annual International Computer Software and Appliations Conference. (2001) 215–224

[15] McUmber, W.E., Cheng, B.H.C.: A general framework for formalizing UML with formal languages. In: 23rd IEEE International Conference on Software Engineering (ICSE01). (2001) 433–442

[16] Riel, A.J.: Object-Oriented Design Heuristics. Addison-Wesley (1996)

[17] Campbell, L., Cheng, B.H.C., McUmber, W., Stirewalt, R.E.K.: Automatically detecting and visualizing errors in UML diagrams. Requirements Engineering Journal (2002)

[18] Briand, L.C., Daly, J.W., Wüst, J.: A unified framework for cohesion measurement in object-oriented systems. Empirical Software Engineering: An International Journal **3** (1998) 65–117

[19] Chae, H.S., Kwon, Y.R.: A cohesion measure for classes in object-oriented systems. In: 5th International Symposium on Software Metrics. (1998) 158–166

[20] Erni, K., Lewerentz, C.: Applying design-metrics to object-oriented frameworks. In: 3rd International Software Metrics Symposium. (1996) 64–74

[21] Muthanna, S., K.Ponnambalam, Kontogiannis, K., Stacey, B.: A maintainability model for industrial software systems using design level metrics. In: 7th Working Conference on Reverse Engineering. (2000) 248–257

# Reliability Prediction in Model-Driven Development

Genaína N. Rodrigues[1], David S. Rosenblum[1], and Sebastian Uchitel[2]

[1] London Software Systems
Department of Computer Science
University College London
Gower Street
London WC1E 6BT
United Kingdom
{g.rodrigues,d.rosenblum}@cs.ucl.ac.uk
[2] Department of Computing
Imperial College London
180 Queen's Gate
London SW7 2RH
United Kingdom
su2@doc.ic.ac.uk

**Abstract.** Evaluating the implications of an architecture design early in the software development lifecycle is important in order to reduce costs of development. Reliability is an important concern with regard to the correct delivery of software system service. Recently, the UML Profile for Modeling Quality of Service has defined a set of UML extensions to represent dependability concerns (including reliability) and other non-functional requirements in early stages of the software development lifecycle. Our research has shown that these extensions are not comprehensive enough to support reliability analysis for model-driven software engineering, because the description of reliability characteristics in this profile lacks support for certain dynamic aspects that are essential in modeling reliability. In this work, we define a profile for reliability analysis by extending the UML 2.0 specification to support reliability prediction based on scenario specifications. A UML model specified using the profile is translated to a labelled transition system (LTS), which is used for automated reliability prediction and identification of implied scenarios; the results of this analysis are then fed back to the UML model. The result is a comprehensive framework for addressing software reliability modeling, including analysis and evolution of reliability predictions. We exemplify our approach using the Boiler System used in previous work and demonstrate how reliability analysis results can be integrated into UML models.

## 1 Introduction

The evaluation of system specifications early in the software development lifecycle has increasingly gained attention from the software engineering community. Early evaluation of software properties, including non-functional ones, is important in order to reduce costs in software development before resources have been allocated and decisions have been made. *Dependability* is one example of an important non-functional property and represents the ability to deliver service that justifiably can be trusted. One

L. Briand and C. Williams (Eds.): MoDELS 2005, LNCS 3713, pp. 339–354, 2005.
© Springer-Verlag Berlin Heidelberg 2005

of the attributes encompassed by dependability is reliability, which is concerned with the correct delivery of software system service.

There has been growing interest in closing the gap between commercial design tools and quantitative evaluation of software systems. However, techniques available to validate a design against non-functional properties often require significant effort and expertise unrelated to the usual business of developing software. The UML 2.0 Specification itself has augmented the previous UML version so that software system characteristics, and in particular the dynamic aspects of software behaviour, can be represented more accurately [14]. As a result, mechanisms to represent various aspects of system design and analysis can be expressed within one consistent language for specifying, visualising, constructing and documenting the artifacts of software systems. As a result of the task force to make UML more comprehensive to cover all aspects and concerns of the software development lifecycle, UML extension mechanisms (particularly UML profiles) have been used to introduce capabilities for representing non-functional concerns in UML models [15, 16].

The UML Profile for Modeling Quality of Service and Fault-Tolerance (henceforth referred to as the QoS Profile) defines a set of UML extensions to represent dependability concerns (including reliability) and other non-functional requirements using the lightweight extension mechanisms of UML [15]. However, we believe the QoS Profile is not comprehensive enough to support reliability analysis, as it does not address the modeling of dynamic aspects (such as scenarios, component interactions, and operational profiles) often required in modeling reliability. On the other hand, dynamic aspects have been defined in the UML Profile for Schedulability, Performance and Time Specification (henceforth referred to as the SPT Profile), but they were not incorporated into the QoS Profile. Because a system consists of a set of interacting components such that the interactions can reveal faults [1], modeling and annotating these interactions appropriately can assist us in predicting software reliability.

In previous work, we defined a technique to predict software system reliability based on scenario specifications [19]. The technique relies on LTSA, the Labelled Transition Systems Analyser tool [21], which provides scenario-based model synthesis and model checking capabilities to support the analysis. In this work, we define a profile for reliability analysis by extending the UML 2.0 specification to support reliability prediction using our LTSA-based approach. Following this principle, our approach to meta-modeling using the UML lightweight extension mechanisms (i.e., profiles) is consistent with the MDA white paper [11], which defines basic mechanisms to structure models consistently and to express formally the semantics of the model in a standardised way. The result is a framework for systematically and pragmatically addressing software reliability modeling, including reliability analysis and prediction, with analysis results integrated back with the UML modeling environment to support system reliability enhancement. We point out here that it is not our intent to propose a new, independent UML profile. To the contrary, our purpose is to contribute towards a more comprehensive profile for reliability modeling premised on existing directions sanctioned by the OMG [15]. We exemplify our approach using the Boiler System used in previous work and demonstrate how the analysis results can be applied back into the UML models.

This paper is structured as follows: In Section 2 we present the basic concepts related to our technique for software reliability prediction. In Section 3 we introduce our model-driven development framework for reliability prediction. In Section 4 we present the core steps of our MDA-compliant model-driven reliability prediction approach. We illustrate the application of our profile in Section 5. Related work is presented in Section 6, and we conclude in Section 7 with a discussion of future directions for our work.

## 2   Background

In this section we present a succinct description of our reliability prediction technique based on *scenario specification*, presented in detail in previous papers [19, 18].

Scenarios are partial descriptions of how components interact to provide system functionality. A scenario specification is formed by composing multiple scenarios possibly from different stakeholders. To support reliability prediction, we annotate a scenario specification with probability annotations and use LTSA to process the annotated scenarios. LTSA is a tool that allows using behaviour models of distributed systems as prototypes for exploring system behaviour, and for automated checking of model compliance to properties (i.e., model checking) [21].

### 2.1   Reliability Prediction

In Figure 1 we depict the major steps our reliability prediction approach comprises. The steps are applied to a scenario specification expressed as a collection of *Basic Mes-*

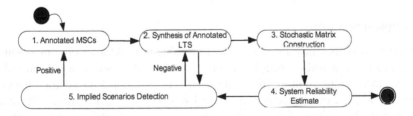

**Fig. 1.** The Steps of Our Reliability Prediction Approach.

*sage Sequence Charts* (henceforth BMSCs) and *High-Level Message Sequence Charts* (henceforth HMSCs). HMSCs provide sequential, conditional and iterative composition of BMSCs and other HSMCs, while BMSCs describe the message exchange between components on a time-line basis.

In the first step, we annotate the scenarios with two kinds of probabilities, *the probability of transitions between scenarios* $PTS_{ij}$, and *the reliability of the components* $R_C$. $PTS_{ij}$ is the probability that the system will execute scenario $S_j$ after executing scenario $S_i$. This information would be derived from an operational profile for the system [9] and is annotated on the HMSCs. The sum of the probabilities $PTS_{ij}$ for all successor scenarios $S_j$ must equal one. As for the component reliabilities $R_C$, they are annotated on the BMSCs. For the purposes of our approach, we interpret the reliability of a component $C$ as being the probability of successful completion of an invocation of any service offered by $C$, irrespective of the execution time of the service.

The second step of our method is to synthesise a probabilistic Labelled Transition System (LTS) from the annotated scenario specification. This step is an extension of the synthesis approach of Uchitel et al. [22], in which a separate LTS is first synthesised for each component, and then the *system architecture* is taken as the parallel composition of the component LTSs. Our extension involves enhancements to this synthesis approach and exploits recent probabilistic extensions to the LTS formalism [2]. The enhancements have the effect of mapping the probability annotations of the scenario specification into probability weights for transitions in the synthesised architecture model. The probability weights of the composed LTS are computed according to the notion of *generative parallel composition* defined by D'Argenio et al. [5]. At the end of this step, it follows that for each state $i$ of the synthesised architecture model and for all successor states $j$ of $i$, $\sum_{j=1}^{n} PA_{ij} = 1$, where $n$ is the number of states in the LTS architecture model and $PA_{ij}$ is the probability of transition between state $s_i$ and $s_j$ of the composed LTS; $PA_{ij} = 0$ if the transition $(s_i, s_j)$ does not exist.

In the third and fourth steps of our reliability prediction method, the architecture model synthesised in the second step is interpreted as a Markov model, and we apply the method of Cheung to compute the reliability prediction [3]. In particular, the probability weights of the architecture model are mapped into a square transition matrix whose row entries sum to one. To conform to Cheung's model, we extend the scenario specification to ensure that it contains exactly one initial and one final scenario. At this stage we can also perform sensitivity analysis of the prediction [18].

## 2.2   Implied Scenarios

Given a scenario specification, it may be impossible to build a set of components that communicate exclusively through the interfaces described and that exhibit only the specified traces when running in parallel [23]. The additional unspecified traces that are exhibited by the composed system are called *implied scenarios* and are the result of specifying the behaviour of the system from a global perspective while expecting the behaviour to be provided by components having only a local system view.

From the reliability prediction point of view, the existence of an implied scenario means that the system produces a trace that reveals a mismatch between behaviour and architecture. In that case, the model can exhibit behaviour (an implied scenario) that has not yet been validated and that, depending on whether it describes intended or unintended system behaviour, can impact system reliability. If we decide that the occurrence of the trace is desirable, we then need to appropriately place the *positive scenario* containing the trace into the scenario specification and annotate it with probabilities as described above. If we consider the occurrence of the trace as undesirable, then the scenario is a *negative scenario*, and the synthesised model must be constrained to prevent the occurrence of the negative scenario; this is accomplished by composing the synthesised model with an LTS that encodes the constraint [23]. We refer to the model where we apply such constraints as the *Constrained Model*, while the unconstrained model we refer to as the *Architecture Model*. In both cases, a new reliability prediction is computed from the revised model.

## 3    The Reliability Prediction Domain

Our framework for reliability prediction in model-driven development is based on the process depicted in Figure 2. The contribution presented in this paper is for steps 1, 2 and 3. The other steps constitute the work described in the previous section.

The framework consists of a UML profile for reliability prediction, plus a translation from the UML diagrams to LTSA. Reliability prediction is carried out as described before, as is the validation of the model by LTSA for implied scenarios. The result of this analysis provides a specification that has been elaborated through detection and validation of implied scenarios. Additionally, the results provide guidance to which software elements modeled in the UML profile the system is more sensitive. The rationale be-

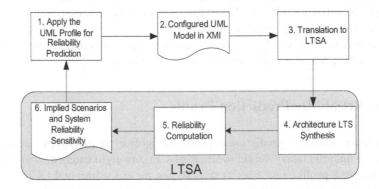

**Fig. 2.** The Model Processing Framework for Reliability Prediction.

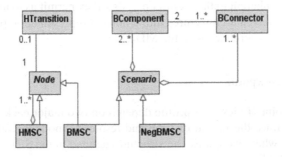

**Fig. 3.** The Domain Model of the Reliability Prediction Technique.

hind our approach is that the reliability of the system depends on two key pieces of information, as explained in Section 2: (1) scenario transition probabilities and (2) the reliability of the components. In order to support this approach within the MDA, we devise the conceptual model of reliability prediction depicted in Figure 3.

From Figure 3 it can be noticed that there are two main abstract constructs in our domain model: the *Node* and the *Scenario*. A *Node* represents the nodes of an *HMSC*. These nodes can be specialized as a *BMSC* or another *HMSC*, in case of a hierarchical HMSC. A *BMSC* corresponds to a Basic Message Sequence Chart describing the interactions between components participating in a scenario, and an *HMSC* corresponds to the high-level structure representing the composition of *BMSC*s. A *Node* element may be associated to an *HTransition* element, which represents the probability of transition to a node representing one of a set of alternative choices of behaviour. In that case, each node representing an alternatives is stereotyped as an *HTransition*.

A *Scenario*, the other main abstraction of our domain model, is an aggregation of at least two *BComponents* and at least one *BConnector*. A *BComponent* represents a software component, while a *BConnector* represents the logical or physical connection between two *BComponents*. The number of *BConnectors* associated to a *BComponent* is equal to the number of other components connected to that *BComponent*. A *Scenario* can be specialised as a *BMSC* or a *NegBMSC*, with the latter corresponding to a negative scenario as previously explained in Section 2.2.

In the next section, we delve more deeply into the processes depicted in Figure 2 and present the UML viewpoint of the structures in Figure 3.

# 4   Our Reliability Prediction Profile

Our profile for reliability prediction exploits the lightweight extension mechanisms of UML rather than the heavyweight mechanisms. Lightweight extensions of UML consist in defining a profile, i.e., a set of stereotypes, tagged values and OCL constraints. Heavyweight extensions of UML work in a higher level of abstraction by extending the Meta-Object Facility with new UML modelling constructs [13]. These extension features present in UML allow us to express the design and analysis domains seamlessly using the concepts inherent to these domains. Also, they permit us to map the behaviour of distributed component architectures into a domain representation preserving the semantics of UML in accordance with the MDA.

## 4.1   The UML Viewpoint

From the UML point of view, our profile depends on two major packages: (1) the SPT Profile, which defines the notion of time and resources modeling, and (2) the UML 2.0 Specification, where we realise the structures defined in the SPT domain and those required to model reliability.

In Figure 4 we show how the elements of our domain model relate to the elements that constitute the SPT Profile. The elements in Figure 4 in italicised font are part of the SPT Profile. A *Scenario*, in the SPT Profile, is an ordered series of steps called *action executions*, and a step, at one level of abstraction, can be decomposed further into a set of finer-grained steps. As can be noticed, all the elements in our domain model, except for *Node* and *Scenario*, extend elements of the SPT Profile. The abstract element *Node* of our domain, depicted in Figure 3, can be represented as a *Scenario* in the SPT profile or as coarse-grained *ActionExecutions*. A *Scenario* of our domain, depicted in Figure 3, can be represented as fine-grained *ActionExecutions* in the SPT profile. A *Scenario* in the SPT profile is specialized as an *HMSC* and an *ActionExecution* class is specialised as a *BMSC* or as an *HTransition*. The specialisation of the *ActionExecution* as an *HTransition* happens whenever the *ActionExecution* represents a choice of behavior. The *HTransition* also holds an association with *Resource Service Instance*, meaning that an *HTransition* keeps the reference of the resource service.

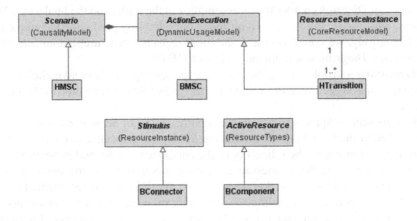

**Fig. 4.** Relationship between our Reliability Profile and the SPT Profile.

In SPT, resources are categorised being *passive* or *active*. Passive resources cannot generate their own behaviour, but only react to the occurrence of a stimulus, while active resources are those capable of spontaneous unprompted behaviour. The *BConnector* is a kind of passive resource, while the *BComponent* is an active resource.

Table 1 describes the elements constituting the UML profile for reliability modeling.

**Table 1.** Stereotypes and Tag Definitions for the Reliability Profile.

| Stereotype | Base Class | Tags |
|---|---|---|
| ≪ HMSC ≫ | Interaction Activities | HName |
| ≪ BMSC ≫ | Interaction | BName |
| ≪ NegBMSC ≫ | Interaction | BName |
| ≪ HTransition ≫ | Interaction | PTS |
| ≪ BComponent ≫ | Classifier Component Instance | BCompRel |
| ≪ BConnector ≫ | Stimulus Message | BConnRel |
| ≪ Stop ≫ | Interaction | N/A |

| Tag | Type | Multiplicity |
|---|---|---|
| PTS | Real (0,1] | [0..1] |
| BCompRel | Real (0,1) | [0..1] |
| BConnRel | Real (0,1) | [0..*] |
| HName | String | [0..1] |
| BName | String | [0..1] |

The stereotypes our profile comprises correspond to the concrete classes of our domain model depicted in Figure 3. Those stereotypes apply to UML 2.0 domain elements as follows:

- *BMSC* – Applies to *Interactions* of *Sequence Diagram* type.
- *NegBMSC* Applies to *Sequence Diagrams* with a *CombinedFragment* having *neg* as its *InteractionOperator*.
- *HMSC* – Applies to the *Interaction Overview Diagram*, which is the structure that best suits the modeling of an HMSC. *Interaction Overview Diagrams* focus on the overview of the flow of control where the nodes are *Interactions* or *InteractionOccurrences* [14]. Also, as a structure to represent the flow of control, the *Interaction Overview Diagram* enables the representation of the initial and the final states of the flow, which are also structures required in our reliability prediction technique [19]. Alternatively, we could use the *CombinedFragments* structure, but an *Interaction Overview Diagram* is semantically closer to HMSCs.
- *HTransition* – Applies to an *Interaction* representing an alternative choice of behaviour. It is tagged with the value *PTS*, the probability of transition to the *Interaction*.
- *BComponent* – Applies to components participating in *Sequence Diagrams* to be analysed by the model processor. The tag *BCompRel* associated to the *BComponent* stereotype represents the reliability of the component, as defined in Section 2.
- *BConnector* – Applies to messages exchanged between two *BComponents* in an *Interaction*. The tag *BConnRel* associated to the *BConnector* represents the reliability of the connector enabling the communication between the components. The reliability of the connector is regarded as the probability of success of a message transition, irrespective of the transition execution time.
- *Stop* – Due to the assumption in our prediction technique that there must be one final scenario in the scenario specification [19], it is required that no more than one *Interaction* connects to the *final node* of the HMSC *Interaction Overview Diagram*. The *Stop* stereotype applies to the *Interaction* with that feature.

The following are constraints defined in our Reliability Profile package:

1. Every *HMSC* and *BMSC* must be uniquely named.
2. Within an *Interaction Overview Diagram* stereotyped as an *HMSC*, every node must be either a *BMSC* or another *HMSC*.
3. Every *BMSC* is an *Interaction* of type *Sequence Diagram*.
4. Every *HMSC* must have one *Activity initial node* and one *Activity final node*.
5. *HMSC* nodes must have at least one incoming and one outgoing transition, except the *initial node* and *final node*.
6. The *PTS* values of *HTransition*-stereotyped nodes connected to the same *Decision* node within an *HMSC* must sum to one.
7. In an *HMSC*, there must be one (and only one) *Interaction* stereotyped as *Stop* and connecting to the *final node*.

Each of these constraints can be expressed easily in OCL, but for space reasons we do not present their OCL rendition.

## 4.2   Mapping from UML to LTSA

Once our profile is applied to a UML model, the translation from UML to LTSA is carried out. The transformation consists of (1) parsing the XML Metadata Interchange (XMI) form of the UML model, which is the standard representation of UML models in XML [12], and (2) generating the XML input format accepted by LTSA.

Current UML tools provide only partial conformance with the UML 2.0 specification, which has forced us to make some workarounds in our implementation. The major problem we encountered was to apply the stereotype *HTransition* and its *PTS* tagged value to the nodes (i.e., *Interaction Occurrences*) within *Combined Fragments* within *Interaction Overview Diagrams*. To get around this problem, we had to associate the *HTransition* stereotype with the transitions between nodes rather than to the nodes themselves. This solution is temporary, and we will evolve the implementation of our profile as tool support improves to properly accommodate the UML 2.0 specification.

We implemented the transformation of our UML profile to LTSA in XSLT [24]. XSLT describes rules for transforming a source document in a tree format (such as an XML file) into a result document described also by a tree. It therefore suits our need to transform the XMI representation of a UML model into the XML format accepted by LTSA. The transformation process is rather straightforward as long as the following conditions are satisfied:

1. An HMSC in LTSA cannot have multiple nodes that correspond to the same BMSC. In case there are multiple *Interaction Occurrences* of the same *Sequence Diagram* in a UML *Interaction Overview Diagram*, those multiple occurrences are reduced to just one node of the LTSA HMSC during the transformation process, keeping the same set of transitions contained in the *Interaction Overview Diagram*.
2. LTSA does not support hierarchically nested HMSCs at the moment. In case an *Interaction Overview Diagram* is specified in multiple hierarchical levels, it should be flattened before transformation is carried out.

## 4.3   Mapping Analysis Results Back to UML

After analysis has been carried out in LTSA following the approach presented in Section 2, we have the system reliability prediction and the detection of implied scenarios. In particular, we can use this analysis to provide answers to the following questions: Do we have any implied scenarios in our system architecture model? What is the impact of the implied scenarios on the system reliability? What is the sensitivity of the system reliability to changes in individual probability values?

If an implied scenario is a positive scenario, which means that the detected trace is to be included in the scenario specification, then a new Sequence Diagram is constructed for the trace and annotated with our profile for reliability prediction. This new *Interaction* is then incorporated appropriately as a node in the *Interaction Overview Diagram*. Incoming and outgoing transitions must be manually attached to the new positive scenario. If an implied scenario is a negative scenario, i.e., a trace to be avoided, it needs to be incorporated into a *NegBMSC*, with the undesirable message traces specified inside an *Interaction Fragment* having *InteractionOperator* type *neg*.

As for the sensitivity analysis, the purpose is to study the impact of components and usage profiles on system reliability [18]. For this purpose, the analysis reveals how the system reliability is sensitive to (1) the *component reliabilities*, and (2) the *scenario transition probabilities*. These two analyses can help in identifying components and scenario transitions that could threaten the reliability of the software system. The results produced by the sensitivity analysis can then be used by system designers to decide on mechanisms to use for enhancing the system reliability.

## 5   Example

We exemplify our approach using a variant of the Boiler Control system presented by Uchitel et al. [23]. As shown in the Interaction Overview Diagram of Figure 5, the Boiler Control system composes five Sequence Diagrams *Initialise*, *Register*, *Analyse*, *Terminate* and *Shutdown*, which are are depicted in Figure 6.

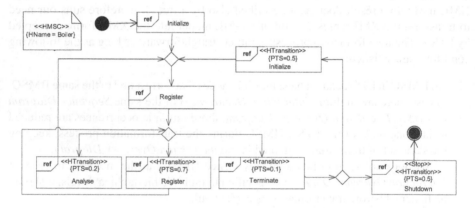

**Fig. 5.** The Interaction Overview Diagram of the Boiler System.

As presented in Section 4, the stereotype *HTransition* is tagged with the probability of transition between scenarios, *PTS*, as shown in Figure 5. The values for the *PTS* are based on the assumption that the system executes the scenario *Register* (which causes sensor readings to be entered into the database) far more frequently than the scenarios *Analyse* and *Terminate*, and that when it does execute *Terminate* there is an equal probability of either reinitialising or shutting down completely. As shown in the figure, it may be necessary to specify multiple references to the same Sequence Diagram if they are to be tagged with different scenario transition probabilities.

Inside the *BMSC*-stereotyped Sequence Diagrams, the components' reliabilities are annotated by applying the stereotype *BComponent* with its tagged value *BCompRel*, as depicted in Figure 6. Without loss of generality, we use coarse-grained, single values for the overall component reliabilities. In general, we can also associate finer-grained values for reliability through annotation of individual messages and segments of component timelines. The *BConnector* element of our profile suits the use of finer-grained

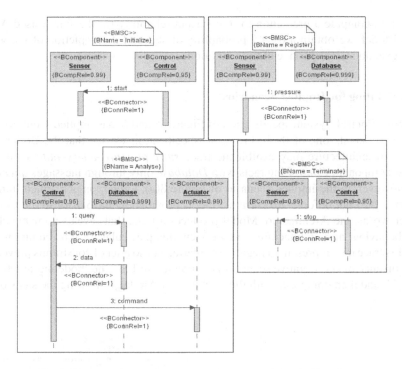

**Fig. 6.** The Annotated Sequence Diagrams of the Boiler System.

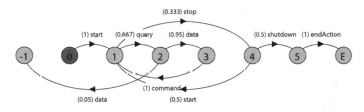

**Fig. 7.** The Synthesised Label Transition System for Component Control in LTSA.

values where individual messages can also be associated with a communication reliability value; in the example, these values are all set to 1.0. The values in Figure 6 for
the reliability of the components reflect the assumption that the *Database* is a highly
reliable, mature commercial software product, that the *Sensor* and *Actuator* are components whose hardware interface to the sensed/actuated phenomena will eventually wear
out and fail, and that *Control* is a newer, complex software subsystem that still contains
latent faults. Notice that the *Shutdown* Sequence Diagram is not present in Figure 6, as
it has traces identical to those in the *Terminate* scenario.

Following the steps of our reliability prediction technique [19], the LTS model for
each component participating in the scenarios is generated; for instance, the LTS for
component *Control* is depicted in Figure 7. Then, the *Architecture Model* of the system is synthesised as the parallel composition of the component LTSs. Using Cheung's

approach to compute a prediction for the system reliability for the synthesised Architecture Model, we obtain a 64.9% probability of successful completion of the whole system execution, irrespective of time duration.

## 5.1 Validating for Implied Scenarios

The Boiler Control System specification of Figures 5 and 6, has implied scenarios, and Figure 8(a) depicts one of them. From the specification we see that the Boiler Control system architecture may exhibit the trace *start–pressure–query–data–command*, and that component *Control* interacts with *Database* only through messages *query* and *data*. However, in the implied scenario of Figure 8(a), a *query* is performed immediately after *start* but before a *pressure* reading is provided by the *Sensor* to the *Control*. In other words, the Architecture Model produces a trace that reveals a mismatch between behaviour and architecture, and we view this particular trace as being undesirable. This trace thus represents a negative scenario, and so a set of constraints preventing the occurrence of the negative scenario is expressed in FSP, the modeling notation of LTSA [7], and then composed with the Architecture Model. Following the steps of our

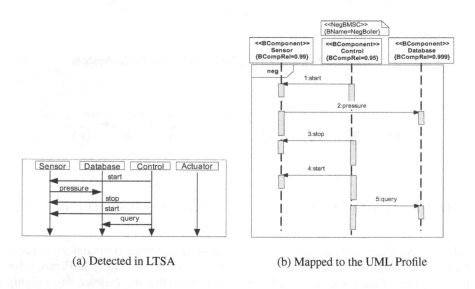

(a) Detected in LTSA                    (b) Mapped to the UML Profile

**Fig. 8.** An Implied Scenario.

reliability prediction technique, a *Constrained Model* of the system is then synthesised as the parallel composition of the constraints with the Architecture model previously obtained. Calculating the reliability of the resulting Constrained Model, we obtain the value of 86.2% probability of successful completion of the whole system execution, irrespective of time duration. Figure 8(b) depicts the implied scenario detected in LTSA as it would be mapped back to UML as a *NegBMSC*.

## 5.2   Sensitivity Analysis

Sensitivity analysis consists of determining how the system reliability varies as a function of the components' reliabilities and scenario transition probabilities, with the purpose of identifying probabilities that have the greatest impact on the reliability of the software system [18]. For component reliabilities, the method consists of varying the reliability of one component at a time and fixing the others to 1. Then, computing the system reliability, we obtain the results presented in Figure 9.

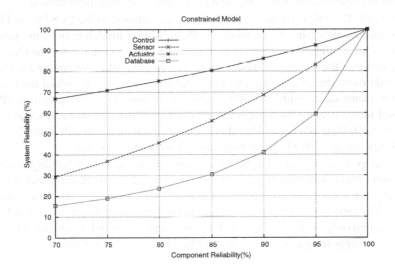

**Fig. 9.** The System Reliability as a Function of the Component Reliabilities.

The graph shows the system reliability of the Constrained Model as a function of the component reliabilities. The analysis shows that the reliability of the Boiler System is most sensitive to component *Database*, followed by components *Sensor*, *Control* and *Actuator*. Note that the *Control* and the *Actuator* curves coincide, meaning that they have an identical impact on system reliability.

## 6   Related Work

Using UML profiles to support modeling of non-functional aspects of software systems following a model-driven approach is not a new idea. The approaches for model-driven non-functional analysis are distinguished mostly by the way they support analysis of annotated UML models.

Majzik et.al. provide a profile for modeling fault-tolerant mechanisms, particularly redundancy, in UML diagrams [8]. Transformations are done in a sound manner through graph transformation, from UML to their analysis platform. Approaches in this category do not follow a standardised MDA approach. As a result, the key benefit of a standards-based approach is lost, i.e., interoperability of applications enabling a market in robust industrial tools that support the approach.

There has been work following the MDA approach for non-functional requirements modeling by extending the SPT Profile with regard to performance [6, 20]. Gu et.al. implement a transformation by parsing the XMI output of profile-mapped UML diagrams [6]. The approach of Skene et.al. resembles that of Gu et.al. but provides a more formal elaboration of the profile via OCL constraints [20]. Our approach follows in the same standards-based spirit, but with regard to reliability modeling. At the end of the day, any standards-compliant UML tool is capable of storing these models.

Recently, Cortellessa et.al. [4] proposed an amendment to the QoS Profile [15] with the purpose of addressing issues related to the reliability modeling of component-based systems. Our profile follows a similar structure as their extension for the QoS Profile, but we differ in the way we compose scenarios. In particular, we consider it important to provide more structure to a scenario specification and thus to model the interaction between scenarios through the *HMSC* structure of our profile. This feature allows us to model larger systems, as a greater number of scenarios can be analysed more easily through the *HMSC* structure. Therefore, we believe that our profile provides gains in modularity for modeling large systems and their reliability issues.

In our profile, we use of UML 2.0 constructs to support reliability analysis for component-based software systems. Constructs in UML 2.0 make easier the task of modeling non-functional requirements due to its richer expressiveness compared to previous UML versions. Reliability modeling using new concepts introduced in UML 2.0 are not commonly found in the literature. We believe that wider availability of modelling tools supporting UML 2.0 will stimulate new work in this area.

# 7    Conclusion

We present in this paper a UML profile to aid reliability prediction and analysis of software systems. We define a framework based on the UML 2.0 specification and the SPT Profile to support a reliability prediction technique that takes into account component structure exhibited in scenarios and the concurrent nature of component-based systems.

Following a compliant MDA process, a UML model specified using the profile is translated to a labelled transition system, which is model-checked by the LTSA tool to identify implied scenarios and is used to compute a reliability prediction according to the method of Cheung. Sensitivity analysis is also used to highlight components and scenario transitions that have a high impact on system reliability. The analysis results are integrated back with the UML modeling environment to support system reliability enhancement. Our purpose with the profile is to contribute towards a more comprehensive profile for reliability modeling consistent with the direction of the OMG [15].

We may acknowledge some shortcomings of our UML profile. We have implemented our profile using the MagicDraw UML tool version 9.0 Community Edition [10], and the XSLT stylesheet we implemented was based on the XMI version 1.2 the tool generates for the UML diagrams. The problem is that Magic Draw provides just partial support to UML 2.0, and the XMI output is out of date. Future versions of the tool are expected to be fully compliant with UML 2.0, as well as the XMI counterpart.

Future directions of our work include extending the profile to support modelling of fault-tolerance mechanisms. The first steps towards this goal were initiated in previous work [17] and by others in the literature, including the OMG itself [15]. By doing this, we intend to support code generation with assessed reliability, enhanced via fault-tolerance mechanisms present in current distributed component platforms. Additional work is also needed to explore methods and techniques that can fully reveal the impact of implied scenarios on system reliability. Finally, we plan to apply our approach on case studies of larger, more realistic systems to evaluate its scalability and the accuracy of the predictions it produces.

### Acknowledgments

David Rosenblum holds a Wolfson Research Merit Award from the Royal Society. Sebastian Uchitel was partially funded by EPSRC grant READS GR/S03270/01. Genaína Rodrigues was funded by CAPES, grant 108201-9. Vittorio Cortellessa provided several valuable comments that improved our understanding of reliability modeling in UML and the state of current efforts with relevant UML profiles. We also thank the anonymous referees for their helpful suggestions on improving the manuscript.

### References

[1] A. Avižienis, J. Laprie, and B. Randell. Fundamental Concepts of Dependability. In *Proc. IARP/IEEE-RAS Workshop on Robot Dependability*, May 2001.

[2] T. Ayles, A. Field, J. Magee, and A. Bennett. Adding Performance Evaluation to the LTSA Tool (Tool Demonstration). In *Proc. 13th Performance Tools*, September 2003.

[3] R. C. Cheung. A User-Oriented Software Reliability Model. In *IEEE Transactions on Software Engineering*, volume 6(2), pages 118–125. IEEE, Mar. 1980.

[4] V. Cortellessa and A. Pompei. Towards a UML profile for QoS: a contribution in the reliability domain. In *Proc. of the $4^{th}$ WOSP*, pages 197–206. ACM Press, 2004.

[5] P. R. D'Argenio, H. Hermanns, and J.-P. Katoen. On Generative Parallel Composition. In *Electronic Notes in Theoretical Computer Science*, volume 22. Elsevier, 2000.

[6] G. P. Gu and D. C. Petriu. Early Evaluation of Software Performance Based on the UML Performance Profile. In *Proc. of the 2003 CASCON*, pages 66–79. IBM Press, 2003.

[7] J. Magee and J. Kramer. *Concurrency: State Models and Java Programs*. Wiley, NY, 1999.

[8] I. Majzik, A. Pataricza, and A. Bondavalli. Stochastic Dependability Analysis of System Architecture Based on UML Models. In *Architecting Dependable Systems, LNCS–2667*, pages 219–244. Springer, 2003.

[9] J. D. Musa. Operational profiles in software-reliability engineering. *IEEE Software*, 10(2):14–32, 1993.

[10] NoMagic Inc. MagicDraw UML. http://www.magicdraw.com/.

[11] OMG. *Model Driven Architecture*. http://www.omg.org/mda/, July 2001.

[12] OMG. *XMI Specification*. http://www.omg.org/cgi-bin/doc?formal/2002-01-01, Jan 2002.

[13] OMG. *MOF 2.0 Specification*. http://www.omg.org/cgi-bin/doc?ptc/2003-10-04, Oct 2003.

[14] OMG. *UML 2.0 Superstructure*. http://www.omg.org/cgi-bin/doc?ptc/2004-10-02, 2003.

[15] OMG. *UML Profile for Modeling Quality of Service and Fault Tolerance Characteristics and Mechanisms*. http://www.omg.org/docs/ptc/04-09-01.pdf, Sep 2004.

[16] OMG.  *UML Profile for Schedulability, Performance and Time Specification.*
http://www.omg.org/technology/documents/formal/schedulability.htm, Jan 2005.

[17] G. Rodrigues, G. Roberts, and W. Emmerich.  Reliability Support for the Model Driven
Architecture. In *Architecting Dependable Systems II.* Springer, LNCS 3069, 2004.

[18] G. Rodrigues, D. Rosenblum, and S. Uchitel.  Sensitivity Analysis for a Scenario-Based
Reliability Prediction Model. In *Proc. ICSE 2005 Workshop on Architecting Dependable
Systems,* pages 73–77, May 2005.

[19] G. Rodrigues, D. Rosenblum, and S. Uchitel.  Using Scenarios to Predict the Reliability
of Concurrent Component-Based Software Systems. In *Proc. ETAPS 2005 Conference on
Formal Approaches to Software Engineering,* pages 111–126. Springer, LNCS 3442, 2005.

[20] J. Skene and W. Emmerich.  A Model Driven Architecture Approach to Analysis of Non-
Functional Properties of Software Architecture.  In *Proc. of the* $18^{th}$ *ASE. Toronto, CA.*
IEEE Computer Society, Oct. 2001.

[21] S. Uchitel, R. Chatley, J. Kramer, and J.Magee.  LTSA-MSC: Tool Support for Behaviour
Model Elaboration Using Implied Scenarios. In *Proc. of* $9^{th}$ *TACAS, Warsaw,* Apr. 2003.

[22] S. Uchitel, J. Kramer, and J.Magee.  Synthesis of Behavioral Models from Scenarios. *IEEE
Transactions on Software Engineering,* 29(2):99–115, Feb. 2003.

[23] S. Uchitel, J. Kramer, and J.Magee.  Incremental Elaboration of Scenario-Based Specifications and Behavior Models Using Implied Scenarios. *ACM Transactions on Software
Engineering and Methodologies,* 13(1):37–85, Jan. 2004.

[24] W3C. *XSL Transformations (XSLT).* http://www.w3.org/TR/xslt, November 1999.

# Model-Based Scalability Estimation in Inception-Phase Software Architecture

Steve Masticola[1], Andre Bondi[1], and Mark Hettish[2]

[1]Siemens Corporate Research, Inc.
755 College Road East
Princeton, NJ 08520
stephen.masticola@siemens.com
andre.bondi@siemens.com

[2]Siemens Communications, Inc.
1700 Technology Drive
San Jose, CA 95110
mark.hettish@siemens.com

**Abstract.** Scalability is one of the crucial nonfunctional requirements that must be evaluated in the Inception Phase of the Rational Unified Process [9]. This is the phase in which the least information is generally available to form a principled evaluation. We demonstrate how an estimate of user scalability can be formed using sequence diagrams of the common user scenarios, together with experimentation (ranging from simple timing measurements to more complex architectural prototypes), published study data, and performance data from baseline systems. Despite being quite inexpensive, the techniques used by our team enabled us to identify and guide corrective actions for major bottlenecks before they became serious design flaws in the Elaboration and Construction phases of the Unified Process. The same techniques also allowed us to quickly evaluate the effects of high-level architecture and technology alternatives on user scalability and response time.

## 1. Problem Statement

This study concerns a large-scale commercial server-based software product (denoted by LSCSP[1]) based on the Microsoft C# platform [6]. The system is partitioned into concurrent processes that communicate using socket-based communication transmission of SOAP messages.

An effort is underway to develop version N+1 of LSCSP based on Java technology, including elements of J2EE. The migration to Java was undertaken for two reasons.

---

[1] The name of the product, the scenarios it supports, and all other identifying information, have been changed to protect Siemens intellectual property.

L. Briand and C. Williams (Eds.): MoDELS 2005, LNCS 3713, pp. 355–366, 2005.

First, the LSCSP marketers wanted to reach customers who find the C# platform unacceptable. Second, it was hoped that the mapping could increase the number of users supported by each server. The LSCSP architects thought that the SOAP messaging scheme was inefficient and that they could get significant scalability with respect to the number of users ("user scalability") gains from a more tightly-coupled messaging mechanism. In this context, user scalability has two components, load scalability, which concerns scalability with respect to the use of active resources such as processors, bandwidth, and I/O devices, and space scalability, which concerns scalability with respect to passive resources such as memory [8]. The LSCSP architects were primarily concerned with load scalability.

The architecture team realized early that, to achieve these gains, LSCSP's modules would have to be mapped onto Java containers of various types (servlet/JSP, EJB etc.) differently from the way they were mapped onto .NET processes and threads. The architecture team identified at least ten reasonable ways to do this. They needed to evaluate the effect that each mapping would have on user scalability. Additionally, within each possible mapping, several technology options were also possible for communications between different pairs of modules. These, too, could potentially affect the scalability of the system.

The two problems we faced, then, were:

- to estimate user scalability for each of the reasonable process-to-container mappings and for each of the possible communication technology alternatives,
- to estimate the increase in user scalability that could be expected from the migration to the new architecture and the Java platform.

This paper presents the lessons learned in creating these estimates. Our purpose is to show a set of useful estimation techniques, rather than to present normative performance data or experimental studies. We therefore omit all detailed description of the experimental procedure, which was intended purely to provide "first-look" data for our own use. Any data here is shown only for descriptive purposes, and should not be taken as normative.

## 2. Nonfunctional Requirements in the Forthcoming System

The forthcoming version of LSCSP had several ambitious performance goals as nonfunctional requirements. Determining whether these goals could be met was the major motivation for doing performance analysis.

First, LSCSP N+1 had a goal of increasing the number of users supported on a "standard server" by an order of magnitude. An example of a "standard server" is a dual Pentium PC with a substantial amount of RAM and hard disk.

In addition, enterprise-level scalability was desired. The intent was to scale to systems of collaborating servers to support increasing numbers of users. Another goal was to support failover between servers with minimal interruption in service.

Achieving both of these goals will require system resources and thus affect user scalability.

## 3. Anticipated Performance Impacts of Some Implementation Choices

LSCSP relies on "server push" technology[2] to periodically update one particular frame. Server push requires the client to periodically poll the server for updates. This further increased the server workload. It was thought that server-push would cause serious scaling problems. Therefore, we wanted to investigate updating technologies other than server push, and their effect on user scalability.

A certain amount of off-server traffic was expected to support cross-server request handling and data replication during normal operation to support failover handling. We wished to get a precise estimate of how much extra load would be caused by server-to-server communication in a large-scale scenario. We acknowledge, therefore, that the resource utilization of these scenarios should be modeled, but that we have not as yet examined this in detail.

### 3.1. The Need for Model Parameterization

Early in the scalability estimation effort, we decided to develop a spreadsheet-based model of user scalability. This would allow us to decide at the Inception Phase of the Rational Unified Process [9] (or at a similarly early stage in other processes) whether the nonfunctional requirements could likely be simultaneously met, or whether the architecture and/or choice of technologies needed to be revised.

Additionally, the team recognized that there were other factors that could not easily be predicted or determined through experimentation or existing data. These included, but were not limited to, per-user resource demands for various usage scenarios, the performance gain in the LSCSP business logic from parallel processing, and the language-dependent performance of Java versus C#. We parameterized the spreadsheet model to allow architects to see the performance impacts of different choices of technologies under different sets of assumptions about their associated processing costs. In the end, our model had twenty-three different parameters.

## 4. Procedure

Our procedure to conduct the analysis was to specify each architectural alternative under consideration in sufficient detail that UML sequence diagrams of the most common scenarios, and experimental data from architectural prototyping, could be

---

[2] This is the conventional terminology, though in fact the client pulls the content.

used to derive expected consumptions of server resources. Our methodology was very similar to that of Smith and Williams [7]. We adapted their techniques in two key ways: we used no special-purpose performance analysis extensions to the UML, and we also employed only commercial UML modeling tools (mainly the UML features of Microsoft Visio), rather than special-purpose tools for performance analysis such as Smith and Williams' SPE*ED.

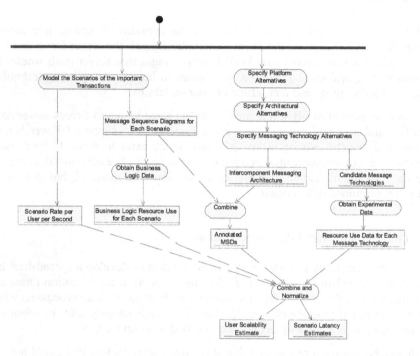

**Figure 1:** The model-based scalability estimation process used by the team.

**Figure 1** shows an abstract overview of the process that was used to estimate user scalability. The team modeled each of the important transaction use cases of LSCSP, producing a message sequence diagram (MSD) for each scenario and an estimated scenario repetition rate (transaction rate) per user per second. Once the scenarios were modeled, resource use data was obtained from the LSCSP performance analysts for most of the business logic used in the scenarios.

Simultaneously, the team specified the platform, architectural, and messaging technology alternatives that they wished to evaluate. This effort produced a list of candidate messaging technologies, and a set of inter-component messaging architectures (i.e., maps from the communication relationships between components to these technologies.) The latter was combined with the scenario MSDs to produce MSDs that had been annotated with the size and technology of each message.

Once the candidate message technologies had been identified, the relationship between message size and resource usage could be determined experimentally for each technology. The annotated MSDs could then be combined with this data to produce an estimate of resource usage for each instance of each scenario. Business logic resource usage could be added as well. With these data in hand, we would be in a position to determine the maximum sustainable transaction rates for given mixes of scenarios.

We note that other performance measures of interest, e.g., a lower bound on the latency for the scenarios, can be estimated using the same data, by finding the length of the critical path through the MSD.

## 4.1. Architectural Alternatives Under Consideration

We wished to analyze the user scalability of several different possible architectural alternatives. In each alternative, a choice was made for platform technologies, mappings of system components to those platforms, and inter-component communications technologies within each mapping.

### 4.1.1. Platform Technologies

LSCSP version N is based on a tiered architecture, consisting of client, presentation, business logic, integration, and resource tiers. Many of the tiers would undergo changes to their platform technology in version N+1.

- The presentation tier platform on LSCSP version N is Microsoft Internet Information Server, including Active Server Pages. In version N+1, this would probably change to Apache Tomcat and Java Server Pages. There is also an option for a tight integration of the presentation tier platform with the business logic tier platform.
- The business logic tier platform in LSCSP version N is simply the Windows runtime, since the LSCSP components run as processes. In LSCSP N+1, the business tier would run on EJB, a lightweight platform (called LWP here), or some architectural alternative that combines the two. Additionally, some non-real-time business logic could be implemented as servlets and run in the servlet container.
- In LSCSP N, there is no integration tier as such. The Java Connector Framework could potentially serve as an integration tier in LSCSP N+1.

The major decisions on platform technology for LSCSP N+1 involved mapping the components of LSCSP to these technologies, possibly with some repartitioning. Additionally, there was a question of whether to use Tomcat standalone or some other technology.

### 4.1.2. High-Level Architecture Options

We considered eight proposed LSCSP package architectures. Ad-hoc diagrams showed the embedding and communication of the business-logic software components within and between the proposed container technologies. These diagrams established partial constraints on the mappings from inter-component messages to specific technologies.

### 4.1.3. Inter-component Communications Technology Options

Within each high-level architecture option, it was clear that a LSCSP implementation could use many different communication technologies. We wanted to evaluate the effect of each of these technologies upon system performance. The technologies identified for study included:

- HTTP (for communicating between the client and presentation tiers.)
- Java Messaging Service.
- EJB calls (local and remote.)
- Lightweight component-to-component calls.
- Serialized Java objects over TCP.
- SOAP-serialized objects over TCP.
- Web services invocation via Jboss Mbean technology.

### 4.2. Scenario Modeling

For the Inception Phase performance modeling, the architecture team extrapolated the inter-component call sequences of LSCSP Version N to LSCSP Version N+1. These sequences were captured in the form of UML sequence diagrams. Figure 2 is an example of one of these scenario diagrams.

### 4.3. Experimentation

While part of the architecture team was capturing scenarios as MSDs, a second part of the team started a program of experimentation with the communication technologies listed in Section 4.1.3. These experiments were an early phase of architectural prototyping, and were intended to produce rough timings for internal use rather than benchmarks for engineering and sizing purposes. Creating a publishable benchmark was outside the scope of our activities.

To obtain reasonably accurate timings on a Windows XP platform from inside of Java, we used Vladimir Robutsov's com.vladium.utils timing utilities [1], [2]. Most of our timing experiments were timed using the sub-microsecond PC wall-clock timer. We standardized on using the wall-clock time to execute a scenario as the basis for resource consumption, for two reasons. First, using CPU time alone would hide idle time and delays due to non-CPU resource utilization. Second, CPU time as measured on Windows XP includes only the immediate process and kernel time, and wouldn't include CPU used by system processes that are called into action indirectly while executing the scenario.

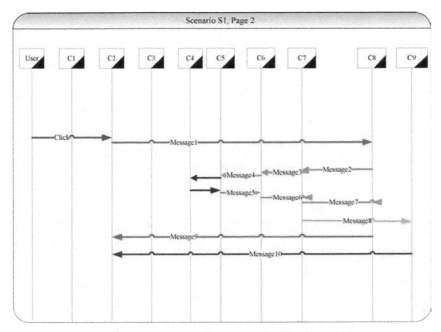

**Figure 2:** Sample MSD from one LSCSP scenario (S1).

Message transmission timings were performed by sampling the performance timer at six instants in the handling of each message: (sender) start of process, marshalling completed, send done; (receiver side) start of reception, message received, message unmarshaled. Synthetic messages with payload lengths varying from one byte to one megabyte were generated and marshaled. Ten messages of each length were sent and received.

Two special concerns were queuing artifacts and JVM optimization. To avoid message queue problems, transmission of any test message was held off until the previous test message had been received and unmarshaled. Since the beneficial effect of JVM optimization only comes into play after the corresponding code has been executing without being optimized, a "warm-up" run was completed before the test run was performed with measurement turned on.

Figure 3 is an example plot of experimental data for a light-weight service call, which confirmed our beliefs that this mechanism is fairly efficient. The upper plot shows that the average elapsed time for handling and light-weight service call is of the same order of magnitude for all message payload sizes. The lower plot contains the same data. Its vertical scale has been expanded to show that the processing time of the light-weight message handling mechanism is quite insensitive to the size of the payload field. Moreover, the average observed processing time is visibly low compared with the displayed points, indicating that the distribution of values is skewed below the average. We did observe some spikes in wall-clock time. We believe that they might be caused by uncontrolled activity by other processes executing under Windows XP.

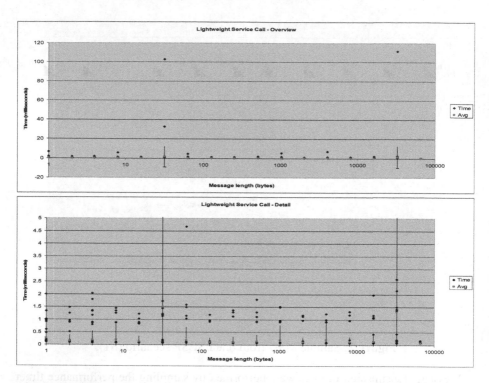

**Figure 3:** Sample data for a light-weight service call. Error bars are at one standard deviation from the mean.

| Mechanism | Latency (msec) with 1024 bytes | Latency (msec) with 2048 bytes | Latency (msec) with 4096 bytes | Latency grows with message size? |
|---|---|---|---|---|
| HTTP server-side response (Tomcat) | 8.60 | 14.70 | 27.07 | Yes |
| Java local call (intraunit) | 0.05 | 0.05 | 0.05 | No |
| Java Messaging Service (JBoss) | 511.80 | 494.38 | 468.43 | Yes[3] |
| Light-weight service call (LWS-Impl) | 0.19 | 0.11 | 0.19 | No |
| Remote session EJB, same container (JBoss) | 0.20 | 0.24 | *0.17 | No |
| Local session EJB, same container (JBoss) | *0.25 | 0.25 | *0.15 | No |
| Serialized objects over TCP | 0.34 | 0.74 | 0.36 | No |
| SOAP messages over TCP (send time) | 0.78 | 1.19 | 1.66 | Yes |
| SOAP messages over TCP (receive time) | 1.26 | 2.13 | 2.18 | Yes |
| Web services using JBoss.NET MBeans | 10.04 | 10.80 | 11.86 | Yes |

**Table 1:** Summary of experimental results at 1024, 2048, and 4096 bytes.

---

[3] The Jboss implementation of JMS showed three different operating regions with respect to message size.

Table 1 shows a summary of the experiment results with message payload sizes of 1024, 2048, and 4096 bytes (a common expected message size) for each of the messaging technologies we considered.

For some messaging mechanisms, such as HTTP and SOAP over TCP, we saw that the elapsed time increased as the message length increased. For other messaging mechanisms, such as EJB inter-bean calls in Jboss and light-weight inter-service calls in LWS-Impl, there was no such trend. These results are indicated in the "Latency grows with message size?" column of Table 1. The asterisks indicate that the data may reflect unexplained experimental error for those measurements and that we have used a conservative estimate instead. (Again, these latency values should not be viewed as normative, since that was not their intent.)

Interestingly, we found that the light-weight service technology LWS-Impland Jboss EJB [5] had about the same message transmission time, probably because they are using similar underlying mechanisms for separating Java namespaces and passing object references between them. The data also shows that the Java Messaging Service (JMS) would not be fast enough to use as an internal communication mechanism within LSCSP. This observation alone saved the team from taking a wrong direction, since JMS was being advocated within the team as a high-speed inter-component communication mechanism.

It is worth noting that the latency for transmitting serialized Java objects over TCP within the same server did not grow much with increasing message size. We conjecture that there is some optimization within the platform (at the Java and possibly the Windows XP layers) that avoids memory copying for these messages.

### 4.4. Use of Published Data

A literature search was undertaken early in the Inception Phase to find any published timing benchmark data that would be relevant to the project. In particular, we wanted to find any existing benchmarks relating business logic performance in Java and C#. Many claims and counterclaims have been made about the performance of these platforms by their proponents, but little data is available comparing communications mechanisms and business logic. One exception is [3]; while this data did not pertain directly to our needs, it served to reinforce our belief that the two languages would have roughly equivalent performance in business logic. Our experimental data later supported this belief.

### 4.5. Baselining the Existing System

Baseline data on CPU usage was available for LSCSP N for each of several scenarios. The usage figures included inter-component messaging, which we wished to exclude in order to baseline the cost of handling business logic irrespective of which option we chose. We therefore ran an experiment to estimate the CPU overhead in messaging.

Following this, the CPU time on the LSCSP N experimental machine was normalized to wall-clock time on the LSCSP N+1 experimental machine, using ratios of CPU clock rate on the two machines and Amdahl's Law [5] to normalize with respect to the number of processors. The ratio of CPU time to wall-clock time and the fraction of parallelizable business logic are engineering estimates that are settable parameters in the spreadsheet model.

We also needed to understand how the performance of the application in C# would compare with that in Java, other things being equal. For this purpose, we created a non-recursive "Towers of Hanoi" program in both languages and ran it with tower sizes from one to twenty. While the experiment is certainly not normative, it reinforced our impression that the business logic would probably not get a significant performance increase in the migration from C# to Java.

### 4.6. Spreadsheet Model

A spreadsheet model was created to summarize the scenarios of Section 4.2. Each worksheet in the spreadsheet corresponded to one scenario. One line on each sheet counted all the messages of a given communication technology and approximate message length in one of the MSDs in the scenario. Since the process of translation from the Visio MSDs to the spreadsheet was manual, checksums for the number of messages were included to check for errors in the transcription of the diagrams.

## 5. Discussion of the Performance Results and Their Architectural Implications

The pie chart in Figure 4 illustrates how the data gathered in the spreadsheet contributed to our understanding of resource usage for a particular group of parameter settings. It clearly shows that the business logic in two particular scenarios (labeled S1 and S2 in Figure 4) would the biggest contributors to system load in LSCSP N+1's expected operation, for a total of 89% of the system load. The total contribution of all messaging in all scenarios to the system load was less than one tenth of the total CPU usage.

We used a partial UML model of LSCSP N+1 (the MSDs of the most important scenarios) along with other experimental and published data and engineering estimates to approximately predict single-server user scalability with good effect. Moreover, we constructed a model which allows architects to vary the engineering estimates as parameters and derive best-case and worst-case user scalability estimates.

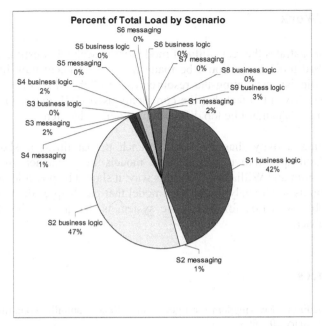

**Figure 4:** Breakdown of load by scenario and load type (inter-component messaging vs. business logic).

The effort to construct these inception-phase estimates, excluding the experimentation, was less than one person-month. Getting the experimental data for message transmission time comprised most of the effort involved in the estimation. This data can now be reused for other projects, greatly reducing the effort needed to get scalability estimates.[4] Moreover, the same technique can be applied to estimate other architectural information of interest in the Inception Phase, such as latency and enterprise-wide user scalability.

Examples of two useful results that came out of our effort were:
- the identification of JMS as being unsuitable for use in LSCSP on performance grounds, and;
- the observation that LSCSP N+1 would be bottlenecked by business logic (especially scenarios S1 and S2), rather than by inter-module communications as was previously expected. This implies that the project goal of a five-fold improvement in users per server would require major attention to business logic performance.

These timely and inexpensively obtained results prevented later embarrassment. They could be used to focus architecture and development activity in LSCSP N+1.

---

[4] The experimentation required about five person-months. It must be emphasized, though, that the data can be re-used for other estimation. Therefore, the cost of the experiments should be amortized over other estimations.

# 6.  Future Work

This paper demonstrates the feasibility of model-based scalability estimation based on industry-standard tools, but it could be made far more efficient with improved tool support. In particular, estimating the resource usage of the MSD edges was tedious and error-prone. Given the fact that the commonly-used UML diagramming tools all support plug-ins, it shouldn't be too difficult to automate this step.

By annotating activity diagrams with branch probabilities, it should also be possible to form quantitative performance models in a manner similar to that suggested by Smith and Williams [7]. In this way, it should be possible to use activity diagrams as inputs to an analytic queuing model that can help evaluate performance over all possible scenarios for which the system is designed, rather than just an enumerated subset.

# 7.  References

[1 Robutsov, Vladimir. "My kingdom for a good timer! Reach submillisecond timing in Java." *JavaWorld*, January 10, 2003.

[2] Robutsov, Vladimir. "Profiling CPU usage from within a Java application. *JavaWorld*, November 8, 2002.

[3] Wilson, Matthew. "C# Performance: Comparison with C++, C, D, and Java, Part 1." Windows Developer Network, Fall 2003,

[4] JBoss, Inc. "JBoss Administration and Development Guide, JBoss 3.2.6." http://docs.jboss.org/jbossas/admindevel326/html/ , 2004.

[5] Gunther, Neil. *The Practical Performance Analyst*, iUniverse Inc., 2000.

[6] Robinson, S. et. al. *Professional C#*. Wrox Press, 2001. ISBN 1861004990.

[7] Smith, C.U. and Williams, L.G. *Performance Solutions: A Practical Guide to Creating Responsive, Scalable Software*. Addison Wesley, Boston, 2002. ISBN 0-201-72229-1.

[8] Bondi, A.B. "Characteristics of scalability and their impact on performance." *Proc. WOSP 2000*, 195-200, Ottawa, September  2000.

[9] Kruchten, Philippe. *The Rational Unified Process: An Introduction, Third Edition*. Addison-Wesley, 2003. ISBN 0-321-19770-4.

# Explicit Platform Models for MDA

Dennis Wagelaar* and Viviane Jonckers

Vrije Universiteit Brussel, Pleinlaan 2, 1050 Brussels, Belgium
dennis.wagelaar@vub.ac.be, vejoncke@info.vub.ac.be

**Abstract.** The main drive for Model-Driven Architecture is that many software applications have to be deployed on a variety of platforms. The way MDA achieves this is by transforming a platform-independent model of the software to a platform-specific model, given a platform model. In current MDA approaches, the model transformations implicitly represent this platform model. Therefore, the number of different target platforms is limited to the number of supported model transformations. We propose a separate platform model, based on description logics, that can can be used to automatically select and configure a number of reusable model transformations for a concrete platform. This platform model can be extended to describe the relevant platform information, including concrete platform instances as well as platform constraints for each model transformation. This separates the model transformation concern from the platform concern and, since the model transformations are no longer limited to targeting one platform, more platforms can be supported with the same set of transformations.

## 1 Introduction

The Model-Driven Architecture (MDA) allows for "separating the specification of the operation of a system from the details of the way that system uses the capabilities of its platform." [1]. This enables the deployment of software applications on a variety of different platforms. The MDA pattern involves modelling the software in a platform-independent model (PIM). This PIM should then be transformed to a platform-specific model (PSM), given a platform model (PM). In current model transformation approaches for MDA [2], the model transformations themselves implicitly represent this platform model. As such, each platform requires one or more corresponding model transformations, which are specifically configured for that platform only. Because the platform concern is not separated from the model transformation concern, the number of supported target platforms is limited to the number of supported model transformations.

In practice, this means that only a relatively small number of general platforms can be targeted, e.g. Java, EJB [3] or C++. Targeting very specific platforms, e.g. Qtopia Palmtop Environment[4] or J2ME Mobile Information Device

---

* The author's work is part of the CoDAMoS project, which is funded by the Institute for the Promotion of Innovation by Science and Technology in Flanders (IWT-Flanders)

L. Briand and C. Williams (Eds.): MoDELS 2005, LNCS 3713, pp. 367–381, 2005.

Profile 1.0 [5], is not feasible because of the maintenance overhead, even though such precise targeting can result in a better optimised PSM in terms of memory footprint, available features, etc. Especially in a world where constrained computing devices become more commonplace every day [6], getting the most out of such a platform is very important.

On the other hand, most model transformations are reusable over multiple platforms and it is only how they are configured that makes them applicable only to one specific platform. For example, one model transformation could target all Java 2 platforms by transforming UML "to-many" association ends to attributes using the Java 2 Collections framework. If this transformation is configured to be applied in combination with a transformation that targets the Java Swing framework, the target platform is already limited to J2SE for the desktop computer [7]. The fact that each configuration of model transformations is also maintained by hand, makes that the problem of limited platform support remains.

We propose a separate platform model, which can be used to automatically select and configure a number of reusable model transformations for a concrete platform. This platform model is expressed in the Web Ontology Language (OWL) [8], which is an extensible language for describing ontologies. Furthermore, we use the OWL-DL variant, which corresponds to description logics [9], such that computational completeness can be guaranteed. This platform model forms a basis for describing platforms in general and can be extended to include the specific platform information that is relevant for a particular application domain. The model transformations can be augmented with a platform constraint that refers to the platform model. This way, the model transformations are no longer limited to one platform, but can instead be used for a well-defined class of platforms. An automatic reasoner, such as RACER [10] or Pellet [11], can be used to verify whether a concrete platform satisfies the platform constraints of a model transformation.

Section 2 explains in detail how platforms can be modelled. The definition of platform dependency constraints is discussed in section 3 and is illustrated by an example PIM and example model transformations. Section 4 explains how relevant model transformations are selected, based on their platform constraints and the concrete platform description. Section 5 discusses related work and section 6 concludes this paper.

## 2   Modelling Platforms

In order to reason about platforms and platform constraints, an ontology of platforms is used. Ontologies can serve as a common vocabulary for a domain [12]. The relationships between the ontology elements can be used to reason about elements based on that ontology, even if those elements aren't related directly. A platform ontology allows one to base expressions about a platform on the vocabulary expressed by the ontology. By using a shared model of platforms, we can reason about the relationship between a platform description and a platform constraint, even if the two do not have a direct relationship. An example platform constraint is that the Java 2 Collections framework needs to be present. An example of a platform description is a Sharp Zaurus hand-held computer. Since both the platform constraint and the platform description refer to the platform ontology to explain what the Java 2 Collections framework and the Zaurus hand-held computer are, one can derive whether the Zaurus hand-held computer platform satisfies the Java 2 Collections framework constraint.

## 2.1   A Platform Vocabulary

Before modelling any specific platforms or platform properties, a basic structure needs to be defined, into which platform extensions can be fitted. We will use a predefined ontology for describing computing context [13], which includes the platform. This ontology is in turn inspired by the User Agent Profile specification (UAProf) [14] and Composite Capability/Preference Profiles (CC/PP) [15], both of which are standards intended to describe target platforms. The ontology is expressed in OWL, an extensible standard for describing ontologies. OWL has a variant, called OWL-DL, that corresponds to description logics, allowing for automated reasoning about the ontology. The ontology used complies to this OWL-DL variant. The part of the ontology that models platforms is shown in Fig. 1.

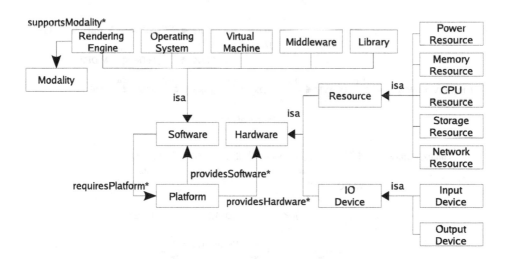

**Fig. 1.** Part of the context ontology for describing platforms

The platform concept in this ontology can provide software and hardware. A '*' next to the relationship names denotes a one-to-many relationship. Software and hardware are broken down into different sub-concepts. This is denoted by the special "isa" subsumption relationship, e.g. the set of operating systems subsumes the set of software in general. The software can impose requirements on the platform, e.g. the need for a network resource, a particular virtual machine or a user interface rendering engine that supports voice communication. This is denoted by the "requiresPlatform" relationship, which points to a description of the required platform.

The ontology can be extended for particular domains of platforms, such as Java virtual machines. Fig. 2 shows part of such an ontology. Above the line is a taxonomy of the Java virtual machines themselves. The "VirtualMachine" concept starts with "context:" to indicate it refers to the "VirtualMachine" concept from the main context ontology. The "JavaVM" can be subdivided in many different configurations. The "JDK" was the first Java configuration. "J2SE" refers to the virtual machines based on JDK 1.2 or up. "PersonalJava" is an early version of Java for mobile devices, which was later re-done as "J2ME". "J2ME" offers two main configurations, "CDC" and "CLDC", which are in turn refined by several sub-profiles. Each of these virtual machine classes implies a specific set of libraries and rendering engines. This is shown below the line: the "JDK" includes a simple "AWT" rendering engine, whereas "JDK1.1" already supports event-driven AWT, as does "CDC". "J2SE" includes "Swing" in addition and "MIDP" has its own rendering engine, named "LCDUI". Similarly, different versions of the java.util library are included in the "CLDC", "JDK", "CDC" and "J2SE" virtual machines.

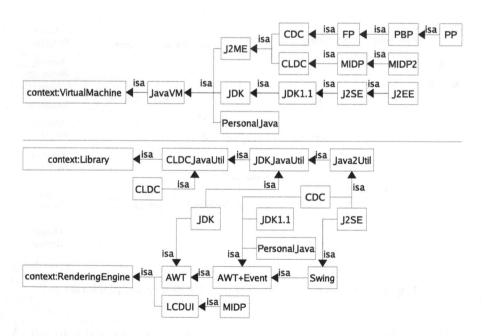

**Fig. 2.** Part of an ontology describing Java virtual machines

## 2.2   Modelling Concrete Platforms

Given the base context ontology and the extensions for the relevant domains, we can model concrete platforms as ontology instances. The Sharp Zaurus PDA, for example, has a J2ME PP virtual machine. The ontology extension that describes this is shown in Fig. 3.

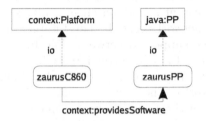

**Fig. 3.** Partial platform description for the Sharp Zaurus PDA

The concepts "Platform" and "PP" are taken from the context and Java ontologies. The instances, "zaurusC860" and "zaurusPP", are depicted as rounded rectangles and are instances of the "Platform" and "PP" classes. This is depicted by the "io" relationships. Finally, the "zaurusC860" platform has a "providesSoftware" relationship with the "zaurusPP" Java Personal Profile virtual machine.

## 3   Modelling Platform Dependencies

The platform dependencies for a particular model transformation can be modelled by defining new, *completely specified* concepts. Such concepts have *necessary-and-sufficient* constraints in addition to any *necessary* constraints. A *necessary* constraint is depicted by the "isa" relationship: whereas it is *necessary* that each "JDK" instance is also an instance of "JavaVM", being a "JavaVM" instance is not *sufficient* for also being a "JDK" instance (see Fig. 2). We will use the notation for describing conditions as used in the Protégé ontology modelling tool [16]. A constraint that requires a platform with an "AWT" rendering engine can be defined as a concept "JavaAWTPlatform", which is a sub-concept of "Platform" (*necessary*) and provides an "AWT" rendering engine (*necessary-and-sufficient*):

$$JavaAWTPlatform \sqsubseteq context : Platform$$
$$\equiv \exists \, context : providesSoftware \, java : AWT$$

Whenever a "Platform" instance fulfils the condition of providing an "AWT" rendering engine, it can be classified as an instance of "JavaAWTPlatform". This classification can be performed by automatic reasoners. This way, concrete platform instances can be matched against a completely defined constraint concept.

If the platform instance classifies as an instance of the constraint concept, then the constraint holds for that instance. For example, the "zaurusC860" platform from Fig. 3 classifies as an instance of "JavaAWTPlatform", since "zaurusPP" is an instance of "PP", which is a sub-concept of "AWT".

## 3.1   Example PIM

Fig. 4 shows the UML class diagram of part of the PIM for a simple instant messaging client. The instant messenger client is able send and receive messages over different kinds of networks (e.g. Jabber/Internet or SMS)[1]. It also keeps a list of contacts for each supported network. The InstantMessagingClient both uses and implements the ErrorReporter interface: it reports raised exceptions either on the command line or on a Network that implements ErrorReporter (e.g. a Loopback network). The design is split up in a model, edit, view and networking part, each in their own package. Concrete view and network types are not shown in the class diagram and will not be considered for the purpose of our example.

The example PIM contains several elements that are not available in the programming language used for the target platform. These elements are the "Applet", "Observer", "Observable", "subscribe" and "Singleton" stereotypes, the "String", "Integer", "Exception" and "OclAny" data types, association relationships and specifications of operations (e.g. in OCL, a dynamic diagram or an Action Language). Model transformations can be defined to translate each of these elements to one or more elements that are available in the target programming environment. Examples of some of these model transformations will be discussed below. The ATL transformation language [17], which has a simple, rule-based syntax, will be used to express these examples.

## 3.2   Example Model Transformations

A common way for transforming UML 1.5 [18] associations to corresponding attributes in Java is to use the Java 2 Collections framework to implement a one-to-many association. The following transformation rules use the `java.util.List` interface and the implementing `java.util.ArrayList` class to achieve a one-to-many association[2]:

```
rule AssocToSingleAttr {
  from s : INMODEL!AssociationEnd (
    s.isNavigable and
    s.multiplicity.range->select(r|r.upper<>1)->isEmpty())
  to t : OUTMODEL!Attribute mapsTo s (
    name <- s.name,
    owner <- s.association.connection->select(x|x<>s)->first().participant,
```

---

[1] The Network class in the model actually represents a network connection; this is why InstantMessagingClient "owns" Network

[2] Note that, in ATL, additional headers are needed and rules are necessary for each model element that needs to be copied/transformed. Only the rules that perform actual transformation are shown here for brevity.

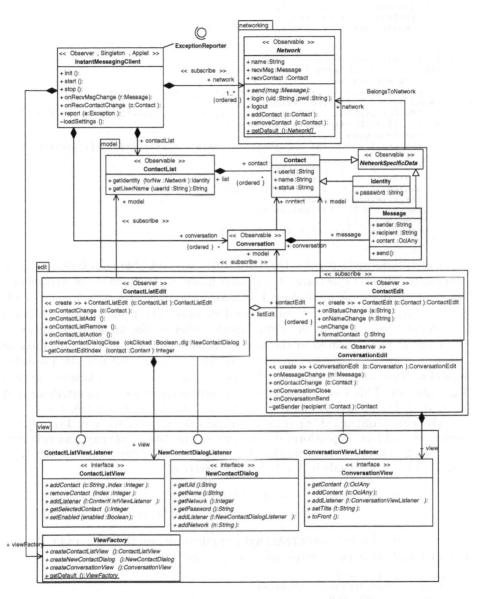

**Fig. 4.** Example PIM class diagram for a simple instant messaging client

```
      type <- s.participant ,
      visibility <- s.visibility ,
      ownerScope <- s.targetScope ,
      changeability <- s.changeability)
}

rule AssocToArrayList {
  from s : INMODEL!AssociationEnd(
    s.isNavigable and
    not s.multiplicity.range->select(r|r.upper<>1)->isEmpty())
  using { list : INMODEL!Interface =
    INMODEL!Interface.allInstances()->select(c|c.name='List')->first(); }
  to t : OUTMODEL!Attribute mapsTo s (
    name <- s.name,
    owner <- s.association.connection->select(x|x<>s)->first().participant ,
    type <- list,
    visibility <- s.visibility,
    ownerScope <- s.targetScope,
    changeability <- s.changeability,
    initialValue <- value),
  value : OUTMODEL!Expression (
    language <- 'java',
    body <- 'new java.util.ArrayList();')
}
```

The transformation rules translate only the navigable association ends to attributes. The first rule translates all association ends with an upper multiplicity range of "1" to simple attributes. The second rule translates all association ends with an upper range other than "1" to Java Lists. The **from** keyword indicates the element to read from the source model, whereas the **to** keyword indicates the element to be created in the target model. The INMODEL and OUTMODEL in the transformation refer to the meta-models used, which is the UML 1.5 meta-model in both cases. The second rule has a **using** clause, which locates the Java List interface. This List interface is then used as the type of the attribute that is created. The ArrayList class is used for initial value of this attribute.

The AssocToSingleAttr transformation rule does not use any Java-related elements, and has no platform dependencies. The AssocToArrayList rule uses the Java 2 Collections framework, which is part of the "Java2Util" library from Fig. 2. This corresponds to the following constraint:

$$Java2UtilPlatform \sqsubseteq context : Platform$$

$$\equiv \exists\, context : providesSoftware\ java : Java2Util$$

An alternative for the AssocToArrayList rule could use the java.util.Vector class to implement the one-to-many association:

```
rule AssocToVector {
  from s : INMODEL!AssociationEnd(
    s.isNavigable and
    not s.multiplicity.range->select(r|r.upper<>1)->isEmpty())
  using { vector : INMODEL!Class =
    INMODEL!Class.allInstances()->select(c|c.name='Vector')->first(); }
  to t : OUTMODEL!Attribute mapsTo s (
    name <- s.name,
    owner <- s.association.connection->select(x|x<>s)->first().participant ,
    type <- vector,
    visibility <- s.visibility,
    ownerScope <- s.targetScope,
    changeability <- s.changeability,
    initialValue <- value),
```

```
    value : OUTMODEL!Expression (
    language <- 'java',
    body <- 'new java.util.Vector();')
}
```

Because the Java Vector class is already available in the "CLDCJavaUtil" library from Fig. 2, the platform constraint can be relaxed to only requiring a "CLDCJavaUtil" library:

$$JavaUtilPlatform \sqsubseteq context : Platform$$
$$\equiv \exists\, context : providesSoftware\ java : CLDCJavaUtil$$

# 4   Selecting Model Transformations

In order to select which model transformations need to be applied, the transformations are grouped into sets of alternatives that represent the same functionality. This grouping can be (partially) automated, based on a heuristic that checks the input specification of the transformation rules. If certain transformation rules have the same input specification, then they are considered alternatives. The transformation rules `AssocToArrayList` and `AssocToVector`, given in subsection 3.2, have the same input specification (represented by the `from` part). Hence, they are considered to be alternatives belonging to one group. The groups that are formed in this way can be adapted manually afterwards. The grouping information is reusable over multiple PIMs and PMs: it only has to be re-computed if the set of transformation rules changes. An example grouping for the model transformations needed for our example PIM is shown in Table 1.

| AssocToArrayList \| AssocToVector |
|:---:|
| Observer \| JavaObserver |
| Accessors \| Java2Accessors |
| Applet \| MIDlet |
| Singleton |
| DataTypes \| Java2DataTypes |

**Table 1.** Example model transformations grouping

The `AssocToArrayList` and `AssocToVector` transformations have already been discussed and form one group.The `Observer` and `JavaObserver` transformations both implement the "Observer", "Observable" and "subscribe" stereotypes. The first transformation requires no Java API, while the second uses the Java 1.0 `java.util.Observer` interface and the `java.util.Observable` class. The `Accessors` transformation creates accessor operations (getters and setters) for each public attribute. `Java2Accessors` does the same, but uses the Java 2 Collections data types. The `Applet` transformation transforms all classes with the "Applet" stereotype into Java applets, whereas the `MIDlet` transformation transforms the same classes into J2ME MIDlets. The `Singleton` transformation adds the singleton infrastructure to each class with the "Singleton" stereotype. Finally, the `DataTypes` and the `Java2DataTypes` transformations translate the OCL data types into Java data types and Java 2 Collections data types respectively.

Since some model transformations may depend on the result of other model transformations, they need to be ordered. The transformation dependencies can also be checked (semi-)automatically by a heuristic that checks if the input specification of a transformation may overlap with the output specification of another (represented by the **to** part). The output specification of the `Java2Accessors` transformation states that it creates new operations. If another model transformation, `JavaObserver`, adapts all setter accessor operations for each Observable, then its input specification could match elements generated by `Java2Accessors`. Hence, `Java2Accessors` has to be placed before `JavaObserver`. If no decision can be made on whether to put one transformation before another, the order is left unchanged. This way, the developer can already pre-sort the groups of transformations manually. The sorting information is, again, reusable over multiple PIMs and PMs: it only has to be re-computed if the set of transformation rules changes. The sorted list of transformation groups is shown in Table 2.

| AssocToArrayList \| AssocToVector |
|---|
| Accessors \| Java2Accessors |
| Observer \| JavaObserver |
| Applet \| MIDlet |
| Singleton |
| DataTypes \| Java2DataTypes |

**Table 2.** Example model transformations grouped and sorted

From each group, at most one model transformation is selected. This selection is based on platform relevance. The platform relevance is determined by subsumption of constraint concepts. If a constraint concept defines a subset of another constraint concept, then that constraint is considered more platform-specific[3]. Consider the following platform constraint:

$$CLDCUtilPlatform \sqsubseteq context : Platform$$
$$\equiv \exists \, context : providesSoftware \; java : CLDCJavaUtil$$

---

[3] This criterion is based on the "Do the Most Specific" conflict resolution strategy in Forward Chaining reasoners such as OPS5 [19] and successors.

Compared to the "Java2UtilPlatform" constraint, this constraint requires the "CLDCJavaUtil" library instead of the "Java2Util" library. Since "Java2Util" subsumes "CLDCJavaUtil" (see Fig. 2), "Java2UtilPlatform" also subsumes "CLDCUtilPlatform". Reasoner engines, such as RACER, can automatically determine a taxonomy of constraints using such inference rules. Note that this taxonomy can be determined without knowledge of any concrete platform (i.e. the platform instances). As such, this taxonomy can be pre-computed and only needs re-computing if the set of constraints changes.

One can imagine that there are cases in which one cannot determine whether a constraint concept subsumes another constraint concept. Consider the following constraint:

$$AWTUtilPlatform \sqsubseteq context : Platform$$
$$\equiv \exists\ context : providesSoftware\ java : CLDCJavaUtil \land$$
$$\exists\ context : providesSoftware\ java : AWT$$

When comparing this constraint to "Java2UtilPlatform", no conclusion can be made on which is more specific. While "CLDCJavaUtil" is subsumed by "Java2Util", nothing can be said about "AWT", since no comparable rule occurs within the "Java2UtilPlatform" constraint. It is very unlikely that functionally equivalent model transformations (i.e. alternatives from one group) will have orthogonal (parts of) constraints (e.g. one constraint requires "AWT" whereas another requires nothing of the sort). However, to cope with this case, one can manually order a group of model transformations, such that the first most-specific is chosen.

When selecting the model transformations for a specific platform, (1) the local constraint taxonomy is taken for each group of alternative transformations and (2) pruned such that all constraints that do not hold are removed. Note that, if no transformations are left for a particular group after this step, no PSM can be generated for the given platform. Then, (3) the first model transformation for which the constraint forms a leaf in the taxonomy tree is chosen. All of the steps 1-3 are of linear complexity[4], so the selection mechanism in its entirety also performs in linear time.

The list of chosen transformations for the example platform from Fig. 3 is shown in Table 3.

The `AssocToArrayList` transformation was chosen over the `AssocToVector` transformation, because it requires a "Java2Util" library instead of a "CLDC-JavaUtil" library. For the same reason, the `Java2Accessors` transformation is chosen over `Accessors`. The `JavaObserver` transformation is chosen over the `Observer` transformation, because it requires a "JDKUtil" library instead of just any "JavaVM". `Applet` is chosen over `MIDlet` because the constraint of the latter did not hold (a MIDlet requires J2ME MIDP). Finally, `Java2DataTypes` is chosen over `DataTypes`, because it again requires a "Java2Util" library instead of a "CLDCJavaUtil" library.

---

[4] the set of transformations and the set of constraints are constant at this time

**Table 3.** Example selection of model transformations

## 5   Related Work

Model transformations are subject to similar configuration management issues as regular software components [20]. Transformation dependencies can be made explicit through their input and output specifications. Limited versioning support is provided by the platform constraints: one can discriminate on platform-specificness of different versions of a transformation.

In Generative Programming [21] and Step-Wise Refinement [22], *features* and *feature models* are used to model a family of software systems instead of a single system. Features can be optional or mandatory for a software system, depending on the presence of other features. In our framework, features are implicitly generated by model transformations, which are chosen based on platform constraints. Feature models can be used to verify if the chosen transformations represent a valid set of features.

The lack of explicit platform models is also discussed in [23]. They introduce *abstract platforms*, which describe a set of elements to model a PIM against. This set of elements includes design artifacts that are available in a target platform (classes, interfaces) and design constructs that can be mapped to that platform (stereotypes, profiles), e.g. with model transformations. The goal of abstract platforms is to ease platform-independent modelling, whereas our platform models are meant to decouple model transformations from concrete platforms.

In [24], platform selection rules are discussed, which allow for pre-selecting a number of target platforms. In that way, less platforms need to be supported. In our case, platform selection rules can be used to narrow down the amount of platform domain aspects (e.g. Java virtual machines) that need to be modelled for a particular application domain (e.g. instant messaging). This does not conflict with the envisioned scenario [6] that targets an open-ended infrastructure of unanticipated devices, since this is supported by in-depth modelling of platform domain aspects, not the amount of aspects that are modelled.

In [25], an infrastructure for combining UML/MOF models and ontologies is introduced. Such an infrastructure can be useful for a better integration of platform constraints into model transformation languages that are based on MOF.

# 6   Conclusion and Future Work

This paper has introduced a platform modelling framework that can describe platform constraints as well as instances of concrete platforms. By separating the platform concern from the model transformation configuration and moving it to an explicit platform model, the model transformations can be reused over several platforms. Our framework can automatically select a number of applicable model transformations for a specific platform. This is done by matching platform constraints for each model transformation against a concrete platform description. Both of these are based on a common ontology, described in OWL-DL, such that an automatic reasoner can determine whether the platform matches the constraint. In this way, more than one concrete platform can be supported with the same set of model transformations.

Note that the reusability of the individual model transformations remains the same. Only the configurations of model transformations, which are far less reusable than an individual transformation, are now automatically derived by means of an explicit platform model. As such, the separation of the platform concern from the model transformation concern is not complete, since each model transformation must include the local platform information that it is supposed to add to the PSM.

The chosen ontology for modelling platforms may not be general enough for all cases and it may also not be specific enough in some cases. Experience will have to show how far we can go with the current ontology. However, we expect that our mechanism can also be applied to different ontologies, since it only requires that the constraints are expressed in description logic.

For the selection mechanism, all the potentially expensive calculations are done in advance (i.e. transformation grouping and sorting and calculating the subsumption taxonomy of constraints). Only if the set of transformations or the set of constraints on those transformations changes, these calculations need to be redone. When transforming a PIM to a PSM, using a concrete platform model, three steps are performed to select which model transformations need to be applied. Each of these steps are of linear complexity, such that the mechanism in its entirety also performs in linear time. As such, the proposed mechanism should scale sufficiently.

Using the current ordered lists of model transformation groups, only a limited set of model transformation dependencies can be expressed. The example used in this paper shows a group containing the `AssocToArrayList` and `AssocToVector` transformations and another group containing `Accessors` and `Java2Accessors`. While we can express that the second group depends on the first, we cannot express that, for the sake of type consistency, `AssocToArrayList` may only be applied in combination with `Java2Accessors`. Recent work on feature modelling [26, 27] and product families [28] provides promising approaches for modelling such complex dependencies and do automatic reasoning on them. We will also investigate if we can map these feature modelling approaches to description logic in order to integrate feature modelling with our platform modelling approach.

## Acknowledgement

The author would like to thank Ragnhild Van Der Straeten, Bruno De Fraine and Wim Vanderperren for reviewing a draft of this paper. Furthermore, the author would like to thank the CoDAMoS project user committee for discussing their ideas for the Instant Messaging scenario, which were useful for the example PIM in this paper.

## References

[1] Miller, J., Mukerji, J.: MDA Guide. Object Management Group, Inc. (2003) Version 1.0.1 (omg/03-06-01).
[2] Czarnecki, K., Helsen, S.: Classification of Model Transformation Approaches. In: OOPSLA 2003 Workshop on Generative Techniques in the context of Model Driven Architecture. (2003)
[3] DeMichiel, L., Ümit Yalçinalp, L., Krishnan, S.: Enterprise JavaBeans™Specification. Sun Microsystems, Inc. (2001) Version 2.0.
[4] Trolltech: Qtopia application platform for embedded Linux. (2005) [Online] http://www.trolltech.com/products/qtopia/.
[5] Sun Microsystems, Inc.: Java 2 Micro Edition website. (2005) [Online] http://java.sun.com/j2me/.
[6] Ducatel, K., Bogdanowicz, M., Scapolo, F., Leijten, J., Burgelman, J.C.: Scenarios for Ambient Intelligence in 2010. IST Advisory Group (ISTAG). (2001) [Online] ftp://ftp.cordis.lu/pub/ist/docs/istagscenarios2010.pdf.
[7] Sun Microsystems, Inc.: Java 2 Standard Edition website. (2005) [Online] http://java.sun.com/j2se/.
[8] Smith, M.K., Welty, C., McGuinness, D.L.: OWL Web Ontology Language Guide. World Wide Web Consortium. (2004) W3C Recommendation 10 February 2004.
[9] Baader, F., Calvanese, D., McGuinness, D.L., Nardi, D., Patel-Schneider, P.F.: The Description Logic Handbook: Theory, Implementation and Applications. Cambridge University Press, Cambridge, UK (2003)
[10] Möller, R., Haarslev, V.: Description Logics for the Semantic Web: Racer as a Basis for Building Agent Systems. Künstliche Intelligenz (2003) 10–15
[11] Parsia, B., Sirin, E., Grove, M., Alford, R.: Pellet website. Mindswap. (2005) [Online] http://www.mindswap.org/2003/pellet/.
[12] Gruber, T.R.: A Translation Approach to Portable Ontology Specifications. Knowledge Acquisition 5 (1993) 199–220
[13] Preuveneers, D., den Bergh, J.V., Wagelaar, D., Georges, A., Rigole, P., Clerckx, T., Berbers, Y., Coninx, K., Jonckers, V., Bosschere, K.D.: Towards an extensible context ontology for Ambient Intelligence. In: Proceedings of the Second European Symposium on Ambient Intelligence, Eindhoven, The Netherlands, Springer-Verlag (2004) 148–159
[14] Open Mobile Alliance: User Agent Profile 2.0 Specification. (2003) Version 20-May-2003.
[15] Klyne, G., Reynolds, F., Woodrow, C., Ohto, H., Hjelm, J., Butler, M.H., Tran, L.: Composite Capability/Preference Profiles (CC/PP): Structure and Vocabularies 1.0. World Wide Web Consortium. (2004)
[16] Stanford Medical Informatics, Stanford University School of Medicine Stanford, CA, USA: Protégé Project website. (2005) [Online] http://protege.stanford.edu/.

[17] Bézivin, J., Dupé, G., Jouault, F., Pitette, G., Rougui, J.E.: First experiments with the ATL model transformation language: Transforming XSLT into XQuery. In: OOPSLA 2003 Workshop on Generative Techniques in the context of Model Driven Architecture. (2003)

[18] Object Management Group, Inc.: Unified Modeling Language Specification. (2003) Version 1.5 (formal/03-03-01).

[19] Brownston, L., Farrell, R., Kant, E., Martin, N.: Programming expert systems in OPS5: an introduction to rule-based programming. Addison Wesley, Reading, Massachusetts, USA (1985)

[20] Larsson, M.: Applying Configuration Management Techniques to Component-Based Systems. Licentiate thesis, Department of Information Technology, Uppsala University, Uppsala, Sweden (2000) Also published as report MRTC 00/24 at Mälardalens högskola.

[21] Czarnecki, K., Eisenecker, U.: Generative Programming: Methods, Tools, and Applications. 1st edn. Addison Wesley, Reading, Massachusetts, USA (2000)

[22] Batory, D., Sarvela, J.N., Rauschmayer, A.: Scaling Step-Wise Refinement. In: Proceedings of the 25th International Conference on Software Engineering (ICSE 2003), Portland, Oregon, USA, IEEE Computer Society (2003) 187–197

[23] Almeida, J.P., Dijkman, R., van Sinderen, M., Pires, L.F.: On the Notion of Abstract Platform in MDA Development. In: The 8th International IEEE Enterprise Distributed Object Computing Conference, Monterey, California, USA, IEEE Computer Society (2004) 253–263

[24] Tekinerdoğan, B., Bilir, S., Abatlevi, C.: Integrating Platform Selection Rules in the Model-Driven Architecture Approach. In Aßmann, U., ed.: Proceedings of Model Driven Architecture: Foundations and Applications (MDAFA 2004), Linköping, Sweden, Research Center for Integrational Software Engineering, Linköping University (2004) 184–200

[25] Bézivin, J., Devedžić, V., Djurić, D., Favreau, J., Gašević, D., Jouault, F.: An M3-Neutral infrastructure for bridging model engineering and ontology engineering. In: First International Conference on Interoperability of Enterprise Software and Applications (INTEROP-ESA'05), Geneva, Switzerland, Springer-Verlag (2005)

[26] Benavides, D., Trinidad, P., Ruiz-Cortés, A.: Automated Reasoning on Feature Models. In: Proceedings of the 17th Conference on Advanced Information System Engineering (CAiSE'05), Porto, Portugal (2004)

[27] Klint, P., van der Storm, T.: Reflections on Feature Oriented Software Engineering. In: OOPSLA Workshop on Managing Variabilities Consistently in Design and Code (MVCDC 2004), Vancouver, Canada (2004)

[28] Liu, J., Batory, D.: Automatic Remodularization and Optimized Synthesis of Product-Families. In: Proceedings of the Third International Conference on Generative Programming and Component Engineering (GPCE 2004), Vancouver, Canada, Springer-Verlag (2004) 379–395

# Integrated Model-Based Software Development, Data Access, and Data Migration

Behzad Bordbar[1], Dirk Draheim[2],
Matthias Horn[3], Ina Schulz[3], and Gerald Weber[4]

[1] School of Computer Science, University of Birmingham
Edgbaston, Birmingham B15 2TT, UK
B.Bordbar@cs.bham.ac.uk
[2] Institute of Computer Science, Freie Universität Berlin
Takustr. 9, 14195 Berlin, Germany
draheim@acm.org
[3] IMIS Projekt, Condat AG
Alt-Moabit 91d, 10559 Berlin, Germany
{horn,schulz}@condat.de
[4] Department of Computer Science, The University of Auckland
38 Princes Street, Auckland 1020, NZ
g.weber@cs.auckland.ac.nz

**Abstract.** In this paper we describe a framework for robust system maintenance that addresses specific challenges of data-centric applications. We show that for data-centric applications, classical simultaneous roundtrip engineering approaches are not sufficient. Instead we propose an architecture that is an integrated model-based approach for software development, database access and data migration. We explain the canonical development process to exploit its features. We explain how the approach fits into the model-driven architecture vision. We report on experiences with the approach in the IMIS environmental mass database project.

## 1 Introduction

It is well-known that maintenance cost regularly is the largest share of software expenditure [4]. Software development does not end after deployment of the initial system version at the customer site. On the contrary, changing functional and non-functional requirements enforce changes in the system and its structure. Software development process models tended to underemphasize the importance of maintenance [28], and are only recently targeting easy maintenance. More seriously and often overlooked, data migration is an issue in software maintenance.

In a model-based approach, simultaneous roundtrip engineering can add value to software development and assist in system maintenance. For data-centric applications however, classical simultaneous roundtrip engineering approaches are not sufficient: during a system's lifetime data have been gathered that must be transported from the old system version to the new system version. This means that you have to deal with database reorganization [24].

L. Briand and C. Williams (Eds.): MoDELS 2005, LNCS 3713, pp. 382–396, 2005.

In practice [26], vendors have started to integrate database mapping facilities into CASE tools and integrated development environments that are capable of model-based development, but this does not solve the data migration problem. As a matter of fact, data migration is still mostly done by hand-coded SQL scripts. This is not a legacy problem of relational databases. Please note that the advanced features of object-relational database management systems [27] for altering database schemas do not help with data migration problems. In practice, relational database technology is here to stay [5]. Therefore a well-defined object-relational mapping mechanism is needed. Hand-coding SQL scripts for data migration is tedious and error-prone in a model-based scenario with object-relational mapping: the abstraction level achieved by model-orientation is broken and the developer has to understand all details of the object-relational mapping.

In this paper we describe a comprehensive framework that provides a solution for the problem posed. We present an integrated model-based approach to (i) object-oriented software development and simultaneous roundtrip engineering, (ii) transparent database access and (iii) data migration. It employs object-relational mapping and novel features like automatic model change detection, and data migration API generation. The paper describes the design rationales of the framework.

The framework incorporates technology that tightly integrates from scratch model evolution, programming language type evolution, database schema evolution and customer data migration [7, 9].

The described framework basically consists of a generator for data migration APIs. For each combination of a current model and an intended new model a specialized data migration API is generated. On the one hand the generated data migration API is intended to be as complete as possible with respect to automatically inferring a schema mapping from the two models under consideration, on the other hand it provides as many hooks as needed to fully customize the data migration. With this approach guidance for the implementation of the data migration is provided. Furthermore, the customizations can be done on the level of transparent database access.

Our framework realizes a persistent object-oriented programming environment. Although relational database technology is employed in the back end, our framework enables us to discuss problems of schema evolution and migration of customer data solely on the level of the object-oriented system model: changes in the object model have a defined footprint in the database schema, and existing data are transformed into the new system accordingly.

In Sect.2 we discuss an introductory example of model evolution with respect to persistent data. We describe how we achieved our goals in Sect. 3. In this paper we take for granted the advantages of transparent database access and do not delve into a discussion under which circumstances transparent database access may infringe the best practice of data independency as provided by mature modern database technology, with, for example, respect to performance tuning. Actually, our approach of lifting data migration to the transparent database access level has proven in the IMIS project to stabilize the development and speed up the development cycles. We report on the IMIS project and its experiences with our approach in Sect. 4. The paper finishes with a discussion of related work and a short conclusion in Sects. 5 and 6.

## 2   The Model Evolution Problem

Figure 1 shows the model evolution of a Company class with an address attribute and some further attributes. The modified model has a new Address class with a new street attribute, city attribute and zip attribute. The address attribute is removed from the Company class. Furthermore there exists an association between the Company class and the Address class. This way the schema migration is uniquely defined. However the data migration is more complicated and depends on the semantics of the changes. In the current example new objects of Address type have to be created and linked to the correct Company objects, whereas their attributes have to be computed properly from the old address attributes.

In a working framework solution the developer must have the capability to define the data migration based on his or her semantic knowledge about the information base. However, at the same time the developer should be supported with respect to canonically given parts of data migration, which can be generated. In our simple example the framework can assume that the remaining attributes of the Company class, i.e. the non-address attributes, are intended to have the same semantics in the new model as in the old model. Based on this assumption the data migration is conceptually just a copying for these attributes. Of course an elaborated approach has to provide means to override the default behavior of such simple data migration parts, too.

## 3   The Proposed Integrated Approach

### 3.1   The Solution Framework

In our approach applications are developed by simultaneous roundtrip engineering of Java programs and UML diagrams. The approach provides transparent database access to a relational database and support for data migration. Figure 2 shows the components of the approach and their interplay. The solution consists of the following new components, which we have implemented in the IMIS project – see Sect. 4.1 – and which encompass a total of 90 kLOC of documented Java code:

- Extensions to the case tool Together:
  - *Modules for model annotations.* The new model annotations allow for specifying the persistent classes of the model and the typical customizations needed for object-relational mapping [23].

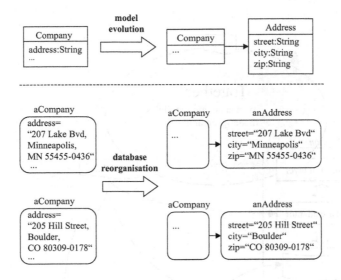

**Fig. 1.** Non-trivial data migration.

- *Model generator.* The so-called model generator creates a *model representation* of the annotated UML model that is appropriate as input for the *generic database adaptor* and *upgrader generator*, which are explained below. In our implementation model representations consist of serialized Java objects. These representations are stored in files named model.dat in Fig. 2.

- *Generic database adaptor.* For each concrete model this generic component [9] realizes the transparent database access layer for the application. It exploits the information in the model representation by inspection and generates the necessary SQL queries.

- *Arbitrary SQL query API.* Note that our approach offers full-fledged support of typical mapping tools, i.e., the developer is able to formulate arbitrary SQL queries to the database that go beyond the canonically generated access methods. Our approach offers an API for this purpose.

- *Upgrader generator.* The upgrader generator takes an old model representation, a new model representation, and an auxiliary property file. It generates an upgrader program API. Next we explain, how database reorganization is supported with the upgrader generator mechanism.

If database reorganization becomes necessary, three steps are undertaken in our approach: (i) database cloning, (ii) schema evolution, and (iii) data migration. Please consider the middle tier of Fig. 2:

(i) *Database cloning.* First a complete copy of the old database is done. This clone has to be adapted by schema evolution and data migration to fit the new model.

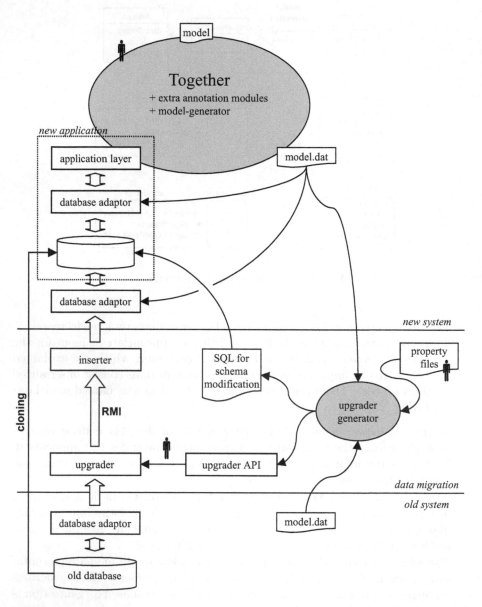

**Fig. 2.** The proposed integrated approach. Developer activity is denoted by a little icon. Developers work with a simultaneous round trip engineering tool. If database reorganization becomes necessary they are supported by the upgrader generator that compares the new model and the old model, detects changes and generates a data migration program with customizable hooks – the upgrader API. The developer can influence the upgrader generator with property files.

(ii) *Schema evolution.* Then the schema of the clone is changed so that it correctly implements the new model with respect to object-relational mapping. For this purpose the upgrader generator compares the new model with the old model and detects changes. This means that the upgrader generator constructs a schema morphism along the lines of a defined set of rules. For example classes with same name are identified in both models. Based on that, the upgrader generator can detect, for example, new attributes of a class. Of course, entirely new classes can be detected as well as deleted classes. Sometimes the default mechanism must be customized. This can be done by the developer via property files, where he or she partly defines an own schema morphism that overrides the default morphism. For example, the developer can define the renaming of a class or attribute. From the detected and defined changes the upgrader generator generates SQL code that can modify the database appropriately.

(iii) *Data migration.* Finally, the data of the old database have to be migrated to the new database. Now cloning the database earlier pays off. For all classes that are not affected by the model evolution step data migration is already completed. For each of the other classes the upgrader generator creates an update class. All the generated upgrade classes form the upgrader API mentioned above. For some of the affected classes the upgrader generator cannot generate the correct default data creation – here the property file mechanism comes into play again: the developer can, for example, specify the movement of classes in the class hierarchy, or the movement of an attribute from one class to another. The generated data migration code reads necessary data in the old database via the old database adaptor. It sends data for the new database via RMI to an inserter component that writes the data via the new database adaptor into the new database. The chosen RMI mechanism is a technical detail that prevents name conflicts by employing two different JVMs for the old and the new system. The developer can override all generated default data migration code. In cases, where the upgrader generator cannot guess a solution, data migration code must be implemented by the developer. Consider our example in Sect. 2: the upgrade API does not possess default behavior for the creation of new Address objects – the Address class is entirely new and the splitting of the old address attribute into the new attributes street, city, and zip is not trivial and must be provided by the developer.

Our approach addresses two objectives with respect to database reorganization: (i) development speed and robustness and (ii) technical speed:

(i) *Development speed and robustness.* A major part of canonically given data migration is generated automatically. The developers have to customize only those parts for which semantic knowledge is required. This speeds up the development needed and therefore stabilizes the database reorganization process. Furthermore, the customizations are done on the level of *transparent database access*, i.e., on the application programming level, and the developers don't have to be aware of the details of the underlying object-relational mapping all the time during data migration customization.

(ii) *Technical speed.* The first step in the database reorganization process is schema migration and there are several ways to do it. One way would be the creation of a new and empty schema. This could be done easily by generating DDL statements from the object model. But creating an empty schema implies that a lot of unchanged data have to be moved from the old into the new schema. The more efficient way is to keep the data in the original schema. The schema is to be modified step by step until the structure fits the new model requirements by dropping, adding and modifying tables or columns etc. Only tables that are related to changed model elements are touched. However, modifying the existing data has also its pitfalls. Some object transformation processes may need information of other objects and these objects may be subject to change, too. With a copy it is not necessary to take dependencies into account, because all the information is still accessible in the old schema. The most efficient and easiest way is to duplicate the database – our tests have shown that it is at least twenty times faster as an SQL based transport solution.

In the past, all constraints and indices were deactivated during evolution. This step was necessary in order to avoid that the evolution process is infringed while it is processing the objects class by class. Since most of the tables and therewith most of the constraints and indices are not involved in the evolution process, a more sophisticated treatment of constraints and indices was developed. This way, in the future it will be possible to deactivate only the few constraints that really interfere with the upgrade process.

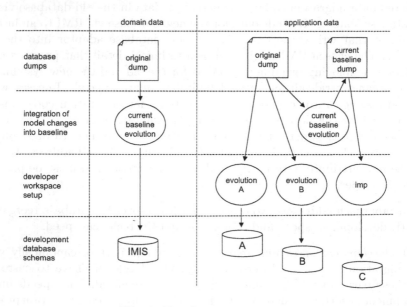

**Fig. 3.** Development process.

## 3.2   The Development Process

At regular intervals, in particular after each installation, the database is dumped from the production system for all used schemas – consider Fig. 3. The dumps are used as a basis for database schema setup during development. During development the same evolution mechanism is used that is used for installing a new software version on the production system. Upgrader code always has to be integrated into the project workspace together with the appropriate model and code changes. This way, the consistency of model, application code and evolution code is enforced. To allow faster setup times, the number of data records is reduced in the dumps that are used during development.

During integration of model changes into the project workspace the commonly used database schema is setup with the new upgrader. During setup of a developer workspace the schema is not affected. In order to prevent that the work of other developers is affected during setup of a new schema, a second database instance is used for the new schema. Developers can decide on there own when to switch to the new schema.

The developer schemas (developers A and B) are set up using the evolution that corresponds to the model changes the developer has done so far. If no model changes have been done by a developer (developer C) a dump of repository data that have already passed through the evolution in the current project workspace is used for developer workspace setup. This way, most of the developers can setup there workspace by importing a database dump. As soon as a developer integrates a model change of the repository data model into the project workspace the current workspace dump is updated using the evolution code just integrated.

At customer site two systems are installed – see Fig. 4. The production system is accompanied by a so called reference system which is used for testing purposes. The evolution process is used in two cases: (i) installation of a new release for testing onto the reference system; and (ii) installation of a new release onto the production system. In addition to the target database, the evolution process always uses a second database as source for the upgrader.

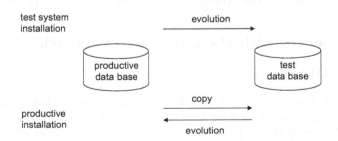

**Fig. 4.** Installation at the customer site

### 3.3  On the Integrated Approach and Model Driven Architecture

IMIS draws on the vision promoted by the MDA [25]. In the MDA, the platform independent model (PIM), which is a high-level abstraction independent of any technology and platform specific model (PSM), which is the transformation of the PIM into a specific platform. In our approach, the PIM is captured as a UML model in the Together CASE tool, which is transferred by the model generator component to a model.dat file, which is just another way of representing the PIM. This file is transformed into code consisting of Java, SQL DDL and eventually SQL DML. Our approach is based on marking PIMs and direct transformation to code – see Sects. 3.5. and 3.7 of the MDA Guide [16]. However, it is noticeable that the transformation in our approach takes a special shape. Simultaneous roundtrip engineering keeps the model and the code in synch by continuous tool support. Furthermore, the transformation explicitly makes use of an old PIM (and for technical speed even of an old implementation), because there are parts in the generated code, i.e., schema manipulating SQL code and customized Java data migration code, that depends on a notion of PIM model difference. As a result, the transformation takes into account the information layer, i.e., existing data, on a conceptual level.

There are different forms of model transformation in the MDA [6, 11]. Round trip engineering points out an important class of transformations, too. There are two main advantages in using this kind of transformations. Firstly, code may include platform specific information added by the developer. In particular, it may include part of the code that cannot be created automatically. In a rigid ad-hoc MDA scenario we either (i) have to discard such information, i.e., re-include them into the code generated from the new model – which is wasteful and error-prone – or (ii) we have to reverse engineer [3] the entire code to create a system which mirrors the old system – which is impractical and can create possible inconsistencies.

In our approach, it is particularly important that the new and the old system share persistent data. The model goes through evolution, but the persistent data are cloned and adapted under the umbrella of a defined model transformation. In a conventional MDA model transformation, there is no defined coupling between the persistent data and the evolution from the old model to the new one.

## 4  Experiences with the Integrated Approach

### 4.1  The IMIS System

Following the nuclear accident in Chernobyl the German federal government established a program targeting radiation protection and precaution in 1986. By the end of 1986 the respective federal law StrVG (Strahlenschutz Vorsorge Gesetz) was adopted. Besides other rules the StrVG contains guidelines for the installation of an information system for monitoring and prediction of radioactivity in the environment. The first version of IMIS was developed between 1989 and 1993 and it has been in use till March 2005. In this paper we describe the entirely new IMIS system, which has been developed by Condat AG in Berlin, Germany. IMIS gathers environmental data, for example, from air, sea, lakes, ground water, plants, soil, food, feed, sewage, waste. IMIS has the following characteristics:

- − 2000 measurement stations;
- − more than 160 deployed clients;
- − 60 client locations;
- − 7 days and 24 hours operation.

From the end user's viewpoint the IMIS system has to be understood as a collection of rather loosely coupled client applications that together provide a broad range of features: data collection (automatic and manual), data export, data import (in particular from the forecast system PARK), data analysis (browsing with different views, domain specific visualization capabilities), document generation (automatic and manual), document retrieval.

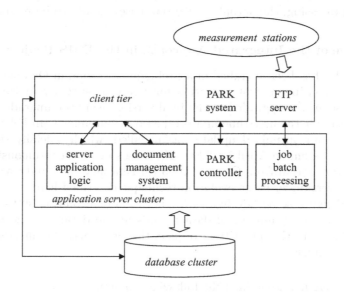

**Fig. 5.** The IMIS Integrated Measurement and Information System.

The system architecture of the IMIS system is depicted in Figure 5. A central Oracle9i database stores the data for evaluation and further processing. Configuration data for the different functions of IMIS are stored in the same database instance. It is running on a Sun V880 high availability cluster server consisting of two nodes. For data storage two Sun T3 storage subsystems are used. Server and communication processes are hosted on four Sun Fire 280 application servers. They are redundant and can replace each other in case of failure. All servers are located at the German federal office for radiation protection BfS (Bundesamt für Strahlenschutz) in Munich.

PCs are used as client systems. The client software follows a straightforward fat client approach. While most of the clients are connected via ISDN to the server LAN, the clients located on site in Munich are connected directly via Ethernet. Most of the new data that are stored into the IMIS database stems from the measurement stations. These provide data by uploading it to an ftp server. From there the data are written by bulk data transfers, in normal operation mode on a daily basis and on a two hour basis in emergency operation mode.

Further data are stored into the database by the external PARK system through the PARK controller. Further data are entered manually by the user. Nearly all the data stored in the IMIS system are long-lived, almost all the data stay unchanged. There is no heavy transaction load on the IMIS system. IMIS is estimated to store data about approximately one million measurements per year - this is equivalent to several million records. This leads to a forecast of approximately 50 GB of measurement data after 10 years – if certain data transforms become necessary due to changing requirements, e.g. for reasons of analytical processing, the actual needed database size has to be reestimated.

## 4.2   Usage of the Integrated Approach in the IMIS Project

The new IMIS has been installed in a preliminary version in October 2003 and was used for continuous test operation until November 2004. At this point in time the system was upgraded to the final version using the upgrade technique described here for the first time in a production environment. In February 2005 an improved and optimized update was installed, which officially substituted the old IMIS system on April 1st 2005. The data stock has continuously evolved during the test period from October 2003 till February 2005 and was migrated to each new version with the evolution technique described here.

Figure 6 shows some key figures for both major evolution steps. For each installation the total number of data records in the database, the number of model changes and the quantity of objects that were actually affected by data migration are given.

Besides these figures we gained the following experiences:

- The actual evolution step, which is copying objects between the old and the new database, takes only three to five minutes on our target hardware. Therefore the mechanisms that has been implemented to reduce the necessity of object copying can be considered as working.
- The usage of evolution code during development leads to a reliable data migration at customer site. We encountered no data corruption or misses caused by evolution.
- Both uses of the evolution technique performed on the real system has shown that auxiliary steps that accompany the actual evolution are much more time consuming. Dump importing was rather costly and took up to three hours. Currently we change the database cloning step to use the data backup and

| total number of data records | | 11-22-04 | 02-26-05 |
|---|---|---|---|
| IMIS | | 14.1M | 20.8M |
| repository | | 6.0M | 8.5M |
| | | 20.1M | 29.3M |
| **number of tables** | | | |
| IMIS | 134 | 152 | 152 |
| repository | 278 | 280 | 279 |
| **model changes (oo)** | | | |
| classes created/deleted | | 28 | 9 |
| attributes/associations created/deleted | | 69 | 23 |
| **model changes (relational)** | | | |
| tables created/deleted | | 32 | 5 |
| columns created/deleted/modified | | 87 | 33 |
| **data modifications** | | | |
| objects updated/inserted | | ~ 4700 | ~ 3600 |
| associations updated/inserted | | ~ 270 | ~ 1300 |

**Fig. 6.** Results of IMIS tool support for data migration.

restore routines of the Oracle recovery manager to copy the old content between the databases.

– Most of the model changes are more or less trivial like attribute insertion or deletion. Changes that require one of the more sophisticated evolution techniques offered by our framework are rather seldom.

– However, the offered sophisticated techniques are particularly useful for complex model changes. For example, during the last installation a new table was created that normalizes a set of three columns that were contained in two other tables before. The new table was filled and the attribute columns were replaced by foreign keys.

## 5   Related Work

ORION [10, 2] is an object-oriented database. It provides a solution to data migration based on dynamic schema evolution that targets the physical level. It is possible to change the schema in a deployed instance of the ORION database. The ORION data migration mechanism is adaptional. This means, that data and application code are adapted to a new model in the evolution cycle.

The TSE [20] solution never deletes parts of the defining model. Schema versioning is based on a view mechanism and all changes, i.e., in particular deletes, are recorded in view changes.

Schema versioning [22] is combined with an adaptional mechanism in the O2 [8] system. O2 minimizes needed application reconstructions.

OTGen [13] is based on a generator for data migration programs. Input to the generator is a declarative definition of an object-relational mapping. The successor of OTGen is the Tess [12] system. The Tess generator also takes into account an existing old schema so that it can generate an initial schema mapping itself.

Clio [18, 17] is an exemplary system for automatic schema matching [21], which is supported by a correspondence engine. The mapping generator of Clio gets source and target schemas as input.

The analysis in [15] clarifies the relationship between data migration and model evolution, given a scenario with a relational schema and a semantic data model.

The approach in [1] succeeds in representing relational views in OCL, whereas [14] discusses extensions to UML for database design taking into account the object-relational features of modern database technology.

The approach in [19] shows that it is possible to specify consistencies for legacy data sources in OCL.

# 6    Conclusion

A round-trip engineering can play the role of an integrated development environment. If cohesion in work product management is the goal support for object-relational mapping should be integrated into each CASE tool that is used in a typical multi-tier setting. Improving schema evolution and data migration with respect to an object-relational mapping has subtle issues, because object-relational mapping is a practical challenge on its own. If an MDA tool does not support data migration it stops supporting the developer of a data-centric application adequately after the first version of the system has been deployed at the customer site.

We can summarize the problem we are addressing in this paper as the problem of combining software maintenance with data migration. This problem is challenging from the standpoint of the MDA. In terms of the MDA, roundtrip engineering tools are traditionally restricted to the model layer. Database reorganization however targets the model layer as well as the information layer below this, i.e., the layer of the model instances. The database metadata belong to the model layer, the persistent data live on the information layer.

We argue that our approach benefits from adding a transparent database access layer between application logic and backend. The code for the layers on the backend side is maintained completely automatically by code generation into heterogeneous technologies. The generated code is not subject to white box reuse. Initially, there would be no need of roundtrip engineering. The need for providing transition support is solely created by the data migration problem.

# References

[1] Herman Balsters.   Modelling Database Views with Derived Classes in the UML/OCL-Framework. In *UML*, pages 295–309, 2003.
[2] Jay Banerjee, Won Kim, Hyoung-Joo Kim, and Henry F. Korth. Semantics and Implementation of Schema Evolution in Object-Oriented Databases. *ACM SIG-MOD Record*, 15(4), February 1987.

[3] Elliot J. Chikofsky and James H. Cross. Reverse Engineering and Design Recovery: A Taxonomy. *IEEE Software*, pages 13–17, January 1990.

[4] Don Coleman, Dan Ash, Bruce Lowther, and Paul Oman. Using Metrics to Evaluate Software System Maintainability. *IEEE Computer*, 27(8):44–49, August 1994.

[5] Graham Colleen. DBMS Software Market: Flat but Not Calm, Dataquest Alert. Gartner Group, May 2002.

[6] Krzysztof Czarnecki and Simon Helsen. Classification of Model Transformation Approaches. In *2nd OOPSLA Workshop on Generative Techniques in the context of Model Driven Architecture*, 2003.

[7] Dirk Draheim, Matthias Horn, and Ina Schulz. The Schema Evolution and Data Migration Framework of the Environmental Mass Database IMIS. In *Proceedings of SSDBM 2004 - 16th International Conference on Scientific and Statistical Database Management*. IEEE Press, 2004.

[8] Fabrizio Ferrandina and Sven-Eric Lautermann. An Integrated Approach to Schema Evolution for Object Databases. In *3rd International Conference on Object-Oriented Information Systems*, pages 280–294. Springer, December 1996.

[9] M. Horn, V. Triestram, and J. van Nouhuys. Data Evaluation Using the Generic Selection Component of the New IMIS System. In *EnviroInfo 2003 - 17th International Conference Informatics for Environmental Protection*. Metropolis, 2003.

[10] J.Banerjee, H. Chou, J.Garza, W.Kim, D.Woelk, and N.Ballou. Data Model Issues for Object-Oriented Applications. *ACM Transactions on Information Systems*, 5(1), January 1987.

[11] I. Kurtev and K. van den Berg. Unifying Approach for Model Transformations in the MOF Metamodeling Architecture. In *1st European MDA Workshop*. University of Twente, March 2004.

[12] Barbara Staudt Lerner. A Model for Compound Type Changes Encountered in Schema Evolution. *ACM Transactions on Database Systems*, 25(1):83–127, 2000.

[13] Barbara Staudt Lerner and A. Nico Habermann. Beyond Schema Evolution to Database Reorganization. *SIGPLAN Notices*, 25(10):67–76, 1990.

[14] Esperanza Marcos, Belén Vela, and José María Cavero. Extending UML for Object-Relational Database Design. In *UML*, pages 225–239, 2001.

[15] Victor M. Markowitz and Johann A. Makowsky. Incremental Reorganization of Relational Databases. In *13th International Conference on Very Large Data Bases*, pages 127–135. Morgan Kaufmann, 1987.

[16] J. Miller and J. Mukerji. MDA Guide Version 1.0.1. Technical Report omg/2003-06-01, Object Managment Group, 2003.

[17] R. J. Miller, L. M. Haas, and M. Hernandez. Schema Mapping as Query Discovery. In *Proceedings of the International Conference on Very Large Data Bases*, pages 77–88. Morgan Kaufmann, 2000.

[18] Renée J. Miller, Mauricio A. Hernández, Laura M. Haas, Lingling Yan, C. T. Howard Ho, Ronald Fagin, and Lucian Popa. The Clio Project: Managing Heterogeneity. *SIGMOD Record (ACM Special Interest Group on Management of Data)*, 30(1):78–83, 2001.

[19] Jan Pettersen Nytun and Christian S. Jensen. Modeling and Testing Legacy Data Consistency Requirements. In *UML*, pages 341–355, 2003.

[20] Young-Gook Ra and Elke A. Rundensteiner. A Transparent Object-Oriented Schema Change Approach Using View Evolution. In *11th IEEE International Conference on Data Engineering*. IEEE Press, 1995.

[21] Erhard Rahm and Philip A. Bernstein. A Survey of Approaches to Automatic Schema Matching. *VLDB Journal: Very Large Data Bases*, 10:334–350, 2001.

[22] J. Roddick. A Survey of Schema Versioning Issues for Database Systems. *Information and Software Technology*, 37(7):383–393, 1995.

[23] Devang Shah and Sandra Slaughter. Transforming UML Class Diagrams into Relational Data Models. In *UML and the Unified Process*, pages 217–236. Idea Group Publishing, 2003.

[24] Gary H. Sockut and Robert P. Goldberg. Database Reorganization - Principles and Practice. *ACM Computing Surveys*, 11(4):371–395, 1979.

[25] Richard Soley. Model Driven Archtitecture, white paper formal/02-04-03, draft 3.2. Object Managment Group, November 2003.

[26] Ruth Sterto. White Paper: Persistent Data Development Tools Validate the Model Driven Architecture Approach. Technical report, Progress Software Corporation, 2004.

[27] Can Türker. Schema Evolution in SQL-99 and Commercial (Object-)Relational DBMS. In *9th International Workshop on Foundations of Models and Languages for Data and Objects - Database Schema Evolution and Meta-Modeling*, volume 2065 of *LNCS*. Springer, 2000.

[28] Edmond VanDoren. Maintenance of Operational Systems - An Overview. In *Software technology Roadmap*. Carnegie Mellon Software Engineering Institute, 1997.

# Invited Presentation I:
# Lessons Learned, New Directions, and Migration Plans for Model-Driven Development of Large Scale Software Based Systems

Michael J. Marich and Haig F. Krikorian

The Boeing Company
{michael.j.marich|haig.f.krikorian}@boeing.com

## Abstract

Model-driven development of software-based systems has only recently witnessed significant progress attributable to the application of approaches such as the Unified Modeling Language (UML) to the task of capturing the architecture details of a system. However, industry has experienced a shortfall in approaches available to architects of large scale distributed, dynamic, and mobile software-based systems. This shortfall is characterized in a number of recently published articles; chief among the reasons highlighted is the lack of precise semantics in available modeling tools.

This talk presents an experience-based look at the lessons learned in model-driven development from the perspective of practicing systems and software engineering professionals. Here we explore the measures that we believe should be undertaken to increase the usefulness of modeling tools. In providing direction, we extend an urgent call to the academic community for assistance in developing and refining formal grammars necessary for the development of large-scale, software-based systems. Based on our experience, we offer guidance to the modeling community that we believe could improve the current state of affairs regarding the use of tools as well as promote the evolution of future tool development. Additionally, we offer insight into the problems associated with migrating the use of modeling tools into the software process for companies that employ several hundred systems and software engineers. While the focus of this presentation is biased toward large-scale systems, medium- and small-scale system developers should also be able to achieve considerable benefit from many of the aspects we propose.

L. Briand and C. Williams (Eds.): MoDELS 2005, LNCS 3713, pp. 397–397, 2005.
© Springer-Verlag Berlin Heidelberg 2005

# Concepts for Comparing Modeling Tool Architectures

Colin Atkinson[1] and Thomas Kühne[2]

[1] University of Mannheim
atkinson@informatik.uni-mannheim.de
[2] Darmstadt University of Technology
kuehne@informatik.tu-darmstadt.de

**Abstract.** As model-driven development techniques grow in importance so do the capabilities and features of the tools that support them, especially tools that allow users to customize their modeling language. Superficially, many modeling tools seem to offer similar functionality, but under the surface there are important differences that can have an impact on tool builders and users depending on the tool architecture chosen. At present, however, there is no established conceptual framework for characterizing and comparing different tool architectures. In this paper we address this problem by first introducing a conceptual framework for capturing tool architectures, and then—using this framework—discuss the choices available to designers of tools. We then compare and contrast the main canonical architectures in use today.

## 1 Introduction

Given the growing interest in Model Driven Development (MDD), modeling tools are becoming an increasingly central and important element of software development environments. As a result, software project managers are increasingly faced with the issue of deciding what modeling tool(s) to use in a project and what role the chosen tool(s) should play. Until recently this was not an issue of great import because modeling has traditionally played a secondary, supportive role in software engineering. The primary artifact of software development has until recently always been code, leaving models, if used at all, to play the role of supporting, non-essential documentation. Even when models are used to generate code skeletons, as is often the case today, they are essentially viewed as accelerators of the coding process rather than as a part of the critical path of software development. However, if the vision of model driven development is even partially successful this situation will change and modeling will become the dominant, critical path activity in software development.

At present however there is no established way of characterizing and comparing the capabilities of modeling tools beyond a superficial comparison of feature lists. This makes it difficult to select a tool for a specific project on a serious technical basis. Without the availability of concrete comparison concepts and evaluation criteria, decisions for modeling tools will be more or less random and at best based on irrelevant or secondary properties.

The lack of a tool evaluation framework not only affects tool users but also tool builders. Unless tool builders are aware of all the architectural options available to

L. Briand and C. Williams (Eds.): MoDELS 2005, LNCS 3713, pp. 398–413, 2005.
© Springer-Verlag Berlin Heidelberg 2005

them and are able to evaluate and compare their tool architecture against other alternatives, they will make their choices in a restricted design space, usually heavily
influenced by tradition rather than by objective criteria. The problem is not that there
is a lack of different (meta-) modeling infrastructure models or metaphors. On the
contrary, quite a number of different approaches exist, such as the famous OMG four-
layer architecture [1], powertype-based approaches [2], two-level approaches [3],
Domain Specific Languages [4], and the orthogonal classification approach [5]. The
problem is that each of these on its own is not a suitable basis for a tool evaluation
framework. While each approach has certain advantages in its own right, none
provides a general perspective for capturing the properties of a particular tool
architecture. In fact, the very number of different notations and modeling metaphors
compounds the problem of enabling an objective tool architecture comparison.

Unfortunately, even the venerable OMG four-layer architecture cannot serve as a
reference architecture against which to compare the design of modeling tools. Not
only is it the subject of much debate on what its different levels actually mean and
how they are related to one another, it is also difficult to map it to other modeling
metaphors. Furthermore, it is a high-level architecture and therefore does not lend
itself to explaining or discriminating between architectures used in current tools.

Consequently, in this paper we provide a conceptual basis for describing and
distinguishing different tool architectures. These concepts allow us to compare the
main realization approaches in use today and to provide a reinterpretation of the OMG
four-layer architecture which more precisely characterizes how it is implemented in
most modeling tools. One of the main contributions of the paper is an enumeration
and trade-off analysis of the architectural options tool designers should consider when
developing a tool. These can be thought of as tool architecture patterns for tool
developers. Finally, we analyze the advantages and disadvantages of some existing
architectures in use today.

## 2  Conceptual Foundations

Before discussing the various architectures that can be used to
realize modeling tools we first need to establish ways to precisely and exhaustively capture the associated design space.

**Fig. 1.** Classification.

### 2.1 Types and Instances

The basic building block for constructing modeling tool architectures is the
relationship between a type and its instances. This is not only the foundation for many
metamodeling infrastructures, but also the foundation for the object-oriented
implementation technology most widely used in mainstream software development
today, e.g., that of Java.

Fig. 1 shows how we depict the relationship between types and instances. We use
the concept of a classification frame split into two compartments—a type compartment and an instance compartment. To distinguish the type compartment from the
instance compartment we draw the former with a darker shade of color than the latter

and typically on the top or to the left. Note that in general one frame may have more than two compartments, in which case the additional ones simply extend the classification hierarchy linearly. Between any two adjacent compartments we always have type / instance relationship.

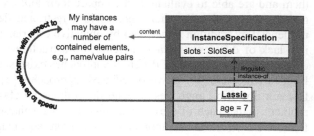

**Fig. 2.** Form Classification.

## 2.2 Form Versus Content

To fully capture an architectural design it is insufficient to use just one general notion of "instance-of". An architecture presented in this way will admit many different interpretations and thus possibly allow consensus where there should be none. We therefore need to be more precise in order to explicitly distinguish between two fundamentally different kinds of instance-of relationships (see also [6] for a similar discussion).

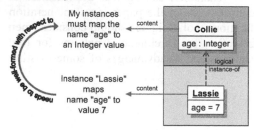

**Fig. 3.** Content Classification.

We refer to the kind of instance-of relationship used in Fig. 2 as "linguistic" instance-of. When it is used, the type (e.g., "Instance Specification") is part of a language definition and the instance (e.g., "Lassie") constitutes a language usage. Hence, we can check whether an element, (e.g., "Lassie") can be regarded as an instance of a *form*, e.g., "InstanceSpecification". The elements "age" and "7" of "Lassie" only need to be representable by the "Slot" classifier, i.e., be in a required *form* (e.g., "string" and "string" respectively). Whether e.g., "7" is an integer or not is irrelevant at this stage. Fig. 2 shows how we depict form-classification by *embedding* a frame within an instance compartment, and starting a new color scheme for the embedded frame. In the following, we will use form-classification to denote the representation format used to store elements, e.g., in a repository. The word "form" is used deliberately in the previous definition to distinguish this kind of "instance-of" relationship from the second kind of instance-of relationship which we refer to as "logical" instance-of (see Fig. 3).

Whether "7" needs to be of type "Integer" or an alternative type must be specified along the logical classification dimension (see Fig. 3). Here we may check whether the *content* (i.e., information expressed by "Lassie") can be regarded as an instance of the *content* expressed by "Collie". In other words, the type "Collie" contains information that is intended to define well-formedness rules which the content of instance "Lassie" must obey. We depict logical-classification by *stacking* compartments on top of each other. Thus, in summary, "form" and "content" are about the difference between *how* information is stored (form) and *what* information is stored (content). From now on, in contrast to Figs. 2 & 3, we will not use labels "linguistic" / "logical" for classification arrows anymore, because it will be clear from the frame notation (e.g., embedding) which kind is implicitly applicable.

## 2.3 Level Spanning

Figs. 2 & 3 show two different ways of combining frames which we refer to as *embedding* and stacking respectively. In order to effectively capture all the level relationships that may occur in tool architectures, we need a third frame combination concept which we refer to as *spanning*. Fig. 4 shows

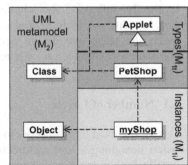

Fig. 4. Stacking versus Spanning.

an example of level-*spanning*, in terms of the OMG's classic four-layer architecture.

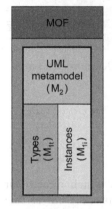

Fig. 4 (a) shows the usual depiction of the $M_2$ and $M_1$ levels in this architecture, where level $M_1$ is regarded as a monolithic level, even though it contains user instances (e.g., objects) and user types (e.g., classes), which are in a logical instance-of relationship to each other[1]. Fig. 4(b) makes this explicit by dividing level $M_1$ into two sublevels $M_{1t}$ and $M_{1i}$. The reason for not *embedding* levels $M_{1t}$ and $M_{1i}$ within the instance compartment of frame $M_2$, is that we assume the contents of both $M_2$ and $M_1$ to be represented as MOF-data. Hence, we have only one representation format (MOF) and all three frames shown in Fig. 4(b) contain data that must be well-formed logically with respect to each other. However, none is the other's representation format.

Fig. 6. Embedding & Spanning.

The complete picture is depicted by Fig. 5, using embedding, spanning and stacking[2] to reinterpret the linear OMG four-layer design as an architecture in which the MOF is the common representation format for all other levels, the latter just establishing logical instance-of relationship with each other[3]. Note that the logical instance-of relationship from $M_{1i}$ to $M_{1t}$ is defined within $M_2$. In other words, level $M_2$ *spans* both levels $M_{1t}$ and $M_{1i}$, meaning that elements from both levels must be well-formed with respect to the rules expressed in $M_2$.

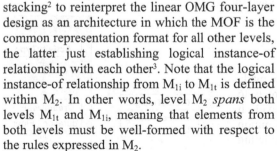

Fig. 5. Type Specialization.

---

[1] We are referring to the corrected four-layer architecture, in which level $M_0$ is no longer part of the modeling stack, but represents the modeled system.

[2] One can think of Fig. 5 as a flat projection of a three-dimensional diagram.

[3] In section 4 we will further discuss possible interpretations of the four-layer architecture.

## 2.4. Generalization

Classification is not the only way of deriving new elements from existing elements. Instead of differentiating an element by *instantiating* it from a *type* of another metalevel, it is sometimes more appropriate to *specialize* it using a *supertype*

Fig. 6 shows an example, where a "PetShop" class is defined to have "Applet" instances, by deriving it from superclass "Applet", as opposed to giving it a special "Applet" property through instantiation. Depending on the purpose of the model, one of these alternatives might be more appropriate than the other, but both are available and a detailed architectural description technique must be able to distinguish and express both cases.

As we are typically not interested in individual element relationships when describing tool architectures, the typical use of a generalization layer to specialize from will be depicted in the way shown in Fig. 7. The generalization dimension is orthogonal to all other types of instance-of relationship kinds and may be used in any combination within a frame.

Note that the orientation of the frames carries no semantics and can thus be used to emphasize certain perspectives, such as the linguistic, logic or generalization dimension.

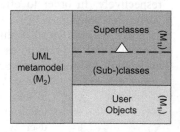

**Fig. 7.** Generalization Layer.

# 3  Architectural Options

Any tool architecture embodies a number of design decisions which directly or indirectly influence the challenge faced by the tool builders as well as the functionality available to tool users. The purpose of the following subsections is to make the respective design decisions more explicit and to provide a checklist to compare tool architectures against each other.

## 3.1  Number of Levels

One of the most basic choices to be made when designing a tool architecture is to decide how many type/instance levels it directly supports. A very common approach is to support two user modeling levels only. This is probably a vestige of traditional technologies such as data-bases (schema / data distinction) and object-oriented languages (type / instance distinction).

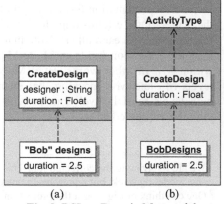

(a)                              (b)

**Fig. 8.** DSL vs Domain Metamodel.

Even tools referred to as *meta*-modeling tools (e.g., MetaEdit+ [7]) often only support two user levels. Such tools allow users to first define a domain specific language (see Fig. 8(a), top part) and then build models using that new language (Fig. 8(a), bottom part). By allowing users to define their own languages they justify their name as "meta"-modeling tools, since the language definition is regarded as a model for the domain models. In other words, the language definition represents a (linguistic) model for models.

However, the existence of just two logical levels (Fig. 8(a)) already causes a problem for a tool based on a two-level implementation technology because it means that two logical levels have to be implemented within just one instance level. In general, one may even desire more than two logical levels: Fig. 8(b) demonstrates how users might want to model at three domain levels using the UML with a domain metalevel added on top of the usual instance and type levels. Such an additional metalevel is useful for making the class level dynamic as it is able to support the creation and deletion of classes even while the (modeled) system is running. Moreover, it lets one easily assign information to classes (e.g., whether an activity type appears in a certain workflow plan or not) by declaring corresponding attributes at the metalevel-types[4].

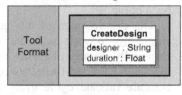

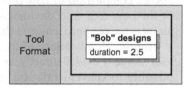

**Fig. 9.** Two Level Implementation.

Fig. 9 illustrates the above mentioned problem by showing an object-oriented (two-level) implementation in which the class level has to be used for defining the tool format in which the user data is modeled. The remaining object level then needs to represent the user models. Fig. 9 shows that both the user's domain specific language (DSL) *and* the corresponding user models must be represented within the tool. As none of the mainstream programming languages natively support more than two levels one cannot simply represent the user models in terms of the user language. However, creating user models only makes sense if the corresponding well-formedness rules are available at the same time. One way of having the models and rules available as data in the tool format is described in the next subsection.

The other approach uses code generation techniques to cast the information of the top part of Fig. 9 into a hard-coded, domain specific metamodel of a generated modeling tool. Fig. 10 depicts this process. Fig. 10(a) corresponds to Fig. 9's top part. Fig. 10(b) shows the architecture of the generated tool which is specifically tailored to deal with the user's DSL. Note that user models are directly represented in the format defined by the DSL definition.

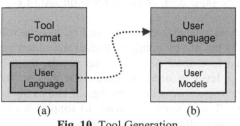

**Fig. 10.** Tool Generation.

---

[4] Similar to the tagged value concept in the UML, but in more uniform way that simply extends the principles of the lower two levels.

The advantage of this generative approach is that any well-formedness rules governing the creation of user models are directly enforced by the underlying data structure. It is not necessary to write a generic checking algorithm which needs to be parameterized with the definition of the user's DSL. Also, such a tool offers an API for accessing and manipulating user models that is specifically tailored to the DSL used. An access method might thus be called "getDuration()" yielding a result of type "Float" instead of some generic access like "getFeatureWithName('duration')" yielding a result with a generic type, e.g., of type "String". A generated tool will also be very efficient in dealing with user models, as all the generated code will be specific to the DSL defined and will have been compiled.

The disadvantage of this generative approach is that it is not possible to use a single tool to work on several levels (language definition + language usage) at once. Especially in early phases, when the DSL is still being defined, it is very convenient to switch back and forth between the levels without going through a change-generate-compile-validate cycle every time. An interpreted language, such as Java, which allows compilation of new code to be done in the background and supports reloading of the new code into the running tool, blurs the boundaries between a generative and an integrative approach from the point of view of the user of the tool.

Another disadvantage of two-level based tools is that they potentially cannot use a user domain model directly as input for a new DSL. In other words, it may not be possible to conveniently use such a tool repeatedly in order to create a cascade of definition-usage pairs, thus creating a (meta-) modeling stack (e.g., MOF ← UML ← Classes ← Objects). The only way for tools with such a limitation to support more than two levels is "level compaction".

## 3.2 Level Compaction

An alternative way to support multiple modeling levels with just one instance level is to abandon the idea that one modeling level (e.g., user classes) automatically defines the representation *format* for the level below (e.g., user objects). Instead, the native tool representation format is used for both user modeling levels. Fig. 11 shows how the situation of Fig. 9 can

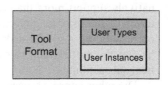

**Fig. 11.** Logical Stacking.

be resolved by keeping both datasets in the same tool, *stacking* them on top of each other.

With *stacking* we express the fact that one level ("User Types" in Fig. 11) controls another level ("User Instances" in Fig. 11) but not by being its format definition but by specifying the rules that it's controlled level must obey. In other words, the tool needs to look up data in the controlling level in order to check the data in the controlled level with respect to well-formedness. The scheme in Fig. 11 can easily be extended to include another level (above "User Types") in order to support a user domain metalevel and hence enable modeling as illustrated in Fig. 8(b).

The architecture shown in Fig. 11 can be extended not only by increasing the innermost stack, but also by using *spanning*. In this way, a tool can be promoted from being specialized for one language (e.g., UML) only, to supporting many user-definable languages. Fig. 5 shows how spanning can be used to build such a (MOF-based) UML tool.

The advantages of an integrative, level-compaction approach are manifold: User instance data can be manipulated independently of user type data. This allows for un-limited freedom in experimentation with what e.g., user domain models should look like. Note that a generative approach (Fig. 10) only allows domain models that adhere to the rules of the user DSL. When the DSL is changed the models formerly created with it are in an outdated format. In contrast, in an integrative approach—although the user instances will no longer conform to the DSL—there will be no need to migrate them to the new format. No representation change is ever needed as long as all levels that may change are in a logical content-controlling relationship with each other.

From the point of view of tool builders, levels belonging to the same level stack can be treated in a uniform way. Multiple-level support only needs to be provided once and can then simply be scaled up to support any number of levels. Levels belonging to the same representation format can be treated uniformly with respect to many operations, such as serialization to output formats.

Another important difference introduced by level compaction is the fact that a tool builder no longer has to replicate model data. Fig. 10 makes it clear that a cascading approach necessitates model data to be stored twice: Once as instance data (e.g., "User Language" in Fig. 10(a)) and another time as type data ("User Language" in Fig. 10(b)). Level compaction uses the same set of data for both purposes at the same time (see, e.g., "User Types" in Fig. 11).

A potential disadvantage of level compaction is that access and modification of the supported levels has to occur in a generic manner, i.e., all levels are treated the same and thus the advantages of level-specific APIs are lost. Yet, this need not necessarily be the case. It is of course possible to provide special views onto each of the levels, by using adapters, for example, so that APIs can be made available that are identical to those of a two-level cascading approach.

## 3.3 Language Versus Library Metaphor

The previous section demonstrated how level compaction can be used to move control from the format-language to a logically controlling

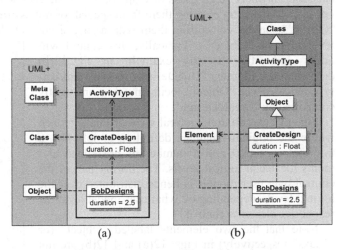

Fig. 12. Language vs Library Metaphor.

language. However, the issue of whether one supports multiple levels within one instance level (level compaction) is orthogonal to whether one uses a very liberal format language or not. A modeling tool with a built-in UML metamodel (see

Fig. 12(a)) is an example of the simultaneous use of both level compaction (for user types & instances) and a confined language space. In order to make our next point more clearly we have added a domain metalevel and hence named the corresponding metamodel "UML+" instead of just "UML". As can be observed from Fig. 12(a), user elements are controlled by two dimensions: First, their *form* must conform to the UML+ metamodel (through linguistic instantiation). Second, their *content* must conform to the next logical level higher up in the stack. The top level of the stack is not content controlled in any way and just needs to obey the format rules imposed by the UML+ metamodel.

As discussed in the previous sections the approach shown in Fig. 12(a) has some trade-offs: Users may only model within the limits of the language defined at the UML+ level. This may be regarded as an advantage (in order to enforce a standard) or a disadvantage (since it is then impossible to use any kind of concept). Hence, any language extension will have to be accomplished by altering the built-in language metamodel "UML+". This is a direct consequence of using, what we call the *language metaphor* for defining valid syntax for user models. Even if the UML+ metamodel were kept as modifiable data, one still needed to perform language meta-modeling and, thus, alter the modeling language standard when trying to create more domain specific models. This is of course the reason why the UML language designers chose to introduce stereotypes as a "lightweight" way of metamodeling. Hence, stereotypes represent another, third way of supporting one more level, in addition to "two-level cascading" (section 3.1) and "level compaction" (section 3.2). Note however the difference in providing a domain metamodel (as in Fig. 8(b)) versus allowing (strictly limited) extensions to the language definition (using stereotypes).

Fig. 12(b) demonstrates an alternative to the *language metaphor* which we refer to as the *library metaphor*. In comparison to Fig. 12(a), the language definition has been reduced to a bare minimum. User elements are not distinguished by their form classifier anymore (e.g., Class or Object), but by an assigned level number. They are not differentiated by creating them from special form-classifiers (e.g., UML+ element "Object"), but by controlling them with a special content-classifier (e.g., user type-level element "Object"). Typically, this control will occur indirectly, as the example in Fig. 12(b) demonstrates: Element "BobDesigns" is only indirect-ly controlled via "Object", being much more tightly controlled by "CreateDesign".

Fig. 13 gives an architectural view of this approach where the original language definition is split into a minimal *core* part and a number of predefined elements located at logical levels. The *library* part of the control over user models is hence distributed over the logical levels, depending on what user-model level the respective elements control.

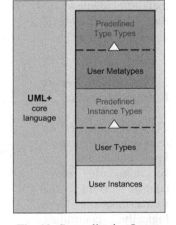

**Fig. 13.** Generalization Layer.

Note that the two elements labeled "Object" (or "Class" respectively) in Figs. 12(a) and 12(b) are not identical. They not only differ with respect to their location in the architecture but also with respect to the way in which they control elements. Element "Object" in Fig. 12(a) enables its instances (e.g., "BobDesigns") to have a certain *form*. Element "Object" in Fig. 12(b) does not need to do that as this is already accomplished by "Element" at level "UML+", albeit in a much more generic way. Element "Object" in Fig. 12(b) restricts this genericity by exerting content-control over, e.g., "BobDesigns" yet this control is considerably strengthened by element "CreateDesign". The latter will be much more specific about the allowed properties of "BobDesigns" as any of the "Object" elements of Fig. 12(a) or 12(b) could ever be.

Note that element "Object" in Fig. 12(a) represents a tool builder's perspective and will support operations for model management. In contrast element "Object" in Fig. 12(b) may contain operations of relevance to the modeling tool user, such as "equals()" for comparing objects based on domain principles, instead of model management principles.

The advantages of using the library metaphor to controlling user models are:
- a simplified core language definition allowing experimentation with model concepts at all logical modeling levels,
- a stable core language definition even in the event of users wishing to extend their "language", and, hence,
- maximum flexibility for users with respect to domain specific modeling.

If the predefined libraries (see Fig. 13) are made immutable and fixed, this flexibility is even reconciled with the desire to retain a common core standard modeling approach, which may only be extended but not completely redefined.

The reduction of the core language to a minimal set of features can be compared to reducing the BNF definition of a programming language's syntax to a bare minimum and letting all removed rules (such as the difference between arithmetic and Boolean expressions) be enforced by static semantics checking. This makes the syntax definition more immune to changes to the language definition at the cost of shifting the change-burden to the definition of the static semantics (the library in our example). The library metaphor has indeed proven to be very successful for languages such as Smalltalk and Java which have a rather small language definition and provide the bulk of their utility through the availability of standardized libraries.

The disadvantages of the library metaphor is the unfamiliarity of the approach to most users and the need for creating machinery that deals with all possible logical levels generically. In particular one needs to implement a generic well-formedness checking algorithm to be applied to a level by parameterizing it with the content of the level above. However, tool builders then only need to define the basic principles of modeling, such as instantiation, specialization, and association once in the core language. These will work uniformly for all levels and there is no need for tool builders to use different checking algorithms for different level crossings or replicate the basic mechanisms time and again so that they are available to the next level. This replication is typically unnecessary, unless one specifically desires these features to work differently for each language level incarnation[5].

The next question to address with respect to tool architectures is therefore the choice of the appropriate number of linguistic levels.

---

[5] The MOF and the UML represent a typical counter-example. Here, one desires as much as uniformity between the UML core and the MOF as possible.

## 3.4 Language Definition Stack Depth

The use of specialization, rather than instantiation, can also be put to use in the core language definition (in the linguistic dimension). Fig. 14 shows a very rough conceptual sketch of how the Fujaba [8] metamodel is composed of several specialization layers. Instead of creating a language definition stack in the sense of "MOF ← UML ← UserModels", the Fujaba developers opted to have a number of languages which refine each other, as opposed to being instantiations of each other. In this way, they have built up the resulting metamodel, step by step, and have alternative views (e.g., as AbstractSyntaxGraph elements or UML elements) on the same set of user data.

The design shown in Fig. 14 of course begs the question as to why the OMG has not opted to cast MOF as a *super*-model, i.e., use generalization rather than a classification, on top of languages such as UML or CWM?

The purpose of the MOF is to provide a common basis for defining all other OMG languages. One way to provide such a common basis is to define a language that *classifies* all the languages one is interested in, as is done by the MOF in its $M_3$-level role. The more diverse the set of languages to be captured under a common umbrella, the more linguistic levels are useful. At each language definition level, more languages fitting into the paradigm currently addressed can be properly described, a process that continues to the very top of the language stack. In the OMG's case we just have

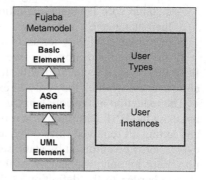

**Fig. 14.** Language Layers.

a language describing all user models (the UML metamodel) and another language on top of this (the MOF), describing object-oriented approaches to modeling. This makes sense if one is interested in a standardized meta-meta-*language* for creating metamodels (such as the UML) and providing the corresponding tools along with this capability.

However the same effect, and more in this example, can be achieved by using a standardized *library* of metamodeling superclasses. Instead of specifying the element "Component" to be a "Class" (in contrast to, e.g., a "Data Type") by assuming it to be an *instance* of a $M_3$-level MOF-element "Class", it could also be differentiated as such by letting it *subclass* from an $M_2$-level element "M-Class". In this way, "Component"-usages would still be different to other UML concept usages, and they would immediately be accessible through this "M-Class" interface. We use the prefix "M-" (for MOF) in order to distinguish this element from the ordinary $M_2$-level UML element called "Class". In other words, the desired repository access to elements in user models can directly be achieved through corresponding metamodel superclasses. A double role as played by the MOF (as a $M_3$-level meta-metamodel & as a general repository format for all levels) would therefore not be necessary.

Note, however, that the above described library approach in the linguistic dimension only works if one is able to find a (MOF-)*super*-model for all the language defining metamodels (such as UML and CWM) that one would like to include. It is the distinguishing advantage of using a classifying language (as the MOF in its $M_3$-

level role) that it can abstract from the metamodels to be captured, without requiring them to share a common (super-)structure.

Summarizing, through "level compaction" and/or using repository superclasses in a language defining metamodel, it is possible to remove language definition levels in the linguistic dimension. Fig. 13 shows an extreme case, where one could do away with a MOF format as well and integrate other modeling approaches, such as CWM, as modeling libraries within the logical levels.

The appeal of a minimal length language stack (in the linguistic dimension) is the simplicity of the associated architecture and the resulting lack of redundancy. All levels can be treated uniformly and neither data nor basic modeling principles have to be replicated.

In favor of a language stack with two or more levels it can be noted that each language introduced makes the associated storage format more concrete and more tailored to the paradigm one aims to cover. Hence, the representation can be more compact and easier to read and write for both humans and tools.

# 4   Canonical Architectures

We will now use the concepts, notation, and architectural options previously introduced to characterize and evaluate the three main canonical architectures currently underpinning modeling tools. This is not intended to be an exhaustive characterization, but to layout the major reference architectures against which other more specialized architectures can be compared.

## 4.1   Four-Layer Architecture

Certainly today's most prominent architecture for metamodeling infrastructures or tool designs is the OMG's four-layer architecture (see Fig. 15(a)).

Since this architecture is not unambiguously specified we can only offer interpretations of it. One alternative, visually suggested by Fig. 15(a), is a logical language stack of "MOF ← UML ← $M_1$"[6], but that would neglect the MOF's role as a repository format for all the levels. However, just casting the MOF as a pure repository format would neglect the

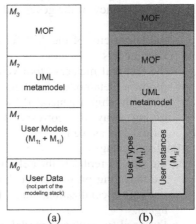

(a)                          (b)
**Fig. 15.** Four-Layer Architecture.

MOF's role as a logical language definition for the UML metamodel at $M_2$., Fig. 15(b) therefore best seems to capture the apparently intended dual role of the MOF and hence best captures the spirit of the whole architecture. Note that it explicitly shows the MOF's ability to represent itself.

---

[6] We are using M1 as a shortcut for M1t and M1i combined, in part because the OMG does not explicitly distinguish between M1t and M1i.

A non-technical but nonetheless very real advantage of the four-layer architecture is that it defines a standard, including standard implementation technologies. It furthermore allows several modeling standards such as the UML and CWM to be fitted under one (MOF-based) architecture.

Its main drawback is the lack of support for more than two user modeling levels. While the architectural style does not prevent an extension of the user modeling levels (within $M_1$), the standardized UML metamodel restricts them to two. Although the UML's solution for providing a language extension feature to modelers—the stereotype mechanism—has been improved from version 1.5 to 2.0, it still does not offer the same power for user domain metamodeling as another user modeling level would offer (as exemplified in Fig. 8(b)).

## 4.2 Two-Level Cascading

The popularity of the two-level cascading approach is testified by the many practical examples of its use. Fig. 16(a) informally depicts the approach of providing a format for creating user defined languages and then, after a generation step, using the user language definition to create user models.

Fig. 16(b) uses our notation to more precisely capture the promotion of the "User Language" instance data to "User Language" types that then can be used to create models. Tools such as MetaEdit+ [7] and Fujaba [8] use this approach. Also the MDR approach using JMI technology [3] and the Software Factories approach [4] use the same underlying principle.

The advantages of this approach are:
- the efficiency of the generated modeling facilities.
- the specificity of the API for accessing user models.
- the fact that metacase tool vendors may produce metamodels for their customers and only ship a generated tool, without giving away the corresponding meta-model data as well.

Its disadvantages are:
- the need to replicate the definition of basic modeling primitives, such as instantiation, specialization, etc. time and again.
- the need to duplicate model content by keeping it both as user instance data (for manipulation during the language definition phase) and as tool type data (for creating user models).
- an inconvenient "edit-generate-compile-validate"-cycle when developing the modeling language (e.g., a DSL).

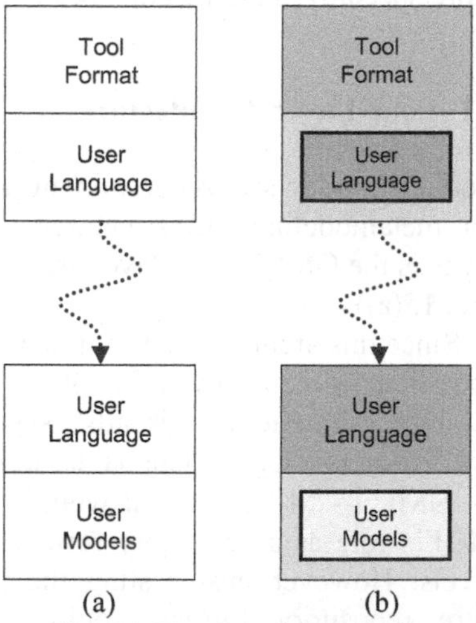

**Fig. 16.** Two-Level Approach.

## 4.3 Orthogonal Classification Architecture

Perhaps the antithesis to the two-level cascading approach described above is the so called orthogonal classification architecture (OCA) based on level-compaction [5]. Fig. 17(a) shows the two (linguistic and ontological[7]) dimensions of this approach featuring just one format level ($L_1$) used for representing an unbounded number of ontological levels. Although the OCA does not dictate any particular number of linguistic or ontological levels, it lends itself to be used with a single (MOF-like) universal format and an unbounded number of user domain modeling levels based on the library metaphor (see section 3.3 and Fig. 17(b)). A tool with this architecture as its basis is ConceptBase [9]. The one format level in ConceptBase is based on the Omega level of Telos [10]. Any other modeling data in ConceptBase is expressed as instances of this one "format" level. In ConceptBase terminology all model data is expressed as propositions.

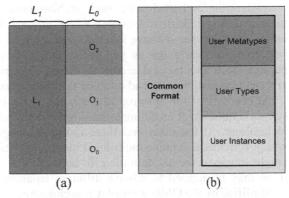

(a)                                    (b)

**Fig. 17.** Orthogonal Classification Approach.

The advantages of the OCA are:
- the complete uniformity with which all ontological levels can be treated. One does not need to consider various kinds of level boundaries except logical stacking.
- the completely redundancy-free storage of modeling data. No single level has to be represented twice so as to use it in two roles.
- a single tool can be used to manipulate all levels in the same manner. There are no limits to experimenting with content in levels since the basic representation format virtually allows unlimited expressiveness. Well-formedness conformance to a higher logical level, of course, is a different matter and may also need to be supported. Locking mechanisms could be used to prevent users altering data in levels they are not supposed to change or even see.

Its disadvantages are:
- the unfamiliarity of the library approach to the majority of modelers
- the fact that current established technologies and market rules are better suited to standardize languages, rather than libraries.

---

[7] For the purpose of this discussion we can equate "ontological" with "logical" instantiation.

# 5 Conclusion

As model-driven development gains popularity, supporting tools are becoming an increasingly important part of software development. The internal architecture of such tools is not only of concern to tool builders but also to tool users since it determines the basic functionality available. Unfortunately, at present there is no framework for characterizing and evaluating such architectures, as previous work on clarifying metamodeling infrastructures has never attempted to include tool representation issues. In this paper we have laid the foundation for such a framework by introducing concepts—including the as yet undistinguished "embedding" and "spanning"—to capture core architectural elements. Using this framework we then discussed the architecture design space and outlined the main canonical architectures in use today.

At one end of the spectrum there is the "Two-level Cascading" approach which supports multi-level modeling technology in terms of classic two-level object-oriented technology. At the other end there is the "Orthogonal Classification Architecture" which provides a genuine multi-level modeling platform, typically in the context of a single linguistic format definition. In between these two extremes, various combinations may be applied to achieve different balances between their pros and cons, as exemplified by the OMG's four-layer architecture.

We believe that an evaluation framework for tool architectures, allowing concrete technical comparisons to be made will be an invaluable help for making strategic decision in the near future, and we hope that our contribution in the form of this paper represents a useful step in this direction.

## Acknowledgements

We would like to thank Andy Schürr and his group and Pierre-Alain Muller for stimulating discussions and for information on Fujaba, and TopModL respectively.

## References

[1]   OMG: Unified Modeling Language, v1.5. OMG document formal/03-03-01, (2003)
[2]   Gonzalez-Perez, C. and Henderson-Sellers, B.: Templates and Resources in Software Development Methodologies. To appear, Journal of Object Technology, May/June (2005)
[3]   Matula M.: Netbeans Metadata Repository. http://mdr.netbeans.org/ (2003)
[4]   Greenfield, J., Short, K.L., Cook, S. and Kent, S.: Software Factories: Assembling Applications with Patterns, Models, Frameworks, and Tools. Hungry Minds Inc. (2004)
[5]   Atkinson, C., Kühne, T., Model-Driven Development: A Metamodeling Foundation. IEEE Software, vol. 20, no. 5 (2003) pp. 36-41
[6]   Bézivin, J., Gerbé, O.: Towards a Precise Definition of the OMG/MDA Framework. Proceedings of ASE'2001, San Diego, USA (2001)
[7]   Kelly, S., Lyytinen, K. and Rossi, M.: MetaEdit+: A fully configurable multi-user and multi-tool CASE and CAME environment. In Proceedings of the 8th International Conference CAISE'96, Springer-Verlag (1996) pp. 1-21

[8]  Klein, T. Nickel, U.A., Niere, J., Zündorf, A.: From UML to Java And Back Again, Tech. Rep. TR-RI-00-216, University of Paderborn (1999)
[9]  Jeusfeld, M.A. et al.: ConceptBase: Managing conceptual models about information systems. Handbook of Information Systems, Springer-Verlag (1998) pp. 265-285
[10] Mylopoulos, J., Borgida, A. Jarke, M. Koubarakis, M.: Telos: representing knowledge about information systems. Vol. 8. No. 4, ACM Trans. on Information Systems (1990)

# Scenario Construction Tool Based on Extended UML Metamodel

Michał Śmiałek[1,2], Jacek Bojarski[1], Wiktor Nowakowski[1], Tomasz Straszak[1]

Warsaw University of Technology[1] and Infovide S.A.[2], Warsaw, Poland
smialek@iem.pw.edu.pl

**Abstract.** Scenario based notations are becoming more and more popular as means for user requirements elicitation. They can be used in more formal specifications as part of detailed use case templates or in agile processes to capture informal user stories. Despite their significance in software engineering, scenarios seem not to be properly supported by appropriate tools. This paper describes a scenario construction tool that offers clear separation of the actual story from notions used therein. The tool is constructed as an extension to visual notation of UML's use cases. It is based on an extended UML metamodel in the area of activities and classifiers. This formal basis makes the tool capable of supplying the existing UML tools with an additional layer of requirements models based on scenarios and notions. This layer makes it possible to transform requirements directly into design-level models. The tool offers such transformation capabilities based on a simple model mapping. This transformation supports human efforts to keep the system's design consistent with the user's needs expressed through scenarios.

## 1 Introduction

Writing a good film scenario is difficult. Apart from being based on an interesting idea, it has to tell a coherent and logical story, and it also has to describe precisely the environment for this story. Such a scenario defines requirements for the film producer. It describes what elements of scenography and what actors are needed. It also tells the filmmakers about the desired "dynamics" of the film. Film scenarios seem to be a good metaphor for structuring software requirements. By writing certain scenarios, the users can tell the developers stories (defined as an "account of incidents or events"[1]) about the functionality of the prospective system. These stories would start with an initial event and end with a happy or sad ending.

Being a good metaphor, scenarios are becoming more and more popular as means for eliciting and writing user requirements [1]. Two of the most widely known scenario-based requirements artifacts are use cases [2] and user stories [3]. Depending on the approach taken by the scenario writers, use case scenarios can be as formal as in [4] or as light as in [5]. User story approach gives an even lighter notation.

---

[1] Merriam-Webster On-line Dictionary

L. Briand and C. Williams (Eds.): MoDELS 2005, LNCS 3713, pp. 414–429, 2005.

Despite their popularity, scenarios can cause significant problems for their writers. Writing a set of good scenarios for a software system seems to be equally hard as writing a good scenario for a film. It can be argued that these problems are caused by the fact that scenarios are written by and for different audiences. On one hand, scenarios should be informal and comprehensible by "ordinary people" (i.e. the users and stakeholders). On the other hand, they should be very precise in order to be implemented correctly by the developers. This leads to numerous propositions of notations for scenarios which causes confusion among people trying to choose an approach that is appropriate for them (see [6] for an insight on this).

The above mentioned plethora of notations for stories calls for some unification. According to what we said above, this unified notation would need to accommodate informality with necessary precision (see [7]). Informality can be assured by writing scenario steps with very simple sentences composed eg. of a subject, a verb and one or two objects (see [8] for an initial idea). In turn, precision can be accomplished by unifying the syntax of scenarios and allowing them to constitute models with well defined semantics. Precise model of requirements would allow for their easier transformation into models associated with the development of the final system (architectural and design models). This brings the requirements models into the mainstream of software development activities.

The activity of writing scenarios calls for some significant tool support. Unfortunately, lack of more precise semantics for scenario steps makes this support quite weak. General requirements management tools can be used only to organize scenarios written in free-form text. Some tools [9] propose more structured approach, offering compliance with some standard templates [2]. Other tools allow for generating scenarios from some formally defined action models [10], [11]. In this paper we propose a tool that allows for creating semantically precise scenario-based models. This precision is based on a very simple notation and thus allows for building textual descriptions that can be easily understood by the users (see also [12]). At the same time, this simple notation can be automatically transformed into a precise model that clearly separates the structure of the problem from its dynamics. This separation on the requirements level allows for transformation into more design-specific models.

The above uniform modeling notation used in the tool, puts it in the context of model-driven development, based on standard modeling notation of UML [13] and the concepts of MDA [14]. Efforts to unify the notation for scenarios lead to extending the UML's UseCase metamodel package. The tool presented in this paper adds the extended metamodel to existing UML tools by offering an appropriate plug-in component. Unified notation for scenarios makes it possible to define appropriate transformations from the requirements level model to the design-level models. By using a plug-in to a UML CASE tool we make this transformation possible thus leading to more flexible development lifecycles leading from the initial user's needs to the resulting code.

In the following sections we describe the concepts behind the tool in more detail. First, we update the UML 2.0 metamodel to accommodate for precise notation and semantics in the area of use cases. We also define an additional metamodel package that contains notions used in the scenario content. Finally we describe the application of the proposed tool in the software development lifecycle.

## 2    Introducing Use Case Scenarios with Notions to UML

Execution of a scenario is a sequence of actions forming a dialog between one or more objects outside of some system and that system. This sequence is performed on behalf of a single primary object (primary actor). This primary object triggers the scenario by interacting with the system. The initial trigger is followed by a sequence of actions performed by the system and by the outside objects (including the primary object). The sequence is controlled by the system and leads to a single goal of significant value to the primary object. This goal can constitute a change in the system's state or change in the state of outside objects or can mean revealing the current state of the system to the primary object. When the above sequence of actions fails to reach the goal, the system returns to the initial state or reaches some error state. When writing-down individual scenarios it makes sense to group them by the initial triggering actions and the final goals for the primary actors. We can call such a group of scenarios having the same trigger and the same goal - a use case (see [2]).

While designing a notation for the above defined scenarios and use cases, we constantly have to bear in mind their diverse audience. This means, that scenarios have to be readable and informal yet precise. Users and stakeholders are used to free-form textual notations for requirements. On the other hand, developers would prefer to have a precisely defined flow of control. This means that we should have in fact two notations easily transformable one into another (see [7]).

In order to combine informality with precision we can write scenarios as sequences of textual sentences. To be precise, these sentences would need to have very simple grammar. A bare minimum for a full sentence is a subject, a verb and an object. With this notation, a scenario might look like this:

1. Superuser chooses to add a user.
2. System shows user data dialog.
3. Superuser enters user data.
4. System validates user data.
5. System adds user to user list.

Sometimes we also need a second object in the sentence (see: "user list" above) which has to be associated with the rest of the sentence with a preposition ("to" in the last sentence above). This gives us a simple, yet powerful grammar for individual actions in a scenario. Every action sentence consists of a **S**ubject, a **V**erb, and one or two **O**bjects (SVO[O] grammar - see [8]).

If we treat the above scenario as part of a full use case (here: "Add user"), we could define also some other scenarios that are initiated with the same triggering action (Superuser chooses to add a user) and lead toward the same goal (a user gets added to the user list). Another such scenario could look as follows:

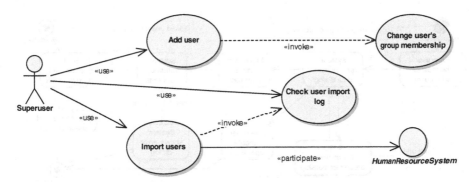

**Fig. 1.** Example use case model

1. Superuser chooses to add a user.
2. System shows user data dialog.
3. Superuser enters user data.
4. System validates user data.
5. System shows error dialog.

The only difference between the two scenarios is the last sentence. We suspect that the alternative scenario is caused by a failed validation of the entered user data. We can note that although the final goal is not reached, the second scenario is part of the same "Add user" use case. We can treat this type of scenarios as failure scenarios.

Having several scenarios within a use case necessitates some ordering of the control flow. We also need some explanation about the conditions that cause different scenarios to be evoked. This leads us to introducing precise control flow semantics for use cases (see [15], [16]). This precision is also needed when we want to express control flow relationships between different scenarios («include» and «extend» relationships in UML). It can be argued that interleaving this flow of control is harmful (see [17], [18]). Thus, we will assume invocation type of control flow here, ie. control flow returns to the invoking use case only after performing one of the final actions in the invoked use case.

We will illustrate the flow semantics by elaborating on the example scenarios already presented above. Our example will consist of four use cases illustrated on Figure 1. Three of these use cases can be «used» directly by the "Superuser" actor. The fourth use case can only be «invoked» from the "Add user" use case. One of the use cases needs additional «participation» of an external interface (interface to another system). It can be noted, that in addition to being «used» directly, the "Check user import log" use case can be also «invoked» from "Import users".

The details of this use case model can be revealed by showing scenarios of individual use cases. This time, instead of writing only sequences of SVO(O) sentences we will use graphical notation of UML's activities ([13], p. 317). With this notation we can precisely describe control flow semantics for alternative flows and inter-use case invocations (see [15]). Figure 2 presents an appropriate

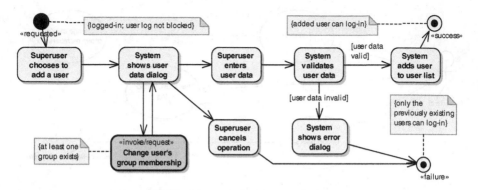

**Fig. 2.** Activity for the "Add user" use case

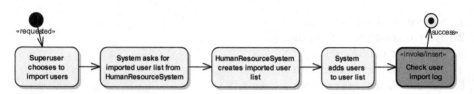

**Fig. 3.** Activity for the "Export users" use case

activity with scenarios for the "Add user" use case. The initial node contains a precondition that guards the usage of this use case, ¡¡requested¿¿ by the actor. There are also two final nodes that denote ¡¡success¿¿ and ¡¡failure¿¿ of appropriate scenarios. These final nodes contain postconditions describing the desired system state in case of use case success or failure respectively.

It can be noted that flow in a use case can be controlled in four ways:

- The user can decide on performing one action or another ("enters user data" or "cancels operation").
- The system might decide on further actions ("user data valid" or "user data invalid").
- The user may ¡¡request¿¿ invoking another use case ("Change user's group membership").
- The system may invoke a use case by ¡¡inserting¿¿ its activity.

The fourth of these possibilities is illustrated on Figure 3. The invoked use case is inserted directly into the flow of the base use case without any user intervention. It can be observed that ¡¡inserting¿¿ a use case has a slightly different semantics than ¡¡requesting¿¿ it from within another use case or ¡¡using¿¿ it directly. This difference in semantics is illustrated on Figure 4. When the "Check user import log" use case is ¡¡requested¿¿, this is done through initial user action ("Superuser chooses to check import log"). When use case is invoked by ¡¡inserting¿¿ it into the flow of another use case, this initial action is omitted. Such duality of invocation is reflected by introducing two types of initial nodes.

Having resolved ambiguity of control flow we still face another source of misunderstanding. With simple SVO(O) sentences formed into an activity with

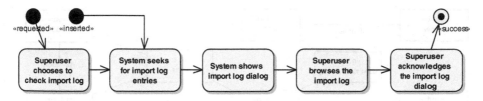

**Fig. 4.** Activity for the "Check import log" use case

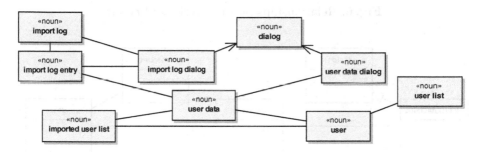

**Fig. 5.** Fragment of the noun vocabulary

different scenarios, we only tell a story. We don't have the means to describe the environment. For instance, we would like to know what "user data" is, and how it is related to "user" and "user data dialog". We thus need some way of expressing the vocabulary that is used when writing scenarios.

An appropriate vocabulary of nouns is illustrated on Figure 5. Relationships between nouns can get reflected in their textual definitions, as presented below (where links to other notions are denoted with square brackets):

- User - contains basic information about the user (login/password), detailed in [user data]; can be inserted into a [user list] or [imported user list].
- User data - detailed information about a [user]; includes user's personal data; user data is part of [imported user lists], gets registered as [import log entry], and is presented to the user through [user data dialog].

Additionally to defining all the nouns, we can also define verbs that can be related to appropriate nouns, thus forming operations on them. Such relationships for our example model are illustrated on Figure 6. Verbs (like "show" or "validate") are treated as behavioral ¡¡features¿¿ of related nouns. Some verbs may also ¡¡compose¿¿ a "complex verb" together with another noun.

The relationships between nouns and verbs form a complete vocabulary. This vocabulary specifies an environment for stories defined through use case scenarios. Such a clear separation of stories from notions used therein gives a very coherent model which can be transformed into other models. As a first step towards designing a system based on developed scenarios we can generate a simple class model (see Fig. 7). Having some simple transformation rules, such a model can be generated automatically from textual scenarios.

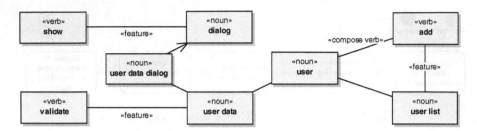

**Fig. 6.** Relationships between verbs and nouns

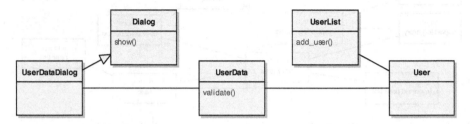

**Fig. 7.** Class model after transformation from the vocabulary

Apart from being a good basis for model transformation, the "scenarios with notions" model can be used just for writing unambiguous and semantically precise requirements specifications. Notions used consistently throughout different scenarios make this task relatively easy. While writing the stories we constantly extend our vocabulary of notions. We describe all the sentence objects and verbs that might cause ambiguity when developing the stories. We also define relations between the notions. This gives us a static map of the "user's territory", which is illustrated on Figures 5 and 6.

Unfortunately, UML does not introduce the notion of a scenario in the use case package ([13], p. 641). It also gives a very vague semantics of such a fundamental modeling element as use case is. On the other hand, introducing clear semantics to the UML's UseCase metaclass seems to be crucial if we want to define transformations from use case based requirements specifications to design level models. This could also allow for applying the concept of MDA [14] to requirements models.

UML, as an extensible modeling language, gives us two ways to clarify the use case semantics through adding scenarios, SVO sentences or notions. The first way is to introduce certain profiles (see [19]) and use existing modeling elements to represent eg. sentence subjects, verbs and objects. Another way is to extend the language's metamodel. This second method seems to be better suited for our purpose, as we want to add new notation and create a plug-in tool that would extend the capabilities of an existing UML-based tool. Extending the UML metamodel gives us also an opportunity to fix numerous problems with the metamodel related to use cases, raised by various authors (see eg. [18], [20]).

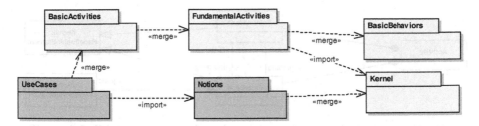

**Fig. 8.** Changes and additions to UML metamodel package dependencies

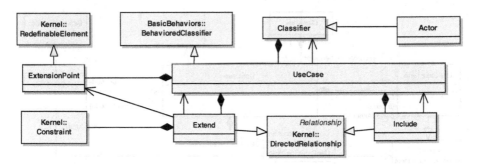

**Fig. 9.** Initial use case metamodel taken from the UML 2.0 specification

These considerations lead us to defining an extension to the UML metamodel. We shall redefine the UseCase package substituting the vague semantics of "behaviored classifiers" with more precise "activities". We also add a separate Notions package which defines specific classifiers that form the notion vocabulary. The two affected packages are illustrated on Figure 8. The concrete syntax of contained elements is based on the notation of use cases, activities (with textual SVO variant) and classes, as presented in this section. Semantics is defined by introducing appropriate new activity nodes, and by specifying transformation of these nodes into vocabulary notions and then - into more design-specific domain model. The abstract syntax and more detailed description of semantics is presented in the following sections.

## 3   Extending UML Activities and Use Cases for Scenarios

The initial UML metamodel for the UseCase package is presented (in a slightly simplified form) on Figure 9 (see [13], p. 642). UseCase metaclass is kind of BehavioredClassifier. UseCase is owned by a Classifier that has its behavior defined with this UseCase. UseCases can be related through Extend or Include DirectedRelationships. They can be also related to Actors. The Extend relationship can be attached to several ExtensionPoints defined within the UseCase.

This metamodel seems to cause several problems pointed out in [20]. The first problem is with UseCase being a specialization of BehavioredClassifier (a Classifier

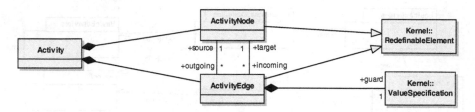

**Fig. 10.** Fragment of the activity metamodel taken from the UML 2.0 specification

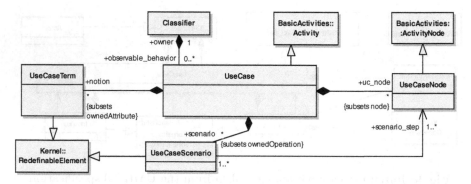

**Fig. 11.** Use case metamodel modified for scenarios, terms and activities

with attached Behavior - see description in [13], p. 469). It is very unclear how semantics of UseCase metaclass relates to semantics of BehavioredClassifier metaclass. Especially considering the fact that the Behavior metaclass is a Classifier itself (even more specificaly - a Class)! Another problem is with the semantics of Extend and Include relationships and ExtensionPoints. ExtensionPoints relate only to Extend relationships. It seems that Include relationships have no defined points of inclusion in the base UseCase. This asymmetry in treating two UseCase relationships seems not to be justified. Extend relationships can have several associated ExtensionPoints. This could be acceptable, however, the semantics of the Extend relationship ([13], p. 647) indicates that ExtensionPoints are actually points of interleaving (similar to GOTO and COMEFROM statements) which was highly criticized in [18] and [17].

Our proposition is that UseCase metaclass would specialize Activity from BasicActivities (see Figure 10 for a short extract from this UML package). It would then be composed of several UseCaseNodes that are kind of ActivityNode. Figure 11 shows, that UseCase, according to our proposition, is composed of several UseCaseScenarios and also contains UseCaseTerms (denoting subjects, verbs and objects in SVO sentences). UseCaseScenarios and UseCaseTerms inherit from RedefinableElement which should clarify the semantics of generalization relationship between UseCases.

Types of UseCaseNodes are presented on Figure 12. We have SentenceNodes (denoting SVO sentences) and ControlFlowNodes. ControlFlowNodes have an as-

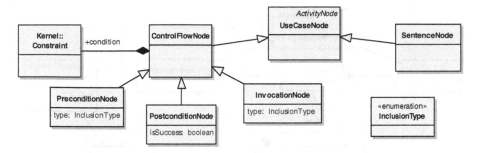

**Fig. 12.** Extended metamodel for ActivityNodes

sociated (optional) Constraint. PreconditionNodes and PostconditionNodes are the initial and final nodes of the activity. A constraint is set that PreconditonNodes can have only a single outgoing ActivityEdge. PostconditionNodes can have one or more incoming ActivityEdges only.

InvocationNode denotes the invocation of another UseCase instance from within the current UseCase instance. InvocationNodes are semantically related to PreconditionNodes. This relation is denoted by the node's type, which can be either request or insert. In the UseCase's activity there can be only a single request and a single insert PreconditionNode (or one of them). The request node can be connected to a SentenceNode that has no other incoming ActivityEdges. The insert node has to be connected to a SentenceNode that is a target of an ActivityEdge connected with SentenceNode being connected with a request node. This reflects the situation shown on Figure 4.

To complete the UseCase metamodel we define appropriate relationships as shown on figure 13. We introduce Usage and Participation relationships that connect a UseCase with external Classifiers (eg. Actors or Interfaces - see. Fig. 1). We also have a single Invocation relationship that can have several associated InvocationNodes that denote points of invocation within the UseCase's activity. This relationship substitutes the Include and Extend relationships from the current UML metamodel. Structure of a SentenceNode is presented on Figure 14.

## 4   Extending UML Kernel for Vocabulary

The structure of vocabularies is shown on Figures 15 and 16. The syntax of the vocabulary model is quite simple. A Vocabulary is kind of Package and contains several Notions that can be Nouns or Verbs. Every Notion has a textual description. Nouns can be of type: actor, object or system. This type determines the relation of a Noun to terms in SentenceNodes of the UseCase metamodel (see also Fig. 14). Nouns and Verbs can be related through NounAssociations and NounVerbAssociations. NounAssociations relate two Nouns. Such associations can have associated NounLinks. Every such link points to a position in the source Noun's description where the target Noun is referenced. Noun associations can be

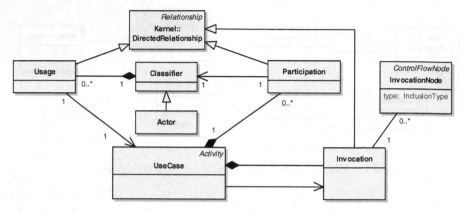

**Fig. 13.** Use case metamodel modified for relationships

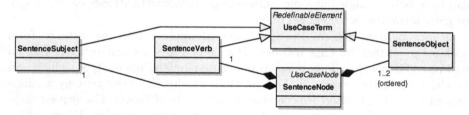

**Fig. 14.** Detailed structure of SentenceNodes

of type: regular or generalization. NounVerbAssociations relate Nouns with Verbs. Every Verb can be related to a maximum of two Nouns. One of these relationships can be of type feature, and another one of type compose verb. The semantics of these types of relationships was described in section 2.

Figure 17 shows transformation mappings between UseCaseTerms, Notions and other Classifier-based models. These mappings allow for automatic generation of class models directly from use case and vocabulary definitions. All SentenceVerbs are mapped to Verbs in the vocabulary. SentenceSubjects and SentenceObjects map into Nouns of appropriate type. NounVerbAssociations can be generated from SentenceNodes (see Fig. 14) through appropriate transformation rules. These rules determine how to relate nouns and verbs depending on the position of related UseCaseTerms in SentenceNodes. For example, when a sentence has two objects, the rule might say that the first object with the verb form a ¡¡compound verb¿¿ and together they form a ¡¡feature¿¿ of the second object. Such rules might be used to perform automatic transformations. NounAssociations are determined by hand by the model developer. This is done simply by adding appropriate NounLinks in the Noun descriptions (i.e. while using other noun's name when defining the current noun). Having determined NounVerbAssociations and NounAssociations, the transformation to a class model is quite straightforward. Every NounAssociation maps to a Generalization or Association

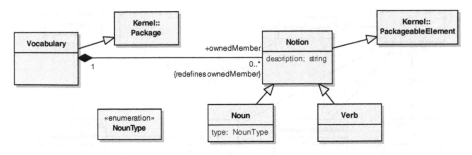

**Fig. 15.** General structure of the vocabulary

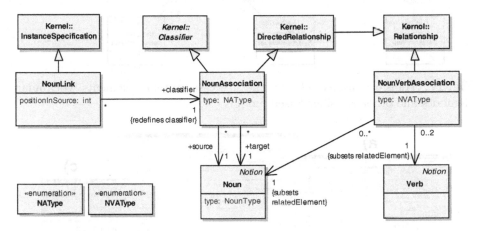

**Fig. 16.** Relationships between vocabulary elements

kind of Relationship. Nouns got mapped to Classifiers (Classes) or their Structural Features (Properties). This distinction has to be made by hand by the model developers before the transformation. Verbs alone and Verbs with Nouns having compose verb relationships translate into BehavioralFeatures (Operations). These operations are inserted into appropriate Classifiers.

## 5   Supporting the Software Lifecycle with a Scenario Construction Tool

The presented notation and metamodel with appropriately defined semantics can be the basis for creating a scenario construction tool. The requirements for such a tool would include adding scenarios and individual sentences, adding and using the vocabulary notions inside scenarios, and transforming scenarios with notions into class models. Experience from using a similar tool (see [12]) shows that developers are reluctant to use "point and click" method for writing scenarios. Instead, they strongly prefer traditional word processor style. Thus, the tool allows for typing directly all the subjects, verbs and objects in consecutive sen-

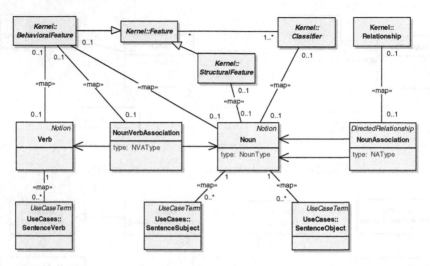

**Fig. 17.** Transformations between the use case sentence elements, vocabulary elements and other classifier-based models

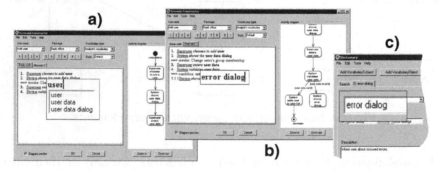

**Fig. 18.** Using the scenario tool for writing scenarios and constructing a vocabulary

tences. However, during typing, the tool checks for appropriate nouns and verbs from the vocabulary, offering instant verification (see Fig. 18a,b). If a noun or a verb is not present, the tool introduces the new word into the vocabulary (Fig. 18c). Words can be also introduced directly (outside of typing scenarios).

The scenario tool is closely integrated (as a plug-in) with a UML CASE tool[2], and uses its model repository. Scenarios can be inserted into appropriate use cases as activity diagrams. The vocabularies, according to the proposed metamodel are kept inside the repository as separate packages. Nouns, verbs and relationships between them are inserted into these packages as simple classes with associations. This notion model is the basis for automatic transformation into

---

[2] The base tool is Enterprise Architect from SparxSystems which offers very extensive and comprehensive programmer's interface.

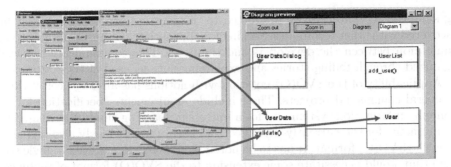

**Fig. 19.** Using the scenario tool to create domain class models

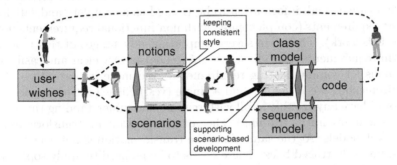

**Fig. 20.** Using the scenario tool in a simple iterative development process

a full class model with nouns transformed to classes or properties, and verbs transformed into operations (see Fig. 19). With such automatic transformations possible, we can support the development lifecycle as illustrated on Figure 20. User wishes can be transformed into a coherent repository of SVO scenarios with notions. This repository can be transformed into domain level class models, and then into design and code. This transformation might also involve dynamic models (transforming scenarios into interaction or activity models), although this is outside of scope of this paper. A coherent requirements repository unambiguously mapped onto design level models can significantly enhance the capability to react to changes in user's needs.

## 6    Conclusions

The described story writing tool is based on an extended UML metamodel in the area of use cases. It supports creation of semantically precise models already on the requirements level. Having precise semantics allows for creating requirements models that can be the basis for further transformation during software development. It might be argued that the proposed formalism constrains the requirements specifiers by enforcing specific format of their products. However, experience shows that this constrain leverages discovery and innovation. By writing simple SVO sentences we are forced to discover notions that could not be discovered with other techniques. Seeking for appropriate notions facilitates communication between the developers and the users. This communication is well organized through telling stories and explaining notions used in these stories.

Applicability of the SVO(O) notation with notions has already been verified in several commercial projects. These include requirements specification for an economic information system and for a university teaching support system. The requirements for the currently described tool itself were obviously also prepared using the SVO(O) format. It has to be noted that there was not even a single scenario that would necessitate some extension to the SVO(O) format of sentences (i.e. introduction of more complex grammar). It seems (although it would need some further investigation) that SVO(O) scenarios together with the vocabulary model capture enough information to be treated as a complete and satisfactory model of requirements (complemented with non-functional requirements not covered by this work). There are several important advantages of this model over free-form requirements. The clients see this model as very clear and easily accept it as means for communicating requirements (and more importantly - changes to requirements). We haven't found a single (yes!) client (out of couple of tens) that would have any trouble at all with reading and understanding this notation (even without any initial training). The notation is ready for transformation into design level models. At the same time, the transformation is not overly complex and can be easily traced back. There seems to be no need to apply sophisticated transformations based eg. on general natural language processing, like it would be needed for traditional requirements specifications.

With the use of the presented tool, the transformation from requirements into static domain model is automatic but not completely automatic. The designers still need to support the transformation with certain information that in not available in SVO stories, like navigability between classess, multiplicities, etc. However, even with the current level of automation, the transformation gives a noticeable effect of reduction of time from formulating the requirements (and most importantly - changes in requirements) to creating a solution (or changes to the solution). It has to be stressed that the current tool adds to traditional requirements tools two significant characteristics: coherence of the underlying metamodel and transformability into other models. With these characteristics, the tool seems to be able to resolve the problem of detailed specifications that are too heavy to be effectively used in development. Instead of a typical requirements tool we have a tool that allows for creating models that can be relatively easy transformed into analytical domain models and then into design and code. This means that writing detailed requirements becomes the first step in "real" (in contrast to "paper based") software development.

# References

[1]  Alexander, I., Maiden, N., eds.: Scenarios, Stories, Use Cases. John Wiley (2004)
[2]  Cockburn, A.: Writing Effective Use Cases. Addison-Wesley (2000)

[3] Cohn, M.: User Stories Applied. Addison-Wesley (2004)
[4] Gelperin, D.: Precise use cases. Technical report, LiveSpecs Software (2004)
[5] Constantine, L.L.: What do users want? Engineering usability into software. Windows Tech Journal (1995) revised in 2000, http://www.foruse.com/ articles/whatusers.htm.
[6] Hurlbut, R.R.: A survey of approaches for describing and formalizing use cases. Technical Report XPT-TR-97-03, Expertech Ltd. (1997)
[7] Śmiałek, M.: Accommodating informality with necessary precision in use case scenarios. Journal of Object Technology **4** (2005) – to be published.
[8] Graham, I.: Object-Oriented Methods Principles & Practice. Pearson Education (2001)
[9] McCoy, J.R.: Requirements use case tool (RUT). In: OOPSLA '03. (2003)
[10] Alexander, I.: Goal patterns generate scenarios. In: RESG Scenarios Day. (1999) http://easyweb.easynet.co.uk/ iany/consultancy/goalpatt/goalpatt.htm.
[11] Sutcliffe, A.G., Maiden, N.A.M., Minocha, S., Manuel, D.: Supporting scenario–based requirements engineering. IEEE Transactions on Software Engineering **24** (1998) 1072–1088
[12] Gryczon, P., Stańczuk, P.: Obiektowy system konstrukcji scenariuszy przypadków uzycia (Object-oriented use case scenario construction system). Master's thesis, Warsaw University of Technology (2002)
[13] Object Management Group: Unified Modeling Language: Superstructure, version 2.0, Revised Final Adopted Specification, ptc/04-10-02. (2004)
[14] Miller, J., Mukerji, J., eds.: MDA Guide Version 1.0.1, omg/03-06-01. Object Management Group (2003)
[15] van den Berg, K.G., Simons, A.J.H.: Control flow semantics of use cases in UML. Information and Software Technology **41** (1999) 651–659.
[16] Metz, P., O'Brien, J., Weber, W.: Specifying use case interaction: Types of alternative courses. Journal of Object Technology **2** (2003) 111–131
[17] Simons, A.J.H.: Use cases considered harmful. In: Proceedings of the 29th Conference on Technology of Object-Oriented Languages and Systems-TOOLS Europe'99, Nancy, France, IEEE Computer Society Press (1999) 194–203
[18] Metz, P., O'Brien, J., Weber, W.: Against use case interleaving. Lecture Notes on Computer Science **2185** (2001) 472–486
[19] Śmiałek, M.: Profile suite for model transformations on the computation independent level. Lecture Notes on Computer Science **3297** (2005) 269–272
[20] Genova, G., Llorens, J., Metz, P., Prieto-Diaz, R., Astudillo, H.: Open issues in industrial use case modeling. Lecture Notes in Computer Science **3297** (2005) 52–61

# Invited Presentation II:
# Experiences in Applying Model Based System Testing Generation

Marlon Vieira

Siemens Corporate Research
marlon.vieira@siemens.com

## Abstract

The goal of this presentation is to illustrate the benefits of using an automated, model-based approach for improving system test design and generation. Our approach, TDE/UML, automatically generates system tests from behavioral models of an application using the Unified Modeling Language (UML.). TDE/UML builds on and combines existing techniques for data coverage and graph coverage. We focus here on the results of applying TDE/UML in diverse Siemens projects: its cost benefits and its fault detection capabilities.

System testing, which ensures the functional compliance of an application with its requirements, is a well-defined process within Siemens. However, in many cases, it remains a manual process. Test designers typically derive their system input and expected output information from a variety of sources including textual use case specification and business process rules. They then create a set of test procedures comprising of individual test steps, which are executed manually by test executors against the system under test. Whenever an automated test environment is available, these test executors are also responsible for translating these textual test procedures into executable test scripts. To automate and formalize this process as much as possible, our research uses model based system test generation.

Our approach makes use of UML Use Case diagrams to describe the relationship among the diverse use cases implemented by the system and the actors who interact with the system through those use cases. UML activity diagrams are used to model the logic captured by a single use case and between use cases. The set of activity diagrams represents the overall behavior specified for the system and it is the basis for testing the different functionalities and business rules described in the use cases specification. Tests are automatically generated from those models following three phases. During the first phase, a test designer manually annotates the UML models based on SCR Test Specification Language (TSL), which implements the category-partition methodology. In the second phase, the test generation tool (TDE/UML) automatically creates a set of textual test procedures (test cases) or executable test scripts. In the third phase, a test executor runs these against the system under test using a commercial UI testing tool.

L. Briand and C. Williams (Eds.): MoDELS 2005, LNCS 3713, pp. 430–430, 2005.

# The Impact of UML 2.0 on Existing UML 1.4 Models

Julie A. Street, Robert G. Pettit IV

The Aerospace Corporation
15049 Conference Center Drive
Chantilly, Virginia 20151 (USA)
[julie.street, rob.pettit]@aero.org

**Abstract.** The Unified Modeling Language (UML) is the accepted standard for object-oriented modeling across the software design industry. Version 2.0 of the UML represents a major new revision to this standard and includes many changes to the current industry state of the practice (UML 1.4). These revisions include the removal or renaming of some existing features as well as the addition of several new capabilities. As tool vendors and software engineers begin to adopt UML 2.0, there is a potential to greatly impact legacy systems and practitioners employing UML 1.4. This report aims at providing an understanding of the changes made in UML 2.0 and their potential impacts, both positive and negative, to the UML 1.4 modeling community.

## 1. Overview

The Unified Modeling Language (UML) is the accepted standard for object-oriented modeling across the software design industry. Since its introduction there have been many positive reviews as well as criticisms of UML. In 2004, a major new revision to the UML standard was released to address the problems and limitations reported. UML version 2.0 consists of many changes and enhancements from the current industry state of the practice, version 1.4. During the revision of UML 2.0, it was decided to break the specification up into two complementary parts; the UML 2.0 Infrastructure and the UML 2.0 Superstructure. The infrastructure specification contains information on the architectural foundations for UML. The user level constructs are described in the superstructure specification. These two specifications combined create the complete specification for UML 2.0 [1].

This paper will specifically focus on the changes to the UML constructs in the UML 2.0 Superstructure. These changes include the removal or renaming of some existing features as well as the addition of several new capabilities. UML 2.0 has the potential to enhance UML 1.4 models. However, not all changes are backward compatible, which could potentially cause problems when transiting legacy designs. The changes made to the UML constructs for modeling the static structure and dynamic behavior will be examined along with their impacts when migrating legacy UML 1.4 models to the new UML 2.0 specification. Table 1 contains a summary of the additions, changes, and deletions in UML 2.0 and each will be addressed in further detail in the paper.

L. Briand and C. Williams (Eds.): MoDELS 2005, LNCS 3713, pp. 431–444, 2005.
© Springer-Verlag Berlin Heidelberg 2005

**Table 1.** Summary of UML 2.0 changes from UML 1.4

| Construct | Additions | Changes | Deletions |
|---|---|---|---|
| Use Case | ☐ None | ☐ None | ☐ None |
| Class | ☐ Redefinition | ☐ Interface notation<br>☐ Active class notation | ☐ None |
| Component | ☐ Ports | ☐ Component notation<br>☐ Connector defined<br>☐ Realization defined | ☐ None |
| Composite | ☐ New construct | ☐ N/A | ☐ N/A |
| State | ☐ Action Blocks<br>☐ State Lists<br>☐ Terminate Pseudostates<br>☐ Submachines<br>☐ Redefinition<br>☐ Protocol Conformance | ☐ Protocol state machine defined<br>☐ Multiple Entry/Exit Points | ☐ None |
| Sequence | ☐ Fragments<br>☐ Diagram Name | ☐ Structure Based on International Telecommunication Union Standard<br>☐ Arrow head notation | ☐ N/A |
| Communicatio n | ☐ Diagram Name | ☐ Name Change From Collaboration Diagram to Communication Diagram | ☐ Transient Links |
| Activity | ☐ Pre & Postconditions<br>☐ Data Stores<br>☐ Activity Groups<br>☐ Pins and Parameter Set<br>☐ Enhanced Partitioning<br>☐ Expansion & Interruptible Regions | ☐ Petri-Net like metamodel<br>☐ Petri-Net like semantics | ☐ State machine metamodel<br>☐ State machine semantics |
| Interaction Overview | ☐ New construct | ☐ N/A | ☐ N/A |
| Timing | ☐ New construct | ☐ N/A | ☐ N/A |

## 2. Structural Impacts

The static model is used to define what entities are participating in the system and the relationships between them. In UML 1.4, the static model is commonly captured using use case diagrams, class diagrams, and component diagrams.

Use case diagrams did not receive any changes in UML 2.0, therefore there will be no impact on existing use case diagrams. Class diagrams, which are used to help define the structure of the objects in the system, did undergo some modifications in UML

2.0. A new feature added is the concept of redefinition, which can be applied to behaviors, classifiers, operations, properties, state machines and templates. Redefinition is the ability to augment, constrain, or override an element within a classifier whose context changes in a specialization. In class diagrams, redefinition is intended to help specialize the properties of a child class when they are originally defined within the context of the parent class [2]. For example, a child class's method can be modified using the redefinition syntax of {redefines method-name}. UML 2.0 also made notational changes to the interfaces and active classes. The short hand notation for interfaces has changed slightly from lollipop to ball and socket notation [1, 4]. The active class notation has also changed slightly from a bold border to a regular border with double vertical lines [3]. To demonstrate the potential impact of the changes to legacy class diagrams, consider a portion of the static structure for a temperature control system modeled in UML 1.4 and UML 2.0 shown in Figure 1.

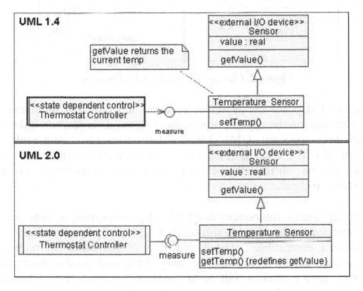

**Figure 1.** Difference in Class Diagram Notation

The most obvious differences are the notational changes to the interface 'measure' and active object 'Thermostat Controller'. This may cause some initial confusion to UML 1.4 practitioners, while they are still learning the new notation. Another change made to the diagram, was the use of redefinition in the 'Temperature Sensor'. Redefinition was used to rename the method 'getValue' to 'getTemp' to help clarify what the specialized sensor returns. Note that redefinition is not required, however legacy models may benefit from using redefinition to help create clearer and more precise visual representations. Redefinition can easily lead to errors and the specification is not clear how redefinition interacts with association specialization and subsetting [2]. Therefore redefinition should be used only when necessary and avoided in designs that use specialization associations and subsetting to prevent confusion. Overall the changes to class diagrams were relatively minor, however, making the required notational updates to legacy UML 1.4 models, without automated CASE tool support, could prove to be an onerous and error prone task.

Another UML construct used to define the static structure is the component diagram, which is used to model components with complex implementations. One of the most noticeable changes to component diagrams is the new notation for components. UML 1.4 used a rectangle with two protruding blocks to represent a component. This notation, however, did not scale well, therefore it changed in UML 2.0. Components now use the <<component>> stereotype, the protruding blocks were removed, and a small icon similar to the UML 1.4 component notation appears in the upper right hand corner [1]. These differences are shown in Figure 2. Ports are a new concept that can be used to add a named set of provided and required interfaces to a component. Ports are created and destroyed with the object that owns them and an object can have any number of ports.

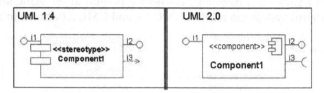

**Figure 2.** Component Notation Differences

A port's behavior depends on its set of required and provided interfaces [1]. To distinguish between interfaces and ports, a small rectangle is placed on the border of the port and the component. UML 2.0 also formalizes some commonly accepted practices used in UML 1.4. The semantics of realization now explicitly include components and the difference between delegation connectors and assembly connectors is now official.

When migrating legacy component diagrams, it is important to note that the old notation for component diagrams is still legal in UML 2.0, therefore making existing designs backward compatible. The formalizing of semantics for realization and connectors will not impact legacy models, only clarify and legalize their usage. The only impact on legacy designs will be if the decision is made to introduce ports, which has the potential to become a substantial amount of work.

UML 2.0 also introduced a new diagram for modeling static structure called the composite structure diagram. This diagram shows the internal structure of a structured object or collaboration. Composite structure diagrams can be used to replace class diagrams of complex objects, since composite structure can additionally include collaborations. Using composite structure diagrams, internal structure can be described with parts, connectors, and ports. It is important to note that structured classes are not made up of type associations, rather each part has its own context, usage and relationships to different parts. Parts are the pieces, not necessarily classes, that a structured class is composed of and each part has a name, type, multiplicity, and role. Connectors are used to define the communication path between roles. Unlike associations, connectors between elements are only valid in the context of the structured class that owns them [2]. To see how this new construct can be utilized consider an elevator station with four elevators. In UML 1.4 only relationships between the classes can be modeled in class diagrams, as shown in left portion Figure

3. It is unclear how many 'Elevators' each 'Elevator Controller' will control. In UML 2.0 this can be remedied by using roles and role relationships in a composite structure diagram as depicted on the right of Figure 3. The roles removed any ambiguity of the number of elevators each controller is to control.

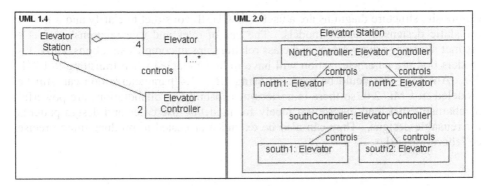

**Figure 3.** Class Diagram vs. Composite Structure Diagram

The models can also be augmented with collaborations to show how the communicating elements collectively accomplish a task or tasks. Collaborations are a new concept introduced in UML 2.0 and not the same as UML 1.4 collaboration diagrams. Collaborations are composed of roles and connectors that together provide a desired functionality [1]. Roles and connectors are only meaningful within the context of the collaboration that owns them and are not valid for the entire system. A collaboration may be used to describe an operation, a use case, a behavior, and even an implementation of a class[2]. Since collaborations define structure and do not use messages, they are different from interaction diagrams. The introduction of collaborations as part of a structured object has made parameterization of UML 1.0 no longer needed. Thus classifier role, association role, and association end role have been removed from UML 2.0 [2]. Collaborations have the potential to greatly enhance legacy design. To illustrate this, consider an inventory control system. In the use case 'Order Inventory' an inventory item must be ordered by a company from another company. This relationship and one to one mapping cannot be captured in the class diagram. Therefore, a collaboration diagram of this functionality can be used to define this relationship using roles as on the left side of Figure 4. The roles of

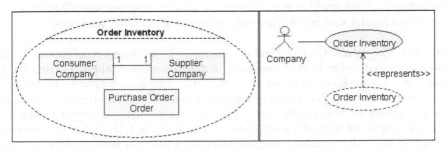

**Figure 4.** UML 2.0 Collaboration and Collaboration Use

'Consumer' and 'Supplier' are both played by the 'Company' class and there is one to one mapping between the roles. To show where the 'Order Inventory' collaboration is used, it can be attached back to its corresponding use case as depicted on the right of Figure 4.

Composite structure diagrams are a useful new UML construct to clarify and improve the static designs in legacy models. The use of roles and role relationships has a distinct advantage over classes and class relationships in complex situations. UML 1.4 models that use parameterization will have to be remodeled when transiting to UML 2.0. Anything that could be modeled using UML 1.4 parameterization can still be modeled in UML 2.0, so there is no loss of capability. Collaborations are powerful mechanisms that lend themselves nicely for modeling use cases and design patterns for reusable designs. They can also be extended or nested to produce more precise collaborations [2].

## 3. Behavioral Impacts

The dynamic behavior view of a model defines how the system will behave over time and in reaction to events. The dynamic behavior is commonly captured using the UML constructs for state machine diagrams, activity diagrams, and interaction diagrams.

State machine diagrams are used to define the internal behavior of the object in terms of its potential states and transition between states. Action blocks were introduced in UML 2.0 to enable a sequence of actions to be shown in a transition [1]. Action blocks can be used in conjunction with signals to help model complex transitions with more precision. UML 2.0 also modified the available pseudostates for modeling complex transitions. Multiple entry and exit points are now legal, which allows different places to enter or leave a state machine diagram [1]. Often state machines can suffer from scalability problems and can have similar states that appear in multiple diagrams. To help remedy this problem, UML 2.0 introduced state lists in which multiple states with the same transition to the same target can be modeled using only one state [1]. This shorthand notation can help simplify state machine diagrams and make them more scalable. Another feature added to help scalability are submachines. A submachine is a reference to another state machine diagram which appears as a regular state block with "state name : diagram referenced name".

UML 2.0 also enhanced state machine diagrams by allowing redefinition, a new feature discussed earlier in class diagrams. Redefinition can be applied to transitions, states, and submachine states of extended state machine diagrams in order to specialize them with respect to the extended diagram. When a transition is redefined, only its content or target state can change, its source state or trigger cannot [1]. Although it was not officially part of the specification, in UML 1.4 it was common practice to use a state machine diagram to create a protocol state machine diagram, which specifies the legal sequence of events. UML 2.0 formalized and included the concept of protocol state machine diagrams as part of the specification [2]. Protocol conformance is a new concept in UML 2.0 and relates to the idea of specialization. Protocol conformance exists between the general and specialized protocol state machine if every rule and constraint in the general case applies to the specialized case [1]. The UML specification is unclear how to denote protocol conformance, but it could be captured in a note or in the design document itself.

Since no existing features were removed from the state machine construct, there is complete backward compatibility to UML 1.4. Therefore there will be no issues when transitioning UML 1.4 state machine diagrams to UML 2.0. There is an opportunity to improve legacy diagrams by taking advantage of the new features available to improve clarity and precision. For example, consider a banking system with an ATM machine. There is a variety of different states the banking system can be in, which can result in a very large state machine diagram. The left side of Figure 5 shows some of the states involved in an ATM machine when a customer first begins to use the ATM machine. In UML 2.0, the details of processing a customer's input can be abstracted out into another diagram and referenced via a submachine state as shown on the right side of Figure 5. The three states involved in processing a customer input are abstracted into a separate state machine diagram called 'Processing Customer Input Diagram', which has three distinct exit points with unique names to show the three different possible exits from the abstracted state. Submachine references such as this can help alleviate the scalability of the large diagram without losing the necessary details.

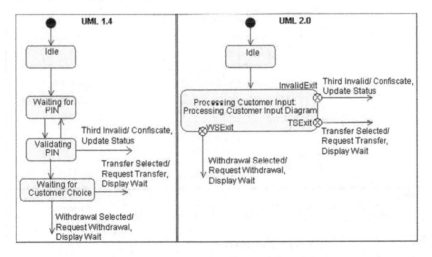

**Figure 5.** Submachine example

Interactions diagram are another means to model dynamic behavior. UML provides two contracts for this purpose, sequence diagrams and communication diagrams (formerly known as collaboration diagrams in UML 1.4). The sequence diagram received significant on improvements in UML 2.0. Sequence diagrams were modified to be aligned with the structure based on International Telecommunication Union (ITU) Standard Z.120 – MCS-2000 and most changes made stemmed from this. A new change to sequence diagrams is the notation of the arrow heads on messages. In UML 1.4 asynchronous messages were represent by half stick arrow heads, but in UML 2.0 they now are represented as full stick arrow heads. Synchronous message were formerly full stick arrow heads, but are now full filled arrow heads. Return messages have also changed slightly from having a solid line to a dashed line [1, 2]. The notational changes may sound small, however they have significant impact on UML 1.4 designs since this new notation is not backward compatible.

Sequence diagrams can quickly grow very large and become cumbersome as the number of objects involved grows. To help combat this problem, UML 2.0 offers the ability for one sequence diagram to reference another via fragments. A fragment is inserted into a diagram as a large rectangle spanning the time period it is active. In order to facilitate fragments, all sequence diagrams are required to have names, which appear in the top left hand corner and all interaction diagrams are marked with "sd" next to their name[1]. Fragments can also be used to add complex control structures such as loops, alternative paths, and concurrent paths. The top left hand of the fragment will denote which type it is and additional information is captured inside the rectangle [1]. For example, if it is a loop control structure fragment, the loop conditional and body are captured inside the rectangle.

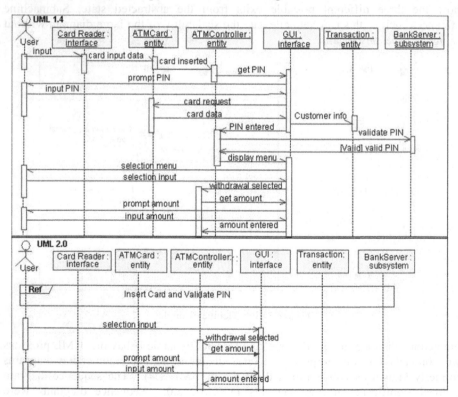

**Figure 6.** Sequence Diagram Comparison

To demonstrate the impact of the changes to sequence diagrams, consider the banking system again. An ATM user may choose to transfer, withdraw, or deposit money as their initial transaction. The steps to process their card must be completed in all cases. In UML 1.4, the sequence of messages involved in processing their card would have to appear in the three separate diagrams. In UML 2.0, this could be modeled more efficiently using a reference fragment, this comparison is shown in Figure 6. Notice that in UML 2.0 using the reference fragment to another sequence diagram called 'Insert Card and Validate PIN' significantly reduces the overall size and complexity of the diagram. In addition to reducing size, reference fragments can also help eliminate redundancy, promote reuse, and consequently ensure consistency among diagrams. Changes made to the 'Insert Card and Validate PIN' will only need to be made in one sequence diagram rather than in every diagram that uses that the sequence. The sequence diagram for 'Insert Card and Validate PIN' was also enhanced in UML 2.0 to include an alternate control fragment to model the various responses possible when validating a PIN number, shown in Figure 7. Notice the fragment is marked with the key word "alt" and the different alternatives are separated by a dashed line.

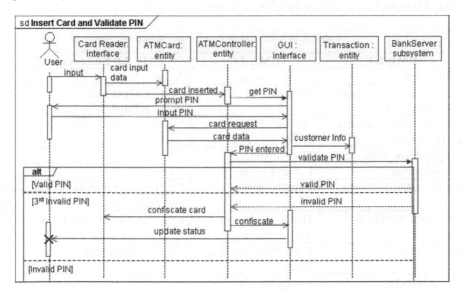

**Figure 7.** Insert Card and Validate PIN Sequence Diagram in UML 2.0

While using fragments has the potential to greatly enhance designs as outlined above, they are optional. However, legacy UML 1.4 diagrams must add diagram names and convert all their arrow heads to the new UML 2.0 semantics. The process of ensuring that every message arrow head is properly changed is critical to ensuring the model's fidelity. Synchronous messages that are not properly updated will be presumed to be asynchronous messages in UML 2.0, which can result in potentially serious design flaws. Without automated CASE tool support, the task of correcting the arrow heads will be tedious and must be done with great diligence.

Communication diagrams focus on modeling the communication between objects across multiple scenarios. One of the most noticeable changes to collaboration diagrams is the name change to communications diagrams. Besides the name change, communication diagrams did not receive many significant changes. The ability to create transient links was removed and the same diagram naming notation used for sequence diagrams was added in UML 2.0 [3, 1]. Communication diagrams did not receive any of the same new structuring mechanisms as sequence diagrams [1]. This is unfortunate because it will make sequence diagrams a more appealing choice for interaction diagrams, so the use of communication diagrams may start to diminish. Since no major new features were added, updating existing communication diagrams to UML 2.0 should be a simple process.

Activity diagrams are a construct to help model flow of control among the activities in a workflow. In UML 1.4 activity diagrams were viewed as a special type of state machine and the flow of control was limited. In UML 2.0 there was an effort to break this mentality, so a significant number of changes were made including use of new metamodel with semantics similar to that of Petri nets. Table 2 shows which new UML 2.0 metaclasses replace the UML 1.4 metaclasses [1].

**Table 2.** Activity Diagram Change Summary

| UML 1.4 | UML 2.0 | UML 2.0 Enhancements |
|---|---|---|
| State Vertex | Activity Node | None |
| Action State, Call State and Subactivity | Actions | Add local pre and postconditions |
| Transition and Control & Data Links | Activity Edge | - |
| Object Flow State | Object Node | - |
| Pseudostates | Control Node | - |
| Final State | Final Nodes | Final nodes for individual flows and diagrams |
| Decision and Merge | Decision Node and Merge Node | Consolidation allowed |
| Fork and Join | Fork Node and Join Node | Consolidation allowed |
| Jump Handler | Exception Handler | - |
| Partitions | Partitions | Multidimensional & hierarchal |

Additionally, activity diagrams were enhanced with several new features to enhance control flow modeling. Data stores were introduced to show persistent data and activity groups are a new mechanism that allows modelers to group nodes and edges. To explicitly show data flows, pin and parameter sets were introduce. Pins represent connection points where input or output data and are modeled as rectangles attached to an activity node with their name. Parameter sets provide the modeler with the ability to group pins to represent various combinations of data flow [1]. Pins and parameter sets are useful for providing a quick visual differentiation of which activities require or produce data. To improve the ability of activity diagrams to model nested regions, expansion region were introduced. They provide the modeler the ability to select a collection of elements that will execute multiple times corresponding to type of region. UML 2.0 introduced the concept of interruptible regions to increase the flexibility and control of modeling interrupts. Interruptible regions define the activity nodes and edges that will terminate if an interrupt occurs and will show where control is reinitiated to handle the interrupt.

Even though the metaclasses and semantics changed, the notation remained the same. The new metaclasses improve the ability to handle multiple flows and helps establish activity diagrams as the construct for modeling control flow. To see how the changes will affect legacy UML 1.4 models, consider an activity diagram for the banking system with ATM. Figure 8 demonstrates the impacts on an activity diagram where the user is entering their card and selecting to view transactions made on their account. Although the notation looks similar it is important to note that meaning is quite different. In UML 2.0 the initial state creates a token and passes it via the activity edge. The activities consume tokens when they are active and pass them back along the activity edge when they are done. A subtle difference in the UML 2.0 model is the combined merge and join nodes. Notice in UML 1.4 two separate nodes are used, which can clutter the model as the diagram grows. UML 2.0 simplifies this structure to use only one node, which provide a more visually clear model. The old notation is still compatible in UML 2.0, but diagrams can be greatly clarified by combining nodes. Another subtle difference in the two diagrams is the use of pins on the 'Get Transactions' and 'Display Default Transactions' activities. The output and input pins are used to clearly show that data is traversing the edge with the token. Pins are not required; however they provide a quick visual distinction between transitions with data and transitions without. Partitioning is another common practice in activity diagrams. In the UML 1.4 example in Figure 8 swim lane partitioning is used to group activities by location. Often times swim lane partitioning is not sufficient, so UML 2.0 introduced multilevel and hierarchal partitioning. The UML 2.0 example in Figure 8 uses hierarchical partitioning to group activities by location and within each location activities are further grouped by the entities performing the activities. Figure 8 demonstrates just some of the many enhancements available in UML 2.0. Although the notation in activity diagrams is similar, all diagrams should be reviewed to ensure the flow is unaffected. UML 2.0 activity diagrams provide a lot more flexibility with their enhancements so legacy diagrams can greatly benefit from taking advantage of the new features.

To enhance UML's ability to model dynamic behavior, interaction diagrams were introduced to provide a mix of sequence diagrams and control flow. Interaction diagrams allow the modeler to model sequence diagram fragments linked using control nodes found in activity diagrams. Although they are officially interaction diagrams and should be maked with "sd" in their diagram name, they are tagged with "intover" [1]. Interaction overview diagrams are an alternative way to show flow of control and interaction within a system. Since they are a new UML construct, 1.4 practitioners are not required to use them and activity diagrams are probably a better construct than interaction overview diagrams for representing control flows.

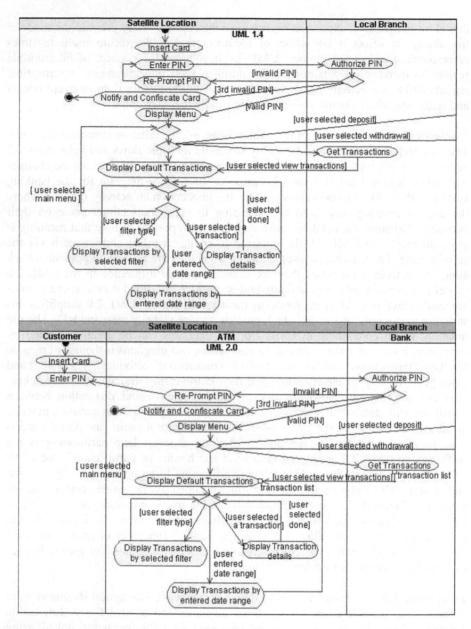

**Figure 8.** Activity Diagram Comparison

Timing diagrams are a new type of interaction diagram introduced in UML 2.0. They are intended to show changes in state of an object over time. They are a special type of sequence diagram that help modelers analyze timing. Timing diagram have the same diagram name notation as sequence diagrams; however the objects involved are modeled as horizontal rows with their name. To see the potential use of timing diagrams, consider a temperature control system that receives temperature data every five seconds as shown in Figure 9. The three participants are listed along the right with their potential states and the ticks along the bottom of the diagram to represent time, which runs concurrently through all blocks [1]. The lifeline for each participant moves vertically up and down to shown a change in state. In Figure 9 it can be seen that every five seconds the 'Temperature Sensor' moves to the sending state to pass a message to the 'Thermostat Controller', which is indicated by the message arrow 'Temp'. Alternatively states can also be more compactly shown on the lifeline itself, as done for the 'Heater' [1].

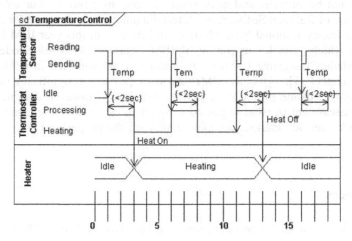

**Figure 9.** Timing Diagram for Temp Control System

Time diagrams also allow time or duration constraints be added, which can be useful for real-time modeling [2]. In the example, a duration constraint is placed on the processing time for the 'Thermostat Controller', which states that processing must be competed in less than two seconds. Timing diagrams are a relatively simple concept, but have the potential to be a powerful construct when modeling real time and embedded systems. They can provide a different view of the system, that sequence diagrams alone cannot do.


# 4. Conclusions

UML 2.0 received many changes and enhancements from the current industry state of the practice, version 1.4. Legacy UML 1.4 models could be greatly improved by taking advantage of the numerous enhancements, such as redefinition and fragments. UML 2.0 also includes several new diagrams that practitioners can take advantage of. It is unclear how useful or well liked these new modeling constructs will become, but that should not dissuade practitioners for trying them. However, since some changes in UML 2.0 are not backward compatible with UML 1.4, they will have direct impact when converting legacy UML 1.4 models. Before the decision is made to convert legacy models to UML 2.0, practitioners should consider the amount of time and effort required to change the model versus what is truly gained. One factor that will influence time and effort is the learning curve associated with understanding and mastering UML 2.0. Extra time and training classes should be allotted to aid in the smooth transition to UML 2.0.    Another equally important factor involved in converting legacy models is vendor tool support. Practitioners should investigate the amount of support for UML 2.0 that their current vendor provides. Special attention needs to be paid to not only support of the UML 2.0 notation, but also the tool's ability to convert legacy diagrams. Without automated tool support, the process of updating all the required notational changes, such as the arrow heads in sequence diagrams, could be onerous and error prone if done by hand.    For example the original release of Rational Software Architect did not provide a feature for importing and updating legacy Rational Rose Models. In February of this year IBM released a new feature which "enables migration of IBM® Rational® Rose® models to the Unified Modeling Language (UML) 2.0 model format supported in IBM Rational Software Architect"[7].    Overall, UML 2.0 does provide a significant number of opportunities to enhance and improve UML 1.4 designs. However, designers should conduct an assessment of what is gained versus the cost of updating legacy models. All trademarks, service marks, and trade names are the property of their respective owners.

# 5. References

1. OMG. Unified Modeling Language Superstructure Specification, Version 2.0, August 2003.

2. J. Rumbaugh, I. Jacobson, and G. Booch.  *The Unified Modeling Language Reference Manual, Second Edition.* Boston, MA:  Addison-Wesley, 2005.

3. M. Fowler.  *UML Distilled Third Edition: A Brief Guide to the Standard Object Modeling Language.* Boston, MA:  Addison-Wesley, 2004.

4. OMG. Unified Modeling Language Specification, Version 1.4, September 2001.

5. B. Selic.  *Tutorial 3: An Overview of UML 2.0.*  UML 2004 Conference.  Lisbon, Portugal, October 2004.

6. B. Selic.  *Modeling Real-Time System Architectures with UML 2.0.* 2nd Estonian Summer School on Computer and Systems Science (ESSCaSS'03).  Taagepera Castle, August 2003 <http://www.cs.ioc.ee/yik/schools/sum2003/lecturenotes/selic3.pdf>

7. "Rational Rose Model Import Feature for Rational Software Architect V6.0" IBM Downloads and Support, 8 February 2005.  <http://www-1.ibm.com/support/docview.wss?rs=2044&context=SSCM72&dc=D426&uid=swg24008877&loc=en_US&cs=utf-8&lang=en>

# Towards UML 2 Extensions for Compact Modeling of Regular Complex Topologies

Arnaud Cuccuru, Jean-Luc Dekeyser, Philippe Marquet, and Pierre Boulet

Laboratoire d'Informatique Fondamentale de Lille
Université des sciences et technologies de Lille
France

**Abstract.** The MARTE RFP (Modeling and Analysis of Real-Time and Embedded systems) was issued by the OMG in February 2005. This request for proposals solicits submissions for a UML profile that adds capabilities for modeling Real Time and Embedded Systems (RTES), and for analyzing schedulability and performance properties of UML specifications. One of the particular request of this RFP concerns the definition of common high-level modeling constructs for factorizing repetitive structures, for software, hardware and allocation modeling of RTES. We propose an answer to this particular requirement, based on the introduction of multi-dimensional multiplicities and mechanisms for the description of regular connection patterns between model elements. This proposition is domain independent. We illustrate the use of these mechanisms in an intensive computation embedded system co-design methodology. We focus on what these factorization mechanisms can bring for each of the aspects of the co-design: application, hardware architecture, and allocation.

## 1 Introduction

The MARTE RFP [1] (Modeling and Analysis of Real-Time and Embedded systems) has been recently voted by OMG. This request for proposals solicits submissions for a UML profile that adds capabilities for modeling real time and embedded systems, and for analyzing schedulability and performance properties of UML specifications. MARTE is not the OMG's first attempt to define a UML standard for the embedded systems community. The SPT profile (Scheduling, Performance and Time analysis) has been adopted and in use for 2 years. However, other OMG standards having significant implications for the SPT profile (such as UML 2 [2,3,4,5] and QoS [6])) have been adopted during that time. Moreover, the use of the profile has led to a significant number of suggestions for improvement and consolidation, that are now part of the MARTE requirements.

Working in the field of intensive computation embedded systems, some requirements expressed in the MARTE RFP are of primary concerns for us. Application domains such as signal processing, image processing or mobile devices usually require intensive data computation to be performed, possibly in parallel, with the help of several computation units. For this kind of applications,

L. Briand and C. Williams (Eds.): MoDELS 2005, LNCS 3713, pp. 445–459, 2005.
© Springer-Verlag Berlin Heidelberg 2005

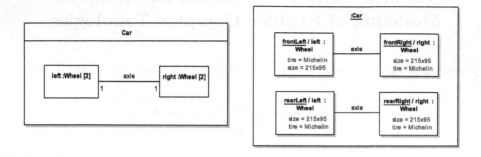

**Fig. 1.** Composite structure definition and instance examples

the RFP requires common high-level modeling constructs for factorizing repetitive structures for both hardware (available parallelism) and software (potential parallelism) and their allocation (temporal and spatial mapping of the software onto the hardware architecture). This paper addresses this particular requirement. Several OMG profiles (already adopted [7] or still under standardization process [8,9]) are more or less oriented toward the embedded systems domain. However, none of them proposes particular modeling constructs for factorizing repetitive structures. UML 2 proposes some mechanisms, though.

We show in this paper that these mechanisms are not suited to the needs expressed in the MARTE RFP, and that extensions are clearly required. We believe that the extensions we propose could be useful in other contexts than the modeling of embedded systems. That's why we introduce them independently of any domain consideration. Finally, we illustrate how we have experimented the use of these extensions in the context of an embedded systems co-design framework: Gaspard. Particularly, we will show that the same mechanisms are used for a compact modeling of the software, hardware and software/hardware allocation parts of the co-design methodology.

## 2   UML 2 Mechanisms for Compact Structural Modeling

Early versions of UML (1.x) already included such mechanisms enabling to express in a compact way the structure of a system, and the relations between entities that compose it. Relationships (associations, compositions and aggregations) can be specified between entities that exist at design-time (such as classes), and define the roles that will be played by instances of these entities at run-time (such as objects) in the context of these relations. Via a multiplicity mechanism, it also enables to specify in a compact way the potential number of occurrences concerned by these relations at run-time.

UML 2 goes further, and enables to refine the description of these relations in the context of composite structures. Composite structures refer to a composition of interconnected elements, representing potential run-time instances collaborating over communication links to achieve some common objectives. In this kind of structures, elements are actually instantiated within the structure of a containing classifier. The number of potential occurrences of these elements and the number of communication links can also be specified with multiplicities (Fig.1).

## 2.1 Multiplicity UML 2 Metamodel Subset

According to UML 2 infrastructure, a multiplicity is a definition of an inclusive interval of non-negative integers beginning with a lower bound and ending with a (possibly infinite) upper bound. It specifies the range of allowable cardinalities that a set may assume. In the kernel package of UML 2 metamodel (Fig.2), the abstract concept of *MultiplicityElement* is introduced to embed this information.

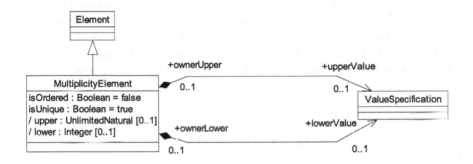

**Fig. 2.** Multiplicity diagram (from the UML 2 superstructure)

## 2.2 Limitations

However, this compact way of modeling carries very few (or no) information concerning topologies of links. In the context of composite structures, this fact can bring ambiguities in the models. Basically, two kinds of connection patterns can be considered as deterministic: The "array connector pattern" (Fig.1), or "one to one pattern", and the star connector pattern (Fig.3), or "one to all pattern". In other words, designers can have a clear idea of the topologies they are modeling only in the cases where the multiplicities of ends are equal to 1 and the different roles have the same multiplicity (array connector pattern) or when they match the multiplicities of the roles they are attached to (star connector pattern).

The general rule applied is the following: "Links will be created for each instance playing the connected roles according to their ordering until the minimum connector end multiplicity is reached for each end of the connectors". In

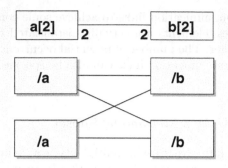

**Fig. 3.** Star connector pattern in a composite structure

the case illustrated in Fig.4, connectors are specified between 3 potential instances of "a" and 2 potential instances of "b". Each "a" is connected to at least
1 "b", and each "b" is connected to at least 2 "a". Applying the general rule
for links creation[1], we obtain two different topologies whether we start drawing
links from "a" instances or "b" instances. The number appearing on each link
shows the order in which links are created. Note that the two interpretations are
valid.

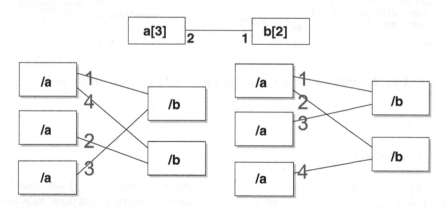

**Fig. 4.** Ambiguous specification of a composite structure

   If we also take into account ports (another essential kind of structural feature
appearing in composite structures) and their associated multiplicities, the problem is even more ambiguous. Moreover, we have shown that these mechanisms
do not exhibit any topological information. The topologies modeled are a consequence of a building process rather than an identified property of the models.

---

[1] if we have correctly understood the ambiguous sentence that defines it...

If a designer wants to specify a particular topology, this information should be easily extracted from the model.

# 3  Extensions for Compact Structural Modeling

From the observations done in section 2.2, we propose powerful extensions inspired by the Array Oriented Language [10] that delete ambiguity problems and increase expression power of UML 2 structural modeling mechanisms. The extensions we propose enable to specify at design time all the links that will exist at run time in a deterministic way. The basic idea is to identify the relations between all the potential link ends concerned by each potential link. These extensions are used for the modeling of complex topologies, and concern basically multiplicities, connectors and dependencies, in the context of composite structures. An extension at the level of structured classifiers is also introduced to simplify the use and understanding of our repetition mechanisms. Even though the final architecture of the MARTE profile is not yet defined, we suppose that it will introduce a package containing common mechanisms for RTES modeling, such as the GRM (General Resource Modeling) package of the SPT profile. The extensions presented in the next sections are supposed to be defined in this package, and to be shared by the other parts of the profile[2].

## 3.1  Multi-dimensional Multiplicities

In section 2.1, we have defined the concept of multiplicity as an inclusive interval of non-negative integers beginning with a lower bound and ending with an upper bound. In Fig.2, we see that the *MultiplicityElement* metaclass carries an *IsOrdered* attribute which specifies whether the "collection" of elements is ordered or not. In the case where it is ordered, this "collection" can be seen as a mono-dimensional array, where elements are implicitly indexed.

The first extension we propose for topology modeling is to take into account multi-dimensional arrays for the description of "collections". Multiplicities UML 2 metamodel subset is extended with the introduction of the *MultiDimensionalMultiplicityElement* concept (Fig.5). Lower and upper bound attributes are defined by *Vectors* instead of *Integers*[3]. In other words, the *MultiplicityElement* is seen as a particular case of the *MultiDimensionalMultiplicityElement* concept: lower and upper bounds attributes contain only one integer value. In Fig.6, we illustrate the use of multi-dimensional multiplicities to specify a cube topology (2×2×2). Each potential instance of "a" implicitly owns an index that identifies its position in the multi-dimensional array described by "a"'s multiplicity.

---

[2] such as Analysis

[3] The *Vector* datatype is an ordered set of integer values. Here, each element of the *Vector* gives the size of the corresponding dimension of the multi-dimensional array.

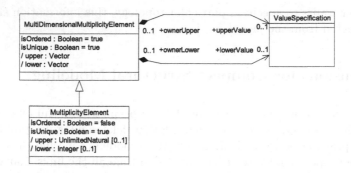

**Fig. 5.** Extended Multiplicity UML 2 metamodel subset for multi-dimensional aspects

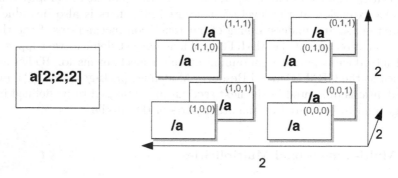

**Fig. 6.** Multi-dimensional multiplicities for the specification of a cube topology

## 3.2    Extended Relationships for Multi-dimensional Multiplicities

In order to handle modeling of links topologies, we introduce the abstract concept of *LinkTopology*. The *LinkTopology* is an optional information set that can be associated to a relationship between potential instances. It takes into account the multi-dimensional aspects introduced in the previous section. Two use cases are identified: links between several potential instances playing the same role, or playing different roles. These two use cases lead respectively to two refinements of *LinkTopology*: *InterRepetitionLinkTopology* and *RepetitiveLinkTopology*. Fig.7 is a simplified diagram[4] summarizing the extensions introduced.

**InterRepetitionLinkTopology.** The systems concerned are composed of a repetition of a single element, such as in a grid or a cube topology. Each po-

---

[4] Only *Connectors* and *Dependencies* are concerned by the *LinkTopology* extensions. In the context of a *Connector*, the *Elements* represent the *ConnectorEnds* associated to the *Connector*. In the context of a *Dependency*, the *Elements* represent the source and target ends of the *Dependency*.

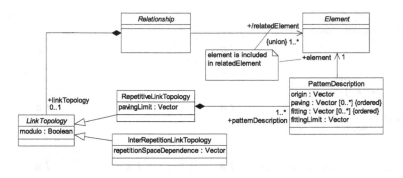

**Fig. 7.** Simplified diagram of the extensions for link topology description

tential instance of this element is connected to other potential instances of the same element, in a regular way. For example, in the case of a cyclic grid, each element instance is connected to neighbors located at north, south, east, and west. The first extension we propose via the *InterRepetitionLinkTopology* enables to specify the relative position of the "neighbors" of each potential instance of an element that carries a multi-dimensional multiplicity. Each potential instance is implicitly associated to one point of the multi-dimensional array described by the multi-dimensional multiplicity of the element. The *repetitionSpaceDependance* attribute is a translation vector on the space of the multi-dimensional array that identifies the position of a given neighbor. The *modulo* attribute (inherited from *LinkTopology*) indicates if the translation is applied modulo the size of the multi-dimensional array. If it is not the case, the translation is not applied on the borders of the array, and the corresponding link will not be created. In Fig.8, we illustrate the use of this mechanism for the modeling a 2d cyclic grid topology. Each connection is supposed to be bi-directional[5].

**RepetitiveLinkTopology.** Complex topologies have to be modeled between different potential instances, playing different roles. Each repeated element typing each potential instance owns a multi-dimensional multiplicity. Each point of the multi-dimensional arrays identified by the multi-dimensional multiplicities corresponds to a potential link end. In the case where the repeated element owns ports and a connection is expressed on one of these ports, the ports are considered as the link ends and the multi-dimensional array is based both on the multiplicity of the repeated element and the multiplicity of the port. The mechanism we introduce via the *RepetitiveLinkTopology* enables to specify in a compact way all the correspondences that exist between the ends contained into two multi-dimensional arrays, and so all the links that will exist at run-time. Basically, the idea consists in identifying regular patterns inside of each of the

---

[5] That's why two connectors only are used to specify the relative position of the four neighbors.

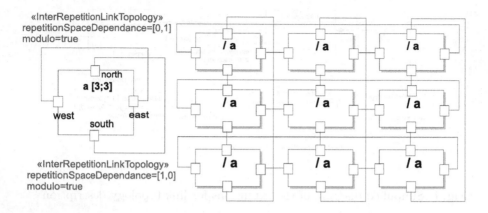

**Fig. 8.** A 3×3 cyclic grid topology modeled with *InterRepetitionLinkTopologies*

arrays, and to relate the points (and so the link ends) contained in these patterns. In the general case, a *PatternDescription* is associated to each of the relationships ends[6] to identity the link ends belonging to a pattern. The *paving* attribute is a set of vectors that enable to identify the origin of each pattern inside of the array corresponding to a relationship end. The number of patterns contained inside of the array is determined by the *pavingLimit* attribute[7]. Identifying the origin of each pattern can be seen as an iterative process, where the iteration limits are given by the *pavingLimit* vector. Each pattern origin is computed by multiplying each iteration index by each paving vector, adding the related *origin* vector. From each of the identified origins, the points belonging to the patterns are identified with the *fitting* vectors. The *fittingLimit* attribute determines the number of points that belong to the patterns, or in other words, the shape and size of the patterns. Each point belonging to a pattern is computed by multiplying the *fitting* vectors by each index of the iteration space defined by the *fittingLimit* attribute, adding the origin of the current pattern.

For a given repetition index, $i, 0 \leq i < pavingLimit$, the pattern is composed of the points indexed by the following set

$$\{ origin + paving.i + fitting.j \mid 0 \leq j < fittingLimit \} \tag{1}$$

if the *modulo* attribute is false and by

$$\{ origin + paving.i + fitting.j \mod shape \mid 0 \leq j < fittingLimit \} \tag{2}$$

if *modulo* is true. In that case, *shape* is the shape of the multidimensional array the patterns belong to. The points of the left $i$ pattern are linked to those of the right $i$ pattern.

---

[6] A particular case is presented in section 3.3.

[7] The number of patterns is the same for all the arrays concerned by the relationship.

In Fig.9, we illustrate the use of this mechanism with the definition of a "perfect shuffle connection pattern"[8].

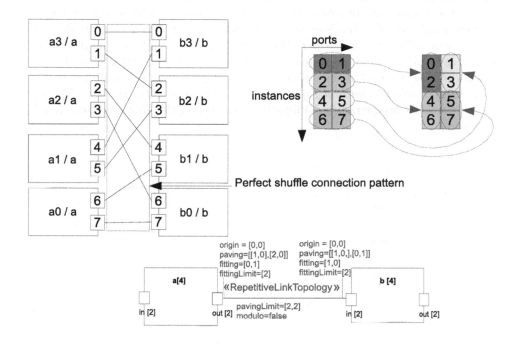

**Fig. 9.** Perfect shuffle modeling via a *RepetitiveLinkTopology*

## 3.3   Repetitive Structured Classifiers

To simplify the use of the *RepetitiveLinkTopology*, we introduce the concept of *RepetitiveStructuredClassifier*. It contains a single element with a multi-dimensional multiplicity. This element is connected to ports with multi-dimensional multiplicities on the boundary of the *RepetitiveStructuredClassifier* that contains it[9].

In the previous section, we have introduced the concept of repetition (or iteration) space, via the *pavingLimit* and *fittingLimit* attributes of *RepetitiveLinkTopology* and *PatternDescription*. The *RepetitiveStructuredClassifier* represents a repetition space. The shape and size of the repetition space is determined by the multi-dimensional multiplicity of the element it contains. In other words,

---

[8] This kind of topology is found in multistage networks such as the Omega interconnection network [11].
[9] A *RepetitiveStrucuturedClassifier* is necessarily strongly encapsulated and requires the usage of ports.

each potential instance of the repeated element is implicitly associated to one point of the repetition space. Links concern ports on the boundary of the classifier and ports of each potential instance of the repeated element.

In the context of *RepetitiveStructuredClassifiers*, *RepetitiveLinkTopologies* can own only one *PatternDescription*, related to the port on the boundary of the *RepetitiveStructuredClassifier*. The *pavingLimit* is given by the multi-dimensional multiplicity of the repeated element and the *fittingLimit* is given by the multi-dimensional multiplicity of the concerned port on the repeated element. Note that *InterRepetitionLinkTopologies* can still be used in the context of *RepetitiveStructuredClassifiers*. Fig.10 illustrates the use of the *RepetitiveStructured-Classifier*.

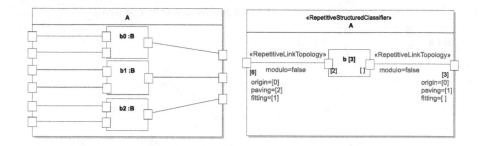

**Fig. 10.** *RepetitiveStructuredClassifier* example

# 4    Using Extensions for Embedded System Co-design

The extensions presented in the previous sections have been experimented in the context of a prototype framework: Gaspard [12,13] (Graphical Array Specification for PARallel and Distributed computing). Gaspard is an MDA (Model Driven Architecture) oriented environment for computation intensive embedded systems co-design. It follows a "Y" approach, and enables automatic model to model transformations and code generations, for various abstraction levels, from high level UML models, through the use of the MDA transformation tool ModTransf [14].

At the top level of the "Y", software, hardware architecture and allocation abstract syntaxes are described by 3 different metamodels. However, these metamodels share common modeling constructs, such as a component oriented approach, or especially the mechanism for compact modeling we have introduced in this paper. After a brief presentation of the Gaspard metamodels and their implementation in UML profiles, this section illustrates the use of this common mechanism for the three parts of the co-design, and emphasizes on what it can bring for each of these aspects.

## 4.1    Gaspard Metamodels and Profiles

Software and hardware architecture metamodels share a common component
oriented approach[10] (Fig.11). Components are described by a composition of
other component potential instances (parts), via connections between their ports.
Ports enable to encapsulate the structure and the behavior of a component in
order to make it independent of its environment, and increase its reusability.
Interfaces are associated to ports, and a connection can be expressed between
two ports only if their interfaces are compatible. The *ElementaryComponent* is
a particular kind of component that does not own any structural or behavioral
description. Its implementation is supposed to be available in the language that
will be targeted by the Gaspard transformations.

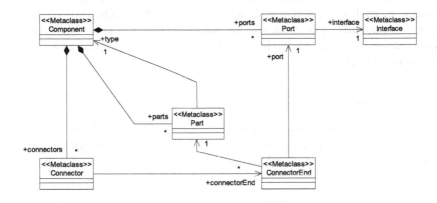

**Fig. 11.** Common component metamodel

In the software metamodel, the *Component* concept is refined into the *Ap-
pComponent* concept. Application components can be interpreted as functions,
that performs some computations on data coming from their environment trough
their provided ports[11] and sending the results to their environment trough their
required ports[12]. Computations are delegated to the parts of the components,
or actually performed by the elementary components. Interfaces basically define
the data types that can be handled by an application component.

In the hardware architecture metamodel, the *Component* concept is refined
into the *HwComponent* concept. Hardware components are abstractions of physical hardware resources. Elementary components are refined in three categories,
according to their function. *HwPassiveComponent*, *HwActiveComponent* and
*HwInterconnectComponent* respectively represent resources able to store data

---

[10] The concepts introduced are near to the concepts of UML 2 composite structures.

[11] e.g ports with provided interfaces

[12] e.g. ports with required interfaces

(all kind of memories), perform some data transfers with or without data transformation (CPU, DMA...) and interconnect other hardware resources[13]. Interfaces associated to ports define a communication protocol between resources.

The allocation metamodel introduces concepts enabling to express the spatial mapping of a software onto a hardware architecture[14]. Some special dependencies can be expressed between ports of software parts and hardware architecture passive parts to model a mapping of the data (*DataAllocation*) and between software parts and hardware architecture active parts to express a mapping of computations (*TaskAllocation*).

The concrete syntax of these metamodels are implemented in UML profiles, with nearly a "one to one" equivalence between the concepts of the metamodels and the stereotypes of the profiles. The *Component* concepts are implemented via stereotyped *StructuredClasses*. Components structures are defined via internal structure diagrams. Application modeling follows a simple design pattern: One interface for each port, and one signal for each interface. The type of the signal represents the data type that can be handled by an application component. Dependencies from the allocation metamodel are implemented in stereotyped UML dependencies.

### 4.2   Case Study

In this section, we illustrate the use of the factorization mechanisms presented in section 3.2 for each part of the co-design modeling. The extensions have been implemented in a separate UML profile.

**Application Example: Contour Detection.** An image is an array of elementary values, named pixels. A contour detection of an image may be realized with a convolution. A convolution is a simple operation which produces each pixel of an output image from a linear combination of some pixels of the input image. The coefficient of the linear combination are given in a coefficient matrix.

The convolution `ContourDetection` is realized as a *RepetitiveStructuredClassifier* that can receive from its environment $514 \times 514$ signals[15] representing the pixels composing the image, and $2 \times 2$ signals[16] representing the values of the coefficient matrix. It can send to its environment $512 \times 512$[17] signals representing the pixels of the computed image. Each potential instance of `t` is connected to ports on the boundary of `ContourDetection`. Basically, each `t` is able to emit one pixel via its `dataOut` port when all its input signals have been received. The order in which pixels are produced[18] is determined by the order in which

---

[13] Refinements of these concepts, with particular attributes, are also defined but will not be presented in this paper.

[14] Temporal aspects are not presented in this paper.

[15] from its $514 \times 514$ `dataIn` provided ports.

[16] from its $2 \times 2$ `coeff` provided ports

[17] via its $512 \times 512$ `dataOut` required ports

[18] or The order in which the behavior associated to each $t$ is executed

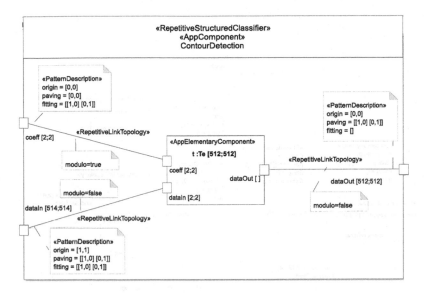

**Fig. 12.** Repetitive application example

signals are received from `ContourDetection` provided ports. In opposition to a classical sequential loop, the specification of `ContourDetection` does not induce any artificial execution order for the production of pixels.

**Hardware Architecture Example: Bi-SPMD.** We target a parallel architecture made of two sets of PE (processor elements) sharing a global memory `global:RAM` (Fig.13). Each set is made of 64 PE linked together in a ring via `east` and `west` communication channels as defined by the *InterRepetitionLink-Topology*. Each PE is associated to an element of a set of 2×64 local memories `local:ScratchPad`. The use of *RepetitiveLinkTopology* allows to specify both the link of each PE with the global memory and the link of each PE with its particular local memory.

**Allocation Example: Bloc Mapping.** We specify the distribution of the 512×512 potential instances of t on the 2×64 potential instances of pe so that each pe receives a bloc of 512×4 t (Fig.14). Note that the *RepetitiveLinkTopology* is here applied to a *Dependency*.

## 5   Conclusion

We have presented an answer to the MARTE RFP requirement concerning the definition of common high-level modeling mechanisms for factorizing repetitive structures. We have illustrated the use of these mechanisms with the embedded

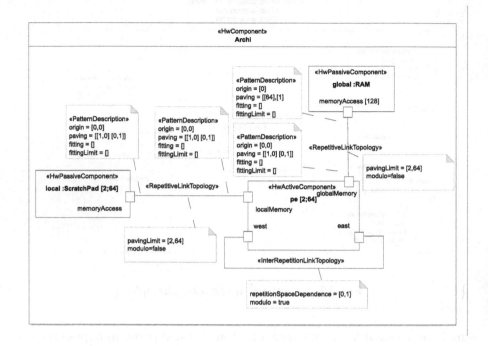

**Fig. 13.** Repetitive hardware architecture example

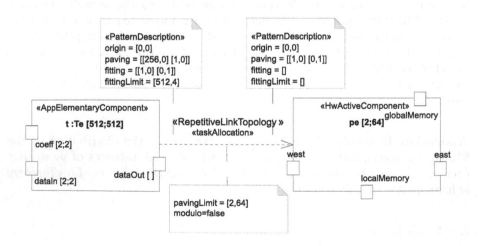

**Fig. 14.** Association example

systems co-design environment Gaspard, for the modeling of software, hardware and software/hardware allocation parts of a sample application. The extensions we have proposed concern only structural aspects of UML 2, and are designed to be easily integrated in a global answer to the RFP. We are now studying if the scope of these mechanisms can be extended to behavioral aspects of UML 2 (feasibility, usefulness). This work is in progress in the context of the Carroll PROTES project [15], which initiated the definition of the MARTE RFP.

# References

1. Object Management Group, Inc., ed.: UML Profile for Modeling and Analysis of Real-Time and Embedded systems (MARTE) RFP.
   http://www.omg.org/cgi-bin/doc?realtime/2005-02-06 (2005)
2. Object Management Group, Inc., ed.: UML 2 Infrastructure (Final Adopted Specification). http://www.omg.org/cgi-bin/doc?ptc/2003-09-15 (2003)
3. Object Management Group, Inc., ed.: UML 2 Superstructure (Available Specification). http://www.omg.org/cgi-bin/doc?ptc/2004-10-02 (2004)
4. Object Management Group, Inc., ed.: UML 2 Diagram Interchange (final adopted specification). http://www.omg.org/cgi-bin/doc?ptc/2003-09-01 (2003)
5. Object Management Group, Inc., ed.: UML 2 OCL (Final Adopted specification). http://www.omg.org/cgi-bin/doc?ptc/2003-10-14 (2003)
6. Object Management Group, Inc., ed.: UML Profile for Modeling Quality of Service and Fault Tolerance Characteristics and Mechanisms.
   http://www.omg.org/cgi-bin/doc?ptc/2004-09-01 (2004)
7. Object Management Group, Inc., ed.: (UML) Profile for Schedulability, Performance, and Time Version 1.1.
   http://www.omg.org/technology/documents/formal/schedulability.htm (2005)
8. Object Management Group, Inc., ed.: UML Extension Profile for SoC RFC.
   http://www.omg.org/cgi-bin/doc?realtime/2005-03-01 (2005)
9. Object Management Group, Inc., ed.: SysML v0.9.
   http://www.omg.org/cgi-bin/doc?ad/05-01-03 (2005)
10. Demeure, A., Lafage, A., Boutillon, E., Rozzonelli, D., Dufourd, J.C., Marro, J.L.: Array-OL : Proposition d'un formalisme tableau pour le traitement de signal multidimensionnel. In: Gretsi, Juan-Les-Pins, France (1995)
11. D.A., L.: Access and alignment of data in an array processor. IEEE Trans. Comput. C-24 (1975) 1145–1155
12. Dekeyser, J.L.: Model driven co-design for system on chip. In: MDE for Embedded System Summer School, Brest, France (2004)
13. Laboratoire d'informatique fondamentale de Lille: Gaspard home page.
    http://www.lifl.fr/west/gaspard/ (2005)
14. Dumoulin, C.: ModTransf: A model to model transformation engine (2004)
    http://www.lifl.fr/west/modtransf.
15. The Caroll Research Programme: (2005) http://www.carroll-research.org/.

# Using UML 2.0 Collaborations for Compositional Service Specification

Richard Torbjørn Sanders[1], Humberto Nicolás Castejón[2], Frank Alexander Kraemer[2], and Rolv Bræk[2]

[1] SINTEF ICT, N-7465 Trondheim, Norway
richard.sanders@sintef.no
[2] NTNU, Department of Telematics, N-7491 Trondheim, Norway
{humberto.castejon, kraemer, rolv.braek}@item.ntnu.no

**Abstract.** Collaborations and collaboration uses are features new to UML 2.0. They possess many properties that support rapid and compositional service engineering. The notion of collaboration corresponds well with the notion of a service, and it seems promising to use them for service specification. We present an approach where collaborations are used to specify services, and show how collaborations enable high level feature composition by means of collaboration uses. We also show how service goals can be combined with behavior descriptions of collaborations to form what we call semantic interfaces. Semantic interfaces can be used to ensure compatibility when binding roles to classes and when composing systems from components. Various ways to compose collaboration behaviors are outlined and illustrated with telephony services.

## 1 Introduction

Service development or service engineering is currently receiving considerable attention and starting to become a discipline in its own right. Driven by the belief that future revenues will have to come from new services, a tremendous effort is being invested in new platforms, methods and tools to enable rapid development and incremental deployment of convergent services, i.e. integrated communication, multimedia and information services delivered transparently over a range of access and transport networks. The Service Oriented Architecture (SOA) and Service Oriented Computing (SOC), building on web services, are exponents of this trend in the business domain. A general challenge for service engineering, be it business or ICT applications, is to enable services and service components to be rapidly developed, and to be deployed and composed dynamically without undesirable service interactions. This is a challenging problem largely due to fundamental properties of services, i.e.:

- A service is a *partial functionality*. It can be combined with other services to provide the full functionality offered to a user.
- A service execution normally involves several *collaborating* components (i.e. a service is not simply an interface to an object).
- Components can participate in several services, simultaneously or alternately.

L. Briand and C. Williams (Eds.): MoDELS 2005, LNCS 3713, pp. 460–475, 2005.

– Services are partially dependent on each other, on shared resources and on user preferences.

In order to support model driven service engineering, corresponding modeling concepts are needed. This is where UML 2.0 collaborations come in, since they possess many properties that make them attractive for this purpose.

First of all the concept of UML collaboration corresponds closely with the concept of a service as explained above. We actually define a *service* as a collaboration between *service roles* played by objects that deliver functionality to the end users. Note that this definition is quite general and covers both client-server and peer-to-peer services as described in [1].

Secondly, UML collaboration uses provide a means to structure complex collaborations and give an overview not provided by other notations, while at the same time being precise. Collaborations have much the same simplicity and appeal as use cases, and can be used for the much same purposes, but provide additional benefits for service engineering, as will be presented in the following. Service specification using collaborations and collaboration uses fits well with the preferred view of marketers and end-users, while at the same time supporting the difficult engineering tasks of service and system designers.

Thirdly, a collaboration role can be bound to several different classifiers by means of collaboration uses. This provides the desired flexibility to bind service roles to components, the only UML requirement being that the classifier is *compatible* with the type of the role(s) bound to it. A precise definition of compatibility is left as a semantic variation in UML 2.0, but it is clear that this should entail the observable behavior on interfaces of a component.

This leads to a fourth motivation for collaborations – they lend themselves nicely to the definition of so-called *semantic interfaces* [2]. As we shall see, a two-party collaboration can define a pair of complementary semantic interfaces. Compared to traditional syntactical interfaces known from web services, CORBA, Java and UML, semantic interfaces also define the visible interface behavior and the goals of the collaboration. This extends the notion of compatibility beyond static signature matching to include safety and liveness properties. It also provides an efficient means to perform such compatibility checks at design time and even at runtime.

Finally, it may be argued that the crosscutting view of collaborations is valuable in its own right [3]. It enables us to focus on the joint behavior of objects rather than on each object individually and, not the least, to focus on the purposes and goals of the joint behavior in terms of desirable global states, called service goals in [4]. A service goal can be expressed in OCL, and is a property that identifies essential progress, thus characterizing a desired or successful outcome of a service invocation. It can be argued that service goals are closer to capturing and expressing the user needs than specifying how they are achieved in terms of detailed interactions. Moreover, goal expressions define liveness properties that must be satisfied by compatible components.

Fig. 1 provides a principal overview of service engineering using collaborations.

Our service engineering approach is both collaboration-oriented and compositional. It is collaboration-oriented because we model services as collaborations between roles played by distributed components, and it is compositional because we build services

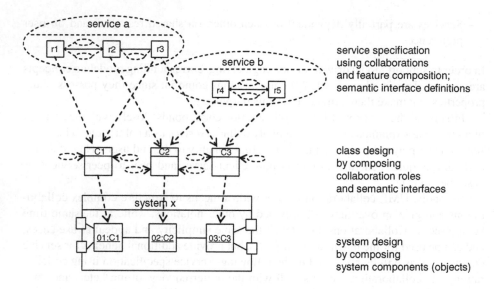

**Fig. 1.** Service engineering overview

from other smaller services. We treat collaborations and collaboration roles as units of reuse.

We consider the following composition cases:

1. Composition of two-party services and semantic interfaces from two-party collaborations.
2. Composition of multi-party services from two-party or n-party collaborations.
3. Class design by composing service roles and semantic interfaces.

Class design is out of the scope of this paper. Here we focus on the use of collaborations for service specification. It is our belief that class design can become a more mechanical process supported by tools if it takes collaborations and semantic interfaces as input. Our experience so far indicates that this is the case [5, 6]. However, further work is still needed to confirm this with certainty.

### 1.1   Structure of the Paper

In section 2 we present how service structures can be described in UML, and how service behavior can be described. We introduce the concept of service goals, and discuss how they can be defined in service structures and in the behavioral descriptions. We introduce what lies in a semantic interface, and discuss compatibility between roles and classifiers.

In section 3 we discuss the composition of two-party collaborations used for defining semantic interfaces, as well as composing multi-party services from subordinate collaborations, and indicate directions toward class design. Finally we conclude.

## 2   Collaborations, Goals and Semantic Interfaces

### 2.1   Collaboration Structure

When used for service specification, the structure of a collaboration identifies the service roles that collaborate to provide the service, as well as their multiplicity and interconnections. Fig. 2 depicts a collaboration called UserCall specifying the structure of a classical telephone call service. This collaboration diagram tells us that exactly two roles, A and B, of type Caller and Callee respectively, are needed to provide a UserCall service, and that a communication path between instances playing those roles must exist.

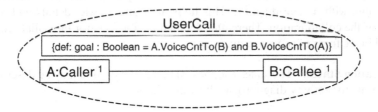

**Fig. 2.** The UserCall service specified as a collaboration with a goal expression

Specifying a service as a collaboration enables roles to be identified and described without introducing undue bindings to implementation details. Thus a service can be specified and understood as a behavioral component of its own, independent of systems components that implement them.

As we shall see, the behavior of collaborations can be described at several levels of detail. Furthermore, collaborations can themselves be used as components in collaboration compositions, thus becoming units of reuse.

### 2.2   Collaboration Goals

The diagram in Fig. 2 also shows a goal that should be reached by the UserCall collaboration. It is represented by an OCL predicate over properties of the two participating roles. In this case it is a simple logical addition of the role goals of A and B, to show that A has a voice connection to B and B has a voice connection to A:

VoiceCnt(A,B)  =  A.VoiceCntTo(B)  and  B.VoiceCntTo(A)

Goal expressions like this can be made very high level, protocol independent and close to the essential purpose of a service as seen from a user point of view. They are actually formal requirements expressions. In this respect they are not new; the novelty lies in the natural binding to the different service specification diagrams, such as collaborations and sequence diagrams. Furthermore, a goal expression represents a liveness property that should hold in actual collaboration uses and therefore constitutes part of the required compatibility of role binding. This illustrates one asset of UML collaborations: they are natural places to express crosscutting properties of services.

## 2.3   Collaboration Behavior

Since UML collaborations inherit from both structured classifiers and behaviored classifiers, they have a large range of expression forms at their disposal. In addition to expressing structural relationships, it is possible to express all forms of behavioral aspects of collaborations, such as interactions, activities and state machines. The UML standard [7] and reference book [8] focus mainly on the structural features of collaborations, and provide few guidelines on how the behavior of a collaboration is described, nor do they explain how collaboration behavior is related to the behavior of its constituent parts, i.e. the roles and role classifiers.

In the following we suggest how the behavior of a collaboration can be described for the purpose of service specification. We first specify the main states a collaboration goes through with a state diagram. This helps to abstract away details and focus on the goal of the collaboration. Thereafter detailed interactions for the collaboration are provided in the form of sequence diagrams.

**Collaboration States.**   The states (or phases) of a collaboration may be described in a state diagram (or activity diagram), as illustrated in Fig. 3.

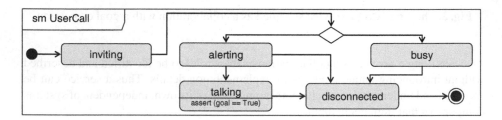

**Fig. 3.** State machine diagram for collaboration UserCall

This state diagram describes well known situations in the progress of a basic telephone call. The transitions between the states are represented by arcs, but we have chosen not to define exactly what causes them. For instance the transition from alerting to disconnected can be due to the caller hanging up, the callee not answering before a timeout, or the network malfunctioning. Leaving such details undefined can be desirable in a high level service specification.

But what do states of a collaboration mean? Given that a collaboration is not instantiated as an object, no entity is ever in a collaboration state. Rather, a collaboration state is a conceptual state expressing certain situations or conditions on the combined states of the roles A and B during the collaboration, see Fig. 4. It may be considered as a liveness property of the collaboration.

The possibility to focus on the joint behavior and goals rather than the individual role behavior is an important asset of collaborations. The role behaviors must somehow be aligned with each other; we indicate a way of doing so in Fig. 4. One must ensure that the role behaviors are dual, i.e. they are fully compatible with respect to safety properties, and that they can reach the joint collaboration states and goals and thereby satisfy liveness properties. A two-party collaboration satisfying these properties defines a pair of semantic interfaces [2].

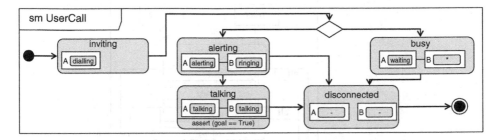

**Fig. 4.** State machine diagram for `UserCall` with role states and service goal expression (UML enhancement illustrating role states in collaboration states)

By describing state machines for both the collaboration and the role classifiers, a certain amount of redundancy is added, and the question of compatibility between them arises. This can either be considered as a problem to be avoided, or as a feature that can be put to use. In our view validating consistency between the role behavior and the collaboration behavior is an opportunity that should not be missed.

**Interactions.** Interaction diagrams are often partial descriptions that are not meant to describe complete behavior, unlike state machine diagrams. For the purpose of service specification interactions for a collaboration should at least focus on the successful cases, i.e. those that lead to the achievement of service goals.

In Fig. 5 we have described interactions that lead to the achievement of the service goal of a collaboration called `Invite`. The goal of this collaboration is to bring the collaborating instances to the `talking` state. The goal is indicated by an adornment in the continuation label `talking`.

### 2.4 Semantic Interfaces and Compatibility

In principle, components can participate in any service as long as they can play their part of the service. Therefore, the specification of a service should not bind the service roles to specific classifiers [9]. In [10] we used association classes to specify services, but they fail to meet the requirements for flexible role binding. This is because with associations the binding is determined by the classifiers at the association ends. Collaborations do not have this limitation. With the help of collaboration uses, collaborations roles can be bound to any classifiers that are compatible with the role types. This is shown in Fig. 6, where the same classifier, `UserAgent`, is bound to two different roles, A and B. This is possible as long as the `UserAgent` class is compatible with both collaboration roles. Our interpretation of compatibility is that the `UserAgent` must have visible interface behavior that is goal equivalent with the behavior of both roles, implying that the roles of the collaboration can be achieved.

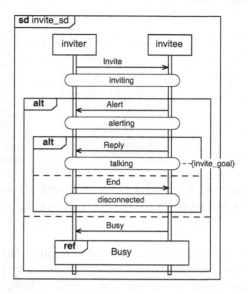

**Fig. 5.** Sequence diagram for collaboration `Invite`

**Fig. 6.** Binding roles to component classes in a collaboration use

This can be put to use by defining a pair of *semantic interfaces* in a two-way collaboration like `UserCall`, as proposed in [2]. The semantic interfaces include goal expressions and role behaviors for the two collaboration roles. Such role behavior can be seen as a kind of protocol state machine specifying only the input/output behavior visible on the interface. It can be derived from a general state machine by making a projection of its behavior on the interface in question. In the case of the `UserAgent` in Fig. 6, compatibility can be checked in two steps. First we verify that the collaboration goals of `UserCall` are reachable given the roles A and B. Then we check that the projected behaviors of `UserAgent` on each side of the connection defined by `UserCall` are goal equivalent to the respective behaviors of A and B. This enables a compositional and scalable validation approach where the most computation intensive work (making projections and comparing behaviors) can be done at design time. When dynamically binding roles to system components at runtime, validation need not be repeated.

The UML standard [7] says that "a collaboration is often defined in terms of roles typed by interfaces". Unfortunately an interface typing a role can only describe either a *provided* interface, or a *required* interface, but not a combination. This is a limitation. We want role classifiers to describe both the required and the provided interface behavior in a single modeling unit. Typing a role by two interfaces, a required and a provided one, is not legal in the current version of UML, nor would this result in a unified interface description. Similarly, a protocol state machine attached to an interface only constrains the sequence of operation calls to a component, and can not be used to describe a two-way interface.

The limitations of interfaces may be overcome, however, if UML allowed describing interface behavior in terms of state machines that model the (projected) input/output behavior of a component on the interface, such as the Port State Machines (PoSM) proposed by Mencl [11]. This is indeed close to the port state machines of ROOM [12], and should be included in UML. Goal compatibility between a component and a port state machine could then be defined in terms of behavior projection.

Given that the behavior of a collaboration role is described in a state machine diagram enriched with service goals, it is relatively straightforward to validate safety and liveness compatibility between a classifier and a semantic interface to which it is bound [6, 13, 10], thus ascertaining goal equivalence between objects and roles.

## 3  Composition from Collaborations

### 3.1  Composition of Two-Party Services and Semantic Interfaces from Two-Party Collaborations

With collaboration uses we can express how services can be composed from elementary service features, as illustrated in Fig. 7.

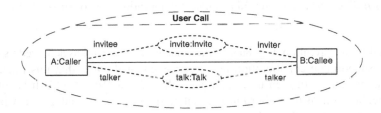

**Fig. 7.** UserCall composed of elementary features (subordinate collaboration uses)

In Fig. 7 the UserCall collaboration is decomposed into smaller features, invite and talk, represented as collaboration uses. These are related to the distinct states of the UserCall service (see Fig. 3) and to the sequence diagram for Invite (see Fig. 5). To simplify the example, we have grouped the states for UserCall so that the goal of the invite collaboration is to bring the UserCall collaboration to the state talking, upon which the talk collaboration use takes over. However, it is not clear from Fig. 7 what relationship there is between invite and talk, that is, if their interactions are interleaved or if they represent a sequence.

It is of central importance to service engineering to make the sequence of goals and the relationships between collaborations explicit. This may be done in several ways. One possibility is showing dependencies between the subordinate collaboration uses and/or their roles in the collaboration diagram itself. Another possibility is to utilize pre- and post-conditions. A third possibility is to use interaction overview diagrams or activity diagrams to express goal sequences, as suggested in Fig. 8a below.

Interaction overview diagrams are a form of activity diagram, and thus the token passing semantics of the latter apply. To express goal relationships, the following interpretation of the tokens is employed: a token being passed represents that a goal is achieved, while an input token implies that a subsequent collaboration use (i.e. a service) is enabled. This can be exploited by mechanisms supporting the dynamic discovery of service opportunities [2, 4]. Note that what happens if the goal is not achieved is not described – the focus is on the achievement of goals. However, if the goal is not achieved in a referenced collaboration, the goal sequence is interrupted.

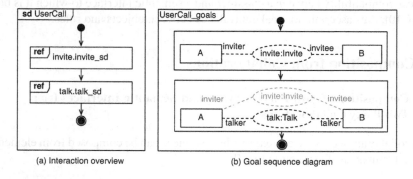

(a) Interaction overview        (b) Goal sequence diagram

**Fig. 8.** Overview of the subordinate collaboration uses of `UserCall`

With this interpretation, Fig. 8a specifies that after `invite` has achieved its service goal, the subordinate collaboration use `talk` is enabled. Note that this relationship applies in the context of their use, i.e. in the collaboration `UserCall`. It is not stated in the specification of the subordinate collaborations `Invite` and `Talk`, which are thus free to be used in other collaboration contexts.

A minor diagrammatic enhancement to UML, which is to include an illustration of the situation with respect to the involved collaborations (see Fig. 8b), seems attractive. This is what we have called a *goal sequence diagram* [10]. The second rectangle in Fig. 8b illustrates how the roles of `Invite` and `Talk` are bound in the context of `UserCall`. They are statically bound in the `UserCall` collaboration of Fig. 7, and simply referred to in Fig. 8b. Goal sequence diagrams do not change the semantics of UML, and what is illustrated in Fig. 8b corresponds to what is expressed in Fig. 8a. Goal sequence diagrams illustrate the evolution of the collaboration structure. For instance, two shades of coloring are employed for the referenced collaboration uses: black color (e.g. for `talk`) illustrates that the collaboration use is active, while grey color (e.g. for `invite`) is for preceding collaboration uses that do not have to exist any longer. For the simple example in Fig. 8 the added value of the goal sequence diagram is not striking; Fig. 10 is perhaps a more convincing case.

Illustrating situations has been also suggested by Diethelm & al. [14]; they use communication diagrams to illustrate use cases and to illustrate do-actions in states.

Two-party collaborations can be composed to form semantic interfaces, which define role behavior and goals of a pair of complementary roles. Limiting such collaborations to a pair of roles is chosen to simplify the validation approach, which is based on validation of object behavior projections and goals over a binary association, as mentioned previously. It also simplifies composition, as components can be composed of composite states that correspond to the semantic interfaces [15].

This restriction does not hinder multi-party services to be defined; they can be composed from two-party collaborations with semantic interfaces, as well as from subordinate multi-party collaborations, as shown below. However, this complicates the validation and composition process, as several interfaces have to be validated or composed, and the relationships between the interfaces must be known. Goal sequence diagrams seem to be promising when it comes to composition, as illustrated in the next section.

### 3.2  Composition of Multi-party Services

An example that illustrates the potential of composing collaborations from subordinate collaborations is found in Fig. 9, where the `UserCall` service with the call transfer feature is described.

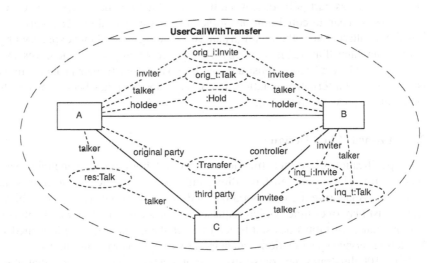

**Fig. 9.** The collaboration `UserCallWithTransfer`

Fig. 9 demonstrates how subordinate collaborations such as `Invite` and `Talk` may be reused in new settings, due to the flexible role binding of collaboration uses. Such reuse is a very attractive aspect of collaborations, and can help to give an intuitive understanding of a complex situation, as illustrated here. Call transfer is a classical challenge for service designers to understand and describe succinctly. From Fig. 9 it is apparent that several call invitations are involved. However, the precise ordering of the subordinate collaboration uses can not be understood from Fig. 9 alone. A goal sequence diagram for the UserCallWithTransfer service, as suggested in Fig. 10a, is one possibility of describing this.

Fig. 10a describes the ordering of collaboration uses required for the overall service goal of the transfer feature to be achieved. The goal sequence diagram combined with the collaboration diagram of the service (see Fig. 9) provides a compact and fairly intuitive description of a complex service. It has been common practice among telecom service engineers to make informal sketches to the same effect as an aid in service design. UML collaborations provide an opportunity to formalize and better support this practice. The goal sequence demonstrates how UML promotes reuse of units of behavior in the form of collaboration uses, and documents the evolution of the static structure depicted in the collaboration diagram. One particularly interesting aspect of the goal sequence diagram in Fig. 10a is that it shows situations in which a role, e.g. B, is simultaneously playing two or more sub-roles, e.g. holder and inviter in the fourth step of the sequence. Note that the simplicity of collaboration structures may be deceiving. Call transfer may look simple in Fig. 9, but when fully elaborated the underlying sequences and role behaviors can be quite complex.

There are limits to what goal sequence diagrams are capable of expressing. For instance, it is not possible to describe goal dependencies among overlapping collaborations. This is the case, for example, of a log-on collaboration that requires a user authentication as part of its operation. It is desirable to model log-on and authenticate as separate collaborations to achieve reuse, and allow log-on to be combined with alternative authentication patterns. However, we cannot express with goal sequence diagrams that authenticate is enabled when log-on achieves a sub-goal, and that authenticate must achieve its goal before further progress in log-on is possible. An alternative notation, Use Case Maps [16], has been shown to have the necessary expressive power [5].

### 3.3   Towards Class Design

The specification of service functionality in collaborations is beneficial beyond the specification phase and can have direct influence on the design of classes and state machines. Analyzing the collaborations and the goal sequences tells us which roles a class must play over time, which requests for roles can arrive in which situations and which connections must be established to reach the goals of the implemented services. Modeling service specifications can help class design, as we now shall see.

Fig. 10b illustrates the coarse structure of a class Participant that implements all three roles A, B and C of UserCallWithTransfer. The sub-roles invitee and inviter are implemented as separate state machines, since call requests can arrive at any time. When a call request from another component is received, invitee creates a new instance of the state machine callsession to handle the request. The sub-roles talk, hold and transfer can be implemented by composite states inside callsession, as these roles are played alternately. The figure also illustrates the connections between the state machines of the components and how they evolve as the service progresses towards the achievement of its goal.

To complete class design one must consider all collaboration roles bound to the class. The Participant class, for example, may take part in several collabora-

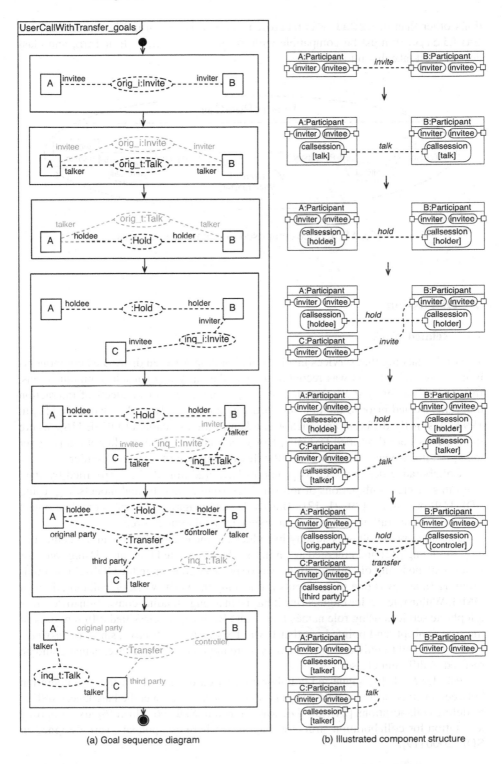

(a) Goal sequence diagram          (b) Illustrated component structure

**Fig. 10.** Goal sequence for `UserCallWithTransfer` with related component structure

tions other than `UserCallWithTransfer`, as it is shown in Fig. 11. In that case `Participant` must be compatible with the four roles ua, A, B and ub, and class design must take this into account.

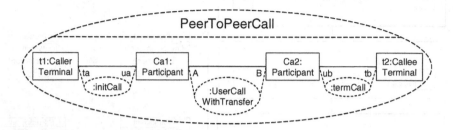

**Fig. 11.** Service composed of elementary services

# 4  Discussion

## 4.1  Related Work

The understanding that services involve collaboration between distributed components is not new; indeed, this was recognized since the early days of telecommunications. In terms of modeling the interaction of collaborations, various dialects of interaction diagrams existed prior to the first standardization of the ITU-T MSC language [17] in 1994. A slightly different approach was taken in the use cases of OOSE [18], where interactions were described textually. However, interactions alone do not really cover the structural aspects of the roles and the flexible binding of roles to classifiers.

Collaborative designs such as protocols have traditionally been specified by state diagrams, using combinations of informal descriptions and formal models, e.g. using SDL [19] or similar ([20, 21, 12]). But while state diagrams describe complete object behavior, the overall goals and the joint behavior tend to be blurred.

The concept of role was already introduced in the end of the 70's in the context of data modeling [22] and emerged again in the object-oriented literature. Using roles for functional modeling of collaborations was of primary concern in the OORAM methodology [23], and was one of the inputs influencing the UML work on collaborations in OMG. Within teleservice engineering it has been a long-standing convention to describe telephone services using role names like A and B. In [9] we classified different uses of the role concept, and pointed out that UML 1.x was too restrictive, since a *Classifier-Role* could bind to only one class, so they were not independent concepts that could be re-used in different classes.

Rössler & al. [3] suggested collaboration based design with a tighter integration between interaction and state diagram models, and created a specific language, CoSDL, to define collaborations [24]. CoSDL was aligned to SDL-96. Floch [6] also proposed a notation for collaboration structure diagrams, where components were designed in SDL-2000 [19].

With UML 2.0, it is now possible to model collaborations in a standardized language, increasingly supported by tools. Modeling collaborating services with UML 2.0 collaborations has earlier been suggested by Haugen and Møller-Pedersen [25]. They pointed out that there might be limitations in binding collaboration uses to classifier parts; these issues must be clarified, and binding to parts should preferably be supported. In the FUJABA approach described in [26], so-called coordination patterns are used for similar purposes as our semantic interfaces. They use a model checker to provide incremental verification based on the coordination patterns.

## 4.2  Further Work

A number of issues presented in this article need to be clarified and researched, and experiments in real projects must be undertaken before all problems are solved. We are currently applying these techniques on several practical service engineering cases including access control services, call control, and mobile information services. Compatibility rules between role classifiers and the objects and classes bound by collaboration uses is a semantic variation point in UML. The research on semantic interfaces [2] is a promising starting point for compatibility checking between complementary roles. Additional work on validating compatibility between roles and class designs, with tool support for composition, is being undertaken.

An experimental tool suite is currently being developed as part of the Teleservice Lab at the department of Telematics at NTNU, based on the Eclipse platform. The EU funded project *Semantic Interfaces for Mobile Services*, SIMS, to commence in 2006, will develop tool support for designing and validating collaborations, taking existing prototypes [27] as a starting point and validating the approach among industrial users.

## 5  Conclusion

This article has suggested ways of exploiting UML 2.0 for service engineering, and has discussed opportunities and limitations that lie in the current standard [7] in that respect. Our conclusion is that UML 2.0 collaborations seem to be a very useful expression form, as it allows one to define pieces of collaborating role behavior that can be bound to role players in a very flexible way.

Useful validation opportunities arise once criteria for role compatibility have been defined. Collaborations can be used to define semantic interfaces, which in turn can be used for compatibility checks and to support composition. We have argued for the inclusion of port state machines in UML as a more general description of semantic interface behavior than the existing protocol state machine mechanisms that have been defined in UML 2.0.

Furthermore we have suggested how minor notational enhancements can be introduced to represent collaboration situations in order to support high level feature composition; this is more of a tool issue than a language issue, but has methodological implications that are important. Finally, we have demonstrated how collaboration uses provide means to define complex multi-party services on a high level.

In contrast to the common practice of modeling complete service sequences involving all participating roles, our approach encourages decomposition into interface behaviors represented as two-way collaborations. The result is smaller and more reusable interface behaviors that can be validated separately, thereby addressing compositionality and scalability. The disadvantage is that behavior composition needs special attention, e.g. using goal sequences as elaborated in [5].

# References

[1] Bræk, R., Floch, J.: ICT convergence: Modeling issues. In: Proc. of the 4th Int. SDL and MSC (SAM) Workshop, Ottawa, Canada, LNCS 3319, Springer (2004)

[2] Sanders, R.T., Bræk, R., von Bochmann, G., Amyot, D.: Service discovery and component reuse with semantic interfaces. In: Proc. of the 12th Int. SDL Forum, Grimstad, Norway, LNCS 3530, Springer (2005)

[3] Rößler, F., Geppert, B., Gotzhein, R.: Collaboration-based design of SDL systems. In: Proc. of the 10th Int. SDL Forum, Copenhagen, Denmark, LNCS 2078, Springer (2001)

[4] Sanders, R.T., Bræk, R.: Discovering service opportunities by evaluating service goals. In: Proc. of the 10th EUNICE and IFIP Workshop on Advances in Fixed and Mobile Networks, Tampere, Finland (2004)

[5] Castejón, H.N.: Synthesizing state-machine behaviour from UML collaborations and Use Case Maps. In: Proc. of the 12th Int. SDL Forum, Norway, LNCS 3530, Springer (2005)

[6] Floch, J.: Towards Plug-and-Play Services: Design and Validation using Roles. PhD thesis, Dep. of Telematics, Norwegain Univ. Sci. and Tech., Trondheim, Norway (2003)

[7] Object Management Group: UML 2.0 Superstructure Specification. (2004)

[8] Rumbaugh, J., Jacobson, I., Booch, G.: The Unified Modeling Language Reference Manual. 2nd edn. Addison-Wesley (2004)

[9] Bræk, R.: Using roles with types and objects for service development. In: IFIP 5th Int. Conf. on Intelligence in Networks (SMARTNET), Pathumthani, Thailand, Kluwer (1999)

[10] Sanders, R.T., Bræk, R.: Modeling peer-to-peer service goals in UML. In: Proc. of the 2nd Int. Conf. on Soft. Eng. and Formal Methods (SEFM'04), IEEE Computer Society (2004)

[11] Mencl, V.: Specifying component behavior with port state machines. Electr. Notes Theor. Comput. Sci. 101 (2004) 129–153

[12] Selic, B., Gullekson, G., Ward, P.T.: Real-Time Object-Oriented Modeling. John Wiley & Sons (1994)

[13] Floch, J., Bræk, R.: A compositional approach to service validation. In: Proc. of the 12th Int. SDL Forum, Grimstad, Norway, LNCS 3530, Springer (2005)

[14] Diethelm, I., Geiger, L., Maier, T., Zündorf, A.: Turning collaboration diagram strips into storycharts. In: Workshop on Scenarios and state machines: models, algorithms, and tools; ICSE'02, Orlando, Florida, USA. (2002)

[15] Floch, J., Bræk, R.: Using SDL for modeling behavior composition. In: Proc. of the 11th Int. SDL Forum, Stuttgart, Germany, LNCS 2708, Springer (2003)

[16] ITU-T Draft Recommendation Z.152: URN - Use Case Maps notation (UCM). (2004)

[17] ITU-T Recommendation Z.120: Message Sequence Charts (MSC). (2004)

[18] Jacobson, I., Christerson, M., Jonsson, P., Øvergaard, G.: Object-Oriented Software Engineering: A Case Driven Approach. Addison-Wesley (1992)

[19] ITU-T Recommendation Z.100: Specification and Description Language (SDL). (2002)

[20] International Organization for Standardization (ISO): Estelle: a formal description technique based on an extended state transition model. ISO9074. (1989)

[21] Harel, D.: Statecharts: A visual formalism for complex systems. Sci. Comput. Program. **8** (1987) 231–274

[22] Bachman, C.W., Daya, M.: The role concept in data models. In: Proc. of the 3rd Int. Conference on Very Large Data Bases, Tokyo, Japan, IEEE Computer Society (1977)

[23] Reenskaug, T., Wold, P., Lehne, O.A.: Working with Objects: The OOram Software Engineering Method. Prentice Hall (1996)

[24] Rößler, F., Geppert, B., Gotzhein, R.: CoSDL: An experimental language for collaboration specification. In: Proc. of the 3rd Int. SDL and MSC (SAM) Workshop, Aberystwyth, UK, LNCS 2599, Springer (2002)

[25] Haugen, Ø., Møller-Pedersen, B.: The fine arts of service modeling. Technical report, Internal report. ARTS (2003) http://www.pats.no/projects/ARTS/arts.html.

[26] Burmester, S., Giese, H., Hirsch, M., Schilling, D.: Incremental design and formal verification with UML/RT in the FUJABA real-time tool suite. In: Proc. of the Int. Workshop on Specification and Vaildation of UML models for Real Time and embedded Systems (SVERTS), associated with UML2004, Lisbon, Portugal (2004)

[27] Alsnes, R.: Role validation tool. Master's thesis, NTNU (2004)

# Model-Driven Engineering in a Large Industrial Context — Motorola Case Study

Paul Baker[1], Shiou Loh[2], and Frank Weil[3]

[1] Motorola Labs, Jays Close, Viables Industrial Estate, Basingstoke, Hampshire, RG22 4PD, UK
Paul.Baker@motorola.com
[2] Motorola Inc, 1301 E. Algonquin Rd., Schaumburg, IL 60196, USA
Shiou.Loh@motorola.com
[3] Motorola Global Software, 1303 E. Algonquin Rd., Schaumburg, IL 60196, USA
Frank.Weil@motorola.com

**Abstract.** In an ongoing effort to reduce development costs in spite of increasing system complexity, Motorola has been a long-time adopter of Model-Driven Engineering (MDE) practices. The foundation of this approach is the creation of rigorous models throughout the development process, thereby enabling the introduction of automation. In this paper we present our experiences within Motorola in deploying a top-down approach to MDE for more than 15 years. We describe some of the key competencies that have been developed and the impact of MDE within the organization. Next we present some of the main issues encountered during MDE deployment, together with some possible resolutions.

## 1 Introduction

Motorola employs over 13,000 software engineers and has been applying initiatives such as the Software Engineering Institute Capability Maturity Model to improve the quality and productivity of software and system development. However, given increasing system complexity, these initiatives are not enough by themselves. As a result, Motorola began to deploy Model-Driven Engineering (MDE) as a means of introducing automation into the development process. After more than 15 years, Motorola has matured and deployed its MDE process with impressive results. This paper introduces some of Motorola's experiences and issues during MDE usage. We conclude by presenting some high-level strategies Motorola is pursuing to further enhance MDE deployment and success.

## 2 Experience

Motorola's experience in MDE crosses a wide spectrum of activities, tools, and modeling languages in the telecommunications domain. Typical applications range from protocol implementations on hand-held devices (pagers, cell phones, etc.) to network controllers in infrastructure components (base stations, radio

L. Briand and C. Williams (Eds.): MoDELS 2005, LNCS 3713, pp. 476–491, 2005.

network controllers, etc.) This section describes this experience, covering languages and standards, development processes, and the automatic generation of tests and application code. In addition, we discuss MDE successes and failures and the impact that MDE has had.

## 2.1   Languages and Standards

Motorola began using standard modeling languages over 15 years ago with Structured Analysis and Structured Design (SA/SD) [9]. This was followed by the introduction of the Specification and Description Language (SDL) [12] to Motorola Europe for the modeling and validation of the design of communication protocols. These positive experiences led to the large-scale deployment of an MDE approach using languages such as Message Sequence Charts (MSC) [11], SDL, and TTCN-2 [13] for the development of large telecommunication systems. MSCs were typically used for requirements specification, SDL for design, and TTCN-2 for test specification.

Following this wider deployment with MSC and SDL, Motorola increased its involvement and leadership within the standards communities, especially the International Telecommunications Union (ITU-T), the European Telecommunication Standards Institute (ETSI), and the Object Management Group (OMG). For example, the MSC language was extended to allow the parameterization of any data language, thereby making it possible to develop test models as a basis for automatic test generation. In general, these languages were very well suited to the domain of telecommunication systems, and their precise semantic foundations gave a clear and unambiguous interpretation for users.

To broaden the application domains for MDE, gain wider user acceptance, and harmonize languages, Motorola pursued the development of UML 2.0 [16] and testing notations. In doing so, MSC and SDL were incorporated into UML 2.0 to provide a language with a wider application scope which preserves those capabilities needed for communication system development.

Together with European telecommunication companies, ETSI pursued the evolution of TTCN-2 to define a test specification language that could be used in a wider context (e.g., CORBA, web-based systems, etc.). The result was TTCN-3 [7], a powerful and well defined abstract test specification and execution framework. Motorola promoted the use of TTCN-3 to harmonize testing across different engineering teams, thereby leading to transferable skills and tool reuse. To bridge the gap between TTCN-3 and UML 2.0, Motorola pursued the development of the UML 2.0 Testing Profile [3] for graphical test modeling.

Motorola is an active participant in the OMG Platform Technology Committee and in the ITU-T SDL Committee (Study Group 17), including the ITU-T efforts to unify SDL and UML (Question 13/17 - System Design Languages Framework and Unified Modeling Language).

## 2.2   Process Overview

Since its adoption of MDE, Motorola has followed a rigorous, top-down process. Typically, the process starts with the development of requirements using scenario-based models (defined using MSCs or UML 2.0 Interaction Diagrams), thereby capturing normative and exception behaviors. Next, architectural requirements are developed to define the main system components and the interactions between them. In addition to refining scenario-based models, interface specifications detailing the data passed between system components are developed in either proprietary or standard languages such as ASN.1. Finally, detailed design models are developed, using either SDL or UML 2.0, for each system component. Data from the system or architectural requirements are transformed either into SDL or UML 2.0 data types. These models are then tested and subsequently transformed into code for the target application.

To support this process, a number of technologies and tools have been developed and deployed. Firstly, Motorola developed a proprietary specification technique for data because standard languages such as ASN.1 [10] could not readily capture the bit-level data layout schemas used in the existing protocols. In doing so, Motorola also developed automatic code generation tools that would not only provide efficient data marshaling (see Sect 2.3), but would also facilitate data reuse between design and testing activities. Motorola also institutionalized the notion of model testing using co-simulation techniques. For example, an executable SDL or UML 2.0 design model[4] is run as a simulation against an executable test suite. This has proven to be a very effective means of ensuring the correctness and quality of models, as other verification techniques (e.g., model checking) are not tractable for such large-scale models. After the model correctness has been determined, automatic code generation is used to generate the necessary code for the target implementation. Finally, for component, integration, and system testing, Motorola introduced automated test generation tools [4] that produce test suites from scenario-based requirements.

## 2.3   Automatic Code Generation

Motorola has been involved in automatic code generation from models for over 15 years [5,6]. The original work was done with Structured Design models, relying on an internally developed action language for the process specifications. These design models were transformed to code through a transformation system written in Smalltalk. While this system worked well for small projects, the original implementation of the code generator proved not to scale well to large infrastructure components encompassing many applications each consisting of several hundred thousand lines of source code and was re-architected.

After the viability of modeling and automatic code generation was established, several factors came into play:

---

[4] Most models are currently in SDL or UML 1.x, but a general transition to UML 2.0 is being made, and products have been developed and shipped using UML 2.0.

- the desire to use standardized and non-proprietary modeling languages,
- the desire to scale to large projects,
- the desire to target small embedded systems such as pagers and cell phones,
- the desire to fully leverage the models for testing.

Modeling notations such as LOTOS and Z never gained popularity in the United States, and commercial tool support for them was minimal. In addition, the telecommunications systems being modeled were largely state-based. The decision was therefore made to adopt SDL as the primary modeling language.

At this point, the automatic code generation efforts in Motorola split into three separate but related paths: code for infrastructure components such as Base Site Controllers, code for subscriber components such as pagers and cell phones, and code for encoding and decoding communications protocols (also called packing and unpacking, or *marshaling*).

**Infrastructure and Subscriber Components** While the basic modeling needs for infrastructure and subscriber development are the same (i.e., state machines, concurrent communicating processes, messages, etc.), the needs of the generated code are vastly different. Infrastructure components typically have powerful processors, large amounts of memory, and no power constraints. In contrast, subscriber components typically have minimal processing power, small amounts of memory, and severe power and battery life constraints. In addition, the infrastructure components have strict throughput, latency, capacity, and reliability requirements, often requiring the simultaneous handling of several thousand calls in a fault-tolerant environment. Subscriber components just have to be fast enough to handle one call, and reliability requirements are not as strict (that is, an entire cell site cannot go down without major consequences, but it is not catastrophic if a cell phone drops a call).

For infrastructure components, entire subsystems are modeled in the design language, including the detailed functionality. The models are tested and de-bugged (see Sect. 2.4), and complete code is generated. While it is sometimes the case that the generated code must be debugged, it is expected that the generated code is *never* modified—if a defect is found, the model is updated and the code is generated again from scratch. This follows the full MDE vision.

Subscriber components generally follow more of a "round-trip" approach. The component is modeled, but the detailed functionality is added to the model in the target language itself (C, C++, Java, etc.). The code is generated with the target code left in place, and the testing is done on the resulting code in a separate application test environment. Changes are never made to the parts of the code that are actually generated, but may be made to the embedded target code. Once debugged, these changes are loaded back into the model.

While it could be argued that round-trip development does not truly follow MDE concepts, there is a fine line between writing target code in a model and writing the same functionality in a modeling language such as SDL. Often, what is written is identical except for minor notational changes. Currently, the use of round-trip versus "full" MDE is more for historical reasons than technical ones.

Using these techniques, Motorola has shipped many millions of lines of code generated from SDL and UML models.

**Marshaling** The common ground in automatic code generation has been protocol encoding and decoding. This marshaling code entails much low-level bit manipulation of data to decode a buffer into the realization of the abstract data types used in the model, and *vice versa* for the encoding.

These types of algorithms are tedious to represent in most modeling languages, and implementation-specific details are best left out of the models. We have found that code generators are much better than humans at finding optimal and correct sequences of bit-manipulation instructions for performing the marshaling and dealing with data from different endian machines.

Motorola makes extensive use of marshaling code generators based on external specifications written in standard languages such as ASN.1 and on internal specifications using a proprietary language. One major advantage, especially for internal protocols, is that once a protocol is specified, all components using that protocol get the generated marshaling code with no additional effort.

Motorola uses generated marshaling code integrated with hand-written C and C++ code, with application code generated from SDL and UML models (both from internal tools and from various vendor tools), with TTCN-2, and with TTCN-3.

**Mousetrap** Motorola has developed its own automatic code generation tool suite called Mousetrap. The Mousetrap tool suite takes as input SDL, UML, ASN.1, and ISL (a proprietary protocol language) and produces highly optimizing code customized for a product platform and a set of performance constraints. Mousetrap is a rule-based code transformation system driven by a vast programming knowledge base. Application code has been generated for and shipped in both infrastructure and subscriber components.

Field data has shown that code generated by Mousetrap has fewer defects than hand code or code generated by vendor tools. This is largely due to Mousetrap's ability to detect model problems that most vendor tools cannot catch, and its ability to generate more complete code than vendor tools (e.g., all of the platform interface code is generated). Code generated by Mousetrap is also higher performance than code generated by vendor tools. The main reasons for this are better optimization techniques in Mousetrap and the luxury of knowing the target platform and being able to customize the code generation for it.

## 2.4    Automation Test Generation

When Motorola first deployed MDE it was observed that users were taking scenario-based requirements and manually translating them into conformance test suites. Hence, an automatic test script generation tool called ptk [4] was developed that would process system and architectural scenario-based models, described using MSCs or UML 2.0 Interactions Diagrams, to generate conformance and load tests. During the development and deployment of requirements-based test generation a number of factors came into play:

**Lack of rigorous models for test generation.** Even though it is common for system architects and designers to use scenario-based notations, they typically do not contain the rigor needed for machine processing. We also found that architects and designers were reluctant to invest the extra effort needed to develop rigorous models since the benefit of automated test generation did not immediately justify the extra effort within their project scope. Hence, Motorola has been pursuing a strategy of providing static analysis and automated construction tools [2,15] for scenario-based models that help reduce appraisal costs and improve productivity. Specifically, these tools enable system architects to detect errors, such as pathologies and feature interactions in the designs, and at the same time to infer new and consistent scenarios.

**Correctness of scenario-based models.** It was often the case that requirements specifications contained semantic inconsistencies leading to tests that yield invalid results. Subsequently, research effort was directed to tools to detected these inconsistencies so that they could be corrected before the application of ptk. Pathological behaviors caused by inconsistencies in communication semantics were prevalent among the issues identified during various Motorola case studies. Hence, it was decided to concentrate research effort on tools that detected these kinds of pathologies. Initially research was directed at characterizing inconsistencies in terms of standard UML behavioral semantics. However, practitioners often develop systems with implicit domain-specific communication semantics that are not formally incorporated within their model. As a result, the initial version of the tool reported many errors that practitioners regarded as false positives. It became clear that the understanding of these communication semantics was important. Hence, research has been directed at automatically inferring semantic constraints needed to resolve inconsistencies in scenario-based models in a manner that can be incorporated with little effort from the practitioner. In addition, it is possible to automatically resolve certain pathological behaviors in the same way. This allows the practitioner to concentrate more on the conceptual aspects of the design and to enable a more agile and lightweight development process overall.

**Test generation versus test specification.** During our experience in deploying test generation, it became very clear that users often did not understand the differences between test generation and test specification. For example, even though Motorola practitioners use test generation tools, they typically use them as test specification tools and hence do not gain the full benefits (improved test coverage, abstraction, etc.). To this end, Motorola pursued the development of the UML 2.0 Testing Profile and the deployment of TTCN-3. The intention is to provide a well-defined test specification and execution framework with an optional graphical modeling front-end which enhances the distinction between test specification and the generation of tests from requirements. [1]

In general, test generation has proven to be very successful in: (1) the reduction of effort in developing tests, either through the use of abstraction and test generation techniques or through the reuse of test models for different test contexts, (2) the improvement of test coverage, and (3) the reduction of In-Process Faults (IPF) that classifies the number of defects introduced during the test development process.

## 2.5   Successes and Failures

The initial roll-out of MDE using SDL and MSC within Motorola Europe proved to be successful in obtaining an approximate 2.3X reduction in effort through the use of co-simulation, automatic code generation, and model testing. As a result, MDE gained traction within other teams within Motorola.

In general, the use of scenario-based test generation tools yields an approximately 33% reduction in the effort required to develop test cases. However, in some cases where complex modeling has been required, the use of scenario-based models has not been appropriate. For example, using a scenario to describe the behavior of a set of concurrent components that form part of a complex and dynamic system can be problematic. In such cases, specifying end-to-end scenarios can tend toward complex scenario specifications, whereas scenarios that specify single component behavior can lead to better reuse and understanding.

The *integrated Dispatch Enhanced Network* (iDEN) infrastructure division has seen a steady trend of MDE adoption over the past nine years. Starting with the use of SDL for one network element, iDEN has expanded its MDE usage to 9 out of 12 major network elements. Most of those network elements have achieved 65%–85% code-generation, which has contributed to significant productivity and quality improvement. The degree of modeling maturity has evolved from informal "whiteboard" modeling to formal modeling with simulation to code generation to test-case reuse and automated marshaling code generation. iDEN is now looking into more seamless and integrated MDE approaches with the emphasis on providing a smoother transition between system engineering and downstream development. At the same time, iDEN is moving from SDL to UML 2.0. This move is consistent with tool vendor and industry trends.

In addition to the overall productivity and quality gains, Motorola has seen tremendous gains in some phases of the development process. For example, it is not unusual to see a 30X–70X reduction in the time needed to *correctly* fix a defect detected during system integration testing. This reduction is attributed to the ability to add a model test that illustrates the problem, fix the problem at the model level, test the fix by running a full regression test suite on the model itself, regenerate the code from scratch, and run the same regression test suite on the generated code. The time it takes to do this is typically 24 hours or less, while achieving the same quality with several hundred thousand lines of hand code can easily take one to two months. The time needed to find the root cause of a defect has been improved in some case and worsened in others. For example, platform interface issues can be difficult to diagnose since the observed behavior may have no obvious correlation to the model, but subtle logic problems in system behavior are easier to uncover in the model simulation.

One pilot project that did not succeed involved an integrated transition from hand code to automatic code generation. The project looked into the possibility of "cleaning up" informal SDL models, generating the code for the process and state machine infrastructure, and directly incorporating the legacy C code for the state machine transitions. The main reasons that the project did not succeed is that (1) the hand code made no clear distinction between these behavioral aspects, so the effort to refactor the hand code far outweighed any potential benefits, and (2) the informal models no longer corresponded to the actual behavior of the hand code since there was no compelling reason to have kept the model up to date.

## 2.6 Impact

Overall, Motorola has seen a positive impact from the adoption of MDE. The detailed results are mixed, however, and are very difficult to use for planning purposes. The main issue in determining impact is the lack of a common baseline. For large-scale development projects, it is unrealistic to try to set up parallel development environments using code generation and hand coding. Even if the required resources for this were available, it would be difficult to account for several factors, including experience levels in the product itself, experience in the modeling language versus the target language, legacy code that must be included, learning curves associated with understanding how to model, reuse of model test cases during product testing, reuse of model components in later development projects, and maintainability of the model versus the hand code.

In spite of the inability to determine and apply an appropriate normalizing factor due to the above issues, Motorola has seen consistent benefits from MDE and code generation. Typical results collected over the past few years have shown the following benefits when compared to hand code:

**Quality:** a 1.2X–4X overall reduction in defects and a 3X improvement in phase containment of defects. Also, more defects are found earlier in the development process where they are less costly to fix. The overall Cost of Quality has also decreased due to a decrease in inspection and testing times.
**Productivity:** a 2X–8X productivity improvement when measured in terms of equivalent source lines of code.

## 3   Issues Encountered

The adoption of MDE within Motorola has not been without challenges. This section lists some of the main issues encountered and the impacts they have had.

## 3.1    Lack of Common Tools

The ready availability of third-party and internal tools for modeling and code generation has led to a wide diversity of processes, languages, etc. Even within a "single" language such as UML, there are several issues such as the inability to completely transfer models between tools, use of vendor-specific extensions, lack of complete UML support, and code generation support for different subsets of UML. In practice, models and skills are only marginally transferable between different development groups.

Our experience is also that testing teams tend toward the development of their own test tools. This leads to a variety of testing solutions which are often duplicated, not well defined, and poorly supported. The skills developed are not always transferable between development groups.

## 3.2    Lack of Abstraction

During requirements modeling we have encountered three main issues:

**Platform Specifics:** Often we find that system architects and designers develop requirements that contain either implicit or explicit assumptions about the implementation. We are addressing this through the promotion of Model Driven Architecture (MDA) [14] approaches.

**Incompleteness:** Typically requirements are defined either through use cases or through scenario-based models. Since only partial models are developed, there are implications on whether technologies such as model checking can be used to determine the correctness of requirements.

**Quality:** Determining the adequacy of requirements is a common concern. We are addressing this through the promotion of a top-down process and the use of metrics and reliability models to determine the quality of requirements [8].

## 3.3    Lack of Well Defined Semantics

Motorola projects have encountered issues with language semantics with virtually every modeling language used. For example, SA/SD had no defined process language and advocated natural language, tool vendors have added their own language extensions, and even UML 2.0 contains *semantic variation points*. The situation has improved drastically over the past decade, but local conventions are still used and the exact meaning of a model often is dependent on the tool in which it was created.

During the construction of models, implicit assumptions are also made about domain semantics. For example, the type of semantics given to the communication between system components may be token passing, First-In First-Out, synchronous/asynchronous, etc. To this end, a mechanism is needed to allow the user to define domain-specific communication constraints that are considered during the construction and transformation of models. An initial UML 2.0 profile, called the Communication constraint UML Profile (CUP) [2], has been developed by Motorola Labs and can be used for specifying domain-specific communication constraints with UML 2.0 Composite Structure Diagrams. CUP is still being developed, but the intention is to standardize this within the OMG.

## 3.4 Coupling of Data and Behavior

With modeling languages such as SDL and MSC, the specification of data values is tightly coupled with the behavior specification. For example, when an SDL signal is sent between processes, the value of the signal is defined within the behavior of each process. This means that when the signal type is modified, each behavior definition must also be modified, resulting in a very large maintenance burden for engineering teams. This also means that value definitions cannot be reused between specification, design, and testing. By providing mechanisms for decoupling data from behavior specification, we have seen very positive results. With UML 2.0 we promote the use of instance modeling as a key strategy for data reuse and reduced model maintenance. An instance is a run-time entity with an identity that is distinguishable from other run-time entities. Hence, instance modeling refers to the creation of "signal" instances as objects that can be referenced and defined in an independent manner.

## 3.5 Poor Performance of Tools and Generated Code

Third-party MDE tools often do not scale well to the sizes needed for modeling real telecommunications systems. We have encountered issues with the ability of tools to load, save, compare, and generate code from large models. This has become less of an issue as computing power increases, but it is far from solved.

We have also encountered performance issues with the generated code. When using third-party tools with limited ability to customize the code generation, it can be extremely frustrating to address performance bottlenecks.

## 3.6 Lack of Integrated Tools

No single tool supports a comprehensive MDE environment, allowing full use of current tools and processes. To this end, integration of modeling concepts and tools becomes problematic. For example, during the transformation of models to code, how is traceability handled if a separate traceability tool is used?

## 3.7 Team Inexperience

We have observed that many teams encounter major obstacles in adopting MDE due to the lack of a well defined MDE process, missing skill sets, and inflexibility in changing the existing culture. Without a well defined MDE process, teams that adopt MDE tend to use a "trial and error" approach and encounter the same set of pitfalls others have already experienced. Skill sets related to MDE includes mastery of formal languages, modeling, simulation, tools, code generation, model performance improvement, testing automation, and proper partitioning of architectural and design views (specific MDE training requirements are being identified as part of the effort described in Sect 4.3). Often the perceived required skill set is daunting for many teams; some do not even attempt MDE due to lack of the required skill sets. Adopting MDE without an appropriate cultural change has also caused many "painful" experiences. While some development process changes could be documented and enforced, other management and development cultural changes are hard to identify and much harder to enforce. One example of inflexibility in cultural changes is the tendency to tune performance through embedding pointer-manipulation code in the models, thus opening the door to the same problems encountered in hand code.

### 3.8   Lack of Migration Tools

Motorola is migrating from SDL-based modeling to UML-based modeling. However, a large number of legacy SDL-based models exist from more than a decade of SDL-based development. To facilitate the move to UML, migration tools are needed that support not only the main behavioral models, but also the associated modeling artifacts such as test cases and MSCs. The current migration tools are inadequate, and this impacts software development.

There is a significant cost of migration which is difficult to justify in terms of return on investment (ROI). Migrating existing software already in the field is in general a risky endeavor with low ROI. The lack of comprehensive migration tools exacerbates the problem.

There is also a limit to the benefit of MDE under a heterogeneous development environment. With large software system consisting of both legacy SDL and new UML models, there is no tractable way to co-develop the entire system. Because of this, it is difficult to achieve consistent benefits from simulation and consistency checking.

### 3.9   Lack of Scalability

We have observed that the current state of corporate MDE usage is characterized by isolated models. For example, even in a highly coupled system such as iDEN, each model exists separately. That is, they interact with each other only in the target network and are neither currently being modeled as a whole nor being leveraged for simulation and consistency checking as a whole.

The challenges of MDE with respect to model scalability are:

**Distributed development:** Almost all large systems are developed by separately managed teams that are also geographically separated. MDE adds another dimension to the distributed development because in order to take advantage of MDE at the whole system level, one needs to build the subsystems interfaces at the model level (not just at the target level). The model-level subsystem interfaces are new and often ill-defined mainly because of the difficulty in abstracting only model-level messaging without complications from lower-levels transport and network layers.

**Information Overload:** Modeling a large system such as the entirety of a cellular network is usually very complicated mainly because there are no straightforward ways of hiding detailed information at the right place in design, simulation, and presentation.

**Legacy Software:** Modeling a large system often requires the new models to interact with legacy software. It is normally not feasible to model a whole system such as cellular network because it is too costly to create stubs that replace the existing legacy software during modeling.

**Tool Performance:** Most MDE tools suffer from modeling performance when the system under development is large. The problem most often appears in simulating a large system such as an entire cellular network.

# 4   Addressing the Issues

This section presents some strategies Motorola is pursuing to optimized its use of MDE while addressing some of the shortcomings presented earlier.

## 4.1   UML 2.0 Profiles

Profiles provide a powerful tool for the specialization of UML 2.0. In particular, to address issues raised earlier in the paper, Motorola is currently using and/or creating several profiles:

**SDL Profile** This profile fills the semantic variation points in UML 2.0 and provides continuity with development that has been based on SDL.

**Testing Profile (U2TP)** This profile provides a means for defining test specifications that can be mapped onto TTCN-3 and JUnit test cases. In doing so, our aim is not only to provide testing tools that are tightly integrated with UML 2.0 model construction tools, but also to enable reuse of UML 2.0 models within the construction of tests.

**System Engineering Profile (SysML)** This profile provides common notations for systems engineering applications.[5]

**Domain Specification Communication Constraints (CUP)** This profile allows system architects and designers to specify domain-specific constraints explicitly as part of their models.

## 4.2   MDE Technical Advisory Board

The Motorola MDE Technical Advisory Board (MDE TAB) is the leadership organization for an effort focused on the tool/software development discipline

---

[5] SysML is not (yet) a UML 2.0 Profile in the strict definition.

deployed within Motorola. The focus of the MDE TAB is to provide a coordinated point of interaction with MDE tool vendors regarding their modeling and software development tools for Motorola global operations and to provide a central organization responsible for collecting and distributing MDE-related standards, metrics, etc.

The purpose of the MDE TAB is to:

- Develop enterprise technical requirements and Motorola-wide solutions.
- Identify and prioritize long-term deployment problems and enhancements.
- Determine the best approaches for addressing problems and requirements.
- Identify training, best practices, policies, and procedures related to MDE tools and processes.
- Determine business impact metrics to measure the prioritized efforts.
- Identify and prioritize tool integration requirements.
- Coordinate with other Motorola teams related to MDE tool usage.
- Manage the supplier relationships.

### 4.3   Modeling Challenge Levels

As discussed in Sect. 3, we have encountered many MDE-associated challenges such as ill-defined process, lack of required skill sets, etc. To overcome the challenges, an organization needs wide-ranging capabilities. However, it is not realistic for any organization to acquire those capabilities in one single effort. Most, if not all, development organizations need time to build their maturity with respect to the deployment of MDE.

Over the years, MDE practitioners have found that they went through different stages of modeling experiences, each stage with its distinctive benefits, challenges, and opportunities. Most MDE teams go through these stages before truly mastering MDE and its process. However, the documentation of those stages is incomplete or nonexistent, causing difficulty in sharing modeling experience among development organizations across the corporation. The planned continued growth of MDE in Motorola drives the need to define a framework of these stages (or levels). This framework must facilitate the sharing of experience, which includes tools, methodologies, best practices, processes, etc.

The framework Motorola is developing, called Modeling Challenge Levels (MCL), is created under a task force sponsored by the MDE TAB (see Sect. 4.2). The main purposes of the MCL are:

- To provide a framework for sharing MDE experience across the corporation. This is accomplished through defining the levels of modeling maturity based on the collective recommendation of MDE expert practitioners. The MCL provides an environment to promote the best practices in MDE, relying on local innovation for best practices while providing access to a corporate-wide experience base.
- To provide guidelines for creating a local MDE roadmap.

– To serve as a self-assessment tool with respect to an organization's modeling maturity. A solid understanding of the current MDE capabilities of an organization enables it to acquire the right MDE resources, plan improvements through gap analysis, understand anticipated challenges and benefits, and share experience effectively with other groups.

MCL describes modeling maturity in six levels (from least to most mature):

1. No Modeling
2. Informal Modeling
3. Formal Modeling
4. Model-Centered Design
5. Model-Driven Engineering
6. Optimized Model-Driven Engineering.

### 4.4   MDE Qualification

Existing qualification approaches such as UML 2.0 certification only assess a level of knowledge about a particular modeling language. The purpose behind MDE qualification is to provide a formal structure, as well as incentives, for the education and sharing of MDE skills and experience in a more systematic manner. It attempts to do this in a staged and generic fashion, thereby allowing managers and developers to learn and practice key skills that are appropriate to their application and development domain. For example, verifying model correctness is a generic and fundamental MDE activity, but how this is performed can depend upon the context of a particular development project. Hence, the emphasis is to build an appreciation of and experience with the core concepts needed for successful MDE while at the same time allowing flexibility on the specific techniques and technologies used. By introducing formality into the education of MDE, Motorola can build up a network of MDE experts that collectively provide feedback for future MDE strategies.

The plan is to build formalized MDE expertise through the introduction of staged MDE qualifications. This provides a formal means for sharing knowledge and experiences between development teams, thereby reducing the risk in adopting MDE technologies. For example, it could be that for the first trial of MDE within a particular development team, the project should be supported by at least one experienced MDE expert. We do not present a comprehensive list of ideas in this paper, but we do provide some idea of what we consider important criteria for the staged qualification of MDE expertise:

**Stage 1** Core MDE concept training and experience, including modeling, verification and validation, and process and measurement.
**Stage 2** Further specialized training and experience, including several MDE languages, hardware and enterprise modeling, formal verification techniques, transformation techniques, and mentoring of Stage 1 projects.
**Stage 3** Advanced training and experience, including demonstrations of modeling within different contexts, leadership in evaluating new MDE technologies, mentoring, and knowledge sharing.

## 4.5  Corporate-Level Tool Selection Committee

Motorola formed a one-time tool selection committee to evaluate the UML tools from third-party vendors and provide a recommendation on which one(s) should be used within Motorola. Each Motorola group engaging in MDE had representation on the committee, and it was the responsibility of the representatives to collect and prioritize the requirements from their respective groups. Based on the collated requirements, tools from the major vendors were evaluated on how well they met the few-hundred weighted requirements. The committee was able to narrow the officially sanctioned modeling tools to two choices. The evaluation of new and updated MDE tools is initiated through the MDE TAB (see Sect 4.2).

## 4.6  MDE Technology Improvement

Motorola continues to invest in MDE technology improvement ranging from automation technologies (including secure code generation, test generation, and model testing), metrics, profile development, meta-modeling, and analysis tools.

## 5  Conclusion

We have presented an overview of the MDE-related activities in Motorola. In one form or another, Motorola has been active in MDE for nearly two decades and has seen incredible successes and glaring failures. We have found that through the coordinated and controlled introduction of MDE techniques, significant quality and productivity gains can be consistently achieved, and the issues encountered can be handled in a systematic way.

## References

1. Baker, P.: Test Generation towards TTCN-3. ETSI TTCN-3 User Conference (2004)
2. Baker, P., Burton, S., Bristow, P., King, D., Jervis, C., Mitchell, B., Thomson, R.: Detecting and Resolving Semantic Pathologies in UML Sequence Diagrams. ACM ESEC-Foundations of Software Engineering (2005)
3. Baker, P., Dai, Z., Grabowski, J., Haugen, O., Samuelsson, E., Schieferdecker, I., Williams, C.: The UML 2.0 Testing Profile. In: Proc. of the Conf. on Quality Engineering in Software Technology 2004. Nuremberg, Germany (2004)
4. Baker, P., Jervis, C., King, D.: An Industrial use of FP: A Tool for Generating Test Scripts from System Specifications. In: Trinder, P., Michaelson, G., Loidl, H-W. (eds.): Trends in Functional Programming, Vol. 1. Intellect (2000) 126-135
5. Boyle, J., Harmer, T., Weigert, T., Weil, F.: Knowledge-Based Derivation of Programs from Specifications. In: Bourbakis, N. (ed.): Artificial Intelligence And Automation. World Scientific Press (1996)
6. Dietz, P., Weigert, T., Weil, F.: Formal Techniques for Automatically Generating Marshalling Code from High-Level Specifications. In: Proc. of the 1998 Workshop on Industrial-strength Formal Specification Techniques. Boca Raton, FL (1998)

7. European Telecommunications Standards Institute: Methods for Testing and Specification; The Testing and Control Notation version 3 (TTCN-3); Part 1: TTCN-3 Core Language. ETSI ES 201 873-1 (2001)
8. Gras, J., McGaw, D.: End-to-End Defect Prediction. In: IEEE International Symposium on Software Reliability Engineering (ISSRE). Saint Malo, France (2004)
9. Hatley, D., Pirbhai, I.: Strategies for Real-Time System Specification. Dorset House, New York (1988)
10. International Telecommunications Union: Abstract Syntax Notation One (ASN.1): Specification of Basic Notation. ITU-T Rec. X.680 (2002)
11. International Telecommunications Union: Message Sequence Chart (MSC). ITU-T Rec. Z.120 (2000)
12. International Telecommunications Union: Specification and Description Language. ITU-T Rec. Z.100 (2000)
13. International Telecommunications Union: TTCN-2 standard, Conformance Testing Methodology and Framework: Part 3: The Tree and Tabular Combined Notation (TTCN). ITU-T Rec. X.292 (1997)
14. Kleppe, A., Warmer, J., Bast, W.: MDA Explained: The Model Driven Architecture: Practice and Promise. Addison-Wesley (2003)
15. Mitchell, B., Thomson, R., Jervis, C.: Phase Automaton for Requirements Scenarios. In: Feature Interactions in Telecommunications and Software Systems VII. IOS Press (2003) 77–84
16. Object Management Group: Unified Modeling Language (UML): Superstructure, Version 2.0 (2003)

# Using a Domain-Specific Language and Custom Tools to Model a Multi-tier Service-Oriented Application — Experiences and Challenges

Marek Vokáč[1] and Jens M. Glattetre[2]

[1] Simula Research Laboratory, P.O.Box 134, 1325 Lysaker, Norway
marekv@simula.no,
http://www.simula.no/
[2] SuperOffice ASA / ICT Norway**, Drammensveien 211, 0212 Oslo, Norway
jens.2005@superoffice.com,
http://www.superoffice.com

**Abstract.** A commercial Customer Relationship Management application of approx. 1.5 MLOC of C++ code is being reimplemented, in stages, as a service-oriented, multi-tier application in C# on Microsoft .NET. We have chosen to use a domain-specific language both to model the external service-oriented interfaces, and to manage the transition to the internal, object-oriented implementation. Generic UML constructs such as class diagrams do not capture enough semantics to model these concepts. By defining a UML Profile that incorporates the concepts we wish to model, we have in effect created a Domain-Specific Language for our application. The models are edited using Rational XDE, but we have substituted our own code generator. This generator is a relatively generic text-substitution engine, which takes a template text and performs substitutions based on the model. The generator uses reflection to convert the UML and Profile concepts into substitution tags, which are in turn used in the template text. In this way, we can translate the semantics of the model into executable code, WSDL or other formats in a flexible way. We have successfully used this approach on a prototype scale, and are now transitioning to full-scale development.

## 1   Introduction and Problem Definition

Many companies are faced with a transition from an object-oriented programming model that implements a rich client, to a service-oriented architecture and an increasing emphasis on Web-based clients. A service-oriented architecture (SOA) requires application components to be structured in a way that is different from traditional, in-process object-oriented models.

Service-oriented architectures also prescribe a different approach than that of earlier Remote Object or Remote Procedure Call architectures, such as CORBA

---

** Supported by the Norwegian Research Council ICT Programme "FAMILIER", and "FAMILIES", ITEA project ip02009 of the EU Eureka $\Sigma$! 2023 Programme.

L. Briand and C. Williams (Eds.): MoDELS 2005, LNCS 3713, pp. 492–506, 2005.

or DCOM. One of the main tenets of SOA is to make boundaries between systems and services explicit, to promote interoperability and to encourage their proper use. Remote invocation is inherently orders of magnitude more expensive than local execution, and the architecture and granularity of the interfaces and messages must reflect this.

At the same time, the actual business and data access logic is generally implemented using object-oriented languages such as Java or C#. It may be desirable to reuse existing code, which typically represents a significant investment by the organization.

A coherent SOA requires modelling—it is not enough to simply go ahead and define services freely; this will result in a large set of disparate services that do not work well together. The design of a large object-oriented implementation will also benefit from modelling.

We are thus faced not only with the need to separately model a coherent SOA and an object-oriented implementation, but also to model the transition between the two—the connection between interfaces and their implementation. Ultimately, this set of models should result in the generation of executable code (including service definitions in WSDL or other appropriate description languages, and at least the skeletons of the implementations), as it will otherwise be hard to realize benefits that justify the investment in the modelling effort.

This experience report is written from the perspective of an industrial development project. We are looking for workable, pragmatic solutions that can be used in a full scale development project at the present time. Our approach to related work, tools and methods reflects this perspective.

We have conducted interviews with architects and developers in our organization to extract the knowledge presented here. The developers' experience with modelling ranges from minimal to extensive (more than 5 years), and their time with the company from 7 years down to just a few months. We are therefore able to present experience from a number of different viewpoints.

The rest of this experience report is organized as follows: section 2 summarizes the different approaches and tools we have considered. In section 3 we present our chosen solution, in the form of a Domain-Specific Language and its related Code Generator. Section 4 reports on our experience from using this approach for a modest, yet commercial and marketable, Collaborative CRM product. Finally, section 5 concludes and outlines our future work.

## 2   Tools and Approaches to Modelling SOA and OO

Several approaches to modelling at roughly the level needed for a Service-Oriented Architecture and its object-oriented implementation have been presented. A lot of effort has been spent on the Unified Modelling Language (UML), and Model-Driven Architecture (MDA) has been pushed as a concept and a trademark of the Object Management Group (OMG).

From the standpoint of a practitioner facing a choice of approach and a deadline, good tool support is perhaps the single most important factor. Manual, paper-based modelling, or the use of prototype academic tools is not a sufficient basis for an industrial project of significant size and complexity. For instance, the MDA specification published by OMG (1) contains a bare three pages on the subject of transformations from the platform-independent to the platform-specific models.

Czarnecki (2) has proposed a taxonomy of transformations, as well as an overview of existing techniques. For our needs, a template-based approach seemed to provide the optimum balance between flexibility, power and readability (2, Ch. 3.1.2).

Our organization is a fairly small one, with six developers being considered a fairly large team. Contrary to the practice in many large (especially North American) companies of having strictly defined roles—such as architect, designer, developer, tester—most of our developers at one time or another assume almost every role, according to the stage of the development process and personal competence. This also influences our approach to modelling, since we do not have a division between modellers and implementers, or between domain and application engineers (3, Ch. 2).

Our evaluation of the state of the art therefore focused on available tools, either released or in a late beta stage, rather than on academic publications and methods therein. In practice, this restricted our choices to UML-based tools such as Rational XDE (4), Telelogic Tau (5), Borland Together (6), and Microsoft Visio (7). A further, important constraint is that our future development will be on the Microsoft .NET platform, using the C# language and Microsoft Visual Studio as the development environment.

A tempting alternative was to use tools designed for Software Factories (8), an approach where separate Domain-Specific Languages are used for different viewpoints within the total model. Transformations from model/viewpoint to C# code, SQL DDL or other artefacts can then be defined.

However, our search did not turn up any tools that we considered to be sufficiently advanced, robust and scalable to support the kind of modelling we wished to undertake. Microsoft's initiative on Software Factories and extensible modelers is interesting (9), but it is still at an early stage and not suitable for production.

Our need was (and still is) for a tool that we can use to span from a data dictionary, via simple object-oriented counterparts to relational tables, through composition and business logic up to a service-oriented set of interfaces that are not merely advanced CRUD operations; and to be able to generate the interfaces, descriptions and skeletons needed for both local and remote (e.g., via Web Services) invocations of the interfaces. It follows that reliance on the tools' built-in code generators would be too restrictive, as the transformations between the different viewpoints are not trivial.

It bears repetition that good tool support is absolutely essential in an industrial project; otherwise the model will quickly turn into more bureaucracy than help. Certainly, if the development process model uses concepts from the Agile/XP domain, with multiple, short iterations, we must expect the models and the transformations to change. An inflexible tool would push the process towards a more strict waterfall pattern, which we do not desire.

# 3    A Domain-Specific Language and Code Generator

While UML has become a *de facto* standard for modelling OO software, the generic UML constructs such as classes, class diagrams and association have relatively low semantic content. Simultaneously, there are constraints on what one can model; for instance, an association cannot be set up between a specific attribute in one class and an attribute in another class.

For modelling an SOA, we need a modelling language that can capture concepts such as a *Data Contract*, a *Message Contract* and a *Service Contract*. We need to be able to group these concepts, inherit, extend and reuse them. Our organization has also made a considerable investment in its data dictionary, which describes (both at a table and an entity level) the data model underlying the whole application. When modelling services, we wish to leverage this investment.

At the same time, the service interfaces should not be mere repetitions of the underlying physical data model. This could very easily lead to a situation reminiscent of DCE, CORBA or DCOM, where the remoteness of a service call is hidden—the approach is to conceal the fact that a method invocation is actually on a remote object. This leads to unwanted dependencies, where internal behaviour (such as data types) is exposed, and often also to performance problems, since iteration over remote, low-level CRUD operations is easy to program but impossible to make fast and reliable.

Service-Oriented Architectures explicitly try to avoid sharing classes, since there are bound to be platform differences; instead, Data, Message and Service Contracts are used to specify messages and their associated content. The mapping from these types to the platform dependent types at each end is incidental and may not be predictable.

As an example, a data type specifying an integer with no upper limit may on some platforms be transformed into a string internally, if the platform lacks native unlimited-precision data types. Sharing class across platforms would require the correspondence to be known in advance, which cannot be taken for granted.

## 3.1    Using UML Profiles to Define a Domain-Specific Language

UML is a modelling language for which there is quite extensive tool support. In UML it is possible to define *Profiles* that add semantic content to the generic mechanisms of UML itself, effectively making it possible to use it as a platform for developing Domain-Specific Languages (DSL). This is not the only possible approach; for instance, van Deursen (10) described a DSL for financial engineering that was used to generate several different kinds of artefacts (VSAM, CICS and COBOL items). It uses the MetaEnvironment tools (11) for the transformation/generation. However, UML and UML Profiles are open standards, and therefore attractive by not locking the organization into a particular tool or tool vendor.

Of course, implementing a profile in a particular tool is dependent on the tool, but the concepts of the profile can in principle be transferred to another tool if needed, together with the models. The facilities provided by Rational XDE for defining profiles are fairly rudimentary, but have so far proven adequate to our needs.

In order to define our DSL, we have taken the minimum set of concepts needed to capture our modelling requirements, and translated them into a UML profile. These concepts cover both the service layer, the data dictionary, and the transition between the Service-Oriented and Object-Oriented worlds. It is critical to us that these two viewpoints are well integrated, since we will be implementing the services using object-oriented languages and tools. Figure 1 shows a simplified example of a service interface and how some of its data fields are derived from the data dictionary.

## 3.2    Generation of Code and Other Artefacts

A model is useful in itself, as a design and documentation tool. However, its value is significantly increased if it can also be used to generate code, tests and embedded documentation. Such use is also a powerful incentive to keep the model up to date, as a working tool, and not just as a construct that was made early on in the development cycle and then quietly abandoned.

By definition, a model is an abstraction, and thus a simplification of the underlying reality. If a model contains enough information to fully generate the implementation, its complexity can easily become of the same order of magnitude as that of the implementation and its usefulness becomes doubtful. We therefore did not set out to find or create a tool that would generate the *content* of our implementations.

However, the structure of the services, the structure and skeleton of the implementation, and the "glue" logic required to technically define, deploy and put together services and their interfaces and implementations, are prime candidates for automated generation from models. The fact that these technologies change significantly over time, as new standards, tools and frameworks are adopted, provides a further powerful incentive for generating them.

Modelling and managing the transition between services and OO implementations is important, because best practices for design and grouping of them can be quite different. From our experience we believe that this is best done at the modelling level, and that generation of a skeleton for the implementation is extremely useful.

## 3.3    Code Generation by Text Substitution

Commercial UML tools such as Borland Together or Rational XDE include code generators for several languages, such as C++, Java or C#. To a greater or lesser degree, architects and developers can influence how the code generator works, i.e., what the emitted code looks like. Generally, however, what is a class in the UML diagram becomes a class or class-like construct in the code, and the adjustments one can make are more in the realm of coding style than semantics. One is also limited to generating the artefacts for which there is built-in support.

With the addition of semantic content through UML Profiles, this situation becomes untenable. The whole purpose of the profile is to capture semantics, that should then be reflected in the code. A UML "class" object that is assigned to a certain stereotype may not represent a class at all, but rather a service, a data contract, or a field with many descriptive attributes in a data dictionary. The standard code generators are not designed to handle this level of content.

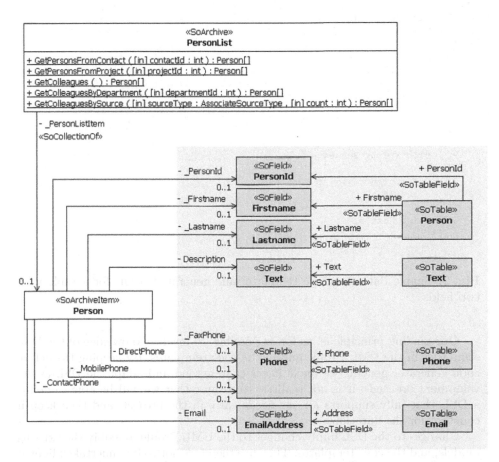

**Fig. 1.** Interface example: The shaded items come from the data dictionary model, while the clear items are service interfaces. The <<SoArchive>> stereotype denotes a list-like data set, while an <<SoArchiveItem>> is a single row in such a list.

We have therefore created a generic code generator that works by text substitution. It takes as its input a template text, and replaces recognized tags in the text with values from the model. The generator uses reflection on the UML profile and the UML tools' data model to define the tags; the (human) template author can then compose templates that translate into relevant, executable code. Simple looping and conditional constructs provide additional flexibility, while we do try to avoid the definition of an entire new programming language and environment within the code generator itself. Figure 2 shows a simple example, where we generate a C# object that corresponds to one database table and its fields; the lower half shows the result for a trivially simple table that has two fields. Syntax coloring is provided by a custom version of the Notepad++ editor (12).

```
1  [@With(Tables)]// [@Table.Description]
2  public struct [@Table.PublicName]
3  {
4  [@With(Table.Fields)]
5      // [@TableField.Field.Description]
6      [@TableField.Field.DataType.CSharp] [@TableField.Field.PublicName];
7  [@Loop(Table.Fields)]
8  };
9  [@Loop(Tables)]
```

```
1  // next_id to be used for each table
2  public struct Sequence
3  {
4      // Sequence-id of host table
5      int Id;
6      // Next id to be used for table
7      int NextId;
8  };
9
```

**Fig. 2.** Simple data structure template, and generated result for a table with two fields

Our guiding principle is, as far as possible, to localize knowledge of the DSL semantics in the UML Profile and in the code templates. By keeping the actual code generator generic, we make it easier to extend and adapt the DSL as development proceeds: it is not realistic to assume that we will be able to define a DSL that fully supports all our needs early in the project, and then keep it constant for the duration.

Changes to the DSL imply changes to the UML Profile, possibly the existing models, and the code templates. They are therefore not to be undertaken lightly, but as long as we confine ourselves to extensions the cost is manageable. A breaking change to existing constructs would be costly; however, this is a problem common to all DSL tools that we know of—and most do not handle even simple extensions to the DSL.

As the problem domain is explored and the language matures, the rate of change over time decreases and languages become more stable. However, if a new aspect or a new domain needs to be modelled, we should expect to have to make changes to the DSL. It is therefore critical that the tool chain supports at least extensions to the DSL in a straightforward manner.

## 3.4 Other Uses for "Code" Generation

Having a text-based code generator that works by text substitution opens the possibility of generating other artifacts than executable code. The generator effectively becomes a simple transformation engine, and can be used to generate HTML documentation, WSDL service definitions, or deployment configuration files.

For instance, we can use the generator, together with a suitable template, to generate an HTML documentation file that contains service signatures, their descriptions (from documentation in the model), and cross-referencing tags that make it possible to seamlessly integrate the documentation into an existing development environment such as Visual Studio.

Another use is to generate WSDL service descriptions. Since the UML Profile contains concepts that make it possible to distinguish a public service from a private service from a simple RPC interface, it is relatively straightforward to use these attributes in the template text and generate WSDL only for the model elements that actually model services at the desired level.

A third use, illustrating the advantages of a template-based approach, is that we can also generate unit test skeletons from the same model either in C#, or in some other language suited to the testing framework used.

## 3.5 Model Transformation by Code Generation and Reverse Engineering

A conventional approach in Model-Driven Architecture (MDA) is to start with a platform-independent model (PIM), transform it through a a set of rules to a platform-specific model (PSM) and from there to code. Examples can be found in (13; 14; 15), with some specifications in (1). However, the practical matter of setting up the transformation rules and tools to manage this in an automated manner is difficult—and if the transformation is performed manually, the overhead repeating it whenever the PIM or the transformation changes quickly becomes prohibitive.

For us, the SOA model, expressed in our DSL is the PIM, while its implementation in an object-oriented form in C#, and using Web Services (16) as a technical vehicle, is the corresponding PSM. That is, we define our DSL and external, service-oriented interface to be "platform-independent". Note that at this level we hold no opinion as to the manner in which the service interfaces are to be accessed. This corresponds to the standard MDA view (1, Ch. 4.1.2).

Changing to use, for instance, Microsoft Indigo as the service access mechanism, would mean changing the transformation from the PIM to the PSM; since the underlying C# execution platform is the same, we would expect to be able to reuse the actual implementations with few changes. A more radical change, for instance to a Java/Corba platform, would of course involve much more work, but we would still expect to generate the service definitions, interfaces and implementation skeletons.

Instead of performing a model-to-model transformation at a modelling-language level, we have chosen to perform the transformation directly from the PIM—which primarily models services—to the OO implementation (effectively the result of generating code from a PSM) directly.

The transformation rules are embedded in the code template that is half of the input to the code generation, the other half being the model and the semantics encoded in its use of the concepts from the UML Profile. Effectively, the template *is* a transformation rule—and it could have been a model-to-model transformation by setting up a template whose end product were valid XMI or some other, relevant metadata format. However, since our emphasis as a commercial development team is on creating a software product, we chose to concentrate on generating code.

Thus, our code templates actually combine two roles: transformation of the model from a platform-independent to a platform-dependent level; and transformation from a model to code (or similar-level artefacts such as WSDL). This combination is intentional, the main reason being efficiency.

Once the implementation code skeleton has been generated, it can be reverse-engineered using the standard functionality of the UML tool. The resulting UML model then becomes the result of applying the semantics of our UML Profile to our PIM, i.e., the PSM. Since it is reverse-engineered it always reflects the code, which is what is ultimately shipped to the customer. It therefore becomes a useful documentation and verification tool, rather than an intermediate step in the development process. A disadvantage of this approach is that the stereotypes from the PIM are lost, unless the generated code is somehow tagged, and the reverse-engineering mechanism recognizes the tags. Such recognition of extra tags is currently not available in Rational XDE.

## 4    Practical Experience

Initially, the designer and user of the modelling tools and code generator was the same person (J. M. G.). As the project matured from a prototype / technology demonstration project to a full-scale development project with six developers, we have gathered more experience with both the technology and the organizational side effects.

We have conducted interviews with all the developers, ranging from the senior architect (M.V.) to recently hired developers with little modelling experience. In general, increased modelling experience correlates with an increased perception of the benefits of the approach.

## 4.1   Positive Experiences

Perhaps the single most positive consequence of using a model is to raise the general consciousness level about the need for well-designed, thought through interfaces. By making the separation between a service interface and its object-oriented implementation explicit, the developer is forced to take the difference into account.

Standardization is also an important benefit. Our code-generation templates contain and enforce a certain pattern for how a service, its messages and data should be related, and how they should be implemented for local and remote calls. Since all of this is generated, it will always be the same and consistent between services. "Standard" items, such as authentication tickets, are automatically added, again in a consistent way.

When new developers are added to an already established team, it may take some time to learn all the written and unwritten rules for design and coding styles. The combination of modelling and generation helps by codifying and enforcing the "standard" way of doing things.

Simultaneous generation of remote interfaces, local implementations, data and message contracts as well as unit test skeletons and documentation pages from a single model ensures that all of these artefacts are actually created. While we cannot force people to actually write good documentation or comprehensive tests, there is at least little excuse for not doing so—and empty tests or documentation pages are highly visible in code reviews. This increases the consistency of the work across developers

Generation also increases the visibility of "auxiliary" tasks such as documentation and testing. The importance of this rises with the approach of a deadline and the temptation to skip testing in order to finish in time.

While "local" changes—changes that affect just one or a few interfaces—do not benefit much from code generation, "global" changes that involve changes to how *all* interfaces or implementations are defined become much simpler to perform, usually by making changes to the template. Since they are applied equally to all relevant objects, consistency is easier to attain.

The fact that the code generator is an in-house tool is generally considered to be a positive factor. The tool quickly becomes central to the development process, and being dependent on a vendor's release plan for fixes or changes could easily become a bottleneck. While the availability of the few developers who can update the tool can also become a limiting factor, it is at least under the team's control. Open source tools are a possible alternative in this situation.

## 4.2   Challenges and Pitfalls

While there are important benefits to be realized from modelling and generation, there are also costs and challenges involved. We have chosen to divide these into the purely technical, and those that are more cultural or organizational in character.

**Technical Challenges** Currently, our model resides in a single file, and the code generator runs on the entire model every time. In practice, this means that only one developer at a time can have the model locked in the version control system (merging of multiple versions is not practical). It also means that all target files are regenerated for every change. While the version control system will recognize and filter out submissions of files that have not actually changed, this still causes problems when scaling up to a team of six developers.

The problem is periodic in nature—typically, there is a period in each iteration where new services are designed and defined, followed by a period of actual implementation. The design period is one of high contention for the model, while the implementation and testing/debugging is independent of the model and therefore does not suffer.

The problem can mostly be solved by dividing the model into separately controlled packages, and by revising the code generator so it can be run on single packages, instead of the whole model. However, changes to templates or the UML profile will still force regeneration of the whole system.

To a certain degree, this problem is also related to the way our teams are organized. A team that has only a few designed architects/interface designers will have much less contention for the models, and can also afford to increase the amount of special knowledge and skills required to manipulate the models. Our teams are organized in the opposite direction, with most of the developers assuming most of the roles during one complete cycle.

A different challenge is posed by the size and complexity of the entities being modelled, and the way they are modelled. Since we are using UML as our basic modelling language, and the Association concept can only connect two Classes (as opposed to connecting specific attributes within or between classes), we ended up modelling service interface *attributes* as separate *classes*, with specific stereotypes. This gives us the flexibility and power we need, for instance by making it possible to reuse an attribute in multiple interfaces.

At the same time, this approach increases the visual complexity of the model and the screen real estate needed to contain it. When each attribute of an interface becomes a separate box with a line going to it, it is easy to run out of space on a screen. The model shown in Figure 1 was simplified for this paper, to make it a reasonable size—in reality, there about three times as many boxes of various kinds in the diagram. Even with dual 20-inch displays on each workstation, this can become an irritating problem. In the near term we do not see any easy solution; in the longer term, a modelling tool that is not based on UML, but is instead built to handle DSL's should provide a solution.

The template language is fairly straightforward, but since it is a proprietary language there is little tool support for it, in the form of syntax highlighting or word completion. We are currently looking at ways of adding these features to Visual Studio, to make template editing easier. Most of the suggestions for improvements—from the developers using the model—relate to details of the template language and tool support for editing templates.

Two of the developers have prior experience using XSLT expressions to transform models. Their perception is that the readability and traceability problems (which part of the template causes a certain output to appear) were larger in XSLT, and that they usually had to actually run a transformation or generation to see the output. With a template language based on simple substitution of textual tags, it is much easier to predict the output. This agrees with the experience of others, such as Czarnecki (2).

Tool support for transitioning from one version of the Profile to the next is largely nonexistent. We have created our own tool to bridge the gap, but serious use of any kind of DSL will be much hampered by the absence of such support. Ideally, a tool should provide an analysis of the consequences of a language change (such as an estimate of the number of modelled entities or associations affected or made invalid), as well as support for mapping concepts in the two language versions, and an application of that mapping to models made using the language.

**Organizational Challenges** Even though we consider our template language to be simple, it still *is* a language, and it raises the learning threshold for new members of the team. It has to be learned, understood and worked with in order to be able to realize the full power of the approach. The alternative, where only one or two "master developers" understand the whole system, is both inefficient (they can become bottlenecks) and risky (in case they leave). The associated training costs are significant but acceptable.

The "extra" work involved in modelling an interface—using the Rational XDE GUI to draw interfaces, create or retrieve attributes and connect them, and attach the various stereotypes and parameters needed, may seem to be a drawback. A possible consequence is that this work is postponed, or that weaknesses in an interface are not corrected because the effort needed to do so is perceived as excessive. This may not actually be a big drawback: if it is very easy to change or create service interfaces, they will proliferate, likely with a decrease in the generality, stability and quality of each interface. Since our service interfaces will be used by partners, customers and consultants for many years, they have to be stable and of a high quality.

Generated code will often contain repetitions—the same template is used to generate skeletons and (partial) implementations for many objects in the model. At one level this may be considered a disadvantage; after all, refactoring to *avoid* repeating an algorithm in multiple places is a well established practice. If we view template as the "code", it contains the algorithm only once, and changes to the algorithm are performed in the template, not the generated code. On the other hand, tools such as source browsers will show all the repetitions. Whether this is actually a problem on a significant scale remains to be seen, and we suspect it to be a matter of personal viewpoint and preference.

**Costs and Benefits** Since we have not performed parallel development using models and code generation versus a more traditional approach, we do not have hard data on the costs and benefits. However, many of the features developed by this project have equivalents in existing code in the company, and those were implemented some time ago, mostly without modelling.

The costs are the most visible—it has taken one senior developer approximately two years to develop the Profile, the code generator and associated tools, and implement both a table- and entity-level database abstraction layer, plus a significant amount of infrastructure code. This is roughly comparable to the effort required for comparable development when the previous generation of the system was implemented.

The benefits, in terms of stability, error frequency or functionality, are harder to characterize. There is no doubt that the model-based approach encourages a much greater test coverage, and that it automatically leads to a degree of consistency that would otherwise require strict enforcement of the company styleguide and standards. We believe that the main benefits will accrue as we scale up the development both in complexity and in volume.

Since the costs associated with this approach are significant, we do believe that small or one-off projects are not likely to realize a net benefit. Our project will now scale up to six developers for approximately one year; we expect this to be large enough to realize a benefit, though we also expect the benefit to be more in terms of increased code quality and functionality, rather than reduced cost and time.

## 5   Conclusions and Future Work

Current modelling tools based on UML reflect the fact that UML semantics are informal, while specific enough to point clearly in the direction of an object-oriented target language. Since service-oriented architectures are not necessarily object-oriented, while their implementations often are, the standard code generators included in UML tools cannot be used for modelling both SOA interfaces and OO implementations directly.

At the same time, tools that support the creation of Domain-Specific Languages, are not yet ready for heavy industrial use. However, we view the DSL approach as perhaps the most promising to date and have adopted it for our development project.

Our solution has been to create a simple code generator based on text substitution, and to use a UML Profile to define the additional semantics we need in the modelling language. We thus transform our chosen UML tool (Rational XDE) into a simple DSL tool, albeit with limited functionality. The metadata that represent the model are reflected into the code generator, and the model-to-code transformations are provided by writing a code template that incorporates substitution tags matching the model metadata.

Our experience so far is that the approach works quite well for those lower layers of the application that express similar functionality repeatedly, such as Data Access Objects for individual tables. Here, "mass production" of functionality based on a template, repeated for each table, makes good sense.

When modelling more high-level services, the emphasis is more on the standardization of naming and behaviour, and the generation of skeletons rather than complete functionality. While the Data Access layer exhibits close to 80% generated code, the service layer has less than 40% generated content—and this percentage may decrease as the implementation complexity increases.

However, it is the generated content that defines the interfaces and the implementation patterns, including the particular technology used to implement services. This is important, since the current emphasis on Web Services will surely be superseded by some other—hopefully compatible—technology within a time span that overlaps the lifetime of our product (typically 10 years). When this happens, regeneration of interfaces and "glue" logic should save a lot of effort, and provide a faster time to market for solutions compatible with new standards.

## 5.1   Future Work

In the near future, our work will concentrate on making the template language more readable, as well as extending support for it into our development environment. Features such as syntax highlighting and auto-completion of reserved words, variables and other constructs is today taken for granted. The absence of such support makes editing of the templates unnecessarily tedious. Similarly, accessing the code generator from within the integrated development environment is desirable.

Further major development will probably wait for the availability of more sophisticated tools, for instance the Software Factory modellers announced by Microsoft. By being designed for customization and implementation of DSL's such tools should be more suitable than using profiles to force foreign semantics into existing UML tools.

We continually strive to find the correct balance between investment in in-house tools and dependence on external tools. In-house tools offer full control, at the price of full cost for the tools' development and maintenance. External tools reverse the equation, offering low cost but also a lower degree of control.

For a tool that is central to our development process, and using a technology that is not yet mature, we believe the in-house approach to be the correct one at this time. In the future, a switch to externally developed tools is quite probable, when sufficiently mature and well-supported tools are offered. Availability of the source code will probably be a distinct advantage, since it offers a "safety valve" in the case of problems that would otherwise threaten a development project.

## Acknowledgements

Thanks are due to Guttorm Nielsen, Director of research & development of SuperOffice ASA for providing the time for writing papers in an otherwise hectic project timetable. Thomas Schjerpen, Martin Valland, Trond Nilsen and Jørund Myhre generously shared their insight and experience.

Our work has also been supported by the Norwegian Research Council ICT Programme "FAMILIER", and participates in FAMILIES, ITEA project ip02009 of the EU Eureka $\Sigma$! 2023 Programme.

# References

[1] Object Management Group: **Model Driven Arhictecture Home Page** (2004) http://www.omg.org/mda/.

[2] Czarnecki, K., Helsen, S.: **Classification of Model Transofrmation Approaches**. In: **2nd OOPSLA'03 Workshop on Generative Techniques in the Context of MDA**, Anaheim, USA (2003)

[3] Czarnecki, K.: **Overview of Generative Software Development** (2005) http://www.swen.uwaterloo.ca/ kczarnec/gsdoverview.pdf.

[4] IBM: **Rational XDE** (2005) http://www-306.ibm.com/software/awdtools/developer/rosexde/.

[5] Telelogic: **Telelogic Tau** (2005) http://www.telelogic.com/products/tau/index.cfm.

[6] Borland Inc: **Together** (2005) http://www.borland.com/together/.

[7] Microsoft Inc: **Visio 2003** (2005) http://office.microsoft.com/en-gb/FX010857981033.aspx.

[8] Greenfield, J., Short, K., Cook, S., Kent, S.: **Software Factories**. Wiley, Indianapolis, USA (2004) ISBN: 0-471-20284-3.

[9] Microsoft Inc: **Microsoft Grows Partner Ecosystem Around Visual Studio 2005 Team System** (2004) http://www.microsoft.com/presspass/press/2004/oct04/10-2600PSLAEcosystemPR.asp.

[10] Deursen, A.v.: **Using a Domain-Specific Language for Financial Engineering**. ERCIM News (1999)

[11] CWI: **ASF+SDF MetaEnvironment** (2005) http://www.cwi.nl/htbin/sen1/twiki/bin/view/SEN1/MetaEnvironment.

[12] Ho, D.: **Notepad ++, Version 2.8** (2004) http://notepad-plus.sourceforge.net/.

[13] Judson, S.R., France, R.B., Carver, D.L.: **Specifying Model Transformations At the Metamodel Level** . In: **UML 2003 - Workshop in Software Model Engineering**, San Francisco, USA (2003)

[14] Pires, L.A.F., Sinderen, M.v., Farias, C.A.R.G.d., Almeida, J.A.P.A.: **Use of Models and Modelling Techniques for Service Development**. In: **3rd IFIP International Conference on E-Commerce, E-Business and E-Government (I3E 2003)**, GuarajÃ, Brazil, Kluwer (2003) 441–456

[15] Solberg, A., Oldevik, J., Aagedal, J..A.: **A Framework for QoS-Aware Model Transformation, Using a Pattern-Based Approach**. In Meersman, R., Tari, Z., eds.: **On the Move to Meaningful Internet Systems 2004: CoopIS, DOA, and ODBASE**. Volume 3291., Agia Napa, Cyprus, Publisher: Springer-Verlag GmbH (2004) 1190

[16] W3C: **Web Services Activity** (2004) http://www.w3.org/2002/ws/.

# Invited Presentation III:
# The Architects' Workbench — Research in the Trenches

Doug Kimelman

IBM, USA
dnk@us.ibm.com

## Abstract

IT architects know how hard it is to collect architectural information in an engagement and keep it all clear and organized in their minds. Transforming that information into models of a viable architecture and keeping the associated documents consistent and up to date is an even greater challenge. The Architects' Workbench (AWB) supports the creative process of architectural thinking and modeling. With AWB, architects capture informal notes, unstructured information and existing documents during customer meetings or at any time throughout an engagement. They proceed to progressively structure, formalize, and refine the information using the AWB modeling and refactoring tools. In this way, AWB users opportunistically build up models to achieve a viable architecture. At any time, users can automatically generation consistent, up-to-date documents from customizable templates. Developed by IBM Research in collaboration with IBM Global Services, AWB has been used in production by IT architecture practitioners, and the response has been very enthusiastic. While customizable to other methods and metamodels, it is tailored to the practice of IBM Global Services. This talk presents key AWB innovations, along with experience from production use of the AWB.

L. Briand and C. Williams (Eds.): MoDELS 2005, LNCS 3713, pp. 507–507, 2005.

# Uniform Support for Modeling Crosscutting Structure

Maria Tkatchenko and Gregor Kiczales

University of British Columbia
{tkatch, gregor}@cs.ubc.ca

**Abstract.** We propose bottom-up support for modeling crosscutting structure in UML by adding a simple join point model to the meta-model. This supports built-in crosscutting modeling constructs such as sequence diagrams. It also facilitates adding new kinds of crosscutting modeling constructs such as role bindings, inter-type declarations, and advice. A simple weaver produces a uniform representation of the crosscutting structure, which can then be displayed or analyzed in a variety of ways.

## Introduction

UML provides support for modeling a system from different perspectives [20]. Some of these perspectives have a hierarchical relationship to each other, such as package and class diagrams. Others have a *crosscutting* relationship [14, 18] – a sequence diagram can crosscut a class diagram, in that it may include calls to methods from multiple classes [10]; collaboration diagrams can crosscut class and sequence diagrams [23]; statecharts can crosscut all the others. There have also been proposals to extend UML with new crosscutting modeling constructs such as advice, inter-type declarations (ITDs) and role bindings [1, 15, 22, 24, 27].

This paper aims to support modeling of crosscutting relationships by building on the join point model[1] (JPM) mechanism used in aspect-oriented programming [18]. We propose bottom-up support for aspects in UML, by adding a simple JPM to the UML meta-model. Our enhanced meta-model supports display and analysis of both pre-existing and new forms of crosscutting structure in UML.

Our work is partly motivated by observing the difficulty of adding pattern composition support to existing UML tools. Prior work in AOP has shown that many patterns are easier to implement using AspectJ [8]. We aim to achieve the same kind of benefits for patterns during modeling by introducing a JPM to the UML meta-model. We also aim to support other forms of crosscutting structure in UML. So rather than using modeling to support AOP [11, 12, 20], our focus is on using the central mechanism of AOP to support modeling.

In aspect-orientation, weaving is defined as coordinating the interaction between the crosscutting concerns. In AOP languages like AspectJ, this involves ensuring that

---

[1] In the context of this paper, the term join point model can cause confusion with the meta-model of the modeling language, and the models written in the language. To help avoid confusion we use the JPM abbreviation throughout the paper.

L. Briand and C. Williams (Eds.): MoDELS 2005, LNCS 3713, pp. 508–521, 2005.
© Springer-Verlag Berlin Heidelberg 2005

advice runs when it should and defining inter-type declarations. We present a weaver that provides simple coordination of crosscutting structure in UML models. By providing a uniform representation of the interactions between crosscutting concerns, our weaver makes it easier to implement model analysis and display tools. The weaver records its results by associating with each model element a set of other model elements with which it crosscuts. Once the pair-wise crosscutting structure is collected into the sets, it can be analyzed and presented in a variety of ways.

The contributions of this work are to show that (i) the crosscutting structure of several traditional modeling relationships, as well as newer aspect-oriented modeling relationships, can be supported by a meta-model enhanced with a simple JPM, (ii) weaving the model to collect the crosscutting structure is straightforward, and (iii) the combination of (i) and (ii) makes it easy for modeling tool implementers and modelers to access, analyze and display crosscutting relationships of interest. We also present (iv) AOP-like advice and inter-type declaration constructs for UML.

## Related Work

There are two streams of research related specifically to our work. The first looks at explicitly adding aspects or AOP concepts to UML, either by using provided extension mechanisms, or by changing the UML meta-model. The second looks at improving the design process by providing means to compose different diagrams, which helps alleviate problems associated with some forms of crosscutting.

### Standard Extension Mechanisms

These proposals use the standard extension mechanisms provided by UML to support aspects or aspect-oriented extensions.

Stein et al. [24] introduce weaving in UML through the use of stereotypes. As a result, sequence diagrams that crosscut each other can be merged to display the final expected behavior (this may require the set of calls in a sequence to be totally ordered, which is computationally expensive). The modeler has to specify the crosscutting elements by means of explicit weaving instructions. By contrast, in our system weaving is implicit and crosscutting is treated on-par with other kinds of structural relations in the model.

Pawlak presents a notation for designing AO programs [21]. In his work, an aspect-class is a new element which extends the semantics of base classes, and contains both regular- and aspect-methods. Pointcut relations link aspect-methods to points in the base class.

Other work also looks at introducing aspects into UML using extension mechanisms such as stereotypes [9, 11].

**Meta-model Changes**

The work discussed in this section uses extensions to the UML meta-model to support aspects or aspect-oriented extensions.

Kande argues that aspects need to be first-class elements in UML [12]. He claims that the composition of a standard UML model with an aspect model does not do a good job of modularizing the separate concerns – the elements in the design model are coupled more than they are in the code. In addition, the model does not communicate the ability to plug and un-plug aspects from the core functionality. He shows that some of the concerns which can be well-separated in an AO program instead end up scattered throughout the design model.

Citing the restrictions that arise when using stereotypes and profiles to extend UML, Lions proposes introducing AOP into UML using meta-modeling [17]. Coupled with our meta-model's uniform support for various kinds of crosscutting, this supports our view that extending the UML meta-model to include AO concepts should be done from the bottom-up.

**Composing Diagrams**

Straw et al. look into composing primary and aspect class diagrams [26]. In their mechanism, conflicts and undesirable emergent properties can be identified during analysis of the composed model. However, the composition directives require developers to already be aware of the potential conflicts in the model, instead of helping them discover this information through analysis of the model.

Clarke and Walker [5] propose the use of composition patterns, which are implemented using UML templates, to specify crosscutting concerns. This approach requires explicit identification of aspects and binding specifications, and can produce composed diagrams, which show the result of bindings applied to the base design.

One important difference between these approaches and our work is that we make weaving implicit, or automatic, and allow the modeler to select which view to take on the woven structure.

Stein and Hanenberg use UML collaborations to specify the details of crosscutting in a given decomposition, which can be either structural or behavioral [25]. The crosscut and crosscutting elements, the composition strategy, and the join points can all be specified independently. The modeler is required to explicitly state all the crosscutting relationships and join points while designing the system.

In Caesar [19] Mezini and Ostermann propose a higher-level module concept on top of join point interception which allows reuse of aspects. They develop the model based on aspect collaboration interfaces, which decouple an aspect into independently specified aspect implementation and aspect binding modules. These two parts must be composed in a weavlet before the aspect can be deployed, which activates its pointcuts and advice.

# Running Example

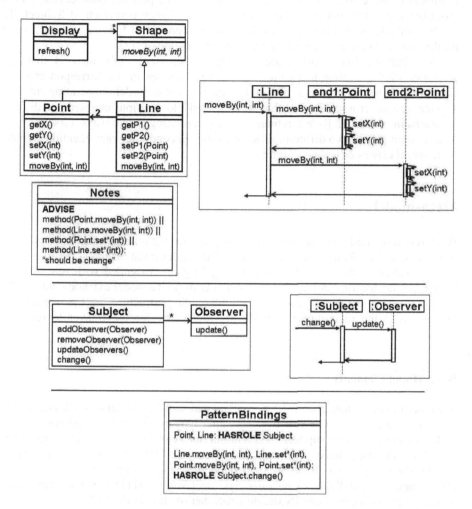

**Figure 1:** Shape example

The paper uses a single running example, adapted from the graphical shapes example discussed in [13, 14, 18], and shown in Figure 1. Three simple model fragments are shown. The first two fragments each contain a class and sequence diagram. The top fragment models the main functionality of Point and Line shapes, including a design note that makes use of the advice construct we have defined. The middle fragment models the Observer design pattern [7]. The bottom fragment models the role bindings between the shape classes and the design pattern.

This model also uses two new kinds of model elements. First, *advice* [13] makes it possible to advise model elements – for example, the moveBy and setter methods of Point and Line. The syntax used in the figure serves only to illustrate the meaning, and is not a concrete proposal for advice syntax.

Second, role bindings bind classes to roles they play, and class members to members of those roles. In the example Point and Line play the Subject role, and the moveBy and setter methods play the role of the change operation in Subject. The binding of roles is not the same as the standard concept of binding in UML, where binding refers to the creation of an element from a template [3].

Note that the class and sequence diagrams crosscut each other in that each sequence diagram refers to methods in multiple classes in the corresponding class diagram. The new advice and role binding elements also model crosscutting structure. Advice can be crosscutting in that it may apply to multiple elements in different diagrams in the model. Role bindings can be crosscutting in two ways. First, they may refer to elements in two different class diagrams. Second, they may mention elements in different classes of a class diagram.

# Meta-model

We have developed a simple implementation of our meta-model weaver based on the Eclipse Modeling Framework (EMF) [6]. The implementation has three main parts. First, a subset of the UML-based modeling language extended with role bindings, inter-type declarations and advice. Second, a UML meta-model extended with a JPM. Finally, a weaver which coordinates crosscutting structure in the model. The extensions to the meta-model provide the foundation for the weaver to record its results.

### Base Model Elements

A model in our system is formed from class and sequence diagrams. Classes in class diagrams are extended with role bindings, inter-type declarations and advice.

In class diagrams we support class and interface elements with generalization, each of which can also have attributes and operations. We do not currently support relationships such as collaboration, dependency, aggregation, realization, etc. We allow methods and fields to be *inter-type declarations* (ITDs) in that they can be placed in one class, but actually define a member of another class [2, 4].

Advice declarations are based on AspectJ, and consist of a pointcut and a string. A pointcut is a predicate that matches certain model elements. An advice declares that elements matched by the pointcut are advised by the advice. This means that the model element is modeled as being annotated by the string specified in the advice. So in the example in Figure 1, the advice means that all model elements that match the pointcut are annotated with the string "should be change".

Role bindings declare the binding of a class to a role or of a class-method to a role-method. Roles and role-methods are modeled as ordinary classes and methods. So in Figure 1 the role bindings mean that Point and Line are modeled as playing the role of Subject, and all the setter and moveBy methods of Point and Line are modeled as playing the role of the change method of Subject.

A sequence consists of a series of method calls, each of which in turn leads to another (possibly empty) sequence. We represent the sequence associated with a call as the focus of control of the target object of the call.

The inclusion of role bindings, inter-type declarations (ITDs) and advice in our modeling language leads to an interesting semantic question. We would like ITDs and advice to be able to depend on role bindings when appropriate. Specifically, we would like an ITD onto a role to have the same effect on classes performing the role as members defined directly in the role. Similarly, we would like pointcuts to be able to depend on role bindings and ITDs.

This semantics is easy to achieve with a simple linear weaving of model elements in which role bindings are handled before ITDs, which are handled before advice. But if we also wanted role bindings to be able to depend on ITDs, then we would have to adopt some sort of a fixed-point approach in our weaver. So far, we have been unable to come up with a sufficiently compelling example that would require the more complex semantics.

## The Join Point Model (JPM)

JPMs are the central mechanism that supports crosscutting in aspect-oriented programming [18]. A JPM can be described in terms of three characteristics: the nature of the join points, a means of identifying the join points, and a means of affecting semantics at join points.

### Join Points
The join points of our JPM are the model elements in the various UML diagrams.

From class diagrams the join points are class, method, field, inter-type, advice and role binding declarations. From sequence diagrams the join points are method call declarations and sequences. If we extended our meta-model to include method return or method call reception elements from the sequence diagram, they would be join points as well. Because our join points are all model elements, we will often refer to a join point as a model element.

### Means of Identifying Join Points
Our system includes several means of identifying join points. In any model element that includes a signature of some form, that signature serves to identify join points. For example, a method call element has a signature which includes the object's type and the name of the method being called. This signature labels the call itself, and will be used to match signatures of method, sequence, and other method call model elements. Similarly, signatures of method model elements identify matching method call and sequence elements.

Advice declarations include a pointcut construct similar to the pointcuts in AspectJ. Pointcuts are predicates that match certain join points. We support several primitive pointcuts, including: class, field, method, call, and sequence, which match the corresponding kind of model element. We also support contextual pointcuts such as within, cflow and cflowbelow which correspond in meaning to the pointcuts with the same name in AspectJ. The syntax and semantics for all the pointcuts we provide are described in Table 1.

**Table 1:** Pointcuts

| Pointcut | Model elements matched |
|---|---|
| class(*class signature*)<br>field(*field signature*)<br>method(*method signature*)<br>methodCall(*method signature*)<br>sequence(*method signature*) | corresponding type of element by signature pattern |
| withinClass(*class signature*)<br>withinSequence(*method signature*) | any element syntactically contained within model elements that match the signature |
| withinClassDiagram(*name*)<br>withinSequenceDiagram(*name*) | any element   syntactically contained within diagrams that match the name pattern |
| cflow(*pointcut*)<br>cflowbelow(*pointcut*) | any element within the control flow of sequences or method calls matched by the inner *pointcut* |
| *pointcut1 && pointcut2* | any element that matches both pointcuts |
| *pointcut1 ǁ pointcut2* | any element that matches at least one of the pointcuts |
| *! pointcut* | any element that doesn't match the pointcut |

**Semantic Effect at Join Points**

Our system preserves the original declaration semantics of each model element. These semantics are extended to make crosscutting structure explicit in a woven model. Each element records all the other model elements which crosscut it.

Because our semantics simply extend the existing meta-model and semantics, it should be possible to incorporate this proposal into other meta-models, but we have not done this yet.

# Weaver

The weaving process takes the model elements and computes a simple uniform representation of the crosscutting among them. For this woven structure, we use a meta-model that incorporates our JPM into the existing UML meta-model. Each model element is treated as a join point, and for each join point the weaver records a set of all other join points it crosscuts. We call this the *crosscut by set* of a join point. For example, a method in a class diagram will have in its crosscut by set all sequence and method call elements with a matching signature, as well as any other crosscutting elements.

Crosscutting is treated symmetrically, so the crosscut by set of a sequence includes the method declarations it crosscuts and vice versa. Table 2 shows, for each kind of join point, all join point kinds that it can crosscut.

Using the crosscut by sets, a modeling tool can display crosscutting structure in a variety of ways. The left side of Figure 2 shows a straightforward visualization of advice applicability overlaid onto standard UML format, whereas the right side shows

**Table 2:** Join points, along with the kinds of join points that each can be in a crosscutting relationship with

| Join point | Join points with which it can crosscut |
|---|---|
| Class | Class role binding, advice |
| Field | Advice |
| Method | Method call, sequence, method role binding, advice |
| Method Call/ Sequence | Method, method call, sequence |
| Class role binding | Class |
| Method role binding | Method |
| ITD | Class, advice |
| Advice | Class, method, method call, sequence, advice |

the internal crosscut by sets produced by the weaver. The complete crosscutting sets produced by the weaver can be used for different kinds of analysis and display of the model.

Weaving starts with a representation of the complete model, which includes all the kinds of model elements discussed above. The weaver processes the model as follows:

1) *Initial inheritance structure.* The weaver traverses all class diagrams, using the class, method and field elements to build up a representation of the inheritance structure, which will be used later for operation and property lookup. In this stage role bindings, ITDs, and advice are simply collected into separate lists for later semantic processing.

2) *Role bindings.* The role bindings are processed by modifying the inheritance tables so that classes appear as sub-types of roles they play, and methods match the signature of the role-method to which they are bound. Each role binding is added to the crosscut by sets of the classes or methods participating in the binding, and those classes and methods are added to the crosscut by set of the role binding.

3) *Inter-type declarations.* New class members are introduced into the model as specified by the ITDs. The inheritance tables are modified accordingly. The inter-type declaration elements themselves are added to the crosscut by sets of the target class, and vice versa.

4) *Sequence diagrams.* All sequences are traversed, and at each sequence or call element the class and method specified in the signature of the sequence/call are looked up in the inheritance tables. If a matching method is found, the sequence/call is recorded in the crosscut by set of the method, and vice versa. If the sequence/call matches other sequences/calls, this crosscutting is recorded in their crosscut by sets, as well.

5) *Advice.* For each advice, all model elements that match the pointcut specified in the advice are added to the crosscut by set of the advice, and vice versa.

## Declarative Crosscutting and Implicit Weaving

Our system is based on a *declarative* semantics for crosscutting modeling elements coupled with *implicit weaving*.

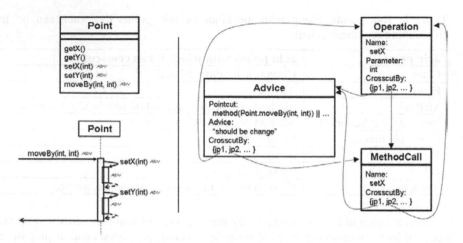

**Figure 2:** The left side of the figure shows a possible visualization of crosscutting advice structure, while the right side shows the internal crosscut by sets. The ADV annotation on some elements on the left indicates that advice applies to them. In this visualization clicking on the ADV would bring up a list of those advice model elements. This is similar to the support Eclipse AJDT provides for understanding advice in AspectJ programs.

Classes, sequence diagrams and other model elements simply model structure, and the weaver runs automatically to compute the crosscut by sets. This is in contrast with other proposals in which crosscutting model elements have a transformational semantics [5, 25, 26]. In those approaches, the modeler selects specific crosscutting model elements to apply, and then explicitly runs the weaver to transform the model.

The declarative semantics and implicit weaving are similar to the semantics of AOP tools like AspectJ, where aspects have a simple declarative semantics, and compilation or some other implicit weaving process simply implements that semantics. The advantage we see for declarative crosscutting semantics in a modeling tool is that when model elements change (i.e. the Observer design pattern), the new semantics can be immediately reflected in the model and any views of the model.

## Implementation

The prototype implementation of our tool is based on the Eclipse Modeling Framework (EMF) version 2.0.0 [6], which allows us to create and display class diagrams. Through extensions to the EMF implementation of the UML meta-model, we have added support for sequence diagrams, role bindings, inter-type declarations, and advice, as well as properties to store crosscut by sets. Of the 24 extensions to the meta-model, over half were simple additions of individual pointcuts elements (one for each pointcut in Table 1). We also implemented a simple weaver consisting of approximately 2100 loc in 42 classes.

The weaver runs after changes to the model, and is not currently optimized for speed. The weaver starts its work by traversing the model and collecting separate lists of class diagrams, sequence diagrams, role bindings, ITDs, and advice. This means that each of the five passes described above only needs to loop through the appropriate lists to do its work.

To provide feedback about crosscutting structure, we took advantage of an EMF feature whereby it displays textual properties of every metaobject. Our weaver not only computes crosscut by sets for model elements, it also computes a textual summary of each of those crosscut by sets. Since EMF automatically displays textual properties of model elements, this lets us see whether elements are advised, participate in role bindings, appear in sequence diagrams, etc.[2]

## Evaluation

Our main goals were to (i) simplify display and analysis of existing crosscutting structure in UML by a modeling tool, and (ii) make the addition of new kinds of crosscutting model elements easier. We sought to do this through a UML meta-model with a built-in JPM, and a weaver that coordinates the crosscutting structure in the various diagrams comprising the model. In this section we use the example from Figure 1 to demonstrate the degree to which the enhanced meta-model and weaver meet these goals.

### Display

We first consider implementing the ADV annotations in Figure 2. The following code implements the underlying test based on our model. It simply walks through the crosscut by set of an element to see whether it contains any advice. The IDE can call the predicate when it is displaying a model element to determine whether to display the annotation.

```
boolean hasAdvice(Decl decl) {
   for (Decl otherDecl : decl.getCrosscutBySet())
     if (otherDecl instanceof Advice)
       return true;
   return false;
}
```

A more sophisticated version of this functionality might display the name of the class enclosing the advice (the aspect in AspectJ terminology), instead of just an ADV. A version of hasAdvice that returns a set of class names is only slightly more complex; it must fetch the enclosing class of each advice and return a set of those classes.

A more complex visualization would be to overlay roles and role members onto classes and class members that play them. The underlying model query required to support this functionality is a getRoles method similar to the second version of hasAdvice.

---

[2] Ideally, EMF would just display the contents of the crosscut by set itself, but version 2.0.0 does not allow us to do that easily.

## Analysis

In the running example, one application of the meta-model is to confirm whether the model elements comply with design specifications. In this case, we would want to check that all the model elements annotated with the advice were designated as a change through the role binding, and that the role binding applied only to the elements to which the advice was attached.

The simplest implementation for this compares the crosscut by lists of the advice and the role binding. We need to check for two things. First of all, that all the elements marked by the advice are bound by the role binding. And second, that no other elements are bound by the role binding. These two conditions guarantee that the model exactly satisfies the design specifications laid out by the advice.

## Adding New Modeling Constructs

EMF has built-in support for class diagrams, but not sequence diagrams, and certainly not role bindings, ITDs or advice. Building on EMF, our implementation starts with just a JPM-enhanced meta-model, class diagrams, and a weaver framework. Sequence diagrams, role bindings, ITDs, and advice are all extensions to our core implementation. Because of this, we can use our experience to address how our meta-model and weaver support our second goal, which was to simplify the addition of new kinds of crosscutting model elements. We do this by looking at the amount of work required to implement support for sequence diagrams, role bindings, ITDs, and advice in our system.

The EMF implementation we started with consisted of approximately 350 classes and over 80 kloc. The work required to add support for the JPM weaver and new model elements is modest. The following discussion describes the implementation, and Table 3 summarizes the discussion. The phases referred to in the discussion are the ordered phases we have described in the section The Weaver.

The first set of additions is to extend the meta-model with the JPM described above and implement the core weaver framework.

The second set of additions defines sequence diagrams, which requires new model elements for sequence diagram, sequence, and method call elements. The weaver is modified so that phase 1 collects these elements. A new phase weaves sequence and class diagrams by recording the sequences and calls in the crosscut by sets of methods and vice versa (the final phase 4). It also weaves all the sequence diagrams by recording crosscutting among calls and sequences.

The third set of additions defines role bindings, with new model elements to represent class and method bindings. It requires modifications to the class model element to allow role bindings as class members. Phase 1 is modified to collect role binding elements. A new weaver phase records the effects of role bindings in the inheritance tables (phase 2). The results of a role binding will affect matching in other stages as well.

Support for ITDs requires changes to the existing field and method model elements, in order to allow a target class which may differ from the containing class. Phase 1 of the weaver is modified to collect ITDs. A new weaver phase implements the addition of ITDs to the target class (phase 3).

**Table 3:** New code required to add support for sequence diagrams, role bindings, ITDs and advice to the meta-model and weaver. (loc numbers represent non-blank, non-commented lines of code)

| Construct | loc | New classes | Edits to EMF meta-model | Edits to weaver |
|---|---|---|---|---|
| Initial weaver with class diagrams | 1094 | 17 | 0 | n/a |
| Sequence diagrams | 1323 | 21 | 4 (create sequence diagram, sequence and method call elements, sequence diagram to model) | 2 (add collector, add new processing phase) |
| Role bindings | 119 | 4 | 3 (create role binding elements, add role binding to class) | 2 (add collector, add new processing stage) |
| ITDs | 43 | 0 | 2 (add target property to field, method) | 2 (add collector, add new processing phase) |
| Advice | 52 | 3 | 2 (create advice element, add advice to class) | 2 (add collector, add new processing phase) |
| Pointcuts | 538 | 14 | 14 (pointcuts) | |

The final set of additions defines advice and pointcuts, with new model elements to represent advice, as well as each of the pointcuts. It also requires modifying the class element to add advice as a class member. Phase 1 is modified to collect advice, and a new weaver phase records advice at each element to which it applies (phase 5). The implementation of pointcut matching is well decoupled from the core of the weaver.

In general, the addition of a new kind of crosscutting model element requires a new phase of processing if the element is not subsumed by any of the above phases. In addition, the position of the new phase in the ordering has to be determined. However, only the first phase of the weaver needs to be modified in order to collect all the new model elements into a list. None of the other existing phases should need to be modified to accommodate this change.

## Future Work

Our first priority is to develop a more sophisticated role binding construct. Mezini et. al. have developed a set of mechanisms for binding aspects to classes that may provide a good basis for our next role binding design [19].

We also want to add other kinds of crosscutting model elements to test the flexibility of our meta-model. In particular, we would like to add statecharts and collaboration diagrams. Statecharts model class states and transitions, which can crosscut the methods of the class. The structure and messages modeled by collaboration diagrams crosscut classes much as sequence diagrams do [7].

Currently, our weaver needs to run over the complete model in order to build up the crosscut by sets, and must run again completely after even small changes to the model. In order for our approach to scale we will have to develop an incremental weaver instead. This problem is similar to the problem of incremental weaving for AspectJ, and incremental model-checking [16], so we hope to be able to apply similar techniques to develop an incremental model weaver.

## Summary

We propose bottom-up support for crosscutting structure in UML by adding a simple JPM to the UML meta-model. This meta-model simplifies implementation of tool support for working with crosscutting structure, addition of new kinds of crosscutting structure, and also makes models of crosscutting structure more declarative.

Using our meta-model, adding new role binding, ITD and advice constructs is a relatively simple task, and those constructs integrate smoothly into the JPM. This makes us optimistic that we will be able to support statecharts, collaboration diagrams, and other kinds of crosscutting model structure, as well.

## Acknowledgments

Thanks to Marcellus Mindel, Branislav Selic, Paul Elder, Charles Riballe and other participants of the IBM Ottawa CASTLE Poster Session for their feedback on this work. We would also like to thank the participants of the AOM workshop at AOSD'05 for their ideas for future directions of this work. Finally, we would like to thank Gail Murphy and the anonymous reviews for their comments and suggestions.

This work is partially supported by IBM Center for Advanced Studies and the Natural Sciences and Engineering Research Council of Canada (NSERC).

## References

1.     Andersen, E.P. and Reenskaug, T., System Design by Composing Structures of Interacting Objects. in *Proceedings of ECOOP*, (London, UK, 1992), Springer-Verlag, 133 - 152.
2.     AspectJTeam. The AspectJ Programming Guide, http://eclipse.org/aspectj/.
3.     Booch, G., Rumbaugh, J. and Jacobson, I. *The Unified Modeling Language User Guide*. Addison-Wesley, 1999.
4.     Cannon, H. Flavors: A non-hierarchical approach to object-oriented programming, Symbolics Inc, 1982.
5.     Clarke, S. and Walker, R.J., Composition patterns: an approach to designing reusable aspects. in *Proceedings of the 23rd International Conference on Software Engineering*, (Toronto, Ontario, Canada, 2001), 5-14.
6.     EclipseProject Eclipse Modeling Framework. http://download.eclipse.org/tools/emf/scripts/home.php.
7.     Gamma, E., Helm, R., Johnson, R. and Vlissides, J. *Design Patterns: Elements of Reusable Object-Oriented Software*. Addison Wesley, 1995.

8.    Hannemann, J. and Kiczales, G., Design Pattern Implementation in Java and AspectJ. in, (2002), ACM, 161-173.

9.    Ho, W.-M., Jezequel, J.-M., Pennaneac'h, F. and Plouzeau, N., A toolkit for weaving aspect oriented UML designs. in *Proceedings of the 1st international conference on Aspect-oriented software development*, (Enschede, The Netherlands, 2002), ACM Press, 99-105.

10.   Jacobson, I. and Ng, P.-W. *Aspect-Oriented Software Development with Use Cases*. Addison Wesley Professional, 2004.

11.   Jezequel, J., Plouzeau, N., Weis, T. and Geihs, K., From Contracts to Aspects in UML Designs. in *Aspect-Oriented Modeling with UML workshop at AOSD*, (2002).

12.   Kande, M.M., J. Kienzle and A. Strohmeier From AOP to UML - A Bottom-Up Approach. *Aspect-Oriented Modeling with UML workshop at the 1st International Conference on Aspect-Oriented Software Development*.

13.   Kiczales, G., Hilsdale, E., Hugunin, J., Kersten, M., Palm, J. and Griswold, W.G., An Overview of AspectJ. in *European Conference on Object-Oriented Programming (ECOOP)*, (Budapest,Hungary, 2001), Springer, 327-355.

14.   Kiczales, G. and Mezini, M., Aspect-Oriented Programming and Modular Reasoning. in *ACM International Conference on Software Engineering*, (2005 (to appear)).

15.   Kim, D.-K., France, R., Ghosh, S. and Song, E., A role-based metamodeling approach to specifying design patterns. in *Proceedings of COMPSAC*, (2003), COMPSAC 2003, 452-457.

16.   Krishnamurthi, S., Fisler, K. and Greenberg, M. Verifying aspect advice modularly. *Foundations of Software Engineering (FSE)*. 137 - 146.

17.   Lions, J.M., Simoneau, D., Pitette, G. and Moussa, I., Extending OpenTool/UML Using Metamodeling: An Aspect Oriented Programming Case Study. in *Workshop on Aspect-Oriented Modeling with UML at the UML Conference*, (2002).

18.   Masuhara, H. and Kiczales, G., Modeling crosscutting in aspect-oriented mechanisms. in *European Conference on Object-Oriented Programming (ECOOP)*, (2003), Springer, 2-28.

19.   Mezini, M. and Ostermann, K., Conquering aspects with Caesar. in *International Conference on Aspect-Oriented Software Development (AOSD)*, (2003), ACM Press, 90-100.

20.   OMG, T. Unified Modeling Language (UML), Version 1.5. *www.uml.org*.

21.   Pawlak, R., Duchien, L., Florin, G., Legond-Aubry, F., Seinturier, L. and Martelli, L., A UML Notation for Aspect-Oriented Software Design. in *Aspect-Oriented modeling with UML workshop at AOSD*, (Enschede, The Netherlands, 2002).

22.   Reifer, D. Doubts and hopes for AOP. *COMMUNICATIONS OF THE ACM, 45* (3). 11-12.

23.   Selic, B., Using UML for Modeling Complex Real-Time Systems. in *Languages, Compilers, and Tools for Embedded Systems: ACM SIGPLAN Workshop LCTES*, (Montreal, Canada, 1998).

24.   Stein, D., Hanenberg, S. and Unland, R., Designing Aspect-Oriented Crosscutting in UML. in *Workshop on Aspect-Oriented Modeling with UML at AOSD*, (Enschede, The Netherlands, 2002).

25.   Stein, D., Hanenberg, S. and Unland, R., Position Paper on Aspect-Oriented Modeling: Issues on Representing Crosscutting Features. in *Workshop on Aspect-Oriented Modeling at AOSD*, (2003).

26.   Straw, G., Georg, G., Song, E., Ghosh, S., France, R.B. and Bieman, J.M., Model Composition Directives. in *Conference on the Unified Modeling Language*, (Lisbon, Portugal, 2004).

27.   Tamai, T., Ubayashi, N. and Ichiyama, R. An adaptive object model with dynamic role binding. *http://www.graco.c.u-tokyo.ac.jp/~tamai/pub/epsilon/rolemodel.pdf*.

# Modeling Crosscutting Services with UML Sequence Diagrams

Martin Deubler[1], Michael Meisinger[1], Sabine Rittmann[1], and Ingolf Krüger[2]

[1] Technische Universität München
Boltzmannstr. 3
85748 München, Germany
{deubler, meisinge, rittmann}@in.tum.de
[2] Department of Computer Science
University of California, San Diego
La Jolla, CA 92093-0114, USA
ikrueger@cs.ucsd.edu

**Abstract.** Current software systems increasingly consist of distributed interacting components. The use of web services and similar middleware technologies strongly fosters such architectures. The complexity resulting from a high degree of interaction between distributed components – that we face with web service orchestration for example – poses severe problems. A promising approach to handle this intricacy is service-oriented development; in particular with a domain-unspecific service notion based on interaction patterns. Here, a *service* is defined by the interplay of distributed system entities, which can be modeled using UML Sequence Diagrams. However, we often face functionality that affects or is spanned across the behavior of other services; a similar concept to aspects in Aspect-Oriented Programming. In the service-oriented world, such aspects form *crosscutting services*. In this paper we show how to model those; we introduce aspect-oriented modeling techniques for UML Sequence Diagrams and show their usefulness by means of a running example.

## 1 Introduction

Today's software systems get increasingly complex. Complexity is observed in all software application domains: In business information systems, technical and administrative systems, as well as in embedded systems such as in avionics, automotive and telecommunications. Often, major sources of the complexity are *interactions between system components*. Current software architectures increasingly use distributed components as for instance seen when using web services [11] and service-oriented architectures [7].

Traditionally, system design focuses on the components that structure the system physically or logically. Components are modeled and implemented in their entirety and mostly independent from each other; they are integrated in subsequent steps. In situations as we face them today with large distributed systems composed of a multitude of interacting components, significant portions of the components' functionality

L. Briand and C. Williams (Eds.): MoDELS 2005, LNCS 3713, pp. 522–536, 2005.

are determined by handling these interactions appropriately. Specifying separate components correctly and completely is a very difficult task. Additionally, when it comes to expressing system-wide concerns like certain Quality-of-Service properties such as end-to-end timing deadlines, component oriented models fall short.

More appropriate for the development of interaction intensive distributed systems are therefore approaches which put interaction modeling in the center of concern. Viewing systems entirely and explicitly modeling the interactions between the components that constitute the system addresses the before mentioned issues with arbitrary and exceptional interaction combinations and overarching system aspects. In interaction centric system specifications, the components are described by the interactions they have to provide; a black-box view that hides internal component complexity. Considering the different functions, features, or services that the system offers provides a straightforward structuring of such interaction models. For today's large multi-functional distributed systems, such approaches provide the necessary flexibility in decoupling the separate functions while still modeling systems in their entirety.

We strongly propose service-oriented software development approaches that place the different functions or services of a system in the center of interest – as for instance introduced by [14] or in [13]. We combine this with an interaction-centric development approach and specify the system services in terms of the interactions between the components involved [21]. We in particular use interaction-centric description techniques such as UML Sequence Diagrams or Message Sequence Charts [19], [22].

**Problem Statement.** When specifying a system in terms of services, it is often desirable to specify certain aspects of behavior contributing to or overlapping several existing services. We view such behavior again as services of the system, namely as *crosscutting services* or *aspects*. Examples for such crosscutting services are authentication, logging and synchronization. It is highly desirable to specify these crosscutting services separately in order to ensure a better comprehensibility, reusability, traceability and evolvability of the software models.

We achieve this by specifying each spread concern within one single unit, called aspect. These aspects – or crosscutting services – can then be modified independently from the rest of the system specification. These concepts are directly based on aspect-oriented programming and modeling techniques [18], [35].

Currently, UML sequence diagrams do not provide such aspect-oriented modeling techniques and are therefore not fully suited for systematic service-based software development. If a system needs to be specified precisely and without redundancy, more powerful notations and description techniques are required.

**Contribution.** In this paper, we address the mentioned problem by introducing an extension of UML Sequence Diagrams motivated by the ideas of aspect-orientation. We model a system based on interaction-based services using UML Sequence Diagrams. We extend the UML 2.0 Sequence Diagram Notation to enable the modeling of crosscutting behavior that is spread over the basic system interactions (services). Our approach is *independent of a specific domain*. We use a running example to explain and evaluate our notation. A more extensive version of this material can be found in [33].

In this paper, we initially assume a control-flow oriented, RPC-style (remote procedure call) communications paradigm for the execution of system services. This is a very common communication scenario that can be often observed for instance when using web services. We have shown in [19], [21] that our service-oriented approach also generalizes for asynchronous communication.

**Outline.** The remainder of the paper is structured as follows. In Section 2 we introduce our service notion and the sequence diagram based description techniques we use. Section 3 introduces our modeling approach and explains the extensions to the UML we propose. Section 4 discusses our approach in the context of related work. In Section 5, we present a conclusion and give an outlook on further steps.

## 2   Service-Oriented Development

In this section we briefly introduce our notion of service and service-oriented development. We specify services in terms of interaction patterns between system components and model those using UML Sequence Diagrams. Our UML extensions for specifying service aspects on top of existing system services are based thereon.

### 2.1   Services and Service Notion

We define a service as follows:

*"A service is defined by the interaction among entities involved in establishing a particular functionality."*

A *service* therefore is a *piece of behavior* or *functionality* which is provided by the collaborative inter-working of system entities. Hereby, an *entity* is an abstract, logical, structural part of the system. Depending on the level of detail it can stand for a component, module, package, or class. The *interaction* is described by interaction patterns that capture the message exchange between the system entities involved in establishing the service. As a consequence of the definition above, a service – and therefore functionality – can be spread across several entities or components. Note that in this paper we use the terms *entity* and *component* equivalently. Analogously, we speak of *functionality* or *behavior* when referring to a *service*.

Consider for instance the central locking system of a modern luxury car. It provides the service of unlocking the car remotely by pressing on the open button of the remote key. On doing so, the doors are unlocked, the alarm device and the anti-theft device are disabled, the exterior lights flash, the interior lights are turned on, the driver's seat is positioned, etc. As we can see, the remote unlocking service is provided by the collaborative work between the entities remote key, the door locks, the security devices, the exterior lights, the interior lights and the motor managing the driver's seat. They communicate with each other using messages.

In addition to capturing interactions between system entities, we also specify *local actions* of entities – for instance a computation of a certain result in reaction to the receipt of a message, to be sent to another entity. Note that a simple form of a service might not involve an interaction of multiple entities; services can be provided by just one entity. For instance, consider the service of adjusting the front seats individually by moving them forth and back.

Because our interaction-based service definition is founded only on the abstract interaction relationship between entities, we profit from the following advantages:

☐ Our service notion can be used independently from a specific domain. A single methodology and supporting tool set can be applied in many different contexts.

☐ Our service notion can be used throughout the overall development process – from requirements elicitation to implementation. Services are first class modeling elements that drive the entire process and that can be traced from requirements to implementation.

☐ Our service notion goes beyond notions that define services by a callable list of procedures only. This is often seen when defining web services or network protocol stack service access points (SAPs). Our service notion instead enables elaborate behavioral specifications containing quality-of-service attributes.

## 2.2   Service Specification with UML Sequence Diagrams

In this section we show how services can be modeled by means of UML sequence diagrams. These and similar graphical notations and languages such as Message Sequence Charts and variants are well-suited ways of modeling interactions, by which our services are specified.

The Unified Modeling Language (UML) [42] has become the de-facto standard for modeling systems. The version 2.0 of the UML enhances the possibility of modeling complex and hierarchical interactions. It provides flexible and powerful constructs and operators to express conditions, parallel execution, repetition and hierarchy. We use UML Sequence Diagrams, to specify our services.

Figure 1 shows the simplified specification of a service of an automotive central locking system. The service is responsible for locking the trunk and all four doors. After pressing the central lock button (which is located inside the car), messages are sent to the trunk lock and the door locks, respectively. The figure shows the application of operators within the sequence diagram to express more complex interactions. In the example, locking the trunk happens in parallel (*par*) to locking the door. By design choice, all doors are locked in sequence. We could also have applied another parallel operator here. The service is established by the inter-working of the components CenterLockButton, TrunkLock and the four doors locks which communicate with each other by exchanging messages. The interaction between these system entities is captured in the interaction pattern that makes up the service.

We interpret the sequence diagram that is assigned to the service universally. This means, once the service is executed, the specified pattern of interactions must occur. In case of alternatives, the respective operator (*alt*) must be applied. Besides sequential and parallel composition of messages and alternatives, there are also loops, optional interactions and references to other interaction diagrams that can be expressed. More complex services can be composed by the use of interaction overview diagrams.

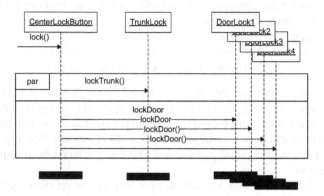

**Figure 1:** LockDoorsService

Note that with the UML 2.0 [42], sequence diagrams have converged much closer to the ITU standard of MSCs which have the advantage to be precisely defined; there is work existing that associates formal semantics to MSCs as well as distinct extensions that make MSCs even more suitable to service-based development approaches [19], [20], [22]. In this work, we focus on UML 2.0 Sequence Diagrams, because UML is more popular than MSCs in the context of modeling object-oriented systems, web services and synchronously communicating systems. Besides, there are many similarities and notational elements are directly transferable.

In this section we presented the notion of service we use as basis of our work. Methodological work around this notion of service can be found in [23], [33]. A formalization of services and service-oriented software architectures based on the mathematical model of streams can be found in [9].

## 3    Modeling Crosscutting Services with Aspects

Well structured software is usually divided into modules with certain responsibilities. This is in accordance with the separation of concerns principle simplifying reusability and a better maintenance of design and implementation. However, some behavior crosscuts these so-called primary modules as it affects several modular entities. In object-oriented programming, the units of modularity for example are classes; a crosscutting concern is spanned across several classes. If the implementation of such a concern is scattered and tangled up with the core functionality, it is difficult to reason about, implement and change. This problem is called the tyranny of the dominant decomposition [39].

Aspect-oriented programming (AOP, cf. [1], [8]) is an implementation level technology that allows to isolate pieces of behavior into single units – called *aspects*; it allows to specify at which locations in the code the aspects should later be inserted.

This ensures the encapsulation of cross-cutting behavior, such as logging or synchronization and therefore results in a better comprehensibility, reusability, traceability and evolvability of the code.

Aspect-oriented modeling (AOM) is a consequence of aspect-oriented programming; it raises the ideas of separation of concerns to the level of software models. To date, most of the work on aspect-orientation has concentrated on the implementation level. How aspects can be modeled appropriately is still not investigated sufficiently. This is particularly true in the area of service-oriented modeling where we face the before mentioned problems. However, in order be able to create more powerful, more elaborate system models, it is inevitable to also model crosscutting services. Therefore it is necessary to have a way to apply aspect-orientation in models.

In the following we explain what aspects are in the service-oriented world; we list the goals and principles that are relevant when modeling aspects. In Section 3.3 we introduce our approach to model crosscutting services using an extended Sequence Diagram notation.

## 3.1   Crosscutting Services

The notion of *aspect* has emerged during the last years (cf. [3], [4], [5]). E.g. in [27] an informal definition for the term aspect is given. The author describes an aspect as a "crosscutting concern". Here, a concern is a "property of interest to a stakeholder" and crosscutting means "intertwining, interdependent, interacting, [or] overlapping".

In component-based software development approaches, the modular entities are components (or classes, packages, etc. depending on the level of examination). A crosscutting concern therefore is overlapping or affecting several components. In our service-oriented point of view, services are by definition overlapping several components. Therefore, each service would be an aspect, which renders the above definition of crosscutting concerns impractical. Instead, in the service oriented world, the basic building blocks are services. Consequently, an aspect – or crosscutting service – is a service that is spanned across or that influences the behavior of other services.

It shows that our definition of crosscutting concerns in the context of service-oriented development follows a similar idea as aspects in a component-oriented approach. We allow specification of modular pieces of behavior and separate crosscutting concerns in aspects. However, our approach retains all before mentioned advantages and benefits from interaction based modeling.

In the following we distinguish between *crosscutting* and *crosscut* behavior. Crosscutting behavior is the functionality that is spread over several services. It affects behavior of existing services which in turn are the *crosscut* functionality.

## 3.2   Principles and Goals for Modeling Crosscutting Services

Introducing a notation for modeling of crosscutting services should comply with the following principles and goals:

☐ *Model crosscutting services like basic services with additional characteristics*: A crosscutting service is a service that affects the behavior of other services. Therefore, it is suggestive to model crosscutting behavior similar to basic services: with Sequence Diagrams. However, we have to take additional care of the special characteristics that make up the nature of service aspects.

☐ *Cleanly modularize crosscutting services*: In order to enable reuse and a better maintenance of design (and later: implementation) we have to cleanly modularize the crosscutting service. Each aspect needs to be located within one model.

☐ *Leave crosscut service untouched*: An aspect might affect several services. However, if a crosscut service should be reused in another system or configuration without the crosscutting service, it will not be influenced by the crosscutting service anymore. Therefore, the specification of the crosscut service must remain independent and unchanged by the aspect. The dependency is unidirectional: the crosscutting service depends on the execution context of the crosscut service.

☐ *Attend to clear illustration of crosscutting relationships*: Crosscutting relationships can be very complex. For example, if several services are affected by several other services or aspects that are crosscut by aspects in turn. A modeling technique to capture/specify aspects must illustrate these complex dependencies concisely.

Additionally, a good modeling approach should provide both a coarse-grained (more abstract) and a fine-grained (more concrete) view on crosscutting relationships. In the next section we will introduce a modeling approach that is in accordance with the listed principles. However, we will not show how aspects can be incorporated in *structural* diagrams such as UML Class Diagrams; the focus of our work lies on the *behavioral* part.

### 3.3 Modeling Crosscutting Services with Sequence Diagrams

Crosscutting services differ from basic services as explained before. We need to specify additional characteristics when modeling aspects. Plain sequence diagrams do not provide enough flexibility and expressiveness. Consequently, we have to introduce additional modeling elements that provide the required expressiveness. In the following we will introduce our modeling elements step by step by means of an example.

#### Modeling Join Points

In contrast to basic services, crosscutting services model *when* the crosscutting behavior takes *place in reference to the behavior of affected services*. We have to specify the points in the system execution where an aspect starts, affects and ends.

In order to define the places where two concerns crosscut one another, we introduce elementary **join points.** We adapt AspectJ [2] nomenclature here. Nonetheless, the concept used permits the use of various AOP flavors. We do not show how our modeling concepts can be translated into AspectJ as they are independent of a particular programming language. Join points mark well-defined, single points in the execution flow at which two concern models are (inter)connected with each other. Join points correspond to messages and local activities of sequence diagrams.

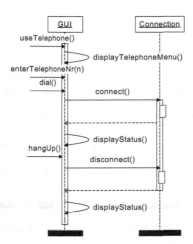

**Figure 2:** UseTelephoneService

In particular, we specify when a crosscutting concern should be executed. We face the following possibilities: Before, After, Around or Instead of a certain action. Actions can be local activities or message send or receive events. We introduce graphical elements to specify when an aspect is invoked – namely *before, after, wrapping* and *overriding* join points. In the following we will explain them with the aid of examples: Figure 2 shows a simple telephone service which can be found for instance in a modern luxury car. When the telephone menu is selected via the car's user interface (MMI), the user can enter a phone number, and connect to this number. The system establishes the connection and displays the call status until the user hangs up. The system disconnects the call and updates the status display.

Now assume that the telephone costs should be charged to individual users. This can be done by enabling an *AccountService*. An account has to be chosen before the actual TelephoneMenu can be used. How can this be realized? One possibility would be to insert the new behavior – the choice of a specific account prior to the use of the telephone – directly in the *UseTelephoneService*. However, it is better to modularize the account service in a separate module as it can be enabled and disabled.

**Before Join Points.** We have to model the point in the execution flow where the behavior is affected. For our example, we choose to insert the new behavior when the telephone service is called, but *before* it is actually performed. Figure 3 shows the introduction of the before join point symbol. The message *useTelephone()* is divided by an axis starting from a before join point (a circled *"B"*). The semantics is that the message *useTelephone()* is not delivered to the axis *GUI*. Instead, the crosscutting behavior is performed: The current display settings are saved (*saveSettings()*) and an account menu is shown (*displayAccountMenu()*). After an account has been chosen (*chooseAccount()*), the display is reset to the saved settings (*resetDisplay()*). The very last, unlabeled arrow indicates that the control flow is given back to the before join point. This means that the afore interrupted message *useTelephone()* is now actually delivered to the *GUI*. That is the point in the execution where the crosscutting behavior ends and the crosscut behavior is continued.

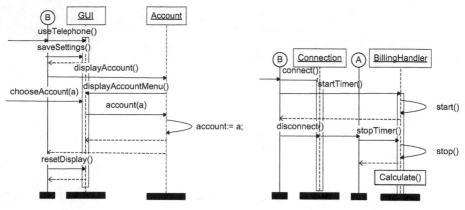

**Figure 3:** AccountService          **Figure 4:** BillingService

*After and Wrapping Join Points.* The *BillingService* (see Figure 4) shows the modeling elements for after and wrapping join points. This service has two parts: (1) When a connection is requested (*connect()*), a timer is started, and (2) When the connection is closed (*disconnect()*), the timer is stopped. Then, some calculation is performed.

In the first part we again make use of a *before* join point. In the second part we introduce an after join point having the following semantics: After the message *disconnect()* is sent to Connection, the message *stopTimer()* is sent. When the timer is stopped, the control flow is returned to the after join point. The behavior being crosscut continues its execution.

In the above example we introduced not only before and after join points. In fact we specified a wrapping aspect which has defined start and end points, respectively. The issue of modeling overriding join points is currently being investigated. Affecting local activities can be obtained similarly to messages.

### Combination of Join Points – Point Cuts

Of course, we also could have modeled the crosscutting behavior as part of the *UseTelephone* service. However, we cleanly isolated the aspect in a separate model. The advantage is evident if we also introduce an internet service (cf. Figure 5).

Applying the account service also to the internet service is now simple by adding a combination of join points (point cuts in AspectJ nomenclature) to the aspect specification. Figure 6 shows how the account service is specified so that it is applicable to either the telephone or the internet service. The *alt*-box defines a logical combination of join points – to be more precise: the logical "OR" between two *before* join points. Either before the message *useTelephone()* or before the message *useInternet()* is sent to the *GUI*, the behavior is interrupted.

Another possibility for the specification of point cuts (combinations of join points) is the use of *parallel-boxes,* etc. The concept of point cuts allows us to model the logical combination of several points in order to specify more complex points in the program execution. Point cuts pick out certain join points in the program flow and values at those points. Investigating this in more detail is one of our next goals.

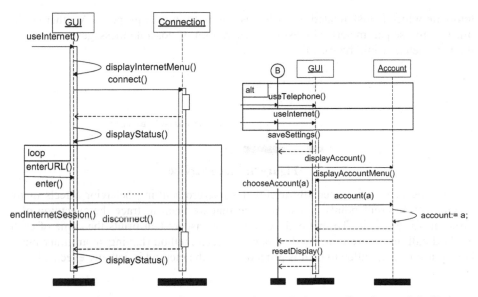

**Figure 5:** UseInternetService          **Figure 6:** AccountService w. Join Point

## Modeling of Execution Context

To provide aspect services with higher flexibility and expressiveness, we expose the execution context of the affected services in point cuts. The aspect thus can make use of it. In the sequence diagrams, we add OCL-style notes to the arrows. Figure 7 shows a report service that reports how much an account has to be charged for. For this purpose, the *sum* (which are the costs of the internet or telephone session) and the *account* (which is to be charged for) are available to the reporting service. They can be seen as parameters being provided to the report service.

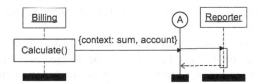

**Figure 7:** Report Service

## Name-Based and Property-Based Specification

In the examples above, we explicitly specified concrete message and activity names when determining the crosscut behavior. We call this *name-based crosscutting*. Sometimes, crosscutting behavior affects many other services. In this case it would mean much effort to specify all places where the aspect makes an appearance. A more powerful way to specify the location of join points within sequence diagrams is *property-based crosscutting*. For example we can use wildcards to specify a group of messages, activities or even axes. Instead of using the *alternative-box* in Figure 6, we could just write *use\*()*. A property-based crosscutting service can be seen as a template which is instantiated by each message fulfilling the property. Another possibility is to use parameterized messages. Then a set of possible messages substituting the parameters would be specified.

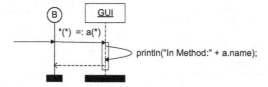

**Figure 8:** Trace Service

This mechanism is especially useful if some crosscutting behavior affects many services at different points. Let us assume that we want to trace the execution of a program for example. To that end, we define an aspect that prints the name of each method call. In Figure 8 the method name of each method (having an arbitrary number of arguments) called to *GUI* is printed *before* the method is actually executed.

# 4 Discussion and Related Work

In this section, we put the service notion and our introduced aspect-oriented description techniques that we have presented in the preceding sections into perspective; in particular, we discuss our approach in relation to others known from the literature.

As noted in [40], the term *service* is used in a variety of meanings, and on various levels of abstraction in the Software Engineering community. The notion and model of service we use in this document captures the interplay of multiple components collaborating to achieve a particular function or feature of the system under consideration. This encompasses the various "traditional" notions of service used in the telecommunications [41] and business information systems domains, but also the emerging uses of the term service in the context of "web services" [11], and service-oriented architectures (SOAs) [7].

In the telecommunications domain, the notion of feature is well established and researched – as pointed out in [41]. Features can be defined as "reusable, self-contained services" [30]; they encapsulate individual pieces of functionality of limited scope, typically used to structure the interfaces or internals of components. Feature-oriented software design and development [31] makes use of features as principal modeling elements. According to [17] features are units of "observable behavior", and "requirements modules" serving as "units of incrementation as systems evolve."

On the other hand, web services [11], [34] at first glance define simple call/reply relationships between the consumer and the provider of the web service. At closer inspection, however, it becomes apparent that web services and their supporting architectures are more loosely-coupled than traditional layered architectures. In particular, web-services typically emerge from the interplay of multiple components – a call upon one web service, in general, results in calls upon multiple other (web) services provided by other components or applications. A web service thus acts as an orchestrator for the collaboration of the components implementing the functionality "behind" the service. This view of services as orchestrators of collaboration is becoming increasingly popular [28], [14]; it transcends the realm of web services – where it is prominently recognized, for instance, by the business process execution language for web services (BPEL4WS) and takes root also in the domain of complex embedded systems as found in the automotive [6] and avionics domains [32].

We have demonstrated the use of UML Sequence Diagrams as graphical description techniques for services. Because Sequence Diagrams capture interaction behaviors that cut across multiple components, we view services and their graphical representations in the form of UML Sequence Diagrams as modeling aspects in analogy to the implementation aspects captured by aspect-oriented programming languages such as AspectJ [18], [2]. In fact, we have shown in [21] that services can be translated immediately into corresponding AspectJ programs; the weaving mechanism of AspectJ can then be exploited to integrate the services defined as Sequence Diagrams into a correct set of component implementation.

Unfortunately, the modeling of aspects is not supported by MSCs or UML sequence diagrams. Although work on including aspect-oriented concepts in the UML has recently been published (cf. [8], [9], [10], [35], [12] and [36]), no elaborate notational elements exist in order to model aspect-orientation adequately. Furthermore, the cited work mainly introduces concepts for class diagrams. Therefore, we give some first ideas on how the modeling of cross-cutting services by means of interaction diagrams can be done.

Recent work has been published that relates aspect-orientation to requirements engineering and design phases, and modeling, cf. [1], [26], [43], [36], [37]. Our service notion can be seen as precisely formulated requirements specified as sequence diagrams. We put our focus in particular on the architecture definition and design phase. The work in [1] mainly sees aspects as crosscutting non-functional requirements or in particular quality attributes [26], while we show how to model crosscutting functional behavior (services) in a similar way to basic services, using cautiously extended sequence diagrams. Similar to [43], we see aspects as interaction patterns. However, we focus on service executions with RPC-style communication semantics which are often used for web service combinations; we also introduce explicit notations to model before, after, around and instead join points within sequence diagrams. In this way we differ from [36] that uses standard UML concepts to represent basic and crosscutting behavior, which we consider too limiting and less intuitive for our purposes. The work in [37] focuses on structural concerns in aspect-oriented design with UML and aspect information interchange using XML, while we focus on behavior models and put the notion of service in the center of concern.

Our approach is related to Model-Driven Architecture (MDA) [25], Model-Integrated Computing [38], aspect-oriented modeling (AOM) [15] and architecture-centric software development (ACD) [42]; similar to MDA and ACD we also separate the software architecture into abstract and concrete models, as for instance shown in [21]. In contrast to the cited model-driven development approaches, however, we consider services and their defining interaction patterns as first-class modeling elements of all our models throughout the different development phases.

In Section 3.2 we mentioned the importance of having both a coarse-grained (more abstract) and a fine-grained (more concrete) view on crosscutting relationships. In this paper we only showed the detailed view of the intertwined relationships. The other case can for instance be achieved by introducing additional stereotypes for UML Use Case Diagrams (cf. [33] for more information).

## 5  Summary and Outlook

In this paper we have shown the significance of an interaction-oriented development approach to address the always increasing complexity of current software systems. Because significant sources of software complexity stem from the interactions among interacting components, an interaction-based model targets the problem at its source. We explained service-oriented development as an approach to specify and develop systems in terms of services as first class modeling elements. Services are defined in terms of interaction patterns between components that participate in the service. Services as such realize crosscutting behavior that spans multiple components.

In analogy to the introduction of aspect-oriented technologies for component or object-oriented software development approaches, we showed its usefulness also for service-oriented development. Retaining all advantages of system specifications using services, we provide means to separate specific pieces of behavior that affect multiple services into aspects. Aspects again are services: crosscutting services. We introduced a notation as an extension to UML 2.0 Sequence Diagrams to model services and services that cross-cut services using aspect-oriented techniques.

We have explained our notation using a running example that is representative for many different domains, including telecommunications, automotive and web service based applications. It is representative for similar situations such as the composition of systems out of interacting web services. We showed that our approach is well suitable to model the traditional RPC-style interactions that occur when composing a system out of a number of separate services.

In the future, further investigations have to be done in how to specify non-functional crosscutting concerns, such as performance or timing constraints. Also, we want to investigate how to identify and resolve contradictory aspect specifications. To prove the value and efficacy of our approach, we plan to apply it to case studies of significant size within the automotive domain as well as in the web services area.

In our work, we concentrate on the *behavioral* part of aspects. The *structural* part – for instance how aspects can be modeled in class diagrams – is not focus of our work. However, the relation between behavioral and structural modeling of aspects has to be investigated in the future, too.

## Acknowlegements

Our work was partially supported by the Deutsche Forschungsgemeinschaft (DFG) within the project *InServe* and by the Bavarian high-tech funding program (High-Tech Offensive) within the project *MEWADIS*. Further funds were provided by the UC Discovery Grant and the Industry-University Cooperative Research Program, as well as by the California Institute for Telecommunications and Information Technology (Calit2). We are grateful to the anonymous reviewers for insightful comments.

# References

[1]  J. Araujo, A. Moreira, I. Brito, A. Rashid: Aspect-oriented requirements with UML. In Proceedings of the Workshop on Aspect-oriented Modeling with UML, UML 2002, Dresden, Germany, October 2002.

[2]  AspectJ Team: The AspectJ Programming Guide. Available at http://eclipse.org/aspectj/.

[3]  Aspect-Oriented Software Development. Proceedings of the 1st international conference on Aspect-oriented software development. ACM Press, 2002.

[4]  Aspect-Oriented Software Development. Proceedings of the 2nd international conference on Aspect-oriented software development. ACM Press, 2003.

[5]  Aspect-Oriented Software Development. Proceedings of the 3rd international conference on Aspect-oriented software development. ACM Press, 2004.

[6]  Automotive Open System Architecture, www.autosar.org

[7]  L. Baresi, R. Heckel, S. Thone, D. Varro: Modeling and validation of service-oriented architectures: Application vs. style. In Proc. of ESEC/FSE, 2003.

[8]  M. Basch, A. Sanchez: Incorporating aspects into the UML. In Proceedings of the International Conference on Aspect-Oriented Software Development, March 2003.

[9]  M. Broy, I. Krüger, M. Meisinger: Services and service-oriented software architectures – methodological foundations. To appear.

[10]  S. Clarke , R.J.Walker. Composition patterns: An approach to designing reusable aspects. In Proceedings of the 23rd International Conference on Software Engineering, pp. 5–14, May 2001.

[11]  A. Colin: Why web services? The Web Services Industry Portal, February 2002. Available at http://www.webservices.org/index.php/article/articleprint/75/-1/61/.

[12]  C.A. Constantinides. A case study on making the transition from functional to fine-grained decomposition. In Proc. of ECOOP 2003 Workshop on Analysis of Aspect-Oriented Software (AAOS 03), July 2003.

[13]  M. Deubler, J. Grünbauer, G. Popp, G. Wimmel, C. Salzmann. Tool Supported Development of Service Based Systems. In 11th Asia-Pacific Software Engineering Conference (APSEC 2004), IEEE Computer Society, Korea, 2004.

[14]  E. Evans: Domain-Driven Design: Tackling Complexity in the Heart of Software. Addison-Wesley, 2003.

[15]  G. Georg, R. France, and I. Ray: Composing Aspect Models. The 4th AOSD Modeling With UML Workshop, 2003.

[16]  C. Ghezzi, M. Jazayeri, R. France. Fundamentals of Software Engineering. Prentice Hall, 1991.

[17]  P. Gibson, D. Méry: Formal Modelling of Services for Getting a Better Understanding of the Feature Interaction Problem. In Bjorner, Broy, Zamulin (eds): Perspectives of System Informatics, Lecture Notes in Computer Science. Volume 1755, Springer, 2000.

[18]  G. Kiczales, E. Hilsdale, J. Hugunin, M. Kersten, J. Palm, W. Griswold: An overview of AspectJ. In Proceedings of the 15th European Conference on Object-Oriented Programming ECOOP 2001, LNCS vol. 2072, pp. 327–353, Springer, June 2001.

[19]  I. Krüger. Specifying services with UML and UML-RT. In Electronic Notes in Theoretical Computer Science, volume 65 (7). Elsevier Science B. V., 2002.

[20]  I. Krüger: Service specification with MSCs and roles. In Proceedings of IASTED International Conference on Software Engineering, Innsbruck, 2004.

[21]  I. Krüger, R. Mathew: Systematic development and exploration of service-oriented software architectures. In Proceedings of the 4th Working IEEE/IFIP Conference on Software Architecture (WICSA 2004), 2004.

[22]  I. Krüger: Towards precise service specification with UML and UML-RT. In Proceedings of the Workshop at UML, Critical Systems Development with UML (CSDUML), 2002.

[23] R. Mathew: Systematic definition, implementation and evaluation of service-oriented software architectures. Master Thesis at University of San Diego, California, 2004.

[24] Message Sequence Chart (MSC 96), ITU-T. Recommendation Z.120. ITU-T, 1996.

[25] Model Driven Architecture. Object Management Group. Available at http://www.omg.org/mda/, 2003.

[26] A. Moreira, J. Araujo, and I. Brito: Crosscutting Quality Attributes for Requirements Engineering. Software Engineering and Knowledge Engineering Conference (SEKE), 2002.

[27] B. Nuseibeh: Crosscutting Requirements. AOSD 2004, The Open University, UK, 2004.

[28] C. Peltz: Web Services Orchestration and Choreography. IEEE Computer 36(10): pp. 46-52, 2003.

[29] D.S. Platt, K. Ballinger: Introducing Microsoft .NET. Microsoft Press, 2001.

[30] C. Prehofer: Plug-and-Play Composition of Features and Feature Interactions with Statechart Diagrams. In Proc. of the Seventh International Workshop on Feature Interactions in Telecommunications and Software Systems, Ottawa, 2003.

[31] C. Prehofer: Feature Oriented Programming: A fresh look at objects, In Proceedings of ECOOP 1997, Springer LNCS 1241, 1997.

[32] Realtime CORBA Joint Revised Submission, Object Management Group, OMG Document orbos/99-02-12 ed., March 1999.

[33] S. Rittmann: Exploring Service-Oriented Software Development for Automotive Systems. Diplomarbeit, Technische Universität München, 2004.

[34] J. Snell, D. Tidwell, P. Kulchenko: Programming Web Services with SOAP. O'Reilly, 2002.

[35] G. Sousa, S. Soares, P. Borba, J. Castro: Separation of crosscutting concerns from requirements to design: Adapting an use case driven approach. In Proc. of Early Aspects 2004: Aspect-Oriented Requirements Engineering and Architecture Design. Workshop at AOSD 2004, March 2004.

[36] D. Stein, S. Hanenberg, R. Unland: Designing aspect-oriented crosscutting in UML. In Proceedings of Aspect-Oriented Modeling with UML. As part of the 1st International Conference on Aspect-Oriented Software Development, April 2002.

[37] J. Suzuki, and Y. Yamamoto: Extending UML with Aspects: Aspect Support in the Design Phase. AOP Workshop at ECOOP'99, Lisbon, Portugal, 1999.

[38] J. Sztipanovits, and G. Karsai: Model-Integrated Computing. IEEE Computer, Apr. 1997, pp. 110-112.

[39] P. Tarr, H. Ossher, W. Harrison, and S.M. Sutton: N degrees of separation: Multidimensional separation of concerns. In Proceedings of the 21st International Conference on Software Engineering, May 1999.

[40] D. Trowbridge, U. Roxburgh, G. Hohpe, D. Manolescu, E.G. Nadhan: Integration Patterns. Patterns & Practices. Available at www.microsoft.com, 2004.

[41] K. J. Turner: Relating Services and Features in the Intelligent Network. In Proc. of the 4th International Conference on Telecommunications, pp. 235-243, Zagreb, June 1997

[42] UML 2.0. Object Management Group. Available at http://www.omg.org/uml.

[43] J. Whittle, and J. Araujo: Scenario Modeling with Aspects. IEE Proceedings - Software, Special Issue on Early Aspects: Aspect-Oriented Requirements Engineering and Architecture Design, August 2004.

# A Formal Enforcement Framework for Role-Based Access Control Using Aspect-Oriented Programming

Jaime Pavlich-Mariscal, Laurent Michel, and Steven Demurjian

Department of Computer Science & Engineering, The University of Connecticut,
Unit-2155, 371 Fairfield Road, Storrs, CT 06269- 2155
jaime.pavlich@uconn.edu, {ldm,steve}@engr.uconn.edu

**Abstract.** Many of today's software applications require a high-level of security, defined by a detailed policy and attained via mechanisms such as role-based access control (RBAC), mandatory access control, digital signatures, etc. The integration of the design/implementation processes of access-control policies with runtime enforcement mechanisms is crucial to achieve an acceptable level of security for a software application. Our prior research focused on formalizing the concept of a role slice, which is a unified modeling language (UML) artifact that captures RBAC security requirements by defining permissions in the form of allowable or prohibited methods, and by specifying roles as specialized class diagrams that contain those methods. This paper augments this effort by introducing a formal framework for the security of software applications that supports the automatic translation of a role-slice access-control policy (RBAC requirements) into aspect-oriented programming (AOP) enforcement code that is seamlessly integrated with the application. The formal framework provides the necessary underpinnings to automate the integration of security policies into software. A prototyping effort based on Borland's UML tool Together Control Center for defining role-slice diagrams and the associated AOP code generator is under development.

## 1   Introduction

Security has become a very important issue in the development of software applications. Definition and realization of access control policies, along with other security requirements, must be an integral part of the development process, to ensure that the proper level of security in an application is attained. Since access-control requirements tend to change across the entire life-time of a software system, it is very important to have mechanisms that allow the developers or the security administrators to understand and evolve the policies seamlessly. To realize the integration of security in an application, it is necessary to consider several key elements: the access-control approach, the means to represent the access-control information during the analysis and design of the system, and

L. Briand and C. Williams (Eds.): MoDELS 2005, LNCS 3713, pp. 537–552, 2005.

the access-control mechanisms to translate those specifications to enforcement code during the implementation (or update them after deployment).

In terms of access control, there are several popular approaches: *mandatory access control* (MAC) [1, 2], *discretionary access control* (DAC) [3], and *role-based access control* (RBAC) [4, 5, 6]. In MAC, permissions are assigned to users based on the objects they can access in a system. Each object is labeled with a *classification level* (e.g., *top secret*, *secret*, *confidential*, and *unclassified*) that represents the sensitivity of their information. To constrain the access to information, each user has a *clearance level* that defines the access to objects based on its relative order with the classification level of each object. In DAC, permissions are defined between users and objects, but there are also privileges to delegate rights to other users, i.e. a user can be granted the permission to delegate a subset of its own permissions to another user. RBAC is a more general approach where permissions are grouped in independent units called *roles*, which represent the role that a user assumes in an organization. Thus, roles, rather than permissions, are assigned to users when they initiate an interactive session with the software system. The set of privileges granted to a user is defined by the set of permissions assigned to its corresponding role.

To represent access-control information, regardless of the approach utilized, it is crucial to use a formalism that allows developers to clearly understand the security policies that they are defining, and to evolve them easily as requirements change. In this regard, visual languages can be very powerful tools; a well-designed visual representation can conceptualize the security information to developers in an intuitive fashion, facilitate changes, and hopefully reduce errors in the definition of the policy. A CASE tool that incorporates that notation for modeling, and that can automatically check the consistency of the generated models is also critical to ensure a proper security definition. Ongoing work by Doan et al. [7, 8, 9] is focusing on creating a framework for the definition of security policies by enhancing UML to support RBAC and MAC, and defining rules for checking the consistency of the models as an application and its security are defined and changed over time. Their focus is on extending use-case, class and sequence diagrams with tagged values representing access-control attributes, such as classification and clearance levels, lifetimes (legal time intervals for accessing elements in the model), etc. Their work associates roles with UML actors, and defines permissions as actor-use-case associations, actor-object associations, and actor-method associations (in sequence diagrams).

While their approach utilizes a visual modeling language to represent security policies, it does not provide a global view of the permissions. A security policy modeled by this method can be hard to understand by developers and security administrators, since such a policy is distributed across many UML elements rather than organized in a single UML artifact. To complement this work, and to provide a more seamless transition from an access-control policy definition to its implementation, a new visual notation was introduced, the *role slice* [10], that can be used to represent roles and their permissions for RBAC. The underlying premise is to define permissions as the *ability to invoke a method of a class*. Roles are represented as stereotyped packages, and their permission assignment is represented by a specialized class diagram containing the assigned methods. Role hierarchies are also supported; they are represented by stereotyped dependency arrows, using model composition[11] to obtain the permissions of each role based on its position in the hierarchy.

The purpose of this paper is to detail and formalize the process that translates an access-control policy into code, via an architecture that emphasizes *separation of concerns* to reduce software complexity, significantly extending our prior work on the definition of a role slice [10]. To do so, this paper introduces a specialized formalism for representing security policies which is instrumental in modularizing security concerns at design time. One contribution of this paper is to separate, at development time and through the use of *aspect-oriented programming* (AOP), the security enforcement code from the rest of the application. Without this type of support, access-control enforcement code is often scattered and tangled in the application's code, making it difficult to track an entire policy as a logical entity. For example, using a traditional object-oriented decomposition, access control code may be added at the beginning of every method, which results in modifications to many classes that are otherwise unrelated to security issues. Using aspects, that code can be isolated, resulting in a complete modularization of the security concern. The transition from security specifications to code is automated with aspect-oriented security code generation. In this regard, a second contribution of this paper is the formalization of this compilation process, where AOP generated security code is included as part of an application's software. The formalisms that we present utilize a functional notation based on structural operational semantics [12].

This paper is organized into five sections. Section 2 explains background concepts on RBAC and AOP. Section 3 formalizes the elements needed for implementing access control: the underlying object-oriented and aspect-oriented models, and role slices. Section 4 formalizes the generation of aspect-oriented access control code from a role-slice specification. Section 5 summarizes related work. Section 6 concludes the paper and reviews on-going prototyping and future work.

## 2  Background on RBAC and AOP

This section provides background information about the integration of access control into software applications by using RBAC, and AOP to create a software architecture that modularizes security. To begin, role-based access control (RBAC) assumes that an organization itself owns the data and not the users (who require access to the data). Access control can be established with respect to the tasks that each user performs inside the organization [13]. Thus, in RBAC permissions are assigned to roles that exist within an organization. A user can assume a role and utilize its permissions for the duration of the authorization.

Since in an organization, the set of functions associated with each role is much more stable than the users who are assigned to those roles[5], the approach limits changes to the security policy and the impact on end-user authorizations. The basic RBAC concepts used in this paper are:

**Permissions** represent the ability to perform a task over some part of the system. The NIST standard[6, 14] deliberately leaves them as uninterpreted symbols, allowing the developers to decide the chosen interpretation according to a particular realization of the security policy. A *positive (negative) permission* explicitly grants (denies) the right to perform an action over the system. Our approach uses negative permissions only to provide overriding capabilities to the role hierarchies.

**Methods** of an object-oriented application are the unit of permission for our approach, allowing each role to be statically associated with the methods that are positive permissions and negative permissions. The use of methods as the level of privilege assignment has been utilized as part of our foundational security work on the object-oriented paradigm [15], our efforts on security for distributed environments [16, 17], and for the integration of MAC and RBAC into UML [7, 8, 9].

**Roles** are the entities that represent the set of permissions to perform task in a system. Users represent individuals who interact with a system. To initiate an interaction, a user obtains a role and all its associated permissions. Roles are organized in hierarchies similar to class hierarchies in object-oriented systems; each role is associated to a set of parent roles and inherits all the permissions from them. Role hierarchies can be used for classifying roles, i.e. grouping them according to common sets of permissions. For that purpose *abstract roles* can be used, which in a role hierarchy cannot be assigned to any user. *Concrete roles* represent roles that can be assigned to a user, and are normally associated to organizational roles.

*Aspect-oriented programming* (AOP) is an approach for isolating *crosscutting concerns*, i.e., requirements orthogonal to the application structure whose implementations are invariably *scattered* and *tangled* throughout the entire application. An AOP *aspect* is a code fragment that modularizes the orthogonal concern. An *aspect weaver* is a compiler that integrates the aspects with the rest of the application. Each aspect specify where and how to inject its own code in the application. Standard terminology includes:

**Advices** An advice is a code fragment that implements a part of an aspect (e.g., access control), and is intended to be woven with the main program.
**Join Points** A join point is a location within a program where the aspect weaver integrates an advice.
**Pointcuts** A pointcut is a set of join points sharing specific static properties. For instance, in AspectJ [18], pointcuts are defined with quantified boolean formulas over method names, class names, control flow or lexical scopes and capture specific event occurrences such as method calls, access to attributes or exceptions to name a few.

**Aspect Weaving** is a compilation technique that identifies join points in point cuts and modifies the code at that site according to the specified advice.

# 3   Formal Definitions

In this section, we detail a formal framework for modeling an object-oriented application (Section 3.1), role slices (Section 3.2), and aspect-oriented concepts (Section 3.3). The formalism employs a functional notation based on [12] to specify the operational semantics of the program transformation. The functional notation used for the program transformation is structure-driven and promotes a concise, yet precise, specification of the compilation process. For uniformity, the following conventions are used throughout the section:

- Most of the definitions use records of the form $\langle l_1 = v_1, l_2 = v_2, ..., l_n = v_n \rangle$, where each $l_i$ is the label of the $i^{th}$ field of the record and $v_i$ is its value.
- The dot operator ("."") is used with the label name to project on the corresponding value. For example, for a record $person = \langle name = Joe, age = 20 \rangle$, the expression $person.name$ denotes the value $Joe$

In addition, some definitions, such as the composition function (see Def. 11), or the weaving function (see Def 15), use higher-order functions such as map and foldl. For completeness, the specification of map and foldl are: Foldl is a higher-order function that takes a function of two arguments, an initial value, and a list, and returns the result of applying the function recursively over every element of the list, in a left-associative way; and, Map is a function that takes a rewriting function and a list, and returns a list that consists of all the transformed elements.

$$\text{foldl} = \lambda f.\lambda v.\lambda l.\,\text{if}\,\text{nil}\,\,l\,\,\text{then}\,\,\,v\,\,\text{else}\,\,(\text{foldl}\,\,f\,\,(f\,\,v\,(head\,\,l))\,\,(tail\,\,l))$$
$$\text{map}\quad = \lambda f.\lambda l.\,\text{if}\,\text{nil}\,\,l\,\,\text{then}\,\,\,\text{nil}\,\,\text{else}\,\,(f\,(head\,\,l)) :: (\text{map}\,\,f\,(tail\,\,l)))$$

## 3.1   Object-Oriented Definitions

This section formalizes an object-oriented application via an abstraction of a full blown object-oriented language that only retains features that are relevant to the discussion of security concerns. The top-level element *application*, contains classes and inheritance relationships. Each *class* contains a set of methods, and each *method* contains an *implementation*, which is a sequence of *method invocations*. A *subsystem* is a subset of the classes and will be used to separate secure and non-secure portions of the system.

The execution of a program is carried out by an interpreter that chains method invocations on object instances. One important element of the execution schema is that for every method executed, an extra argument representing an *environment* function is passed to every method invocation. The environment keeps the state of variables, such as the return value of a method, the credentials for the authenticated (active) role, the access control policy (available roles and role hierarchy), and the exit value of the program.

**Definition 1 (Interpreter Function).** *An interpreter $I : M \rightarrow S \rightarrow Arg \rightarrow \mathcal{N}$ is a function that, given a method, an environment (see Def. 2), and a method argument, performs a sequence of method invocations (reduction steps) and terminates with the output of an exit status (natural number):*

$$I = \lambda m.\lambda s.\lambda arg. \ (evalCall \ \langle m, s, arg \rangle) \ 'exit'$$

To define its behavior the interpreter uses the auxiliary function `evalCall` that, given a method invocation (see Def. 4), recursively evaluates the implementation of the method, executing control flow statements, performing method invocations, and altering the environment. At the end it returns a new environment. We deliberately avoid a more detailed definition of this function, because it would unnecessarily increase the complexity of our definitions, and because the interpreter and its semantics are not affected by techniques proposed herein.

**Definition 2 (Environment Function).** *An environment $S : Id \rightarrow T$ is a function that tracks global information during the execution of the application, by associating an identifier of type $Id$ (e.g. a string) to an object of type $T$.*

Note that $T$ is a sum type capable to hold a value of any type that exist within the application. An example of the values that S can assume during the execution of a program is $['exit' \mapsto 0, 'activeRole' \mapsto R, 'policy' \mapsto P]$, where 'exit' represents the exit value of the execution of the application (see Def. 1), 'activeRole' is mapped to the object representing the active role of the application (see Eq. 3 and Eq. 7), and 'policy' is mapped to the access control policy (see Def. 10 and Eq. 3). The environment is also used to store the return value of a method after its invocation (e.g. $['returnValue' \mapsto 5]$). For convenience, the auxiliary function

$$set = \lambda s.\lambda i.\lambda v.\lambda x.\text{if } x = i \text{ then } v \text{ else } s \ x$$

will be used to update the environment. It takes an environment $s$, an identifier $i$ and a value $v$, and returns a new environment that contains the association $i \mapsto v$ in addition to the original ones.

**Definition 3 (Method).** *A method is a record $\langle name, impl \rangle$, where name is the name of the method and impl is the implementation of the method.*

When the method is evaluated, the interpreter obtains the functional implementation of the method, which is of the form $\lambda s.\lambda arg.b$, where $s$ is the environment function, $arg$ is the argument passed to the method [1] and $b$ is the method implementation. This function returns a new environment containing the changes done by the execution of the method. During compilation time, the implementation of the method is treated as a sequence of the form shown in Def. 5.

**Definition 4 (Method Invocation).** *A* method invocation *is a record of the form* $\langle m, s, arg \rangle$, *where m is the invoked method, s is the environment, and arg its argument.*

The interpreter function `evalCall` is responsible for the evaluation of a method and returns a new environment that reflects all the changes and side effects resulting from the execution of the method. For example, a Java method invocation of the form `a.method(p1,p2,p3);` is expressed as $\langle method, s, \langle a, p1, p2, p3 \rangle \rangle$.

**Definition 5 (Implementation).** *An* implementation $(inv_1, ..., inv_n)$ *is a sequence of method invocations.*

This definition *purposefully abstracts away several elements from a real implementation* (e.g., control flow statements, builtin instructions or side-effects operations such as assignments) that would add complexity to the formalization but do not affect the framework.

**Definition 6 (Class).** *A* class *is a set of methods. Because attributes are not necessary to explain our approach, we do not include them in the definition of class.*

**Definition 7 (Application).** *An* application *is a record* $\langle C, H \rangle$, *where C is the set of classes and* $H \subseteq C \times C$ *is the inheritance relation between classes in C, with each pair* $\langle a, b \rangle \in H$ *indicates that a is a subclass of b.*

**Definition 8 (Subsystem).** *A* subsystem *of an application* $\langle C, H \rangle$ *is a record* $\langle SC, SH \rangle$, *where* $SC \subseteq C$ *and SH is the projection of H onto SC.*

## 3.2   Role Slices

In this section, we review and formalize the role-slice artifact as it relates to RBAC and permission assignment, using a university application illustrated in Figure 1, that depicts a simplified class model that manages information about courses and students, providing access for different types of users (e.g., teachers, students, administrators, etc.). The `Course` class stores information about syllabus, credits, and enrolled students, while `StudentRecord` stores the information about a student's id number, name, and enrolled courses. The `Catalog`

---

[1] An argument can also be a tuple of values

class shows all of the public information on the courses offered. To grant access through RBAC, we define two roles: *Teacher* is able to manage a course, define its syllabus, and obtain the list of enrolled student names; and, *Student* is able to get the basic information on a courses s/he is enrolled in, obtain their syllabus, and the number of credits. A *role slice* is used to define an *access-control policy*. A role

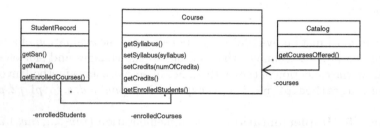

**Fig. 1.** Class diagram of the Courseware Application

slice denotes the set of class methods that a given role can access, and represents the separate concern that captures permissions for roles. Since a role may not require access to every class, the role-slice permission assignment is defined with respect to a subsystem. Pictorially, a role slice is represented in UML as a stereo-typed package containing a specialized class diagram (see Fig. 2), that is a subset of the class model; each class present in the role slice has only the methods that are assigned to the corresponding role as positive or negative permissions. The diagram in Fig. 2 is defined over the subsystem ⟨{Course,StudentRecord}, {}⟩. Catalog represents publicly-accessible information and does not appear in any role slice. The two concrete role slices are Teacher and Student. Each inherit permissions from the abstract role slice AcademicPeople that holds the common set of permissions. Note that positive and negative permissions (methods) are represented, respectively, with the stereotype ≪ *pos* ≫ and ≪ *neg* ≫. The *role-slice composition relationship* captures inheritance among roles in a role hierarchy. Visually, it is represented as a stereotyped dependency arrow that starts from the child and points to the parent. To obtain the complete set of permissions for a role in a hierarchy, a specialized version of the *composition with override integration* defined by Clarke [11] composes two class diagrams by unifying their classes and methods. For role slices, the names of the classes are matched (i.e., classes with the same name in both role slices compose into one class in the final diagram), and the child overrides any permission definition in the parent. For the role-slice diagram in Fig. 2, a full composition operation produces the diagram shown in Fig. 3. In this new role-slice diagram, only concrete role slices are shown. To illustrate overriding, the method getEnrolledStudents is positive in AcademicPeople, and negative in Student. The composed role slice for Student shows this method as negative. Formally, a role-slice is defined as follows.

**Definition 9 (Role Slice).** *A role slice is a record* $\langle PP, NP, abstract \rangle$, *where* $PP$ *is the set of methods with positive permissions, $NP$ is the set of methods with negative permissions, and abstract indicates whether the role slice is abstract or concrete (see definition of Roles in section 2).*

**Definition 10 (Access-Control Policy).** *An* access-control policy *represents the sets of roles and permissions for a specific subsystem containing the classes requiring access control, and is a record* $\langle RS, CR, S \rangle$, *where $RS$ is the set of role slices defined over the subsystem $S$, and $CR \subseteq RS \times RS$ is the* role-slice composition relation *that defines the role hierarchy. Each pair in $CR$ is of the form $\langle a, b \rangle$, where $a$ is the child role slice and $b$ is the parent role slice.*

**Definition 11 (Full composition).** *Full composition* $fc : RS \rightarrow CR \rightarrow RS$ *is a function that takes a role slice and a composition relation as arguments, traversing the role-slice hierarchy to return the role slice composed with all its ancestors. For space reasons, no further details are given for this function.*

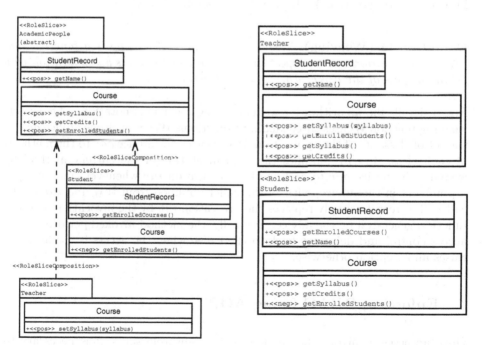

**Fig. 3.** Composed Role Slice Diagram

**Fig. 2.** Role Slice Diagram

### 3.3  Aspect-Oriented Definitions

This section details the formal definitions of the aspect-oriented elements needed for specifying access-control code. The concepts that are introduced are abstractions of real AOP constructions that only capture the features necessary to describe the compilation of the security design. For example, join points only reference method calls initiated in specific methods, and there are no attribute-based join points and advices only represent the **around** construct.[2]

**Definition 12 (Point Cut).** *A* point cut *represents a set of specific locations in the code of the application that are used to integrate the aspect code. It is represented as a record* $\langle caller, callee \rangle$, *where* caller *is a method where all invocations of* callee *must be modified to include the aspect code.*

**Definition 13 (Advice).** *An* advice *is a record* $\langle PC, T \rangle$, *where* $PC$ *is a set of point cuts and* $T$ *is a rewriting function that modifies the method invocations specified in* $PC$.

**Definition 14 (Aspect).** *An* aspect *is a set of advices.*

**Definition 15 (Weaving).** Weaving $W : App \rightarrow A \rightarrow App$ *is a function that takes an application and an aspect as arguments, and outputs an application with all the advices of the aspect woven to its structure.*

Fig. 4 details the algorithm for weaving using $\lambda$-calculus notation. The aspect-weaving function $W$ uses three auxiliary functions. $W_C$ weaves one advice *adv* to the set of classes $C$ of the application. $W_M$ weaves one advice *adv* to the methods of each class. $W_{IMPL}$ modifies the implementation of the current method by weaving the advice *adv* to each method invocation *inv* whenever $\langle m, inv.m \rangle$ is a point cut in the advice, with $m$ the caller obtained from $W_M$ and $inv.m$ the callee. The rewrite simply replaces the invocation *inv* by the invocation of a new function generated by the advice. Typically, the method invoked performs some access control and delegates back to the callee when the access is granted and raises an exception otherwise.

## 4  Enforcing RBAC Using AOP

Once an access-control policy is defined by using role slices, it is necessary to translate that specification to enforcement code. This process is done automatically by a code generator, currently under development at UConn. This program takes as input a role-slice access-control policy (see Def. 10) and outputs:

---

[2] before and **after** constructs can easily be emulated in the rewriting function

$$W_{IMPL} = \lambda m.\lambda inv.\lambda adv. \text{ if } \langle m, inv.m \rangle \in adv.PC$$
$$\text{then } adv.T \text{ } inv$$
$$\text{else } inv$$
$$W_M \quad = \lambda m.\lambda adv.\langle m.name, \text{map } (W_{IMPL} \text{ } m) \text{ } m.impl \rangle$$
$$W_C \quad = \lambda c.\lambda adv.\text{map } W_M \text{ } c$$
$$W \quad = \lambda app.\lambda a.\langle \text{foldl } (\lambda c.\lambda adv. \text{ map } W_C \text{ } c \text{ } adv) \text{ } app.C \text{ } a, app.H \rangle$$

**Fig. 4.** Weaving Algorithm

- A *policy database*, containing the access control policy, and an authorization schema to store user instances and their assigned roles. The assumption is that every user is assigned only one role per session with the system. In our example, this information is accessed through the environment using the id string 'policy'.
- An *access-control aspect* that intercepts every call to the set of classes which access needs to be controlled and grants or deny access depending on the permissions stored in the policy database.

Formally, to implement access control for an application *app*, a subsystem *subs* is defined for controlling access, i.e., for the university application in Sec. 3.2 $subs = \langle \{StudentRecord, Course\}, \{\} \rangle$. The access-control aspect is defined as:

$$ac = \{adv_{\text{login}}, adv_{\text{enf}}\} \tag{1}$$

To enforce access control, the aspect uses the active role of the user currently logged in. The method that obtains the active role remains application dependent. In this example assume that when a user initiates a session in the system, a `login` method is invoked to obtain a tuple $\langle u, r \rangle$ representing an instance of the logged user ($u$) and his/her active role ($r$). The $adv_{\text{login}}$ advice intercepts the login method and stores the active role in the environment.

$$adv_{\text{login}} = \langle \{ \langle m, \text{login} \rangle : m \in ( \bigcup_{c \in app.C} c) \backslash \{\text{login}\}\}, T_{\text{login}} \rangle \tag{2}$$

The pointcut of $adv_{\text{login}}$ references all calls to the `login` method that do not occur within the `login` method itself. $T_{\text{login}}$ is the rewriting function that retrieves the user's role from the return value of the `login` method, applies full composition to it (see Def. 11), and stores it into the environment as the 'activeRole'.

$$T_{\text{login}} = \lambda inv.\langle (\lambda s.\lambda arg.\text{let } y = ((inv.m \text{ } s \text{ } arg) \text{ } 'returnValue') \text{ in} \tag{3}$$
$$\text{set } s \text{ } 'activeRole' \text{ } (fc \text{ } y.r \text{ } (s \text{ } 'policy').CR)), inv.s, inv.arg \rangle$$

The $adv_{\text{enf}}$ advice enforces the security policy. It intercepts external calls to the subsystem *subs* (calls to methods in *subs* originating outside *subs*).

$$adv_{\text{enf}} = \langle \{ \langle a, b \rangle : a \in M_{\text{ext}}, b \in M_{\text{in}}\}, T_{\text{enf}} \rangle \tag{4}$$

$M_{ext}$ is the set of methods outside the subsystem *subs*, and $M_{in}$ is the set of methods within subsystem *subs*.

$$M_{ext} = \bigcup_{c \in (app.C \setminus subs.SC)} c \tag{5}$$

$$M_{in} = \bigcup_{c \in subs.SC} c \tag{6}$$

$T_{enf}$ is the method invocation rewriting function that checks positive permissions. It receives a method invocation *inv* and produces a new invocation record whose first member $m$ is a new function that performs the access control and possibly delegates to the original function implementation when the access is granted.

$$T_{enf} = \lambda inv.\langle(\lambda s.\lambda arg.\, \texttt{if}\ inv.m \in (s\ \text{'activeRole'}).PP \tag{7}$$
$$\texttt{then}\ (inv.m\ s\ arg)$$
$$\texttt{else Exception}), inv.s, inv.arg\rangle$$

Notice that negative permissions are not checked explicitly, because they are implicitly enforced by this implementation; the main purpose of negative permissions is to provide overriding when doing role slice composition.

To illustrate the ideas discussed above, we first model the university application and a secure subsystem:

$$app = \langle\{StudentRecord, Course, Catalog\}, \{\}\rangle \tag{8}$$

$$subs = \langle\{StudentRecord, Course\}, \{\}\rangle \tag{9}$$

The security policy for the subsystem *subs* is defined by the composed role slices *Teacher* and *Student* (see Fig. 3); the *Student* role slice is:

$$Student = \left\langle \left\{ \begin{array}{c} getEnrolledCourses, getName \\ getSyllabus, getCredits \end{array} \right\}, \{getEnrolledStudents\} \right\rangle \tag{10}$$

Security enforcement of the university application is implemented by an access control aspect as shown in Eq. 1. For space reasons, we only give details of the advice $adv_{enf}$ (Eq. 4), defined with respect to the sets of external and internal methods, as:

$$M_{ext} = \{getCoursesOffered\} \tag{11}$$

$$M_{in} = \{getSsn, getName, getEnrolledCourses, getSyllabus, setSyllabus,$$
$$getCredits, setCredits, getEnrolledStudents\} \tag{12}$$

To illustrate the effects of the weaving function, we show the details of the method $getCoursesOffered$:

$$\left\langle getCoursesOffered, \left( \begin{array}{c} \langle getSyllabus, s, \langle thecourse \rangle \rangle, \\ \langle getCredits, s, \langle thecourse \rangle \rangle \end{array} \right) \right\rangle \tag{13}$$

For brevity, assume that its implementation has only two method invocations, which are executed over an instance of *Course*, called *thecourse*. Since the method *getCoursesOffered* is external, all its invocations to internal methods are woven to advice $adv_{enf}$. The functional implementation of the invocation to *getSyllabus* after the weaving is:

$$\langle(\lambda s.\lambda arg. \text{ if } getSyllabus \in (s \text{ 'activeRole'}).PP \tag{14}$$
$$\text{then } (getSyllabus \ s \ arg)$$
$$\text{else Exception}), s, \langle thecourse\rangle\rangle$$

This woven invocation now calls *getSyllabus* only if the active role has permissions to do it.

# 5   Related Work

There have been previous attempts to use AOP for enforcing access control. One such approach is [19], which contains an example of composition of access-control behavior into an application by using aspect-oriented modeling techniques, with the aim of integrating security into a class model that allows designers to verify its access-control properties. Their approach takes a generic security design and instantiates it in a model tied to the domain of the application. In contrast, our code generation also requires the instantiation of the design, but only the access control aspect has dependencies with the domain class model. In addition, the role-slice notation provides a language to represent the policy that can be implemented using the aspect-oriented paradigm.

Another effort is [20] that provides a general framework for incorporating security into software via AOP, presenting a particular example access control via aspects. Their approach is similar to ours in the way they constrain method invocations based on permissions, but it differs in permission definition; in theirs, each permission is represented as a specific method tied to a framework of server objects that define them and a set of client objects that invoke them, while in ours, permissions are defined over any method in the class diagram, with a formal mapping between policy definition and code to set the base for automatic code generation. In terms for formalizing AOP, [21] proposes a monadic formal model for dynamic join points and AOP. Their notation is complete and general enough for representing AOP. Our approach is simpler (sufficient for our needs) and with the specific purpose of representing access-control enforcement.

Regarding the UML notation, [22] has proposed a Network Enterprise Framework using UML for representing RBAC requirements without separation of duty. Permissions are represented using UML packages and interfaces; role hierarchies are achieved by interface inheritance. This approach inspired the role-slice model, which in contrast uses classes, supports permission overriding, and role hierarchies, which are defined over a special grouping unit (the role slice).

Another effort that relates to role slices is [23], which defines a metamodel to generate security definition languages. SecureUML [23] is an instance defined by this approach; a platform-independent security definition language for RBAC. The syntax of SecureUML has two parts: an *abstract syntax* independent from the modeling notation; and, a *concrete syntax* which can be used as an extension to a modeling language, such as UML. The abstract syntax defines basic elements to represent RBAC: *roles*, which can be assigned to *users* or *groups* of users; *permissions*, which are assigned to roles based on specific associated *constraints*; and, *actions*, which are associated with *permissions*, where a role can have a permission to execute one or more actions. SecureUML's concrete syntax is defined by mapping elements in the abstract syntax to concrete UML elements [23]. We note that our role-slice diagram and associated concepts can be an instance of the concrete-syntax of the SecureUML notation, and that our syntax and associated mappings to UML elements differ from their approach. We also note that the role-slice diagram is only one component of our overall research. Specifically, our usage of composition in the role-slice diagram and the subsequent transition of the composed diagram into AOP enforcement code, is significantly different than the approach in SecureUML.

# 6    Conclusions and Future Work

This paper has formalized a compilation mechanism for security specification, that is able to support the automatic transition of a new UML artifact, the *role slice* (based on our previous work), into aspect-oriented code for security enforcement. Based on background on RBAC and AOP in Section 2, we have presented a formal functional model that captured an object-oriented application, aspect-oriented modeling, and role slices (see Section 3). This model facilitates the formalization of aspect-oriented access control generation from role slices, as presented in Section 4. Overall, we believe that our efforts to formalize the security definition and enforcement processes can be instrumental in attaining precise and accurate security specifications that can be evolved over time.

In terms of ongoing research, the effort presented in this paper is occurring concurrently with work underway at UConn to extend UML with MAC and RBAC [7, 8, 9], as mentioned in the introduction. As part of this effort, a team of graduate students has been integrating both that work and the work presented herein as part of Borland's UML tool Together Control Center (TCC). TCC has an open API and plug in architecture that has allowed us to extend UML diagrams to support security definition, and to define a new role-slice diagram. In addition to this prototyping effort, we are continuing our research into the role-slice model as presented in this paper. Specifically, we are interested in enhancing our model with additional security concerns, including: MAC to be able to handle security against methods based on classification and clearance; delegation to provide the ability to pass on authority (role) from one user to another; and, instance-based security that expands our work to control access to methods based on object instances in addition to our current class-based approach. Our intent is to extend the formalisims of Sections 3 and 4 with each additional access control capability.

# References

[1] Bell, D., LaPadula, L.: Secure computer systems: Mathematical foundations model. Technical report, Mitre Corporation (1975)

[2] Biba, K.: Integrity considerations for secure computer systems. Technical report, Mitre Corporation (1977)

[3] DoD: Trusted Computer System Evaluation Criteria. 5200.28-STD. DoD (1985)

[4] Ting, T.C.: A user-role based data security approach. In Landwehr, C., ed.: Database Security: Status and Prospects. (1988)

[5] Sandhu, R.S., Coyne, E.J., Feinstein, H.L., Youman, C.E.: Role-based access control models. IEEE Computer **29** (1996) 38–47

[6] Ferraiolo, D.F., Sandhu, R., Gavrila, S., Kuhn, D.R., Chandramouli, R.: Proposed NIST standard for role-based access control. ACM Trans. Inf. Syst. Secur. **4** (2001) 224–274

[7] Doan, T., Demurjian, S., Ting, T., Phillips, C.: RBAC/MAC security for UML. In Farkas, C., Samarati, P., eds.: Research Directions in Data and Applications Security XVIII. (2004)

[8] Doan, T., Demurjian, S., Ting, T., Ketterl, A.: MAC and UML for secure software design. In: Proc. of 2nd ACM Wksp. on Formal Methods in Security Engineering, Washington D.C. (2004)

[9] Doan, T., Demurjian, S., Ammar, R., Ting, T.: UML design with security integration as a first class citizen. In: Proc. of 3rd Intl. Conf. on Computer Science, Software Engineering, Information Technology, e-Business, and Applications (CSITeA'04), Cairo (2004)

[10] Pavlich-Mariscal, J.A., Doan, T., Michel, L., Demurjian, S.A., Ting, T.C.: Role slices: A notation for rbac permission assignment and enforcement. In: Proceedings of 19th Annual IFIP WG 11.3 Working Conference on Data and Applications Security. (2005)

[11] Clarke, S.: Composition of object-oriented software design models. PhD thesis, Dublin City University (2001)

[12] Plotkin, G.: A Structural Approach to Operational Semantics. Technical Report DAIMI FN-19, CS Department, University of Aarhus (1981)

[13] Ferraiolo, D., Kuhn, R.: Role-based access controls. In: 15th NIST-NCSC National Computer Security Conference. (1992) 554–563

[14] Sandhu, R., Ferraiolo, D., Kuhn, R.: The NIST model for role-based access control: Towards a unified standard. (2000) 47–64

[15] Demurjian, S.A., Ting, T.C.: Towards a definitive paradigm for security in object-oriented systems and applications. Journal of Computer Security **5** (1997)

[16] Phillips, C., Demurjian, S., Ting, T.: Security assurance for an rbac/mac security model. In: Proc. of 2003 IEEE Info. Assurance Workshop, West Point, NY (2003)

[17] Phillips, C., Demurjian, S., Ting, T.C.: Safety and liveness for an rbac/mac security model. In di Vimercati, S., Ray, I., eds.: Database and Applications Security XVII: Status and Prospects. (2004)

552     Jaime Pavlich-Mariscal, Laurent Michel, and Steven Demurjian

[18] AspectJ-Team: The aspectj programming guide. http://dev.eclipse.org/viewcvs/ indextech.cgi/ checkout /aspectj-home/doc/progguide/index.html (2003)

[19] Song, E., Reddy, R., France, R., Ray, I., Georg, G., Alexander, R.: Verifiable composition of access control features and applications. In: Proceedings of 10th ACM Symposium on Access Control Models and Technologies (SACMAT 2005). (2005)

[20] Win, B.D., Vanhaute, B., Decker, B.D.: Security through aspect-oriented programming. In: Proceedings of the IFIP TC11 WG11.4 First Annual Working Conference on Network Security, Kluwer, B.V. (2001) 125–138

[21] Wand, M., Kiczales, G., Dutchyn, C.: A semantics for advice and dynamic join points in aspect-oriented programming. In Leavens, G.T., Cytron, R., eds.: FOAL 2002 Proceedings. (2002)

[22] Epstein, P., Sandhu, R.: Towards a uml based approach to role engineering. In: Proceedings of the fourth ACM workshop on Role-based access control. (1999) 135–143

[23] Basin, D., Doser, J., Lodderstedt, T.: Model driven security, Engineering Theories of Software Intensive Systems. (2004)

# A Domain Model for Dynamic System Reconfiguration

D'Arcy Walsh, Francis Bordeleau, Bran Selic

Carleton University, Ottawa, Canada
{jdwalsh@acm.org, francis@zeligsoft.com, bselic@ca.ibm.com}

**Abstract.** In this paper, a domain model of dynamic system reconfiguration is presented. The intent of this model is to provide a comprehensive conceptual framework within which to address problems and solutions related to dynamically reconfigurable systems in a systematic and consistent manner. The model identifies and categorizes the various types of change that may be required, the relationship between those types, and the key factors that need to be considered and actions to be performed when such changes take place. A rigorous formal methodology, based on the Alloy language and tools, is employed to specify precisely and formally the detailed relationships between various parts of the model.

## 1 Introduction

Predicting future user requirements or anticipating changing domain imposed requirements for software systems [1, 2] is extremely difficult and error prone, often resulting in over- or under-engineered solutions. This leads to the notion of software systems that can evolve dynamically [3]. This paper describes a *domain model* of dynamic system reconfiguration that provides a well-defined context for a systematic treatment of different approaches to the problem of evolving software systems.

The proposed domain model defines the core concepts that make up a reconfigurable system. It is *component based* since it represents a software system as a configuration of autonomous cooperating components [6,7]. Dynamic reconfiguration is therefore viewed as a run-time realignment of that configuration [3, 8-11]. The particular kinds of realignment are represented as *types of change*.

A change to a system may be either *user driven* or *domain imposed*. In either case, there will be new or augmented functional and non-functional requirements on the system. Importantly, it may be required that the functional change must not violate the original non-functional conditions (e.g., response time, availability) or vice-versa. A change may either be *expected*, and therefore planned for within the design of the system, or *unexpected*, and therefore involving more fundamental and possibly more pervasive behavioral and structural changes. Finally, the time to enact the required change may be *bounded* or *unbounded* compared to other conditions for evolution [4, 5].

The essentials of the proposed domain model are first expressed in the form of a conceptually simple feature model [12, 13]. This is used as a basis for deriving a more refined formal model expressed using the Alloy language [14-18]. This allows the

L. Briand and C. Williams (Eds.): MoDELS 2005, LNCS 3713, pp. 553-567, 2005.
© Springer-Verlag Berlin Heidelberg 2005

proposed domain model to be formally validated for consistency. Finally, the feature and Alloy models are used to produce a UML class model [13, 19-21] that combines the various aspects into a single comprehensive metamodel of dynamic reconfiguration.

The rest of this paper first identifies the types of change that occur in a dynamically evolving system. Section 3 describes the feature model, while the Alloy model is described in section 4. Finally, the main elements of the UML class model are described in section 5.

# 2 Types of Change

The type of a change defines, at an abstract level, how a system evolves to adapt to new conditions. The evolution of a particular system conforms to one or more of these general types but within the context of the particular conditions that motivated the change and the concrete representations of that system.

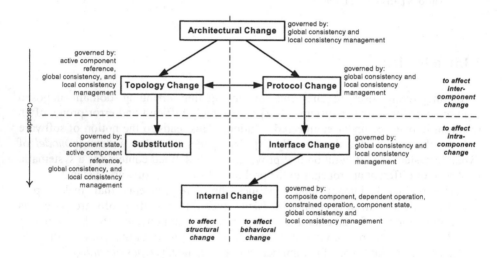

**Fig. 1.** Types of change and their dependencies

Figure 1 shows the six types of change that could be applied to a running system and their mutual relationships. Together they provide a comprehensive dynamic reconfiguration capability. Each type is described below in terms of whether structural or behavioral change is affected, whether inter-component or intra-component change is required, and its dependencies on other change types. The types of change determine whether the behavioral or structural signature of a system must change, which in turn determines whether a system's internal behavior or external interactions need to be realigned.

The diagram also identifies the system integrity characteristics that govern each change type and which ensure global and local consistency across the system in the face of change. Depending upon the combination of change types needed, the same integrity characteristics may apply for different types of change (such as global and local consistency constraints).

The types of system change are the following:

- *Substitution* replaces a particular component by another within a given system topology. This is a structural intra-component change. It does not require any other types of change;
- *Internal Change* changes the internal implementation of a component. This is an intra-component type of change that can be either behavioral, structural, or both. It does not require any other types of change;
- *Interface Change* changes the externally observable behavior of a component. It is a behavioral intra-component change. Ultimately, it may require internal change of one or more components to realize the new behavior;
- *Protocol Change* changes the control flow and/or data flow of components. This is a behavioral inter-component change. Ultimately, it may require a topology change or an interface change;
- *Topology Change* changes the topology of a system through component addition and/or removal. This is a structural inter-component change. Ultimately, it may drive substitution or protocol changes; and
- *Architectural Change* changes global and/or local system properties. It is an inter-component change that may be structural, behavioral, or both. Ultimately, it may require topology and/or protocol changes.

The system integrity characteristics are:

- *Active Component References* ensure that any active client that is bound to a changing component has a valid binding after the change is completed (the binding may have to be dynamically updated);
- *Component State* indicates that any needed transfers of state from the changing component to its replacement component(s) occurred through appropriate mechanisms;
- *Constrained Operations* ensure that any operation with a dependency on a component's state element would not be enacted until the given state element's life cycle was restored as necessary after its component's change;
- *Dependent Operations* ensure that any change to a given operation was valid with respect to any client operations that had a direct dependency on the operation about to change;
- *Composite Components* ensure that any change to a given component was valid with respect to any composed components that had a direct dependency on the changing component;
- *Global Consistency* ensures the preservation of any global architectural invariants of a system, as implied by its specification; and
- *Local Consistency* ensures the preservation of any local architectural invariants of a system, as implied by its specification.

The change types and system integrity characteristics are more fully described in [22], including case studies.

# 3 The Feature Model

A dynamically re-configurable component-based system must provide adequate capability to:

- Respond to run time change stimuli;
- Identify the nature of change that would be required as global or local properties (including their reconciliation);
- Enact the types of change that may be required; and
- Govern the change to ensure overall system integrity.

The extent to which these capabilities are provided depends on the particular environment in which the system is running.

To understand how to do this, a domain model of dynamic reconfiguration is defined in three steps. First, a model of the primary concepts of a component-based system is defined. Next, a model of the primary concepts of the *context* of dynamic change is defined. Finally, the two models are combined to produce the desired domain model of dynamic reconfiguration. The feature modeling technique [12] was chosen for these models because of its conceptual simplicity and ease of mapping to an Alloy representation. In this formalism, a complex feature is decomposed into one or more sub-features. The sub-features can be designated as being *mandatory*, *mandatory-and*, *mandatory-or*, *optional*, *optional-and*, or *optional-or*.

## 3.1 Component-Based System Feature Model

Figure 2 shows the decomposition of the concept of a Component-Based System. External Interactions is an example of a mandatory feature. Required Service and Provided Service are examples of mandatory-and features. Connection is an example of an optional feature.

This separation of features is intended to ease the understanding of a complex system from the viewpoint of dynamic reconfiguration. It allows, at the modeling level, the internal implementation of components to be viewed independently of component interactions, and it enables dependencies that drive internal implementations to be considered separately from those that drive external interactions. There are, of course, dependencies between the various sub-features, but this decomposition enables better focus on the areas most directly related to dynamic reconfiguration. As one example of a sub-feature dependency not shown, a component may be recursively composed of other components. Dependencies between the various sub-features are represented in the Alloy specification.

A Component-Based System is decomposed into:

- *External Interactions* that represent the cooperating components of a system;
- *Internal Behavior* that represents the encapsulated implementation of capabilities required to satisfy a component's external interaction obligations; and
- *Dependencies* that represent the configuration of a component with respect to other components.

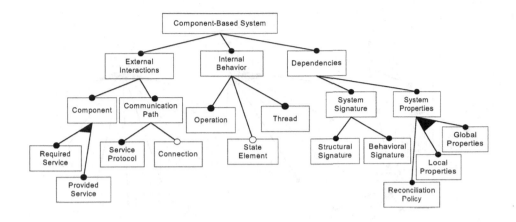

**Fig. 2.** Feature model of a component-based system

*External Interactions* is further decomposed into components and communication paths that connect required services to provided services and which conform to service interaction protocols. This decomposition is consistent with the concepts found in various architecture description languages (ADLs) [23].

*Internal Behavior* is further decomposed to enable modeling of internal computation (as operations, state elements, and threads), systematic management of system integrity (by managing dependencies between operations, state elements, and threads) and mapping of internal behavior to external interactions (by linking certain operations to required or provided services).

*Dependencies* is further decomposed to allow the specification of global or local system properties as constraints [18], the reconciliation of these constraints, and the specification of system profiles that constrain external interactions and internal behavior.

The following sequence determines the constraints hierarchy in a component-based system:

- The system specification constrains *System Properties*;
- System Properties constrain the *System Signature*;
- The *Structural Signature* constrains *External Interactions*; and
- The *Behavioral Signature* constrains *Internal Behavior*.

### 3.2 Context of Change Feature Model

Figure 3 shows the decomposition of the concept Context of Change. The specific system integrity characteristics are examples of optional-and features.

This separation of features allows different aspects of the context of change to vary independently and causal flow to be modeled in a fashion more easily understood.

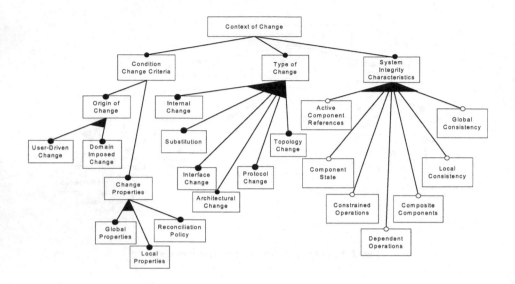

**Fig. 3.** Feature model of context change

*Context of Change* represents software evolution as a feature that will enable the system model to be dynamically reconfigurable. It is decomposed into:

- *Condition Change Criteria* that represent conditions under which a system evolves;
- *Type of Change* that represents the different kinds of dynamic reconfiguration already noted in Figure 1; and
- *System Integrity Characteristics* that represent the different system characteristics that must be managed to help ensure overall system integrity.

*Condition Change Criteria* is further decomposed to indicate that a change may be user driven and/or domain imposed and to allow a direct mapping of change properties to system properties when changing a running system. *Type of Change* is further decomposed to represent the six types of change defined in section 2. *System Integrity Characteristics* is further decomposed to represent the seven system integrity characteristics described in section 2.

The following sequence determines how a context of change is defined:

- Changing the system specification determines the *Origin of Change*;
- *User-Driven* and/or *Domain Imposed Change* determine *Change Properties*;
- *Change Properties* determine *Type of Change*; and
- *Type of Change* determines *System Integrity Characteristics*.

### 3.3 Dynamic Reconfiguration Feature Model

The two previous models are combined to produce the overall domain model of a dynamically reconfigurable component-based system, by adding *Context of Change* as a feature of a component based system, as shown in Figure 4.

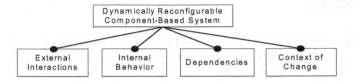

**Fig. 4.** Feature model of a dynamically reconfigurable component-based system

The process of dynamic reconfiguration progresses as follows (see Figure 5):

1. Determine whether *User-Driven Changes* and/or *Domain Imposed Changes* are required;
2. Interpret the particular *Origin of Change* and represent it as appropriate *Global Properties* and/or *Local Properties* with an associated *Reconciliation Policy* (this would include reconciliation with existing *System Properties*);
3. Determine what feasible subsets of *Type of Change* (if any) would satisfy the *Condition Change Criteria*;
4. If necessary, realign *Dependencies* and, possibly, *External Interactions* and *Internal Behavior*; and, finally, ensure *System Integrity Characteristics* are maintained when enacting change.

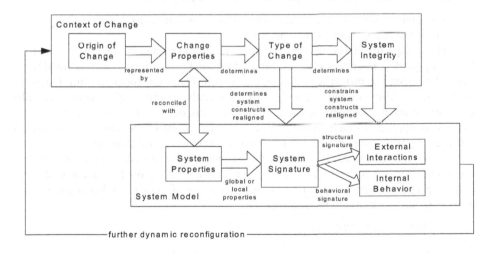

**Fig. 5.** Primary feature interactions of dynamic reconfiguration

The diagram in Figure 5 also shows that further dynamic reconfiguration may occur after a given kind of change has been enacted. For example, architectural change may lead to topology change and so on. Depending upon the change type, different aspects of the system model would be realigned, constrained by different subsets of integrity characteristics that help ensure overall system consistency. The complete description of the feature model including a description of change groupings and change sequences is given in [22].

## 4 The Alloy Model

In [22], the intent of formulating a more formal model is to refine the feature model in a precise way and to use this formal model as a bridge to a UML Platform Independent Model (PIM) of dynamic reconfiguration.

A rigorous methodology is employed to specify the primary feature interactions among the context of change and the system model. Alloy, a purely relation-oriented language, is used to describe the feature model as a formal specification. The Alloy Analyzer is then used to automatically validate its consistency, generate snapshots, execute operations, and check various properties of the model. Alloy was chosen because it is a relatively simple yet powerful language for expressing executable specifications. At the time of writing, Alloy version 2.1 was used [14-17].

The following outlines the general approach taken:

- Each feature defined in the feature model is specified as a signature in Alloy;
- Based upon these signatures, containment relations are then specified to formally relate these features to each other;
- Based upon these containment relations, Alloy facts and assertions are specified as further constraints; and
- Based upon these facts and assertions, Alloy checks and functions are specified to generate snapshots, execute operations, or check properties.

With this approach, the feature model is transformed to a semantically richer Alloy model that specifies many constraints.

The complete model, given in [22], is partitioned into separate Alloy modules based upon dependencies (for example, the condition change criteria module is dependent upon the properties module, and so on). These dependencies build until the highest-level Alloy module specifies a dynamically reconfigurable system as fully constrained by the signatures, facts, and assertions defined in constituent modules. With this approach, each module may be independently checked for consistency representing well-formed building blocks of the complete specification.

At the root of the Alloy model is the assumption that a system specification may be represented by a set of constraints [18]. Given this, global or local system or change properties can be specified as constraints. The following Alloy signatures are used to specify system or change properties:

```
sig SpecificationAsConstraint {}

sig Property {constraint: SpecificationAsConstraint}

disj sig GlobalProperty, LocalProperty extends Property {}

sig ReconciliationPolicy {disj compatibleProperties,
incompatibleProperties: Property -> Property}
```

This means that *SpecificationAsConstraint* is contained by *Property*. *Global Property* and *Local Property* are specified as extensions to *Property* as disjoint signatures. *Reconciliation Policy* is specified as containing the disjoint relations *compatibleProperties* and *incompatibleProperties*. These relations specify compatible or incompatible properties as *Property* to *Property* relations.

The following are some example Alloy facts from the complete model related to properties:

```
fact{no p: Property | some rp: ReconciliationPolicy | p -> p
in rp.compatibleProperties || p -> p in
rp.incompatibleProperties}

fact{no p1, p2: Property | some rp: ReconciliationPolicy | p1
->    p2 in rp.compatibleProperties && p1 -> p2 in
rp.incompatibleProperties}

fact{no p1, p2: Property | some rp: ReconciliationPolicy | p1
-> p2 in rp.compatibleProperties && p2 -> p1 in
rp.incompatibleProperties}
```

These particular facts indicate: (i) a given property may not be related to itself as compatible or incompatible properties, (ii) if *p1* is related to *p2* as a compatible property, *p1* may not be related to *p2* as an incompatible property, and (iii) if *p1* is related to *p2* as a compatible property, *p2* may not be related to *p1* as an incompatible property.

Figure 6 shows a visual representation generated by the Alloy Analyzer when run for three properties. This represents one valid solution.

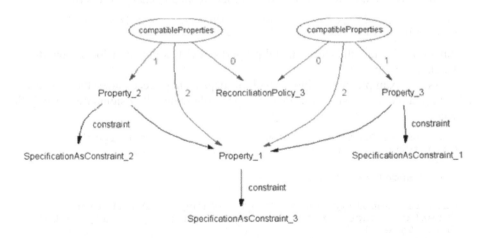

**Fig. 6.** Example visual representation generated by the Alloy analyzer

Figure 7 shows the *Change Properties* feature model fragment:

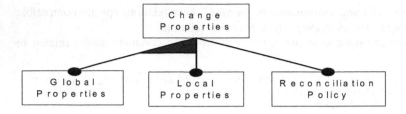

**Fig. 7.** Change properties feature model fragment

Dependent upon the properties module, the following Alloy signature specifies *Change Properties*:

```
sig ChangeProperties {globalProperties: set GlobalProperty,
localProperties: set LocalProperty, reconciliationPolicy:
ReconciliationPolicy}
```

If, for example, *ReconciliationPolicy* was an optional sub-feature (which it is not) it would be specified as optional in the Alloy model:

```
sig ChangeProperties {globalProperties: set GlobalProperty,
localProperties: set LocalProperty, optional
reconciliationPolicy: ReconciliationPolicy}
```

The following is a fact from the complete model related to change properties:

```
fact{all p: Property | some cp: ChangeProperties | p in
cp.globalProperties || p in cp.localProperties}
```

This particular fact indicates that all properties exist as global or local properties of some change properties.

As an example of a higher-level of dependency, reconsider the *Context of Change* feature model shown in Figure 3. The following Alloy signatures specify the concept:

```
sig ContextOfChange {context: ConditionChangeCriteria ->
ChangeType -> SystemIntegrityCharacteristics}

sig ChangeType {}

disj sig TopologyChange, InternalChange, Substitution,
InterfaceChange, ProtocolChange, ArchitecturalChange extends
ChangeType {}

sig SystemIntegrityCharacteristics {integrityCharacteristics:
set SystemIntegrityCharacteristic}

sig SystemIntegrityCharacteristic {}

disj sig ActiveReference, ComponentState,
ConstrainedOperation, DependentOperation, CompositeComponent,
LocalConsistency, GlobalConsistency extends
SystemIntegrityCharacteristic {}
```

The Alloy model fragment above specifies *Context of Change* as containing a *ConditionChangeCriteria* to *ChangeType* to *SystemIntegrityCharacteristics* relation. *ConditionChangeCriteria* is defined in a separate module (not shown). Types of change are specified as disjoint signatures, one for each of the six kinds of change described previously. Specific system integrity characteristics are each specified as disjoint signatures one for each of the seven kinds of system integrity previously described.

When analyzed, *ContextOfChange* resolves to a relation that associates particular instances of *OriginOfChange* (which itself contains particular instances of user-driven and/or domain-imposed change related to an instance of ChangeProperties) with a particular change type with a set of system integrity characteristics (which may be empty since its sub-features are optional-or).

Based on the information shown in Figure 1 (see [22] for details), the following is a fact, related to context of change, that constrains certain integrity characteristics from being related to certain change types:

```
fact{all c: ContextOfChange | some ccc:
ConditionChangeCriteria | some ac: ArchitecturalChange | some
si: SystemIntegrityCharacteristics | no ar: ActiveReference |
c.context = ccc -> ac -> si && ar in
si.integrityCharacteristics}
```

This particular fact indicates that active references are excluded from being an integrity characteristic of architectural change.

As a final example, consider Figure 8 showing the feature model fragment of the concept *Dependencies*:

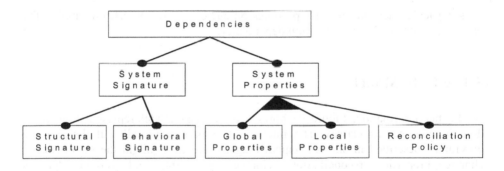

**Fig. 8.** Feature model of dependencies

The following Alloy signature specifies the concept:

```
sig Dependencies {systemProperties: SystemProperties,
systemSignature: SystemSignature}
```

Similar to the concept ChangeProperties, discussed above, the following Alloy signature specifies SystemProperties:

```
sig SystemProperties {globalProperties: set GlobalProperty,
localProperties: set LocalProperty, reconciliationPolicy:
ReconciliationPolicy}
```

The following Alloy signatures specify *SystemSignature:*

```
sig SystemSignature {structuralSignature:
StructuralSignature, behavioralSignature:
BehavioralSignature}

sig StructuralSignature {requiredDependencies: Operation ->
RequiredService, providedDependencies: Operation ->
ProvidedService}

sig BehavioralSignature {operationDependencies: Operation ->
Operation, stateElementDependencies: Operation ->
StateElement, compositeComponentDependencies: Operation ->
Service}
```

In this example, beyond the straightforward feature-to-signature mapping, the Alloy specification formally constrains the structural and behavioral profile of a system. *StructuralSignature* is specified as relations between operation and required or provided service. *BehavioralSignature* is specified as relations between an operation and another operation, an operation and a state element, or an operation and a service (in this context provided by a composite component).

The following is a fact from the complete model related to dependencies:

```
fact{some op1, op2: Operation | some b: BehavioralSignature |
op1 in op2.operations || op2 in op1.operations => op1 -> op2
in b.operationDependencies}
```

This particular fact indicates: if op1 relies on op2 or op2 relies op1, this implies that op1 is related to op2 as an operation dependency.


## 5 The UML Model

As further information, Figure 9 shows a basic class model representation of the domain concepts as classes. The intent is to represent visually all the concepts previously described in one convenient diagram and to highlight the importance of change properties reconciliation, change enactment, and further dynamic reconfiguration concerns. As a work in progress, this model will be further constrained when the UML model more completely represents the Alloy specification.

With respect to change properties reconciliation, the classes *SystemProperties* and *ChangeProperties* represent the current system properties and (new) change properties, respectively, as global and local constraints. Each grouping of properties is internally reconciled according to reconciliation policies. In addition, these groupings are reconciled with respect to each other. The overall reconciliation is modeled as a binary association linking *SystemProperties* and *ChangeProperties*. The reconciled change properties in turn determine which subsets of change types are required to perform the necessary system reconfiguration.

With respect to change enactment, the association class *ChangeEnactment* specifies how the required change types, as constrained by system integrity characteristics, realign the system model. Depending upon the types of change required, the structural and/or behavioral signature of the system may have to be re-aligned, which, in turn, may impact its internal behavior or external interactions.

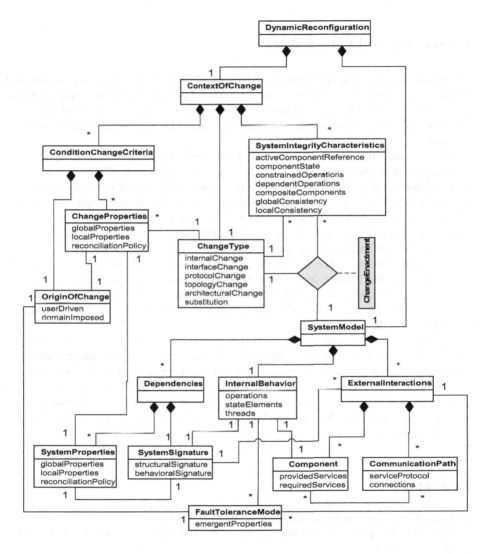

**Fig. 9.** Domain concepts as UML classes

With respect to further dynamic reconfiguration, given the internal behavior or external interactions of a system have changed, the system may reach a failure state or require further change based upon emergent properties. This is represented by the group of classes *ExternalInteractions*, *InternalBehavior*, *FaultToleranceMode*, and

*OriginOfChange*. *ExternalInteractions* and *InternalBehavior* are related to *FaultToleranceMode* upon failure (or emergent properties). *FaultToleranceMode* then drives OriginOfChange (which ultimately may be user driven or domain imposed) which in turn indicates needed change properties. This completes the cycle of system dynamic reconfiguration described by this domain model.

# 6 Summary and Future Work

This paper presents a domain model of dynamic reconfiguration for component-based software systems. Its purpose is to provide a well-formed and comprehensive conceptual framework (i.e., a reference model) within which it is possible to study various problems and solutions related to dynamic software evolution in a systematic manner.

First, the full set of domain-independent types of change and their interdependencies is identified. They define, at an abstract level, which factors need to be considered and what needs to be done in a dynamically reconfigurable system for a particular type of change. These types are factored into a feature model of dynamic change that is combined with a general model of component-based software systems. The resulting model of dynamically reconfigurable component-based systems is then converted into a formal Alloy model and refined further. This allows much more precise specification of the semantics of the domain model whose consistency is formally validated. Finally, for convenience, the domain model is also rendered in the form of a single comprehensive UML model. Size and scope limitations preclude a more complete reporting on the results of this research. However, [22] provides a more complete description.

Continuing work is investigating a model execution environment that encodes the PIM at the meta-level within a reflective substrate and then demonstrates domain-specific base-level dynamic reconfiguration using a number of case studies from three diverse domains. The model execution environment serves to validate the PIM to determine if it is comprehensive and/or explicit in its coverage. Ultimately, this indicates whether the feature model significantly characterized a dynamically reconfigurable system or not.

# References

1. Jarke, M., Meta models for requirements engineering. 1996.
2. Jarke, M., Requirements Tracing (Introduction). Communications of the ACM, 1998. **41**(12): p. 32-36.
3. Georgiadis, I., J. Magee, and J. Kramer. Self-Organising Software Architectures for Distributed Systems. in ACM WOSS '02. 2002. Charleston, SC: ACM.
4. Oreizy, P., Issues in Modeling and Analyzing Dynamic Software Architectures. 1999, Information and Computer Science, University of California, Irvine: Irvine, California.
5. Oreizy, P., N. Medvidovic, and R.N. Taylor. Architecture-Based Runtime Software Evolution. in Proceedings of the International Conference on Software Engineering. 1998.

6.  Szyperski, C., Component Software: Beyond Object-Oriented Programming Second Edition. Component Software Series. 2002, New York, N. Y.: Addison-Wesley.
7.  Deployment-and-Configuration-Draft-Adopted-Specification,       Deployment       and Configuration Draft Adopted Specification. 2003, OMG: Needham, MA.
8.  Oreizy, P., et al., An Architecture-Based Approach to Self-Adaptive Software. IEEE Intelligent Systems, 1999: p. 54-62.
9.  Appavoo, J., et al., Enabling automatic behavior in systems software with hot swapping. IBM Systems Journal, 2003. **42**(1): p. 60-76.
10. Lopes, A., M. Wermelinger, and J.L. Fiadeiro, Higher-Order Architectural Connectors. ACM Transactions on Software Engineering and Methodology, 2003. **12**(1): p. 64-104.
11. Whisnant, K., Z.T. Kalbarczyk, and R.K. Iyer, A system model for dynamically reconfigurable software. IBM Systems Journal, 2003. **42**(1): p. 45-59.
12. Czarnecki, K. and U.W. Eisennecker, Generative Programming: Methods, Tools, and Applications. 2000, New York, N.Y.: Addison-Wesley.
13. Gomaa, H., Designing Software Product Lines with UML From Use Cases to Pattern-Based Software Architectures. Object Technology Series, ed. G. Booch, I. Jacobson, and J. Rumbaugh. 2004, New York, N.Y.: Addison-Wesley.
14. Jackson, D., I. Schechter, and I. Shlyakhter, Alcoa: The Alloy Constraint Analyzer. 1999, Massachusetts Institute of Technology: Cambridge, Massachusetts.
15. Jackson, D., Alloy: A Lightweight Object Modelling Notation. 2001, Massachusetts Institute of Technology: Cambridge, Massachusetts. p. 32.
16. Jackson, D., Micromodels of Software: Ligthweight Modelling and Analysis with Alloy. 2002, MIT Lab for Computer Science: Cambridge, Mass. p. 1-58.
17. Vaziri, M. and D. Jackson, Some Shortcomings of OCL, the Object Constriant Language of UML. 1999, MIT Laboratory for Computer Science: Cambridge, Mass. p. 1-17.
18. Marriott, K. and P.J. Stuckey, Programming with Constraints An Introduction. 1998, Cambridge, Mass.: MIT Press.
19. Duffy, D.J., Domain Architectures Models and Architectures for UML Applications. 2004, Hoboken, N.J.: John Wiley and Sons.
20. Fowler, M., UML Distilled Third Edition A Brief Guide to the Standard Object Modeling Language. Object Technology Series. 2004: Addison-Wesley.
21. Warmer, J. and A. Kleppe, The Object Constraint Language Second Edition Getting Your Models Ready for MDA. Object Technology Series. 2003, New York, N.Y.: Addison-Wesley.
22. Walsh, D., Ph.D. Work in Progress, in School of Computer Science, Carleton University. 2005, Ottawa-Carleton Institute for Computer Science: Ottawa, Canada.
23. Medvidovic, N. and R.N. Taylor, A Classification and Comparison Framework for Software Architecture Description Languages. IEEE Transactions on Software Engineering, 2000. **26**(1): p. 70-93.

# Exceptional Use Cases

Aaron Shui[1], Sadaf Mustafiz[1], Jörg Kienzle[1], and Christophe Dony[2]

[1] School of Computer Science, McGill University, Montreal, Canada
aaron@rome.com, sadaf@cs.mcgill.ca, Joerg.Kienzle@mcgill.ca
[2] LIRMM, Université de Montpellier, Montpellier, France
dony@lirmm.fr

**Abstract.** Many exceptional situations arise during the execution of an application. When developing dependable software, the first step is to foresee these exceptional situations and document how the system should deal with them. This paper outlines an approach that extends use case based requirements elicitation with ideas from the exception handling world. After defining the actors and the goals they pursue when interacting with the system, our approach leads a developer to systematically investigate all possible exceptional situations that the system may be exposed to: exceptional situations arising in the environment that change user goals and system-related exceptional situations that threaten to fail user goals. Means are defined for detecting the occurrence of all exceptional situations, and the exceptional interaction between the actors and the system necessary to recover from such situations is described in handler use cases. To conclude the requirements phase, an extended UML use case diagram summarizes the standard use cases, exceptions, handlers and their relationships.

## 1 Introduction

Most main stream software development methods define a series of development phases – requirements elicitation, analysis, architecture and design, and finally implementation – that lead the development team to discover, specify, design and finally implement the main functionality of a system, which dictates the system's behavior most of the time. However, there are also many exceptional situations that may arise during the execution of an application. When using a standard software development process there is no guarantee that such situations are considered during the development. Whether the system can handle these situations or not depends highly on the imagination and experience of the developers. As a result, the final application might not function correctly in all possible situations.

When developing dependable systems, i.e. mission- or safety-critical systems where a malfunction can cause significant damage, nothing should be left to chance. Following the idea of integrating exception handling into the software life cycle [1, 2], this paper describes an extension to standard *use case*-based requirements elicitation that leads the developers to consider all possible exceptional situations that the system under development might be exposed to. We

L. Briand and C. Williams (Eds.): MoDELS 2005, LNCS 3713, pp. 568–583, 2005.

believe that thinking about exceptional behavior has to start at the requirements phase, because it is up to the users of the system to decide how they expect the system to react to exceptional situations. Only with exhaustive and detailed user feedback is it possible to discover and then specify the complete system behavior in a subsequent analysis phase, and decide on the need for employing fault masking and fault tolerance techniques for achieving run-time reliability during design.

The rest of the paper is structured as follows. Section 2 provides background information on use cases and exceptions. Section 3 defines some terminology and outlines the proposed extensions to standard UML use cases. Section 4 describes our proposed process, and illustrates the ideas by means of an elevator control case study. Section 5 presents related work in this area, and the last section draws some conclusions.

## 2   Background

### 2.1   Exceptions

An exceptional situation, or short *exception*, describes a situation that, if encountered, requires something exceptional to be done in order to resolve it. Hence, an *exception occurrence* during a program execution is a situation in which the standard computation cannot pursue. For the program execution to continue, an extraordinary computation is necessary [3].

A programming language or system with support for exception handling, subsequently called an *exception handling system* (EHS) [4], provides features and protocols that allow programmers to establish a communication between a piece of code which detects an exceptional situation while performing an operation (a *signaler*) and the entity or context that asked for this operation. An EHS allows users to signal *exceptions* and to define *handlers*. To *signal* an exception amounts to:

1. identify the exceptional situation,
2. to interrupt the usual processing sequence,
3. to look for a relevant handler and
4. to invoke it while passing it relevant information about the exception.

*Handlers* are defined on (or attached to, or associated with) entities, such as data structures, or *contexts* for one or several exceptions. According to the language, a context may be a program, a process, a procedure, a statement, an expression, etc. Handlers are invoked when an exception is signaled during the execution or the use of the associated context or nested context. To *handle* means to set the system back to a coherent state, and then:

1. to transfer control to the statement following the signaling one (*resumption model* [1]), or
2. to discard the context between the signaling statement and the one to which the handler is attached (*termination model* [1]), or
3. to signal a new exception to the enclosing context.

## 2.2   UML and Use Cases

The Unified Modeling Language (UML) [5] defines a *notation* for specifying, constructing, visualizing, and documenting the artifacts of a software-intensive system. UML is intentionally process-independent. However, it offers a variety of diagrams that unify the scores of graphical modeling notations that existed in the software development industry in the 80's and 90's. The diagram we are focussing on in this work is the *use case diagram*.

Since their introduction in the late 80's [6], *use cases* are a widely used formalism for discovering and recording behavioral requirements of software systems [7]. A use case describes, without revealing the details of the system's internal workings, the system's responsibilities and its interactions with its environment as it performs work in serving one or more requests that, if successfully completed, satisfy a goal of a particular stake-holder. The external entities in the environment that interact with the system are called *actors*.

In short, use cases are stories of actors using a system to *meet goals*. The standard way of achieving a goal is described in the *main success scenario*. Alternatives or situations in which the goal is not achieved are usually described in *extensions*. Use cases are in general text-based, but their strength is that they both scale up or scale down in terms of sophistication and formality, depending on the need and context. They can be effectively used as a communication means between technical as well as non-technical stake-holders of the software under development.

Use cases can be described at different levels of granularity [8]. *User-goal* level use cases describe how individual user goals are achieved. Optional *summary* level use cases provide a general overview of how the system is used. Finally, *subfunction* level use cases can be written that encapsulate subgoals of higher level use cases.

Some development methods, for example the object-oriented, UML-based development method Fondue [9], define a textual template that developers fill out when elaborating a use case. Using a predefined template forces the developer to document all important features of a use case, e.g. the *primary actor* (the one that wants to achieve the goal), the *level*, the *main success scenario* and the *extensions*. Fig. 1 shows an example Fondue use case.

Whereas individual use cases are text-based, the UML use case diagram provides a concise high level view of all (or a set of) use cases of a system. It allows the developer to graphically depict the use cases, the actors that interact with the system, and the relationships between actors and use cases.

## 3   Terminology and Proposed Extensions

### 3.1   Goals, Exceptional Goals and Failure to Achieve Goals

Each user-level use case describes a unit of useful functionality that the system under development provides to a particular actor. It details all interaction steps that an actor has to perform in order to achieve his / her goal. Typical goals are, for instance, withdrawing money from a bank account, placing an order for a book on an online store, or using an elevator to go to a destination floor (see Fig. 1).

Sometimes, however, *exceptional situations arising in the environment*, i.e., situations that cannot be detected by the system itself, might cause actors to interact with a system in an exceptional way. The situations are exceptional in the sense that they occur only rarely, and they change the goals that actors have with the system, either temporarily or permanently. Sometimes even new actors – *exceptional actors* – start interacting with the system in case of an exceptional situation.

Very often, such situations are related to safety issues. In an elevator system, for example, a fire outbreak in the building causes the elevator operator, an exceptional actor, to activate the fire emergency mode (see Fig. 5), in which all elevator cabins go down to the lowest floor to prevent casualties or physical damage in case the ropes break. Activating the emergency behavior is an *exceptional goal* for the elevator operator, since this happens only in very rare occasions.

But even if all actors interact with the system in a normal way, *system-related exceptional situations* might prevent the system from providing the desired functionality to the actor. For example, insufficient funds can prevent a successful withdrawal, an order might not be fulfillable because the book is currently out of stock, or a motor failure might prevent a user from taking the elevator. In such cases, the goal of the actor cannot be fulfilled.

In general, the exceptional situation triggers some exceptional interaction steps with the environment. One of the steps is (or should be!) to inform the actor of the impossibility to achieve the goal. Once informed, the actor can decide how to react to the situation. The system itself might also be capable of *handling* the problem, for instance by suggesting to withdraw a smaller amount of money, or by suggesting to buy some other book, or by activating the emergency brakes and calling the elevator operator (see Fig. 6).

## 3.2   Exceptions in Use Cases

It is important to discover and then document all possible exceptional situations that can interrupt normal system interaction. Any exceptional situation that is not identified during requirements elicitation might potentially lead to an incomplete system specification during analysis, and ultimately in an implementation that lacks certain functionality, or even behaves in an unreliable way.

Use cases describe the interaction that happens between actors and the system under development to achieve the primary actor's goal. In Fondue, the standard way of achieving the goal is called the *main success scenario*. Use cases also offer the possibility to add extensions to the main success scenario in case the interaction takes a different route. Certain extensions can still be considered "normal" behavior, since they represent alternate ways of achieving the actor's goal.

Exceptional situations in use cases are situations that *interrupt* the flow of interaction leading to the fulfillment of the actor's goal. From now on, we'll use the word *exception* to refer to such exceptional situations[3]. An exception occurrence endangers the completion of the actor's goal, suspending the normal interaction temporarily or for good. We propose to give names to all exceptions that can occur while interacting with the system under development, and to document them in a table together with a small textual description. As mentioned in section 3.1 we will distinguish between exceptions arising in the environment, subsequently called *actor-signaled exceptions*, and exceptions internal to the system that prevent the system from providing the requested service, subsequently called *system-detected exceptions*.

## 3.3   Handler Use Cases

Just like it is possible to encapsulate several steps of normal interaction in a separate subfunction-level use case, an exceptional interaction that requires several steps of handling can be described separately from the normal system behavior in a *handler use case*. The major advantage of doing this is that from the very beginning, exceptional interaction and behavior is clearly identified and separated from the normal behavior of the system. This distinction is even more interesting if it be extracted at a glance from the use case diagram.

In a use case diagram, standard use cases appear as ellipses (see Fig. 10), associated to the actors whose goals they describe. We propose to identify handler use cases with a <<handler>> stereotype, which differentiates them from the standard use cases. To allow developers to identify exceptional behavior at a glance, handler use cases can be represented in the use case diagram with a special symbol or using a different color. Handler use cases for actor-signaled exceptions, i.e. handlers that describe exceptional goals, are self-contained, just like standard use cases. Handlers that address system-detected exceptions on the other hand may not necessarily be meaningful by themselves, but only within the context of a normal use case. However, handlers are full-fledged use cases in the sense that they can include sub-level handler use cases, or have themselves associated handlers that address exceptions that might occur during the processing of an exception.

Separation of handlers also enables subsequent reuse of handlers. Just like a subfunction-level use case can encapsulate a subgoal that is part of several user goals, a handler use case can encapsulate a common way of handling exceptions that might occur while processing different user goals. Sometimes even, different exceptions can be handled in the same way. Associating handler use cases to other use cases is described in section 3.4.

---

[3] It is important to point out that the meaning of exception at the requirements level is *not* directly related to exceptions as defined by modern programming languages. The term exception is used at a higher level of abstraction here.

## 3.4  Linking Exception, Handlers and Use Cases

Just like in standard exception handling, where exception handlers are associated to exception handling contexts, handler use cases apply to a base use case, in this case any standard use case or other handler use case. We suggest to depict this association in the use case diagram by a directed relationship (dotted arrow) linking the handler use case to its base use case.

This relationship is very similar to the standard UML <<extends>> relationship. It specifies that the behavior of the base use case may be affected by the behavior of the handler use case in case an exception is encountered. Similar to the explicit extension points introduced in UML 2.0, the base use case can specify the specific steps in which the exception might occur (see Fig. 7 step 4a), but does not need to. In the latter case, the exceptional situation can affect the base processing at any time.

In case of an occurrence of an exceptional situation, the base behavior is put on hold or abandoned, and the interaction specified in the handler is started. A handler can temporarily take over the system interaction, for instance to perform some compensation activity, and then switch back to the normal interaction scenario. In this case, the relationship is tagged with a <<interrupt & continue>> stereotype. Some exceptional situations, however, cannot be handled smoothly, and cause the current goal to fail. Such dependencies are tagged with <<interrupt & fail>>. This is similar to the resumption and termination models reviewed in section 2.1.

The <<interrupt & continue>> and <<interrupt & fail>> relationships also differ from the <<extends>> relationship in the sense that they apply also to all sub use cases of a base use case. In the elevator example presented in the next section, for instance, an *Emergency Override* can interrupt *Take Elevator*, and therefore also any of the included use cases of *Take Elevator*, namely *Call Elevator*, *Ride Elevator* and *Elevator Arrival*.

Finally, the exceptions that activate the handler use case are added to the interrupt relationship in a UML comment. The notation follows the notation that was introduced in UML 2.0 to specify extension points for use cases. An example of an extended use case diagram for the elevator system with all exceptions, handler use cases and relationships is shown in Fig. 10.

# 4  Exception-Aware Process and Elevator Case Study

This section introduces our exception-aware requirements elicitation process and illustrates it based on a case study, a reliable and safe elevator system. For the sake of simplicity, there is only one elevator cabin that travels between the floors. There are two buttons on each floor (except for the top and ground floors) to call the lift, one for going up, one for going down. Inside the elevator cabin, there is a series of buttons, one for each floor.

The job of the development team is to decide on the required hardware, and to implement the elevator control software that processes the user requests and

**Use Case:** TakeElevator
**Scope:** Elevator Control System
**Primary Actor:** User
**Intention:** The intention of the *User* is to take the elevator to go to a destination floor.
**Level:** User Goal
**Frequency & Multiplicity:** A *User* can only take one elevator at a time. However, several *Users* may take the elevator simultaneously.
**Main Success Scenario:**
    1. User **CallsElevator**.
    2. User **RidesElevator**.
**Extensions:**
    1a. The cabin is already at the floor of the *User* and the door is open. *User* enters elevator; use case continues at step 2.
    1b. The user is already inside the elevator. Use case continues at step 2.

**Fig. 1.** TakeElevator Use Case

coordinates the different hardware devices. So far, only "mandatory" elevator hardware has been added to the system. The approaching of the cabin at a floor is detected by a sensor. The elevator control software may ask the motor to go up, go down or stop, and the cabin door to open or close.

## 4.1    Describing Normal Interaction

To start off the requirements elicitation phase, the use cases that describe the interaction with the system under *normal* conditions are elaborated. In the elevator system there is initially only one primary actor, the *User*. A user has only one goal with the system, namely to take the elevator to go to a destination floor, described in the user-goal level use case *TakeElevator* shown in Fig. 1.

As we can see from the main success scenario, the *User* first calls the elevator (step 1), and then rides it to the destination floor (step 2). The potential concurrent use of the elevator is documented in the *Frequency & Multiplicity* section [10].

The *CallElevator* and *RideElevator* use cases are shown in Fig. 2. To call the elevator the *User* pushes the up or down button and waits for the elevator cabin to arrive. To ride the elevator the *User* enters the cabin, selects a destination floor, waits until the cabin arrives at the destination floor and finally exits the elevator.

*CallElevator* and *RideElevator* both include the *Elevator Arrival* use case shown in Fig. 3. It is a subfunction level use case that describes how the system directs the elevator to a specific floor: once the system detects that the elevator is approaching the destination floor, it requests the motor to stop and opens the door.

The use cases that describe the normal interaction between the user and the elevator control system can be summarized in a standard UML use case diagram as shown in Fig. 4.

**Use Case:** CallElevator
**Primary Actor:** User
**Intention:** *User* wants to call the elevator to the floor that he / she is currently on.
**Level:** Subfunction
**Main Success Scenario:**
1. *User* pushes button, indicating in which direction he / she wants to go.
2. System acknowledges request.
3. System schedules **ElevatorArrival** for the floor the *User* is currently on.
**Extensions:**
2a. The same request already exists. System ignores the request. Use case ends in success.

**Use Case:** Ride Elevator
**Primary Actor:** User
**Intention:** The *User* wants to ride the elevator to a destination floor.
**Level:** Subfunction
**Main Success Scenario:**
1. *User* enters elevator.
2. User selects a destination floor.
3. System acknowledges request and closes the door.
4. System schedules **ElevatorArrival** for the destination floor.
5. *User* exits the elevator at destination floor.
**Extensions:**
1a. *User* does not enter elevator. System times out and closes door. Use case ends in failure.
2a. *User* does not select a destination floor. System times out and closes door. System processes pending requests or awaits new requests. Use case ends in failure.
5a. *User* selects another destination floor. System acknowledges new request and schedules **ElevatorArrival** for the new floor. Use case continues at step 5.

**Fig. 2.** *CallElevator* and *RideElevator* Use Case

**Use Case:** ElevatorArrival
**Primary Actor:** N/A
**Intention:** System wants to move the elevator to the *User*'s destination floor.
**Level:** Subfunction
**Main Success Scenario:**
1. System detects elevator is approaching destination floor.
2. System requests motor to stop.
3. System opens door.

**Fig. 3.** *ElevatorArrival* Use Case

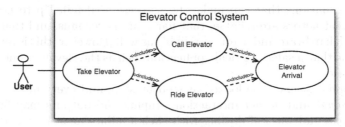

**Fig. 4.** Standard Elevator Use Case Diagram

## 4.2  Actor-Signaled Exceptions

The next step in our process consists in identifying exceptional situations that arise in the environment that make actors deviate from their initial goal, or change their goals completely. Sometimes actors change their goals spontaneously, sometimes changes in the environment influence the behavior of actors. In any case, the system has to interrupt its current processing and try to fulfill the new goal.

Exceptions arising in the environment are communicated to the system by special actions of actors – hence their name *actor-signaled exceptions*. A dependable system must react to actor-signaled exceptions in a well-specified way. If the handling requires exceptional interaction steps with the primary actor or other secondary actors, then a handler use case must be defined. The handler is then linked to the context, i.e. the use case in which th exception can occur.

**Actor-Signaled Exceptions in the Elevator Case Study** In the elevator case study we identified two actor-signaled exceptions. *EmergencyStop* is signaled by the *User* actor pushing the emergency button in the elevator in case he wants to interrupt the movement of the cabin. *EmergencyOverride* is signaled by an exceptional actor, the elevator operator, using the emergency override key on the ground floor in case of an emergency, for example a fire outbreak in the building. In our case, both exceptions can interrupt the normal system operation at any time, so their context is *TakeElevator*.

Fig. 5 shows the handler *UserEmergency* that handles the exception *EmergencyStop*. The system immediately activates the emergency brakes. Subsequently, the *User* can toggle off the emergency button to reactivate the elevator. The system then resumes the original use case because the relation between *TakeElevator* and *UserEmergency* is `<<interrupt & continue>>`.

The *EmergencyOverride* exception is handled by the *ReturnToGroundFloor* handler use case, also shown in Fig. 5. *ReturnToGroundFloor* interrupts and fails the *TakeElevator* use case.

## 4.3  System-Detected Exceptions

Each use case must now be examined to see if there are any system-related exceptional situations that can make the use case goal fail. Up to now we have assumed that actors are reliable, that hardware never fails, and that communication with hardware and actors is reliable as well. However, this is an unrealistic assumption that a safety-critical application such as the elevator control software cannot make.

Each use case must be looked at step by step, and every interaction classified into *input* and *output* interactions. Inputs and outputs may fail, and the consequences and ways of dealing with such a failure must be identified. If the consequences endanger the accomplishment of the user goal, then the system must detect the failure – hence the name *system-detected exception* – and address the situation. Detection might require additional hardware or timeouts.

**Use Case:** UserEmergency < <handler> >
**Contexts & Exceptions:** TakeElevator{EmergencyStop}
**Primary Actor:** User
**Intention:** *User* wants to stop the movement of the cabin.
**Level:** User Goal
**Frequency & Multiplicity:** Since there is only one elevator cabin, only one *User* can activate the emergency at a given time.
**Main Success Scenario:**
   1. System initiates **EmergencyBrake**.
   2. *User* toggles off emergency stop button.
   3. System deactivates brakes and continues processing requests.

**Use Case:** ReturnToGroundFloor < <handler> >
**Contexts & Exceptions:** TakeElevator{EmergencyOverride}
**Primary Actor:** Elevator Operator
**Intention:** Elevator Operator wants to call the elevator to the ground floor because the elevator operation is too dangerous.
**Level:** User Goal
**Frequency & Multiplicity:** Only one ReturnToGroundFloor use case can be active at a given time.
**Main Success Scenario:**
   1. System clears all requests and requests motor to go down.
   2. System detects that elevator is approaching the ground floor and requests motor to stop.
   3. System opens elevator door.

**Fig. 5.** *UserEmergency* and *ReturnToGroundFloor* Handler Use Case

Once the exception is detected, ways of addressing the exception have to be investigated. Very often, actors – especially humans – are "surprised" when they encounter an exceptional situation, and are subsequently more likely to make mistakes when interacting with the system. Exceptional interactions during exception handling must therefore be as intuitive as possible, and respect the actor's needs. Again, all interaction steps addressing an exception have to be recorded in handler use cases.

*Input Problems* If omission of input from an actor can cause the goal to fail, then, once the omission has been detected, different options of handling the situation have to be considered. For instance, prompting the actor for the input again after a given time has elapsed, or using default input are possible options. Safety considerations might make it even necessary to temporarily shutdown the system in case of missing input. Invalid input data is another example of input problem that might cause the goal to fail. Since most of the time the actors are aware of the importance of their input, a reliable system should also acknowledge input from an actor, so that the actor realizes that she is making progress in achieving her goal.

*Output Problems* Whenever an output triggers a critical action of an actor, then the system must make sure that it can detect eventual communication problems or failure of an actor to execute the requested action. For example, the elevator

**Use Case:** RedirectElevator < <handler> >
**Context & Exception:** ElevatorArrival{MissedFloor}
**Primary Actor:** N/A
**Intention:** System redirects the elevator to a different floor because the destination floor is unreachable.
**Level:** Subfunction
**Main Success Scenario:**
1. System cancels request to stop at destination floor.
2. System detects elevator is approaching a floor.
3. System requests the motor to stop.
4. System detects elevator is stopped at floor.

**Use Case:** EmergencyBrake < <handler> >
**Context & Exception:** TakeElevator{MotorFailure}
**Primary Actor:** N/A
**Intention:** System wants to stop operation of elevator and secure the cabin.
**Level:** Subfunction
**Main Success Scenario:**
1. System stops motor.
2. System activates the emergency brakes.
2. System turns on the emergency display.

**Fig. 6.** *RedirectElevator* and *EmergencyBrake* Handler Use Case

control software might tell the motor to stop, but a communication failure or a motor misbehavior might keep the motor going. Again, additional hardware, for instance, a sensor that detects when the cabin stopped at a floor, or timeouts might be necessary to ensure reliability.

**System-Detected Exceptions in the Elevator Case Study** To illustrate the process, let us go step by step through the use case *ElevatorArrival* (see Fig. 3). The first step involves the floor sensor informing the system that the elevator is approaching a floor. A floor sensor defect might cause the elevator to miss a destination floor. In this case, the corresponding handler *RedirectElevator*, shown in Fig. 6, stops the cabin at the next floor.

In Step 2 of *ElevatorArrival* the system requests the motor to stop. In case the motor malfunctions and does not stop, the emergency brakes have to be activated immediately. This is done by the *EmergencyBrake* handler, also shown in Fig. 6.

Finally, in step 3 of *ElevatorArrival*, the system requests the door to open. This output can only be sent *after* a successful stop of the motor. For reliability reasons, a "stop detection" mechanism, such as an additional sensor that monitors the cabin speed, must be added to the system. Additionally the door might fail to open in step 3. In this case, the elevator could move to a different floor and try to open the door there. Without threatening reliability, we can also choose to ignore the failure and continue processing the next request, and hence leave it up to the user in the elevator to decide to either retry the floor, go to a different floor or push the emergency button. Fig. 7 shows the updated, reliable version of the *ElevatorArrival* use case.

**Use Case:** ElevatorArrival
**Primary Actor:** N/A
**Intention:** System wants to move the elevator to the *User*'s destination floor.
**Level:** Subfunction
**Main Success Scenario:**
1. System detects elevator is approaching destination floor.
2. System requests motor to stop.
3. System detects elevator is stopped at destination floor.
4. System opens door.

**Extensions:**
4a. Exception{DoorStuckClosed}
System continues processing the next request (it is up to the user to select a new destination floor or press the emergency button). Use case ends in failure.

**Fig. 7.** Updated *ElevatorArrival* Use Case

**Use Case:** DoorAlert < <handler> >
**Primary Actor:** N/A
**Context & Exception:** TakeElevator{DoorStuckOpen}
**Intention:** System wants to alert the passengers that there is an obstacle preventing the door from closing.
**Level:** Subfunction
**Main Success Scenario:**
1. System displays "door open".
2. System turns on the buzzer.
3. System requests the door to close.
*Step 3 is repeated until the door closes.*
4. System detects that the door is now closed.
5. System turns off the buzzer.
6. System clears the display.

**Use Case:** OverweightAlert < <handler> >
**Primary Actor:** N/A
**Context & Exception:** RideElevator{Overweight}
**Intention:** System wants to alert the passengers that there is too much weight in the elevator.
**Level:** Subfunction
**Main Success Scenario:**
1. System displays "overweight".
2. System turns on the buzzer.
3. System detects that the weight is back to normal.
4. System turns off buzzer.
5. System clears display.

**Fig. 8.** *DoorAlert* and *OverweightAlert* Handler Use Case

Looking at the *CallElevator* and *RideElevator* use case, we can detect a common problem that might prevent the goals from succeeding: the elevator door might be stuck open, for instance because an obstacle prevents it from closing. This case is handled by the *DoorAlert* handler use case. Another exceptional situation occurs when there are too many passengers in the elevator. The *OverweightAlert* handler addresses this exception. The *DoorAlert* and *OverweightAlert* handlers are shown in Fig. 8.

**Use Case:** CallElevatorOperator < <handler> >
**Context & Exception:** EmergencyBrake{ElevatorStoppedTooLong],     Overweigh-
tAlert{OverweightTooLong}, DoorAlert{DoorStuckOpenTooLong}
**Intention:** The system wants to alert the elevator operator, so that the elevator operator can come and assess the damage.
**Level:** Subfunction
**Main Success Scenario:**
   1. System cancels all pending requests.
   2. System displays "calling operator ".
   3. System calls operator.

**Fig. 9.** *CallElevatorOperator* Handler Use Case

The step-by-step analysis of the use cases must then be recursively applied to
all the handlers, because handlers may themselves be interrupted by exceptions.
In our system, the *EmergencyBrake*, *OverweightAlert* and *DoorAlert* handler
use cases all wait until the situation is resolved. In case the problem persists for
a certain amount of time, the elevator control system should notify an elevator
operator. The elevator operator can then evaluate the situation and, if necessary,
call a service person. This functionality is described in the handler use case
*CallElevatorOperator* shown in Fig. 9.

### 4.4   Requirements Elicitation Summary

In parallel to the elaboration of the individual use cases and handlers, we propose to build an extended exception-aware use case diagram providing a detailed
and precise summary of the partitioning of the system into normal and exceptional interactions. The diagram follows the syntax described in sections 3.3
and 3.4. User expectations of handling exceptional situations are documented in
handler use cases identified with the < <handler> > stereotype, and attached to
their respective contexts with < <interrupt & continue> > or < <interrupt &
fail> > relationships. For traceability and documentation reasons, the diagram
should also be accompanied with a table that records all discovered exceptions,
together with a small textual description of the situation, the exception context,
the associated handler, and the mechanism of detecting the situation.

The extended use case diagram for the elevator control system is shown in
Fig. 10. The aforementioned exception table for the elevator system with the
detailed descriptions of each exception is not shown here for space reasons.

## 5   Related Work

Main stream software development methods currently deal with exceptions only
at late design and implementation phases. However, several approaches have
been proposed that extend exception handling ideas to other parts of the software
development cycle.

De Lemos et al. [2] emphasize the separation of the treatment of requirements-
related, design-related, and implementation-related exceptions during the software life-cycle by specifying the exceptions and their handlers in the context

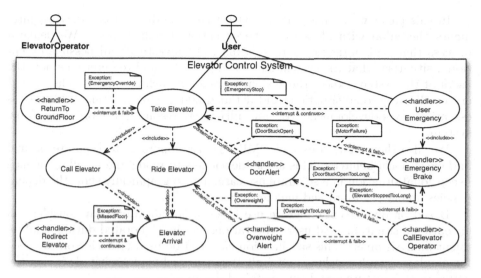

**Fig. 10.** Reliable Elevator Use Case Diagram

where faults are identified. The description of exceptional behavior is supported by a cooperative object-oriented approach that allows the representation of collaborative behavior between objects at different phases of the software development.

Rubira et al. [11] present an approach that incorporates exceptional behavior in the development of component-based software by extending the Catalysis software development method. The requirements phase of Catalysis is also based on use cases, and the extension augments them with exception handling ideas.

Our approach is different from the above for several reasons. Firstly, we help the requirements engineers to discover exceptions and handlers by providing a detailed *process* that they can follow. Without a process, the only way a developer can discover exceptions is based on her imagination and experience. Secondly, our process increases reliability even more by helping the developers detect the need for adding "feedback" and "acknowledgement" interaction steps with actors to make sure that there were no communication problems. Additionally, the process recommends adding of hardware to monitor request execution of secondary actors when necessary. Finally, our handler use cases are stand-alone, and can therefore be associated with multiple exceptions and multiple contexts.

# 6   Conclusion

We believe that when developing reliable systems, exceptional situations that the system might be exposed to have to be discovered and addressed at the requirements elicitation phase. Exceptional situations are less common and hence the behavior of the system in such situations is less obvious. Also, users are more likely to make mistakes when exposed to exceptional situations.

In this paper we propose an approach that extends use case based requirements elicitation with ideas from the exception handling world. We define a process that leads a developer to systematically investigate all possible exceptional situations that the system may be exposed to, and to determine how the users of the system expect the system to react in such situations. The discovery of all exceptional situations and detailed user feedback at an early stage is essential, saves development cost, and ultimately results in a more dependable system.

We also show how to extend UML use case diagrams to separate normal and exceptional behavior. This allows developers to model the handling of each exceptional situation in a separate use case, and to graphically show the dependencies among standard and handler use cases.

Based on our exception-aware use cases, a specification that considers all exceptional situations and user expectations can be elaborated during a subsequent analysis phase. This specification can then be used to decide on the need for employing fault masking and fault tolerance techniques when designing the software architecture and during detailed design.

For more information on our exception-aware process, and for details on how we extended the UML 2.0 metamodel to incorporate our extensions, the interested reader is referred to [12].

# References

[1] Goodenough, J.B.: Exception handling: Issues and a proposed notation. Communications of the ACM **18** (1975) 683 – 696

[2] de Lemos, R., Romanovsky, A.: Exception handling in the software lifecycle. International Journal of Computer Systems Science and Engineering **16** (2001) 167 – 181

[3] Knudsen, J.L.: Better exception-handling in block-structured systems. IEEE Software **4** (1987) 40 – 49

[4] Dony, C.: Exception handling and object-oriented programming: Towards a synthesis. In Meyrowitz, N., ed.: 4th European Conference on Object–Oriented Programming (ECOOP '90). ACM SIGPLAN Notices, (ACM Press)

[5] Object Management Group: Unified Modeling Language: Superstructure. (2004)

[6] Jacobson, I.: Object-oriented development in an industrial environment. In: Conference proceedings on Object-oriented programming systems, languages and applications, ACM Press (1987) 183 – 191

[7] Larman, C.: Applying UML and Patterns: An Introduction to Object-Oriented Analysis and Design and the Unified Process. 2nd edn. Prentice Hall (2002)

[8] Cockburn, A.: Writing Effective Use Cases. Addison–Wesley (2000)

[9] Sendall, S., Strohmeier, A.: Uml-based fusion analysis. In: UML'99, Fort Collins, CO, USA, October 28-30, 1999. Number 1723 in Lecture Notes in Computer Science, Springer Verlag (1999) 278–291

[10] Kienzle, J., Sendall, S.: Addressing concurrency in object-oriented software development. Technical Report SOCS-TR-2004.8, McGill University, Montreal, Canada (2004)

[11] Rubira, C.M.F., de Lemos, R., Ferreira, G.R.M., Fliho, F.C.: Exception handling in the development of dependable component-based systems. Software — Practice & Experience **35** (2004) 195 – 236
[12] Shui, A.: Exceptional use cases - Master Thesis, School of Computer Science, McGill' University (2005)

# Modeling Turnpike Frontend System: A Model-Driven Development Framework Leveraging UML Metamodeling and Attribute-Oriented Programming*

Hiroshi Wada and Junichi Suzuki

Department of Computer Science
University of Massachusetts, Boston
hiroshi_wada@otij.org and jxs@cs.umb.edu

**Abstract.** This paper describes and empirically evaluates a new model-driven development framework, called Modeling Turnpike (or mTurnpike). It allows developers to model and program domain-specific concepts (ideas and mechanisms specific to a particular business or technology domain) and to transform them to the final (compilable) source code. By leveraging UML metamodeling and attribute-oriented programming, mTurnpike provides an abstraction to represent domain-specific concepts at the modeling and programming layers simultaneously. The mTurnpike frontend system transforms domain-specific concepts from the modeling layer to programming layer, and vise versa, in a seamless manner. Its backend system combines domain-specific models and programs, and transforms them to the final (compilable) source code. This paper focuses on the frontend system of mTurnpike, and describes its design, implementation and performance implications. In order to demonstrate how to exploit mTurnpike in application development, this paper also shows a development process using an example DSL (domain specific language) to specify service-oriented distributed systems.

## 1. Introduction

Modeling technologies have matured to the point where they can offer significant leverage in all aspects of software development. Given modern modeling technologies, the focus of software development has been shifting away from implementation technology domains toward the concepts and semantics in problem domains. The more directly application models can represent domain-specific concepts, the easier it becomes to specify applications. One of the goals of modeling technologies is to map modeling concepts directly to domain-specific concepts [1].

Domain Specific Language (DSL) is a promising solution to directly capture, represent and implement domain-specific concepts [1, 2]. DSLs are the languages targeted to particular problem domains, rather than general-purpose languages that are aimed at any software problems. Several experience reports have demonstrated that DSLs can improve the productivity in implementing domain-specific concepts [3].

---

* Research supported in part by OGIS International, Inc. and Electric Power Development Co., Ltd.

L. Briand and C. Williams (Eds.): MoDELS 2005, LNCS 3713, pp. 584–600, 2005.

This paper proposes a new model-driven development framework, called Modeling Turnpike (or mTurnpike), which aids modeling and programming domain-specific concepts with DSLs. mTurnpike allows developers to model and program domain-specific concepts in DSLs and to transform them to the final (compilable) source code in a seamless and piecemeal manner. Leveraging UML metamodeling and attribute-oriented programming, mTurnpike provides an abstraction to represent domain-specific concepts at the modeling and programming layers simultaneously. At the modeling layer, domain-specific concepts are represented as a *Domain Specific Model (DSM)*, which is a set of UML 2.0 diagrams described in a DSL. Each DSL is defined as a UML metamodel that extends the UML 2.0 standard metamodel [4]. At the programming layer, domain-specific concepts are represented as a *Domain Specific Code (DSC)*, which consists of attribute-oriented programs. Attributes are declarative *marks*, associated with program elements (e.g. classes and interfaces), to indicate that the program elements maintain application-specific or domain-specific semantics [5]. The frontend system of mTurnpike transforms domain-specific concepts from the modeling layer to programming layer, and vise versa, by providing a seamless mapping between DSMs and DSCs without any semantics loss.

The backend system of mTurnpike transforms a DSM and DSC into a more detailed model and program by applying a given transformation rule. mTurnpike allows developers to define arbitrary transformation rules, each of which specifies how to specialize a DSM and DSC to particular implementation and deployment technologies. For example, a transformation rule may specialize them to a database, while another rule may specialize them to a remoting system. mTurnpike combines the specialized DSM and DSC to generate the final (compilable) source code.

This paper focuses on the frontend system of mTurnpike, and describes its design, implementation and performance implications. In order to demonstrate how to exploit mTurnpike in application development, this paper also shows a development process using an example DSL to specify service-oriented distributed systems.

## 2.  Contributions

This section summarizes the contributions of this work.

- *UML 2.0 support for modeling domain-specific concepts.* mTurnpike accepts DSLs as metamodels extending the UML 2.0 standard metamodel, and uses UML 2.0 diagrams to model domain-specific concepts (as DSMs). This work is one of the first attempts to exploit UML 2.0 to define and use DSLs.
- *Higher abstraction for programming domain-specific concepts.* mTurnpike offers a new approach to represent domain-specific concepts at the programming layer, through the notion of attribute-oriented programming. This approach provides a higher abstraction for developers to program domain-specific concepts, thereby improving their programming productivity. Attribute-oriented programming makes programs simpler and more readable than traditional programming paradigms.
- *Seamless mapping of domain-specific concepts between the modeling and programming layers.* mTurnpike maps domain-specific concepts between the modeling and programming layers in a seamless and bi-directional manner. This

mapping allows modelers[1] and programmers to deal with the same set of domain-specific concepts in different representations (i.e. UML models and attribute-oriented programs), yet at the same level of abstraction. Thus, modelers do not have to involve programming details, and programmers do not have to possess detailed domain knowledge and UML modeling expertise. This separation of concerns can reduce the complexity in application development, and increase the productivity of developers in modeling and programming domain-specific concepts.

- *Modeling layer support for attribute-oriented programs.* Using the bi-directional mapping between UML models and attribute-oriented programs, mTurnpike visualizes attribute-oriented programs in UML. This work is the first attempt to bridge a gap between UML modeling and attribute-oriented programming.

## 3. Background: Attribute-Oriented Programming

Attribute-oriented programming is a program-level marking technique. Programmers can *mark* program elements (e.g. classes and methods) to indicate that they maintain application-specific or domain-specific semantics [5]. For example, a programmer may define a "logging" attribute and associate it with a method to indicate the method should implement a logging function, while another programmer may define a "web service" attribute and associate it with a class to indicate the class should be implemented as a web service. Attributes separate application's core (business) logic from application-specific or domain-specific semantics (e.g. logging and web service functions). By hiding the implementation details of those semantics from program code, attributes increase the level of programming abstraction and reduce programming complexity, resulting in simpler and more readable programs. The program elements associated with attributes are transformed to more detailed programs by a supporting tool (e.g. pre-processor). For example, a pre-processor may insert a logging program into the methods associated with a "logging" attribute.

The notion of attribute-oriented programming has been well accepted in several languages and tools, such as Java 2 standard edition (J2SE) 5.0, C# and XDoclet[2]. For example, J2SE 5.0 implements attributes as *annotations*, and the Enterprise Java Beans (EJB) 3.0 extensively uses annotations to make EJB programming simpler. Here is an example using an EJB 3.0 annotation.

```
@entity class Customer{
   String name;}
```

The @entity annotation is associated with the class Customer. This annotation indicates that Customer will be implemented as an entity bean. A pre-processor in EJB, called *annotation processor*, takes the above annotated code and applies a certain transformation rule to generate several interfaces and classes required to implement Customer as an entity bean (i.e. remote interface, home interface and

---

[1] This paper assumes modelers are familiar with particular domains but may not be programming experts.
[2] http://xdoclet.sourceforge.net/

implementation class). The EJB annotation processor follows the transformation rules predefined in the EJB 3.0 specification.

In addition to predefined annotations, J2SE 5.0 allows developers to define their own (user-defined) annotations. There are two types of user-defined annotations: *marker annotations* and *member annotations*. Here is an example marker annotation.

```
public @interface Logging{ }
```

In J2SE 5.0, a marker annotation is defined with the keyword @interface.

```
public class Customer{
    @Logging public void setName(...){...} }
```

In this example, the Logging annotation is associated with setName(), indicating the method logs method invocations. Then, a developer specifies a transformation rule for the annotation, and creates a user-defined annotation processor that implements the transformation rule. The annotation processor may replace each annotated method with a method implementing a logging function.

A member annotation, the second type of user-defined annotations, is an annotation that has member variables. It is also defined with @interface.

```
public @interface Persistent{
    String connection();
    String tableName(); }
```

The Persistent annotation has the connection and tableName variables.

```
@Persistent(
    connection = "jdbc:http://localhost/",
    tableName = "customer" )
public class Customer{}
```

Here, the Persistent annotation is associated with the class Customer, indicating the instances of Customer will be stored in a database with a particular database connection and table name. A developer who defines this annotation implements a user-defined annotation processor that takes an annotated code and generates additional classes and/or methods implementing a database access function.

## 4. Design and Implementation of mTurnpike

mTurnpike consists of the frontend and backend systems (Fig. 1). The frontend system is implemented as DSC Generator, and the backend system is implemented as DSL Transformer. Every component in mTurnpike is implemented with Java.

The frontend system transforms domain-specific concepts from the modeling layer to programming layer, and vise versa, by providing a seamless mapping between DSMs and DSCs. In mTurnpike, a DSL is defined as a metamodel that extends the UML 2.0 standard (superstructure) metamodel with UML's extension mechanism[3]. The UML extension mechanism provides a set of model elements such as *stereotype* and *tagged-value* in order to add application-specific or domain-specific modeling semantics to the UML 2.0 standard metamodel [6]. In mTurnpike, each DSL defines a set of stereotypes and tagged-values to express domain-specific concepts. Stereotypes

---

[3] An extended metamodel is called a *UML profile*. Each DSL is defined as a UML profile in mTurnpike.

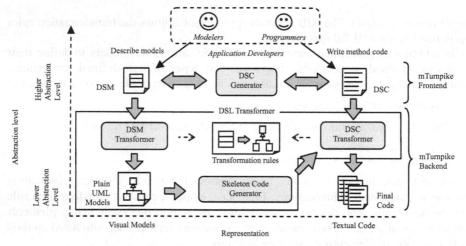

**Fig. 1.** mTurnpike Architecture and its Key Components.

are specified as metaclasses extending UML's standard metaclasses, and tagged-values are specified as properties of stereotypes (i.e. extended metaclasses).

Given a DSL, a DSM is represented as a set of UML 2.0 diagrams (class and composite structure diagrams). Each DSC consists of Java interfaces and classes decorated with the J2SE 5.0 annotations. The annotated code follows the J2SE 5.0 syntax to define marker and member annotations.

The backend system of mTurnpike transforms a DSM and DSC into a more detailed model and program that specialize in particular implementation and deployment technologies. Then, it combines the specialized DSM and DSC to generate the final (compilable) code (Fig. 1).

In mTurnpike, the frontend and backend systems are separated by design. mTurnpike clearly separates the task to model and program domain-specific models (as DSMs and DSCs) from the task to transform them into the final compilable code. This design strategy improves separation of concerns between modelers/programmers and platform engineers[4]. Modelers and programmers do not have to know how domain-specific concepts are implemented and deployed in detail. Platform engineers do not have to know the details of domain-specific concepts. As a result, mTurnpike can reduce the complexity in application development, and increase the productivity of developers in modeling and programming domain-specific concepts.

This design strategy also allows DSMs/DSCs and transformation rules to evolve independently. Since DSMs and DSCs do not depend on transformation rules, mTurnpike can specialize a single set of DSM and DSC to different implementation and deployment technologies by using different transformation rules. When it comes time to change a running application, modelers/programmers make the changes in the application's DSM and DSC and leave transformation rules alone. When retargeting an application to a different implementation and/or deployment technology, e.g. Java RMI to Java Messaging Service (JMS), platform engineers define (or select) a transformation rule for the new target technology and regenerate the final compilable

---

[4] Platform engineers possess expertise in platform technologies on which DSMs and DSCs are deployed. They are responsible for defining transformation rules applied to DSMs and DSCs.

source code. As such, mTurnpike can make domain-specific concepts (i.e. DSMs and DSCs) more reusable and extend their longevity, thereby improving productivity and maintainability in application development.

### 4.1. Mapping Between DSMs and DSCs in the mTurnpike Fontend System

mTurnpike implements the mapping rules shown in Table 1 to transform DSMs to DSCs, and vice versa. Fig. 2 shows an example DSM, the class `Customer` stereotyped as `<<entitybean>>` with a tagged-value. mTurnpike transforms the UML class (DSM) to the following Java class and member annotation (DSC).

**Table 1.** Mapping rules between DSMs and DSCs.

| | **UML Elements in DSM** | **Java Elements in DSC** |
|---|---|---|
| DSL or Profile (M2) | Definition of a stereotype that has no tagged-values | Definition of a marker annotation |
| | Definition of a stereotype that has tagged-values | Definition of a member annotation |
| | Definition of a tagged-value | Definition of a member variable in a member annotation |
| DSM (M1) | Package | Package |
| | Class and interface | Class and interface |
| | Method and data field | Method and data field |
| | Modifier and visibility | Modifier and visibility |
| | Primitive type | Primitive type |
| | Stereotype that has no tagged-values | Marker annotation |
| | Stereotype that has tagged-values | Member annotation |
| | Tagged-value | Member annotation's member variable |

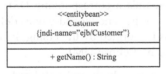

**Fig. 2.** UML Class `Customer` (DSM)

**(1) Java class `Customer` (DSC)**
```
@entitybean(
    jndi-name = "ejb/Customer")
public class Customer{
    public String getName(){} }
```
**(2) Member annotation `entitybean` (DSC)**
```
@interface entitybean{
    String jndi-name(); }
```

### 4.2. Design and Implementation of the mTurnpike Frontend System

The mTurnpike frontend system is implemented by DSC Generator (Fig. 1). It performs transformations between DSMs and DSCs based on the mapping rules described in Section 4.1. The following five steps involve in the transformation.

**(1) Loading a DSM to build a UML tree:** DSC Generator imports a DSM as a representation of the XML Metadata Interchange (XMI) 2.0 [7]. Developers can generate XMI descriptions of their DSMs using any UML tools that support XMI 2.0. Here is an example XMI description showing the class `Customer` in Fig. 2.

```
<UML:Class xmi.id="id_class" owner="id_project" name="Customer"
 appliedSteotype= "profile.xmi#//*[@xmi.id=&quot;id_profile&quot;]">
<UML:Element.ownedElement>
 <UML:Operation xmi.id="id_operation"
  name="getName" owner="id_class">
  <UML:Element.ownedElement>
   <UML:Parameter xmi.id="id_param" type="id_string"
    name="Unnamed" direction="result" owner="id_operation"/>
  </UML:Element.ownedElement>
 </UML:Operation>
 <UML:TaggedValue xmi.id="id_taggedvalue"
  name="jndi-name" owner="id_class">
  <UML:TaggedValue.dataValue>
   ejb/Customer
  </UML:TaggedValue.dataValue>
 </UML:TaggedValue>
</UML:Element.ownedElement>
</UML:Class>
<UML:DataType xmi.id="id_string" owner="id_project" name="String"/>
```

The `<UML:Class>` tag defines a class, and its attribute `appliedStereotype` references, with XPath directives, a stereotype defined in another XMI file (`profile.xmi`). In this example, the stereotype <<entitybean>> is referenced with its identifier `id_profile`. The `<UML:TaggedValue>` tag defines a tagged-value associated with the class `Customer`.

When accepting a DSM, DSC Generator identifies a DSL that the input DSM follows. DSLs are also represented as XMI descriptions. In the above example, a DSL is defined in a file named `profile.xmi`. DSC Generator parses a DSM and its corresponding DSL, as XMI files, to build an in-memory tree structure, called UML tree. A UML tree is an instance of the UML standard metamodel. For building UML trees, DSC Generator follows the data structures provided by the Eclipse Modeling Framework (EMF)[5] and Eclipse-UML2[6].

Once a UML tree is constructed, DSC Generator validates the UML tree (i.e. an input DSM) against the standard UML metamodel. It examines if the DSM follows the syntax and semantics defined in the standard UML metamodel. DSC Generator also validates the UML tree (i.e. an input DSM) against a corresponding DSL. For example, it checks if the DSM uses appropriate stereotypes and tagged-values defined in the DSL. The validation of UML trees (DSMs) is performed by traversing the trees using a visitor class, named `UML2Switch` provided by Eclipse-UML2.

**(2) Building a JAST for a DSL:** Once a UML tree is built and validated, DSC Generator constructs a Java Abstract Syntax Tree (JAST) corresponding to a DSL represented in the UML tree. DSC Generator traverses a UML tree, using `UML2Switch` in Eclipse-UML2, and constructs a JAST node corresponding to each node in the UML tree based on the mapping rules described in Section 4.1.

---

[5] www.eclipse.org/emf/
[6] www.eclipse.org/uml2/. Eclipse-UML2 implements the UML metamodel as a set of Java objects on EMF.

Fig. 3 shows some key data structures to construct JASTs. Annotation represents an annotation. In order to represent a member annotation, Annotation has an association with AnnotationMembers, each of which represents its member variable. AnnotationMember keeps a value of member variable. AnnotationDefinition and AnnotationMemberDefinition represent the definitions of an annotation and an annotation's member variable. They are powertypes Annotation and AnnotationMember, respectively.

**(3) Building a JAST for a DSC:** After constructing a JAST corresponding to a DSL represented in a UML tree, DSC Generator completes the JAST by transforming the rest of the UML tree into JAST nodes. Transformations are performed with the JAST data structures shown in Fig. 3, following the mapping rules described in Section 4.1. In Fig. 3, AnnotatableElement is the root interface for the Java program elements that can be decorated by J2SE 5.0 annotations.

The following code fragment shows how DSC Generator transforms a stereotyped UML class (i.e. a class in DSM) to an annotated Java class (i.e. a class in DSC). The method convertClass() takes a UML class and instantiates the class Class in a JAST, which represents a Java class (see also Fig. 3). Then, the method transforms the stereotypes applied to the UML class to Java annotations by instantiating the class Annotation in resolveStereotypes() and convertStereotype().

```
import edu.umb.cs.dssg.mturnpike.java.ast.*;
Class convertClass( org.eclipse.uml2.Class c_ ) {
  Class c = new Class();        // create a Java class as a JAST node
  resolveStereotypes(c, c_);// create a Java annotation(s), if a UML class is stereotyped.
  return c;
}
void resolveStereotypes( AnnotatableElement annotatableElement,
org.eclipse.uml2.Element element ) {
  foreach( Stereotype s in element.getAppliedStereotypes() ){
    Annotation annot = convertStereotype( element, s );
    annotatableElement.addAnnotation( annot ); }
}
```

**Fig. 3.** Key data structures to construct Java Abstract Syntax Trees

```
Annotation convertStereotype( org.eclipse.uml2.Element element,
org.eclipse.uml2.Stereotype stereotype ) {
  Annotation annotation = new Annotation();
  String name = stereotype.getName();
  annotation.setName( name );
  AnnotationDefinition annotDefinition = getAnnotDefinition( name );
  annotation.setMeta( annotationDefinition );
  foreach( Property p in stereotype.getAttributes() ){
    AnnotationMember annotMember = new AnnotationMember();
    ... // set the name, type and definition of the created annotation member.
    annotation.addMember(annotationMember); }
  return annotation;
}
```

**(4) Building a DSC (annotation definitions):** Once a JAST is constructed, DSC Generator generates annotation definitions in a DSC. Each JAST node has the `toString()` method, which generates Java source code corresponding to the JAST node. DSC Generator traverses a JAST and calls the method on instances of `AnnotationDefinition` and `AnnotationMemberDefinition` (Fig. 3).

**(5) Building a DSC:** Once generating annotation definitions, DSC Generator generates the rest of annotated code in a DSC. DSC Generator traverses a JAST and calls the `toString()` method on each node in the JAST.

After DSC Generator generates a DSC (i.e. annotated code), programmers write method code in the generated DSC in order to implement dynamic behaviors for domain-specific concepts[7]. Please note that the methods in the generated DSC are empty because DSMs specify only the static structure of domain-specific concepts (using UML class diagrams and composite structure diagrams).

In addition to transformations from DSMs to DSCs, mTurnpike can perform reverse transformations from DSCs to DSMs. In a reverse transformation, mTurnpike parses a DSC (i.e. annotated Java code) with a J2SE 1.5 lexical analyzer (J2SE 1.5 parser)[8], and builds a JAST following the data structure shown in Fig. 3. The JAST is transformed to a UML tree and an XMI file using Eclipse-UML2

### 4.3.  Design and Implementation of the mTurnpike Backend System

The mTurnpike backend system consists of three components: DSM Transformer, Skeleton Code Generator and DSC Transformer (Fig. 1).

**DSM Transformer:** DSM Transformer accepts a DSM as a UML tree built by DSC Generator, and transforms it to a more detailed model (Fig. 1). Given a transformation rule that a platform engineer defines, DSM Transformer transforms (or unfolds) DSM model elements associated with stereotypes and tagged-values into plain UML model elements that do not have any stereotypes and tagged-values. In this transformation, a DSM is specialized to particular implementation and deployment technologies. For

---

[7] Please note that the methods in DSC are empty because both DSMs and DSCs only specify the static structure of domain-specific concepts (a DSM consists of class and composite structure diagrams).

[8] mTurnpike's lexical analyzer is implemented with JavaCC (http://javacc.dev.java.net/).

example, if a transformation specializes an input DSM to Java RMI, the classes in the DSM are converted to the classes implementing the `java.rmi.Remote` interface.

DSM Transformer is implemented with the Model Transformation Framework (MTF)[9], which is implemented on EMF and Eclipse-UML2. MTF provides a language to define transformation rules between EMF-based models. mTurnpike follows the syntax of MTF's transformation rule language to specialize DSMs. Each transformation rule consists of conditions and instructions. DSM Transformer traverses a DSM (i.e. a UML tree built by DSC Generator), identifies the DSM model elements that meet transformation conditions, and applies transformation instructions to them. This process generates another UML tree that represents a model specializing in particular implementation and deployment technologies. The following is an example transformation rule.

```
relate class2class(
  uml:Class src when equals(match over src.stereotypes.name, "Service"),
  uml:Class tgt,
  uml:Interface tgt2 when equals(tgt2.name, "Remote")
  ) when equals(src.name, tgt.name){
      implementation(tgt, tgt2)
}
relate implementation(uml:Class c1, uml:Interface c2){
      realize(over c1.implementation, c2)
}
relate realize(uml:Implementation i, uml:Interface c){
      check interfaces(g.contract, c)
}
relate interfaces(uml:Interface c1, uml:Interface c2)
  when equals(c1.name, c2.name)
```

The keyword `relate` is used to define a transformation rule. This example defines four transformation rules. Each rule accepts model elements as parameters and instructs how to transform them. For example, the first rule (`class2class`) accepts the classes stereotyped with <<Service>>, and transform each of them to two classes. One of the two classes has the same name as an input <<Service>> class, and it extends an interface whose name is `Remote`.

**Skeleton Code Generator:** Skeleton Code Generator takes a UML tree created by DSM Transformer, and generates skeleton code in Java (Fig. 1). It traverses an input UML tree, builds a JAST corresponding to the UML tree using the JAST package shown in Fig. 3, and generates Java code from the JAST. Since the mTurnpike frontend system only supports structural UML diagrams (class and composite structure diagrams), the methods in the generated code are empty.

**DSC Transformer:** DSC Transformer accepts a DSC generated by DSC Generator, method code written on the generated DSC by programmers, and skeleton code generated by Skeleton Code Generator. Then, DSC Transformer combines them to generate the final compilable code (in Java). DSC Transformer extracts method code embedded in an input DSC, and copies the method code to an input skeleton code. DSC Transformer analyses a transformation rule, which is used by DSM Transformer, in order to determine where each method code is copied in an input skeleton code.

---

[9] http://www.alphaworks.ibm.com/tech/mtf/

## 5. An Example DSL

This section describes an example DSL to develop service-oriented distributed systems, and overviews a development process using the DSL with mTurnpike.

### 5.1. SOA DSL

Service Oriented Architecture (SOA) is a distributed systems architecture that connects and operates network services in a platform independent manner. SOA models a distributed system as a collection of services. It abstracts distributed systems using two concepts, *service interface* and *connections between services*, and hides the details of implementation and deployment technologies, such as programming languages used to implement services and remoting infrastructures used to operate services. In SOA, each service maintains its own interface that makes its functionality accessible to other services via network. Each connection between services is an abstraction to specify how to interact (or exchange messages) between services.

The proposed SOA DSL focuses on connectivity between services, and allows developers to visually design the connections between services as UML diagrams. It

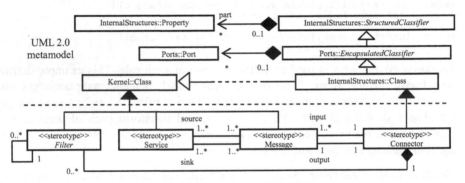

**Fig. 4.** The proposed SOA DSL

is defined as a UML profile extending the standard UML metamodel. Fig. 4 shows the core part of the proposed SOA DSL.

Service and Message are stereotypes used to specify network services and messages exchanged between services. They are defined as a metaclass extending the Class metaclass in the standard UML metamodel.

Connector is used to represent connections between services. It is a stereotype extending the Class metaclass in the InternalStructures package (Fig 4). This metaclass defines a model element used in the UML composite structure diagram. It allows developers to define nested model structures, such as a class composed of several internal (nested) classes. Connector maintains two different semantics: *connection semantics* and *invocation semantics* (Fig. 5). ConnectionSemantics is used to specify how to establish a connection between services. It defines four different semantics (Fig. 5). The Reliability option guarantees that messages are delivered to destinations. The Encryption option instructs that messages are encrypted on a connection. The `Stream` option enables streaming messages. The `Queuing` option deploys a message queue between services to enable a store-and-forward messaging policy. `InvocationSemantics` is used to specify how to invoke a service through a connection. Supported invocation semantics include synchronous, asynchronous and oneway invocations.

A Connector can contain Filters to customize its behavior (Fig. 4). The proposed SOA DSL currently defines four different filters (Fig. 6). MessageConverter converts the schema of messages exchanged on a connection. MessageAggregator synchronizes multiple invocations and aggregates their messages. Multicast simultaneously sends out a message to multiple filters or services. Interceptor is a hook to intercept invocations and examine messages.

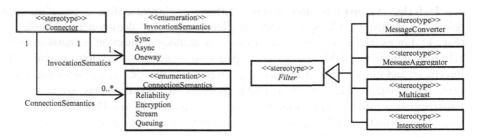

**Fig. 5.** Connector stereotypes          **Fig. 6.** Filter stereotypes

## 5.2. Development Process Using mTurnpike and SOA DSL

Using a SOA DSL described in Section 5.1, this section overviews an application development process with mTurnpike.

**(1) Defining a DSM.** Modelers define a DSM in the UML 2.0 class diagrams or composite structure diagrams. Fig. 7 shows an example DSM using the SOA DSL described in Section 5.1. `Customer` orders a product to `Supplier` by sends out an `OrderMessage`. If a `Supervisor` approves the order by issuing an `Authorization`, `Aggregator` aggregates the `OrderMessage` and `Authorization`, and sends an aggregated message to `Supplier`. `Connection` is responsible for connecting services and delivering messages between them. It establishes a synchronous and secure connection between services.

**(2) Generating a DSC from a DSM.** DSC Generator takes a DSM and generates a DCS (Fig. 1). The following is a DSC (annotated code) for `Supplier`.

```
@Service

public class Supplier{ public onMessage( OrderMessage message){} }
```

**(3) Writing Method Code.** Programmers write method code in the generated DSC in Java (Fig. 1). For example, they write `onMessage()` in the `Supplier` class.

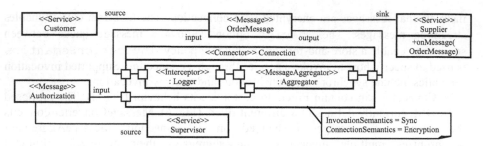

**Fig. 7.** An example DSM using the proposed SOA DSL

**(4) Defining Transformation Rules.** Platform engineers define a transformation rule to specialize a DSM in particular implementation and deployment technologies (Fig. 1). For example, if a DSM specifies a synchronous connection, a transformation rule may transform a UML class stereotyped with <<service>> into several UML interfaces and classes that are required to implement the <<service>> class as a Java RMI object (Fig. 8). If a DSM specifies an asynchronous connection, a transformation rule may specialize the <<service>> class to a JMS object (Fig. 8). The transformation rule also may specialize a <<Message>> class (e.g. OrderMessage) to implement the interface javax.jms.Message.

**(5) Generate Final Code.** DSL Transformer takes a DSM and a DSC as inputs, and generates the final (compilable) code (Fig. 1). It applies a transformation rule described in the step (4) to an input DSM to specialize the DSM. Then, it generates skeleton code in Java from the specialized DSM. Finally, DSL Transformer extracts method code from a DSC, and copies the method code to the generated skeleton code.

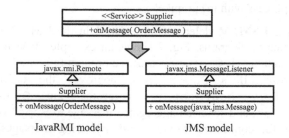

**Fig. 8.** Service implementations with JavaRMI and JMS

# 6.   Preliminary Performance Evaluation

This section empirically evaluates the efficiency and memory footprint of the mTurnpike frontend system. Measurements are obtained with nine configurations (Table 2). For example, in the A1 configuration, mTurnpike loads a DSM that contains 10 classes, each of which has five data fields, one stereotype and five tagged-values (120 model elements in total). Measurements uses a Sun J2SE 5.0.2 VM running on a Windows 2000 PC with an Athlon 1.7 Ghz CPU and 512MB memory.

**Table 2.** Measurement configurations.

| The number of model elements defined in each class | The number of classes | | |
|---|---|---|---|
| | 10 | 100 | 500 |
| 5 data fields and 1 stereotype (5 tagged-values for each stereotype) | A1 (120) | B1 (1200) | C1 (6000) |
| 10 data fields and 2 stereotypes (5 tagged-values for each stereotype) | A2 (230) | B2 (2300) | C2 (11500) |
| 50 data fields and 10 stereotypes (5 tagged-values for each stereotype) | A3 (1110) | B3 (11100) | C3 (55500) |

In order to evaluate the efficiency of the mTurnpike frontend system, Fig. 9 shows the time for mTurnpike to execute each of the five functional steps to transform a DSM to a DSC (see Section 4.2). The numbers placed in the figure depicts how long it takes for mTurnpike to execute functional steps 1, 3 and 5. Fig. 9 shows mTurnpike is efficient enough in the configurations A1 to B2 (its overhead is up to 5 seconds). The transformation overhead is acceptable in small-scale to mid-scale application development. mTurnpike does not interrupt developers' modeling and programming work severely. Fig. 9 also shows that it takes 8 up to 33 seconds for mTurnpike to execute its frontend process in the C1 to C3 configurations. Several optimization efforts are currently underway, and they are expected to reduce the latency.

In order to examine the memory footprint of the mTurnpike frontend system, Fig. 10 shows how much memory space mTurnpike consumes to transform a DSM to a DSC. mTurnpike consumes no more than 15MB memory to handle models produced in small-scale up to large-scale projects (in the configurations A1 to C2). Since the memory utilization of mTurnpike is fairly small, it is not necessary for developers to upgrade their development environments (e.g. memory modules in their PCs).

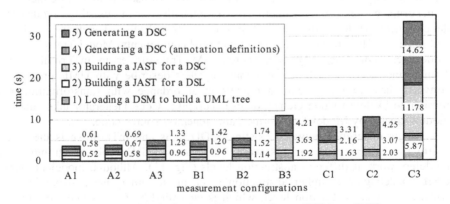

**Fig. 9.** Overhead of mTurnpike to transform a DSM to a DSC.

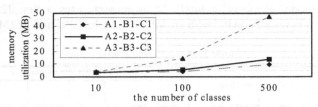

**Fig. 10.** Memory footprint of mTurnpike to transform a DSM to a DSC.

## 7.  Related Work

mTurnpike reuses the J2SE 5.0 syntax to write annotated code (i.e. marker and member annotations). However, mTurnpike and J2SE 5.0 follow different approaches to define transformation rules between annotated code and compilable code. In J2SE 5.0, transformation rules are defined in a procedural manner (i.e. as programs). It allows developers to define arbitrary transformation rules in user-defined annotation processors (see Section 2). A user-defined annotation processor examines annotated code using the Java reflection API, and generates compilable code based on a corresponding transformation rule. Although this transformation mechanism is generic and extensible, it tends to be complicated and error-prone to write user-defined annotation processors. Also, transformation rules are difficult to maintain in annotation processors, since updating a transformation rule requires modifying and recompiling the corresponding annotation processor.

In contrast, mTurnpike allows developers to define transformation rules in a declarative manner. Declarative transformation rules are more readable and easier to maintain than procedural ones. It is not required to recompile mTurnpike when updating transformation rules. Also, transformation rules are defined at the modeling layer, not the programming layer. This raises the level of abstraction for handling transformation rules, resulting in higher productivity of users in managing them.

mTurnpike has some functional commonality with existing model-driven development (MDD) tools such as OptimalJ[10], Rose XDE[11], Together[12], UMLX [8] and KMF [9] They usually have two functional components: Model Transformer and Code Generator (Fig. 11). Similar to DSM Transformer in mTurnpike, Model Transformer accepts UML models that modelers describe with UML profiles, and converts them to more detailed models in accordance with transformation rules. Similar to Skeleton Code Generator in mTurnpike, Code Generator takes the UML models created by Model Transformer, and generates source code.

A major difference between existing MDD tools and mTurnpike is the level of abstraction where programmers work. In existing MDD tools, programmers and modelers work at different abstraction levels (Fig. 11). Although modelers work on UML modeling at a higher abstraction level, programmers need to handle source code, at a lower abstraction level, which is generated by Code Generator (Fig. 11).

---

[10] http://www.compuware.com/products/optimalj/

[11] http://www.ibm.com/software/awdtools/developer/rosexde/

[12] http://www.borland.com/together/architect/

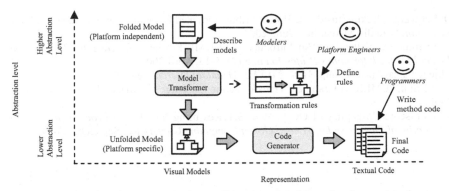

**Fig. 11.** Development process using traditional model-driven development tools.

The generated source code is often hard to read and understand. It tends to be complicated, time consuming and error-prone to modify and extend the source code.

Unlike existing MDD tools, mTurnpike allows both programmers and modelers to work at a higher abstraction level (Fig. 1). Programmers implement behavioral functionalities (i.e. method code) in DSCs, before DSL Transformer transforms DSCs to more detailed programs that specialize in particular implementation and deployment technologies. This means that programmers can focus on coding application's core logic (or business logic) without handling the details in implementation and deployment technologies. Also, DSCs (i.e. annotated code) are much more readable and easier to maintain than the source code generated by Code Generators in existing MDD tools (see Sections 2 and 3.1). Therefore, mTurnpike provides a higher productivity of programmers in implementing their applications.

## 8. Conclusion

This paper describes and empirically evaluates a new model-driven development framework called mTurnpike. In addition to an overview of architectural design, this paper focuses on the frontend system of mTurnpike and describes its design, implementation and performance implications. In order to demonstrate how to exploit mTurnpike in application development, this paper also shows a development process using an example DSL to specify service-oriented distributed systems.

## References

1. G. Booch, A Brown, S Iyengar, J. Rumbaugh and B. Selic, "An MDA Manifesto," In *The MDA Journal: Model Driven Architecture Straight from the Masters*, Chapter 11, Meghan-Kiffer Press, December 2004.
2. S. Cook, "Domain-Specific Modeling and Model-driven Architecture," In *The MDA Journal: Model Driven Architecture Straight from the Masters*, Chapter 3, Meghan-Kiffer Press, December 2004.
3. S. Kelly and J. Tolvanen, "Visual Domain-specific Modeling: Benefits and Experiences of using metaCASE Tools," In *Proc. of Int'l workshop on Model Engineering, ECOOP*, 2000.
4. Object Management Group, *UML 2.0 Superstructure Specification*, Otober, 2004.

5. D. Schwarz, "Peeking Inside the Box: Attribute-Oriented Programming with Java 1.5," In *ON Java.com*, O'Reilly Media, Inc., June 2004.
6. L. Fuentes, A. Vallecillo. "An Introduction to UML Profiles". *UPGRADE, The European Journal for the Informatics Professional*, 5 (2): 5-13, April 2004.
7. Object Management Group, *MOF 2.0 XML Metadata Interchange*, 2004.
8. E. Willink, "UMLX: A Graphical Transformation Language for MDA," In *Proc. of OOPSLA*, 2002.
9. O. Patrascoiu, "Mapping EDOC to Web Services using YATL," In *Proc. of the 8th IEEE International Enterprise Distributed Object Computing Conference*, September 2004.

# Simplifying Autonomic Enterprise Java Bean Applications Via Model-Driven Development: A Case Study

Jules White, Douglas C. Schmidt, Aniruddha Gokhale

Vanderbilt University, Department of Electrical Engineering and Computer Science,
Box 1679 Station B, Nashville, TN, 37235
{jules, Schmidt, gokhale}@dre.vanderbilt.edu
http://www.dre.vanderbilt.edu

**Abstract.** Autonomic computer systems aim to reduce the configuration, operational, and maintenance costs of distributed applications by enabling them to self-manage, self-heal, self-optimize, self-configure, and self-protect. This paper provides two contributions to the model-driven development (MDD) of autonomic computing systems using Enterprise Java Beans (EJBs). First, we describe the structure and functionality of an MDD tool that formally captures the design of EJB applications, their quality of service (QoS) requirements, and the autonomic properties applied to the EJBs to support the rapid development of autonomic EJB applications via code generation, automatic checking of model correctness, and visualization of complex QoS and autonomic properties. Second, the paper describes how MDD tools can generate code to plug EJBs into a Java component framework that provides an autonomic structure to monitor, configure, and execute EJBs and their adaptation strategies at runtime. We present a case study that evaluates how these tools and frameworks work to reduce the complexity of developing autonomic applications.

## 1 Introduction

**Autonomic computing challenges**. Developing and maintaining enterprise applications is hard, due in part to their complexity and the impact of human operator error, which have shown to be a significant contributor to distributed system repair and down time [2]. The aim of autonomic computing is to create distributed applications that have the ability to self-manage, self-heal, self-optimize, self-configure, and self-protect [1], thereby reducing human interaction with the system to minimize down-time from operator error. Although the benefits of autonomic computing are significant [1], the pressures of limited development timeframes and inherent/accidental complexities of large-scale software development have discouraged the integration of sophisticated autonomic computing functionality into distributed applications. Some enterprise application platforms offer limited autonomic features, such as such as Enterprise Java Bean (EJB) [3] application servers clustering capabilities, though they tend to have large development teams and long development cycles.

A key challenge limiting the use of autonomic features in enterprise applications is the lack of design tools and frameworks that can (1) alleviate the complexities stem-

L. Briand and C. Williams (Eds.): MoDELS 2005, LNCS 3713, pp. 601-615, 2005.

ming from the use of *ad hoc* methods and (2) generate code that is correct-by-construction. Some infrastructure does exist, such as IBM's Autonomic Computing Toolkit [4], which focuses on system-level logging and management. System-level autonomic toolkits are inadequate, however, for fine-grained autonomic capabilities, which fix problems early before an entire application must be restarted.

To address the limitations with system-level autonomic toolkits, *component-level* autonomic frameworks are needed to reduce the effort of developing autonomic applications. Component-level autonomic properties support more fine-grained healing, optimization, configuration, monitoring, and protection than system-level toolkits. For example, a mission-critical command and control system for emergency responders should be able to shutdown/restart application component logic selectively as it fails, rather than shutdown/restart the entire application. With existing autonomic infrastructure based on the system-level , the failure of a key component triggers a restart of the entire application [5]. In contrast, a component-level autonomic framework could provide mechanisms to restart only the point of failure.

**Simplifying autonomic system development via MDD techniques.** *Model-driven development* (MDD) [6] tools are a promising means of reducing the cost associated with these activities. Models of autonomic systems developed with MDD tools can be constructed and checked for correctness (semi-)automatically to ensure that application designs meet autonomic requirements. Tools can also generate the various capabilities to move data, coordinate actions, and perform other autonomic functions.

To address the need for component-level autonomic computing – and to avoid *ad hoc* techniques that manually imbue autonomic qualities into distributed applications – we have created the *J3 Toolsuite,* which is an open-source MDD environment that supports the design and implementation of autonomic applications. J3 consists of several MDD tools and autonomic computing frameworks, including (1) *J2EEML*, which captures the design of EJB applications, their quality of service (QoS) [6] requirements, and the autonomic adaptation strategies of their EJBs via a domain-specific modeling language (DSML) [7], (2) *Jadapt*, which is a J2EEML model interpreter that analyzes the QoS and autonomic properties of J2EEML models, and (3) *JFense*, which is an autonomic framework for monitoring, configuring, and resetting individual EJBs [8].

This paper describes the structure and functionality of J2EEML and shows how it simplifies autonomic system development by providing notations and abstractions that are aligned with autonomic computing, QoS, and EJB terminology, rather than low-level features of operating systems, middleware platforms, and third-generation programming languages. We also describe how (1) Jadapt generates EJB and Java code from J2EEML models to ensure that autonomic applications meet their specifications and to reduce implementation time and (2) JFense provides a set of reusable autonomic components that allow developers to plug-in EJB applications and focus on autonomic logic, rather than the glue for constructing autonomic systems. Finally, we evaluate how the J3 Toolsuite reduces the complexity of developing an autonomic EJB application used as a case study to evaluate our MDD tools and processes.

Our case study centers on an EJB-based system that schedules highway freight shipments using the multi-layered autonomic architecture shown in Figure 1. The system has a list of freight shipments that it must schedule. It uses a constraint-optimization engine to find a cost effective assignment of drivers and trucks to shipments.

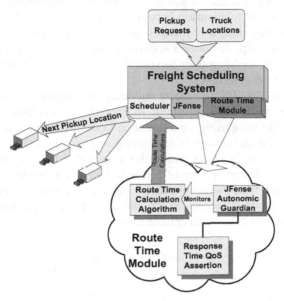

**Fig. 1.** A Multi-Layered Autonomic Architecture for Scheduling Highway Freight Shipments

A central component in Figure 1 is the *Route Time Module* (*RTM*), which determines the route time from a truck's current location to a shipment start or end point. The *RTM* uses a geo-database and the GPS coordinates from the truck to perform the calculation. This module is critical to the proper operation of the optimization engine. A heavy load is placed on the *RTM*, so it is crucial that it maintains its *QoS assertions*, such as maintaining a maximum response time for the *RTM* of 100 milliseconds. QoS assertions are properties that the system can introspectively measure about itself to determine whether the measured value for the property is beneficial to the system. These measured *QoS goals* allow the system to decide whether it is in a good state and predict whether it will continue to remain in a good state.

**Paper organization**. The remainder of this paper is organized as follows: Section 2 describes the MDD J3 Toolsuite for developing autonomic EJB applications; Section 3 gives an overview of J2EEML and describes key challenges we faced when developing it; Section 4 quantifies the reduction in manual effort achieved by using the J3 Toolsuite on our highway freight shipment case study; Section 5 compares our work with related research; and Section 6 presents concluding remarks.

## 2 Modeling Autonomic EJB Applications with J2EEML

J2EEML is a DSML that enables EJB developers to construct models that incorporate autonomic and QoS concepts as first-class entities. J2EEML itself is developed using the *Generic Modeling Environment* (GME) [9], which is a general-purpose MDD environment that we use to simplify the creation of *metamodels* that characterize the roles and relationships in the autonomic computing domain, and *model interpreters* that generate many artifacts required to implement autonomic EJB applications. J2EEML captures the relationship between QoS assertions and application components to address key design challenges of developing autonomic applications. For example, J2EEML helps developers understand which components to monitor in their EJB applications by enabling them to visualize and analyze the relationships between components and QoS assertions.

Developers use J2EEML to capture the design of autonomic systems and the mapping of components to QoS assertions in four phases: (1) they create a structural model of the EJBs composing an autonomic system, (2) they create models of the QoS properties that the system is attempting to maintain, (3) they map these QoS properties to the specific beans within the system that the properties are measured from, and (4) they design courses of action to take when the desired QoS properties are not maintained. This modeling process captures the structure of the system, how the QoS properties are related to the structure, and what adaptation should occur if a QoS property is not within an acceptable range.

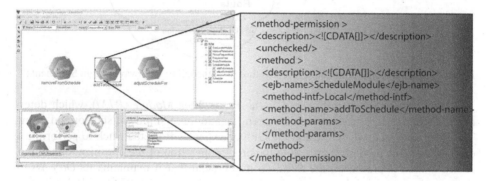

**Fig. 2.** J2EEML Remote Interface Composition Model for the *TruckStatusModule*

## 2.1 Modeling EJB Structures with J2EEML

The first piece of a J2EEML model is its *EJB structural model*, which describes the components of the system that will be managed autonomically. This model defines the beans that compose the system and captures the EJB specifics of each bean, including JNDI names, transactional requirements, security requirements, package names, descriptions, remote and local interface composition, and bean-to-bean interactions. An EJB structural model is constructed via the following steps:

1. Each session bean is added to the model by dragging and dropping session bean atoms into the J2EEML model. Developers then provide the Java Naming and Directory Interface (JNDI) name of the bean, its description, and its state type (i.e., stateful or stateless).
2. For each session bean, a model is constructed of the business methods and creators supported by the bean by dragging and dropping method and creator atoms. Figure 2 shows a model of the remote interface composition of the *TruckStatusModule* from the case study described in Section 1.

3. Entity beans are dragged and dropped into the model to construct the data access layer. These beans are provided a JNDI name/description and properties indicating if they use container managed persistence (CMP) or bean managed persistence (BMP).

4. Persistent fields, methods, and finders are dragged and dropped into the entity beans. Each persistent field has properties for setting visibility, type, whether it is part f the primary key, and its access type (i.e., read-only or read-write).

5. Relationship roles are dragged and dropped into the entity beans and connected to persistent fields. These relationship roles can be connected to other relationship roles to indicate entity bean relationships.

6. Connections are made between beans to indicate bean-to-bean interactions. Capturing these interactions allows Jadapt to later generate the required JNDI lookup code for a bean to obtain a reference to another bean.

After these six steps have been completed, the J2EEML model contains enough information to represent the composition of the EJBs.

Figure 3 shows a J2EEML structural model of the highway freight scheduling system. In this figure, each bean within the freight scheduling system has been modeled via J2EEML. Interactions between the beans are also modeled, thereby allowing developers to understand which beans interact with one another. Figure 3 also illustrates snippets of the XML deployment descriptor and Java class generated for the *Scheduler*.

To support decomposition of complex architectures into smaller pieces, J2EEML allows EJB structural models to contain child EJB models. Beans within the these children show up as ports that can receive connections from the parent solution. This design allows developers to decompose models into manageable pieces and enables different developers to encapsulate their designs.

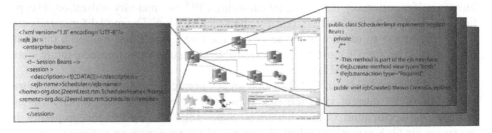

**Fig. 3.** J2EEML Structural Model Showing Bean-to-Bean Interactions

For our highway freight scheduling example, we constructed a structural model of each bean required for the *Route Time Module*, constraint-optimization engine, truck status system, and incoming pickup request system, as shown in Figure 3. The model also includes information on the entity beans used to access the *truck location* and *pickup request* databases.

Using J2EEML provides several advantages in the design phase, including (1) visualization of beans and their interactions, component security requirements, system transactional requirements, and interactions between beans, (2) enforcement of EJB best practices, such as the Session Façade pattern [10], which hides Entity beans from clients through Session beans , and (3) model correctness checking, including checks for proper JNDI naming. J2EEML's visualization benefits significantly decreased the difficulty of understanding system structure and interactions. The correctness checking and enforcement of best design practices facilitated rapid creation of both a correct-by-construction and well-designed solution.

# 3 Designing J2EEML to Address Key Concerns of Autonomic Computing

Autonomic applications require four elements to achieve their assertions: *monitoring, analysis, planning, and execution* [1]. These elements form a *controller* that observes and adapts the application to maintain its assertions. This section describes how the monitoring, analysis, and planning aspects of autonomic systems present unique challenges when designing and building the J2EEML and shows how we addressed each challenge. To focus the discussion, we use the *Route Time Module* (*RTM*) shown in Figure 1 as a case study to illustrate key design challenges associated with autonomic systems.

## 3.1 Monitoring

Monitoring is the phase in autonomic systems where applications observe their own state. Since this state information is used in later phases to control system behaviors it is crucial that the right information be collected at the right times without adversely impact system functionality and QoS. The following are key design challenges faced when developing the monitoring aspects of autonomic systems:

**Challenge 3.1.1: Providing the ability to specify the large range of data that can be monitored by the system.** Developers of autonomic systems must address how to self-monitor key data, e.g., by capturing CPU and memory utilization, exceptions thrown by the applacation, or error messages in a log. The model for specifying what information to capture from the system must be flexible and support a range of data types. The model must also be extensible and support unforeseen future data types that might be needed later.

A core concept behind J2EEML is that an autonomic EJB application can measure properties of its current state introspectively and determine if the property values indicate the application is in a beneficial state. J2EEML models the properties it measures via *QoS assertions*, which determine which properties an autonomic system can measure about itself introspectively and analyze to determine if the properties are in an acceptable assertion range. Each assertion provides properties for setting its name and description. Developers can drag and drop these assertions into J2EEML models.

The J2EEML QoS assertions model is critical for understanding an autonomic system's QoS properties, how they can be measured, what their values should be, and how degradations in them can be corrected. Understanding QoS assertions is also crucial to designing the structural architecture of EJB applications and understanding how they meet those assertions. Capturing and mapping QoS requirements to the appropriate structural architecture have traditionally used natural language descriptions, such as "the service must support 1,000 simultaneous users with a good response time." Due to the lack of an unambiguous formal notation, such descriptions are prone to different interpretations, which result in architectures that do not meet the QoS requirements. Choosing an EJB architecture that best fits the QoS requirements can be complex and error-prone since specification ambiguity and hidden architectural trade-offs make it hard to choose the appropriate design.

For example, deciding whether to use remote interfaces for a J2EE implementation of a service can have a substantial impact on end-to-end system QoS. Remote interfaces allow distribution of beans across servers, which can increase scalability. Distribution can also increase latency, however, since requests must travel across a network or virtual machine boundaries.

With the *RTM* in our case study, one QoS assertion is the average response time. This QoS assertion states that the system will measure all requests to the *RTM* and track the average time required to service each request. If the calculated average response time exceeds 50 milliseconds, the assertion is false, indicating that the *RTM* is taking too long to respond, otherwise the assertion is true, indicating that the *RTM* is responding properly.

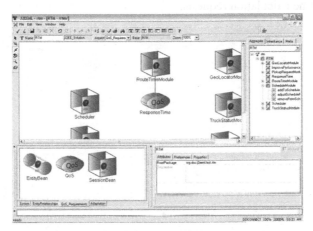

**Fig. 4.** J2EEML Model Associating the *ResponseTime* QoS Assertion with the *RouteTimeModule*

Figure 4 illustrates a J2EEML model of the scheduling system and the association of the *RTM* to the *ResponseTime* QoS property. This model shows J2EEML's ability to model QoS properties as aspects [15] that are applied to a component. When the model is interpreted and the Java implementation generated, the association between the *RTM* and *ResponseTime* assertion will lead to the appropriate monitoring code being generated in the *RTM*'s implementing class.

**Challenge 3.1.2: Building a system to specify where monitoring logic should reside in the system.** The decision of what to monitor directly affects where the monitoring logic will reside. To monitor a log for errors, the logic could be at any level of the application, such as a central control level. For observing exceptions or the load on a specific subcomponent of the application, the monitoring logic must be embedded more deeply. In particular, developers must position the monitoring capability precisely so that it is close enough to capture the needed information, but not so deeply entangled in the application logic that it adversely affects performance and separation of concerns.

In our freight scheduling case study, we must ensure separation of concerns in the application design and find an efficient means of monitoring. The monitoring logic for the *RTM*, however, should not be entangled with the route time calculation logic. Moreover, the time to monitor each request should be insignificant compared to the time to fulfill each route request.

After the structural and assertion models are completed, developers can use J2EEML to map QoS assertions to EJBs in the structural model. This mapping documents which QoS assertions should be applied to each component. It also indicates where monitoring, analysis, and adaptation should occur for an autonomic system to maintain those assertions. For example, to determine the average response time of the *RTM*, calls to the *RTM*s route time calculation method must be intercepted to calculate their servicing time. The relationship between the *RTM* bean and average response time assertion in the model indicates that the *RTM* bean must be able to monitor its route time calculation requests.

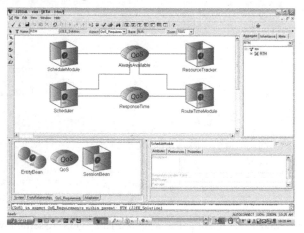

**Fig. 5.** J2EEML Mapping of QoS Assertions to EJBs

J2EEML supports aspect-oriented modeling [11] of QoS assertions, i.e., each QoS assertion in J2EEML that crosscuts component boundaries can be associated with multiple EJBs. For example, maintaining a maximum response time of 100 milliseconds is crucial for both the *RTM* and the *Scheduler* bean. Connecting multiple components to a QoS assertion, rather than creating a copy for each component, produces clearer models. It also clearly shows the connections between components that share common QoS assertions. Figure 5 shows a mapping from QoS assertions to EJBs. Both the *RTM* and the *Scheduler* in this figure are associated with the QoS assertions *ResponseTime* and *AlwaysAvailable*. The *ResourceTracker* and *ShipmentSchedule* components also share the *AlwaysAvailable* QoS assertion in the model.

Components can have multiple QoS assertion associations, which J2EEML supports by either creating a single assertion for the component that contains sub-assertions or by connecting multiple QoS assertions to the component. If the combination of assertions produces a meaningful abstraction, hierarchical composition is preferred. For example, the *RTM* is associated with a QoS assertion called "AlwaysAvailable" constructed from the sub-assertions "No Exceptions Thrown" and "Never Returns Null." Combining "Minimum Response Time" and "No Exceptions Thrown," however, would not produce a meaningful higher-level abstraction, so the multiple connection method is preferred in this case.

## 3.2 Analysis

Analysis is the phase in autonomic systems that takes state information acquired by monitoring and reasons about whether certain conditions have been met. For example, analysis can determine if an application is maintaining its QoS requirements. The analysis aspects of an autonomic system can be (1) centralized and executed on the entire system state or (2) distributed and concerned with small discrete sets of the state. The following are key challenges faced when developing an autonomic analysis engine:

**Challenges 3.2.1: Building a model to facilitate choosing the type of analysis engine and Challenge 3.2.2: Building a model to facilitate choosing how the engine should be decomposed and/or distributed.** To choose a distributed vs. monolithic analysis engine, the tradeoffs of each must be understood. Concentration of analysis logic into a single monolithic engine enables more complex calculations. However, for simple calculations, such as the average response time of the *RTM* component, a monolithic engine requires more overhead to store/retrieve state information for individual components than an analysis engine dedicated to a single component. A monolithic analysis engine also provides a central point of failure. A key design question is thus where analysis should be done and at what granularity.

A model to facilitate choosing the appropriate type of analysis engine must enable developers to identify what data types are being analyzed, what beneficial information about the system state can be gleaned from this information, and how that beneficial information can most easily be extracted. It is important that the model enable a standard process for examining the required analyses and determining the appropriate engine type.

To create an effective analysis engine, developers must determine the appropriate number of layers. A key issue to consider is whether an application should have a single-layer vs. multi-layered analysis engine. At each layer, the original monitoring design questions are applicable, i.e., what should be monitored and how should it be monitored? A model to enable these decisions must clearly convey the layers composing the system. It also must capture what analysis takes place at each layer and how each layer of analysis relates with other layers.

Developers can use J2EEML to design hierarchical QoS assertions to divide-and-conquer complex QoS analyses. A hierarchical QoS assertion is a assertion that is only met if all its child assertions are met. In terms of QoS assertions, this means that all the child QoS assertions must hold for the parent QoS assertion to hold. With respect to the *RTM*, the QoS assertion *GoodResponseTime* only holds if both the child QoS assertions *AverageResponseTime* and *MaximumResponseTime* also hold. This hierarchical composition is illustrated in Figure 6, where *GoodResponseTime* is an aggregation of several properties of the response time.

Modeling QoS assertions hierarchically enhances developer understanding of what type of analysis engine to choose. A small number of complex QoS assertions that cannot be broken into smaller pieces imply the need for a monolithic analysis engine. A large number of assertions – especially hierarchical QoS assertions – imply the need for a multi-layered analysis engine.

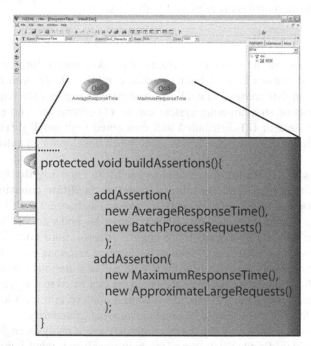

```
protected void buildAssertions(){

    addAssertion(
        new AverageResponseTime(),
        new BatchProcessRequests()
        );
    addAssertion(
        new MaximumResponseTime(),
        new ApproximateLargeRequests()
        );

}
```

**Fig. 6.** J2EEML Hierarchical Composition of ResponseTime QoS Assertion J2EEML Hierarchical Composition of *ResponseTime* QoS Assertion

Modeling QoS assertions hierarchically also enhances developer understanding of how to decompose the analysis engine into layers. The hierarchical model of the QoS assertions corresponds directly to the decomposition of the analysis engine into layers. Developers can use J2EEML to first add complex QoS assertions to their models and then determine if the complex assertion can be accomplished by combining the results of several smaller analyses. If so, developers can add these smaller QoS assertions as children of the original QoS assertion to represent the smaller analyses and then apply this iterative process to the new children.

### 3.3 Planning

Planning is the phase in autonomic systems where applications examine the results of their analysis and decide what actions to take to reach their assertions. For our highway freight scheduling example, this could involve changing the *RTM* to use a less precise but faster algorithm that maintains the minimum response time as demand grows. A typical autonomic application may have hundreds of assertions and planning the correct actions in the face of QoS failures is critical to an autonomic application. The following are key challenges faced when developing an autonomic analysis engine:

**Challenge 3.3.1 Designing a means to specify layered adaptation plans.** As with monitoring and analysis, planning can be implemented with a layered architecture. A simple, one-layer architecture would monitor, reason, and react to all system events at one level, which works well for macro-level events and actions. This simple approach is less suitable for applications that need more flexible and fine-grained control of their behavior. To increase flexibility and fine-grained control, therefore, more layers can be integrated into the system. Layers distribute intelligence throughout the system and support a divide-and-conquer approach to planning.

After the planning is provisioned into layers, each layer must be assigned a responsibility to react to and recover from QoS failures. In our highway freight scheduling example, one layer might ensure that the *RTM* is always available and the next layer down might ensure that a minimum response time is maintained. Intelligent separation of responsibilities can produce hierarchical chains of command that reduce the complexity of accomplishing the overall assertion. Finding these well-proportioned divisions of labor is hard.

J2EEML models adaptation by specifying the actions the system should take when a QoS assertion fails. Each application component may have a group of assertions associated with it. If one assertion does not hold for the component, it indicates a QoS failure that must be fixed. Developers can use J2EEML to specify groups of actions that must be taken to correct these failures.

Once an assertion has failed to hold for a specific component, the application must determine how to fix the problem. To model the appropriate course of action, J2EEML uses the concept of *adaptation plans*, which are groups of actions that can be performed to fix a specific type of QoS assertion failure. For example, if the average response time assertion fails, the *RTM* must change its calculation algorithms to be less precise but run faster.

Figure 7 shows a J2EEML model that associates the *ResponseTime* QoS assertion with the *ChangeAlgorithms* single-layered adaptation plan.

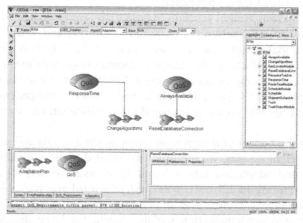

**Figure 7:** J2EEML Model Associating the ResponseTime QoS Assertion with the ChangeAlgorithms Adaptation Plan J2EEML Model Associating the *ResponseTime* QoS Assertion with the *ChangeAlgorithms* Adaptation Plan

### 3.4 Reducing the Complexity of Developing Autonomic Systems with JFense and Jadapt

JFense is a component-level framework that performs autonomic functions, such as monitoring the QoS of EJBs, analyzing system state, communicating between autonomic layers, determining how to adapt to QoS failures, and executing adaptation plans. Jadapt is a J2EEML model interpreter that supports rapid development and verification of autonomic code by generating implementations of EJBs from a structural model. It serves as a bridge between a J2EEML model and the JFense framework, i.e., it generates Java code for (1) a J2EEML structural model and (2) plugging the generated EJBs into the JFense framework. Jadapt generates configurations for JFense to mirror the J2EEML model, stubs for the EJBs, EJB deployment descriptors, and monitoring, analysis, planning, and execution class stubs, which relieves developers from tedious and error-prone coding tasks. Moreover, Jadapt ensures that the code mirrors the system architecture in J2EEML implementation, which reduces problems stemming from misinterpretation of the specification and inconsistencies between interfaces and their implementations.

## 4 Evaluating Development Effort Savings of the J3 Toolsuite

We developed the highway freight scheduling system case study to illustrate the advantages of using the J3 Toolsuite to develop autonomic EJB applications. The initial implementation of this case study required several thousand lines of Java code. The generated EJB implementations accounted for nearly 75% of the complete code base, the test framework accounted for 20%, and the JFense glue code accounted for 5%. Using a traditional development approach, much of this code would have been developed manually. With the J3 Toolsuite, in contrast, all code except for the business logic and testing logic was generated initially by Jadapt from our J2EEML specification, which accounted for approximately one-third of the code required to implement the Java classes for the application.

Using our highway freight scheduling case study, we evaluated the impact of adding new sources of information that required monitoring and where the logic would reside. In our initial design, only response times of the *Scheduling* component were monitored. We then refactored the design to monitor response times of the *RTM* component, as well. Adjusting the design using J2EEML and re-generating the implementation took approximately five mouse clicks and resulted in the generation of ~20 new lines of source code that correctly mirrored the specification and was correct-by-construction.

To evaluate the impact of design refactoring on the analysis and planning layers of the highway freight system, we modified its initial design by changing its response time analysis and adaptation into a hierarchy of average and maximum response times. The refactoring in J2EEML was straightforward and took ~12 mouse clicks. The change generated ~75 new lines of code, which minimized the complexity of the design change and implementation update. Again, for large development projects without MDD tool support, many such changes would occur and hence the manual redevelopment effort would be much higher.

To evaluate the development effort associated with sharing adaptation plans between QoS assertions, we refactored our highway freight system to share the improved response time adaptation plan between both the average response time QoS assertion and the maximum response time QoS assertion. After this change was made to the model and Jadapt regenerated the model artifacts, 36 new lines of code were present that updated the existing adaptation plan to include the new adaptations and changed the adaptation plan of the maximum response time to use its modified adaptation plan. As with other refactorings we analyzed, adjusting the J2EEML model and regenerating the code required ~12 mouse clicks, while developing the equivalent functionality manually required significantly more effort.

As with the autonomic modeling and generation capabilities of the J3 Toolsuite, significant reductions in development complexity were yielded by applying MDD to the implementation of the structural model. For example, when a single `Session-Bean` with one method was added to the J2EEML model, the resulting bean, interfaces, deployment descriptor, and helper classes generated 116 lines of Java code and 80 lines of XML. The model change in J2EEML required two drag and drop operations. As with the autonomic code generated by Jadapt, the code was correct-by-construction and the JNDI name of the bean was also correct. Adding two interactions from existing beans to the new bean generated another ~12 lines of error-prone JNDI lookup/narrowing code that was automatically generated by Jadapt, thereby simplifying developer effort and enhancing confidence in the results.

## 5 Related Work

An increasing number of MDD tools exist for modeling component-based systems. Cadena [16] is an MDD tool for building and modeling component-based DRE systems, with the goal of applying static analysis, model-checking, and lightweight formal methods to enhance these systems. Other tools, such as Rational Rose, provide UML modeling capabilities for component-based systems. In contrast to J2EEML, these tools are not tailored to the domain of modeling autonomic functionality in component-based systems. For example, they lack the ability to establish the critical mapping between QoS properties, components, and adaptations, which forces developers to (1) resort to traditional textual descriptions for specifying QoS properties and (2) maintain separate models for understanding how the QoS, adaptation, and components in the system interrelate. As a result, it is hard to understand how an application will monitor itself and how it will react to QoS failures.

IBM's Autonomic Toolkit [4] addresses the issues of monitoring, analysis, planning, and executing autonomic applications. It includes the Autonomic Management Engine, which monitors events, analyzes them, then plans and executes corrective action on a computing resource; the Generic Log Adapter [13] for Autonomic Computing, which converts existing log files to the Common Base Event format [14]; and the Log and Trace Analyzer for Autonomic Computing, which reads logs in the Common Base Event format, correlates the logs based on different criteria, and displays the correlated log records. These tools do not, however, address the complexity of integrating autonomic functionality into applications, i.e., they do not help developers design their autonomic applications or implementing the logic required by them. In contrast, the J3 Toolsuite is specifically tailored to reducing design and implementation complexity, as well as providing a runtime framework.

# 6 Concluding Remarks

In theory, autonomic systems can minimize the impact of human error in development and management. In practice, however, it is hard to develop the monitoring, analysis, planning, and execution aspects required for autonomic systems reliably and productively. In particular, developers must reason about complex sets of QoS assertions and ensure that applications meet them. Autonomic capabilities provide a means for EJB applications to self-manage and attempt to maintain the QoS assertions. To facilitate self-management, the structure of EJB applications and their QoS assertions must be captured formally so applications can reason about themselves.

The bridge between the QoS assertions of autonomic systems and their structural designs involves mapping these assertions to specific system components. Without this mapping, applications cannot use introspection to determine whether their QoS assertions are being met. The J3 Toolsuite described in this paper provides MDD tools and an autonomic computing framework to support these capabilities to simplify the development of autonomic EJB applications.

The J2EEML MDD tool helps link assertions and structure by allowing developers to specify this mapping via a DSML. J2EEML also includes mechanisms for modeling complex EJB structures, interactions, and architectures and using these models to generate code that is correct-by-construction, which frees developer from reinventing complex autonomic frameworks.

After capturing structural properties, QoS assertions, and assertion to structure mapping in J2EEML, developers still must integrate autonomic features into their - distributed EJB applications. This integration is often complicated due to the lack of component-level frameworks for autonomic systems. To address these concerns, we have developed the Jadapt code generation tool and the JFense autonomic framework. Jadapt allows developers to generate the code needed to plug their application's EJBs into JFense. JFense provides a comprehensive and flexible framework for multi-layered autonomic monitoring, analysis, planning, and execution architectures, which allows developers to focus on the system's business logic and QoS analysis logic.

The following are our lessons learned thus far by developing and using the J3 Toolsuite:

- Developing adaptations for an application is hard. Most developers do not think about designing components that can be adapted, swapped, restarted, or reconfigured to handle errors. Providing a DSML to aid developers in seeing the crosscutting adaptive concerns was hard.
- Creating a model of the mapping from components to QoS properties and adaptive behavior greatly enhances the ability of developers to understand the complex behavior of autonomic systems that would ordinarily be buried in hundreds of source files.
- Constraint checking and code generation can greatly reduce and/or eliminate hard-to-debug JNDI naming errors. Constraint checking of JNDI allows these errors to be detected at design time rather than runtime.

In future work, we are developing increasingly sophisticated autonomic distributed applications using our J3 Toolsuite to serve as a testbed for investigating various autonomic architectures, monitoring strategies, and planning strategies. We are also enhancing these tools to increase their expressive and code generation capabilities. We plan to integrate our MDD tools with CIAO [6], which is an open-source, QoS-enabled CORBA Component Model (CCM) implementation.

The J3 Toolsuite DSMLs, tools, and frameworks are available at www. source-forge.net/projects/j2eeml.

# References

1. Kephart, J., O., Chess, D., M.: The Vision of Autonomic Computing. IEEE Computer. (January 2003).
2. Oppenheimer, D., Ganapathi, A., Patterson, D.: Why do Internet services fail, and what can be done about it?. In: Proc. USENIX Symposium on Internet Technologies and Systems (March 2003)
3. Matena, V., Hapner, M.: Enterprise Java Beans Specification, Version 1.1. Sun Microsystems (Dec. 1999)
4. Autonomic Computing Toolkit, IBM, www106.ibm.com/developerworks/autonomic/overview.html.
5. Candea, G., Fox, A.: Designing for High Availability and Measurability. In: Proc. of the 1st Workshop on Evaluating and Architecting System Dependability (2001)
6. Wang, N., Schmidt, D., Gokhale, A., Rodrigues, C., Natarajan, B., Loyall, J., Schantz, R., Gill, C.: QoS-enabled Middleware. In *Middleware for Communications*, edited by Q. Mahmoud, Wiley and Sons, New York, (2003)
7. Ledeczi, A., Bakay, A., Maroti, M., Volgysei, P., Nordstrom, G., Sprinkle, J., Karsai, G.: Composing Domain-Specific Design Environments. IEEE Computer (Nov. 2001)
8. Eymann, T., Reinicke, M., et al.: Self-Organizing Resource Allocation for Autonomic Networks. In: Proc. DEXA Workshops (2003)
9. Ledeczi, A., The Generic Modeling Environment. In: Proc. Workshop on Intelligent Signal Processing, Budapest, Hungary (2001)
10. Alur, D., Crupi, J., Malks, D.: J2EE Core Patterns. Sun Microsystems Press (2003)
11. Gray, J., Roychoudhury, S.: A Technique for Constructing Aspect Weavers Using a Program Transformation Engine. In: Proc. of AOSD '04, Lancaster, UK, (March 22-26, 2004)
12. Gamma, E., Helm, R. Johnson, R., Vlissides, J.: Design Patterns: Elements of Reusable Object-Oriented Software. Addison-Wesley (1995)
13. Giguere, E.: Create GLA components using Release 2 of the Autonomic Computing Toolkit. IBM Developerworks, (www106.ibm.com/ developerworks/edu/ac-dw-ac-glacomp2i.html? TACT=104AHW20&S_CMP=HP)
14. Specification: Common Base Event. IBMDeveloperworks, (www106.ibm.com/ developerworks/webservices/library/ws-cbe/).
15. Loyall, J., Bakken, D., Schantz, R., Zinky, J., Karr, D., Vanegas, R.: QoS Aspect Languages and Their Runtime Integration. In: Proc. of the Fourth Workshop on Languages, Compilers and Runtime Systems for Scalable Components (1998)
16. Hatcliff, J., Deng, W., Dwyer, M., Jung, G., Prasad, V.: Cadena: An Integrated Development, Analysis, and Verification Environment for Component-based Systems. In: Proc. of the 25th International Conference on Software Engineering, Portland, OR (2003)

# Automated Invariant Maintenance Via OCL Compilation

Kurt Stirewalt[1] and Spencer Rugaber[2]

[1] Computer Science and Engineering
Michigan State University

[2] College of Computing
Georgia Institute of Technology

**Abstract.** UML design models, specifically their declarative OCL invariants, must be refined into delivered code. A key problem is the need to integrate this logic with programmer-written code in a non-intrusive way. We recently developed an approach, called *mode components*, for compiling OCL constraints into modules that implement logic for transparently maintaining these constraints at run time. Specifically, mode components are implemented as nested C++ class template instantiations. The approach makes use of a key device—status variables. The attributes of a component to which other components are sensitive are called its *status*. A *status variable* is a lightweight wrapper on a status attribute that detects changes to its value and transparently invokes a method to handle announcements to dependent components. A mode component is a wrapped code unit containing one or more status variables. The contribution of this paper is a technique for achieving this integration using metaprogramming techniques.

## 1 Problem Statement

Component-based software development attempts to gain productivity and quality benefits by making use of existing code resources. But even if the existing components are themselves reliable, the resulting assembly might not be. We would like to find ways to improve our confidence in the assembly, while retaining the leveraging benefits. Assume that we start with a specified set of behavioral guarantees, called *invariants,* for the target system. Our quality goal is ensure that the invariants are maintained throughout execution. Moreover, we want to achieve this goal while satisfying the following additional, non-functional properties.

- **Transparency:** The solution should refrain from intruding into the components themselves. Transparency separates reasoning about invariants from the details of the components' implementations. Also, it reduces the need to modify the code of the components, thereby lessening the risk of introducing defects.

- **Flexibility:** There are a variety of architectural approaches for combining components. A flexible solution is one in which an architectural approach can be selected by the designer based on other desirable system properties.

L. Briand and C. Williams (Eds.): MoDELS 2005, LNCS 3713, pp. 616–632, 2005.
© Springer-Verlag Berlin Heidelberg 2005

Moreover, flexibility supports reuse, enabling components to be packaged in various ways.

- **Economy:** A goal of the composition process is to avoid additional run-time costs over an *ad hoc* implementation. As a general rule, the more encapsulated and self- contained the components are, the more complex is the composition mechanism required to integrate them. With complexity comes run-time overhead. An economical solution supports collaboration without additional run-time cost.

- **Intentionality:** In order to reason about system behavior, it should be possible to relate the behavioral specification of a desired invariant to its implementation directly. In particular, each invariant should be traceable to the code mechanism responsible for guaranteeing it. Intentionality also supports maintainability— changes to system functional requirements often mean altering system invariants. Invariants implemented intentionally are easier to alter.

This paper describes a mechanism for assembling components into a system whose behavior is guaranteed. The composition and its invariant properties are specified by a designer using a subset of UML and OCL. The specified model is automatically compiled into a set of wrappers that enforce the desired invariant properties. The wrappers make use of the metaprogramming features of C++ to achieve the non-functional goals of transparency, flexibility, economy, and intentionality.

# 2 Solution Approach

## 2.1 Modeling

The component assembly process described in this paper is called DYNAMO, short for Dynamic Assembly from Models. DYNAMO supports model-based specification of component assemblies. What this means is that a designer specifies an assembly in a high-level, declarative notation rather than operationally in a programming language. The notation we have used is the Unified Modelling Language[1] (UML) [12] including the Object Constraint Language (OCL) [21]. Moreover, we have interpreted UML class model constructs in terms of the vocabulary of software architecture[2]. (See Table 1.) Annotations to the class model, in the form of OCL constraints, provide semantics. In particular, handlers for external system events (*stimuli*) are ultimately modelled as methods in a component. OCL pre- and post- condition constraints specify the effect of events on the system. Invariants, initially indicated with natural language annotations, are first translated by the designer into OCL annotations to associations. (The UML rule restricting invariants to classifiers is relaxed for this step only.) As the architecture is refined, associations are subsumed by DYNAMO's layered

---

1    Specifically, UML v1.4.
2    See [11] for a discussion of the use of UML for modelling software architecture.

architecture. At this point, each constraint is assigned to the component responsible for maintaining it.

**Table 1.** DYNAMO UML Interpretation

| UML Concept | DYNAMO Interpretation |
|---|---|
| System | Assembly |
| Package | Layer |
| Class | Component |
| Attribute | Percept |
| Association | Invariant |
| Dependency | Event |

## 2.2 Design Method

A designer using the DYNAMO method constructs a declarative model of the assembly expressed using a graphical UML CASE tool. The DYNAMO design method comprises three phases that refine a conceptual model of a proposed assembly into interrelated components organized into layers. In Phase 0, the environment in which the assembly executes is described in terms of external actors, the assembly itself, and the behavioral properties that the assembly guarantees to maintain. Phase 1 partitions the assembly into its constituent components, assigning responsibility for handling external stimuli and invariant- maintenance to the components appropriately. Finally, Phase 2 asks the designer to layer the constituents, where lower-level components communicate status changes upward, and higher-level components make specific service requests of lower-level components. For more details of the DYNAMO design process and a complete elaboration of an example, refer to [10].

## 2.3 Architecture

In DYNAMO, desired system properties are expressed as invariants using OCL. When an external stimulus perturbs the state of the system, invariants must be re-established. We also wish the process to satisfy the non-functional constraints (transparency, flexibility, economy, and intentionality) described above. We call this process *invariant maintenance.* DYNAMO addresses the invariant-maintenance problem by compiling the OCL invariants into wrappers that transparently notify dependent components when they need to take action to re-establish an invariant. In particular, DYNAMO components are organized into a layered, implicit-invocation architecture. The order of layers is determined by the navigation paths occurring in the OCL constraints, thereby improving intentionally. Implicit invocation, because it is provided by wrappers, enhances transparency. Both improvements add to flexibility and reusability. The implementation approach described in the next section addresses the issue of economy.

A DYNAMO design comprises a layered set of components. For each component, event-handling methods, percepts[3], and OCL constraints are identified. The compilation process takes these three elements as input and produces wrapper code as output. At run-time, the wrappers detect and propagate events and update dependent components, thereby maintaining system invariants.

# 3   Metaprogramming Implementation

DYNAMO implementation takes advantage of the metaprogramming features of C++. Specifically, component wrappers are implemented as layered C++ class template instantiations. A class template is a parameterized class definition, where the parameter is usually another class. Moreover, the parameter can be used as the base class of the template class thereby enabling components to be stacked into layers. When combined with C++'s compile-time inlining mechanism, much run-time overhead can be avoided. This section describes how OCL constraints are realized as generated C++ wrappers. To do so, DYNAMO makes use of two devices—status variables and mode components.

## 3.1   Status Variables

A key concept in our approach to solving the invariant-maintenance problem is that of a status variable. The attributes of a component to which other components are sensitive are called its *status*. A *status variable* is a lightweight wrapper on a status attribute that detects changes to its value and announces them to dependent components.

```
class B {
  protected:
    int b;
  public:
    ...
    void tweak(const int& x) {
      b = x;
    }
    ...
};
```

**Figure 1.** Schematic class template for an independent component

To illustrate how status variables work, consider the trivial example of two components, A and B, with integer status attributes a and b, respectively, such that variable a must hold exactly twice the value of variable b, regardless of how b changes. That is, there is an invariant between A and B such that $a = 2 * b$. Expressed in OCL, this invariant is {context A inv: a = 2 * B.b}. It is assumed that the value of b can change in arbitrary ways. Hence, a C++ schematic for

---

3    A *percept* is a unit of presentation that communicates system state to the end user.

```
( 1) template <typename T>
( 2) class StatusVariable {
( 3)    public:
( 4)       StatusVariable() {}
( 5)       StatusVariable(const T& t) : data(t) {}
( 6)       virtual T& operator= (const T& t) {data = t;}
( 7)       virtual operator T() {return data;}
( 8)    protected:
( 9)       T data;
(10) };
```

**Figure 2.** StatusVariable class

component B is shown in **Figure 1**, where tweak is an arbitrary method representative of the various ways in which the value of b might be altered. When tweak is called, b's status changes, thereby requiring an update to a. A solution to the invariant-maintenance problem requires a means of updating component A whenever tweak is invoked.

We implement a status variable's update behavior by wrapping the definition of the variable's class with a *listening agent*, such as is described in [18], that exports the same abstract interface as the existing class. To do this, status variables take advantage of several C++ features, including its ability to overload the assignment operator. That is, when an overloaded assignment is made to a C++ variable, a programmer-provided method is invoked to perform additional activities. The power of status variables is their use of assignment overload to transparently detect changes of status.

Each status variable has its own class that is produced by instantiating the class template StatusVariable<T> shown in **Figure 2**. The template parameter T is the type of the attribute to be wrapped. In the case of attribute b, the type is int. Status variable classes have one attribute of their own, named data (line 9), protected from external access. This attribute holds the actual value being wrapped. Changes to b are trapped by the assignment overload method (operator=) on line 6. This method is virtual (polymorphic) and will be extended in the derived class by a method that notifies component A that b has been altered. The only responsibility that the assignment overload operator has in the StatusVariable class is to assign the new value to data.

Clients of status variables, such as component A, do not know that attribute b has been wrapped. Hence, when they request the value of b, they must be provided an int, not a StatusVariable<int>. C++ provides a supporting mechanism, called a user-defined conversion, as illustrated on line 7 by operator T(). In the example, T is int, and the int() method is invoked whenever the value of b is requested, either explicitly within the code of B, or implicitly, via compiler-generated conversions. Hence, the int value of data is returned whenever the value of the status variable wrapping b is requested. The StatusVariable<T> class also provides constructors (lines 4 and 5) useful both for initially establishing invariants or in case class B provides an externally visible way to initialize b.

```
( 1)  template <typename T>
( 2)  class SV_B_b : public StatusVariable<T> {
( 3)    public:
( 4)      SV_B_b() {}
( 5)      SV_B_b(const T& x) : StatusVariable<T>(x) {}
( 6)      void setUpdater1(Updaters* sc1P) {
( 7)        updater1P = sc1P;
( 8)      }
( 9)      T& operator=(const T& d) {
(10)        StatusVariable<T>::operator=(d);
(11)        if (updater1P)
(12)          updater1P->update1();
(13)      }
(14)    protected:
(15)      Updaters* updater1P;
(16)  };
```

**Figure 3.** Status change announcement mechanism

## 3.2  Using Status Variables

Given a constraint, its dependent and independent variables can be determined[4]. Changes to the independent variables must be detected and the associated dependent variables adjusted to reflect the change. That is, each independent variable in each constraint must be wrapped as an instance of a class derived from StatusVariable<T>. The name of the class is formed from the name of the status variable and the component containing it, thereby ensuring uniqueness. For variable b of component B, the generated template class has the name SV_B_b. SV_B_b has the form illustrated in **Figure 3**.

Note that SV_B_b derives from StatusVariable (line 2) and overrides the assignment operator (lines 9-13). The override invokes the assignment operator in StatusVariable, thereby storing the assigned value. It then invokes an update method (update1). The update method, which also must be generated, lives in component A, as wrapped, and contains the code to retrieve the new value of b and update a accordingly. When SV_B_b is generated, it must know the name of the update method (update1) and which component it lives in (A). It obtains this information when the setUpdater1 method (lines 6-8) is called by the component containing the status variable (B, as wrapped).

---

4    There are some *non-constructive* constraints for which this may not be possible. They are discussed in section 4.5.

```
( 1)  template <typename T>
( 2)  class B_Top : public T {
( 3)    public:
( 4)      B_Top() {};
( 5)      B_Top(const int& x) : T(x) {}
( 6)      int getValue_b(void) {return(b);}
( 7)      void bind_b_1(Updaters* scP) {
( 8)        b.setUpdater1(scP);
( 9)      }
(10)  };
```

**Figure 4.** Mode component wrapper for component B

### 3.3  Mode Components

It remains to describe how dependent components (such as A) are bound to independent components (such as B). In the example, A is responsible for updating the value of a when b is changed. It does this in a generated method, update1 (line 6 of **Figure 5**) That is, a new method for A (update1) is generated, which is called when b changes. Its responsibility is to request the new value of b and, using it, to recompute the value of a. This raises several questions: Where does the code for update1 live? How does b know to call update1? And how does A know how to obtain the value of b?

The update1 method logically lives in component A. However, as we wish to leave existing components untouched to the extent possible, we generate a new wrapper that extends A with the update method. The other two questions can be resolved by further wrapping B in such a way that the required information is available. Once B is wrapped, it becomes a mode component. A *mode component* is a wrapped component containing one or more status variables. The mode component wrapper for B is named B_Top (shown in **Figure 4**), and it is generated based on the status variables and invariants specified for the assembly[5].

B_Top is a class template. Moreover, it is a *mixin* class template [2]. This means that its template parameter is a class, and that B_Top derives from that class. That is, B_Top is a subclass of the class bound to the template parameter T. Mixins are used as a way to provide behavior to a class in addition to that derived from its normal base class. In the case of B_Top, its parameter is B. If A then refers to B_Top instead of B, it will obtain the extended behavior.

---

5   Note that the _Top and _Bot suffixes on template class names refer to their roles in the layered architecture and not to their roles in the inheritance hierarchy. That is, the _Top wrapper provides services that communicate with a component above it in the layered architecture. The relative nesting of the templates is actually in the inverse order to their position in the layering.

```
(1)  template <typename T>
(2)  class A_Bot : public A,
(3)     public Updaters, private T {
(4)     public :
(5)        A_Bot() {myB.bind_b_1(this);}
(6)        void update1() {a = 2 * myB.getValue_b();}
(7)     protected :
(8)        T myB;
(9)  };
```

**Figure 5.** Wrapping dependent components

B_Top adds two methods to those available in B. Method getValue_b provides access to the status variable b's value. It can be called by A when A is alerted to changes in b. Method bind_b_1 illustrates the mechanism whereby A can inform B of any invariant re-establishment methods that must be called when B's status changes. Specifically, bind_b_1 is the means by which changes to b are communicated in order to maintain the first invariant (1). Its argument is a pointer to the update method in A (update1) responsible for maintaining the invariant. bind_b_1's responsibility is to communicate this pointer to the status-variable wrapper for b (line 8 of **Figure 4**).

The binding between components related by invariants is complex. Dependent components like A must be able to request status variable values, such as b. To do this, A must have access to B, the component that contains b. A straightforward way to do this is to have A contain a pointer to B. But pointers are costly, each access requiring the dereferencing of the pointer. The C++ template mechanism can sometimes avoid this overhead by having A derive from B as a mixin. Then A can have direct access to b, just like it can to its own instance variables.

To summarize: A has four responsibilities that arise due to its interaction with B: 1) It must derive from B in order to access it efficiently; 2) it must let B know how to alert it when changes occur; 3) once alerted, it must access the value of b; and 4) it must re- establish the invariant by recomputing the value of a.

To discharge these responsibilities while maintaining transparency, another wrapper is used (**Figure 5**). A_Bot is a mixin class template. Its template parameter is the component upon which it is dependent, B (as wrapped by B_Top). A_Bot mixes B in via private inheritance, thereby hiding B from subsequent classes derived from A. This inheritance discharges responsibility 1. In addition, A_Bot inherits publicly from two other classes, A and Updaters. Updaters is an interface class containing declarations for the types of updater methods.

The key feature of A_Bot is the update1 method on line 6. This is the method called by the status variable b when it detects a change to its own value. Notice that update1 accesses the value of b by using the getValue_b member function of component B. This method discharges responsibility 3. Line 6 also illustrates how the invariant is re-established to discharge responsibility 4.

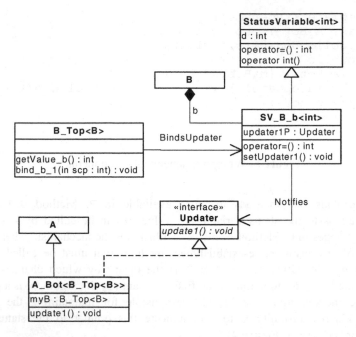

**Figure 6.** Mode component implementation architecture

Responsibility 2 is handled by the wrapper's constructor shown on line 5. When component A is instantiated, the method `bind_b_1` is called in component B, passing the address of component A itself as an argument. The address is passed in turn to the `setUpdater1` method of `SV_B_b`, where it is stored for use when b changes value.

Putting the pieces of the example together requires a nested template instantiation, such as `A_Bot<B_Top> myA;` which declares an assembly myA as the composition of A (as wrapped) with B as wrapped. Notice that stacking components in this fashion easily generalizes. If B itself was dependent on a status variable in component C, another level of nesting could be used.

The overall mode-component architecture is presented in **Figure 6**[6]. Status-Variable<int> contains space for the actual value being monitored and provides default operations for assignment override and type conversion. Actual status variable classes, such as SV_B_b<int>, override the assignment operation to invoke any listeners, such as update1. Updater is an abstract class containing pure virtual methods for each of the constraint update methods. B and A are the original components containing, respectively, attributes b and a. They both must be wrapped in order to become mode components. Because A contains a dependent status variable, a, it is above B in the component layering. Its wrapper, A_Bot, must therefore provide a downward-looking service, update1, for updating status variable a. Conversely, B's

---

6     To simplify the diagram, the template classes themselves and the corresponding «bind» dependencies are not shown.

wrapper, B_Top, must provide upward looking services, such as getValue_b and bind_b_1. GetValue_b enables A to retrieve the updated value of b; bind_b_1 provides a way for letting B know which update service in A to invoke.

### 3.4  Fine Print

In order to clearly explain status variables and mode components, several details of the invariant maintenance process have been glossed over in the description above. Foremost among them is the seeming separation of A's invariant re-establishment wrapper (A_Bot) from B's announcement wrapper (B_Top). In reality, A itself may contain independent status variables participating in other invariants. For example, component Z might depend on variable a of component A. This would imply the need to generate an A_Top wrapper similar to B_Top. Because of the nesting enabled by C++ templates, both A_Top and A_Bot can be used to wrap A.

Other details not discussed are status variable initialization and the initial establishment of any relevant invariants. If, for example, component B provides a way to initialize the value of variable b, then the generated code has to include a memberwise initializer for it that incorporates a call to any relevant updaters. The actual compilation process also includes generating several include files providing access to required names.

Another issue concerns OCL collection classes. The example elaborated on in this section does not make use of any of collections. Actually, collection classes themselves are just another form of value that can serve either a dependent or independent role in an invariant. But we do not want a change to a single element of a collection to alert all components dependent on the collection, but only those dependent on the altered element. C++ template nesting can help address this issue as well. We have experimented with inserting intermediate template class instantiations, called *data transformers*, that can optimize certain invariant-reestablishment operations on collections by intercepting and mediating the corresponding update requests.

The example also made only fleeting use of OCL navigation. In actual practice, OCL constraints can included a cascade of classifier names to relate topologically distant components. Navigation such as this can be handled in DYNAMO by using C++'s name scoping operator ( : : ) to directly access variables in nested components.

### 3.5  Extending the Example

The approach described above illustrated how an invariant dependent on a single status variable can be maintained. Real systems are more complex. This section describes how the example can be generalized.

**Multiple status variables.** For each status variable x of type $T_x$ aggregated by a component K, there is a corresponding generated class SV_K_x. Each x must be defined within K as a normal instance variable, but with type SV_K_x$<T_x>$. There is no limit to how many such variables K can have. Note that it is the responsibility of each component to maintain its own intracomponent invariants.

**Multiple constraints.** A given independent status variable, x, belonging to component K, may be involved in multiple constraints ($C_i$). Hence, multiple updates may have to be performed when the value of x changes. For each such constraint, an update method (updateC$_i$) and a bind method (bind_x_C$_i$) must be generated. Moreover, the code in the SV_K_x class must invoke each of the updater methods (updateC$_i$). Finally, the addresses of the updater methods must be remembered in the SV_K_x class with function pointers (updaterC$_i$P).

**Circularities.** In the example above, component A is notified of changes to component B and then requests new values from it. The mode component mechanism for accomplishing this takes advantage of the C++ ability to nest templates. That is, component A as wrapped has as a template parameter component B as wrapped. This mechanism is inherently asymmetric. That is, it cannot be used to have component A notify component B because of the resultant circularity in the template instantiation ordering.

Several things should be noted about a circular dependency such as this. First, there is no reason why components A and B cannot use traditional intercomponent messaging when A needs to notify B of a change. That is, B can provide an update method that A can call directly. The second observation is that a circularity is often a symptom of a design problem. One manifestation of the problem is an endless loop— B notifying A which notifies B, repeatedly. Hence, any circularity in the dependency graph may be a sign of a design problem and should be carefully examined.

**Multiple components per layer.** Sometimes circular dependencies are inherent but do not lead to an endless loop. This can occur when a status variable (p) in one component depends on a status variable (q) in another, and q depends on a different status variable (r) in the first. While this situation is circular as far as template nesting is concerned, it does not lead to infinite update when one of the variables is changed. As an alternative to the asymmetric mechanism of mode components, both components can be configured as nested classes contained within a single mode component class, such as with mixin layers [16].

## 3.6  Tool Support

DYNAMO designs are expressed using an OCL-capable UML modeling tool such as Rational/IBM [8] or ArgoUML [19]. These tools support the export of diagram content and associated OCL annotations in the industry-standard XMI CASE-data interchange format [13]. We have written tools for extracting relevant information from XMI, representing it in a target-independent abstract syntax tree (AST) and generating code from the AST. Code generation consists of two steps: conversion to an internal representation (IR) and traversal of the IR to generate C++ wrapper templates. Further details concerning the compilation process can be found in reference [14].

# 4   Evaluation

## 4.1   Transparency

What alterations to the source code of existing components are required in order to make them into mode components? Only one change is necessary on the part of a programmer—the types of status variables must be adjusted. That is, member variables of components upon which other components are dependent must be so designated. Two scenarios can be imagined. In the first, the original designer of a component library is seriously concerned with reuse. Components are developed, and potentially interesting status is declared as such in the component code. The second scenario is the adaptation of an existing component into a mode component. In this case, the adaptor must not only decide what facilities of the component are required of other components, but must also locate the definitions of these variables in the code, so that their types may be altered. In both scenarios, the coding effort required of the developer consists of adding some `#include` statements and changing the types of the status variable declarations. Any scheme for intercomponent invariant maintenance must provide access to the constituent state. Hence, we judge the mode component approach to be adequately transparent.

## 4.2   Flexibility

The DYNAMO approach is flexible in several senses. First is the fact that alternative components with the same APIs can be substituted for each other. Moreover, additional component can be inserted to provide optimizations and other enhancements. These added or substituted components simply amount to interpolated templates in the C++ code. DYNAMO is also flexible in a different sense. Mode components are not the only scheme for maintaining invariants. For example, mediators [17] provide many of the same features. More conventional approaches to invariant maintenance in C++, such as aggregated components with embedded pointers and explicit delegation can also be used. The DYNAMO compilation architecture has been successfully applied to these alternative approaches. That is, the DYNAMO compilation approach is flexible with respect to the specific mechanism for updating status to maintain invariants.

## 4.3   Economy

Flexibility normally leads to overhead. Typically, flexibility is achieved by using indirection through pointers. Using pointers implies dereferencing, which, in turn, means an extra operation on every access. Our approach reduces overhead by making use of two features of C++: template classes and inlining.

Components are normally constructed independently and encapsulated in their own classes. This reduces coupling and enhances maintainability. But, because components need to interact, they often hold pointers to each other. Another approach is to have one component be a subclass of another. Then the subordinate can directly access the features of the superordinate component without the pointer overhead. But such an approach is intrusive and unnatural. Mixin inheritance is an alternative to subtyping—a mixin adds a feature to a class without requiring that the mixin be an explicit subtype.

The other C++ feature that can reduce overhead is *inlining*. Normally, the compilation of a method call introduces significant overhead at the calling site. The C++ compiler can detect situations where a copy of the code for the called method can be inserted directly at the call site without the associated overhead. This technique is particularly applicable when the method code is short, such as obtains with instance-variable access routines (getters and setters). In this way, components can retain their encapsulation without engendering normal intercomponent communication overhead. Templates and inlining enable our approach to provide low overhead invariant maintenance.

### 4.4  Intentionality

The overarching goal of the DYNAMO work on component assembly is to increase assurance. It accomplishes this by providing an invariant-maintenance mechanism. Invariants are directly manifest in the code. In particular, each independent variable in each invariant results in the generation of a status-variable wrapper to provide change notification and an update method to re-establish the invariant when one of its constituents changes. Because this code is generated, it is possible for the designer to have confidence that the specification is being met. Hence, the approach is intentional[7].

### 4.5  Limitations

The DYNAMO approach, while satisfying the above-described non-functional goals, is not without limitations. Some of these are described here.

- **Loss of symmetry:** Components nested as template mixins are inherently asymmetric. This loss of flexibility is compensated for by the reduced overhead they require.

- **Constructiveness:** Not every invariant can be expressed as a mode component constraint. Constraints in which a single variable appears on the left hand side[8] are called constructive. This is a theoretical limitation of the approach that has not proven a problem in practice.

- **Circularities:** More serious are cyclically dependent constraints, as for example, happens if variable a depends on variable b in one constraint, and variable b depends on variable a in another. Run-time update of one variable can lead to an infinite cascade of invariant re-establishments. In DYNAMO, such co-dependencies can be grouped into the same mixin layer, providing a symmetric solution.

---

7    *Intentional Programming* [4] is an alternative metaprogramming approach that provides intentionality.

8    Some constraints may be algebraically manipulated to solve for a target independent variable.

- **Code obfuscation:** The DYNAMO metaprogramming approach generates C++. Several difficulties arise if this code needs to be maintained. First, the generated code comprises deeply nested class templates; reading and understanding it requires in-depth knowledge of C++. Also, should the code ever have to be edited and recompiled, any ensuing compiler error messages will be hard to interpret.

## 5   Related Work

There are a variety of design strategies for maintaining invariants among an assembly of components. At one extreme, an invariant can be implemented as an explicit integration component, distinct from the components it integrates (hereafter referred to as its integrands). Under this approach, the integration component might be a peer of its integrands, as is the case with mediators [17], or it might encapsulate its integrands, as with GenVoca layers [1]. Some designs even employ a hybrid of these approaches. For example, Java AWT programmers define containers, which (like layers) encapsulate GUI components but which (like mediators) listen for events from these components [7]. At the other extreme, an invariant can be implemented as a collaboration [20], which distribute the responsibilities for maintaining the invariants among the integrands. An alternative to choosing an invariant maintenance mechanism at the time when the code is written is delaying the decision until assembly time. This has been called the *flexible- packaging* problem, and an approach to providing it is described in [5].

DYNAMO makes use of the template processing mechanism of the C++ compiler to obtain its metaprogramming functions. An alternative approach is provided by the Open C++ project [3]. Open C++ adds the meta-object protocol to the C++ compiler. That is, programmer have the ability to reprogram the compiler by, for example, telling it what to do when it sees a new construct, such as a `MonitoredClass`. This construct might be realized with code that counts method calls or variable updates. The metaprogrammer is responsible for using available features of the Open C++ API to write metaprograms for doing the counting. We have successfully applied this tool to generate DYNAMO status variable updates, so it would seem to provide a viable alternative to the template program approach described in this paper. A survey of other work on invariant maintenance can be found in reference [15].

On the issue of implementation, currently, the most complete OCL compiler comes from the Dresden University of Technology and supports OCL 1.4. To support OCL 2.0, the Dresden development team is redesigning their compiler as described in reference . The Dresden compiler features a MOF (Meta Object Facility) Repository that manages models and meta-models by providing interfaces for their access. The code generator itself is designed to take instances of the OCL metamodel as input and output Java code without altering the state of the environment.

## 6  Summary and Conclusions

A high-assurance system behaves as you expect it to and, just as importantly, you know that it does so. The enemy of assurance is complexity, and the main weapons in fighting complexity are abstraction, transparency and intentionality. DYNAMO uses model-based specifications written in OCL to express system properties at a high level of abstraction. Wrapper code is then generated in such a way that each of the specified invariants are mapped transparently and intentionally into self-contained classes without compromising existing code. Two additional benefits accrue from the DYNAMO approach: flexibility and economy. The code generation architecture and the design of the wrapper code are such that the choice of collaboration mechanism can be made flexibly at assembly time. And the generated code avoids much of the costly indirection common in alternative invariant-maintenance mechanisms.

The DYNAMO approach is one of invariant maintenance. That is, critical system properties are expressed as assembly invariants. An assembly invariant relates aspects of one component with those of others. When the state of the former component changes in such a way that a participant in the invariant is altered, dependent components must be notified and the invariant re-established.

A variety of approaches have been developed for invariant maintenance, and DYNAMO introduces another, called a mode component. Mode components are wrapped components organized into a layered, implicit-invocation architecture. The wrapping is such that changes to the state of the underlying component are detected and notification made to dependent components without explicit coupling to those components.

DYNAMO code generation makes use of the metaprogramming capabilities of the C++ language and compiler. Specifically, DYNAMO expresses the various invariant maintenance mechanisms as templates that are processed at compile time, rather than run-time. Moreover, the templates are organized as mixins, thereby reducing the need for indirection. The resulting code provides a low-overhead approach to solving the invariant-maintenance problem.

## Acknowledgments

The PIs on this project wish to thank the following student participants: Jonathan Gdalevich, Corinne McNeely, Terry Shikano, Patrick Yaner, and David Zook from Georgia Tech and Reimer Behrends and AliReza Namvar from Michigan State. We also wish to thank colleague Laura Dillon from Michigan State. This effort was sponsored by the Defense Advanced Research Projects Agency, and the United States Air Force Research Laboratory, under agreement number F30602-00-2-0618. Other support was provided by Office of Naval Research grant N00014-01-1-0744 and by NSF grants EIA-0000433 and CCR-9984726.

# References

1. D. Batory and S. O'Malley. "The Design and Implementation of Hierarchical Software Systems with Reusable Components." *ACM Transactions on Software Engineering and Methodology,* 1(4):355–398, October 1992.

2. Gilad Bracha and William Cook. "Mixin-based Inheritance." *Proceedings ECOOP/ OOPSLA '90,* October 21-25, 1990, 303-311.

3. Shigeru Chiba. OpenC++ Home Page. http://www.csg.is.titech.ac.jp/~chiba/ openc++.html.

4. Krzysztof Czarnecki and Ulrich W. Eisenecker. "Intentional Programming" Chapter 11 in *Generative Programming.* Addison Wesley, 2000.

5. R. DeLine. "Avoiding Packaging Mismatch with Flexible Packaging." *Proceedings IEEE International Conference on Software Engineering,* pp. 97–106, 1999.

6. David Garlan and Curtis Scott. "Adding Implicit Invocation to Traditional Programming Languages." *International Conference on Software Engineering,* 1993, pp. 447-453.

7. J. Gosling and F. Yellin. *The Java Application Programming Interface, Volume 2: Window Toolkit and Applets.* Addison-Wesley, 1996.

8. International Business Machine Corp. "Rational Software." http://www-306.ibm.com/ software/rational/.

9. Loecher, Sten and Ocke, Stefan. "A Metamodel-Based OCL-Compiler for UML and MOF." Department of Computer Science. Dresden University of Technology. September 2003.

10. Corinne McNeely, Spencer Rugaber, Kurt Stirewalt, and David Zook. "DYNAMO Design Guidebook." Technical Report GIT-CC-02-37, College of Computing, Georgia Institute of Technology, June 27, 2002, ftp://ftp.cc.gatech.edu/pub/coc/tech_reports/2002/GIT-CC-02-37.ps.Z.

11. N. Medvidovic, D. S. Rosenblum, D. F. Redmiles and J. E. Robbins. "Modeling Software Architectures in UML." *ACM Transactions on Software Engineering and Methodology,* 11(1):2-57, January, 2002.

12. Object Management Group. "Unified Modeling Language, Version 1.4." OMG Document Number 01-09-67, Chapter 6, http://www.omg.org/cgi-bin/apps/doc?formal/01-09- 67.pdf.

13. Object Management Group. "XML Metadata Interchange (XMI)." http://www.omg.org/ technology/documents/formal/xmi.htm.

14. Spencer Rugaber and Kurt Stirewalt. "Metaprogramming Compilation of Invariant Maintenance Wrappers from OCL Constraints." Technical Report GIT-CC-03-46, College of Computing, Georgia Institute of Technology, October 28, 2003, http://www.cc.gatech.edu/dynamo/papers/compile.pdf.

15. Spencer Rugaber and Kurt Stirewalt. "Final Project Report / Dynamic Assembly from Models (DYNAMO)". Technical Report, GIT-CC-05-03, College of Computing, Georgia Institute of Technology, March 2005, ftp://ftp.cc.gatech.edu/pub/coc/tech_reports/2005/ GIT-CC-05-03.pdf.

16. Y. Smaragdakis and D. Batory. "Implementing Layered Designs with Mixin Layers." *Proceedings of the 12th European Conference on Object-oriented Programming,* 1998.

17. K. Sullivan and D. Notkin. "Reconciling Environment Integration and Software Evolution." *ACM Transactions on Software Engineering and Methodology,* 1(3):229–268, July 1992.

18. R. N. Taylor *et al.* "Chiron-1: A Software Architecture for User Interface Development, Maintenance, and Run-Time Support." *ACM Transactions on Computer-Human Interaction,* 2(2):105–144, June 1995.
19. Tigris.org. "Welcome to ArgoUML." http://argouml.tigris.org/.
20. M. VanHilst and D. Notkin. "Using Role Components to Implement Collaboration-Based Designs." *Proceedings of OOPSLA 1996,* pp. 359–369, 1996.
21. Jos Warmer and Anneke Kleppe. *The Object Constraint Language.* Addison Wesley, 1999.

# SelfSync: A Dynamic Round-Trip Engineering Environment

Ellen Van Paesschen[1], Wolfgang De Meuter[2], and Maja D'Hondt[2]

[1] Programming Technology Laboratory
Vrije Universiteit Brussel
Pleinlaan 2, 1050 Brussel, Belgium
evpaessc@vub.ac.be
[2] Laboratoire d'Informatique Fondamentale de Lille
Université des Sciences et Technologies de Lille
59655 Villeneuve d'Ascq, Cédex, Lille, France
wdmeuter@vub.ac.be, maja.d-hondt@lifl.fr

**Abstract.** Model-Driven Engineering (MDE) advocates the generation of software applications from models, which are views on certain aspects of the software. In this paper, we focus on a particular setup which consists of a graphical data modeling view and a view on an object-oriented implementation, which can be either textual or graphical. A challenge that arizes in the context of MDE is the notion of *Round-Trip Engineering* (RTE), where elements from both views can be manipulated and thus need to be synchronized. We systematically identify four fundamental RTE scenarios. In this paper, we employ the framework of these scenarios for explaining *SelfSync*, our approach and tool for providing dynamic support for RTE. In SelfSync, the entities of the data modeling view and the corresponding implementation objects are one and the same. Additionally, we present a comparison with related work accompanied by an extensive discussion.

## 1 Introduction

*Model-Driven Engineering* (MDE) advocates generating software applications from models, which are views on certain aspects of the software. One commonly found approach is to support one or more graphical modeling views on the one hand and an implementation view on the other, which can be either textual, i.e. the actual source code, or graphical. In this paper, we focus on a particular setup which consists of a *data modeling* view and a view on an *object-oriented* implementation.

An important issue that arizes in the context of MDE is the notion of *Round-Trip Engineering* (RTE). Several definitions exist of RTE, but all boil down to the following: when there exist at least two views on a software artefact, each view can be used to manipulate the artefact and all the other views need to be synchronized accordingly [1], [6], [12], [20]. RTE often considers a setup similar to the one we outlined above. Therefore, the challenge in this setup is that both

L. Briand and C. Williams (Eds.): MoDELS 2005, LNCS 3713, pp. 633–647, 2005.

the data modeling view and the object-oriented implementation (view) can be manipulated and thus need to be synchronized. In this paper, we identify four fundamental RTE scenarios that cover the range of possible changes to both views.

We provide a very dynamic approach to RTE, where the entities of the data modeling view and the corresponding implementation objects are one and the same [17], [16]. This contrasts with other approaches, which usually employ a synchronization strategy based on transformation [12], [20], [28]. In this paper, we first present our approach and accompanying tool, SelfSync, in Section 2. We then present the four identified RTE scenarios in Section 3. Next we show how our approach and tool address these four scenarios in Sections 4 to 7. We present and discuss related work in Section 8. Finally, we conclude in Section 9.

## 2   SelfSync

SelfSync supports data modeling in an *Extended Entity-Relationship* (EER) diagram [4] and object-oriented programming in the prototype-based language *Self* [21], [26]. In this section we elaborate on these two parts while introducing an example (sections 2.1 and 2.2). We then explain how SelfSync is used to prototype applications rapidly (section 2.3). Finally, we describe the three views that SelfSync synchronizes during Round-Trip Engineering (section 2.4).

### 2.1   EER Modeling

EER diagrams consist of the typical data modeling elements, similar to *Class Diagrams* in the *Unified Modeling Language* (UML) [9]: entities (classes in the UML), attributes and operations[3] in entities, and association and inheritance relations between entities. The associations can be 1-to-1, 1-to-many, and many-to-many. There are some variants of the typical data modeling elements, such as entities and weak entities, and simple, primary and derived attributes. The EER notation we use combines existing approaches: Chen's boxes [4], the relations of the crow's feet notation and the cardinalities of [7] [4]. We use different colours to denote the differences between entities and weak entities, and between simple, primary and derived attributes. We want to stress that our new combined notation is merely a consequence of our choice of development platform.

In Figure 1 an EER model of a moderate banking system is shown. This example is used throughout the paper. A Customer has a primary attribute customerID and simple attributes customerName, customerStreet and customerCity. Customer is in a many-to-many relation with Loan (role borrows) and with Account (role accounts), and in a many-to-one relation with Employee (role banker). Payment is a weak entity that is dependent of Loan. An Account can be specialized into a SavingsAccount or a CheckingsAccount.

---

[3] We extended the standard EER diagram with operations in addition to attributes.
[4] The order of cardinalities is reversed, as in the Object Modeling Technique

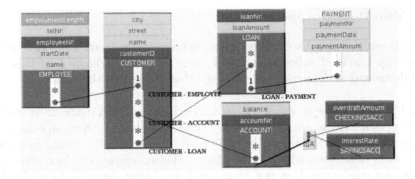

**Fig. 1.** An EER diagram for a moderate banking system.

## 2.2   Self

The object-oriented implementation language we employ is the prototype-based language Self. In general, prototype-based languages can be considered object-oriented languages without classes. As such, a *prototype* is used for sharing data between objects and new objects can be created by cloning a prototype. Self, however, introduces another programming idiom, *traits*, which share behavior among objects and let objects inherit from them, which allows for simulating classes [3]. Note that in Self everything is an object, more specifically prototypes, traits and cloned objects, which can again be prototypes.

The Self development environment provides support for visual programming using *outliners*, graphical views on objects. Objects, attributes and methods can be created and initialized using menus of the outliners. This is depicted in Figure 2 by the two boxes on the top left, labeled *Self code* and *Self outliners*.

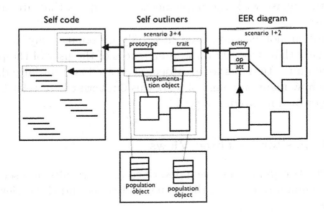

**Fig. 2.** The setup of our tool for supporting Round-Trip Engineering.

## 2.3   Two-Phased Approach

We distinguish two phases when using SelfSync, which are typically but not necessarily executed subsequently. For each phase we indicate how this setup is implemented and provide terminology that is used in the remainder of this paper.

In the first, *active modeling* phase a user draws an EER diagram while corresponding Self objects are automatically created. In reality, these objects *are* the modeled entities: drawing a new EER entity automatically results in an EER entity *view* being created on a new object. Hence, we support incremental and continuous synchronization *per entity* and *per object*: changes to an EER entity are in fact changes to the outliner of an object and thus are automatically propagated to the object via Self's reflection mechanism. Similarly, changes to an object, made via the object's outliner, are automatically propagated to the corresponding EER entity. View-dependent information, such as relationships constraints in the EER diagram and method bodies in the Self objects, is preserved during changes and subsequent synchronization.

Our implementation strategy consists of generating per entity a prototype for sharing the entity's data and a traits object for sharing its behavior. This results in the following setup, again depicted in Figure 2: the top right-hand box in this figure is the *EER diagram*, whose entities are mapped to the corresponding Self outliners. Each entity corresponds to a prototype-traits pair, bounded in a dashed box. This is denoted by the arrow from the entity in the EER model to the dashed box containing prototype and traits outliners. We refer to the prototype-traits pair that implements a certain entity from the EER diagram as an *implementation object*.

The second phase of our approach is an *interactive prototyping* process[5]. This phase allows a user to create and initialize ready-to-use objects from each implementation object created in the previous phase, thus *populating* the application. With the notion of a *population object* we distinguish the objects that result from this phase with the implementation objects that are created in the previous phase.

This phase cannot be supported in a fully automatic way, because choices need to be made that depend on the preferences of the user of the program. For example, when an actual `Customer` object is created and initialized, our system asks the user how many `Account` objects this `Customer` is to refer to, which can be any number or unlimited.

## 2.4   One Repository – Three Views

Performing the two-phase approach described above results in a setup that consists of one common repository, the actual Self code, and three views on it:

---

[5] Note that a *prototype* is a special object in prototype-based languages for supporting data sharing of several objects whereas *prototyping* is the activity of instantiating and initializing a program into a ready-to-use, running system.

- the EER data modeling view: consists of all the information pertaining to entities (attributes and operations) as well as inheritance between entities and associations with multiplicities between entities
- a code-time implementation view: the outliners on the implementation objects, which show everything related to object-oriented programs; programmers can enrich the implementation objects with additional attribute slots, fill in the method bodies, create new implementation objects manually, etc. Note that relations in the implementation view are implicit since these occur when a certain object has one or more objects as attribute.
- a run-time implementation view: (the outliners on) the population objects, which contain actual data for running the application

SelfSync synchronizes the three views, which is partly facilitated because the objects in the three views are actually different views on the same Self code. On the other hand, view-dependent information is not visible in all the views. For example, multiplicities in EER diagrams are not visible in the population objects but are nevertheless enforced by SelfSync.

# 3   Round-Trip Engineering Scenarios

Round-Trip Engineering is especially crucial in the context of MDE, where multiple views of a software application can in principle be manipulated and the other views need to be synchronized accordingly [1], [6], [12], [20]. When considering a graphical model as one view and the (graphical or textual) source code as another, Round-Trip Engineering typically considers *forward* and a *backward* activities. The former consists of changing the graphical model after which the source code needs to be synchronized with the model. The latter denotes changes to the source code and subsequent synchronization steps to the graphical model.

Based on the direction of synchronization we make a distinction between the views the changes take place in: 1) the EER data modeling view and 2) the code-time object-oriented implementation view both described at the end of Section 2.4. The data modeling view represents synchronization in the forward direction, whereas the code-time implementation view represents the inverse. All elements contained in these views can *evolve*, which we use in this paper as a collective term for being created, changed or deleted.

Based on which kinds of elements evolve in a view, we make another distinction in Round-Trip Engineering: 1) changes to entities, attributes and operations in the data modeling view, and changes to implementation objects, data and method slots in the code-time implementation view and 2) changes to association and inheritance relations in the data modeling view, and changes to relations between implementation objects in the code-time implementation view.

Each of the four scenarios corresponds to a particular direction of Round-Trip Engineering and particular elements that are changed and subsequently synchronized as summarized in Table 1:

**Table 1.** The four scenarios that cover synchronization between a graphical data modeling view and an OO code-time implementation view.

| | Entities | Relations |
|---|---|---|
| Data modeling view | Scenario 1 | Scenario 2 |
| OO code-time implementation view | Scenario 3 | Scenario 4 |

**scenario 1:** changes to entities, attributes and operations in the data modeling view, which are synchronized in both the code-time and the run-time implementation view

**scenario 2:** changes to association and inheritance relations in the data modeling view, which are synchronized in both the code-time and the run-time implementation view

**scenario 3:** changes to implementation objects, data and method slots in the implementation view, which are synchronized in the data modeling view

**scenario 4:** changes to (implicit) relations in the implementation view, which are synchronized in the data modeling view

Note that in scenario 1 and 2 when operations or relations in the data model evolve, this can impact the population objects in the run-time implementation view. In Figure 2 the four scenarios are situated in the different views of the SelfSync architecture.

## 4   Scenario 1: Entity Evolution from Model to Code

We use the banking system EER model (see Figure 1) as an example. This model is extended to support simple insurances. We illustrate the scenario with the following steps:

1. Add two new entities `insurance` and `insurer` to the banking system model
2. Add a new attribute `policyNr` to `insurance`
3. Add a new attribute `insuredObject` to `insurance`
4. Add a new operation `checkClaim` to `insurance`

To realize the entity evolution scenario, the following actions are performed in SelfSync at code-time, by the user followed by our automated synchronization mechanism:

1. Add a new blank entity view to the EER diagram via the appropriate menu and name it `insurer`. *Synchronization steps:* First, a new blank entity view becomes graphically visual; since this is a new view on a new implementation object, a new implementation object is automatically created. This newly created implementation object contains no public data slots and an empty traits object to contain methods. The implementation object is automatically saved in the `banking` schema object. The name of the graphical entity view in the diagram is changed to `insurer`, this is propagated automatically onto the viewed implementation object.

2. Analoguously to step 1, the entity view `insurance` is added.

3. Next, we add a new attribute to the graphical entity view `insurance` via the appropriate menu, and name it `policyNr`. *Synchronization steps:* First a blank attribute (dark/light blue) becomes graphically visual inside the `insurance` entity view. Automatically, a new data slot is added to the `insurance` implementation object. The renaming is propagated to the implementation object by renaming the original data slot in the implementation object. This implies that changes to the contents of the data slot in the implementation object are not lost when the corresponding attribute in the entity view is renamed.

4. Similarly, a new operation is added to the `insurance` entity view via the appropriate menu, and is named `checkClaim`. *Synchronization steps:* First a blank operation (red) becomes graphically visual inside the `insurance` entity view. Automatically, a new method slot is added to the traits object of the `insurance` implementation object. The renaming is propagated to the traits object by renaming the original method slot. The body of the method can be viewed and edited from inside the entity view: the changes are propagated to the method body in the implementation object.

Deleting attributes and operations automatically results in deleting the corresponding data or method slot in the implementation object. Deleting an entire entity view automatically results in deleting the implementation object from the banking schema object.

By adding, removing, renaming, and changing an operation to an entity view, all run-time population objects that are created from the entity view's code-time implementation object, are affected. This is a consequence of adding corresponding method slots in the traits object of the code-time implementation objects, that are shared by the code-time implementation object as well as by all its run-time population objects.

## 5 Scenario 2: Relationship and Specialization Evolution from Model to Code

We use the banking system EER model (see Figure 1) as an example. This model is extended to support simple insurances. We illustrate the scenario with the following steps:

1. Specialize the entity `employee` into `insurer` in the banking system model
2. Add a new 1-to-n relation between the entities `customer` and `insurance` in the banking system model

To realize the entity evolution scenario, the following actions are performed in SelfSync at code-time, by the user followed by our automated synchronization mechanism:

1. Add a new specialization to the EER diagram from the entity view `insurer` to the entity view `employee`, via the appropriate menu. *Synchronization*

*steps:* Automatically, the `insurer` implementation object inherits from the `employee` implementation object. Deleting the specialization in the EER model automatically results in removing the inheritance between the two implementation objects.

2. Add a new 1-to-n relationship between the entity views `insurer` and `customer`, via the appropriate menu. *Synchronization steps:* Automatically a slot called `1_to_n_relation_insurer_customer` is added to both viewed implementation objects `insurer` and `customer`. This slot contains a reference to the other partner entity object. Deleting the relationship in the EER model automatically results in deleting the slot.

After the interactive prototyping phase a 1-to-1 or 1-to-n relationship between two entity views also results in satisfying the cardinality constraints imposed by these relations. When two entity views are in a relationship in which the first one has a single reference (one or zero) to the second one, the uniqueness of this reference is enforced in the run-time population objects in two ways. First we ensure that all run-time population objects (i.e. the clones) of the first code-time implementation object's type (i.e. the prototype) have at most one reference to run-time population objects of the second code-time implementation object's type. Secondly, we also ensure that only one run-time population object of the second code-time implementation object's type refers to run-time population objects of the first type. If two entity views are in a 1-to-1 relationship, this is enforced in the two directions. Our system checks for violation of these constraints, each time the slots of a run-time population object are updated.

Adding dependencies between two entity views results in another kind of enforcement. In this case we ensure that when a run-time population object is deleted, all run-time population objects whose corresponding entity view is dependent of the entity view of the deleted run-time population object, are deleted also.

Note that since the multiplicity and dependency information is stored in the traits objects shared by both code-time implementation and run-time population objects, changing relationships and multiplicities or dependencies in the EER diagram affects also existing run-time population objects.

# 6   Scenario 3: Object Evolution from Code to Model

We use the banking system EER implementation as an example. When a new code-time implementation objects is created it is installed in the schema object and its entity view becomes visual. When an entire code-time implementation object is deleted, the entity view automatically dissapears from the EER diagram. The other cases are illustrated with the following steps:

1. Add a new attribute `insurer` to the implementation object `insurance` in the banking system implementation
2. Rename the attribute `insurer` in the implementation object `insurance` to *myInsurer*

3. Add a new method `extendPolicy = ('to be implemented')` to the implementation object `insurance`
4. Change the body of `extendPolicy` in the implementation object `insurance` to `(numberOfInsuredObjects: (numberOfInsuredObjects + 1))`

To realize the entity evolution scenario, the following actions are performed in SelfSync at code-time, by the user followed by our automated synchronization mechanism:

1. Add a new data slot to the `insurance` implementation object via the main Self object menu and name it *insurer*. *Synchronization steps:* Automatically, the `insurance` entity view in the EER model is extended with a new attribute `insurer`. Note that deleting a data slot in an implementation object automatically results in deleting the corresponding attribute in the entity view.
2. Rename the `insurer` data slot in the `insurance` implementation object to *myInsurer* by double-clicking it. *Synchronization steps:* Automatically, the `insurer` attribute in the `insurance` entity view in the EER model is renamed to `myInsurer`.
3. Add a new method slot `extendPolicy = ('to be implemented')` to the implementation object `insurance`. *Synchronization steps:* Automatically, the `insurance` entity view in the EER model is extended with a new method attribute `extendPolicy`. When this method body is viewed or edited in the `insurance` entity view in the EER model via the operation menu, the text `'to be implemented'` becomes visible. Note that deleting a method slot in an implementation object automatically results in deleting the corresponding operation in the entity view.
4. Change the body of `extendPolicy` to `(numberOfInsuredObjects: (numberOfInsuredObjects + 1))` by clicking the method body symbol in the `insurance` implementation object. *Synchronization steps:* When the method body of the `extendPolicy` operation is viewed or edited in the `insurance` entity view in the EER model via the operation menu, the new body `(numberOfInsuredObjects: (numberOfInsuredObjects + 1))` becomes visible.

When these changes are applied to run-time population objects, the entity views of the corresponding code-time implementation objects are not affected.

## 7 Scenario 4: Reference and Inheritance Evolution from Code to Model

We use the banking system EER implementation as an example. We illustrate the scenario with the following steps:

1. Change the contents of the attribute `myInsurer` in the implementation object `insurance` to contain the `insurer` implementation object.
2. Create a new child of the implementation object `insurance`

To realize the entity evolution scenario, the following actions are performed in SelfSync at code-time, by the user followed by our automated synchronization mechanism:

1. Set the contents of the `myInsurer` data slot in the `insurance` implementation object to contain the `insurer` implementation object either via the appropriate Self menu, a user action, or at run-time. *Synchronization steps:* Automatically, a one-to-one relationship link is drawn between the `insurance` entity view and the `insurer` entity view in the EER model, given no 1-to-1 link is drawn between them currently. This synchronization is performed dynamically: when we manually remove the 1-to-1 link in the EER model, it is automatically re-drawn, each time the Self system updates the slots of the `insurance` implementation object and discovers that it (still) contains a reference to the `insurer` implementation object

2. Create a new child of the implementation object `insurance` via the Self main menu. *Synchronization steps:* Automatically, a new entity view is added to the EER model. Simultaneously, a new implementation object has been created, inheriting the slots of the `insurance` implementation object. Next a new "is-a" link is drawn between the new entity view and the `insurance` entity view in the EER model.

When these changes are applied to run-time population objects, the entity views of the corresponding code-time implementation objects are not affected.

# 8    Related Work and Discussion

We situate our approach in the intersection of three domains: Round-Trip Engineering, visual programming and agile development. We discuss Borland's Together (section 8.1) and the Naked Objects approach (section 8.2), respectively, as representatives for the first two domains. A concrete instance of agile modeling and other related work can be found in Section 8.3. In Section 8.4 we compare SelfSync to the related approaches.

## 8.1    Round-Trip Engineering

The state-of-the-art in RTE includes application such as Rational XDE [25], Borland Together [28], and FUJABA [22]. One of the leaders in this domain is Borland's Together. This set of commercial tools provides support for modeling, designing, implementing, debugging, and testing applications. The synchronization mechanism between UML class diagrams and implementation is realized by the *LiveSource* technology. More specifically, the implementation model (i.e. the source code) is parsed and rendered as two views: a UML class diagram and in a formatted textual form. LiveSource is in fact a code parsing engine. The user can manipulate either view and even the implementation model. However, all user actions are translated directly to the implementation model and then translated back to both views. We discuss the relation to SelfSync in Section 8.4.

Other related work in RTE, is mostly concerned with characterizing RTE rather than providing concrete tool support. In [1], RTE is described as a system with at least two views that can be manipulated. Applying the inverse transformation $f^{-1}$ on a view that is transformed using $f$, should again yield the same view. The Automatic Roundtrip Engineering [1] approach advocates the automatic derivation of this inverse transformation function based on the original transformation function. Our approach is based on Model-View-Controller (MVC) [10]. Therefore, a change initiated in a view is not actually performed in the view, but in the underlying implementation element, which results in the relevant views being automatically updated.

In [20] RTE is connected to inconsistency handling. In SelfSync, MVC makes inconsistency handling superfluous since no inconsistencies are introduces for the same reasons explained above. The same work states that RTE is not merely a combination of forward and backward engineering since there is not always a one-to-one mapping between similar elements in different views. In contrast, we deliberately assume such a mapping in order to automate the synchronization bidirectionally.

## 8.2   Visual Programming

At the level of visual programming we compare SelfSync to the Naked Objects [18], [24] approach that also applies MVC, but in one direction: from code to model. Building a business system consists solely of defining the domain business objects (i.e. code-time implementation objects) in Java, which immediately are made visible to and manipulable by the user in a business object model. The Naked Objects Java framework represents classes as icons and uses Java interfaces to determine the methods of any business object and render them visible on the screen by means of a generic viewing mechanism.

With respect to run-time support, the user can visually create new business objects, specify their attributes, add associations between them, or invoke methods on them. The ready-to-use objects are visually represented and automatically created and updated in the Java program.

## 8.3   Other Related Work

In this section we describe other related work that is not discussed in detail but included for completeness.

Since the late eighties, it has been encouraged to combine (E)ER models and object-orientation (OO) [5], [15]. Various approaches and techniques exist for translating EER into object-orientation [8], [14], [11], [13]. Such mappings can be used in the domain of object-relational (O/R) mappers [29], [23], [27]. These tools generate an object implementation from a data model such as (E)ER, and possibly support synchronization of both models. Some of them generate code to enforce constraints on relationships and dependencies between implementation objects, based on the data model. However, these applications do not consider behavior at the level of the datamodel.

Finally, since SelfSync allows rapid prototyping, we consider a concrete example of agile modeling [2]. In this case the stress is less on synchronization and more on rapid prototyping and testing. In [2] applying eXtreme programming to modeling is realized by making UML diagrams executable. Different UML diagrams are translated into Petri-Nets and interpreted by a Petri-Net engine. This engine can be seen as a *UML Virtual Machine* and contains a Java parser. The precise evolution support in this case depends on the environment in which the UML models are created and in which the UML Virtual Machine is integrated. As is, as far as we know, no support for RTE is provided.

### 8.4   Discussion

The ensuing discussion compares SelfSync to the related work introduced above. We distinguish four tracks: (1) UML versus EER, (2) forward RTE support (scenarios 1 and 2), (3) backward RTE support (scenarios 3 and 4), and (4) run-time RTE support.

**UML Versus EER.** There is an almost religious discussion between the (E)ER and the UML communities as to which approach is better. Typical claims are that (E)ER modeling is more formally funded but that the UML is more open [19], [9]. In our work, however, the use of EER does not exclude the transfer of our conceptual results to an UML-based context. In this paper, we describe Round-Trip Engineering on the data modeling level in terms of entities, attributes and operations, and association and inheritance relations. These EER modeling elements have equivalent modeling elements in Class Diagrams of the UML.

**Forward RTE Support.** Forward RTE support, embodied by scenarios 1 and 2, is provided by Together's LiveSource. Naked Objects only provides backward RTE support and some run-time support. We first mention the similarities with SelfSync, and then discuss the differences.

*Similarities.* Both LiveSource and SelfSync provide forward RTE support when evolving the following data modeling elements: entities or classes, attributes, operations, relations and specializations. In LiveSource this is supported by first propagating the changes to the implementation model and then updating the views, i.e. the class diagram and the formatted source code. In SelfSync this is supported because these data modeling elements and the corresponding implementation elements are in reality the same. Although LiveSource uses Java as implementation language, which is class-based, and SelfSync uses Self, originally a prototype-based language, this is not the fundamental difference here. Indeed, a mapping needs to be devized between data modeling and implementation elements, whether this is entities on classes or entities on prototypes and traits.

*Differences.* The only other support offered for cardinalities and dependencies in Together is not inherent to LiveSource but a consequence of the fact that Together supports the technology of Enterprise Java Beans (EJB), the component model for J2EE. EJB 2.0's container-managed persistence specification allows fine-grained control over entity bean relationships. When we add an association between two container-managed entity beans in a class diagram, parameters such as relation name and multiplicities need to be supplied. Automatically a new container-managed relationship is created. To the best of our knowledge, the actual enforcement of cardinalities is only limited and only due to the static typing that is provided by Java. In particular, an attribute cannot contain an object of another type than declared with the attribute. Although we employ a dynamically typed implementation language, we provide this level of enforcement, and more. For example, we also ensure that only one population object of a certain type refers to another population object if the latter is allowed to have a single reference to the first type.

To enforce dependencies using EJB a `cascade-delete` XML tag is used in the description of relationships: when the entity bean is deleted, all its dependents it is in a relationship with, are deleted as well. The difference with SelfSync is that, although we provide similar support for enforcing dependencies, we provide it in the context of an RTE tool and not solely in the implementation technology.

**Backward RTE Support.** Backward RTE support, embodied by scenarios 3 and 4, is provided by Together's LiveSource and Naked Objects. We first mention the similarities with SelfSync, and then discuss the differences.

*Similarities.* LiveSource and SelfSync provide backward RTE support when evolving the following object-oriented implementation elements: classes in the class-based approaches and prototypes or traits in our prototype-based approach, attributes, methods, references between classes or prototypes, and inheritance between classes or traits. Naked Objects support the same except for references and inheritance. In Together's LiveSource and SelfSync the backward RTE support is enabled in an analogous way to the forward RTE support. Naked Objects' support for backward RTE is similar to ours, i.e. through MVC, but an additional compilation step of the changed Java code is necessary.

*Differences.* LiveSource and SelfSync do not differ in the kind of backward RTE support provided, only in the internal strategy, as explained earlier. Naked Objects, however, does not provide support for synchronizing evolving references and inheritance in the Java code.

**Run-Time RTE Support.** Run-time RTE support only makes sense in the forward direction, more specifically changes to the data model are reflected in the run-time population objects. It is nonsensical to automatically synchronize a data model when changes are made to instantiated and initialized objects. Especially since most statically typed, class-based implementation languages such as Java would restrict the possible changes that can be made based on the source code. In dynamically typed languages or prototype-based languages (or both) there are less restrictions to changing the run-time population objects, but even in these cases it is undesirable to reflect them in the data model.

Only SelfSync provides full forward run-time RTE support. This means that evolution of attributes, operations, relations, specializations, cardinalities and dependencies are reflected in the run-time population objects. The main reason SelfSync supports this is primarily due to the dynamic character of the implementation language, Self. Using another dynamically typed language, such as Smalltalk, would allow us to achieve similar results. In a context where a statically typed implementation language is used, such as Java, one would have much less flexibility in changing the data model (or even the source code directly) and synchronizing the corresponding ready-to-use population objects. Another reason why this is supported in SelfSync, is that Self separates state sharing and behavior sharing.

In the Naked Objects approach there is only support at the level of adding associations between instantiated business objects, which is reflected in the corresponding Java objects.

## 9    Conclusion

This paper presents three contributions with respect to Round-Trip Engineering (RTE) in a particular Model-Driven Engineering setup consisting of a data modeling view and a view on an object-oriented implementation. First of all, we identify and describe fundamental set of four Round-Trip Engineering scenarios. These scenarios distinguish between direction, from model to code or vice versa, and kind of elements that evolve, entity views and implementation objects and their elements on the one hand, or relations between them on the other. A second contribution is our tool, SelfSync, which provide very dynamic support for these four RTE scenarios, not only at code-time but in relevant run-time situations as well. This is a direct result of the entities of the data modeling view and the corresponding implementation objects being one and the same in SelfSync. Finally, we describe related work and present a comparison accompanied by an extensive discussion.

## References

[1] U. Assman. Automatic roundtrip engineering. *Electronic Notes in Theoretical Computer Science*, 82.

[2] M. Boger, T. Baier, F. Wienberg, and W. Lamersdorf. Extreme modeling. pages 175–189, 2001.

[3] C. Chambers, D. Ungar, B.-W. Chang, and U. Holzle. Parents are shared parts of objects: Inheritance and encapsulation in SELF. *Lisp and Symbolic Computation*, 4(3):0–, 1991.

[4] P. P. Chen. The entity-relationship model - toward a unified view of data. *ACM Trans. Database Syst.*, 1(1):9–36, 1976.

[5] P. P. Chen. Er vs. oo. In *Entity-Relationship Approach - ER'92, 11th International Conference on the Entity-Relationship Approach, Karlsruhe, Germany, October 7-9, 1992, Proceedings*, volume 645 of *Lecture Notes in Computer Science*, pages 1–2. Springer, 1992.

[6] S. Demeyer, S. Ducasse, and S. Tichelaar. Why unified is not universal? In *UML'99, Fort Collins, CO, USA, October 28-30. 1999, Proceedings*, volume 1723 of *LNCS*, pages 630–644. Springer, 1999.

[7] R. Elmasri and S. B. Navathe. *Fundamentals of Database Systems*. Addison-Wesley World Student Series, 3 edition, 1994.

[8] J. Fong. Mapping extended entity relationship model to object modeling technique. *SIGMOD Record*, 24(3):18–22, 1995.

[9] M. Fowler and K. Scott. *UML distilled: a brief guide to the standard object modeling language*. Addison-Wesley Longman Publishing, Boston, MA, USA, 2000.

[10] E. Gamma, R. Helm, R. Johnson, and J. Vlissides. *Design Patterns: Elements of Reusable Object-Oriented Software*. Addison Wesley, Reading, Mass., 1995.

[11] M. Gogolla, R. Herzig, S. Conrad, G. Denker, and N. Vlachantonis. Integrating the er approach in an oo environment. In *Entity-Relationship Approach - ER'93, 12th International Conference on the Entity-Relationship Approach, Arlington, Texas, USA, December 15-17, 1993, Proceedings*, volume 823 of *Lecture Notes in Computer Science*, pages 376–389. Springer, 1993.

[12] A. Henriksson and H. Larsson. A definition of round-trip engineering. Technical report, Linkopings Universitet, Sweden, 2003.

[13] R. Herzig and M. Gogolla. Transforming conceptual data models into an object model. In *ER'92, Karlsruhe, Germany, October 1992, Proceedings*, volume 645 of *Lecture Notes in Computer Science*, pages 280–298. Springer, 1992.

[14] C.-T. Liu, S.-K. Chang, and P. K. Chrysanthis. Database schema evolution using EVER diagrams. In *Advanced Visual Interfaces*, pages 123–132, 1994.

[15] S. B. Navathe and M. K. Pillalamarri. Ooer: Toward making the e-r approach object-oriented. In *Entity-Relationship Approach: A Bridge to the User, Proceedings of the Seventh International Conference on Enity-Relationship Approach, Rome, Italy, November 16-18, 1988*, pages 185–206. North-Holland, 1988.

[16] E. V. Paesschen, M. D'Hondt, and W. D. Meuter. Rapid prototyping of extended entity relationship models. In *ISIM 2005, Hradec Nad Moravici, Czech Republic, April 2005, Proceedings*, pages 194–209. MARQ, 2005.

[17] E. V. Paesschen, W. D. Meuter, and T. D'Hondt. Domain modeling in self yields warped hierarchies. In *Workshop Reader ECOOP 2004, Oslo, Norway, June 2004*, volume 3344 of *Lecture Notes in Computer Science*, page 101, 2004.

[18] R. Pawson and R. Matthews. Naked objects: a technique for designing more expressive systems. *ACM SIGPLAN Notices*, 36(12):61–67, Dec. 2001.

[19] K.-D. Schewe. UML: A modern dinosaur? In *Proc. 10th European-Japanese Conference on Information Modelling and Knowledge Bases, Saariselkä (Finland), 2000*. IOS Press, Amsterdam, 2000.

[20] S. Sendall and J. Kuster. Taming model round-trip engineering. In *Proceedings of the Workshop on Best Practices for Model-Driven Software Development at OOPSLA 2004, Vancouver, Canada*, 2004.

[21] D. Ungar and R. B. Smith. Self: The power of simplicity. In *OOPSLA '87, Orlando, Florida, USA*, pages 227–242, New York, NY, USA, 1987. ACM Press.

[22] Fujaba: http://wwwcs.uni-paderborn.de/cs/fujaba/.

[23] Llblgen: http://www.llblgen.com/.

[24] Naked objects framework: http://www.nakedobjects.org.

[25] Rational: http://www-306.ibm.com/software/awdtools/developer/rosexde/.

[26] Self: http://research.sun.com/self/.

[27] Simpleorm: http://www.simpleorm.org/.

[28] Together: http://www.borland.com/together/.

[29] Toplink: http://www.oracle.com/technology/products/ias/toplink/index.html.

# UML for Document Modeling:
# Designing Document Structures for Massive and Systematic Production of XML-based Web Contents

Alejandro Bia[1] and Jaime Gómez[2]

[1] Miguel Hernández University, Spain
abia@umh.es
[2] University of Alicante, Spain
jgomez@dlsi.ua.es

**Abstract.** This paper discusses the applicability of modeling methods originally meant for business applications, on the design of the complex markup vocabularies used for XML Web-content production.

We are working on integrating these technologies to create a dynamic and interactive environment for the design of document markup schemes.
This paper focuses on the analysis, design and maintenance of XML vocabularies based on UML. It considers the automatic generation of Schemas and DTDs from a visual UML model of the markup vocabulary, as well as pieces of software, like input forms. Additionally, we integrate these UML design capabilities with other handy tools like automatic Schema simplification and multilingual markup. ♣

## Introduction

Most authors that treated the relationship between UML and XML [1,2] only targeted business applications and did not consider the kind of complex document-structure and metadata modeling required for massive and systematic production of XML contents for the Web. Text digitization projects, like most digital libraries, produce thousands of XML documents for Web publication, accompanied by complex metadata that include bibliographic, historical, processing and format descriptions. This is the case of text based digital library projects like those carried out by the History of Art Department at the University of Malaga[1], and the Miguel de Cervantes Digital Library[2] of the University of Alicante, where we applied UML for XML Schema design and maintenance.

---

♣ This work is part of the METASIGN project, and has been supported by the Ministry of Education and Science of Spain through the grant number: TIN2004-00779.
[1] Development of a Terminological and Conceptual Thesaurus (TTC) of Spanish Artistic Treatises of the Modern Age, including a database of digitized texts (ATENEA).
[2] http://cervantesvirtual.com/

L. Briand and C. Williams (Eds.): MoDELS 2005, LNCS 3713, pp. 648–660, 2005.

Digital Library XML documents that model the structure of literary texts and include bibliographic information (metadata) plus processing and formatting instructions are by far much more complex than the XML data we usually find in business applications. Figure 1 shows a small document model based on the TEI[3]. Although it may seem complex, it is just a very small TEI subset.

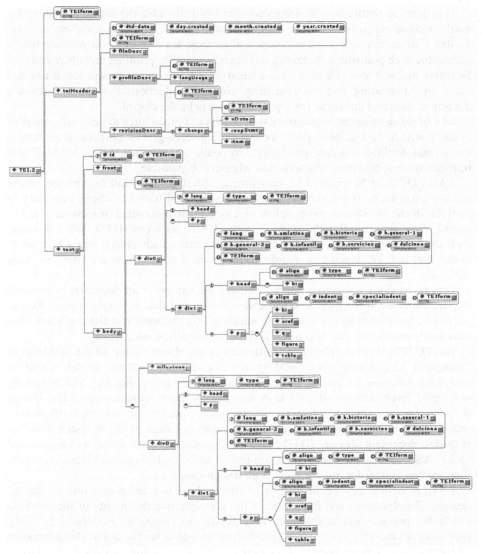

**Figure 1**: a small document model based on the TEI

---

[3] The TEI (Text Encoding Initiative) is a very complete as well as powerful markup vocabulary, both for text and metadata, originally based on SGML but now available in XML format. Different subsets of this markup vocabulary expressed in DTD, Relax NG or W3C Schema formats, can be obtained from a service called "Roma" at he TEI website: http://www.tei-c.org/

This type of markup is not as simple and homogeneous as the typical structured data we find in business applications. In these documents we usually find a wide variety of elements nested up to deep levels, and there are many exceptional cases that can lead to unthinked-of markup situations that also need to be covered. Markup schemes like TEI [3] and DocBook [4] are good examples of this kind of complexity and versatility.

However, no matter how heterogeneous and unpredictable the nature of humanities markup could get to be, software engineers have to deal with it in a systematic way, so that automatic processes can be applied to these texts in order to produce useful output for Web publishing, indexing and searching, pretty printing, and other end user facilities and services. There is also a need to reduce content production times and costs by automating and systematizing content production. For these, software, documentation and guides of good practice have to be developed.

The building of all these automation, methods and procedures to deal with complex content structures can be called Document Engineering. The purpose is to reduce costs, and facilitate content production by setting constraints, rules, methods and implementing automation wherever and whenever is possible.

XML, DTDs or Schemas, XSL transforms, CSS stylesheets and Java programming are the usual tools to enforce the rules, constraints and transformations necessary to turn the document structuring problem to a systematic automated process that lead to useful Web services. But the wide variety of Schema types (DTD, W3C Schema, RelaxNG, to name a few), and the individual limitations/advantages of each of them, make the task of making a standardized production environment like this very difficult.

On one hand we need a markup vocabulary that can cover all document structuring requirements, even the most unusual and complex, but that is simple enough for our purposes. In other words, we need the simplest DTD/Schema that fits our needs. We previously treated the problem of DTD/Schema simplification in [5, 6].

But DTD/Schema simplification, although useful, doesn't solve all the problems of Document Engineering, like building transformations to obtain useful output or assigning behavior to certain structures (like popup notes, linking, and triggering services). Environments of this kind are usually built incrementally. The design information, if any, is dispersed into many pieces of software (Schemas, transformation, Java applets and servlets), or does not exist at all. A system like this includes document design (DTD/Schemas), document production techniques and tools (XSL and Java), document exploitation tools (indexing, searching, metadata, dictionaries, concordances, etc.) and Web design altogether.

UML modeling may be the answer to join all those bits and pieces into a coherent design. The objectives are: to reduce design cost, improve the quality of the resulting products, provide documentation, and finally to simplify maintenance. UML modeling for massive Web content production may also lead to automatic generation of some of components needed. J. Gomez et al [7, 8] have successfully built a CASE tool (VisuaWADE) that allows the modeling of web navigation for web applications, and also generates usable web interfaces.

## Previous Related Work

According to David Carlson [1], the eXtensible Markup Language (XML) and the Unified Modeling Language (UML) are two of the most significant advances from the fields of Web application development and object-oriented modeling. As Kimber and Heintz define it [2], the problem is how we integrate traditional system engineering modeling practice (nowadays based on UML) with traditional SGML and XML document analysis and modeling.

Martin Bernauer et al [9], presented an interesting survey of approaches for representing XML Schema in UML at the ICWE 2004 conference, which they used for comparison to their own approach [10]. According to them, existing work on representing XML Schema in UML has emerged from approaches to platform specific modeling in UML and the transformation of these models to XML Schema, with the recognized need for UML extensions to specify XML Schema peculiarities.

A White Paper from Rational, in 1999 [11] may be the first approach of this kind to model XML schemas using UML. Although it deals with an old version of XML Schema, it introduces UML extensions that address modeling of elements, attributes, model groups, and enumerations, which can also be found in the following approaches. The approach by Carlson [1], which we used as a guide for our current work, uses XMI[4] rules for transforming UML to XML Schema. It defines a UML profile that handles almost all XML Schema components, with some exceptions[5]. Some weaknesses are attributed to the profile concerning its representation of model groups, i.e., sequence, choice, and all. In spite of these limitations, a commercial tool called "hypermodel"[6] has been built based on this profile, which includes a two-way transformation between XML Schema and UML.

Provost [12] has addressed some of the limitations of Carlson's work [1], including the representation of enumerations and other restriction constraints, and of list and union type constructors[7]. Eckstein's approach ([13], in German, based on [14]) also defines a profile similar to Carlson's [1], with some enhancements regarding simple types and notations. Goodchild et al [15] point out the importance of separating the conceptual schema, i.e., the platform independent model, from the logical schema, i.e., the platform specific model (following the guidelines of MDA[8] [16]), a separation that is not considered in the other approaches. In this approach, the logical schema is a direct, one-to-one representation of the XML schema in terms of a UML profile. The profile[9] covers almost all concepts of XML Schema, but several of its representations are not UML conformant.

---

[4] XML Metadata Interchange

[5] Exceptions are: simple content complex types, global elements and attributes, and identity constraints.

[6] http://xmlmodeling.com/hyperModel/

[7] The latter doesn't conform to UML

[8] In the model driven architecture (MDA), a two step integration is assumed, comprising a platform specific model which abstracts from implementation language details, and a platform independent model which abstracts from technology details.

[9] http://titanium.dstc.edu.au/papers/xml-schema-profile.pdf

Bernauer's own approach [10] resembles Goodchild's [15] by aiming at a one-to-one representation of XML schemas in a UML profile. It builds on the existing UML profiles for XML Schema, with some improvements and extensions.

A recent online article by Benoît Marchal [17] also served as an inspiration for our work.

Other related work on mapping conceptual models expressed in UML or EER to XML Schema or DTD, has also identified various options for transforming conceptual-level concepts to XML Schema concepts [1,14,18,19,12]. Most of the transformations are, however, not unambiguously applicable in the reverse direction and would thus only be useful in an interactive transformation process, requiring a user's knowledge of the XML schema to be transformed to UML.

## Advantages of Modeling XML Documents with UML

As a modeling tool,

-   UML applies to several technologies: Python, Java, PHP, SQL, C++, Web design, etc.
-   Its widespread use reduces the training needs, allowing for easy design sharing.
-   UML diagrams can show as much or as little information as needed, so it is possible to build several models with different degrees of sophistication.

Apart from modeling the structure of a class of documents (as DTDs and Schemas do), UML can capture other properties of document elements:

-   Behavior: this is related to event oriented functions (e.g. popup notes)
-   Additional powerful validation features (e.g. validating consistency of certain fields like author name against a database.)
-   Customization of document models to provide different views or subsets of the markup scheme to different users (e.g. DTDs for development of different types of documents)

We believe that the dynamic and interactive environment described here will be very useful to professionals responsible for designing and implementing markup schemes for Web documents and metadata. Although XML standards for text markup (like TEI and DocBook) and metadata markup (e.g. MODS, EAD, RDF, METS) are readily available [20], tools and techniques for automating the process of customizing DTD/Schemas and adding postprocessing functionality are not.

## Description of the Project

We are working on integrating these technologies to create a dynamic and interactive environment for the design and maintenance of document markup schemes (see figure

2). Our approach is to expand the capabilities of Visual Wade[10] to obtain a tool that allows the visual analysis, design and maintenance of XML vocabularies based on UML. Among the targets we are working on, we can mention the automatic generation of different types of DTD/Schemas from a visual UML model of the markup vocabulary, code generation whenever possible (like generating HTML forms or XSLT), generation of documentation, and special enhanced validators that can perform verifications beyond those allowed by DTDs or Schemas (like verification of certain element content or attribute values against a database).

Many mappings are possible between an XML schema and a UML model. UML supports several types of diagram. The most commonly used are class diagrams, use case diagrams, package diagrams, sequence diagrams, and activity diagrams. The most suitable diagram for our purposes is the class diagram, which can represent an object-oriented model. Carlson [1] suggests a method based on UML class diagrams and use case analysis for business applications which we adapted for modeling document markup vocabularies.

A UML class diagram can be constructed to visually represent the elements, relationships, and constraints of an XML vocabulary (see figure 3 for a simplified example). Then all types of Schemas can be generated from the UML diagrams by means of simple XSLT transformations applied to the corresponding XMI representation of the UML model.

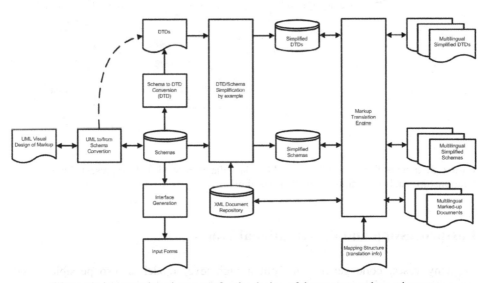

**Figure 2:** integrated environment for the design of document markup schemes

The UML model information can be stored in an XML document according to the XMI standard as described by Hayashi and Hatton [21]: "Adherence to the [XMI]

---

[10] VisualWade is a tool for software development based on UML and extensions. It was developed by our research group, named IWAD (Ingeniería Web y Almacenes de Datos - Web Engineering and Data-Warehousing), at the University of Alicante. This group also developed the OOH Method (for more information see http://www.visualwade.com/)

standard allows other groups to easily use our modeling work and because the format is XML, we can derive a number of other useful documents using standard XSL transformations". In our case, these documents are schemas of various types as well as DTDs. Like Schemas, DTDs can be also generated from the XMI representation of the UML model (doted line), but as DTDs are simpler than Schemas, and all types of Schemas contain at least the same information as a DTD, DTDs can also be directly generated from them.

We choose W3C Schema as the central format for our set of tools. DTDs were discarded as the central format, since they have their own non-XML syntax, which makes them unsuitable for XSTL conversion, and they are the poorest of all the current document validation formats, lacking new features like types.

We use XSLT for round-trip W3C Schema derivation from XMI. We use Trang and some other XSLT (xsd2dtd) to convert the generated W3C Schema to and from DTDs, and RelaxNG (both compact and extended notation). In this way, our set of tools is capable of handling four types of schema notations: W3C, RelaxNG (normal and compact), and the old and widespread DTDs.

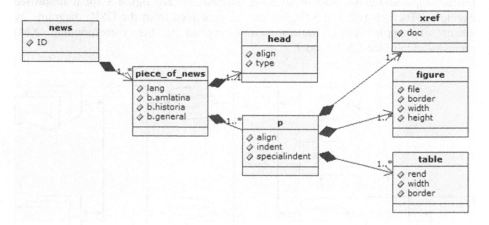

**Figure 3:** a simplified example of a UML class diagram to visually represent the elements, relationships, and constraints of an XML vocabulary

## Postprocessing and Presentational Issues

In many cases, code generation from a high level model is also possible. Code generation may include JavaScript code to implement behavior for certain elements like popup notes, hyperlinks, image display controls, etc. This is the case of HTML input forms that can easily be generated from Schemas as done by Suleman [22].

We have successfully experimented on the generation of XSLT skeletons for XML transformation. Usually XSL transforms produce fairly static output, like nicely formatted HTML with tables of contents and hyperlinks, but not much more. In exceptional cases we can find examples of more sophisticated interaction.

This high level of flexible interactivity is the real payoff from the UML-XML-XSLT-browser chain. This sort of functionality is usually programmed specifically for individual projects, given that it's highly dependent on the nature of the markup in any given document. We aim to provide the ability to specify this at the UML level. For instance, a note could be processed differently according to its type attribute and then be displayed as a footnote, a margin note, a popup note, etc. In certain cases it can be associated to a JavaScript function to be popped up in a message window or in a new browser instance according to attribute values. In this sense, we could provide a set of generic JavaScript functions which could retrieve content from elements and display it in various ways (popup, insertions, etc.) or trigger events (like a dictionary lookup).

We should look for document models that allow al kinds of presentation, navigation and cognitive metaphors.

- Sequential reading
- Text reuse (links and includes)
- Non-sequential reading
- Hyperlinks
- Collapsible text
- Foot notes, margin notes, popup notes
- The folder metaphor
- TOCs, indexes and menus

All the elements in a structured document have an associated semantic and a behavior or function (as in the above example, a popup note must appear on a popup window when a link to it is pressed). This is not reflected in conventional document models: a DTD/Schema may say that a note is a popup note: <note type=popup>...</note> but the behavior of this note is not stated at all. Some postprocessing must be implemented for the popup effect to happen. A UML based document model can incorporate the expected behavior like methods in a class diagram.

## Other Auxiliary Tools for Document Design and Optimization

As additional aiding tools for this project we have incorporated two of our earlier developments:
- First the automatic simplification of DTDs or Schemas based on sample sets of files [5, 6]. This tool can be applied to obtain simplified DTDs and Schemas customized to fit exactly a collection of documents.
- Second, multilingual vocabulary capability: automatic element-name and attribute-name translation to be applied when multilingual markup is required. A detailed explanation of the multilingual markup project can be found in [23].

See figure 2 for an idea of how these tools interact with the UML document modeling. The techniques described here can also be used for modeling metadata markup vocabularies.

## DTD Simplification by Example

We designed and implemented a method for the automatic generation of simplified Schemas from a complex source Schema and a set of sample marked-up files. The purpose is to create the minimum Schema that the sample set of files complies. In this way, new files can be created and parsed using this simplified Schema but still being compliant to the original, more general one. The simplified Schema can be used to make the task of markup easier, especially for non-experienced XML writers.

Our approach is to automatically select only those Schema features that are used by a set of valid documents (validated against the more general Schema) and eliminate the rest of them (the unused ones), obtaining a narrow scope Schema which defines a subset of the original markup scheme. This "pruned" Schema can be used to build new documents of the same markup subclass, which in turn would still comply with the original general Schema.

Using this automated method, the simplified Schema can be updated immediately in the event that new features are added to (or eliminated from) the sample set of XML files (modifications to files of the sample-set must be done using the general Schema for validation). This process can be repeated to incrementally produce a final narrow-scope or customized Schema.

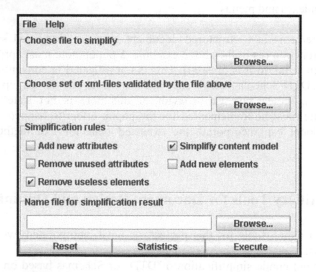

**Figure 4:** Interface of the Schema/DTD simplification module

In this way, we use a complex Schema as a general markup-design frame to build a simpler working-Schema that suits a specific project's markup needs. Another use of this technique is to build a one-document Schema, i.e. the minimum Schema that a given XML document would comply.

Another benefit of this tool is that it produces statistical data that may help markup designers improve their markup schemes like the frequency of use of certain elements within others which is helpful to detect unusual structures that could reflect mark-up mistakes, misuse of the Schema, or Schema features that may allow unwanted generalization.

The user interface of the Schema simplification tool is shown as in figure 4. Two of the five processing rules are chosen by default. The user can then change this initial setup and choose the simplification rules to apply.

## Multilingual Markup Translation Engine

Markup is based on mnemonics (i.e. element names, attribute names and attribute values). These mnemonics have meaning, being this one of the most interesting features of markup. Human understanding of this meaning is lost when the encoder doesn't have a good command of the language the mnemonics are based on. By "multilingual markup" we refer to the use of tags built with mnemonics in one's own language, but still following the rules of the original markup vocabulary. We have built a set of tools to automate the use of multilingual vocabularies, including the translation of Dublin Core and TEI to Catalan, French, German and Spanish. This set of tools translates both XML document instances, and XML document validators (Schemas and DTDs).

We started by defining the set of possible translations of element names, attribute names, and attribute values to different target languages. We stored this information in an XML multilingual translation mapping document.

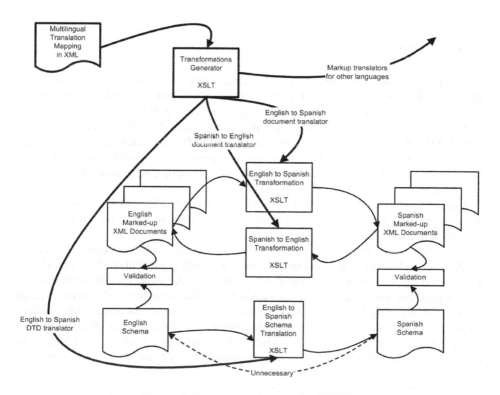

**Figure 5:** Schema translation using XSLT.

This mapping document which contains all the necessary structural information to develop the language converters is read by the transformations generator, which was built as an XSLT script. XSL can be used to process XML documents in order to produce other XML documents or a plain text document. As XSL stylesheets are XML, they can be generated as an XSL output. We used this feature to automatically generate both an English-to-local-language XSL transformation and a local-language to English XSL transformation for each of the languages contained in the multilingual translation mapping file. In this way we assured both ways convertibility for XML documents.

For each target language we also generate a DTD or a Schema translator. In our first attempts, this took the form of a C++ and Lex parser. Later, we changed the approach. Now we first convert the DTD to a W3C Schema, then we translate the Schema to the local language, and finally we can (optionally) generate an equivalent translated DTD. This approach has the advantage of not using complex parsers (only XSLT) and also solves the translation of Schemas as well, which is an interesting goal in itself (see figure 5). In our latest implementation, the user can freely choose amongst DTD, W3C Schema and RelaxNG, both for input and output, allowing for a format conversion during the translation process.

Many other markup translators can be built to other languages in the way described here, as demonstrated by our tests with Catalan and French.

## Conclusions

Concerning the described set of DTD/Schema design tools, the integration of UML design with example based automatic simplification and multilingual vocabulary capabilities, proved to be a very useful and practical design aid.

However, we experienced some limitations in the use of UML. While commercial non UML products like XML Spy or TurboXML use custom graphical tree representation to handle XML schemas, comprising very handy collapsing and navigating capabilities, most general purpose UML design environments lack these specialized features.

One of the downsides of UML is that it is less friendly when working with the low-level aspects of modeling [17]. For instance, it is easy to order the elements of a sequence in a tree, but it is very tricky to do so in UML.

Although UML proves very useful for modeling document structures of small to medium complexity (metadata applications and simple documents), UML models for medium to big sized schemas (100 to 400 elements), like those used for complex DL documents, become practically unmanageable[11]. The diagrams become overloaded with too many class boxes and lines, which end up being unreadable. This problem could be solved, or at least mitigated, by enhancing the interfaces of UML design programs with newer and more powerful display functions. Facilities like intelligent collapsing or hiding of diagram parts or elements, overview maps (see figure 6),

---

[11] The DTD used by the Miguel de Cervantes DL for its literary documents contains 139 different elements. The "teixlite" DTD, a simple and widely used XML-TEI DTD, contains 144 elements.

zooming, 3-D layouts, partial views, and other browsing capabilities would certainly help to solve the problem.

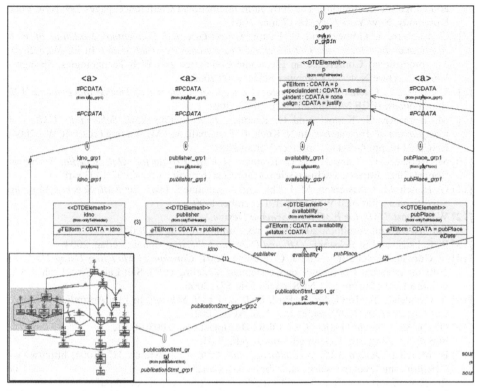

**Figure 6:** A class diagram of the TEI metadata section, the teiHeader. The overview map (bottom left) helps to locate the partial view of the diagram.

# References

[1]  D. Carlson, *Modeling XML Applications with UML*. Object Technology Series. Addison-Wesley, 2001.

[2]  W. Eliot Kimber and John Heintz. *Using UML To Define XML Document Types*. In Extreme Markup Languages 2000, Montreal, Canada, 15-18 August 2000.

[3]  Michael Sperberg-McQueen, Lou Burnard, Syd Bauman, Steven DeRose, and Sebastian Rahtz. *Text Encoding Initiative: The XML Version of the TEI Guidelines*. http://www.tei-c.org/P4X/, 2001. Copyright 2001 TEI Consortium (TEI P4, Guidelines for Electronic Text Encoding and Interchange, XML-compatible edition).

[4]  T. Allen, E. Maler, and N. Walsh. *DocBook DTD*. Copyright 1992-1997 HaL Computer Systems, Inc., O'Reilly & Associates, Inc., Fujitsu Software Corporation, and ArborText, Inc. URL: http://www.ora.com/davenport/

[5]  A. Bia, R. C. Carrasco, and M. Sánchez-Quero. *A Markup Simplification Model to Boost Productivity of XML Documents*. In Digital Resources for the Humanities 2002 Conference (DRH2002)}, pages 13-16, {University of Edinburgh, George Square, Edinburgh EH8 9LD - Scotland - UK, 8-11 September 2002.

[6]  A. Bia and R. C. Carrasco. *Automatic DTD simplification by examples*. In ACH/ALLC 2001. The Association for Computers and the Humanities, The Association for Literary and Linguistic Computing, The 2001 Joint International Conference, pages 7-9, New York University, New York City, 13-17 June 2001.

[7]  C. Cachero, J. Gómez, and O. Pastor. *Object-Oriented Conceptual Modeling of Web Application Interfaces: the OO-HMethod Presentation Abstract Model*. In EC-Web 2000. 1st International Conference on Electronic Commerce and Web Technologies. Springer-Verlag. Lecture Notes in Computer Science, 09 2000.

[8]  J. Gómez, C. Cachero, and O. Pastor. *Conceptual Modeling of Device-Independent Web Applications*. IEEE Multimedia 8(2): 20-32. 2001.

[9]  M. Bernauer, G. Kappel, and G. Kramler. *Representing XML Schema in UML - A Comparison of Approaches*. In N. Koch, P. Fraternali, and M. Wirsing (eds.): ICWE 2004, LNCS 3140, pp. 440-444, Springer-Verlag 2004.

[10] M. Bernauer, G. Kappel, and G. Kramler. *A UML Profile for XML Schema*. Technical Report, 2003. http://www.big.tuwien.ac.at/research/publications/2003/1303.pdf

[11] G. Booch, M. Christerson, M. Fuchs, and J. Koistinen. *UML for XML Schema Mapping Specification*. Rational White Paper, December 1999.

[12] W. Provost. *UML for W3C XML Schema Design*. http://www.xml.com/lpt/a/2002/08/07/wxs_uml.html, August 2002.

[13] R. Eckstein and S. Eckstein. *XML und Datenmodellierung*. dpunkt.verlag, 2004.

[14] R. Conrad, D. Scheffner, and J. C. Freytag. XML *Conceptual Modeling Using UML*. In 19th International Conference on Conceptual Modeling (ER), Salt Lake City, Utah, USA, volume 1920 of Springer LNCS, pages 558–571, 2000.

[15] A. Goodchild N. Routledge, L. Bird. *UML and XML Schema*. In 13th Australian Database Conference (ADC2002), pages 157–166. ACS, 2002.

[16] OMG. *MDA Guide Version 1.0.1*. OMG Document omg/2003-06-01, http://www.omg.org/docs/omg/03-06-01.pdf, 2003.

[17] B. Marchal. *Design XML vocabularies with UML tools*. March 31st, 2004, http://www-128.ibm.com/developerworks/xml/library/x-wxxm23/                          or ftp://www6.software.ibm.com/software/developer/library/x-wxxm23.pdf

[18] R. Elmasri, Y. Wu, B. Hojabri, C. Li, and J. Fu. *Conceptual Modeling for Customized XML Schemas*. In 21st International Conference on Conceptual Modeling (ER), Tampere, Finland, volume 2503 of Springer LNCS, pages 429–443. Springer, 2002.

[19] T. Krumbein and T. Kudrass. Rule-*Based Generation of XML Schemas from UML Class Diagrams*. In Proceedings of the XML Days at Berlin, Workshop on Web Databases (WebDB), pages 213–227, 2003.

[20] D. Megginson. *Structuring XML Documents*. Charles Goldfarb Series. Prentice Hall, 1998.

[21] L. S. Hayashi and J. Hatton. *Combining UML, XML and Relational Database Technologies. The Best of All Worlds For Robust Linguistic Databases*. In Proceedings of the IRCS Workshop on Linguistic Databases, pages 115--124, University of Pennsylvania, Philadelphia, USA, 11-13 December 2001. SIL International.

[22] H. Suleman. *Metadata Editing by Schema*. In Traugott Koch and Ingeborg Solvberg, editors, Research and Advanced Technology for Digital Libraries: 7th European Conference, ECDL 2003, volume 2769, pages 82-87, Trondheim, Norway, August 2003. Springer-Verlag.

[23] A. Bia, M. Sánchez-Quero, and R. Déau. *Multilingual Markup of Digital Library Texts Using XML, TEI and XSLT*. In XML Europe 2003 Conference and Exposition, page 53, Hilton Metropole Hotel, London, 5-8 May 2003. IDEAlliance, 100 Daingerfield Road, Alexandria, VA 22314.

# Metamodel Reuse with MOF

Xavier Blanc, Franklin Ramalho[1] and Jacques Robin[2]

Laboratoire d'Informatique de Paris 6, Université Pierre et Marie Curie (LIP6-UMPC)
8, Rue du Capitaine Scott, 75015 Paris, France
xavier.blanc@lip6.fr, franklin.ramalho@gmail.com,
robin.jacques@gmail.com

**Abstract.** As model-driven development promotes metamodels as key assets it raises the issue of their reuse throughout a model-driven product line life cycle. One recurrent reuse need occurs when metamodeling integrated multi-language platforms: one construct from one language is integrated to constructs from other languages by *generalizing* it, making it more expressive. None of the metamodel assembly facilities provided by MOF and UML (import, merge and combine) or others proposed in previous work adequately addresses this need. We thus propose a new reuse and generalize facility for such purpose.

## 1 Introduction

Model Driven Development (MDD) raises the level of abstraction of the development life cycle by shifting its emphasis from code to models, metamodels and model transformations. It views any software artifact produced at any step of the development process as a valuable asset by itself to reuse across different applications and implementation platforms so as to cut the cost of future development efforts. Since they drive much of the MDD process, metamodels are the first artifact to reuse when an MDD team extends its portfolio of application domains, product requirements or target implementation platforms. However, the issue of metamodel *reuse* has not yet received much attention in the MDD literature. The reuse facilities provided by standards such as MOF 2.0 [11] and UML 2.0 [12] [13] or proposed in previous research on the topic [5][6][9][10] are essentially limited to two simple reuse needs. The first is *reuse as is* through inter-package visibility facilities such as package import in MOF or copy and paste transformations such as package combine in MOF. The second is *reuse as specialization* through inheritance facilities such as package merge in UML 2.0. As larger, more complex metamodels get constructed and then incrementally extended during their lifecycle, a diversity of

---

[1] Now at Departamento de Sistemas de Computação, Universidade Federal de Campina Grande (DSC-UFCG) Campina Grande, PB, Brazil and Centro de Informática, Universidade Federal de Pernambuco (CIn-UFPE), Recife, PE, Brazil.

[2] Now at Centro de Informática, Universidade Federal de Pernambuco (CIn-UFPE), Recife, PE, Brazil.

L. Briand and C. Williams (Eds.): MoDELS 2005, LNCS 3713, pp. 661-675, 2005.
© Springer-Verlag Berlin Heidelberg 2005

more sophisticated metamodel reuse needs is emerging. They prompt the definition of new metamodeling assembly facilties to address them and proposals to incorporate these facilities in MOF.

In this paper, we identify one such more sophisticated metamodel reuse need that we call *reuse and generalize*, and we propose a new metamodeling assembly facility that addresses it. This need is pervasive for various classes of metamodeling tasks. One such class is metamodeling multi-paradigm languages that historically result from successive extensions of a mono-paradigm core with constructs imported from other paradigms and adapted from integration. Another such class is metamodeling integrated multi-language platforms that support development in several languages that are conceptually integrated (as opposed to just loosely coupled through communication interfaces). In such cases, constructs from different languages have been extended or integrated by *generalizing* them so as to subsume constructs from other languages. Historically, such situation occurred many times over for example when defining concurrent or object-oriented extensions of imperative, functional or logic programming languages. It is currently occurring again as distributed, XML-based extensions of many languages are being defined.

The paper is organized as follows. In the next section, we advocate a *compositional* approach to metamodeling multi-paradigm languages or integrated multi-language platforms. With such an approach, metamodels of minimal size with potential for reuse are first built separately and then assembled in a way that mirrors how constructs from each paradigm or language are reused in the integrated whole. We identify and discuss five general benefits of such an approach in subsection 2.3. To make our points concrete, we illustrate these benefits, as well as all the subsequent points we make throughout the paper, on a specific case study: metamodeling the Flora platform [18]. Prior to discussing these points, we thus have to introduce the necessary background on Flora and then motivate having chosen it for the case study. We respectively do so in subsections 2.1 and 2.2. Briefly, metamodeling Flora is an interesting illustrative case study because it supports in an integrated way several languages and paradigms and it is a versatile platform that supports programming, meta-programming, reasoning, meta-reasoning as well as data and metadata definition, updates and queries.

Since Flora is such a comprehensive platform that results from a long, multi-step integration process, starting from section 3, we focus the scope of our illustrative examples on only *one* such step: the integration of first-order logic programming in Prolog with meta-programming based on high-order variables, resulting in HiLog. Subsections 3.1 and 3.2 thus respectively present simplified metamodels of these two languages supported by Flora. Subsection 3.3 then further zooms on only the relevant elements of theses two metamodels that we use to illustrate the general need to *reuse and generalize* metamodel elements. This example involves reusing elements metamodeling first-order predicates to metamodel their generalization as high-order predicates. In the subsequent subsections 3.4 to 3.6 we explain in detail why none of the three package assembly facilities provided the MOF 2.0 and UML 2.0 standard (`import`, `merge` and `combined`) can be used to address such reuse need. In subsection 3.7, we propose a fourth package assembly specifically designed for such need that we thus call `reuse and generalize`. In section 4, we review the literature in metamodel reuse and show that none of the proposals put forward to date address such a need. In section 5, we conclude by summarizing our contributions.

# 2 Metamodeling Integrated Multi-language Platforms

In this section, we first present the main characteristics and historical genesis of the Flora multi-language, multi-paradigm and multi-purpose platform. Metamodeling Flora is the larger case study from which we extracted the examples that we use throughout the paper to illustrate the general points that we make on metamodel reuse. We then motivate the choice of such metamodeling task as illustrative case study. We take the opportunity to point out the mutual synergy that exists between MDD and platforms integrating multiple concepts and services such as Flora. Finally, we advocate a compositional approach to metamodeling such platforms by identifying five benefits that it provides and illustrating each of them on the Flora metamodeling case study.

## 2.1 Flora: An Integrated Multi-language, Multi-purpose Platform

Flora implements a subset of the language Concurrent Transaction Frame Logic (CTFL). Syntactically, CTFL integrates constructors from: (a) logic programming, (b) object-oriented programming, (c) imperative programming and (d) concurrent programming. Semantically, it provides declarative formal accounts of all these constructs by way of logical model theories. Historically, CTFL and Flora result from a 15 year research effort to overcome the failings of ISO Prolog to fulfill the original logic programming ideal: a language with declarative logical semantics that is simultaneously (a) a practical Turing-complete *programming* language, (b) an expressive *knowledge representation* language and (c) a concise *data definition, update and query* language. From its root in Prolog, CTFL evolved incrementally, as a series of largely *orthogonal* extensions, each one providing a semantically well-founded logical alternative to the extra-logical predicates of Prolog that betrayed the original logic programming ideal. This evolution had six main steps:

1. Extending Prolog with the logically *Well-Founded Negation as Failure* (WFNAF) connective;
2. *HiLog (HL)*, extending Prolog with high-order syntax inspired from functional programming for meta-level programming, reasoning and querying but with first-order logical semantics [4]
3. *Transaction Logic (TL)*, extending Prolog with logically well-founded backtrackable knowledge base updates and procedural constructs such as conditionals and loops [2];
4. *Frame Logic (FL)*, extending HiLog with an object-oriented syntax [8] and logical semantics for single-source multiple structural and behavioral inheritance integrated with deduction [17];
5. *Concurrent* Transaction Logic *(CTL)*, extending Transaction Logic with multiple threads, critical sections and inter-thread messages [3].

The Flora platform implements extensions 1-4 above, *i.e.,* *Sequential Transaction Frame Logic* (STFL). It does so reusing the XSB Prolog platform that already implements extensions 1-2. Flora has two main components: the Flora Compiler that transforms an STFL program onto an optimized XSB Prolog program, and the Flora Shell, a front-end for queries in STFL that transforms STFL queries into semantically equivalent XSB queries, calls XSB to answer them and passes the answers back to the user in STFL syntax.

## 2.2 The Synergy Between MDD and Integrated Multi-language Platform

From an MDD perspective, a platform such as Flora that is multi-language, multi-paradigm and multi-purpose is very interesting in that it raises the possibility to rely on a single platform to (a) *run* a prototype to *validate* functional requirements of an application with the users, (b) *run* the same prototype to *test* its correctness on a set of specific cases, but also (c) *query* the same prototype to formally *verify* general properties that abstract from any set of specific cases, thus providing stronger robustness guarantees. Performing such verification on an implementation allows circumventing the major loophole of traditional formal development that relies on two different languages (one formal but non-executable for modeling and one executable but with no clear semantics for programming) and two different platforms (one for model validation and verification, and one for implementation execution and testing): namely the reintroduction of semantic errors while programming a verified model. We are currently exploring this possibility in the on-going MODELOG project [15] which investigates the development of a CASE tool for MDD providing a variety of services. Chief among these services is the fully automated generation of Flora code from UML models that consist of OCL annotated class and activity diagrams linked together through object flows. In order to develop this CASE tool for MDD using MDD itself, the first two steps of the MODELOG project are (1) developing a metamodel of the target platform Flora and (2) specify model transformations as QVT[14] relations between elements of this target metamodel and the source UML and OCL metamodels made available by the OMG. It is while carrying out the first task that we identified and addressed the metamodeling reuse issues presented in this paper.

## 2.3 Compositional Metamodeling and Its Benefits

For metamodeling languages and platforms that tightly integrate multiple paradigms and purposes, we advocate a *compositional approach* that faithfully mirrors their structure as a simple core and a set of largely orthogonal and complementary extensions. With such an approach, one starts by independently metamodeling the core and each extension in a separate package, to then assemble them together. So for example, when we applied this approach to the case of Flora, we developed one separate metamodel package for (1) *First-order logical terms* that are common to Prolog and many other logic and rule-based languages, (2) *Prolog programs and clauses* that reuses the logical terms package, and (3) each *orthogonal extension* of either logical terms or Prolog clauses used in CTFL programs. From such minimal metamodel units, larger metamodels for HL, STL, CTL, FL, SFTL *(i.e.,* for Flora) and CTFL can then be obtained through assembly. This compositional approach brings five clear benefits. The first is *cognitive complexity management* for such large meta-modeling tasks. For example, the fully assembled Flora metamodel contains over 275 elements. Hence, much simplicity was gained by decomposing it into nine packages. The second benefit is the creation of valuable course *didactic assets* that visually contrast basic language concepts and platform services and clarify the many different ways in which they can be integrated. For example, the compositional Flora metamodel is such an asset for teaching the distinct principles and complementary strengths of logic, object-oriented and imperative language concepts for programming, knowledge representation and data manipulation. The third benefit is the *reusability of minimal metamodel units* for other languages or platforms. For example, we have already reused the first-order logical term package of the Flora metamodel to build a metamodel of the language *Constraint Handling Rules* [7]. The fourth benefit is to provide a sound basis for *representing integration semantics* in UML and OCL which are more accessible than the mathematical notations generally used for such task. In the case of Flora, while each of its sub-language possesses denotational and operational semantics, the unification of theses into a single framework is still incomplete; metamodeling the semantics of each sub-language should bring valuable insights towards such unification. The fifth benefit of compositional metamodeling is compiler MDD based on model transformations. For example the Flora to XSB compiler could be specified as a set of declarative QVT relations [14] between elements of the STFL and HiLog metamodels.

These benefits are pervasive since many modern, powerful languages result, like Flora does, from successive and partially orthogonal extensions from an initial simple core. For example, the semantic web language standards put forward by the World Wide Web consortium (W3C) also evolved this way: an initial core, RDF [1] was successively extended to yield RDFS, DAML, DAML-OIL, and finally OWL [16]. In addition, all these languages reuse the syntactic core XML syntax, and DAML-OIL itself resulted from the integration of DAML with OIL.

# 3 Illustrative Case-Study: HiLog as an Extension of Prolog

While we assembled the minimal unit metamodel packages into the whole Flora metamodel, we were confronted several times with the need to reuse metamodel elements from one package while generalizing them in the package assembly. We now explain why such reuse need cannot be addressed by the facilities currently provided by the MOF 2.0 and UML 2.0 standards by focusing on a *single* assembly step: the one that takes as input the Prolog metamodel and a metamodel of high-order predicates and that results in the HiLog metamodel. We first present (simplified) non-compositional versions of the Prolog and HiLog metamodels and explain their main concepts. We then further zoom on only the relevant elements in these metamodels necessary to illustrate the *reuse and generalize* need, and successively show that elements from the Prolog metamodel for first-order predicates *cannot* be reused and generalized to define high-order predicates in the HiLog metamodel by using either

import, merge or combine. We then specify a new reuse and generalize
package facility and illustrate its use for such case.

### 3.1 A Non-compositional Simplified Metamodel of Prolog

The non-compositional, simplified Prolog metamodel is shown in Fig. 1. It shows that
a Prolog program is a set of clauses, with each clause consisting of a premise that is a
Prolog query and a single conclusion that is a first-order logic atom. A Prolog query is
a tree of arbitrary depth which leaves are first-order logic atoms and which non-leaf
nodes are one of the two logical connectives and or or. A first-order logic atom is
also a tree of arbitrary depth which leaves are either constant symbols or first-order
variables, and which non-leaf nodes can only be constant symbols. Each sub-tree is a
called a logical term, which root is called the functor of the term and which depth one
sub-trees are called its arguments. Non-functional terms are depth zero sub-trees and
opposed to functional terms which depth is at least one. A ground term is a sub-tree of
arbitrary depth that is free of variables.

### 3.2 A Non-compositional, Simplified Metamodel of HiLog

High-Order Logic (HiLog) extends Prolog with high-order syntactic sugar while
semantically remaining first-order. At the program, clause and query levels, HiLog
follows exactly the same construction rules as Prolog. The former extends the latter
only at the lower logical atom level. The extension is twofold: (1) HiLog, allows
programs in addition to terms as arguments, and (2) HiLog allows arbitrary terms
(functional or not, ground or not) as functors instead of restricting them to constant
symbols (i.e., non-functional ground terms) as Prolog does.

   For example, P(f(X))(G(Y), (G, c :- X, p(Y(P)))). is a valid HiLog term but not a
Prolog term for three reasons: (1) its functor is a compound term P(f(X)), (2) its first
argument's functor is a variable G and (3) its second argument is a program made of
two clauses, G. and c :- X, p(Y(P)). HiLog extends Prolog with meta-programming,
meta-reasoning and metadata definition and query facilities within the logical
paradigm under well-defined first-order declarative semantics. It brings to logic
programming the high-order syntax that is key to the versatility of functional
programming. In the HiLog metamodel of Fig. 2 the first of the two ways in which
HiLog extends Prolog is reflected by the fact that the functor meta-association
outgoing from the FunctionalTerm meta-class targets the Term meta-class,
instead of the Constant meta-class as in the Prolog metamodel. The second
extension is reflected by the introduction of the new meta-class LogicalArgument
as the target of the arg meta-association outgoing from the LogicalAtom meta-
class. This new LogicalArgument meta-class generalizes the two meta-classes
FunctionalTerm and Program.

## 3.3 Reusing and Generalizing Metamodel Elements from Prolog in HiLog

The relation between HiLog and Prolog can be summarized as follows: "A HiLog program is a Prolog program, *except that,* (a) the functor of the atoms of its clauses can recursively be compound and/or non-ground terms and (b) the arguments of the atoms of its clauses can recursively be HiLog programs." As a language, HiLog thus

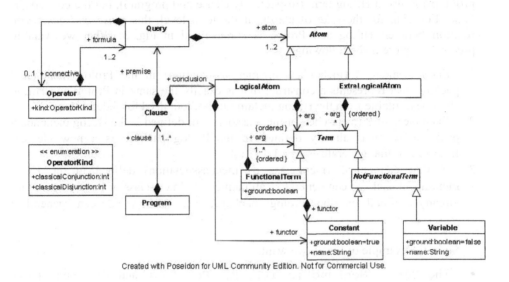

**Fig. 1.** Non-compositional, simplified Prolog metamodel

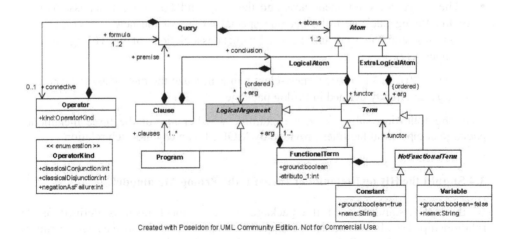

**Fig. 2.** Non-compositional simplified HiLog metamodel.

reuses Prolog in three ways. First it reuses its lexical categories `constant` and `variable`. Second it reuses its functional roles `functor`, `argument` and `connective`. Third it reuses its syntactic rules to build clauses from terms and connectives and to build programs from clauses. However, HiLog reuses Prolog by *generalizing* it: the HiLog syntactic rules to build terms from constants, variables and programs fulfilling the functor and argument roles of a term are less restrictive than the corresponding rules in Prolog. Thus, every Prolog term (respectively clause and program) is also a HiLog term (respectively clause and program), but the converse is false. Focusing for the sake of clarity at the term level, this *reuse and generalize* relation between HiLog and Prolog is summarized in Fig. 3. What we want to precisely capture is the following:

1.  Each element `E` (meta-class or meta-association) in the Prolog metamodel package that represents a construct that is exactly the same in Prolog and HiLog shall be available from the HiLog metamodel without need for redefinition;
2.  Each element `E` (meta-class or meta-association) defined in the HiLog metamodel package that was already defined in the Prolog package is a new element `HiLog::E` that generalizes `Prolog::E`.
3.  A new element `G` (meta-class or meta-association) defined in the Hilog metamodel package can generalize an element `S` (meta-class or meta-association) already defined in the Prolog package, i.e, `HiLog::G` can generalize `Prolog::S`.

So in the example of Fig. 3, we want:

*   The `Term`, `NonFunctionalTerm`, `Constant` and `Program`[3] meta-classes of the Prolog package to be reusable "as is" by elements of the HiLog package;
*   The `LogicalAtom` meta-class and the `arg` and `functor` meta-associations of the Prolog package to be become specializations of the new `LogicalAtom` meta-class and the `arg` and `functor` meta-associations of the HiLog package (respectively).

*   The `LogicalArgument` meta-class can generalize the meta-classes `Term` and `Program` already defined in Prolog package.

In the following subsections, we examine whether any of the three metamodel package composition facilities provided by MOF 2.0 can capture such relation.

### 3.4 Should the HiLog Metamodel `Import` the Prolog Metamodel?

In the MOF standard [11] the package `import` mechanism is defined as "a relationship that allows the use of unqualified names to refer to package members from other namespaces". It is a one-way relationship: when a package P imports a

---

[3] Omitted from Fig. 3 but linked to `LogicalAtom` through association navigation in Fig. 1 and Fig. 2.

package Q, the elements of P can be linked to the elements of Q but not vice-versa. In our case, since we want to reuse Prolog package elements in the HiLog package, the only possible direction is to `import` the Prolog package from the HiLog package. In that direction, `import` fulfills the *reuse* part of our *reuse and generalize* need. However it then also prevents the fulfillment of the *generalize* part. This is illustrated in Fig. 4. The `Term` meta-class of the Prolog package *cannot* be linked as needed to the `LogicalArgument` of the HiLog package meta-class by a specialization association, for it would break the unidirectionality of the `import` dependency between the two packages.

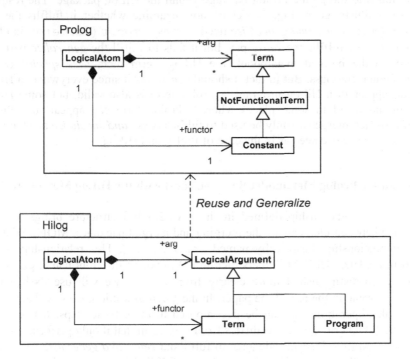

**Fig. 3.** Reuse and Generalize relationship between HiLog and Prolog

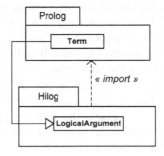

**Fig. 4.** `Import` cannot stand for reuse and generalize.

## 3.5 Should the Prolog Metamodel Be Merged Within the HiLog Metamodel?

The merge mechanism has been first defined in the UML2.0 Infrastructure [12]. Merging a package Q within a package P can be understood as an "alias" equivalent to the following action sequence: (1) for each element (meta-class or meta-association) E of the merged package Q, create a copy E' of E in the merging package P; (2) Import Q from P; and (3) for each copied element E, create an inheritance association that states that its copy E' specializes E.

In our case, since we want to reuse the Prolog package in the HiLog package, our only option is to merge the Prolog package within the HiLog package. The result of doing so is illustrated in Fig. 5. Let us now examine whether it fulfills the two requisites for our *reuse and generalize* need. Just as import (that merge in effect extends), merge fulfills the *reuse* part but it fails to fulfill the *generalize* part. For example, in the merged metamodel, the HiLog::Term meta-class *specializes* the Prolog::Term meta-class. But in fact it should *generalize* it since everywhere a HiLog term can appear in a HiLog program, a Prolog term is also valid, but some HiLog terms are not valid in some places where a Prolog term can appear in a Prolog program. In fact, merge can only be used to fulfill a *reuse and specialize* need, but not a *reuse and generalize* need as in the case of Prolog and HiLog.

## 3.6 Should the Prolog Metamodel Be Combined with the HiLog Metamodel?

As the merge relationship defined in the UML2.0 Infrastructure brings a lot of inheritance between elements of the merging and merged packages, MOF2.0 defined a variant relationship, historically named combine [11]. This relationship is also defined in the latest UML2.0 Superstructure [13], under a different name: package merged. To distinguish it more clearly from merge, we will use its historical combined name in the rest of the paper. In the previous section, we saw that merge is a complex operation that can be decomposed in three basic steps: (a) copy, (b) import and (c) inherit. Combine differs from merge in that it only performs the first "copy" step. At first, it seems adequate to fulfill our *reuse and generalize* need, since we saw that with merge, the *reuse* part was fulfilled by the "copy" step but the *generalize* part was made impossible by the "inherit" step that was in the wrong direction. However, consider the situation where a meta-association A occurs both (a) between meta-classes C and D in the package Q to reuse and (b) between C and a generalization G of D in receiving package P. This a standard situation when using combine to fulfill a *reuse and generalize* need. It is illustrated in Fig. 6. where the same meta-association arg links the meta-class LogicalAtom to the meta-class Term in the Prolog package to reuse, while it links the same meta-class LogicalAtom to the meta-class LogicalArgument that generalizes Term in the receiving HiLog package. In such cases, the package resulting from combining Q with P *is not a valid* MOF 2.0 metamodel since it includes two meta-associations *with the same name* A that links the same meta-class C to *two distinct* meta-classes G and D. This is illustrated in Fig. 7 that shows the package resulting from combining the Prolog and HiLog packages. In this example, two copies of the arg meta-association link        the        meta-class        LogicalAtom        to        two        distinct        meta-classes,

LogicalArgument and Term, and two copies of the functor meta-association also link of LogicalAtom to both the Term and Constant meta-classes. The resulting metamodel is thus invalid.

### 3.7 Our Proposal: A New Metamodel Assembly Facility

Since none of the three metamodel package assembly facilities currently provided either MOF 2.0 or UML 2.0 can satisfactorily fulfill a pervasive need for compositional metamodeling, we propose a fourth one that we call reuse and generalize. It is based on combine but corrects the flaw that we identified in the latter for reusing while generalizing elements of a metamodel package Q into another package P. This facility creates a new resulting package that assembles elements from P and Q by the following action sequence:

1.  For each element (meta-class or meta-association) E appearing in either packages Q and P, create a copy E' of E in the resulting package R.
2.  Whenever this results in conflicting pairs of meta-associations with the same name, one linking a meta-class C to a meta-class G and another linking a meta-class C to specialization D of G, delete the latter.

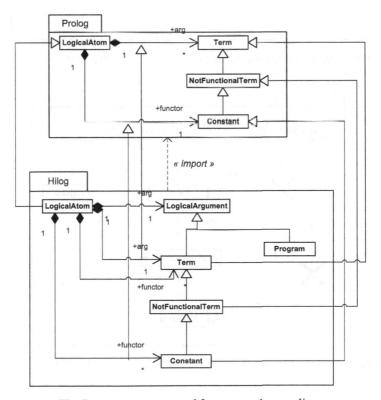

**Fig. 5.** Merge cannot stand for reuse and generalize.

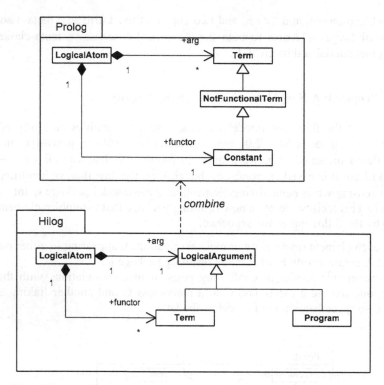

**Fig. 6.** Input packages of `combine` and of `reuse and generalize`.

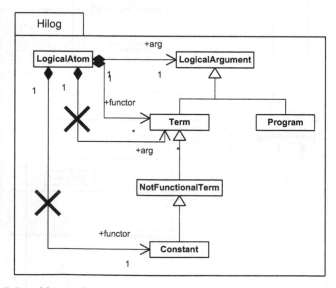

**Fig. 7.** Resulting package of `combine` and of `reuse and generalize`.

The result of reuse and generalize the Prolog package in the HiLog package in shown in the same Fig. 7, together with the result of combined. The difference is the crossed-over links, present with combined but absent with reuse and generalize. The latter thus contains only a single arg meta-association that links the LogicalAtom meta-class to the LogicalArgument meta-class and a single functor meta-association that links LogicalAtom to the Term meta-class. It is thus a valid MOF 2.0 metamodel that reuses the Prolog metamodel while generalizing it elements in the resulting HiLog metamodel. Note that the HiLog *package* that forms the second input to this reuse and generalize transformation is *not* a HiLog *metamodel* for it captures only the constructs *proper* to HiLog that define how it extends Prolog. The current version of the whole Flora metamodel was assembled from nine packages and sub-packages linked together by two instances of import and seven instances of reuse and generalize.

# 4 Related Work

Using a subset of the UML structural infrastructure similar to MOF, Clark et al. [5] proposed two new package assembly facilities. The first that they call "merge", but that is distinct from the merge of MOF, addresses the case of the same meta-class occurring in the two packages to assemble. In the "merging" package, the meta-attributes and meta-associations of such meta-class becomes the union of those in its occurrences in the two "merged" packages. The second facility, called *renaming* allows equating the names of two elements with two distinct names in the two packages prior to a "merge". Later, the same authors [6] proposed a Metamodeling Framework using a language that is distinct from MOF and that allows the definition of parametric model elements templates. This framework includes package *specialization* assembly facilities that deal with such templates.

Addressing the same issue, Ledeczi [9] proposed three assembly facilities: one that is much similar to Clark et al.'s "merge", one that restricts the union of the meta-class elements in the "merging" package to its attributes and containment associations in the "merged" package, and one that restricts it to its complementary non-containment associations.

Mens et al. [10] proposed package assembly facilities for collaborative diagrams. Since such diagrams are not used at the metamodeling level, these facilities do not seem to be easily applicable to metamodel assembly issues.

In short, none of the facilities proposed in these works addresses the specific *reuse and generalize* need that we identified.

# 5 Conclusion

Many powerful computational languages and platforms result from a historical process of gradually extending an initial core with largely orthogonal and complementary constructs inspired from other languages. There are great benefits to metamodeling such languages and platforms in a compositional way that reflects this historical maturation and clearly separates concerns. When doing so, one immediately feels the need for a metamodel package assembly facility that allows both *reusing* the elements of two basic packages, each one focused on a single concern, and *generalizing* them in a resulting package that captures their integration. In this paper, we have shown that none of the three metamodel assembly facilities currently provided by MOF and UML fulfills such need:

- `Import` because it prohibits imported elements to specialize elements of the importing package;
- `Merge` because it implicitly makes the reused elements generalizations instead of specializations of the new ones;
- `Combine` because when a reused meta-class is generalized, its meta-associations are not generalized, but instead *duplicated* at the level of its generalization, resulting in an invalid model.

We thus proposed a new `reuse and generalize` facility that is inspired from `combine` but that correctly generalizes instead of duplicating meta-associations in such cases. The ever widening scope of MDD is likely to reveal many other metamodel reuse needs beyond the "reuse as is" and "reuse and specialize" currently provided by MOF and the "reuse and generalize" addressed in this paper. In future work, we intend to create a catalog of metamodel reuse needs and to identify how these needs can be addressed by a minimal set of primitive reuse operators together with an algebra that defines semantically sound complex compositions of such operators.

## Acknowledgements

The research presented in this paper was sponsored by research grant 371/01 from CAPES-COFECUB, by one doctoral research fellowship from CNPq, by the ModelWare project co-funded by the European Commission under the "Information Society Technologies" Sixth Framework Programme (2002-2006), and by the "Model Driven Development Integration" (MDDi) project from the Eclipse Foundation. We would like to thank Marie-Pierre Gervais for her insightful feedback on a preliminary version of this paper.

## References

[1] Birbeck, M., Ozu, N. et al.: Professional XML. 2nd Ed. Wrox (2001)
[2] Bonner, A. and Kifer, M.: Transaction Logic Programming. Technical Report CSRI-323. Computer Systems Research Institute, University of Toronto (1995)
[3] Bonner, A. and Kifer, M.: Concurrency and Communication in Transaction Logic. Joint International Conference and Symposium on Logic Programming. Bonn, MIT Press (1996).
[4] Chen, W., Kifer, M. and Warren, D.S.: HiLog: A Foundation for High-Order Logic Programming. Journal of Logic Programming. 15(3) (1993) 187-230
[5] Clark, T., Evans, A. and Kent, S.: A Metamodel for Package Extension with Renaming. International Conference on the Unified Modeling Language (2002) 305-320

[6] Clark, T., Evans, A. and Kent, S.: Engineering Modelling Languages: A Precise Metamodeling Approach. Fundamental Approaches to Software Engineering (FASE) International Conference. Lecture Notes in Computer Science, Vol. 2306. Springer-Verlag (2002) 159-173

[7] Frühwirth, T. and Abdennadher, S.: Essentials of Constraint Programming. Series: Cognitive Technologies.Springer. (2003)

[8] Kifer, M., Lausen, G. and Wu, J.: Logical Foundations of Object-Oriented and Frame-Based Languages. Journal of the ACM 42(4). (1995) 741-843.

[9] Ledeczi A, Nordstrom, G., Karsai, G., Volgyesi, P. And Maroti, M.: On Metamodel Composition. Conference Control Applications, IEEE Press. Mexico City, Mexico (2001) 84-90

[10] Mens, T., Lucas, C. and Steyart, P.: Supporting Disciplined Reuse and Evolution of UML Models. PSMT – Workshop on Precise Semantics for Software Modeling Techniques in UML Conference. (1998) 378-392

[11] OMG.: The MOF 2.0 specification. http://www.omg.org/mof (2003)

[12] OMG.: The UML 2.0 Infrastructure specification. http://www.omg.org/uml (2003)

[13] OMG.: The UML 2.0 Superstructure specification. http://www.omg.org/uml (2003)

[14] The QVT-Merge Group. QVT 1.8.: Revised submission for OMG MOF 2.0 Query/Views/Transformations Request For Proposal. 2004.

[15] Ramalho, F., Robin, J. and Schiel, U.: Concurrent Transaction Frame Logic Formal Semantics for UML Activity and Class Diagrams. Electronic Notes in Theoretical Computer Science, 95(17). (2004)

[16] The World-Wide Web Consortium. Web Ontology Language. http://www.w3.org/2004/OWL. 2004 (2004)

[17] Yang, G.: A Model Theory for Nonmonotonic Multiple Value and Code Inheritance in Object-Oriented Knowledge Bases. PhD. Thesis, Computer Science Department, Stony Brook University of New York. (2002)

[18] Yang, G., Kifer, M. and Zhao, C. FLORA-2: A Rule-Based Knowledge Representation and Inference Infrastructure for the Semantic Web. 2nd International Conference on Ontologies, Databases and Applications of Semantics (ODBASE), Catania, Italy. (2003) 671-688.

# Modeling the User Interface of Multimedia Applications

Andreas Pleuß

Institut für Informatik, Ludwig-Maximilians-Universität München
Munich, Germany
andreas.pleuss@ifi.lmu.de
http://www.medien.ifi.lmu.de

**Abstract.** Multimedia applications are a branch of software development with growing importance. Typical application areas are training applications and simulations, infotainment systems - e.g. in cars - or computer games. However, there is still a lack of tailored concepts for a structured development of this kind of application. The current paper proposes a modeling approach for the user interface of multimedia applications with the goal of a model-driven development. We identify the special properties of multimedia application development and the resulting aspects to be covered by the user interface model. Existing conventional user interface modeling approaches are not sufficient, as they do not cover the media-specific aspects of the application. However, a multimedia application usually includes conventional user interface elements as well. Thus, we first propose a solution for the media-specific part. Second, we elaborate an integration of our approach with existing conventional approaches. Finally, we discuss the overall model-driven development approach and outline its benefits.

## 1 Introduction

Multimedia applications are an application domain with still growing importance. In typical application areas, like training and simulation software or computer games, the intensive usage of multimedia is already established since many years. Additionally, in the last years the production of sophisticated user interfaces became more and more common even in other applications areas. Often cited examples are information systems with an emphasis on a pleasing and entertaining user interface, so called infotainment systems. Modern cars contain such applications to provide integrated access on the car's entertainment, comfort and navigation functionality. For a classification of multimedia applications see e.g. [1], [2].

The extract of the most common definitions of the term *multimedia application* postulates an interactive application integrating at least a temporal and a discrete media type. *Discrete media* refers to media which does not change over time, like a still image, while temporal media is time dependent like audio or video. As today a high amount of software is compliant to this definition we

L. Briand and C. Williams (Eds.): MoDELS 2005, LNCS 3713, pp. 676–690, 2005.

restrict this for the purpose of this paper: First, the usage of media objects is a core feature of the application, including also complex media types like video and animation. (Animation refers here to graphics which changes over the time in any way). Second, the application provides sophisticated interaction associated with application logic. Purely document-oriented software, i.e. a (static) hypertext document, is not in the main focus of this paper.

The development of multimedia applications is characterized by the integration of knowledge, tools, and experts from two different areas: software engineering and media design. While requirements analysis is performed analogously to conventional software and the implementation phase is supported by powerful multimedia authoring tools (e.g. *Macromedia Flash* [3]), there is still a lack of concepts to bridge the gap between analysis and implementation. Current multimedia development methods, like described in [4], use mainly informal methods with emphasis on media production and design. Concepts for the structured integration of the application logic and the consideration of software engineering principles are still missing, although they are heavily claimed by various research contributions like [5], [6], [7], [8]. This results in badly structured applications, where maintenance and extension requires exceeding effort, although changes of requirements are also common for this type of application [9]. Common software engineering methods, like UML-based design methods, are not sufficient, as they do not cover media integration and user interface design [2], [10], [11].

Early approaches to address this problem focus on single specific aspects of a multimedia application, in particular synchronization (see [12], [13]), or very specific application domains like [14]. The first comprehensive approach is *OMMMA* (*Object-oriented Modeling of Multimedia Applications*, [10], [15]) which provides a design model for multimedia applications based on UML. Based on OMMMA, we propose in [16] further refinements and enhancements enabling a model-driven development of multimedia applications.

The current paper continues the research in [16], where we described an overall frame for model-driven development of multimedia applications and the relationships between the different views of a multimedia application model. These views are the static structure (i.e. the domain model), the user interface, the interaction, and the overall temporal structure (i.e. coarse-grained program flow). The current paper takes one of these views – the user interface, which is probably the most important and extensive view – and goes into the details.

We first discuss in detail the required aspects to be covered by a user interface model for multimedia applications. While existing work focuses only on the media-specific user interface elements, we take into account, that usually also conventional user tasks are part of a multimedia application. Thus, we consider in addition the existing task-based user interface modeling approaches for conventional widget based applications. On that base we first propose a detailed and platform-independent modeling approach for the media-specific modeling part. Afterwards, we elaborate the integration with the required parts from conventional task-based user interface models. Finally, we discuss the resulting overall model-driven development approach for multimedia applications.

The paper is structured as follows: section 2 introduces conventional approaches for user interface modeling. In section 3 we discuss in detail the requirements for multimedia applications and how they affect the concepts from conventional user interface modeling. On that base, we discuss in section 4 the required model elements for the media-specific part and propose a notation. In section 5 the media-specific part of section 4 is integrated with the required elements from conventional task-based modeling. We discuss the overall model-driven approach in section 6. Section 7 provides the conclusions and the outlook.

## 2   Conventional User Interface Modeling

There is already a good understanding of the basic principles for modeling user interfaces. This section briefly describes the basic concepts based on the detailed overview provided in [17], followed by the introduction of a concrete approach, *UMLi* [18], which we use as base for the further work in this paper.

First work on user interface modeling started already in the 1980's, e.g. [19]. The main problem of early approaches was that they emerged either from the engineering domain or from the UI designer domain (see [11]) – a similar problem as addressed in this paper for multimedia applications. Advanced approaches integrate the both views. They usually base on a conventional domain model, like UML class diagrams, as well as on a task model, like *ConcurTaskTrees* [20]. The task model has its origins in the human-computer-interaction community. It represents the user's tasks and decomposes them hierarchically into subtasks, down to primitive actions on the user interface. Task and domain model are usually modeled during analysis.

The *abstract UI model* describes the user interface in an abstract and platform-independent way. It consists of three different kinds of elements: *Abstract interaction objects* allow primitive user actions like invoking an action or selecting an element from a list. *Information elements* present information to the user, which can be either from the domain model or additional information like a label text. Interaction objects and information elements are assigned to *presentation units*, which represent an abstraction of windows on the screen. The elements are derived from the task model and are related to the domain model either by invoking actions or by presenting or manipulating information.

Finally, a *concrete UI model* is derived from the abstract UI model. It contains concrete user interface elements, usually widgets, and their concrete layout. Often the concrete UI model is realized by specialized implementation tools like user interface builders. The transformation from abstract to concrete UI model can be done semi-automatically, e.g. rule-based like in [21].

In the following we briefly sketch a concrete approach, *UMLi* [18]. It applies the mentioned principles of UI modeling and realizes them as an extension of UML. As today UML is a de-facto standard and widely understood, we use this approach for the further work in this paper.

A presentation unit in the abstract UI model in UMLi contains the following elements: *inputters*, which receive information from the user, *displayers*, which

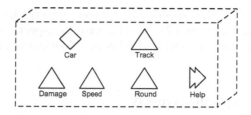

**Fig. 1.** UMLi diagram for the racing game example

provide information to the user, *editors*, which are simultaneously inputters and displayers, and *action invokers*, which receive events from the user (e.g. like a button).

Figure 1 shows an UMLi diagram for the race screen of a racing game application. We use this example, as on the one hand it demonstrates all characteristics of a multimedia application and on the other hand its requirements are easy to understand without specific domain knowledge. During the race the user has to steer the car over the track. In addition to the car and the track the application displays information about the current status, like the car's speed and damage, and the number of completed rounds. Moreover, the user can leave the race to view the application's help. The UMLi diagram consists of a presentation unit representing the race window (dashed lines). It contains the required user interface elements. To display information about the car status and the current round, we use displayers (represented by upward triangles). For the invocation of the help window we use an action invoker (represented by the semi-overlapped triangles). As the user constantly modifies the car's position and orientation, we decide to represent it by an editor (notated as a diamond) and the track by a displayer. (Another decision is also possible, as actually the car stays always in the center of the screen while the track moves, but probably such decisions belong rather to the concrete layout than to the task-based abstract layout modeled with UMLi).

The behavior of the user interface elements, i.e. the dialogue, is modeled in UMLi using UML activity diagrams. To describe the relationships between actions and user interface elements they use Object Flows. The difference between plain UML and UMLi activity diagrams are stereotypes which mainly aim for a more compact notation of constructs frequently occurring for user interfaces.

## 3   Required Aspects to Model

The foregoing section describes the established concepts for modeling a user interface. The focus of those approaches lies only in user interfaces for "conventional" applications, like database applications. Their user interface objects are restricted to standard objects, usually widgets, as explicitly stated e.g. in [17], [18]. As this focus is not sufficient for multimedia applications we discuss in the following section the required aspects for this specific domain.

Section 3.1 discusses the aspects directly related to the heavy usage of media objects. On that base, section 3.2 comes back to the aspects of conventional task based user interfaces and examines whether and how they change in multimedia applications.

## 3.1  Multimedia-Specific Aspects

The requirements are derived from the existing multimedia related modeling approaches described in section 1, as well as from the methods and artifacts mentioned in multimedia development related work like [4], [9].

**Integration of Specific Media Types.** The core characteristic of a multimedia application is the integration of different media types. The choice of a media type specifies, on which perception channels information is presented to the user and how the user can interact with it. Thus, it is a fundamental decision which media type is used to achieve the optimal transmission of a given piece of information to the user. Often the choice of media type is a basic requirement from the customer, e.g. in a medical training application the customer may postulate to have a human organ presented by a 3D animation. It may also be possible that the choice of media type is already obliged by circumstances, like restriction of resources or the media objects available from third parties.

The usage of the complex media types should also be specified as soon as possible within the development process, as the production of media content often takes much effort and time. Dependent on the chosen type of media, the respective experts and tools need to be available.

The media type affects the other parts of the application, e.g. because of its specific interaction behavior. In summary, the model should allow to specify which concrete media objects to use in the application. We propose a solution for this requirement in section 4.

**Inner Structure of Media Objects.** Complex media types often consist of several sub-objects. For example an animation representing a car may consist of sub-animations for doors and wheels, which may move independently. Besides, also the whole car can move. Dependent of the sub-objects, they contain sub-objects themselves.

A user interface model should allow specifying such an inner structure, when the sub-objects have to be accessed by the program code of the application. On the one hand, the media designer has to take into account which parts of a media object should be accessed from code. Typically these parts are designed as sub-components. In the example above typically the wheels themselves are also designed as animations contained within the car animation. On the other hand, the application code programmer has to know how to access the required parts, e.g. their name and their path within the hierarchy of sub-objects. In summary, the specification of the inner structure of media objects is required to define the interface between application code and media objects and should thus be supported by the modeling approach. We propose a solution for this requirement in section 4.

**Spatial User Interface Layout.** An issue to discuss is the spatial user interface layout. A vision of the layout can be the basic motivation for the whole multimedia application. It can be the core of the customer's requirements. For example a customer has the idea of a racing game application, where the screen shows a view on the track and in the foreground a specific instrument board.

On the other hand, it is contentious whether to include the spatial user interface layout into a model. Clearly, the structure of the user interface is important, e.g. which window contains which elements. This aspect is already covered by conventional user interface models in an abstract way. Spatial layout would add information about the size and position of elements. But this information can lead to platform dependent models, as the screen size of the target platforms can change significantly. Moreover, as demonstrated by conventional user interface models, interaction objects are implemented for different platforms using different widgets or probably different modes (e.g. on some devices auditory instead of graphical messages).

Moreover, it is not clear, whether the (semi-)formal specification of size and position adds valuable information to the model. To capture the vision of a screen layout, usually no exact and absolute values are required. Quite contrary, the final pixel precise adjustment is better performed in the implementation tool anyway. To sketch the idea of the layout, informal and quickly to handle methods are more suitable.

In summary, there is no urgent need for specifying the spatial layout in the model. As it usually adds no further (formal) information, it can be viewed as an additional optional view on the existing model. This additional view can be addressed e.g. by layout sketches. The quick creation of optional layout sketches can probably also be supported by an advanced modeling tool.

**Synchronization.** The temporal behavior of different time-dependent media objects can be related to each other. An example is an animation which should be synchronous with sound or a video which should start after another video has finished. Such synchronization issues often affects other parts of the application – e.g. other media objects or the program code – and should therefore be part of the model.

In the meanwhile, UML offers various mechanisms to model temporal behavior. Also activity diagrams, used for behavior modeling in UMLi, are suitable to denote the order of media objects and whether they can be interrupted by events. UML 2.0 also enables an advanced specification of temporal constraints.

## 3.2   Task-Related Aspects

Based on the media-specific requirements, the following section discusses the consequences for the conventional task-based user interface elements from section 2.

**Interaction Objects.** Media objects can act as interaction objects, e.g. the user can click on an animation. However, there is still the need for conventional interaction objects. A multimedia application usually contains also conventional tasks. For example in the racing game application the user should be able to input his name, invoke the help or cancel the application. Such tasks are often outside the customer's media-specific vision of the application. They also usually require no specific media-type. In that case, conventional abstract interaction objects are useful to stay independent of the target platform and even the modality. The interaction may even be without any graphical design, e.g. just pressing a key on the keyboard. The designer should not be forced to make such decisions when it is not mandatory.

Another issue is that time-dependent media objects can invoke actions independently from the user. They can trigger time-related events, e.g. when they are interrupted or have finished. Dependent from the media type additional events are possible, e.g. a moving animation can trigger an event when it touches another animation or reaches a specific region on the screen.

In summary, abstract interaction objects should be part of the model. As media objects may also act as interaction objects, the model must integrate these two kinds of elements. Additionally, it must be considered that media objects can invoke actions independently from the user. We propose a possible solution in section 5.

**Information Elements.** All media objects present information to the user, which can be static or derived from the domain model. Thus, media objects act as information elements. To some extent, all information elements are also media objects, as they provide their information of course using any media type (e.g. text). However, for the same reasons as for interaction objects (see 3.2), the model should also provide abstract information elements. Likewise, the model must integrate media objects and abstract information objects in a consistent way. In section 5 we propose a possible solution for those requirements.

**Presentation Units.** A multimedia application will usually show different presentation units, similar to conventional applications. An extension arises from the dynamic nature of time-dependent media types like animation or video: they add an internal state to the presentation unit. This takes effect, if for example the presentation of the presentation unit is interrupted, e.g. to show a help window, and should be continued afterwards. A video or an animation should then potentially resume the state which it had before the interruption.

A solution for this problem is already proposed in [16]: an extended presentation unit is called *scene*. A scene can have attributes and methods like usual classes in UML diagrams. Attributes are used to realize the internal state of a scene. The methods include special entry-methods, which are invoked when the scene is entered. The initialization of a scene depends on the invoked entry-method and the method's parameters, which allow resuming the internal state.

# 4   Modeling the Media Objects

In section 3 we discussed the required aspects for the modeling approach. This section discusses the different model elements (denoted in italics) to model these aspects for the media-specific part.

## 4.1   Media Objects

As introduced in section 1 media types are classified into *temporal media* and *discrete media*. Some properties, like synchronization, occur only for temporal media objects. Discrete media types are *images*, *graphics* and *text*. The basic temporal media types are *audio*, *video* and *animation*. Further we distinguish *2D animation* and *3D animation*, because of their different structure. The production of 3D graphics and animation usually requires specialized tools and experts while 2D graphic creation is much simpler and even part of several multimedia authoring tools (e.g. Macromedia Flash).

## 4.2   Inner Structure

According to section 3 it is necessary to define the inner structure of media objects, to enable their manipulation through program code. By definition, only temporal media types can have a dynamic, code controlled inner structure. In particular (interactive) animations are usually closely linked to program code. Due to the complexity of 3D animation, several approaches to describe its structure already exist. We take them as base to derive the general concepts for our purpose. Afterwards we briefly sketch the structure of 2D animation, audio, and video.

**Inner Structure of 3D Animation.** A common concept in the 3D community for the description of 3D animation is the so-called *scene graph* (it is important to note that there is no direct relation to the scene concept described in 3.1). In the following we base on our work in [22] where we describe a platform-independent scene graph approach.

The nodes of a scene graph represent the visible, material *3D objects* themselves as well as components affecting their appearance. The latter ones are *light*, the current position of the viewer (referred to as *camera*), and predefined further possible viewer positions (*viewpoints*). The spatial information itself is also represented by a node: a *transformation* node performs one or more transforming operations – i.e. translation, scale, or rotation – to all its assigned sub-nodes. The nodes are connected by directed relationships which define the object hierarchy (usually as a tree). A transformation is always relative to its parent node, i.e. if the parent node is moved, its inner transformations are still valid.

It is important for our purpose that only nodes, which have to be accessed by application logic, are (explicitly) specified in our models. All other parts of the inner structure are omitted as implicit parts of the nodes.

If a node has multiple identical children (i.e. a car owns several wheels), it can be denoted in a compact way by just specifying one of the child nodes together with the actual number of children. Moreover, a keyword assigned to the relationship denotes whether the multiple children nodes are separate copies (keyword `copy`), i.e. can be modified separately, or whether they reference only the same single object (keyword `ref`), i.e. they are always exactly identical.

**Inner Structure of 2D Animation.** The structure of 2D animations can be derived from the 3D animations. Light, camera and viewpoints are not relevant for 2D level. The remaining elements are 2D objects and transformations. The shapes contained in an animation can be animations themselves or static graphics. The latter ones are not relevant for our purpose, as we here specify only nodes which are manipulated through code.

Figure 2 shows the main model elements for the inner structure of 2D and 3D animations.

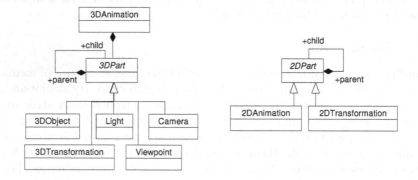

**Fig. 2.** Simplified metamodel for inner structure of 2D and 3D animation

**Inner Structure of Audio and Video.** The content of audio and video is rarely directly manipulated by program code. The general concepts can be summarized as follows: Audio can be composed of several tracks, e.g. for a left and a right speaker. Typical manipulations are the application of filters or the change of volume for one or more tracks. Moreover, an audio object can be composed of several samples, i.e. parts within its local timeline. Most actions on audio are time-related, e.g. jumping to a specific point on the timeline (*cue point*). To be independent from concrete audio objects we specify cue points by the semantics of their name (instead of defining concrete time values). The mapping from a cue point to a concrete time value can then be done during the deployment of the audio object, e.g. by the audio designer. Video can be handled in analogous way.

### 4.3   Example

Figure 3 shows the media-specific part of the racing game example from section 2. The track is represented by an animation. It contains additional animations for obstacles and for the car. We clearly indicate the inner sub-objects here in the diagram by placing them within their topmost parent object. The car animation contains two front wheels. The inner structure is only specified insofar as required for the application code. For example the front wheels should be moved whenever the car drives through a corner. The annotations at the relationship between `Car` and `FrontWheels` specify that there are two front wheels which behave identically (and have thus not to be implemented as two independent objects).

Additionally the application should provide a cockpit view for the user displaying the current status of the car. This is realized by animations for the speedometer and the damage control. Moreover, the car is represented by sound. The other user interface objects of this screen are not contained in the diagram, as they require no specific media type.

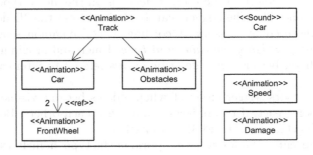

**Fig. 3.** Media-specific user interface elements of a racing game application

# 5   Integration of Media-Specific Aspect and Task-Based Aspects

In this section we integrate the media-specific part of the model from section 4 with the conventional task-based elements from section 2. In particular, we discuss how to fulfill the requirements of section 3.

## 5.1   Media-Objects as Interaction Objects and Information Elements

According to section 3 media objects are related to the conventional task-based user interface elements. All of them act as information elements.

Whether and how a media object can act as interaction element depends on the media type. Audio can usually not act as an interaction object, as it can not be manipulated. Of course it is possible to record and parse audio using a microphone as accomplished at speech recognition. However, this does not relate to playing an auditory media object, and is therefore not discussed in this paper.

The same holds for video, where a camera and gesture recognition are necessary for user inputs.

However, all visual elements, including video, appear on the screen and can therefore receive user events, e.g. when selected by a pointing device. Thus, all visual objects can act as action invokers. As animations can dynamically change their content dependent on the application logic, they can additionally act as editors. An example is the car animation which represents e.g. the current rotation of the car. The user manipulates the animation to edit the rotation value.

## 5.2   Media-Objects as Trigger

As mentioned in section 3, temporal media objects can also invoke actions without direct intervention from the user. It depends on the media type which types of triggers are possible. The triggers can be derived from the 3D domain, where they are represented by *sensors*. According to [22] common sensor types are *touch*, *proximity*, *visibility*, *collision*, and *time*. Touch and proximity sensors are not relevant here, because they describe events related to interaction with the user.

Visibility sensors trigger an event when objects became visible for the user. Collision sensors react, if two objects collide with each others. Both can occur for moving objects, i.e. (2D and 3D) animations.

Time events can occur for every temporal media type, namely when it reaches a specific point on its local timeline. This can be the end of the timeline or a specified cue point. All sensors can be assigned to a whole media object as well as to sub-objects from its inner structure.

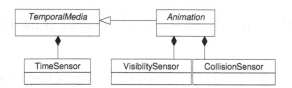

**Fig. 4.** Simplified metamodel for sensors

## 5.3   Modeling Example

The example shows the integration of the task-based user interface elements from figure 1 and the media objects specified in figure 3. The dashed arrows denote that a media object realizes an abstract user interface element. An abstract user interface element can be realized by multiple media objects. If required for clarity, abstract editor elements can be decomposed in inputter and displayer. In the diagram, this would be possible for the car editor (but not shown here in

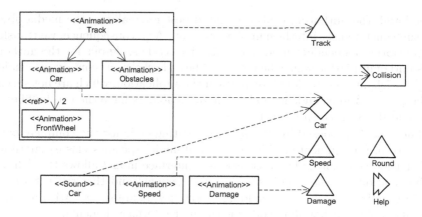

**Fig. 5.** Integration of task-based and media-specific user interface elements for the racing game example

the diagram). Abstract user interface elements, which are not realized by media objects, have to be realized during the implementation phase by appropriate platform specific solutions (e.g. widgets).

To describe the behavior of the user interface elements, the UMLi activity diagrams (see section 2) can used in the same way as before. The only difference are the sensors from media objects. They can be represented by UML *AcceptEventActions* to be used in the activity diagram. For example in figure 5 the Obstacles animation provides a collision sensor, which waits for the occurrence of collision events on the obstacles.

## 6    Model-Driven Development

In [16] we proposed the overall framework for a model-driven approach for multimedia applications. The current paper extends it by a platform-independent user interface model. It can be transformed into platform-specific models, using the concepts of *model driven development* (e.g. [23]).

Typically, multimedia applications are implemented using authoring tools like Macromedia Flash, which emphasize powerful support for the creation, integration, and deployment of media objects. However, they poorly support concepts for structuring the application logic and control. For example, interactive user interface elements often require the assignment of a script snippet to the respective element. As a result, script snippets are scattered all over the application. The consistent application of established software engineering concepts, like e.g. the Model-View-Controller paradigm [24], is often only possible with deep experience and under consideration of implementation "tricks".

Considering the mentioned strength and weaknesses of multimedia authoring tools, they seem to be dedicated to a model-driven approach. The model is much better suited to design the overall application structure and behavior. On the other hand, the authoring tools are suited best for realizing the media objects and the concrete user interface implementation. As a consequence, we transform the platform-independent models directly into code skeletons for the authoring tools and omit platform-specific models. The code skeletons contain placeholders (gaps or default objects) for those parts of the application, which are not specified in the platform-independent model. The placeholders have then to be filled out or replaced within the authoring tool.

The models proposed in [16] allow generating code for the complete overall structure of the application. The structural model specifies classes, attributes, and method signatures. The abstract user interface model allows the definition of the relationships between user interface elements and the structural model. The interaction model (corresponding to activity diagrams in UMLi) allows the generation of event handling code for the user interface elements.

The implementation of the methods from the structural model (i.e. the method bodies) is not part of the model. In multimedia applications methods often affect the user interface. Thus, the purposes of those methods are not only "hard" goals, like the correct computation of a value, but also "soft" goals, like esthetics. For example in a racing game a class `Car` provides methods which are responsible for the user's driving experience. Values and parameters often have to be found out by "trial and error" and should be optimized for the target platform. Thus, the methods are implemented directly within the authoring tool.

The media objects in the model are transformed into placeholders (e.g. bounding boxes), which have then to be replaced in the authoring tool. The abstract user interface objects can be transformed into widgets for the respective target platform. A rule based transformation, like in [21], is well supported by the MDA concepts for transformations, like parameters and constraints, as explained e.g. in [25].

# 7   Conclusion and Outlook

The approach described in this paper proposes a contribution for the model-driven development of multimedia applications. As the user interface is usually the core feature of this type of application, the concepts described in the paper can constitute the basement of multimedia modeling.

Beside the contributions to our modeling approach, the main contributions presented here lie in the general results for multimedia user interfaces. It is not contentious that multimedia applications require specific solutions addressing the heavy usage of media objects, as described by the existing research work. But in addition, the user also has to perform conventional tasks for controlling the application and its content. As a consequence we take here into account the results from conventional user interface modeling and integrate them with the media-specific aspects.

As a second general contribution we provide a fundamental discussion about the involved requirements for modeling user interfaces containing media objects.

On that base we propose an abstract and platform-independent modeling approach for media objects and their inner structure.

As a consequence, the whole multimedia application models are platform-independent. We propose a model-driven approach generating directly code skeletons from the platform-independent models. The code skeletons contain gaps which are completed in the authoring tool. It is fundamental that the completion requires only tool abilities which the authoring tools are best in: the creation and deployment of media objects, the user interface layout and the platform specific definition of code on well-defined places predefined by the platform-independent model.

We have specified a MOF-compliant metamodel for our approach. On that base we have built a modeling tool for our models implemented on *Eclipse* [26] and related technologies like the *Eclipse Modeling Framework*. The tool provides simple tree-editors to create and edit models according to the metamodel. More sophisticated graphical diagram editors are currently under development. Moreover, we have a code generator producing *SVG/JavaScript* code skeletons from our models. At the moment we develop further generators, especially for Flash. For the Flash authoring tool we currently develop a plug-in to provide additional support for processing the generated code skeletons, e.g. navigation between the gaps in the generated skeletons and support for a round-trip engineering.

We are preparing the evaluation of our approach in student projects. In particular we provide an annual teaching course "Multimedia-Programmierung" (multimedia programming) where students have to develop in teamwork multimedia applications of middle size, e.g. in the last year a multiplayer racing game application implemented with Flash.

# References

[1] Tannenbaum, R.S.: Theoretical Foundations of Multimedia. Freeman, New York (1998)

[2] Hannington, A., Karl, R.: Towards a Taxonomy for Guiding Multimedia Application Development. In: 9th Asia-Pacific Software Engineering Conference (APSEC 2002), 4-6 December 2002, Gold Coast, Queensland, Australia. IEEE Computer Society (2002)

[3] Macromedia: Macromedia, http://macromedia.com/ (2004)

[4] Mallon, A.: The Multimedia Development Process, http://ourworld. compuserve.com/homepages/adrian_mallon_multimedia/devmtpro.htm (1995)

[5] Hirakawa, M.: Do Software Engineers Like Multimedia? In: IEEE International Conference on Multimedia Computing and Systems (ICMCS) 1999 Proceedings. Volume 1. IEEE Computer Society (1999) 85–90

[6] Arndt, T.: The Evolving Role of Software Engineering in the Production of Multimedia Applications . In: IEEE International Conference on Multimedia Computing and Systems (ICMCS) 1999 Proceedings. 1 edn. IEEE Computer Society (1999)

[7] Rahardja, A.: Multimedia Systems Design: A Software Engineering Perspective. In: International Conference on Computers and Education (ICCE) 95 Proceedings. IEEE Computer Society (1995)

[8] Bianchi, A., Bottoni, P., Mussio, P.: Issues in Design and Implementation of Multimedia Software Systems. In: Proceedings of IEEE International Conference on Multimedia Computing and Systems (ICMCS '99), Florence, Italy, Volume I. IEEE Computer Society (1999) 91–96

[9] Osswald, K.: Konzeptmanagement - Interaktive Medien - Interdisziplinäre Projekte. Springer, Berlin (2002)

[10] Engels, G., Sauer, S.: Object-oriented Modeling of Multimedia Applications. In Chang, S.K., ed.: Handbook of Software Engineering and Knowledge Engineering. Volume 2. World Scientific, Singapore (2002) 21–53

[11] Trætteberg, H.: Model-based User Interface Design. PhD thesis, Norwegian University of Science and Technology, Oslo (2002)

[12] Hirzalla, N., Falchuk, B., Karmouch, A.a.: A Temporal Model for Interactive Multimedia Scenarios. IEEE MultiMedia **2** (1995) 24–31

[13] Bertino, E., Ferrari, E.: Temporal Synchronization Models for Multimedia Data. IEEE Transactions on Knowledge and Data Engineering **10** (1998) 612–631

[14] Arya, A., Hamidzadeh, B.: Face Animation: A Case Study for Multimedia Modeling and Specification Languages . In Deb, S., ed.: Multimedia Systems and Content-Based Image Retrieval. Information Science Publishing (2003)

[15] Sauer, S., Engels, G.: Extending UML for Modeling of Multimedia Applications. In Hirakawa, M., Mussio, P., eds.: IEEE Symposium on Visual Languages 1999 Proceedings. IEEE Computer Society (1999)

[16] Hußmann, H., Pleuß, A.: Model-Driven Development of Multimedia Applications. In: Talk at 'The Monterey Workshop 2004 - Workshop on Software Engineering Tools: Compatibility and Integration', Submitted for Proceedings. (2004)

[17] Szekely, P.: Retrospective and Challenges for Model-Based Interface Development. In Vanderdonckt, J., ed.: Computer-Aided Design of User Interfaces. Presses Universitaires de Namur, Namur, Belgium (1996)

[18] da Silva, P.P., Paton, N.W.: UMLi: The Unified Modeling Language for Interactive Applications. In Evans, A., Kent, S., Selic, B., eds.: UML 2000 - The Unified Modeling Language. Advancing the Standard. Third International Conference, York, UK, October 2000, Proceedings. Volume 1939. Springer (2000) 117–132

[19] Wiecha, C., Bennett, W., Boies, S.J., Gould, J.D.: Generating Highly Interactive User Interfaces . In Bice, K., Lewis, C.H.a., eds.: Proceedings of the ACM CHI 89 Human Factors in Computing Systems Conference. April 30 - June 4, 1989, Austin, Texas, New York (1989)

[20] Paternó, F., Mancini, C., Meniconi, S.: ConcurTaskTrees: A Diagrammatic Notation for Specifying Task Models. In Howard, S., Hammond, J., Lindgaard, G., eds.: Proceedings Interact'97. Chapman & Hall (1997)

[21] Vanderdonckt, J.: Automatic generation of a user interface for highly interactive business-oriented applications. In Plaisant, C., ed.: Companion Proceedings of CHI'94. ACM Press, New York (1994)

[22] Vitzthum, A., Pleuß, A.: SSIML: Designing Structure and Application Integration of 3D Scenes. In: Proceedings of the tenth international conference on 3D Web technology. ACM Press, New York (2005)

[23] Frankel, D.S.: Model Driven Architecture. John Wiley (2003)

[24] Buschmann, F., Meunier, R., Rohnert, H., Sommerlad, P., Stal, M.: Pattern-Oriented Software Architecture: A System Of Patterns. Volume 1. John Wiley, West Sussex, England (1996)

[25] Kleppe, A., Warmer, J., and, B.W.: MDA Explained. Addison-Wesley (2003)

[26] Eclipse: The Eclipse Project, http://www.eclipse.org/ (2004)

# An Ontology-Based Approach for Evaluating the *Domain Appropriateness* and *Comprehensibility Appropriateness* of Modeling Languages

Giancarlo Guizzardi, Luís Ferreira Pires, Marten van Sinderen

Centre for Telematics and Information Technology,
University of Twente, Enschede, the Netherlands
{guizzard, pires}@cs.utwente.nl, sinderen@ctit.utwente.nl

**Abstract.** In this paper we present a framework for the evaluation and (re)design of modeling languages. We focus here on the evaluation of the suitability of a language to model a set of real-world phenomena in a given domain. In our approach, this property can be systematically evaluated by comparing the level of homomorphism between a concrete representation of the worldview underlying the language (captured in a metamodel of the language), with an explicit and formal representation of a conceptualization of that domain (a reference ontology). The framework proposed comprises a number of properties that must be reinforced for an isomorphism to take place between these two entities. In order to illustrate the approach proposed, we evaluate and extend a fragment of the UML static metamodel for the purpose of conceptual modeling, by comparing it with an excerpt of a philosophically and cognitive well-founded reference ontology.

## 1 Introduction

The objective of this paper is to discuss the design and evaluation of artificial modeling languages for capturing phenomena in a given domain according to a conceptualization of that domain. In particular, we focus on two properties of a modeling language w.r.t. a given real-world domain [1]: (i) *domain appropriateness*, which refers to truthfulness of the language to the domain; (ii) *comprehensibility appropriateness*, which refers to the pragmatic efficiency of the language to support communication, understanding and reasoning in the domain.

The elements constituting a *conceptualization* of a given domain are used to articulate abstractions of certain state of affairs in reality. We name them here *domain abstractions*. Domain conceptualizations and abstractions are intangible entities that only exist in the mind of the user or a community of users of a language. In order to be documented, communicated and analyzed these entities must be captured in terms of some concrete artifact, namely a *model*. Moreover, in order to represent a model, a *modeling language* is necessary. Figure 1 depicts the relation between a conceptualization, domain abstraction, model and modeling language.

L. Briand and C. Williams (Eds.): MoDELS 2005, LNCS 3713, pp. 691–705, 2005.

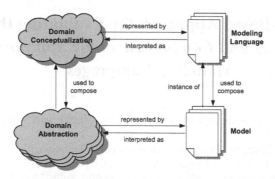

**Figure 1.** Relation between conceptualization, abstraction, modeling language and model.

In this paper, we propose a framework to evaluate the suitability of a language to model a set of real-world phenomena in a given domain. In our approach, *domain* and *comprehensibility appropriateness* can be systematically evaluated by comparing the level of homomorphism between a concrete representation of the worldview underlying the language (captured in a *metamodel of the language*), with an explicit and formal representation of a conceptualization of that domain (a *reference ontology* [8]). Our framework comprises a number of properties that must be reinforced for an iso-morphism to take place between these two entities. If an isomorphism can be guaranteed, the implication for the human agent who interprets a diagram (model) is that his interpretation correlates precisely and uniquely with an abstraction being represented. By contrast, in case the correlation is not an isomorphism there may be multiple unintended abstractions that match the interpretation.

The framework presented here builds on existing work in the literature. In particular, it considers the frameworks proposed in [2], which focus on evaluating the match between individual diagrams and the state of affairs they represent, and the approach of [3], which focuses on the system of representations as a whole, i.e., a language. Although our approach is also centered in the language level, we show that, by considering desirable properties of the mapping of individual diagrams onto what they represent, we are able to account for desirable properties of the diagrams' modeling languages. In this way, we extend the original proposal presented in [3]. We also build here on the work of the philosopher of language H.P.Grice [4] and his notion of *conversational maxims* that states that a speaker is assumed to make contributions in a dialogue which are *relevant, clear, unambiguous,* and *brief, not overly informative* and *true according to the speaker's knowledge.* Finally, in comparison to [2] and [3], by presenting a formal elaboration of the nature of the entities depicted in Figure 1 as well as their interrelationships, we manage to present a more general and precise characterization of the characteristics that a language must have to be considered truthful to a given domain.

The remaining of this paper is structured as follows. Section 2 introduces the evaluation framework proposed here. Section 3 presents a formal characterization of the notions of domain conceptualization and their representing ontologies, as well as their relations to modeling languages and particular models. In order to illustrate our approach, we evaluate and extend a fragment of the UML static metamodel for the purpose of conceptual modeling, by comparing it with an excerpt of a philosophically and cognitive well-founded reference ontology. Section 4 discusses the foundational ontology employed for this purpose. Section 5 discusses the evaluation of the UML metamodel, and the extensions that we propose in order to enforce suitability to conceptual modeling. Section 6 presents some final considerations.

## 2    A Framework for Language Evaluation

Following [2], we define four properties that should hold for an isomorphic correlation to take place: *lucidity*, *soundness*, *laconicity* and *completeness* (see Figure 2). Each of these properties is discussed below.

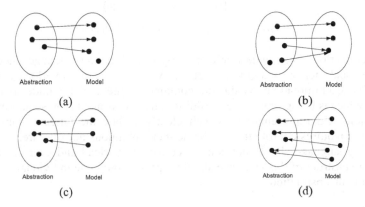

**Figure 2.** Examples of *Lucid* (a) and *Sound* (b) *representational* mappings from *Abstraction* to *Model*; Examples of *Laconic* (c) and *Complete* (d) *interpretation* mappings from *Model* to *Abstraction*.

### 2.1 Lucidity and Construct Overload

A model $\mathcal{M}$ is called *lucid* w.r.t. a domain abstraction $\mathcal{A}$ if a (representation) mapping from $\mathcal{A}$ to $\mathcal{M}$ is *injective*, i.e., iff every construct in the model $\mathcal{M}$ represents at most one (although perhaps none) concept of the domain abstraction $\mathcal{A}$. An example of an injective mapping is depicted in Figure 2(a).

The notion of lucidity at the level of individual diagrams is strongly related to the notion of *ontological clarity* at the language level [3]. The ontological clarity of a modeling grammar is undermined by what is termed in [3] a *construct overload*. A construct overload occurs when a single language construct is used to represent two or more domain concepts. These notions albeit related are not identical. A construct can be overloaded at the language level, i.e., it can be used to model different concepts, but every manifestation of this construct in individual models is used to represent only one of the possible concepts. Figure 3 exemplifies a non-lucid representation. In this case, the construct X is used to represent two entities of the abstraction, namely the numbers 2 and 3. In this case, although the representation system does not have a case of construct overload (since labeled boxes only represent numbers and arcs only represent the less-than relation between numbers) the resulting model is non-lucid. In summary, the absence of construct overload in a language does not directly prevent the construction of non-lucid representations in this language. Additionally, construct overload does not entail non-lucidity. Nevertheless, non-lucidity can also be manifested at a language level. We say that a language is non-lucid according to a conceptualization if there is a construct of the language that when used in a model of an abstraction (instantiation of this conceptualization) stands for more than one entity of the represented abstraction. Non-lucidity at the language level can be considered as a special case of construct overload that does entail non-lucidity at the model level.

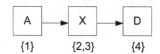

**Figure 3.** Example of a Non-Lucid Diagram.

Construct overload is an undesirable property of a modeling language since it causes ambiguity and, hence, undermines clarity. When a construct overload exists, users have to bring additional knowledge not contained in the model to understand the phenomena which is being represented. Additionally, a non-lucid representation language entails non-lucid representations which clearly violate the Gricean conversational maxim that requires contributions to be neither ambiguous nor obscure. In summary, a modeling language should not contain construct overload and every instance of a modeling construct of this language should represent only one individual of the represented domain abstraction.

## 2.2 Soundness and Construct Excess

A model $\mathcal{M}$ is called *sound* w.r.t. a domain abstraction $\mathcal{A}$ if a (representation) mapping from $\mathcal{A}$ to $\mathcal{M}$ is *surjective*, i.e., iff every construct in the model $\mathcal{M}$ represents at least one (although perhaps several) concept of the domain abstraction $\mathcal{A}$. An example of a surjective representation mapping is depicted in Figure 2(b).

An example of an unsound diagram is illustrated in Figure 4. The arc connecting the labeled boxes D and A does not correspond to any relation in the represented world. Unsoundness at the model level is strongly related to unsoundness at language level, a property that is termed *construct excess* in [3]. Construct excess occurs when a language construct does not represent any domain concept. Although construct excess results in the creation of unsound models, soundness at the language level does not prohibit the creation of unsound models. For example, there is no construct excess in the language used to produce the model of Figure 4.

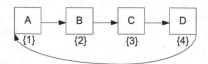

**Figure 4.** Example of an Unsound Diagram.

An unsound diagram violates the Gricean cooperative principle because any represented construct will be assumed to be meaningful by users of the language. Since no mapping is defined for the exceeding construct, its meaning becomes uncertain, hence, undermining the clarity of the model. Users of modeling language must be able to make a clear link between a modeling construct and its interpretation in terms of domain concepts. Otherwise, they will be unable to articulate precisely the meaning of the models they generate using the language [3]. Therefore, a modeling language should not contain construct excess and every instance of its modeling constructs must represent an individual in the domain.

### 2.3 Laconicity and Construct Redundancy

A model $\mathcal{M}$ is called *laconic* w.r.t. a domain abstraction $\mathcal{A}$ if an interpretation mapping between $\mathcal{M}$ and $\mathcal{A}$ is *injective*, i.e., iff every concept in the abstraction $\mathcal{A}$ is represented by at most one (although perhaps none) construct in the representation $\mathcal{M}$. An example of an injective interpretation mapping is depicted in Figure 2(c).

The notion of laconicity at the model level is related to the notion of *construct redundancy* at the language level in [3]. Construct redundancy occurs when more than one language construct can be used to represent the same domain concept. Once again, despite of being related, laconicity and construct redundancy are two different (even opposite) notions. On one hand, construct redundancy does not entail non-laconicity. For example, a language can have two different constructs to represent the same concept, however, in every situation the construct is used in particular models it only represents a single domain element. On the other hand, the lack of construct redundancy in a language does not prevent the creation of non-laconic models in that language. An example of a non-laconic diagram is illustrated in Figure 5. In this picture, the same domain entity (the number 3) is represented by two different constructs ($C_1$ and $C_2$) although the representation language used does not contain construct redundancy.

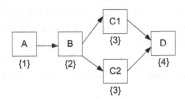

**Figure 5.** Example of a Non-laconic Diagram.

Non-laconicity can also be manifested at the language level. We say that a language is non-laconic if it has a construct that when used in a model of a domain abstraction, causes an entity of this abstraction to be modeled more than once in the resulting representation. For instance, take a version of the labeled boxes language used so far and let the less-than relation between numbers be represented both as the *transitive closure of the is-arrow-connected* and by the *is-smaller-than* relation between labeled boxes. All models using this representation (e.g., Figure 6) are deemed non-laconic. Non-laconicity at the language level can be considered as a special case of construct redundancy that does entail non-laconicity at the model level.

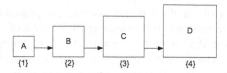

**Figure 6.** Example of a Non-laconic Diagram generated by a Non-Laconic Language.

In [3], the author claims that construct redundancy *"adds unnecessarily to the complexity of the modeling language"*, possibly confusing the users. Therefore, construct redundancy can also be considered to undermine representation clarity. Non-laconicity also violates the Gricean principle, since a redundant representation can be interpreted as standing for a different domain element. In sum, a modeling language should not contain construct redundancy, and elements in the represented domain should be represented by at most one instance of the language modeling constructs.

## 2.4 Completeness

A model $\mathcal{M}$ is called *complete* w.r.t. a domain abstraction $\mathcal{A}$ if an interpretation mapping between $\mathcal{M}$ and $\mathcal{A}$ is *surjective*, i.e., if each concept in a domain abstraction (instance of the domain conceptualization) is represented by at least one (although perhaps many) construct in the representation $\mathcal{M}$. An example of a *surjective* interpretation mapping is depicted in Figure 2(d).

The notion of completeness at the model level is related to the notion of *ontological expressiveness* and, more specifically, *completeness* at the language level, which is perhaps the most important property that should hold for a representation system. A modeling language is said to be *complete* if every concept in a domain conceptualization is covered by at least one modeling construct of the language. Language incompleteness entails lack of expressivity, i.e., there can be phenomena in the considered domain that cannot be represented by the language. Alternatively, users of the language can choose to overload an existing construct in order to represent concepts that originally could not be represented, thus, undermining clarity. Thus, unless some existing construct is overloaded, an incomplete modeling language is bound to produce incomplete models. However, the converse is not true, i.e., a complete modeling language can still be used to produce incomplete models (see example in Figure 7). In Figure 7, a domain element (the 3 < 4 relation) is omitted in the representation.

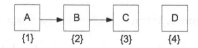

**Figure 7.** Example of an Incomplete Diagram.

In accordance with the detailed account of Grice's cooperative principle (specifically, that all necessary information is included), model and language designers should attempt to ensure completeness. In summary, a modeling language should be complete w.r.t. a domain conceptualization and every element in a domain abstraction (instance of this domain conceptualization) must be represented by an element of a model built using this language.

# 3    Conceptual Modeling, (Meta) Conceptualization and Ontology

According to Figure 1, a modeling language delimits all possible specifications[1] that can be constructed using this language, i.e., it determines all grammatically valid specifications of the language. Likewise, a conceptualization delimits all possible domain abstractions (representing state of affairs) that are admissible in that domain [5]. Therefore, for example, in a conceptualization of the domain of genealogy, there cannot be a domain abstraction in which a person is his own biological parent, because such a state of affairs cannot happen in reality. Accordingly, we can say that a modeling language is truthful to this domain if it has as valid (i.e., grammatically correct) specifications only those that represent state of affairs deemed admissible by a conceptualization of that domain. In the sequel, following [5], we present a formalization of this idea. This formalization compares conceptualizations as *intentional structures* and meta-models as represented by logical theories:

Let us first define a *conceptualization* C as an *intentional structure* $\langle W, D, \Re \rangle$ such that W is a (non-empty) set of possible worlds, D is the domain of individuals and $\Re$ is the set of n-ary relations (concepts) that are considered in C. The elements $\rho \in \Re$ are *intentional relations* with signatures such as $\rho^n:W \to \wp(D^n)$, so that each n-ary relation is a function from possible worlds to n-tuples of individuals in the domain. For instance, we can have $\rho$ accounting for the meaning of the natural kind apple. In this case, the meaning of apple is captured by the intentional function $\rho$, which refers to all instances of apples in every possible world. For every world $w \in W$, according to C we have a *intended world structure* $S_wC$ as a structure $\langle D,R_wC \rangle$ such that $R_wC = \{\rho(w) \mid \rho \in \Re\}$. More informally, we can say that every intended world structure $S_wC$ is the characterization of some state of affairs in world w deemed admissible by conceptualization C. From a complementary perspective, C defines all the admissible state of affairs in that domain, which are represented by the set $S_c = \{S_wC \mid w \in W\}$.

Let us consider now a language $\mathcal{L}$ with a vocabulary V that contains terms to represent every concept in C. A *logical model* for $\mathcal{L}$ can be defined as a structure $\langle S,I \rangle$: S is the structure $\langle D,R \rangle$, where D is the domain of individuals and R is a set of extensional relations; $I:V \to D \cup R$ is an interpretation function assigning elements of D to constant symbols in V, and elements of R to predicate symbols of V. A model, such as this one, fixes a particular *extensional interpretation of language* $\mathcal{L}$. Analogously, we can define an intentional interpretation by means of the structure $\langle C,\Im \rangle$, where $C = \langle W, D, \Re \rangle$ is a conceptualization and $\Im:V \to D \cup \Re$ is an intentional interpretation function which assigns elements of D to constant symbols in V, and elements of $\Re$ to predicate symbols of V. This intentional structure is named the *ontological commitment* of language $\mathcal{L}$ to a conceptualization C. A model $\langle S,I \rangle$ of $\mathcal{L}$ is said to be compatible with *ontological commitment* $K = \langle C,\Im \rangle$ if: (i) $S \in S_c$; (ii) for each constant c, $I(c) = \Im(c)$; (iii) there exists a world w such that for every predicate symbol p, I maps such a predicate to an admissible extension of $\Im(p)$, i.e. there is an intentional relation

---

[1] We have so far used the term *model* instead of specification since it is the most common term in conceptual modeling. In this section, exclusively, we adopt the latter in order to avoid confusion with the term (logical) model as used in logics and tarskian semantics. A specification here is a syntactic notion; a logical model is a semantic one.

$\rho$ such that $\Im(p) = \rho$ and $\rho(w) = I(p)$. The set $I_k(\mathcal{L})$ of all models of $\mathcal{L}$ that are compatible with K is named the set of *intended models* of $\mathcal{L}$ according to K.

In order to exemplify these ideas let us take the example of a very simple conceptualization C such that $W = \{w,w'\}$, $D = \{a,b,c\}$ and $\Re = \{$person, father$\}$. Moreover, we have that person(w) = {a,b,c}, father(w) = {a}, person(w') = {a,b,c} and father(w') = {a,b}. This conceptualization accepts two possible state of affairs, which are represented by the world structures $S_wC = \{\{a,b,c\}, \{\{a,b,c\},\{a\}\}$ and $S_{w'}C = \{\{a,b,c\}, \{\{a,b,c\},\{a,b\}\}$. Now, consider a language $\mathcal{L}$ whose vocabulary consists of the terms `Person` and `Father` with an underlying metamodel that poses no restrictions on the use of these primitives. In other words, the metamodel of $\mathcal{L}$ has the following logical rendering[2] $(T_1)$: {∃x `Person(x)`, ∃x `Father(x)`}. Clearly, we can produce a logical model of $\mathcal{L}$ (i.e., an interpretation that validates the logical rendering of $\mathcal{L}$) but that is not an intended world structure of C. For instance, the model D'={a,b,c}, person = {a,b}, father = {c}, and I(`Person`) = person and I(`Father`) = father. This means that we can produce a specification using $\mathcal{L}$ whose model is not an *intended model* according to C.

We now extend the metamodel of language $\mathcal{L}$ by adding one specific axiom and, hence, producing the metamodel $(T_2)$: {∃x `Person(x)`, ∃x `Father(x)`, ∀x `Father(x)` → ∃x `Person(x)`}. In comparison with $\mathcal{L}$, the resulting language $\mathcal{L}'$ with the amended metamodel $T_2$ has the desirable property that many more of *its valid specifications have logical models that are intended world structures of C*.

A domain conceptualization C describes the set of all possible state of affairs that are considered admissible in the subject domain D. A representation O that has as *valid specifications* only those which represent *admissible state of affairs* according to conceptualization C is named an *Ontology* of domain D according to C. With an *explicit representation of a conceptualization* in terms of a *domain ontology*, one can measure the truthfulness (or *domain appropriateness*) of a language $\mathcal{L}$ to domain D, by observing the difference between the set of valid models of the metamodel M of $\mathcal{L}$ and the set of valid models of the ontology O of D (see Figure 8). In the best case, these two specifications are *isomorphic* and, thus, they share the same set of logical models. Therefore, not only every entity in conceptualization C must have a representation in the metamodel M of language $\mathcal{L}$, but these representations must obey the same axiomatization.

In the example above, we address the domain of genealogical relations. This exemplifies what is named a *material domain* in the literature. Accordingly, a modeling language designed to represent phenomena in this domain is named a *Domain-Specific Modeling Language* [7]. However, we illustrate our approach here by considering a (domain-independent) *general conceptual modeling language* (e.g., EER, ORM, UML). What should be real-world conceptualization that this language should commit to? We argue that it should be a system of general categories and their ties, which can be used to articulate domain-specific common sense theories of reality. This meta-conceptualization should comprise a number of domain-independent theories (e.g., theory of parts and wholes, types and instantiation, identity, existential dependence, etc.), which are able to characterize aspects of real-world entities irrespec-

---

[2] Given a specification S in a modeling language $\mathcal{L}$, the logical rendering of S is defined as the logical theory T that is the first-order logic description of that specification [12].

tive of their particular nature. The development of such general theories of reality is the business of the philosophical discipline of *Formal Ontology* [8]. A concrete arti-fact representing this meta-conceptualization is named a *Foundational Ontology* [9].

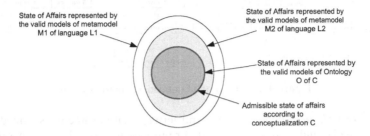

**Figure 8.** Measuring the degree of *domain appropriateness* of modeling languages via an on-tology of a conceptualization of that domain.

## 4    The Unified Foundational Ontology (UFO-A)

In this section, we present a fragment of a philosophically and cognitively well-founded reference ontology (foundational ontology) that has been developed in [10, 12, 13, 14]. In particular, in [14], this ontology is named UFO (Unified Foundational Ontology) and is presented in three compliance sets. Here, we focus the first one (UFO-A), which is an *ontology of endurants*. In the sequel, we restrict ourselves to a fragment of UFO-A, depicted in Figure 9. Moreover, due to space limitations and the focus of the paper we briefly present the ontological categories comprising UFO-A (see aforementioned articles for details).

A fundamental distinction in this ontology is between the categories of *Individual* and *Universal*. Individuals are entities that exist in reality possessing a unique iden-tity. Universals, conversely, are space-time independent pattern of features, which can be realized in a number of different individuals. The core of this ontology exemplifies the so-called *Aristotelian ontological square* comprising the category pairs *Substan-tial-Substantial Universal, Moment-Moment Universal*. From a metaphysical point of view, this choice allows for the construction of a parsimonious ontology, based on the primitive and formally defined notion of *existential dependency*.

**Definition 1** (existential dependence): We have that an individual *x* is *existentially dependent* of another individual *y* iff, as a matter of necessity, y must exist whenever x exists. ■

Existential dependence is a modally constant relation, i.e., if x is dependent of y, this relation holds between these two specific individuals in all possible worlds that x exists.

*Substances* are existentially independent individuals. Examples of Substances in-clude ordinary mesoscopic objects such as an individual person, a dog, a house, a hammer, a car, Alan Turing and The Rolling Stones but also the so-called *Fiat Ob-jects* such as the North-Sea and its proper-parts, postal districts and a non-smoking area of a restaurant.

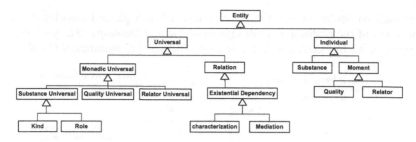

**Figure 9.** Excerpt of the Foundational ontology UFO-A.

The word *Moment* denotes, in general terms, what is sometimes named trope, abstract particular, individualized property or property in particular [9]. Therefore, in the scope of this work, the word bears no relation to the notion of time instant in colloquial language. A moment is an individual that can only exist in other individuals. Typical examples of moments are a color, a connection and a purchase order. Moments have in common that they are all dependent of other individuals (their bearers). Some moments are one-place *Qualities* (e.g., a color, a headache, a temperature); others are relational moments or *Relators* (e.g., a kiss, a handshake, a medical treatment, a purchase order), which depend on several substances.

A *Substantial Universal* is a universal whose instances are substances (e.g., the universal Person or the universal Apple). Within the category of substantial universals, we make a further distinction based on the formal notions of *rigidity* and *anti-rigidity*:

**Definition 2** (Rigidity): A universal U is rigid if for every instance x of U, x is necessarily (in the modal sense) an instance of U. In other words, if x instantiates U in a given world w, then x must instantiate U in every possible world w'. ■

**Definition 3** (Anti-rigidity): A universal U is anti-rigid if for every instance x of U, x is *possibly* (in the modal sense) not an instance of U. In other words, if x instantiates U in a given world w, then there must be a possible world w' in which x does not instantiate U. ■

A substantial universal which is rigid is named here a *Kind*. In contrast, an anti-rigid substantial universal is termed a *Role*. The prototypical example highlighting the modal distinction between these two categories is the difference between the universal (Kind) Person and the (Role) universal Student, both instantiated by the individual John in a given circumstance. Whilst John can cease to be a Student (and there were circumstances in which John was not one), he cannot cease to be a Person. In other words, in a conceptualization that models Person as a Kind and Student as a Role, while the instantiation of the role Student has no impact on the identity of an individual, if an individual ceases to instantiate the kind Person, then it ceases to exist as the same individual. Moreover, in [13], we have formally proved that a rigid universal cannot have as its superclass an anti-rigid one. Consequently, *a Role cannot subsume a Kind in our theory.*

A *Quality Universal* is a universal whose instances are individual qualities (e.g., the objectified color of this apple is an instance of the universal color), and a *Relator Universal* is one whose instances are individual relational moments (e.g., the particular enrollment connecting John and a certain University is an instance of the universal Enrollment). Both quality and relator universals are moment universals. The relation between a substantial universal and quality universal is one of **Characterization**. If a quality universal Q characterizes a substantial universal S, then every instance of Q is existentially dependent of an instance of S. Likewise, a relation between a set of substantial universals and a relator universal is one of **Mediation**. If a relator universal R mediates the substantial universals $S_1...S_n$, then every instance of R is existentially dependent of a plurality of entities, namely, particular instances of $S_1...S_n$.

*Relations* are entities that glue together other entities. In the philosophical literature, two broad categories of relations are typically considered, namely, *material* and *formal* relations [15,16]. Formal relations hold between two or more entities directly, without any further intervening individual. The only formal relations considered in this article are the existential dependence relations aforementioned. Other examples include relations such as *part-of*, *subset-of*, *instantiation*, among others not discussed here [10]. Material relations, conversely, have material structure on their own and include examples such as kisses, conversations, fights and commitments. The relata of a material relation are mediated by relators. For example, an individual *purchase* is a relator that connects a customer and a supplier, and a *treatment* is a relator which connects a patient with a medical unit. The notion of relational moments is supported in several works in the philosophical literature (e.g., [15,16,17]) and, the position advocated here is that, relators play an important role in answering questions of the sort: what does it mean to say that John is married to Mary? Why is it true to say that Bill works for Company X but not for Company Y?

In this paper, we only countenance as relations those of existential dependency discussed above, i.e., characterization and mediation. Thus, by a relation here we mean a formal relation of existential dependency. Material relations are represented by explicitly representing their founding relators. Therefore, according to this theory, formal and material relations are entities of different ontological nature. Whilst a formal relation such as the one between John and his knowledge $x$ of Greek holds directly and as soon as John and $x$ exist, the relation of John being treated in a particular Medical Unit $MU_1$ is a contingent one, and must rely on the existence of a founding entity, such as, for instance, a treatment t in which both John and $MU_1$ participate.

## 5    Evaluating and Extending UML for Conceptual Modeling

In this section we start by constructing representation and interpretation mappings between the concrete metaclasses of the UML metamodel presented in the *UML 2.0 Superstructure Specification* and the ontological categories comprising the foundational ontology employed here.

We start our discussion by focusing on the meta-construct Class. We assume for now a specific notion of class, namely one whose instances are single objects (as opposed to tuples of objects). In this sense, the ontological interpretation of a UML Class is that of a *monadic universal*. However, by carrying on this process, we realize that in UML there are no modeling constructs that represent the leaf ontological categories specializing *monadic universal*, namely, *kind*, *role*, *quality* and *relator*. In other words, there are ontological concepts prescribed by our reference ontology that are not represented by any modeling construct in the language. This is a case of *construct incompleteness* at the modeling language level.

In UML, the association meta-construct is used to represent both formal and material relations. As discussed in Section 4, formal and material relations are considered here as entities belonging to disjoint ontological categories. Therefore, the representation mapping from both formal and material relations to associations in UML can be considered a case of _construct overload_. However, in a different perspective, there are refinements on the category of relations in UFO-A that have no representation in the UML metamodel (characterization and mediation). Here, we have another case of _construct incompleteness_ at the modeling language level.

According to the UML specification, an interface is a declaration of a coherent set of features and obligations. It can be seen as a kind of contract that partitions and characterizes groups of properties that must be fulfilled by any instance of a classifier that implements that interface. In an interpretation mapping from the UML metamodel to the ontology of Figure 9, an interface qualifies as a case of _construct excess_. This means that since the UML interface is merely a design and implementation construct, there is no category in the conceptual modeling ontology proposed here that serve as the ontological interpretation for this construct.

In order to solve the cases of construct incompleteness in reference to the category of monadic universals, we propose a (lightweight) extension to the UML class meta-construct by introducing the stereotypes « kind », « role », « quality » and « relator », representing the respective ontological finer-grained distinctions. The profile formed by these newly introduced stereotypes must also contain a number of constraints that restrict the way the modeling constructs can be related. The goal is to have a meta-model such that all syntactically correct specifications using the profile have logical models that are _intended world structures_ of the conceptualizations they are supposed to represent. Thus, for instance, in a conceptual model using this profile, a class stereotyped as « kind » must not include in its superclass collection one class stereotyped as « role », since it is a postulate of our theory that anti-rigid universals cannot subsume rigid ones.

In general, qualities can be atomic or complex. Atomic quality universals are typically not represented in a conceptual model explicitly but via attribute functions that map each of their instances to points in a given _quality dimension_. For example, suppose we have the universal Apple (a substantial universal), characterized by the universal Weight. Thus, for an arbitrary instance $x$ of Apple there is a quality $w$ (instance of the quality universal Weight) that is existentially dependent of $x$. Associated with the universal Weight, and in the context of a given measurement system (e.g., the human perceptual system), there is a quality dimension _weightValue_, which is a set isomorphic to the half line of positive integers, obeying the same ordering structure. In this case, we can define an _attribute function_ weight(Kg) which maps for every instance of apple (and in particular $x$) to a point in a quality dimension, i.e., its quality value. Due to space limitations we do not discuss here the case of atomic qualities and related notions[3]. A formal treatment of this subject can be found in [12].

An example of a complex quality universal is the universal _Symptom_, characterizing the role _Patient_: every individual Symptom is existentially dependent of an individual patient. Thus, even if the patients John and Paul experience headaches which

---

[3] We emphasize, nonetheless, that the same ontological concept of _attribute functions_ is represented in the UML grammar both by the constructs of _attributes_ and _navigable end names_, thus, amounting to a case of _construct redundancy_ in the language.

are qualitatively indistinguishable, the headache of John is an individual which is only dependent of John. A complex quality universal is the ontological counterpart of the concept of *Weak entity types* in EER diagrams. We propose that they should be explicitly represented in class diagrams (via a class stereotyped as « quality »), or, to use an object-orientation term, *objectified*.

We advocate that associations in UML for the purpose of conceptual modeling should only represent formal relations. Consistently, we extend this construct in the UML metamodel by proposing the stereotypes « characterization » and « mediation » representing the two types of existential dependency considered here. Associations stereotyped as « characterization » must have in one of its association ends a class stereotyped as « quality » representing the characterizing quality universal.

In contrast, we propose to express relational properties explicitly via classes stereotyped as « relator », representing the ontological category of relator universals. The formal relation of mediation that takes place between the relator universal and the universals it mediates is explicitly represented by an association stereotyped as « mediation ». In addition, associations stereotyped as « mediation » must have in one of its association ends a class stereotyped as « relator ».

By representing relational properties explicitly via their founding relator universals, we not only remove the case of construct overload related to associations, but we also produce a representation that is more expressive, conceptually clear and semantically unambiguous. Consider, for example, the models depicted in Figure 10. In the standard UML representation of associations, the cardinality multiplicity of one-to-many between *GraduateStudent* to *Supervisor* is ambiguous and can be interpreted in a multitude of incompatible ways. For example, when stating that *"a supervisor supervises one to many student"* what exactly is being stated? (i) that in a given assignment there is one supervisor advising many students?, or (ii) that only one supervisor and one student are involved, but a supervisor can supervise many assignments? An analogous situation takes place when trying to interpret this association in the converse direction. In particular, due to the lack of expressivity of the traditional UML association, the model of Figure 10(a) cannot differentiate the two different conceptualizations, which are explicitly modeled in Figures 10(b) and 10(c). Finally, as discussed in [12], the problem of ambiguity of multiplicity constraints exemplified in these models only takes place in the case of material relations, in which two different types of constraints are collapsed.

Both *characterization* and *mediation* are directed relations. In the case of the former, the source is a quality universal, and in the case of the latter, the source is a relator universal. In both cases, the target is a substantial universal. Moreover, these two relations are mapped at the instance level to an *existential dependency* relation between the corresponding source individuals and their bearer objects. This has the following consequences for the extended UML metamodel: (i) the association end connected to the target (substantial) universal must have the minimum cardinality constraint of at least one, since moments are dependent entities; (ii) In the case of a « characterization » relation, the association end connected to the target (substantial) universal must have the maximum cardinality constraints of at most one, since qualities inhere in a unique bearer [10]; (iii) the association end connected to the target (substantial) universal must have the meta-attribute *isreadOnly* = *true*, since existential dependency is modally constant; and (iv) existential dependency relations are always binary relations. Finally, since a *relator individual* is dependent (mediates) on at least two numerically distinct entities, we have the following additional constraint: (v) let R be a relator universal, let $\{C_1...C_2\}$ be a set of substantial universals mediated by R (related to R via a « mediation » relation) and let $lower_{Ci}$ be the value of the minimum cardinality constraint of the association end connected to $C_i$ in a « mediation » relation to R, then $(\sum_{i=1}^{n} lower_{Ci}) \geq 2$.

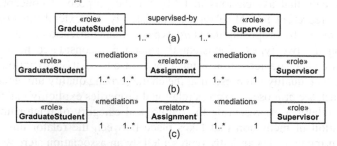

**Figure 10.(a)** Ambiguous representation of material relations using the standard UML notation **(b)(c)** Exemplification of how relators can disambiguate two conceptualizations that in the standard UML notation would have the same representation.

In order to solve the problem of construct excess in the case of UML interface meta-class, we propose to remove this construct from the extended UML metamodel, implying that the use of this construct would be prohibited in order to ensure that the resulting models are ontologically well-founded.

# 6     Final Considerations

In this paper, we present an ontology-based framework for evaluating the *domain* and *comprehensibility appropriateness* of modeling languages. The framework defines a systematic method for comparing the *metamodel* of a language with a concrete representation of a conceptualization of a given subject domain, termed a *reference ontology*. Moreover, the paper illustrates the application of the method by evaluating and extending a fragment of the *UML metamodel*. This has been achieved by comparing this metamodel with a *foundational ontology* that is considered as a suitable meta-conceptualization for domain independent *conceptual modeling*, and proposing stereotypes and usage constraints that make the metamodel isomorphic with the foundational ontology.

The framework presented here builds on existing work in the literature, extending them in important ways. For instance, the approaches of [2] and [3] address solely the relation between ontological categories and the modeling primitives of a language, paying no explicit attention to the possible constraints governing the relation between these categories. Moreover, it does not consider the necessary mapping from these constraints to equivalent ones, to be established between the language constructs representing these ontological categories. Additionally, [3] addresses only the design of general conceptual modeling languages. In contrast, the framework and the principles proposed here can be applied to the design of conceptual modeling languages irrespective to each generalization level they belong, i.e., they can be applied both the level of material domains and corresponding domain-specific modeling languages, and the (meta) level of a domain-independent (meta) conceptualization that underpins a general conceptual modeling language. Finally, as discussed in [11], by explicitly representing the subject domain of a language in terms of a well-founded ontology, we can account for important pragmatic aspects that should be preserved in the design of *concrete visual syntaxes*.

**Acknowledgements.** This work is part of the Freeband A-MUSE Project (contract BSIK 03025). We would like to thank Gerd Wagner, Nicola Guarino and Chris Vissers for fruitful discussions and for providing valuable input to the issues of this article.

# References

1.  Krogstie, J. (2001): *Using a Semiotic Framework to Evaluate UML for the Development of Models of High Quality*, Idea Publishing Group.
2.  Gurr, C.A. (1999): *Effective Diagrammatic Communication: Syntatic, Semantic and Pragmatic Issues*, Journal of Visual Languages and Computing, 10, 317-342.
3.  Weber, R. (1997). *Ontological Foundations of Information Systems*. Coopers & Lybrand, Melbourne.
4.  Grice, H.P. (1975): *Logic and conversation*. In: Syntax and Semantics: Vol 3, Speech Acts (P. Cole & J. Morgan, eds). Academic Press, New York, pp. 43-58.
5.  Guarino, N. (1998): *Formal Ontology and Information Systems*, Formal Ontology in Information Systems. Proceedings (FOIS), Italy.
6.  Ciocoiu, M., Nau D. (2000): *Ontology-Based Semantics*. 7th International Conference on Principles of Knowledge Representation and Reasoning (KR'2000), USA.
7.  Tolvanen, J.-P., Gray, J., Rossi, M., editors (2004): *Domain-Specific Modeling with Visual Languages*, Journal of Visual Languages and Computing, Elsevier Science.
8.  Husserl, E. (1970): *Logical Investigations*, London: Routledge & Kegan Paul.
9.  Masolo, C.; Borgo, S.; Gangemi, A.; Guarino, N.; Oltramari, A. (2003): *Ontology Library*, WonderWeb Deliverible D18.
10. Guizzardi, G., Herre, H., Wagner G. (2002): *On the General Ontological Foundations of Conceptual Modeling*, 21st Intl. Conf. on Conceptual Modeling (ER), Finland, LNCS 2503, Springer-Verlag.
11. Guizzardi, G.; Ferreira Pires, L.; van Sinderen, M. (2002): *On the role of Domain Ontologies in the Design of Domain-Specific Visual Languages*, 2nd Workshop on Domain-Specific Visual Languages, 17th OOPSLA, USA.
12. Guizzardi, G.; Wagner, G.; Herre, H. *On the Foundations of UML as an Ontology Representation Language*, 14th Intl Conference on Knowledge Engineering and Knowledge Management (EKAW), UK, LNCS 3257, Springer-Verlag.
13. Guizzardi, G.; Wagner, G.; Guarino, N.; van Sinderen, M. (2004): *An Ontologically Well-Founded Profile for UML Conceptual Models*, 16th Intl.Conference on Advances in Inf. Systems Eng. (CAiSE), Latvia, LNCS 3084, Springer-Verlag.
14. Guizzardi, G.; Wagner, G. (2005): *On a Unified Foundational Ontology and some Applications of it in Business Modeling*, Ontologies and Business Systems Analysis, Michael Rosemann and Peter Green (Eds.), IDEA Publisher.
15. Heller, B., Herre, H. *Ontological Categories in GOL*. Axiomathes 14: 71-90, Kluwer Academic Publishers, 2004.
16. Smith, B.; Mulligan, K (1986): *A Relational Theory of the Act*, Topoi (5/2), 115-30.
17. Schneider, L. (2003): *Designing Foundational Ontologies: The Object-Centered High-Level Reference Ontology OCHRE as a Case Study*, 22nd Intl. Conference on Conceptual Modeling (ER), LNCS 2813, Springer-Verlag.

# Workshops at the MODELS 2005 Conference

Jean-Michel Bruel

LIUPPA
Université de Pau et des Pays de l'Adour
64000 Pau, France
Jean-Michel.Bruel@univ-pau.fr

## 1   Introduction

It was a tradition in the previous UML series to host a number of workshops. Workshops provide the opportunity for a small group of people to exchange recent or preliminary results and to conduct intensive discussions on a particular topic. They complement in a sense the main conference and are generally very appreciated by attendees, most of them also attending the main conference.

For this new 2005 edition, it has been decided to host 12 one-day satellite events, during the 3 first days of the conference. The 2003 conference held 9 workshops, last year one held 9 workshops and a new Doctorial Symposium. This year, we have chosen to hold the successful Doctorial Symposium and to add a novelty, mainly related to the broader scope of the new series, a Symposium dedicated to models education.

The selection committee that helped me reviewing the proposals was formed by the following researchers:

- Elisa Baniassad (Chinese University of Hong Kong)
- Siobhán Clarke (Trinity College Dublin, Ireland)
- Gregor Engels (U. of Paderborn, Germany)
- Ana Moreira (Universidade Nova de Lisboa, Lisbon, Portugal)
- Ivan Porres (Åbo Akademi University, Turku, Finland)
- Ambrosio Toval (U. of Murcia, Spain)

We have selected 10 workshops which are detailed in the following section. Among the selected workshops, four have been previously held in the previous edition of the conference, one is the merging of two successful workshops from last year, and five are new to the conference series. This novelty has been particularly interesting and we hope that the community will also appreciate it. It reflects the changes at the main conference level itself.

At the time of writing those lines (end of June 2005) we of course have no information in terms of registration or success of each of these 12 events. The reader will find a brief overview of each of them in the following section, and we also invite her/him to consult the Satellite Events Proceedings that is expected to be published and that will contain, among others materials, an abstract of each workshops, written by their organizers, as well as an improved version of a selection of the 2 best papers of each workshops. We hope that this will provide a good idea of the workshops discussions and results.

L. Briand and C. Williams (Eds.): MoDELS 2005, LNCS 3713, pp. 706–714, 2005.

# 2   Detailed List of Workshops

## W1: Tool Support for OCL and Related Formalisms - Needs and Trends

**Organizers:** Thomas Baar (EPFL Lausanne, Switzerland), Dan Chiorean (University of Cluj-Napoca, Romania), Alexandre Correa (University of Rio de Janeiro, Brazil), Martin Gogolla (University of Bremen, Germany), Heinrich Hußmann (University of Munich, Germany), Octavian Patrascoiu (University of Kent, United Kingdom), Peter H. Schmitt (Universität Karlsruhe, Germany), Jos Warmer (Ordina, The Netherlands)

**URL:** See the main conference web site.

**Abstract:** Model-centric methodologies and new technologies such as MDA, MDSE, LDD, or DSL attract now a lot of attention both in academia and in industry. Since they propagate a shift from the implementation code to more abstract but nevertheless detailed and precise models, their successful application in industrial projects heavily depends on matured tools support. The traditional way to make a model more precise is by using a textual constraint language such as OCL. Recently, an increasing amount of work has been spent on OCL tools by various organizations so that software developers has today the choice among more than 10 academic and commercial tools. However, compared to similar tools supporting other textual languages, e.g. integrated development environments (IDEs) for Java, tools for OCL are still rather archaic.

The increasing importance of OCL for model-centric methodologies on one hand and the improving but not perfect tool support for OCL on the other hand naturally raise a lot of questions. Which features should an OCL tool offer to encourage the usage of OCL in practice? Is it feasible to make OCL more executable and to provide an animator for OCL? Which consequences for future tools have the fact that OCL is incorporated in a number of other formalisms? Should we strive for a common architecture of OCL tools which would enable us to reuse standard components? What is the relationship between OCL and similar formalisms such as JML, SQL, or graph-grammar based formalisms? Are there unclear issues in the OCL language descriptions that still prevent a smooth tool support?

## W2: MoDeVA – Model Design and Validation

**Organizers:** Benoit Baudry (INRIA, France), Christophe Gaston CEA/LIST, France), Sudipto Ghosh (Colorado State University, USA)

**URL:** http://www.irisa.fr/manifestations/2005/MODEVA2005/

**Abstract:** Design and validation methods appear to be more and more necessary in an industrial context. This fact is due to several actors. Software systems are more and more complex and cannot be understood by a stand-alone human without a proper standardisation. MDA(Model Driven Architecture) or more generally object/component oriented design methods have been defined in order to overcome a part of this problem. Moreover, systems large scale and complexity induce important risks of bugs or unpredicted behaviours resulting from interactions between subsystems. Formal methods have been intensively applied to evaluate reliability of systems. These methods generally require adequate specification and structuring languages to describe (a part of) the system under validation. For instance, modular first order languages are suitable for this purpose. One of the main problem encountered when trying to combine design and validation features, is that structuring languages suitable for one of the features are generally not suitable for the other. In this way, object-oriented paradigm is suitable for large scale system design, since it allows anthropomorphic design based on services exchanges of basic entities. However, this paradigm is not suitable (without restriction) for validation activities, since any enrichment of a system is likely to cause loss of global properties. In the opposite way, modular paradigm ensures properties preservation but the price to pay is an amount of design difficulties.

The MoDeVa (Model Design and Validation) workshop aims at being a forum for researchers and practitioners with varying backgrounds to discuss new ideas concerning links between model-based design and model-based validation. More precisely, topics of interest include design processes that support complex system modelling and formal or semi-formal refinement mechanisms. In the frame of validation methodology, model-based testing will be considered as "first-class-citizen" since testing is the primary used technique in the industrial context. Design methodologies including considerations on properties preservation (non-regression testing for example) will be appreciated. Languages to describe or validate models include UML and its MDE (Model Driven Engineering) and MDA aspects, algebraic languages, automata-based language, first order language, propositional languages... The considered design paradigm may be inherited from programming language field, like object oriented design, or more abstract, like component or feature based modelling.

## W3: MARTES – Modeling and Analysis of Real-Time and Embedded Systems

**Organizers:** Sebastien Gerard (CEA, France), Susanne Graf (Verimag, Grenoble, France), Øystein Haugen (Univ. of Oslo, Norway), Iulian Ober (Verimag, Grenoble, France), Bran Selic (IBM, Canada)

**URL:** http://www.martes.org/

**Abstract:** This workshop is a merge of the former workshop series SIVOES and SVERTS. The concern of this workshop is the use of MDA in the context of Real-time, distributed and embedded systems, where a particular emphasis is put on modeling, semantic issues and methods and tools for analysis.

## W4: Aspect Oriented Modeling

**Organizers:** Omar Aldawud (Lucent Technologies, USA), Tzilla Elrad (Illinois Institute of Technology, USA), Jeff Gray (University of Alabama at Birmingham, USA), Mohamed Kandé (Condris Technologies, Switzerland), Jörg Kienzle (McGill University, Canada), Dominik Stein (University of Duisburg-Essen, Germany)

**URL:** http://dawis.informatik.uni-essen.de/events/AOM_MODELS2005/

**Abstract:** Aspect-orientation is a rapidly advancing technology. New and powerful aspect-oriented programming techniques are presented at the International Conference on Aspect-Oriented Software Development every year. However, it is not clear what features of such techniques are "common aspect-oriented concepts" and what features are rather language-specific specialties. Research in Aspect-Oriented Modeling (AOM) has the potential to help find such common characteristics from a perspective that is at a more abstract level (i.e., programming language-independent). The ultimate goal of research in AOM is to provide aspect-oriented software developers with general means to express aspects and their crosscutting relationships onto other software artifacts.
This workshop aims to identify and discuss the impacts of aspect-oriented technologies on software modeling, and to set up a shared agenda for future research in aspect-oriented modeling of software systems. To achieve these goals, we invite the participants to present new ideas and discuss the state of research and practice in modeling different kinds of crosscutting concerns at multiple levels: software architecture, detailed design, testing, and mapping models onto aspect-oriented programs. The results of the workshop are expected to contribute towards answering the following key questions:
- How do aspects emerge and appear in models?
- In what respect do they help to understand the problem domain? And how do they help to find "better" software solutions?
- In what regards are current modeling techniques suitable to design aspects?
- In what respect do they fail to do so?
- How could those deficiencies be resolved?

## W5: Model Transformations in Practice

**Organizers:** Jean Bezivin (University of Nantes), Bernhard Rumpe (TU Braunschweig), Andy Schuerr (TU Darmstadt), Laurence Tratt (King's College London)

**URL:** http://sosym.dcs.kcl.ac.uk/events/mtip/

**Abstract:** Model Transformations in Practice is a workshop to be held at the upcoming MoDELS 2005 conference. It aims to provide a forum for the model transformation community to discuss practical model transformation issues. Currently, many different model transformation approaches have been proposed and explored, but there has been too little work on comparing and contrasting various approaches. Without such comparisons, it is hard to assess new model transformation approaches, or to discern sensible future paths and upcoming standards such as the upcoming OMG MOF/QVT recommendation.

The aim of this workshop is to lead to an increased understanding of the relative merits of different model transformation techniques and approaches. A more advanced understanding of such merits is of considerable benefit to both the model transformation and wider modelling communities.

## W6: WiSME – Workshop in Software Model Engineering

**Organizers:** Krzysztof Czarnecki (University of Waterloo), Jean-Marie Favre (University of Grenoble), Martin Gogolla (University of Bremen), Tom Mens (University of Mons-Hainaut)

**URL:** http://planetmde.org/wisme-2005

**Abstract:** Model-Driven Engineering is a form of generative engineering, by which all or at least central parts of a software application are generated from models. Model Driven Engineering should be seen as an integrative approach combining existing software engineering techniques (e.g., testing and refinement) and technical spaces (e.g., 'ModelWare' and 'XmlWare') that have usually been studied in separation. The goal of the workshop is to improve common understanding of these techniques across technical spaces and create bridges and increase the synergies among the spaces. This year's WiSME workshop will concentrate on two complementing themes: Bridging Technical Spaces and Model-Driven Evolution.

## W7: Model Driven Development of Advanced User Interfaces

**Organizers:** Jan Van den Bergh, Hasselt University, Belgium, Heinrich Hussmann, University of Munich, Germany, Andreas Pleuss, University of Munich, Germany, Stefan Sauer, University of Paderborn, Germany

**URL:** http://www.edm.uhasselt.be/mddaui2005/

**Abstract:** The user interface of an application is often one of the core factors determining its success. While model-driven development is gaining popularity in the software engineering community, model-based user interface development is an important line of research in the human-computer interaction community. Both approaches make extensive use of models to develop software, but currently they are still vastly independent. This workshop aims at integrating the knowledge from both domains, leading to a model-driven development of user interfaces. In particular the focus lies on advanced user interfaces corresponding to the current state-of-the-art in human-computer interaction, such as interfaces supporting complex interactions, visualizations, multimedia representations, multimodality, adaptability, or customization.

## W8: NfC – Models for Non-functional Aspects of Component-Based Software

**Organizers:** Jan Øyvind Aagedal (SINTEF ICT, Norway), Geri Georg (Colorado State University, USA), Raffaela Mirandola (University of Roma "TorVergata", Italy), Ileana Ober (IRIT, France), Dorina Petriu (Carleton University, Canada), Wolfgang Theilmann (SAP Research Belfast, Ireland), Jon Whittle (George Mason University, USA), Steffen Zschaler (Technische Universität Dresden, Germany)

**URL:** http://www.comquad.org/nfc05/

**Abstract:** Developing reliable software is a complex, daunting, and error-prone task. Therefore, many researchers are interested in improving the support for developers creating such software. Component-based software engineering has emerged as an important paradigm for handling complexity. In parallel, raising the level of abstraction when reasoning about systems, thus using models, is another technique for lowering the complexity. The goal of this workshop is to look at issues related to the integration of non-functional property expression, evaluation, and prediction in the context of component-based software engineering and finding the best techniques to deal-with non-functional aspects in a model based approach, such as, but not limited to, UML-based approaches. This includes semantic issues, questions of modelling language definition, but also support for automation, such as analysis algorithms, MDA-based approaches, or tool-support for refinement steps. As models are only really meaningful if used in the context of a software development process, we also welcome work in this area.

We expect the workshop to foster cooperation between the various research groups in the field. One important expected outcome is a joint workshop report as well as ongoing discussions, e.g., on a workshop mailing list. The aim of this workshop is to bring together practitioners and academics that are currently working around these topics to highlight the ongoing solutions and the problems encountered. The workshop is organized on two half-day sessions: The morning session is dedicated to invited talks and presentations; followed in the afternoon by working sessions. The number and subject of these sessions will be decided by the organizers depending on the position papers.

## W9: MDD for Software Product-lines: Fact or Fiction?

**Organizers:** Dr. Douglas C. Schmidt (Vanderbilt University, Tennessee), Andrey Nechypurenko (Siemens), Egon Wuchner (Siemens)

**URL:**
http://www.geocities.com/andreynech/MDDandProductLinesWorkshop.html

**Abstract:** key advantages of using model-driven development in conjunction with commonalityvariability analysis (CVA) are (1) rigorously capturing the key roles and responsibilities in a CVA and (2) helping automate repetitive tasks that must be accomplished for each product instance. Often, however, new customer requirements invalidate the results of earlier CVAs, such that a CVA and its derived meta-models, DSMLs, and generators must be modified invasively and intrusively to reflect these new requirements. The primary scope of this workshop will be on theory and methods to reduce the impact of the new unanticipated requiremetns on the (meta)models and model interpretes in order to improve the usability of model-based technologies in real-life large scale applications.

## W10: Use Cases in Model-Driven Software Engineering

**Organizers:** Hernán Astudillo (Universidad Técnica Federico Santa María, Valparaíso, Chile), Gonzalo Génova (Universidad Carlos III de Madrid, Spain), Michal Smialek (Warsaw University of Technology, Poland), Juan Llorens (Universidad Carlos III de Madrid, Spain), Pierre Metz (Darmstadt University of Applied Sciences, Germany), Rubén Prieto-Díaz (James Madison University, USA)

**URL:** http://www.ie.inf.uc3m.es/wuscam-05/index.htm

**Abstract:** The integration of use cases within Model Driven Software Engineering requires a better definition of use case contents, in particular use case description of behavior through sequences of action steps, use case pre- and post- conditions, and relationship between use case model and conceptual model. The UML2 specification allows for several textual and graphical representations of use case behavior, but does not provide any rules for transformations between different representations at the same level of abstraction. It does not provide either any rules for transformations of these representations to other artifacts at levels closer to implementation. With this workshop we hope to show how the resourceful application of use case models help to fill the "requirements gap" in the current resarch and practice of model-driven methodologies.

## W11: Educator's Symposium

**Organizers:** Holger Giese, University of Paderborn, Germany, Pascal Roques, Valtech Training, France, Omar Aldawud, Lucent Technologies, USA, Balbir Barn, Thames Valley University, UK, Leonor Barroca, Open University, UK, Francis Bordeleau, Carleton University Canada, Jean-Michel Bruel, University of Pau, France, Doris Carver, Louisiana State University, USA, Betty H.C. Cheng, Michigan State University, USA, Kendra Cooper, University of Texas at Dallas, USA, Peter Dolog, L3S Research Center, Germany, Robert B. France, Colorado State University, USA, Haim Kilov, Stevens Institute of Technology, USA, Timothy C. Lethbridge, University of Ottawa, Canada, Bruce R. Maxim, University of Michigan-Dearborn, USA, Hossein Saiedian, University of Kansas, USA, Justo N. Hidalgo Sanz, Denodo Technologies, Spain, Perdita Stevens, University of Edinburgh, UK, Xudong He, Florida International University, USA

**URL:** See the main conference web site.

**Abstract:** Model-driven development approaches and technologies for software-based systems, in which development is centered round the manipulation of models, raise the level of abstraction and thus, improve our abilities to develop complex systems. Therefore, a number of approaches and tools have been proposed for the model-driven development (MDD) of software-based systems. Examples are UML, model-driven architecture (MDA), and model-integrated computing (MIC).

Putting the model-driven development vision into practice requires not only sophisticated modeling approaches and tools, but also considerable training and education efforts. To make people ready for model-driven development, its principles and applications need to be taught to practitioners in industry, incorporated in university curricula, and probably even introduced in schools.

The educator's symposium at the MoDELS conference, the premier conference devoted to the topic of model-driven engineering of software-based systems, was intended as a forum in which educators and trainers could meet to discuss pedagogy, use of technology, and share their experience pertaining to teaching modeling techniques and model-driven development.

## W12: Doctoral Symposium

**Organizers:** Jeff Gray, University of Alabama at Birmingham, USA, Aditya Agrawal, IBM TJ Watson Research, USA, Jean Bézivin, University of Nantes, France, Betty Cheng, Michigan State University, USA, Emanuel Grant, University of North Dakota, USA, Jörg Kienzle, McGill University, Canada, Ana Moreira, Universidade Nova de Lisboa, Portugal, Kerry Raymond, DSTC, Australia

**URL:**  See the main conference web site.

**Abstract:** The Doctoral Symposium at the MoDELS conference provided an
international forum for doctoral students to interact with other students and
faculty mentors. The Doctoral Symposium brings together PhD Students
working in areas related to modeling and model-driven engineering. Selected
students had the opportunity to present and to discuss their research goals,
methods and results within a constructive and international atmosphere.
The Symposium organizers provided useful guidance for completion of the
dissertation research and initiation of a research career. The symposium was
intended for students who had already settled on a specific research proposal
and have some preliminary results, but still have enough time remaining before their final defense so that they can benefit from the Symposium discussions. Due to the mentoring aspect of the event, the Symposium was open
only to those students and mentors participating directly in the event.

# Acknowledgements

I would like to thank the members of the selection committee who not only
spontaneously accepted my invitation, but also provided helpful comments in
the selection process. I also would like to thank Geri Georg for her countless
time and help in many aspects of the organization of the Satellite events.

# Tutorials at the MODELS 2005 Conference

Gianna Reggio

DISI - University of Genova
Genova, Italy
reggio@disi.unige.it

**Abstract.** The MoDELS 2005 conference provides six half-day tutorials on advanced topics related to model-driven engineering, presented by recognized worldwide experts. Here, there is a short summary of each tutorial and the list of presenters.

## 1 Introduction

Tutorials will give conference attendees the opportunities to acquire new knowledge, to get some different insights, and to develop abilities on key subjects and related up to date techniques. The tutorial program of the MoDELS 2005 conference seeks to continue this tested tradition. This program is intended for practitioners, reaearchers, educators and students looking for a better and deeper understanding of topics related to the model-driven engineering. It will cover both languages and systems used to create complex applications.

For this conference, we received a very large number of high quality tutorial proposals, but unfortunately we had space only for six. As a result, a large number of good proposals were not accepted as we sought to mantain a strong attendance at each tutorial. In the six that we selected there is a good mixture of tutorials covering areas that are topical and have great appeal and relevance to the modelling community.

We summarize these tutorials in the following section; further details can be accessed at the MoDELS 2005 conference web site:

http://www.modelsconference.org

## 2 Detailed List of Tutorials

**Tutorial T1: Model Driven Development with Eclipse Modeling Framework (EMF)**

**Presenters:** Vladimir Bacvanski and Petter Graf (InferData, Austin, USA)

This tutorial teaches the participants how to use and extend the Eclipse Modeling Framework (EMF). Using a case study and numerous examples, the participants master the EMF framework as a generative tool for model driven

L. Briand and C. Williams (Eds.): MoDELS 2005, LNCS 3713, pp. 715–718, 2005.

development. The tutorial explores all aspects of EMF development, from creation of models for EMF, use of generators, Java Emitter Templates, concluding with an overview of model transformation technologies for EMF.

The conceptual but also non-trivial practical skills gained in this tutorial will enable participants to effectively start developing their model driven applications. The skills apply both to practitioners who need to develop Eclipse tools, as well to researchers who will use Eclipse and EMF as a foundation for their experiments.

## Tutorial T2: Language-Driven Development

**Presenters:** Tony Clark and Andy Evans (Xactium Limited, Sheffield, UK)

Languages provide a unifying and ubiquitous abstraction for systems development. Just as Booch argued that Object-Orientation is based on the things we learn in Kindergarten, we argue that Languages are a more intuitive and powerful representation than Objects. We propose that the Language abstraction is set to become the next major paradigm shift in software development.

In this tutorial we describe how developers can gain siginificant productvity increases in the way they build systems by identifying, capturing and deploying tools that support the right languages for their business domain.

The ideas presented in this tutorial are based on many years experience of contributing to language standards within the Object Management Group, and experience of applying the ideas to large scale industrial projects.

## Tutorial T3: Designing Software Product Lines with UML 2.0: From Use Cases to Pattern-Based Software Architectures

**Presenter:** Hassan Gomaa (George Mason University, Fairfax, USA)

This tutorial addresses how to develop object-oriented requirements, analysis, and design models for software product lines (SPL) using the UML 2.0 notation.

The emphasis throughout is on modeling commonality and variability among the family members of the product line. During requirements modeling, kernel, optional, and alternative use cases define the software functional requirements of the SPL. The feature model is developed to capture common and variable product line requirements, and how they relate to the use case model. During analysis, static models define kernel, optional, and variant classes and their relationships. In dynamic modeling, statecharts define the state dependent aspects of the SPL and interaction models describe the dynamic interaction between the objects that participate in each kernel, optional, and alternative use case.

The tutorial then covers how to develop the component-based SPL architecture using the new UML 2.0 notation for structured classes and composite structure diagrams, which allows components, ports, and connectors to be depicted. The SPL architecture is built using software architectural structure and communication patterns.

The tutorial is based on the prresenter latest book, "Designing Software Product Lines with UML: From Use Cases to Pattern-Based Software Architectures", Addison Wesley, 2005.

## Tutorial T4: Modeling and Analysis of Aspectual Requirements

**Presenters:** Awais Rashid (Lancaster University, UK) and Ana Moreira (Universidade Nova de Lisboa, Lisbon, Portugal)

Aspect-oriented software development (AOSD) techniques have shown promise in dealing with broadly-scoped, crosscutting propertics, i.e., the aspects. However, to date, most techniques have focused on design modelling of aspects and aspect-oriented programming technologies. Aspects, however, exist from the very early stages of problem analysis and hence, should be addressed during requirements engineering. This tutorial highlights the need to identify, model and analyse aspects during requirements engineering. It shows, with the help of practical examples, how to extend existing requirements models, e.g., use-case or viewpoint based models, with abstraction and composition support for aspects. The tutorial also describes how to analyse such models as well as the key role they play in a model-driven development (MDD) lifecycle.

At the end of the tutorial, participants will have a clear understanding of:

- the importance of aspects in the software development process;
- the role of aspect-oriented concepts in requirements modelling and analysis;
- techniques, tools and good practice guidelines for identifying, modelling, composing and analysing crosscutting properties at the requirements-level;
- how aspect-oriented requirements models and their analysis drive development of solution domain models in a model-driven development approach.

## Tutorial T5: An Overview of UML 2.0

**Presenter:** Bran Selic (IBM Software Group - Rational Software, Canada)

The first major revision of the UML standard, UML 2.0, has recently been adopted by the Object Management Group. This version of the language was strongly influenced by the recent maturation of model-driven development (MDD) methods and technologies. The tutorial describes the major new features and capabilities of UML 2.0 with a full explanation of the rationale and design philosophy for each.

The presenter is currently chairing the OMG team responsible for maintaining the standard.

## Tutorial T6: Software Factories: Using Domain Specific Languages, Patterns, Frameworks and Tools to Assemble Applications

**Presenter:** Steve Cook (Microsoft Corporation, Cambridge, UK)

Increasingly complex and rapidly changing requirements and technologies are making application development increasingly difficult.

This tutorial explores this phenomenon, and presents the Software Factory pattern for building languages, patterns, frameworks and tools for specific domains, such as user interface construction or database design. We discuss the forces acting towards increasing industrialization of software development through delivery of knowledge and automation in context. We explore innovations, such as software product lines and model driven development, which reduce the cost of implementing the pattern, making it cost effective for narrower and more specialized domains, such as B2C application development and business process automation. We introduce the concept of the software schema, a network of viewpoints describing artifacts comprising the members of a family of software products, and we show how mappings between these viewpoints can be used to provide constraints supporting model transformation and self organizing processes.

Examples and demonstrations are used throughout to illustrate the concepts.

## Acknowledgements

I would like to thank Bran Selic and João Araújo for their contributions during the selection process.

# Panels at the MODELS 2005 Conference

Siobhán Clarke

Trinity College, Ireland
siobhan.clarke@cs.tcd.ie

## Panel P1: What Would Be the Ideal Meta-modeling Infrastructure?

**Chair:** Pierre-Alain Muller, University of Haute Alsace, France

The goal of this panel is to discuss the requirements for an ideal meta-modeling architecture. The panel will address the following points:

- What is the scope of meta-modeling?
- How to reconcile domain-oriented meta-hierarchies with language-oriented meta-hierarchies?
- What would be a minimal core meta-language?
- What kind of tool support should be available for meta-modeling?

## Panel P2: A DSL or UML Profile. Which Would You Use?

**Chair:** Stuart Kent, Microsoft, Cambridge, UK

In implementing model driven approaches to software development, there is some debate about the languages to use for modelling. On one side, there is the UML, advocates of which might argue that it has everything you'll need and its profiling mechanisms are quite adequate to cope with any customization or specialization you might need. On the other side are those advocating domain specific languages, who might argue that most of the time you're going to need to specialize and customize the language you use for modelling, that UML is not a good starting point for such specialization, and UML profiles are weak mechanism for extensibility anyway. Let's instead put together technology appropriate for building DSLs, they'd say. Of course, within the DSL camp, there's further debate about what is the right technology, but perhaps that's the topic of another panel... we'll see.

## Panel P3: Building Better Systems: Modeling, Verification, and Testing

**Chair:** Clay Williams (Moderator, IBM Watson Research Center, USA)

L. Briand and C. Williams (Eds.): MoDELS 2005, LNCS 3713, pp. 719–720, 2005.
© Springer-Verlag Berlin Heidelberg 2005

**Panelists:** Paul Baker (Motorola Research, UK), Lionel Briand (Carleton University, Canada and Simula Research Labs, Norway) and Sudipto Ghosh (Colorado State University, USA)

A stated goal of model-based software development is that software quality will drastically improve as a result of the use of modeling methods. This hope has been held out repeatedly in the past by other software development movements, including formal methods, computer aided software engineering (CASE), and various process movements, such as the Cleanroom approach to building software. The participants in this panel will explore whether we are reasonable in hoping that modeling as we know it today will significantly assist with quality issues. In doing so, they will discuss what the major technical issues are that need to be addressed in order to achieve higher quality software, and propose a research agenda for addressing these issues. The panelists will pay particular attention to the use of modeling languages to facilitate better testing, as well as how modeling languages can be used as a basis for verification approaches such as model checking and theorem proving.

# Author Index

# Lecture Notes in Computer Science

For information about Vols. 1–3614

please contact your bookseller or Springer

Vol. 3666: B.D. Martino, D. Kranzlmüller, J. Dongarra (Eds.), Recent Advances in Parallel Virtual Machine and Message Passing Interface. XVII, 546 pages. 2005.

Vol. 3665: K. S. Candan, A. Celentano (Eds.), Advances in Multimedia Information Systems. X, 221 pages. 2005.

Vol. 3664: C. Türker, M. Agosti, H.-J. Schek (Eds.), Peer-to-Peer, Grid, and Service-Orientation in Digital Library Architectures. X, 261 pages. 2005.

Vol. 3663: W.G. Kropatsch, R. Sablatnig, A. Hanbury (Eds.), Pattern Recognition. XIV, 512 pages. 2005.

Vol. 3662: C. Baral, G. Greco, N. Leone, G. Terracina (Eds.), Logic Programming and Nonmonotonic Reasoning. XIII, 454 pages. 2005. (Subseries LNAI).

Vol. 3661: T. Panayiotopoulos, J. Gratch, R. Aylett, D. Ballin, P. Olivier, T. Rist (Eds.), Intelligent Virtual Agents. XIII, 506 pages. 2005. (Subseries LNAI).

Vol. 3660: M. Beigl, S. Intille, J. Rekimoto, H. Tokuda (Eds.), UbiComp 2005: Ubiquitous Computing. XVII, 394 pages. 2005.

Vol. 3659: J.R. Rao, B. Sunar (Eds.), Cryptographic Hardware and Embedded Systems – CHES 2005. XIV, 458 pages. 2005.

Vol. 3658: V. Matoušek, P. Mautner, T. Pavelka (Eds.), Text, Speech and Dialogue. XV, 460 pages. 2005. (Subseries LNAI).

Vol. 3655: A. Aldini, R. Gorrieri, F. Martinelli (Eds.), Foundations of Security Analysis and Design III. VII, 273 pages. 2005.

Vol. 3654: S. Jajodia, D. Wijesekera (Eds.), Data and Applications Security XIX. X, 353 pages. 2005.

Vol. 3653: M. Abadi, L. de Alfaro (Eds.), CONCUR 2005 – Concurrency Theory. XIV, 578 pages. 2005.

Vol. 3652: A. Rauber, S. Christodoulakis, A M. Tjoa (Eds.), Research and Advanced Technology for Digital Libraries. XVIII, 545 pages. 2005.

Vol. 3650: J. Zhou, J. Lopez, R.H. Deng, F. Bao (Eds.), Information Security. XII, 516 pages. 2005.

Vol. 3649: W.M. P. van der Aalst, B. Benatallah, F. Casati, F. Curbera (Eds.), Business Process Management. XII, 472 pages. 2005.

Vol. 3648: J.C. Cunha, P.D. Medeiros (Eds.), Euro-Par 2005 Parallel Processing. XXXVI, 1299 pages. 2005.

Vol. 3646: A. F. Famili, J.N. Kok, J.M. Peña, A. Siebes, A. Feelders (Eds.), Advances in Intelligent Data Analysis VI. XIV, 522 pages. 2005.

Vol. 3645: D.-S. Huang, X.-P. Zhang, G.-B. Huang (Eds.), Advances in Intelligent Computing, Part II. XIII, 1010 pages. 2005.

Vol. 3644: D.-S. Huang, X.-P. Zhang, G.-B. Huang (Eds.), Advances in Intelligent Computing, Part I. XXVII, 1101 pages. 2005.

Vol. 3642: D. Ślezak, J. Yao, J.F. Peters, W. Ziarko, X. Hu (Eds.), Rough Sets, Fuzzy Sets, Data Mining, and Granular Computing, Part II. XXIII, 738 pages. 2005. (Subseries LNAI).

Vol. 3641: D. Ślezak, G. Wang, M. Szczuka, I. Düntsch, Y. Yao (Eds.), Rough Sets, Fuzzy Sets, Data Mining, and Granular Computing, Part I. XXIV, 742 pages. 2005. (Subseries LNAI).

Vol. 3639: P. Godefroid (Ed.), Model Checking Software. XI, 289 pages. 2005.

Vol. 3638: A. Butz, B. Fisher, A. Krüger, P. Olivier (Eds.), Smart Graphics. XI, 269 pages. 2005.

Vol. 3637: J. M. Moreno, J. Madrenas, J. Cosp (Eds.), Evolvable Systems: From Biology to Hardware. XI, 227 pages. 2005.

Vol. 3636: M.J. Blesa, C. Blum, A. Roli, M. Sampels (Eds.), Hybrid Metaheuristics. XII, 155 pages. 2005.

Vol. 3634: L. Ong (Ed.), Computer Science Logic. XI, 567 pages. 2005.

Vol. 3633: C. Bauzer Medeiros, M. Egenhofer, E. Bertino (Eds.), Advances in Spatial and Temporal Databases. XIII, 433 pages. 2005.

Vol. 3632: R. Nieuwenhuis (Ed.), Automated Deduction – CADE-20. XIII, 459 pages. 2005. (Subseries LNAI).

Vol. 3631: J. Eder, H.-M. Haav, A. Kalja, J. Penjam (Eds.), Advances in Databases and Information Systems. XIII, 393 pages. 2005.

Vol. 3630: M.S. Capcarrere, A.A. Freitas, P.J. Bentley, C.G. Johnson, J. Timmis (Eds.), Advances in Artificial Life. XIX, 949 pages. 2005. (Subseries LNAI).

Vol. 3629: J.L. Fiadeiro, N. Harman, M. Roggenbach, J. Rutten (Eds.), Algebra and Coalgebra in Computer Science. XI, 457 pages. 2005.

Vol. 3628: T. Gschwind, U. Aßmann, O. Nierstrasz (Eds.), Software Composition. X, 199 pages. 2005.

Vol. 3627: C. Jacob, M.L. Pilat, P.J. Bentley, J. Timmis (Eds.), Artificial Immune Systems. XII, 500 pages. 2005.

Vol. 3626: B. Ganter, G. Stumme, R. Wille (Eds.), Formal Concept Analysis. X, 349 pages. 2005. (Subseries LNAI).

Vol. 3625: S. Kramer, B. Pfahringer (Eds.), Inductive Logic Programming. XIII, 427 pages. 2005. (Subseries LNAI).

Vol. 3624: C. Chekuri, K. Jansen, J.D. P. Rolim, L. Trevisan (Eds.), Approximation, Randomization and Combinatorial Optimization. XI, 495 pages. 2005.

Vol. 3623: M. Liśkiewicz, R. Reischuk (Eds.), Fundamentals of Computation Theory. XV, 576 pages. 2005.

Vol. 3622: V. Vene, T. Uustalu (Eds.), Advanced Functional Programming. IX, 359 pages. 2005.

Vol. 3621: V. Shoup (Ed.), Advances in Cryptology – CRYPTO 2005. XI, 568 pages. 2005.

Vol. 3620: H. Muñoz-Avila, F. Ricci (Eds.), Case-Based Reasoning Research and Development. XV, 654 pages. 2005. (Subseries LNAI).

Vol. 3619: X. Lu, W. Zhao (Eds.), Networking and Mobile Computing. XXIV, 1299 pages. 2005.

Vol. 3618: J. Jedrzejowicz, A. Szepietowski (Eds.), Mathematical Foundations of Computer Science 2005. XVI, 814 pages. 2005.

Vol. 3617: F. Roli, S. Vitulano (Eds.), Image Analysis and Processing – ICIAP 2005. XXIV, 1219 pages. 2005.

Vol. 3615: B. Ludäscher, L. Raschid (Eds.), Data Integration in the Life Sciences. XII, 344 pages. 2005. (Subseries LNBI).